S0-CDO-779

Professional J2EE EAI

Matjaz B. Juric

with

S. Jeelani Basha

Rick Leander

Ramesh Nagappan

Wrox Press Ltd. ®

Professional J2EE EAI

© 2001 Wrox Press

All rights reserved. No part of this book may be reproduced, stored in a retrieval system or transmitted in any form or by any means, without the prior written permission of the publisher, except in the case of brief quotations embodied in critical articles or reviews.

The author and publisher have made every effort in the preparation of this book to ensure the accuracy of the information. However, the information contained in this book is sold without warranty, either express or implied. Neither the authors, Wrox Press, nor its dealers or distributors will be held liable for any damages caused or alleged to be caused either directly or indirectly by this book.

First published December 2001

Published by Wrox Press Ltd,
Arden House, 1102 Warwick Road, Acocks Green,
Birmingham, B27 6BH, UK
Printed in the United States
ISBN 1-861005-44-X

Trademark Acknowledgements

Wrox has endeavored to provide trademark information about all the companies and products mentioned in this book by the appropriate use of capitals. However, Wrox cannot guarantee the accuracy of this information.

Credits

Authors
Matjaz B. Juric
S. Jeelani Basha
Rick Leander
Ramesh Nagappan

Additional Material:
Ivan Rozman
P. G. Sarang
Dave Young

Technical Architect
Craig A. Berry

Technical Editors
Christian Peak
Daniel Richardson
Steve Rycroft
Robert F.E. Shaw

Category Manager
Emma Batch

Author Agent
Nicola Phillips

Project Administrator
Simon Brand

Technical Reviewers
Vishwajit Aklecha
Kapil Anshankar
Rich Bonneau
Virat Chadha
Kyle Gabhart
Phil Powers de George
Mehran Habibi
Romin Irani
Alexander V. Konstantinou
Jim MacIntosh
Nathan Nagarajan
Don Reamey
Raffi Simonian
Madhuri Singampalli
Prabhpreet Singh
Matt Staples
Rick Stones

Production Project Coordinator
Pip Wonson

Illustrations
Emma Eato
Abbie Forletta
Natalie O'Donnell
Matt Clark

Cover
Dawn Chellingworth

Proof Reader
Agnes Wiggers

Index
Martin Brooks
Andrew Criddle

About the Authors

Matjaz B. Juric

Matjaz holds a Ph.D. in computer and information science and is an Assistant Professor at the University of Maribor. His research areas cover all aspects of component technology, with special emphasis on integration, distributed object and component systems (CORBA, EJB, RMI, COM+, .NET), component development, Web Services, performance, analysis, and design. He has gained experience from several large-scale integration projects, and he has been involved in the RMI-IIOP (an integral part of the Java 2 platform) development for performance analysis and optimization.

Matjaz is author of several scientific and professional articles in journals like Java Report, Information and Software Technology, ACM journals, etc. He co-authored the book *Professional EJB (Wrox Press)* and published a chapter in the book *More Java Gems*. He has presented at conferences like OOPSLA, ICPADS, PDCS, Java Development, and SCI. He is also a reviewer, program committee member, and conference co-organizer.

> *My efforts in this book are dedicated to my family. Special thanks go to all my friends at Wrox, at the University of Maribor, and everyone else who has supported me.*

Matjaz contributed 9 chapters to this book: Chapters 1-4, 9-12, and 17.

S. Jeelani Basha

Jeelani is working as a Senior Software Engineer with Infinity Markets, Inc., California. His interest in programming led him from electrical engineering to software programming. He is a certified Java2 Programmer with more than 5 years of experience and has implemented various projects using J2EE.

His current subject of interest is Web Services and he is concentrating his efforts towards making Web Services a viable solution for enterprise applications. He has a bachelors degree in Electrical Engineering from REC Bhopal, India.

> *I would like to thank my parents for their blessings and to my love, Tahaseen, for her continuous help and encouragement. Special thanks to Romin for drawing my attention away from EJBs and towards Web Services! Thanks also to Urooj, Seshu, and Saradhi for their help.*

> *Dedicated to my brother, the late S. Rabbani (Rabs).*

Jeelani contributed Chapter 18 to this book.

Rick Leander

Rick has worked in software development for over twenty-five years and is currently owner of Zeno Street Software, a Denver-based consulting firm. He has gained a wealth of EAI experience while integrating vertical market software for managed healthcare organizations throughout the Unites States and has refined this knowledge with graduate research while completing his M.A. from Webster University. In addition to EAI, his technical interests include EDI, XML, databases, and distributed business application development. He lives in the Denver, Colorado area, with his wife Barb and his dog Freckles.

I'd like to thank Dan Novak of Webster University for steering me towards graduate work in business integration and EAI. Thanks also to the great people at the Aurora Central Library for their large collection of up-to-date technical books, including many Wrox titles. Most of all, special thanks to my wife Barb for all her support and encouragement.

Rick contributed Chapters 5, 6, and 7 to this book.

Ramesh Nagappan

Ramesh is an Architect specializing in Java- and CORBA-based distributed computing architectures. He is a Java evangelist and also an active contributor to open source specifications and implementation. Before he hooked on to Java and CORBA, he worked as a Research Engineer, developing software solutions for CAD/CAM, Computational fluid dynamics solutions, and Aerodynamics applications. In his spare time, he enjoys water sports and playing with his son Roger. He can be reached at nramesh@mediaone.net.

Thanks to Joyce for all the helpful suggestions and advice, which have added great value to this work. A special thanks goes to Sunil Mathew, and my colleagues at Sun Java Center for their continuing encouragement all the way.

To my wife Joyce and our son Roger for all their love, support, and inspiration, and also to my loving parents for brightening my life.

Ramesh contributed 5 chapters to this book: Chapters 8 and 13-16.

Table of Contents

Table of Contents

Table of Contents

Table of Contents

Table of Contents

Table of Contents

Table of Contents

Introduction

Welcome to Professional J2EE EAI. **Enterprise Application Integration (EAI)** refers to the unrestricted sharing of data and business processes among the connected applications and data sources in an enterprise. While the need for EAI is easy to identify, actually accomplishing it is another matter entirely.

By its very nature an enterprise application is unlikely to exist in isolation. Any reasonably large company will have many such applications – probably written using many different technologies. The mergers and acquisitions of businesses is a common occurrence and as a company grows it is vital to tie the existing systems together. The cost of maintaining many disparate systems is large, and the benefits of doing so will surely diminish over time.

This book will demonstrate the fundamental concepts relating to EAI within the architecture of the **Java 2 Platform, Enterprise Edition (J2EE)**. J2EE represents the primary distributed architecture model for creating business applications and is arguably the most mature and robust design for enterprise development. It offers technologies that enable the development of large and scalable applications. It also provides a layer of abstraction that can be applied on top of an enterprise system, promoting a standards-based approach to development. The J2EE architecture also promotes the creation of multi-tier applications, in which developers can break down the mammoth undertaking of enterprise-scale integration into specific, self-contained tasks.

Starting with an audit of the legacy systems that we may encounter, we'll provide a comprehensive study of the choices and strategies available to us when we use the design principles and patterns associated with the J2EE architecture. After familiarizing ourselves with basic data-level integration, we'll venture into situations in which we'll need to get to grips with the business method level integration. From here, we'll cover complex integration issues such as bridging between different technologies and transaction and security management in EAI systems. Finally, we'll examine how we can prepare for emerging integration challenges, such as web services and business-to-business integration.

What's Covered in This Book

We will organize our integration attempts into four parts: integration through data, business method integration (otherwise known as application-to-application integration), presentation integration, and business-to-business (B2B) integration. In each of these sections we will discuss the strategies and methods available to us, and then focus on the technologies used to implement the integration, demonstrating the concepts with complete examples. We will cover the following:

- **Integration through data**
    - JDBC, JDO, and other ways to access data
    - Using XML for data exchange (JAXP)
    - Message brokers (JMS)
- **Business method integration**
    - RMI-IIOP and Java IDL for CORBA integration
    - Using EJBs for integration
    - The J2EE Connector Architecture (JCA)
    - COM bridges for Windows integration
    - Transaction (JTA) and security (JAAS) management
- **Presentation integration**
    - Servlets and JSP pages for client integration
- **B2B integration**
    - XML technologies and vocabularies
    - XML/XSLT for building user interfaces
    - SOAP, UDDI, and WSDL
    - E-Marketplaces and portals

What You Need To Use This Book

Most of the code in this book was tested with the Java 2 SDK version 1.3 (http://java.sun.com/j2se/1.3/) and the Java 2 Platform, Enterprise Edition SDK 1.3 Reference Implementation (http://java.sun.com/j2ee/sdk_1.3/). However, running the examples in some chapters will require some additional software:

Application Servers

As well as the J2EE Reference Implementation, we have used:

- BEA WebLogic Server 6.1 – http://commerce.beasys.com/downloads/weblogic_server.jsp

Of course, it should be possible to test the examples on any enterprise-scale application server, for instance:

- ❏ IBM WebSphere – http://www-4.ibm.com/software/webservers/appserv/
- ❏ JBoss – http://www.jboss.org/jboss-overview.jsp
- ❏ SilverStream – http://www.silverstream.com/
- ❏ Sybase – http://www.sybase.com/products/applicationservers/easerver/

Databases and Drivers

Several of the chapters also require access to a database. For these chapters we have used a mixture of:

- ❏ Cloudscape (an in-process version comes with the J2EE RI) – http://www.cloudscape.com/
- ❏ Sybase SQL Anywhere and jConnect 5.5 JDBC drivers – http://www.sybase.com
- ❏ Microsoft SQL Server 2000 – http://www.microsoft.com/sql/evaluation/default.asp and SQL 2000 JDBC Driver – http://www.microsoft.com/SQL/downloads/2000/jdbc.asp
- ❏ Oracle and Oracle XA drivers – http://www.oracle.com/
- ❏ MySQL (we used version 3.23) and the MM.MySQL JDBC Driver (we used version 2.0.6) – http://www.mysql.org/
- ❏ Drivers for other databases are available from i-net Software at – http://www.inetsoftware.de

Additional Software

Finally, there are several additional and optional pieces of software that a couple of chapters also require:

- ❏ Java 2 SDK version 1.4 – http://java.sun.com/j2se/1.4/
- ❏ A C++ compiler that suits your particular platform. We used Microsoft Visual C++ 5.0 – http://msdn.microsoft.com/visualc/
- ❏ XML Parsers, we have used Apache Xerces – http://xml.apache.org/xerces-j/index.html and the Apache Xalan XSLT processor – http://xml.apache.org/xalan-j/
- ❏ Java Transaction API specification – http://java.sun.com/products/jta/index.html
- ❏ A CORBA implementation, we used Inprise/Borland Visibroker for C++ and Visibroker for Java (both versions 4.5) – http://www.inprise.com/visibroker/
- ❏ A Java-COM Bridge, we used J-Integra – http://www.intrinsyc.com/products/bridging/jintegra.asp
- ❏ Microsoft Visual J++ 6.0 – http://msdn.microsoft.com/visualj/
- ❏ A SAP Resource Adapter – http://www.inqmy.com/download/download.htm
- ❏ Borland Security Service version 4.5 – http://www.borland.com/downloads/
- ❏ Tomcat 4 – from http://jakarta.apache.org/tomcat/index.html
- ❏ Apache SOAP 2.2 – from http://xml.apache.org/soap/index.html

- ❏ IBM's Business Test Registry – from http://www-3.ibm.com/services/uddi/

- ❏ IBM's UDDI4J – from http://oss.software.ibm.com/developerworks/projects/uddi4j

- ❏ IBM's Web Services Toolkit 2.4 – http://www.alphaworks.ibm.com/tech/webservicestoolkit/

- ❏ JDOM API (we used beta 7) – from http://www.jdom.org/

The code in the book will work on a single machine, provided it is networked (that is, it can see http://localhost/ through the local browser).

The complete source code from the book is available for download from:

http://www.wrox.com/

Conventions

To help you get the most from the text and keep track of what's happening, we've used a number of conventions throughout the book.

For instance:

> **These boxes hold important, not-to-be forgotten information which is directly relevant to the surrounding text.**

While the background style is used for asides to the current discussion.

As for styles in the text:

- ❏ When we introduce them, we **highlight** important words.

- ❏ We show keyboard strokes like this: *Ctrl-A*.

- ❏ We show filenames and code within the text like so: doGet()

- ❏ Text on user interfaces and URLs are shown as: Menu.

We present code in three different ways. Definitions of methods and properties are shown as follows:

```
protected void doGet(HttpServletRequest req, HttpServletResponse resp)
                     throws ServletException, IOException
```

Example code is shown:

```
In our code examples, the code foreground style shows new, important,
    pertinent code
while code background shows code that's less important in the present context,
    or has been seen before.
```

Customer Support

We always value hearing from our readers, and we want to know what you think about this book: what you liked, what you didn't like, and what you think we can do better next time. You can send us your comments, either by returning the reply card in the back of the book, or by e-mail to feedback@wrox.com. Please be sure to mention the book title in your message.

How To Download the Sample Code for the Book

When you visit the Wrox site, http://www.wrox.com/, simply locate the title through our Search facility or by using one of the title lists. Click on Download in the Code column, or on Download Code on the book's detail page.

The files that are available for download from our site have been archived using WinZip. When you have saved the attachments to a folder on your hard drive, you need to extract the files using a de-compression program such as WinZip or PKUnzip. When you extract the files, the code is usually extracted into chapter folders. When you start the extraction process, ensure your software (WinZip, PKUnzip, etc.) is set to use folder names.

Errata

We've made every effort to make sure that there are no errors in the text or in the code. However, no one is perfect and mistakes do occur. If you find an error in one of our books, like a spelling mistake or a faulty piece of code, we would be very grateful for feedback. By sending in errata you may save another reader hours of frustration, and of course, you will be helping us provide even higher quality information. Simply e-mail the information to support@wrox.com, your information will be checked and if correct, posted to the errata page for that title, or used in subsequent editions of the book.

To find errata on the web site, go to http://www.wrox.com/, and simply locate the title through our Advanced Search or title list. Click on the Book Errata link, which is below the cover graphic on the book's detail page.

E-mail Support

If you wish to directly query a problem in the book with an expert who knows the book in detail then e-mail support@wrox.com, with the title of the book and the last four numbers of the ISBN in the subject field of the e-mail. A typical e-mail should include the following things:

- ❑ The **title of the book**, **last four digits of the ISBN**, and **page number** of the problem in the Subject field.

- ❑ Your **name**, **contact information**, and the **problem** in the body of the message.

We *won't* send you junk mail. We need the details to save your time and ours. When you send an e-mail message, it will go through the following chain of support:

- ❑ Customer Support – Your message is delivered to our customer support staff, who are the first people to read it. They have files on most frequently asked questions and will answer anything general about the book or the web site immediately.

❏ Editorial – Deeper queries are forwarded to the technical editor responsible for that book. They have experience with the programming language or particular product, and are able to answer detailed technical questions on the subject.

❏ The Authors – Finally, in the unlikely event that the editor cannot answer your problem, he or she will forward the request to the author. We do try to protect the author from any distractions to their writing; however, we are quite happy to forward specific requests to them. All Wrox authors help with the support on their books. They will e-mail the customer and the editor with their response, and again all readers should benefit.

The Wrox Support process can only offer support to issues that are directly pertinent to the content of our published title. Support for questions that fall outside the scope of normal book support, is provided via the community lists of our http://p2p.wrox.com/ forum.

p2p.wrox.com

For author and peer discussion join the P2P mailing lists. Our unique system provides **programmer to programmer**™ contact on mailing lists, forums, and newsgroups, all in addition to our one-to-one e-mail support system. If you post a query to P2P, you can be confident that it is being examined by the many Wrox authors and other industry experts who are present on our mailing lists. At p2p.wrox.com you will find a number of different lists that will help you, not only while you read this book, but also as you develop your own applications. Particularly appropriate to this book are the **j2ee**, and **pro_java_server** lists.

To subscribe to a mailing list just follow these steps:

1. Go to http://p2p.wrox.com/.

2. Choose the appropriate category from the left menu bar.

3. Click on the mailing list you wish to join.

4. Follow the instructions to subscribe and fill in your e-mail address and password.

5. Reply to the confirmation e-mail you receive.

6. Use the subscription manager to join more lists and set your e-mail preferences.

Why This System Offers the Best Support

You can choose to join the mailing lists or you can receive them as a weekly digest. If you don't have the time, or facility, to receive the mailing list, then you can search our online archives. Junk and spam mails are deleted, and your own e-mail address is protected by the unique Lyris system. Queries about joining or leaving lists, and any other general queries about lists, should be sent to listsupport@p2p.wrox.com.

1

Integrating the Enterprise

The growing need for the easy accessibility of information presents new challenges for application development in the modern world. This need is unlikely to be fulfilled by the separate "stand-alone" applications used by the majority of companies, because sharing data between such applications is very difficult. However, these companies cannot afford to write off or replace their stand-alone applications overnight because they are mission-critical, and it is often not cost effective to redevelop their entire information systems from scratch in today's business environment.

In addition, companies need to introduce new applications and systems from time to time. It's important to recognize that these new solutions are usually based on modern architectures, which differ significantly from the architectures used by older **legacy** applications. Often modern applications are bought in the form of components, which are then integrated into a larger application. These new applications need to be integrated into the existing system; and the existing applications need to be integrated together to make the information they contain available and accessible.

Application integration is not an easy task; indeed it has become one of the most difficult problems facing enterprise application development in the last few years. The major challenges relate to the integration of the different domains, architectures, and technologies. If we wish to integrate, we must also find ways to allow the coexistence of different architectures, and solve problems inherent in integrating several different technologies. In addition to all of this, we also have to look closely at application content in order to solve the problems of data redundancy and different views of the same problem. These conceptual challenges may be even more difficult to overcome than the technical ones. To make things even more difficult, there is often a significant investment already in place for a variety of application integration technologies that we must deal with.

Furthermore, the requirements placed on information systems are both growing significantly and changing frequently all the time. Integration projects therefore have to be performed in the shortest possible time, deliver results quickly, and adapt to these ever-changing requirements. Of course, the resources for integration are often limited too.

The total integration of applications within an enterprise is often called **Enterprise Application Integration (EAI)**. EAI has been the driving force behind application and information system development of the last few years. Actually, there are two main forms of EAI. First, it is necessary to allow for application integration within a company (intra-EAI), and second, we may wish to promote inter-EAI (**business-to-business (B2B)**) integration.

In this book, we will focus on integrating the Java 2 Platform, Enterprise Edition (J2EE) architecture and its technologies with other systems, including COM+ and CORBA. We will also discuss integrating legacy architectures, spanning mainframe systems, Enterprise Resource Planning (ERP), and client/server systems.

However, in this chapter we will present the basics. We will define the concept of Enterprise Application Integration, consider the challenges presented by it, and focus on EAI from the perspective of a Java developer and the J2EE platform. Along the way, we will:

- ❑   Define EAI and explain the need for it
- ❑   Discuss the role of existing systems in EAI
- ❑   Consider the architectures for EAI
- ❑   Compare legacy and modern application architectures
- ❑   Define application integration layers
- ❑   Discuss business-to-business (B2B) integration
- ❑   Define the role of middleware in EAI
- ❑   Explain what composite information systems are
- ❑   Discuss Java and other new generation architectures and their role in EAI

What Is Enterprise Application Integration?

EAI is basically a new name for the integration process that companies have been working on for years. EAI addresses integration globally and systematically. With this in mind, let's first discuss the need for integration. This will allow us to pin down the definition of EAI more precisely, and to consider the requirements for successful application integration.

Why Do We Need to Integrate Applications?

In the past, applications were thought of as individual solutions to isolated problems. The architects did not think of those applications as of parts of an enterprise-wide information system. This is why the majority of older applications allow only very limited interoperability with other applications. To modify applications in order to make them more interoperable, a good understanding of the application's development and processes is required, but unfortunately there is often little (if any) application documentation that can provide this information. Even today, some applications are developed with little or no concern given to how to connect them with other systems. For these reasons, EAI is as relevant to both existing legacy systems and to modern solutions.

The reason for EAI lies in business expectations. From the business viewpoint, the goal is to maximize the benefits of each application and the information system as a whole. Separate applications cannot fulfil both of these requirements.

Part of the problem is that the data is partitioned and replicated between the different applications. Each application models the data differently, according to the needs of the application, not the whole company. This makes it difficult to join the data from different applications, since we must use different technologies, applications, and database products to access the data, and we need to understand how the data is modeled in each application. Obtaining the global picture of the data can therefore be very difficult for a "normal" user, so valuable information is often locked away in these applications that could be shared and distributed to all new groups of information consumers: remote employees, business partners and customers, to name just a few.

In addition, separate applications are often unsuitable for supporting modern front-end applications such as web access, business-to-business, and business-to-customer collaborations – for example integrating back-office applications with a front-end customer web-order system.

In order to stay competitive, companies must modernize and improve the functionality of their information systems. Managers see the information system as a tool through which they can maximize the company benefits. They are prepared to invest in it because they know what return of investment they can expect; they can foresee the efficiency increase and the productivity boost.

Improving the functionality of an information system is possible in several ways. The most obvious way is to replace the old applications with a freshly developed solution. Even if, at first sight, this seems an attractive solution, we can easily see why it is inapplicable in most cases. Developing and debugging new software overnight is impossible; also, migration of live (in-use) systems can incur significant costs.

Likewise, it is unfeasible to introduce commercial solutions, like ERP systems, in any great hurry. Each company evolves like a living organism, with a distinctive way of doing business, and its distinctive properties must be reflected in a business' information systems. Adapting commercial solutions to reflect this requires time, and time is money. Introducing new systems also requires training and educating the personnel.

Replacing existing systems with new solutions always requires more time and more money than previously planned, even in the most pessimistic scenarios. Incorporating all the peculiarities and special cases in the software requires time and knowledge. This becomes much easier if the company has its business processes well documented, but there are few companies with detailed documentation for *all* of the business processes applicable to the solution. Often, there is no single person that understands the entire process.

So, it is clear that replacing existing systems with new solutions will often not be a viable proposition. Too much time and money has been invested in the systems, and there is too much knowledge locked into them. Therefore, we need a standard way to reuse existing systems but integrate them into the global, enterprise-wide information system.

Defining EAI

We are now ready to define Enterprise Application Integration a little more accurately. Actually, the definition of EAI varies depending upon your viewpoint.

From the business perspective, EAI is the competitive advantage a company gets when all applications are integrated into a unified information system, capable of sharing information and supporting business workflows. Information must often be gathered from several domains and integrated into a business process. Without EAI, although the required information may well be available and exist in some form somewhere in an application, for typical users it is practically impossible to access it online.

From the technical perspective, EAI refers to the process of integrating different applications and data, to enable sharing of data and integration of business processes among applications without having to modify these existing applications (too much). EAI must be performed using methods and activities that enable it to be effective in terms of costs and time.

As you can see, there is no short and simple definition of what EAI actually is. So, let's consider how others have tried to pin down its definition. The Webopedia (http://www.webopedia.com/) states that:

> *"EAI is the unrestricted sharing of data and business processes throughout the networked applications or data sources in an organization. Early software programs in areas such as inventory control, human resources, sales automation, and database management were designed to run independently, with no interaction between the systems. They were custom built in the technology of the day for a specific need being addressed and were often proprietary systems. As enterprises grow and recognize the need for their information and applications to have the ability to be transferred across and shared between systems, companies are investing in EAI in order to streamline processes and keep all the elements of the enterprise interconnected."*

Furthermore, Whatis.com (http://www.whatis.com) has a similar definition of EAI:

> *"EAI is a business computing term for the plans, methods, and tools aimed at modernizing, consolidating, and coordinating the computer applications in an enterprise. Typically, an enterprise has existing legacy applications and databases and wants to continue to use them while adding or migrating to a new set of applications that exploit the Internet, e-commerce, extranet, and other new technologies. EAI may involve developing a new total view of an enterprise's business and its applications, seeing how existing applications fit into the new view, and then devising ways to efficiently reuse what already exists while adding new applications and data."*

Although these definitions sound reasonably simple, many people believe that EAI is one of the most chaotic fields. They believe that identifying problems and selecting solutions can be time consuming and requires a lot of knowledge and that often even a "sixth sense" is necessary in order to succeed with the integration.

> **Although we shouldn't overlook the fact that integration requires a lot of knowledge and is complex, we will show that with a disciplined and systematic approach, integration can be performed in a controlled manner with very good chance of success – without the need for a "sixth sense".**

The fact is that large companies have several applications that should work together. Integration projects are those that make this happen, and they differ from other projects. They tend to be much more complex. This is probably why companies are spending a lot of money on integration and the predictions just confirm that. The Gartner Group (http://www.gartner.com/), for example, predicts that companies will spend around 5 billion US dollars on integration by 2005. Ovum believes that companies will spend around 1.5 billion US dollars in 2002 just buying the middleware necessary for integration. Other predictions show that companies will have to spend as much as 60% of the total IT budget for integration purposes, which will be distributed equally among consulting, software, and hardware.

There are also several approaches to integration. For example, we could make it on a data level, a point-to-point level (where two applications are sharing 'chunks' of data), or a method level, allowing them to share functionality as well (not only data). In each case, what we aim to do is essentially enable interoperability between different applications – in other words, getting apples and oranges to speak to each other.

EAI projects will have to deal with existing applications, but will also have to provide ways to include recently-developed applications too. Some of the existing applications are older, based on technologies that today are not considered "state-of-the-art", on programming languages that are not used often anymore, and on platforms earlier than current; these are known as legacy applications. We will use the term **legacy application** or **legacy system** for any system that, regardless of age, conforms to the following conditions:

- ❏ Is in use and is useful today.
- ❏ Uses an obsolete/out-of-date system architecture. We will define what we mean by a modern architecture later in this chapter.

In accordance with this definition, there are two main sets of legacy systems:

- ❏ Traditional monolithic, mostly mainframe-based systems
- ❏ Client/server systems, which are mostly PC-based

Other existing applications are newer, and use modern architectures, developed with modern technologies, programming languages and platforms. We will refer to these as **modern applications**. Still, these modern architectures, technologies, languages and platforms often differ from those on which we will base the integration. Therefore they will need to be integrated too. We will refer to all existing applications, legacy applications and modern applications, using the term **existing applications**.

The results of Deloitte and Touche show that, "approximately 75% of the operational information systems are legacy systems". This changes the nature of the integration project somewhat. You can have an integration project that involves only newly developed systems and this situation is what we all would wish to work on. In new systems we have the possibility to design from the ground up and to prepare applications for integration. This is considerably different from an integration project where existing applications are involved. Taking existing applications into account is often difficult. Existing applications probably do not have documentation or interoperability interfaces, and they may be based on technologies that we are not familiar with. Additional constraints are incurred because we should not destabilize existing applications and we must cope with the fact that at least some of the legacy systems will be replaced in the near future.

Requirements for Successful EAI

For application integration to succeed, companies must have an **integration strategy**. Management must support the integration process and provide the necessary priorities to enable a centralized control and management for the integration. There must be clear requirements specifying what is expected from an integrated system so goals can be established.

An important aspect of integration is the relevance of existing applications. Every company has to be aware whether the existing system still meets its requirements and when the time to renew it is. If the application does not meet its requirement anymore, efficient ways have to be found to re-engineer, renew, or upgrade it.

This means that there is a trade-off between the cost of redesigning and reimplementing an application and the cost of maintaining an inadequate one. Maintaining existing systems can become very costly; when to actually replace these systems is now a key business decision. How to replace them on the other hand is a technical decision. However, the overall architecture of the information system should be designed so that it supports easy renewal of selected parts, without influence or with only limited influence on other parts of the information system. This is a very important aspect to bear in mind when defining the integration architecture.

Not all companies will benefit from integration equally. Of course, if a company has only a limited number of systems, which share technology and architecture, integration becomes much easier. Conversely, there may be several different large-scale applications that are widely geographically distributed on several different platforms, some of which have overlapping functionality. In this case, the system will clearly benefit from EAI considerably. This situation is not that rare and can occur when a company has been merged with another company, if it has no strategy for information system development, or if it has experienced uncontrolled growth.

To summarize, to integrate successfully it is necessary to assess the health of existing systems, to analyze the requirements of the system, and to match the current situation with the goals and requirements. This is best done on a case-by-case basis, because it is not easy to define universal metrics.

We have already noted that an understanding of existing systems is vital to successful EAI. Let's now take a closer look at these existing systems.

A Closer Look At Existing Applications

In this section we will set the scene by looking at the different kinds of existing applications that we may be required to work with. We have already identified the distinction between legacy and modern applications. Legacy applications were developed at a time in the past when there was usually little need to consider enterprise architectures. The majority of legacy systems were designed to support the needs of individual functional business domains, not those of the entire enterprise. Such systems have a limited focus and are unable to grow or to evolve easily.

Most legacy systems were developed from technical models rather than from business models. The technical decisions were made on an individual basis because no company-wide strategies were defined regarding which technologies should be used. Often the technology selected was down to individual developers, or even other companies to which the projects have been outsourced. This led to a typical current situation in which many companies have several different open and propriety technologies, such as programming languages, database management systems, operating systems, platforms, networking, and so on. Furthermore, legacy systems are crucial for companies and they therefore cannot afford to write them off. Large amounts of data reside in legacy databases. Another huge problem is the unavailability of source code for many legacy systems, which has been lost or destroyed, mostly accidentally.

Legacy Application Architectures

Most old applications were developed using **monolithic** architectures. A monolithic architecture joins presentation, business logic, and data management into a single monolithic application. Such applications are structurally-oriented and written in one of the structural languages, such as COBOL, Fortran, PL/I, among others. There even exist rare systems that are written in Assembler. In these cases, data is usually stored in files using different binary formats. Systems commonly contain hundreds of thousands of lines of code that has been developed and maintained over the years by different developers. Usually there is no documentation and, worryingly, the source code can often become lost, or nobody really knows if the source code reflects the same executable version that is currently in use. The majority of such systems reside on mainframe computers. It is probably needless to say that initially there was no integration among different monolithic applications. However, integration of those solutions was first performed some three decades ago.

> The healthcare industry was among the first to realize the need to integrate monolithic applications. Healthcare companies are typical for initiating integration: they have a lot of departments that were not managed centrally, and therefore each department had a unique solution, with none of them connected together. The fact is that a patient usually goes to several departments for their treatment. There was therefore a necessity to integrate the partial solutions and to improve the efficiency of work. In addition, healthcare companies usually do not have large budgets for IT, so they could not afford to replace their systems overnight or to outsource the integration. It did not take long for other companies to follow – they quickly realized that integrating different applications could save a lot of work and thus make the company much more efficient.

The first attempts at monolithic integration were to merely link different applications to a central database:

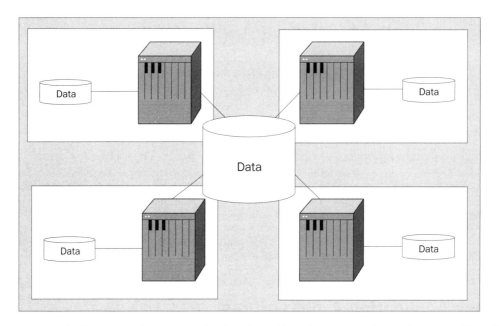

The central database often did not store the data from all applications, so the applications still needed local databases too. The main reasons for this were capacity and performance related. Data thought of as important for the whole company was stored in the central database, and less important data was persisted locally – in many cases, because needs and priorities change over time, the kind of data defined as being important to the whole company changed too. You should note that this type of integration required the reprogramming of each application.

From a technical perspective, such database integration was not too difficult when there was only one platform in the company, possibly a mainframe computer, and if there were not very many applications. However, there were many companies that did not fall into this category. More specifically, even in the era of mainframe systems, some of the larger companies maintained numerous different applications that processed (sometimes related) data from different perspectives. As applications were not initially designed to interoperate, changing them to use the same database was a difficult task.

The process of **downsizing** (replacing the mainframe computers with networks of PCs) made things even more complicated. In the 1980s, there were few companies in which the downsizing was centrally controlled. There was little in the way of standardized information strategies to define which architectures, platforms, and technologies to use. Due to the lack of strategy, the information technologist in each department had a free hand to select the technology, and they usually did so based on personal preferences, not on the objectives of the whole enterprise.

Downsizing brought with it some big changes in application architecture. Monolithic architectures could not fulfill the needs of the user anymore. On one hand there were growing integration needs; on the other hand networked PCs started to replace 'dumb' terminals. As it was necessary to share the data among the users, monolithic applications became unsuitable.

The solution to these problems was the **client/server architecture** that separates applications into two tiers. In the majority of cases, the data management was separated from the rest of the application. This meant that the business logic and user interface were still joined, and in too many cases interconnected. Because the client performed most of the processing involved in the business logic, this kind of client/server applications have become known as thick or fat (or even rich) clients. However the data was separated off, it usually resided on one of several dedicated DBMS (Database Management System) servers:

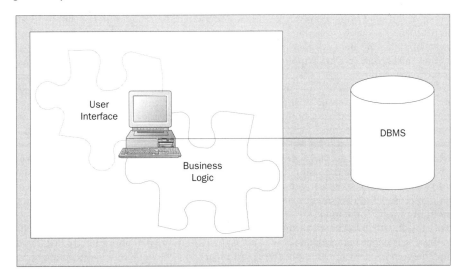

This architecture made access to system data from different applications much easier; however, it relied on correct and consistent business logic implementation across client implementations. Most of the newly-developed applications were using the client/server architecture, but existing monolithic solutions remained too. The need to integrate systems became even more pressing.

The other possibility for client/server systems was to separate the business logic from the client, and put it on the server:

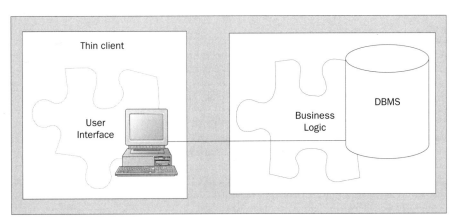

In this scenario the client-side code was obviously much lighter, so this is often called thin client architecture. The business logic was either stored on the DBMS server in the form of stored procedures written as SQL statements, or on a server tightly coupled to the database. Most DBMSs support stored procedures, although there are variations in their syntax and capabilities, creating another potential problem: moving this logic from one DBMS to another is an extremely painful procedure, if not practically impossible. Whatever the case, we can see that the client/server architecture means a tight coupling between the applications and the database.

The number of different applications in a company increased. Although different applications targeted different problems, in many cases there was some functional overlapping between them. For example, the account booking and the customer management applications both required a customer database. Let's say that the account booking application already existed. The customer management application requires more detailed records of customers. Often the developers did not make the effort needed to introduce the new data attributes into the existing customer database. Instead they introduced another customer database, with different attributes. In this case, we not only have similar customer data residing in two separate databases, but the names and data format for the data in each database (such as IDs, primary keys, other attributes) will be different. Resolving this problem can be an arduous job.

However, it was soon realized that accessing the same data is not the solution to all integration problems either. Accessing the data and possibly transferring it between databases is not enough because it is very difficult to analyze such data to get valuable business information for decision support. It is also impossible to reuse all of the functionality from another application. Without reusing functionality the only possibility was to implement the functionality in different applications, thus increasing the complexity again, which becomes particularly visible when dealing with maintenance. Duplicating functionality is also necessary because if we access the data in the database directly, we avoid business rules implemented in the original application; this means that we have to be very cautious because direct database access could threaten data integrity.

To solve the problems of analyzing large amounts of data stored in different applications, and to enable sharing the application functionality, data warehouses and enterprise resource planning systems started to emerge.

Data Warehouses and ERP Systems

At the beginning of the 1990s, integration became an important issue from two distinct viewpoints.

One issue was the use of **data warehouses**. A data warehouses is a central repository for all of the significant data that the company's applications collect. The data from those applications is selectively extracted and organized into the data warehouse. Due to the variety of good structured data contained within them, data warehouses were (and still are) effective as off-line executive and decision support systems, and useful anywhere where raw data has to be analyzed and conclusions need to be derived from such analysis.

The data from application databases is usually moved to data warehouses at certain time intervals, most commonly once per day. Therefore data warehouses are not the perfect choice for integration, especially where we cannot afford to work with data that may be out-of-date. The procedures associated with a data warehouse system might look something like that shown in the diagram opposite, where the data from different databases are extracted, transformed, and loaded to the central data warehouse. The rules for these three stages are defined as meta-data:

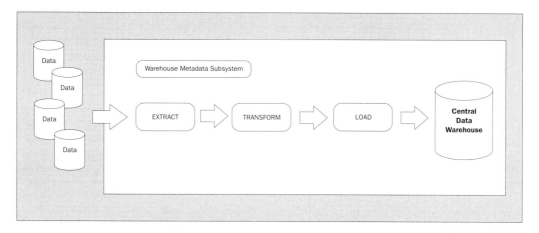

The second issue was the use of **Enterprise Resource Planning (ERP)** systems. ERP systems are business management systems, typically implemented by a single vendor as a set of integrated applications that cover all facets of the business, including planning, manufacturing, sales, and marketing. The idea was to use ERP systems to cover all of the information needs of an enterprise. Several leading manufacturers, including SAP, Baan, PeopleSoft, and others, have worked hard to provide broad coverage of different business domains.

Unfortunately, experience has shown that ERP systems cannot fulfill the information needs of a company completely. ERP systems are very large and very complex. Although source code is available for some of them, vendors do not want customized changes made to it. However, there are so many curiosities and idiosyncrasies in each company that need to be covered on an individual basis, and companies today have to react quickly to adapt to market changes too. This almost always requires modifications or additions in the information system, and waiting for the solutions from large suppliers of ERP systems is not practical. Various market research results suggest that ERP systems typically cover only 25-40% of the information needs of an enterprise (the rest is covered by other application software, including in-house solutions, some of them developed with visual and productivity tools). This may seem a surprisingly low percentage, but the suppliers of ERP systems have become aware of the problem. This is why the majority of them today offer ways to integrate ERP systems with other software.

Reviewing the Current Landscape

If we sum up, the situation today is that companies are faced with a disparate mix of heterogeneous existing systems on which their business depends. Unfortunately this mix of different systems has not been designed in any unified manner – it just grew, and will continue to grow. Heterogeneity thus drains the development resources. Instead of creating solutions to new problems, too many developers spend a considerable amount of time and resources porting old solutions instead. In addition, there are a finite number of computers in most enterprises.

The most critical applications for many companies are the transaction processing applications, such as order entry, shipping, billing, and receivables. These applications have often been developed over many years, the developers have been swapped several times, and today there is hardly anyone who fully understands them. Some of them are still running from mainframe systems, some are even packaged applications, which are very difficult to modify. Companies are understandably reluctant to modify or replace any of these applications. The dilemma then becomes how to modernize them without jeopardizing operations.

On the other hand, there are analysis applications that need to access certain information stored in different databases, according to defined business needs. They should be developed in the shortest possible time; however, this is not always the case. Even seemingly simple analysis applications can be very difficult to write when the relevant data resides in diverse applications in different, incompatible databases and formats, incompatible platforms, and spread over different departments or divisions.

The problem can become even more difficult if the company has been integrated with other companies, whose information systems have not yet been fully integrated and are not understood very well. Fragmented information systems, whether in format, organization, or geography, greatly complicate the development.

As well as different platforms and application systems, most companies have used different programming models over time. This diversity is manifested through:

❑   Combinations of monolithic, client/server, and multi-tier applications

❑   Mix of procedural and object-oriented solutions

❑   Mix of programming languages

❑   Different types of database management systems (relational, hierarchical, object)

❑   Different middleware solutions for communication (message-oriented middleware, object request brokers, remote procedure calls)

❑   Multiple information transmission models, including publish/subscribe, request/reply, and conversational

❑   Different transaction and security management middleware

❑   Different ways of sharing data

❑   Possible use of EDI, XML, and other proprietary formats for data exchange

Differences in programming models make it difficult not only to integrate solutions, but are sometimes an obstacle for communication between developers.

Companies often did not have defined strategies for information systems development. This is manifested in by-product or departmental computing, which means that each department had the freedom to choose technologies and developed solutions on its own. Consequently, multiple "information islands" appeared. Applications in these information islands can be everything up to and including the key business applications. Information islands make the company-wide integration much more difficult than it should be.

By some estimates, it is not unusual for a large company to have over one thousand information islands, and a total of more than five thousand individual applications. Integrating applications, however, means much more than just accessing different DBMS and enabling application interoperability by putting them on the same bus.

Connectivity is not sufficient because information islands were not designed to interoperate. Therefore each island will have its own semantics – its own meaning for business objects such as customer, order, invoice, and so on. There will also be partial redundancy with other information islands. Semantic incompatibilities make the integration particularly challenging.

When implementing the integration, developers will therefore be faced with a diversity of systems, including:

- ❑ Self-developed solutions

- ❑ Custom-built but outsourced solutions

- ❑ Commercial and ERP systems

Another important aspect is any integration that has already been implemented between the legacy systems. This includes everything from simple data exchange to use of middleware products (an obvious choice for integration). In terms of legacy systems the most commonly used middleware are MOM (or messaging systems in general), and RPC (Remote Procedure Call). These integrations have usually been implemented on an application-to-application basis. As the number of applications increased so did the number of integration links between them. The problem with such integration is that it is very difficult to maintain these links when something changes in an involved application. We will address this in more detail in Chapter 2.

In addition to all this diversity of architectures, technologies, platforms and programming languages, companies are introducing new applications, based upon modern application architectures, too.

Modern Application Architectures

Any modern application architecture must fulfill the need for rapid solution development, possibly with the composition of pre-prepared pieces of software. On the other hand, modern application architecture also should support maintainability, flexibility, security, scalability, and other such important properties. The current solution to this is to use multi-tier architectures, the most common of which contain three (or more) tiers:

- ❑ **Presentation or user interface tier**
  Where user services such as input, dialog, and display management are handled

- ❑ **Business logic or middle tier**
  Provides business logic services that are shared by different applications

- ❑ **Data persistence tier**
  Provides database management and other related functionalities

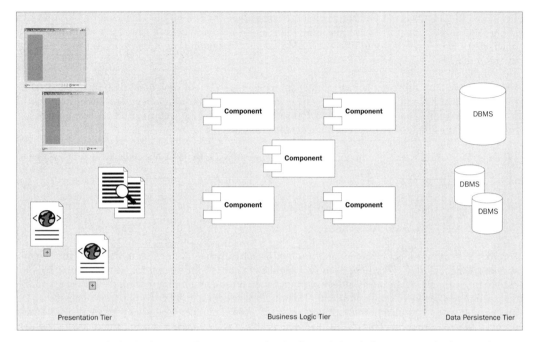

Each tier, particularly the business logic tier, can be further subdivided into several sub-tiers that we refer to in terms of multi-tier logical architecture. We'll now turn our attention to what can be described as the building blocks of each tier – **components**.

Components are pieces of executable code that implement a certain functionality. This functionality is exposed to the rest of the architecture through one or more interfaces. Components are strongly encapsulated; they hide their internal details from their clients. The only way a client can access a component is through the interface.

Other components access the interface of a component using high-level abstraction. They do not need to worry about the implementation of this (in addition to communication and location). Middleware takes care of all the communication details and thus enables seamless interoperability between component A and component B on different tiers, locations, and different platforms. Actually middleware hides the low-level details, providing a unified view on components. This idea is schematically presented in the next figure:

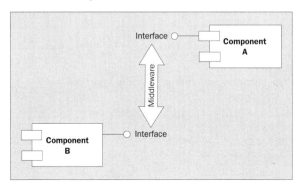

Components are a way of packing the executable code. They are not an implementation technique per se, although components often get confused with objects. It is true that components and objects share many concepts, such as interfaces and encapsulation. However, components differ from objects in that components provide larger, possibly coarser-grained functionality with not too many relations to other components. Any client can use the services provided by the component, no matter what programming language the component is written in, where it is located, or what its internal structure is. It is not necessary for components to be implemented with OO programming languages; although it makes sense to use an OO approach for developing new components, it is not a problem to implement a component using other non-OO (even legacy) approaches. This is particularly important when concerned with EAI, where we are faced with such a diversity of existing and new applications.

We have already mentioned that components can be found in different layers. The components on the user interface tier differ from those on the business logic tier. The most obvious difference is that the user interface tier components will have to provide some kind of visual representation, while the middle tier (or business process tier) components will mainly provide services.

Components are developed using component models. They provide the environment in which components execute. Popular component models for the presentation tier are JavaBeans, and Microsoft ActiveX. Popular business logic tier component models include CORBA (Common Object Request Broker Architecture), EJB (Enterprise JavaBeans), and Microsoft COM+ (Component Object Model). We will talk more about these component models in the later chapters.

Although it requires more effort to build multi-tier component applications, the benefits are obvious and numerous:

❑ **Integration and reusability**
  Business process components perform a set of operations that are described and accessed through the interface. The interfaces enable the interoperability between components and promote the reuse of functionality.

❑ **Encapsulation**
  Components on each tier are strongly encapsulated. The only way to access the component is through the interface. The client of the component does not know and does not have to know the internal details of a component. This encapsulation enables us to replace the implementation of a component without influencing the rest of the system, so long as the interface and the functionality remain unchanged.

❑ **Distribution**
  The access to components is not limited to a single computer or even a single process. They can be distributed (and/or replicated) among computers without modifications in source code of client components. Communication details are handled by the middleware layer, which achieves location transparency.

❑ **Partitioning**
  Moving the functionality into three or more tiers enables us to build thin clients, and solves the problems with tight coupling of the business logic to the persistence layer. By using abstraction layers we can achieve flexible deployment options and configurations.

❑ **Scalability**
  Matching the capacity of the middle tier to the client demands (by implementing performance optimization techniques) and the ability to physically distribute and replicate the critical components, enables good control over scalability over a long time period.

❑ **Enhanced performance**
Applications can take advantages of server-side optimization techniques, like multiprocessing, multithreading, pooling, resource and instance management, and thread management, without changing code and allowing dynamic configuration changes.

❑ **Improved reliability**
Single points of failure, as well as bottlenecks, can be eliminated using replication and distribution.

❑ **Manageability**
With the separation of code into multiple tiers it is much easier to locate the components that need to be modified. Most frequently changed is the business logic, so locating this in a separate tier means that changes there do not require costly and time-consuming reinstallations. Rather, they can be managed centrally.

❑ **Increased consistency and flexibility**
As long as the interfaces between the tiers and the interfaces inside the tier stay unchanged, the code can be modified without impact on other parts of the system. In multi-tier architectures it is much easier to adapt the information system to changing business needs. Another advantage of this is that a change to a business tier component will affect all applications that utilize that component, enhancing consistency.

❑ **Support for multiple clients**
Different kinds of clients can access the business logic through the same interface.

❑ **Independent development**
Components can be developed independently of other components. Interfaces between components define the contract between them, and this enables independent development (as long as the contracts are respected).

❑ **Rapid development**
Application developers can focus on rapidly developing and deploying the business functionality, while remaining transparent to the underlying infrastructure. Components can be used in unpredictable combinations to form applications.

❑ **Packaging**
Components can be packaged in a variety of ways, which provides great flexibility for deployment.

❑ **Configurability**
Different implementations of the same logical component can be readily interchanged at run-time, enabling you to provide the capabilities that you need without redesigning applications.

On the flip side, we've already noted that initially it takes more effort to build multi-tier solutions. There are other disadvantages too:

❑ **Possible poor performance and scalability**
Multi-tier architectures introduce remote invocation operations that pack a considerable performance hit. Also, the large numbers of clients that access business-tier components simultaneously introduce scalability problems. Therefore, unless we understand and address these issues when designing the architecture, multi-tier applications can end up providing poor performance and scalability.

❑ **Security risks**
Since multi-tier architectures are based upon easy access to business logic services, steps must to be taken to see that measures are applied which will prevent unauthorized access to the business logic tier.

❑ **Component management**
Multi-tier architectures require distribution and linking of components, which creates an additional management burden.

Finally, the logical multi-tier architecture described above has to be mapped to the physical architecture. Often, the physical architecture will imitate the logical, physically separating the client tier, the middle tier and the data persistence tier, assigning each tier to one or several computers, depending on the needs, application size, number of clients, and so on. However, we do not have to map each logical tier to a separate physical tier. Gathering the tiers together physically is sometimes beneficial from a performance perspective, because it minimizes communication times.

In web-based systems, we often expose the web component tier (that manages the web presentation logic) as another separate tier, as shown in the diagram below:

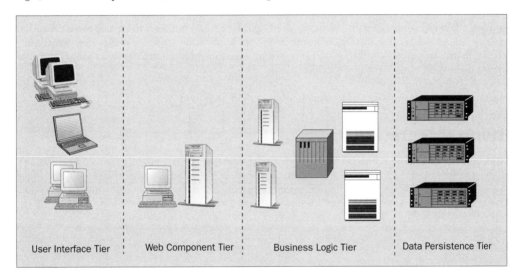

| User Interface Tier | Web Component Tier | Business Logic Tier | Data Persistence Tier |

The reason for doing this is that this tier actually takes over some of the tasks of the presentation tier and some of the business logic tier's tasks too, but it is located near the business logic tier. This is advantageous because the web component tier often requires considerable communication with the business logic tier, and it can provide some security services as well.

Now that we have become familiar with the challenges of EAI, and with the different architectures we will be faced with, let's focus on possible solutions. In the next section we will discuss how we can address the challenges of integration.

Application Integration Layers

There is no simple answer to the demands of EAI. Rather, the integration architecture is built step-by-step in several layers. The idea behind this is to break the problem into several smaller problems and solve each subproblem step-by-step (similar to the way in which network architecture is broken up into layers, as defined by ISO OSI). We have to start building the EAI architecture at the lowest layer and climb, step-by-step. The most important processes in application integration are:

❏ Platform (hardware) integration

❏ Data level integration

❏ Application interface integration

❏ Business method integration

❏ Presentation integration

❏ Inter-EAI or business-to-business (B2B) integration

Omitting a layer is a short-term solution to speed up the process, but we will almost certainly have to pay back this time later in the integration process. Both application interface and business method integration are sometimes combined and referred to as business level integration, because they share some of the concepts, as we will see in Chapter 9.

Let's now examine these layers of application integration individually.

Platform Integration

Platform (hardware) integration is the prerequisite for enabling the overall integration. The goal is to achieve the interoperability of different platforms, for example mainframes with different operating systems like VMS, MVS, and OS/400, PC computers with Windows, Linux, and workstations with Solaris, HP-UX, AIX, among others. Platform integration is schematically shown on the next figure:

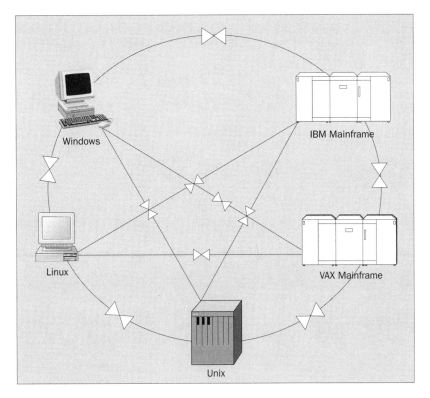

Today, most hardware platforms use open standards, so achieving their interoperability and integration is often not very difficult.

However, difficulties can arise with the integration of old platforms that vendors do not support anymore. Also, systems that have not been maintained over the years and use old versions of operating systems may provide difficulties, because they might not support the required interoperability. The upgrade to new versions may provide unexpected problems when we attempt to execute important applications on them. Platform integration also becomes a concern if some proprietary solutions or products have been used in the past.

Data Level Integration

Data level integration is often the starting point of application integration. Data-level integration enables access to the data shared by other applications and allows data to be moved between different data stores. The following figure schematically presents the integration of three databases through uni- or bi-directional data accesses:

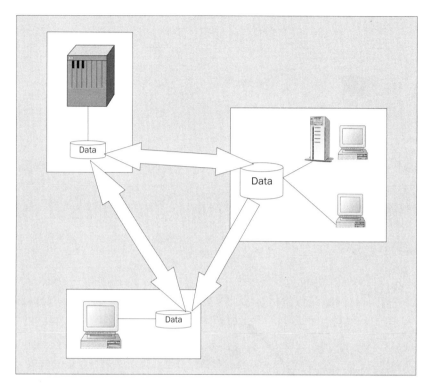

Data-level integration might sound simple, but it can become quite difficult to manage when several hundred data stores are involved. Typical difficulties that we might encounter include understanding the schemas, identifying the data, guaranteeing data consistency, problems with distributed databases, latency with updating them, and so on.

In addition, it is necessary to unify the data model, solving data redundancy and semantic abnormalities that have been introduced in the information systems during their development over the years. This is also called schema integration, and can be a difficult task. We will discuss it further in Chapter 5.

An advantage of data-level integration is that it often does not require changes in the source code of existing applications.

Application Interface Integration

Application interface integration enables a higher-level form of integration, where an application can use some functionality residing in other applications. This is achieved using the application programming interfaces (APIs) that the applications expose. Often, a form of middleware is involved for transferring the requests and results, such as message-oriented middleware (MOM), remote procedure calls (RPC), and even object request brokers (ORB). We will discuss middleware and its role in EAI a little later in this chapter.

It is very important to understand that application integration solves only technical aspects of integration. In other words, the applications are using technology oriented, low-level interfaces to achieve interoperability, not business methods. Application interface integration, however, solves several problems; in particular we can reuse functionality without having to duplicate it. The next figure illustrates the reuse of functionality; applications invoke functions on each other through their APIs:

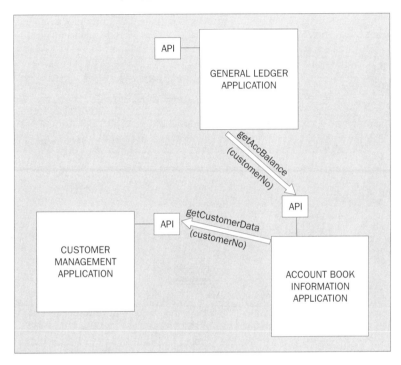

Attempting application interface integration, however, can incur many problems, including the lack of APIs, incompatibilities between them, dependence on a particular middleware technology, and problems with integration of middleware products. We will address these problems in later chapters.

Business Method Integration

As we have seen above, application integration is about low-level, technical integration between applications. It does not concern the higher-level, business method integration. Business method integration enables uncompromised support for business processes in the enterprise, where existing solutions take part in distinctive steps of the business process. It exposes the high-level methods as abstractions of business methods through interfaces.

Business method integration presents the enterprise wide information system as we would like to have it – or as we would build it if we could build it anew, with clear requirements about what we would like to get from the integrated system and with the knowledge and support of modern technologies. This means that information system interfaces are based on a modern architecture. However, the functionalities are not reimplemented; rather, they use existing applications. Those existing applications are remodeled in such a way that they expose the functionality of the business process tier and fit into the modern application architecture.

Achieving business method integration is often connected with business process re-engineering and is not a solely technical problem. It requires the implementation of several technical layers as the foundation and integrates applications at a higher level of abstraction.

The figure below presents a high-level business process component that provides a function through a remote API on the business logic tier: for example, the calculation of the current balance of a cell phone account:

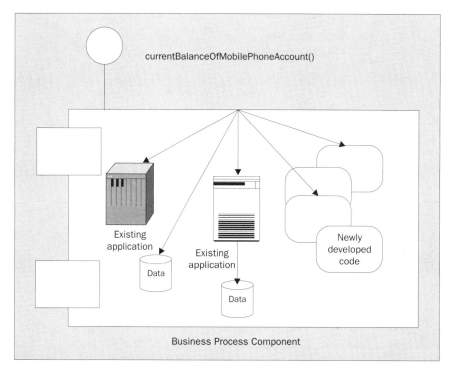

To implement this, the component reuses the functionality of several existing systems and some newly-developed systems. In Chapter 4, we will see that the calculation of the current cell phone account can be a difficult task, because it has to include the information from different applications, including deposits on the account (for pre-paid telephones), domestic and international class, and possible payments performed using the cell phone (parking fee for example). Different applications can use the component to fulfil support for business processes.

Presentation Integration

Often, after achieving business method integration, we will move on to presentation integration. Since existing applications are now remodeled and encapsulated on the middle tier where they expose their functionality through high-level interfaces, it becomes crucial that the user gets a unified view on the information system as well. As long as the user has to switch between legacy applications, they will be aware that they are using old applications.

With the development of a unified presentation tier we hide the fact that in the background different applications, some legacy and others newly developed, are executing. This way we improve the efficiency of end users, because they do not have to switch between different existing applications and use different existing user interfaces. With a unified presentation tier we also provide a way to replace parts of legacy systems in the future without influencing the other parts of the system.

The figure below shows how the user interface components from the presentation tier access the business logic components. Some of them implement their operations through reuse of existing systems, the others use newly-developed components. Both look exactly the same to the presentation tier components:

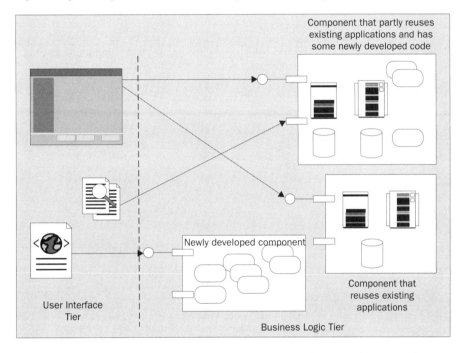

Implementing these integration steps brings us to the desired multi-tier architecture of an integrated enterprise-wide information system. The integrated information system still contains legacy applications, but these are now integrated and take their part in the multi-tier architecture. To achieve this, we will have to use different middleware technologies. We will discuss these a little later on, in the context of the J2EE platform.

Inter-EAI or Business-to-Business Integration

Today even the integration of applications within a company is often not sufficient. There is a growing need to enable inter-enterprise integration, often referred to as **business-to-business (B2B)** integration, or e-business. E-Business poses new challenges for an information system. The requirements today are very high and gone are the days where a company could just publish offline catalogs on their web pages. Online, up-to-date information, delivered with efficiency, reliability, and quality is expected. Even well-known names from traditional businesses cannot expect that their position will be maintained in an e-business environment without effort.

Of course, the prerequisite for efficient e-business or B2B integration is an integrated enterprise information system, possibly on the business process level, which must be implemented at both ends. Only this level of integration allows on-demand processing of requests. Customers today expect immediate response, and are not satisfied with batch processing and several days of delays in confirming orders.

However, these delays are often the case when e-business is not backed by an efficiently integrated enterprise information system. Immediate responsiveness, achieved by the highly-coupled integration of the back end (enterprise information systems) and the front-end (presentation) systems is a key success factor. Although this sounds obvious, research from leading consulting companies such as the Gartner Group shows that today there are very few front-end systems that are efficiently integrated with the back-end. Most of these non-integrated applications will fail to meet business expectations. The primary reason is the lack of enterprise integration, which is the most important prerequisite for both a successful e-business and an efficient company.

In the next figure we can see the typical e-business interaction between four companies:

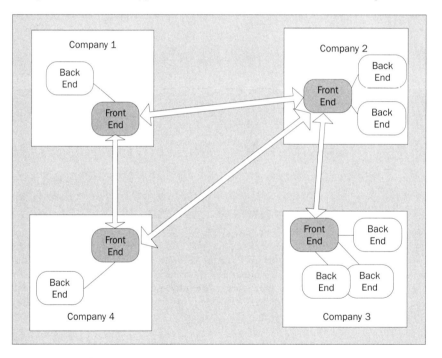

Applications from one company are invoking operations on front-end applications belonging to another company. Only if these front-end systems are satisfactorily connected with back-end systems will the other company will be able to provide an immediate and accurate response, which is a prerequisite for successful B2B collaboration: one company's application will not be willing to wait too long for the result.

Another important fact is that most front-end applications can use existing and legacy systems as back-end solutions. Making the integration between such systems efficient will be the key success factor. In particular, immediate response and immediate propagation of data to all related applications will be the major issue. Front-end applications not efficiently supported by back-end systems will certainly fail to meet all requirements. Although this prediction is reasonable, even by 2005 more than a half of front-end systems will not be adequately integrated, according to prognoses from industry research and advisory organizations such as the GartnerGroup.

To achieve a seamless B2B integration, companies will have to implement intra-EAI first and then using the same or comparable technologies to enable B2B connectivity. As EAI and B2B are closely related, we will focus on using the same technologies for both goals, but in different variations. In Chapter 18 we will also look at specific B2B technologies, like Web Services and e-marketplaces.

The Composite Information System Approach

So far we have seen that EAI is not only relevant to "old stuff". EAI redefines the approaches of integration with the goal of becoming more time and cost effective. To make these approaches work in real life, we have to define the integration architecture that will support the approaches and concepts presented so far. The integration architecture should provide the basis for an enterprise-wide information system that will benefit from the synergy provided by the integration of different applications. We have two goals to fulfill:

❑   We have to define an architecture that will make it possible to reuse existing applications. We should take advantage of the existing system's information and code when developing enterprise architectures.

❑   The architecture should easily accommodate new generation applications, providing a scalable architecture that will allow us to easily make changes and modifications in the future. The new generation and legacy systems must be able to cooperate with each other too.

There is nothing controversial in stating that for new generation systems we should use the multi-tier application architecture that we have identified earlier. The problem is that existing and legacy systems do not comply with this architecture. Legacy systems do not look like components, which are the building blocks of modern applications.

The challenge, therefore, becomes how to make the existing systems look like components. The solution will be to find ways to encapsulate legacy applications into virtual reusable components that will provide several interfaces and expose the functionality in a universal manner. When accessing these components through the interfaces, we will not care whether we are dealing with a newly developed component, or an encapsulated legacy component; we will access both in the same manner. This is shown on the next figure, where on the business logic tier we can see two virtual components that reuse existing systems, as well as a newly developed component, all exposing their functionality through interfaces:

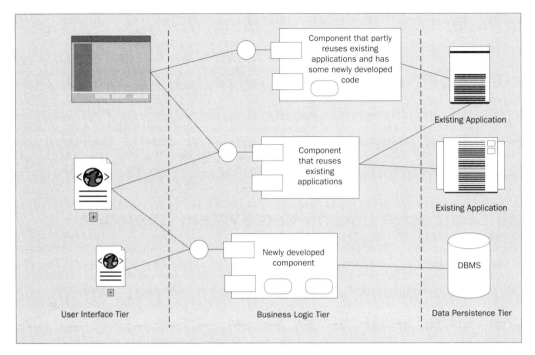

Component that partly reuses existing applications and has some newly developed code

Existing Application

Component that reuses existing applications

Existing Application

Newly developed component

DBMS

User Interface Tier

Business Logic Tier

Data Persistence Tier

Although the proposed idea sounds relatively simple, it is potentially very difficult to implement because of modeling and system issues. If we could find a way of encapsulating existing systems in a way that they would look like new generation components, we would be able to integrate them seamlessly.

In this case, the interface becomes the contract between components in the system, and it abstracts the services provided by the components. From that perspective, the interface has a very important role. As long as the interfaces stay unchanged, we can modify the implementation of the components without influencing the rest of the system. In other words, as long as we use the same interfaces, we can replace existing systems with newly-developed solutions, and none of the clients would ever know that a change has happened. Even better, we will not have to modify the clients in any way.

Therefore it is very important how we define the business logic interfaces. We have to focus on their semantics and define them on a highly abstract level, rather than just exposing the functionality of existing applications, otherwise it would be very difficult to replace existing systems with the new ones and preserve the interface. Consequently, achieving efficient integration is always connected with redesigning the information system as a whole, which is also a good opportunity to perform business process reengineering.

If we follow this process, what we get is a **composite information system**, which reflects the picture of an information system that we would build if we started afresh. On one hand, a composite information system integrates the existing applications, whilst on the other, it reflects the modern application architecture, because it is designed in multi-tier manner and is component-oriented. The big difference is that we will reuse almost all existing applications. The composite information system is a powerful approach for integration that addresses all the requirements of EAI.

To implement the composite information system pattern there are several technology choices, but we will always have to use one or the other form of middleware.

Using Middleware for EAI

Middleware is system services software that executes between the operating system layer and the application layer. It connects two or more applications, providing connectivity and interoperability between the applications. Although middleware has been traditionally used for integration, it is not a silver bullet that can solve all integration problems. Due to over-hyping in the 1980s and early 1990s, the term "middleware" has lost popularity in the last few years. The middleware concept however is today more important for integration than ever, and all integration projects will have to use one or many different middleware solutions.

> **The term "middleware" is used today to denote products that provide glue between applications, distinct from simple data import and export functions that might be built into the applications themselves.**

All forms of middleware are useful for easing the communication between different software applications. The selection of middleware influences the application architecture, because middleware centralizes the software infrastructure and its deployment. Middleware introduces an abstraction layer in the system architecture and thus reduces the complexity considerably. On the other hand, each middleware product introduces a certain communication overhead into the system, which can influence performance, scalability, throughput and other efficiency factors. This is important to consider when designing the integration architecture, particularly if our systems are mission-critical and are used by a large number of concurrent clients.

Middleware products encompass a wide variety of technologies, including:

- ❑ Database access technologies
- ❑ Message-oriented middleware (MOM)
- ❑ Remote procedure calls
- ❑ Transaction processing monitors
- ❑ Object request brokers (ORBs)
- ❑ Application servers
- ❑ Several hybrid and proprietary products

In the following sections, we'll take a closer look at these types of middleware.

Database Access Technologies

Database access technologies provide access to the database through an abstraction layer, which enables us to change the actual DBMS without having to modify the application source code. In other words, it enables us to use the same or similar code to access different database sources.

The technologies differ in the form of the database interfaces they provide. They can offer function-oriented or object-oriented access to databases. The most well-known representatives are JDBC and Java Data Objects (JDO) in the Java platform, and Open Database Connectivity (ODBC) and Active Data Objects (ADO) in the Microsoft platform.

Message Oriented Middleware

Message oriented middleware is a client/server infrastructure that increases interoperability, flexibility and portability of applications. It enables communication between applications over distributed and heterogeneous platforms, and reduces complexity because it hides the communication details and the details of platforms and protocols involved; the functionality of MOM is accessed via APIs. The applications can therefore exchange data without needing to understand the details of the other applications, architectures and platforms involved.

MOM typically resides on both the client and the server side. It provides asynchronous communication, using message queues to store the messages temporarily. Asynchronous communication allows communication even if the receiver is temporarily not available, and these messages can contain almost any type of data. The message waits in the queue and is delivered as soon as the receiver is able to accept it. But asynchronous communication has its disadvantages as well; because the server side does not block the clients, they can continue to accept requests even if it cannot keep pace with them, risking an overload situation.

The figure below shows two applications communicating using MOM. Applications access the MOM through API, and the applications are responsible for constructing and parsing messages, but MOM hides all transport and network details:

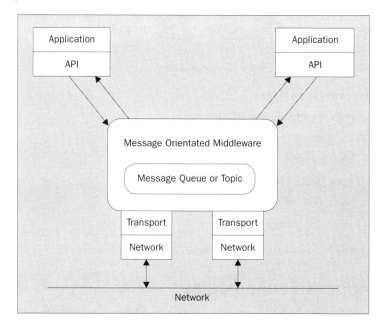

MOM is appropriate for event-driven communication between applications. It is also appropriate for object-oriented systems because it mimics the message sending and receiving communication of OO systems.

MOM products are proprietary products and have been available from the mid-80s, so they are incompatible among each other. Using a single product results in dependence on a specific vendor. This can have a negative influence on flexibility, maintainability, portability and interoperability. The same MOM product must run on each and every platform being integrated. However, not all MOM products support all platforms, operating systems and protocols. We will however see later in the book that the Java platform provides ways how to achieve relatively high independence from a specific vendor through a common interface, used to access all middleware products – the Java Message Service (JMS).

Remote Procedure Calls

Remote procedure calls are also a client/server infrastructure intended to enhance interoperability between applications over heterogeneous platforms. Similar to MOM, it enables communication between software on different platforms and hides almost all of the details of communication. RPC is based in procedural concepts – developers use remote procedure or function calls. First implementations date back to the early 1980s.

The main difference between MOM and RPC is the manner of communication. While MOM supports asynchronous communication, RPC promotes synchronous, request-reply communication (sometimes referred to as "call/wait"), which blocks the client until the server fulfills its requests. The next figure shows two applications communicating using RPC. To achieve remote communication, the applications use procedure calls. RPC middleware hides all of the communication details, which makes using remote procedure calls appear very similar to local procedure calls:

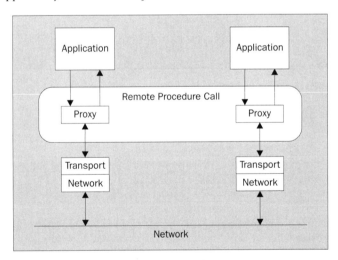

RPC guards against overloading a network, unlike the asynchronous mechanism MOM. There are a few asynchronous implementations of RPC available but they are more the exception than the rule.

RPC is appropriate for client/server applications in which the client can issue a request and wait for the server to return a response before continuing with its own processing. On the other hand RPC requires that the recipient is online to accept the remote call. If the recipient fails the remote calls will not succeed, because the calls will not be temporarily stored and then forwarded to the recipient when it is available again, as is the case with MOM.

Architectural flexibility is enhanced by using RPC, because we can allow a client to use a function call to access a server on a remote system. RPC allows the client remote access without forcing the client to know the network address or any other lower-level information. The semantics of a remote call is the same whether or not the client and server are collocated.

> *RPC is often connected with the Distributed Computing Environment (DCE), developed by the Open Systems Foundation (OSF). DCE is a set of integrating services that expand the functionality of RPC. In addition to RPC the DCE provides directory, time, security, and thread services. Over these fundamental services it places a layer of data sharing services, including a distributed file system and diskless support.*

Transaction Processing Monitors

Transaction processing (TP) monitors are important middleware technology in mission-critical applications. They represent the first generation of application servers. TP monitors are based on the concept of transactions; they monitor and coordinate transactions among different resources. Although the name suggests that this is their only task, they have at least two other very important additional roles:

❑ Performance management

❑ Security services

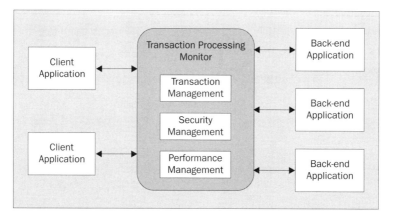

TP monitors provide performance management through load balancing and resource pooling techniques, which enable efficient use of computing resources and therefore a larger number of concurrent clients. TP monitors provide load-balancing, where they map client requests to different back-end applications, depending upon how many client requests have been initiated. For this they use stateless routines, which includes the application transition logic that would otherwise have to be put in a client application.

They also provide security management, enabling us to disable client access to particular data and resources if required. TP monitors can be viewed as middle-tier technology and this is why they are predecessors of today application servers.

TP monitors have been traditionally used in legacy information systems. They are based on the procedural model, using remote procedure calls for communication between applications, and are difficult to program because of complex APIs through which they provide functionality. TP monitors are also proprietary products, which makes migration from one product to another very difficult. In spite of these issues, they have been successfully used for more than 25 years.

Object Request Brokers

Object request brokers (ORBs) are a middleware technology that manage and support the communication between distributed objects or components. ORBs enable seamless interoperability between distributed objects and components without the need to worry about the details of communication. The implementation details of the ORB are not visible to the components. ORBs provide location transparency, programming language transparency, protocol and operating system transparency.

The communication between distributed objects and components is based upon interfaces, and is usually synchronous, although it can also be deferred synchronous communication or asynchronous communication. ORBs are often used with component location services. ORBs are complex products but they manage to hide almost all of the complexity. More specifically, they provide the illusion of locality – they make all of the components appear to be local, while in reality they may be deployed anywhere in the network. This simplifies the development considerably but can have a negative influence on performance.

The next figure shows two components communicating over an object request broker. The components can invoke methods remotely in exactly the same way as they would locally, because ORB hides all of the communication details:

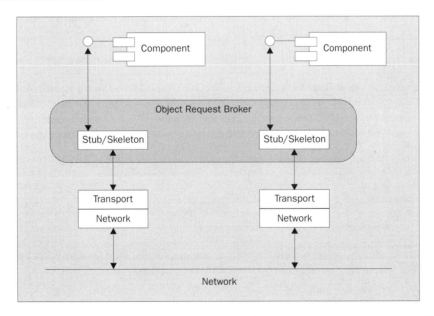

ORB products may implement their functionality according to various different scenarios. They might move some functionality to the client and server components, or they can provide them as a separate process, or integrate them into the operating system kernel.

There are three major standards of ORBs:

- ❏ OMG CORBA ORB compliant
- ❏ Java RMI and RMI-IIOP
- ❏ Microsoft COM/DCOM/COM+

There are many ORB products compliant with both the CORBA ORB specifications and various implementations of RMI and RMI-IIOP. RMI-IIOP is particularly important, because it uses the same protocol for communication between components as the CORBA ORB, namely IIOP (Internet Inter-ORB Protocol). This makes RMI-IIOP interoperable with CORBA.

On the other hand there is only a single implementation of the Microsoft model. The Microsoft model differs from the others in some important concepts, such as the component state for instance.

Interoperability between the RMI-IIOP and CORBA on one hand, and the Microsoft model on the other, is still possible and we will address it in Chapters 11 and 14, respectively.

Application Servers

Application servers are the most recent form of middleware. They handle all (or the majority of) interactions between client tier and the data persistence tier. They provide a collection of the middleware services we have already mentioned, together with the concept of a management environment in which we deploy business logic components – the **container**. In the majority of application servers we can find support for ORBs, MOM, transaction management, security, load balancing and resource management.

Application servers provide a comprehensive solution to enterprise information needs. They are also an excellent platform for integration. Today, vendors often position their application servers as integration engines, or specialize their common purpose application servers by adding additional functionality (such as connections to back-end and legacy systems), so that they can position their products as integration servers. Although such servers can make the configuration of different middleware products relatively easy, it is still worth bearing in mind what is beneath the surface.

Whether used for integration or for new application development, application servers are **software platforms**. A software platform is a combination of software technologies necessary to run applications. In this sense application servers, or more precisely the software platform that they support, define the infrastructure of all applications developed and executed on them. Application servers can implement some custom platform, making them a proprietary solution of a specific vendor (these are sometimes referred to as proprietary frameworks). Such application servers are becoming more and more rare.

On the other hand, application servers can support a standardized, open and generally accepted platform. The following lists the most important aspects of a platform:

- ❏ Technical aspects
- ❏ Openness
- ❏ Interoperability

❑ Cost

❑ Maturity

Let's look at these points in a little more detail.

Technical Aspects

Technical aspects define the software technologies that are included in the software platform, and the architecture of the applications developed for that platform. It also includes interoperability, scalability, portability, availability, reliability, security, client contracts, the ability to grow and accommodate new solutions, and so on. Interoperability with other systems is obviously a very important aspect for integration.

Openness

Openness enables vendors and third-party companies to influence the development of a particular software platform. Different solutions exist, from fully closed platforms that bind us to a certain vendor, to fully open platforms – for example the open-source initiative, where everything (even source code) is free and can also be freely modified. Open platforms are often defined with specifications. These are documents that strictly define the technologies included in the platform and enable different vendors to implement the platform (as application servers for example). A tight specification guarantees consistency; a platform defined in terms of specifications can also have a reference implementation and a set of compatibility tests.

Interoperability

Interoperability among platform implementations is crucial for the adoption of a particular platform. In particular, the way the platform regulates additions and modifications are crucial. The stricter the platform is with the implementation of the core specification, the better the chance it has of being successful and gaining a large market share. However, each platform needs to provide ways for application servers to differentiate their product, possibly through implementing some additional functionality.

Cost

Cost of the platform is also an important factor and it is probably the most difficult to assess because it includes the cost of the application server and other development software, the cost of hardware, the training, and the cost of the maintenance of the applications throughout their life cycle.

Maturity

Last (and perhaps least important) is maturity, from which we can predict how stable the platform is. The more mature the platform is, the more it has been tested in a real-world environment, proving that it is suitable for large-scale applications.

Choosing a Suitable Integration Platform

To implement the integration architecture we have to choose the technologies we will use. We will focus on enterprise software platforms that gather together all of the necessary technologies and middleware solutions needed for building enterprise information systems.

If we would like an open, modern, standardized platform that is based on specifications, we do not have many choices today. The prime choice is clearly the J2EE platform. The other possibilities are CORBA (Common Object Request Broker Architecture) and the Microsoft .NET architecture.

CORBA is a standardized, open architecture managed by OMG (Object Management Group); J2EE and CORBA have been converging in the last years. Although there are rumors that the .NET platform will be standardized and become open, and will eventually be ported to operating systems other than Windows, not much has been done toward this end at the time of writing. If .NET becomes an open platform it will be a valuable contender to Sun's J2EE. However, based on previous experience, this will surely take a long time, if ever.

The J2EE platform, on the other hand, is controlled by the Java Community Process (JCP). The JCP is responsible for the development of the whole Java technology. Anyone can join the JCP and influence the evolution of the Java platform. Modifications to the platform require consensus among the members of the JCP process. This guarantees that there will be no rapid changes that would cut the compatibility with existing software. On the other hand, it gives the members the possibility to influence its development and direction. Sun Microsystems still has the rights on the J2EE trademark and requires licenses to be paid, but it is the JCP, not Sun, who controls the platform.

The J2EE specification, controlled by the JCP, is then implemented by many different application server vendors who compete in a very large market. This means that the customer is free to choose the application server and the vendor, and at a later date to switch to a different vendor if needed, but any existing software should be portable between the different vendor's implementations.

> *Actually, although the goal is that the porting of software should be possible without any modifications, experience shows that minor modifications are often necessary. However, these modifications are much smaller and easier to perform than porting the software to a totally different platform, for example .NET.*

Using J2EE To Integrate Applications

The J2EE platform is a software framework that provides technologies for the design and development of multi-tier business applications. Business applications are almost always complex and require a lot of data manipulation and processing, and they often have to support large numbers of concurrent clients. Particularly complex is the middle or business logic tier, because it requires many supporting services, such as database access, security, transaction support, resource management, and so on. The J2EE platform provides services that ease the development of business applications, and enable the developer to concentrate on the business functions he has to implement, not on the technologies involved.

The J2EE architecture defines a client tier, a middle tier and a back-end tier. The client tier supports different types of clients, from applications and applets to thin web-based and mobile clients.

The middle tier provides the infrastructure for the business services and is subdivided into the **web tier** and the **Enterprise JavaBeans (EJB) tier**. The web tier provides services related to the web and thin clients. The EJB tier provides the environment for executing business logic components.

The back-end tier provides enterprise services such as data persistence, but can also host other existing enterprise information systems (EIS). The architecture of the J2EE platform is illustrated in the following figure:

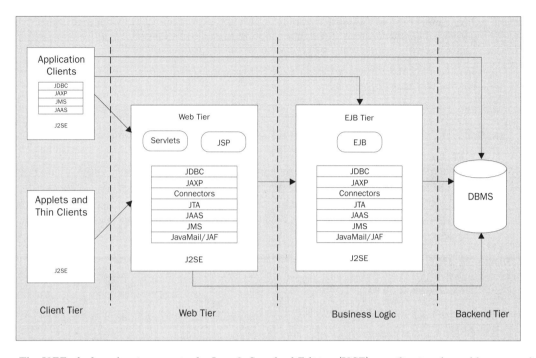

The J2EE platform has its roots in the Java 2, Standard Edition (J2SE) specification, but adds support for many important enterprise technologies. In version 1.3 J2EE supports the following technologies:

- **Enterprise JavaBeans (EJB) version 2.0** provides services for developing, deploying and managing business logic tier components on the EJB tier.

- **JavaServer Pages (JSP) version 1.2** allows development of dynamic web-based user interfaces.

- **Java Servlets version 2.3** provides a mechanism for extending the functionality of the web server to access the business systems.

- **JDBC version 2.0** provides services for connectivity with relational databases.

- **Java Message Service (JMS) version 1.0.2** is a standardized API for accessing message-oriented middleware (MOM), and supports the point-to-point and publish/subscribe models.

- **Java Remote Method Invocation, RMI-IIOP**, part of the Java 2 SDK version 1.3, Standard Edition, provides the ORB services and enables transparent remote method invocation between distributed objects and components. The ORB is protocol-independent and currently supports the RMI native protocol (JRMP) and the CORBA-compliant IIOP protocol.

- **Java Interface Definition Language (IDL)**, part of the Java 2 SDK version 1.3, Standard Edition, is a CORBA compliant ORB that enables interoperability with external CORBA distributed objects using the IIOP protocol.

- **Java Transaction API (JTA) version 1.0.1** and **Java Transaction Service (JTS) version 1.1** provide support for transactions and provides interfaces for application-level transaction demarcation.

❏ **Java Authentication and Authorization Service (JAAS) version 1.0** provides security services, particularly authentication and authorization. It provides the Pluggable Authentication Module (PAM) framework implementation for authenticating users.

❏ **Java Naming and Directory Interface (JNDI) version 1.2** is a standardized API for accessing naming and directory services.

❏ **Java API for XML Processing (JAXP) version 1.1** provides support for handling XML-formatted data. It provides DOM (Document Object Model) and SAX (Simple API for XML) parsers and an XSLT (Extensible Stylesheet Language for Transformations) transformation engine.

❏ **J2EE Connector Architecture version 1.0** is a service provider interface that enables the development of resource adapters through which the access to enterprise information systems is enabled. It defines a standard set of system level contracts between a J2EE compliant server and a resource adapter

❏ **JavaMail version 1.2** provides API for sending e-mails and requires the JavaBeans Activation Framework (JAF).

From the list we can classify different services as middleware solutions, as follows:

❏ Data access middleware: JDBC

❏ Message-oriented middleware: JMS

❏ Object request brokers: RMI-IIOP and Java IDL

❏ Transaction processing: JTA with JTS

We have already identified that middleware support is crucial for integration, and this applies just as strongly to the integration of J2EE-developed applications with existing and new generation applications. However, some other technologies are also important for integration, particularly the Java Connector Architecture for accessing enterprise information systems, JAXP for XML-based integration, JNDI for integrating different naming and directory services, JTA for integration with other transaction systems, and JAAS for integration of security services.

In the following chapters we will discuss all of these technologies, and focus on each one from the perspective of integration. We will also look at client-side integration, discuss the role of servlets and JSP pages, and have a look at Windows client-side integration through COM+ bridges.

Although not yet part of J2EE platform, we will also focus on some important emerging technologies that will probably be playing an important role in integration in the near future. We will look at the Simple Object Access Protocol (SOAP) and show how to use it with J2EE applications for integration. We will also look at the emergence of Web Services, and discuss Universal Discovery, Description and Integration (UDDI) and the Web Services Definition Language (WSDL), showing how to use them particularly for B2B integration.

J2EE Technologies for Legacy System Integration

In this book we will focus on using the J2EE platform for integration with legacy and modern existing applications. For integration with legacy systems we'll be looking at:

❏ Ways to access and exchange data (JDBC, JDO, XML)

- ❏ Transforming data (XSL)

- ❏ Message brokers (JMS)

- ❏ Java Connector Architecture (JCA)

- ❏ Distributed objects (RMI, RMI-IIOP, CORBA)

- ❏ Components (EJB)

- ❏ SOAP (Simple Object Access Protocol)

We will focus particularly on integration techniques that can be applied to minimize the changes in legacy applications as much as possible, and on methods to overcome the disadvantages of point-to-point integration.

Technologies for the Integration of Modern Systems

We will also cover the integration of existing solutions developed in modern architectures, other than J2EE, that need to be integrated too. This can happen between divisions or departments, even in the same departments, or between different companies. Here we are touching on inter-EAI too, but this is not a problem because EAI and inter-EAI (B2B) integration are connected in many ways and it is difficult to draw an accurate boundary between the two.

Today, the most important integration of modern systems (from the perspective of the Java developer) is the integration of Java platform-based applications with the CORBA architecture on one hand and the Microsoft Windows platform on the other.

CORBA architecture is not a competing but a complementary architecture to Java. The Java platform is based on, and supports, many technologies from CORBA, including:

- ❏ Internet Inter-ORB Protocol (IIOP) for communication between objects

- ❏ Java Transaction Service (JTS) and Java Transaction API (JTA), both based on CORBA Object Transaction Service (OTS) for transaction management

- ❏ CORBA Naming Service for obtaining the initial references

- ❏ Accordance between EJB and CORBA Component Model (CCM)

This is why, in this book, we will show how to use CORBA technologies to integrate Java solutions with modern solutions developed in other programming languages. We will discuss advanced topics as well, like integration of transaction and security management between the two architectures.

The other important integration need is the integration of Java-based solutions with the Microsoft Windows platform. The first and most important is the integration of a Microsoft-based user interface tier with a Java business process tier. The Microsoft Windows platform is the dominant platform on the client side, so this question is important. There are several ways that we can achieve this integration:

- ❏ Developing thin web-based clients

- ❏ Using COM and automation bridges

- ❏ Using SOAP for communication between the client and the business process tiers

If it is necessary to integrate business tiers in the Java and Microsoft platforms, then we need to integrate different component models, namely EJB and COM+ (Component Object Model). This can be achieved using:

- ❑ Third-party COM bridges. Sun provides a COM bridge that is called the J2EE Client Access Services (J2EE CAS) COM Bridge, but this is not the only solution.

- ❑ Custom-built bridges between the two component models.

In the near future, the integration of Microsoft .NET-based solutions with the Java platform will certainly become an important topic. The Microsoft .NET platform is partially based on open standards, particularly on SOAP. In Chapter 18 we will look at the role of SOAP when we consider Web Services and B2B integration.

Summary

In this chapter we have defined what EAI actually is and identified the problems associated with application integration. We have seen that only on rare occasions will we be lucky enough to be able to develop applications without the need to consider existing solutions. In the majority of cases we will be forced to integrate newly-developed solutions with legacy systems on one hand, and with new generation systems that are based on different architectures on the other.

Application integration is difficult because there are many factors involved in a successful integration project:

- ❑ We have to deal with semantic problems and be able to unify different information islands
- ❑ We have to solve technical problems

In this book we focus on the integration of the J2EE platform with other applications. The J2EE platform introduces multi-tier application architecture and several other modern concepts, particularly platform independence through the use of virtual machines. That makes it, and the applications developed using J2EE, considerably different from other existing and new generation solutions. Therefore, the technical aspects of integration cannot be neglected. Finally, there are organizational aspects that can ruin integration attempts as well.

We have also stated that we will use a multi-tier integration architecture, and that we will attempt to reuse existing systems' functionality without the need to modify them considerably. In addition, we will try to keep the door open for the replacement of existing systems in future – and we will try to make this process as painless as possible. We have identified that on most occasions we will be faced with legacy systems and new generation systems based on different platforms, architectures, and technologies. Some of these systems will be commercial applications, while others will be self-developed solutions, and yet others will be custom-built but outsourced applications. From this diversity we can see that the modifications we can safely make to applications to prepare them for integration depends on how much knowledge we have about them.

Finally, we have seen that efficient EAI is the prerequisite for a company to be able to take part in B2B integration. To enable efficient front-end B2B systems, we need effective EAI with back-end systems, so companies that wish to take part in B2B must first solve their own internal integration challenges.

In the next chapters we will go into more detail about integration concepts, and will focus on integration methods, techniques and organizational aspects.

2

Choices and Strategies

When deciding to integrate existing applications into a global, enterprise-wide information system, we first have to become familiar with the choices and strategies that are available to us. Often, the first thoughts of how to start an integration project will be confusing, mainly because we have to cope with a lot of complexity in the system. Looking at a global information system is a complex task, and developing an integration strategy from scratch is a very complicated problem. It gets even more complicated when we have to take into account existing systems and try to reuse as much of their functionality as possible.

Even the most efficient companies will have a mix of applications, possibly written in a variety of languages or obtained from a mix of vendors, and some of them may even be partially integrated in one way or another. In many cases, older applications have little, if any, associated documentation. The more unfortunate companies may even rely on applications based on different operating systems.

For an integration project to be successful, we need to plan it accurately and produce a strategy of how to achieve the integration. This strategy has to be accordant to the current situation of the information system from a technical perspective. We also need to take into account the organization's culture and align ourselves with the way the organization works. Finally, the integration project needs support from all parties involved. This includes users, developers, and management. Support from the management level is particularly important because, as we will see, it is not possible to achieve an efficient integration without appropriate authorization.

In this chapter we will review the general guidelines relating to the most important choices and strategies that we must be aware of before starting an integration project. We will discuss how different types of integration may be relevant to different systems. In examining the relevant choices and strategies, this chapter will cover the following:

❏ Application replacement and application extension

❏ Bottom-up and top-down approaches to integration

❏ The significance of a centrally managed integration project

❏ Integration infrastructure

❏ Integration broker pattern and architecture goals

❏ The composite information system approach and multi-tier architecture

❏ Virtual components and component wrapping

❏ The four steps to defining an effective integration architecture:

    ❏ Data-level integration

    ❏ Application interface level integration

    ❏ Business method level integration

    ❏ Presentation-level integration

❏ Re-engineering practices

❏ A brief look at business-to-business (B2B) integration and web services

❏ Integration principles

Let's start with a brief overview of the different ways in which we can implement our integration plans.

The Path To Integration

The ability to instantly access vital information that may be stored in a variety of different information systems may influence the success of a company. For a modern company the presence of an effective information infrastructure that avoids the need for employees to perform numerous manual tasks like filling in paper forms, and other bureaucracy, is of utmost importance. Clearly, employees should not have to contend with such inefficiencies and 'irritations' as switching between different applications to get their work done, re-entering the same data more than once in different applications, or waiting for data to be processed. Ideally, a well-integrated system should offer instant access to information, no matter which part of the system is used.

> **Ultimately, an information system is, by definition, only as effective as the integration between the different applications.**

Readers of this book will recognize the importance of integrating information systems *across* the enterprise first, and then *between* different enterprises. In Chapter 1 we have seen that integration across the enterprise – EAI – is essential because it provides unified and efficient access to relevant, coordinated information from a variety of sources. EAI is also important because it is a prerequisite for integration between enterprises – B2B integration – which can be efficient only if all the involved companies have integrated their back-end information systems.

> **Companies are realizing the importance of integration at different speeds.**

Some businesses are already fully involved in integration projects with many solutions already working – they have seen the advantages of integration and understand how to achieve successful integration. Other companies are aware that integration is important but, although they may have started integration projects, they have not yet seen any positive results, mainly because the integration projects have not been successful.

Further still, some companies are only now realizing the importance of integration, and this could in fact be too late for them. Such companies may be looking for ways to achieve integration fast, without spending too much money, and without assigning too many staff members to the integration project. By cutting corners and attempting to implement only the most urgent parts of integration in the shortest possible time will, most likely, result in only partially working solutions at best.

> **The problem is exacerbated by the fact that managers are often unfamiliar with all the complexity hidden behind the integration process.**

Sometimes even the "IT people" – the architects and developers, do not fully understand the traps behind the integration. Most importantly, managers might not understand that integration is a topic that is related to the company as a whole, and not to the IT department only. All of these potential problems can lead to the so-called **bottom-up** approach to integration, which is discussed in detail in the next section.

Another scenario that leads to the same disorganized approach is when the management of a company does not see the need for integration yet, while the IT department is aware that integration is needed and should be initiated as soon as possible. Therefore, the integration team starts to build a partial solution to solve the most pressing problems. As the integration is not approved from the top, the IT sector does not have enough resources (usually time and money) and, more significantly, it does not have the authorization to start to solve the integration globally. Most developers will agree that these are all-too-familiar situations.

Before we start discussing different approaches to integration let us first have a look at the initial situation and the choices a company can apply to solve the needs for EAI.

The Present Situation

> **Today, companies that have been around for even just a few years are typically faced with a disparate mix of heterogeneous existing systems.**

Companies will usually have several different applications, developed over time. These can include:

❑ Applications developed inside the company

❑ Custom-built outsourced solutions

❏   Commercial and Enterprise Resource Planning (ERP) applications

These applications may have been developed on different platforms, using different technologies and programming languages. As they have been developed over time, different applications probably use different programming models. These differences are manifested through:

❏   Combinations of monolithic, client/server, and multi-tier applications

❏   Mix of procedural and object-oriented solutions

❏   Mix of programming languages

❏   Different types of database management systems (relational, hierarchical, object)

❏   Different middleware solutions for communication (message-oriented middleware, object request brokers, remote procedure calls)

❏   Multiple information transmission models, including publish/subscribe, request/reply, and conversational

❏   Different transaction and security management middleware

❏   Different ways of sharing data

❏   Possible usage of EDI, XML, and proprietary formats for data exchange

Another important aspect is the integration that has already been implemented between the existing applications. This includes everything from simple data exchange to the use of middleware products. In addition to all this diversity of architectures, technologies, platforms, and programming languages the companies have kept introducing new applications – and with new applications they have possibly introduced modern application architectures.

Last but not least, we must not forget that companies depend on their existing applications and, in most cases, cannot survive without them. Thus, in the next section we'll take a quick look at the alternatives to integration.

Alternative Choices

We have seen that EAI is not an easy or quick solution towards an integrated information system. Before deciding on integration we should examine any other possibilities. Generally, these include:

❏   Replacement

❏   Extension

Application replacement is often the intuitive answer to the challenges that integration places in front of us, but extension should also be considered. In this section we will discuss the options of simply replacing or extending existing applications with new solutions.

Sometimes, particularly if management does not understand the problems related with integration of the information system, the IT departments might receive requirements that are tightly connected with integration. Examples of such scenarios include building the web front-end, implementing B2B or B2C collaborations, or building web-based or graphical user interfaces on top of existing applications. Then IT departments might select application extension. Here we will argue that there are no long-term benefits to application extensions – it provides a short-term solution only.

Application Replacement

In the hope of saving time and money, managers will often consider the partial or complete replacement of existing systems. Replacement requires that we make a clean break and stop using the existing applications and turn to a new system.

When we consider replacing applications we can choose to purchase them or to develop them, either in-house or outsourced. The determining factors for choosing between purchase and development are essentially the type of application we are replacing and how well a commercial application could cover our needs. Although, in theory, purchasing is the preferred solution over development because it is much faster, it also has important drawbacks. It is unlikely that a purchased application will cover the business needs as efficiently or as comprehensively as the custom-developed solution. We will also not be able to influence the application development or modify a commercial application to the same extent as a custom-developed solution.

On the other hand, the flexibility of custom-built applications is offset somewhat by the lengthy development time. Furthermore, today's companies rarely have the resources for large in-house developments, and outsourcing the project does not necessarily accelerate its development.

> **Purchasing is a quicker option than development, but development allows for customization. Making the choice will therefore depend upon which option best fits with the company's business plan.**

Then we have to answer the even more important question regarding which applications to replace. Will we simply be replacing one or two old legacy applications, or will we have to replace the whole information system?

If we replace a single or a few applications, we have not actually solved our original problem – the integration.

> **Even if we replace one or two applications, they still stay unconnected and we are faced with similar challenges as before. Thus, in terms of integration, the only sensible decision is to replace the whole information system with a newly developed, integrated solution.**

If we were able to develop an integrated information system that covered all our requirements, this would perhaps offer the ultimate solution. Unfortunately, there are several factors that prevent us from doing just this.

First of all, to develop a new information system from scratch requires time and resources that, in most cases, we simply cannot afford. There have been many years of development invested into the existing applications, and reimplementing all of this functionality would require a lot of knowledge and resources. It is very unlikely that this would be possible in a reasonable or acceptable time.

Companies today are also so complex that it would be almost impossible to buy a commercial application that would cover all their information needs. This is how ERP systems have emerged. However, it was soon realized that ERP systems could not cover all possible needs. Research from leading consulting companies suggests that ERP can only account for 30% to 40% of information needs. The remainder has to be covered by custom solutions. This is also the reason why the majority of ERP suppliers, such as SAP, Baan, or PeopleSoft, have started to introduce interoperability interfaces into their products.

Even if we could develop the new information system in a reasonable time we would still need to deploy it, transfer all data, and teach the users how to use the new system. These are some of the reasons why there will be only a few companies that will attempt to replace their entire information systems. Such companies will soon realize that the replacement is more complex, more time consuming, and more costly than even their worst case scenarios could have predicted.

> **Replacement of the whole information system is not applicable to most enterprise situations.**

In the context of integration and reusing the functionality of existing systems, we should distinguish between replacement of the whole information system and individual applications. Even if the replacement of the whole information systems is not considered as a solution, we should always be aware that for each existing application we may at some point have to make the decision to replace it. This is typically the moment when the costs of maintaining an existing application are larger than its actual benefits. Careful modifications to these applications will prolong their lifetime. Therefore we should also look at the ways in which to replace existing applications as painlessly as possible.

Before we focus on integration let's first examine another alternative – application extension.

Application Extension

We have already identified that IT departments often receive requirements for the information system that are related to integration, such as building the web front-end. In Chapter 1 we identified that requests can be implemented efficiently only if existing back-end applications are integrated.

Often management will not understand the need for integration and will place tight schedules on the IT department. In this case the IT department might opt for extending the functionality of existing applications, rather than fully integrating them.

Indeed, we will see in the next few chapters that application extension can be important for integration. However, here we will consider application extension as a task that is focused on a single or a small subset of the existing applications. Such application extension does not focus on the global application architecture, but instead attempts to modify existing applications so that they can accommodate the changes. It modifies them without determining how they fit into and contribute to the enterprise's overall requirements and information architecture, treating each application as a separate domain.

Application extension is used frequently, because it can provide solutions quickly and with little effort. The most obvious scenarios are when adding a graphical user interface to the old, legacy applications. This was important some ten years ago when moving from mainframes to personal computers. More recently, a comparable problem concerns the addition of a web-based front-end, and implementing B2B and B2C collaborations on top of existing applications.

The way that existing applications have usually been extended is demonstrated in the following diagram:

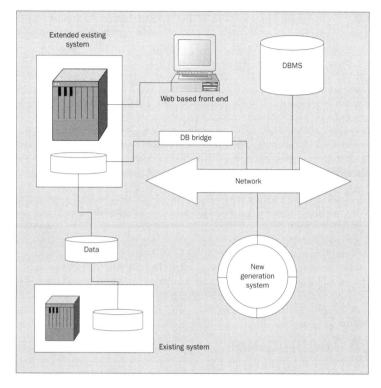

Here we see two existing applications that have had a data exchange implemented. One of the applications is extended with a web-based front-end system that allows web access to some of the functionality. Additionally, there is a database bridge implemented that allows other applications to access the data in this application.

Although at first sight this architecture seems reasonable, it has several drawbacks in terms of integration. Extension, as described above, effectively modifies the architecture of the existing application without thinking of the global picture. Thus, it presents the same disadvantages that can be identified for the bottom-up approach (defined shortly).

> **Extension does not build on the global architecture; it simply modifies the applications to accommodate the required changes.**

We should also consider how other applications can interact with the extended existing application. They have to use the bridge, meaning that they need additional specific code to access the existing application. They will have to use a different bridge for each existing application, which will increase the complexity of the system as a whole.

The previous section identified that eventually there will come a time in the life cycle of a legacy application when we will have to replace it. In the architecture shown before a replacement would mean that all other applications would have to be modified, because access to the application would be different. In fact, even modifications to the application would provoke such changes in the other applications. This is because in this scenario the applications are **tightly coupled**.

Since changes occur often, this approach adds complexity to the system with each change or modification. It is only a question of time before the complexity becomes too great to manage all the changes required.

Nevertheless, extension is a relatively low-cost approach and, because it does not focus on the global information system, it can be accomplished relatively quickly and painlessly. This is why many companies have chosen to extend at least some of their existing applications. Note that we will often be in a situation where the existing systems will have had such extensions implemented.

> **With the above points in mind, application extension should not be considered as a sound approach towards EAI.**

Rather, we should look at integration by defining an architecture that allows us to overcome these disadvantages, while still reusing existing systems. In the next section we will start to look at integration more closely.

Integration Techniques

After discussing replacement and extension of applications, we have seen that in most companies the only choice is a step-by-step integration that will eventually lead to a global enterprise-wide integrated information system. Such an information system would reuse existing applications, but give the illusion to the users that they are using a modern information system that fulfills their needs.

> **Integration is not an easy task – to succeed we will need to plan and architect it carefully.**

Thus, we must first select the applications that we will include in the integration. Applications in each company can be classified into one of the following two classes:

- ❑ **Primary applications**

  These are important for the whole company and used by a large number of employees. They have been developed either in-house, outsourced, or bought and are under the control of IT department.

- ❑ **Subsidiary applications**

  These are often used by a single employee and, most likely, they have been developed without the knowledge of the IT department by the users themselves with a productivity tool, like office applications. Subsidiary applications ease the every-day work of this employee and implement the tasks that this employee has to performed, but are not supported by the primary applications. Examples include printing circular letters, generating specific reports, and so on.

> **When designing the integration architecture it is very important that we include both the primary and the subsidiary applications.**

Clearly, users have developed subsidiary applications because they need the additional functionality, so if we do not implement them as part of the integrated system the users will continue to use their self-developed solutions. This will result in several problems, including manual transfers of data between the primary and subsidiary applications and in important data being stored on local computers in a variety of formats, like word processors and spreadsheets. Accessing such data will be very difficult and the objectives of the integration project will not be met.

> **Before we begin with integration we should perform an analysis of all the applications that have been used in a company, from the large company-wide applications to the small personal solutions of individual employees.**

After we have selected the applications, we have to choose our approach to integration. We will look at two different approaches and discuss their advantages and disadvantages:

- ❑ Bottom-up approach
- ❑ Top-down approach

We will then discuss the integration infrastructure, technologies, architectures, and the steps towards the composite information system. First let's look at the bottom-up approach to integration.

The Bottom-Up Approach

> **The bottom-up approach to integration is focused on individual problems that arise because of the lack of integration between applications. It solves the specific problems through uncoordinated integration projects, avoiding the issues of the global integration architecture.**

In order to define the bottom-up approach to integration, let's consider an example of a cell phone operator that has several separate applications that do not communicate. These applications are as follows:

- ❑ An application for customer management
- ❑ Two different applications for accounting the domestic and international calls
- ❑ An application that manages the accounts of customers
- ❑ An application that prints invoices
- ❑ An application that handles the tariffs and costs of calls

To keep our example simple (for now), let's suppose that there are no connections between the applications. However, it is obvious that there should be many. Due to the lack of integration, users have to re-enter the same information two or three times, which not only makes the work take longer than necessary but also introduces an element of human error through typing mistakes. These can be difficult to track down, thus losing additional time. The IT department and the users of these applications are fully aware that integration would bring important benefits. At the very least, connections are required between the invoice printing application, both call accounting applications, the customer management application, and the account management application.

Let's also presume that in this particularly company, the IT department does not have the authority to make independent decisions and cannot convince the upper management of the necessity of integration. The users of these applications also don't have important positions in the company because they are mostly clerks. Due to regulations, competition between cell phone operators is not a serious issue, so the management does not prioritize the need for complex analysis and other up-to-date information. They are satisfied with information that is several days old, which can therefore be prepared manually.

In this particular scenario it is easy to see that convincing management of the need for integration would be a difficult, if not impossible, task. Now we may wonder why management does not see the need for integration. Unfortunately, too often a business must feel pain before management gives attention to a problem – this is reactive rather than proactive management, and, unfortunately, is very typical. In our scenario, things have not developed far enough for this to happen.

In our case, the IT department can wait until management experiences the negative effects of their inefficient systems, and then starts to look towards integration. Or, the IT department can take things into their own hands and try to implement the most needed integration parts between the applications. Unfortunately both approaches will ultimately lead to the same problems.

If the IT department waits and does nothing regarding the need for integration, the time will come when management starts to feel that there is a problem that can be solved with integration. In our scenario this will most likely be the situation when competition on the market starts to increase. At this point, management will look for ways in which to minimize costs; they will initially identify the lost hours of the workforce, because of the unnecessarily repetitive nature of some of the tasks (for example, re-entering the data, manually changing the structure of the data, and so on). They will also feel the need for accurate and timely information, which can only be effectively produced by an integrated information system.

Given this scenario, it will likely be a little too late by the time management senses the problem. Therefore, they will ask for the IT department to implement the fastest possible solution to see results as soon as possible. The management is not likely to take the time to understand everything that they need from the information system. In our scenario, this would be, say, the potential integration between the invoice printing, call accounting, customer, and account management applications mentioned previously. Furthermore, management will probably not consider anything beyond what satisfies their own narrow view of the problem.

Now most IT departments, because they don't have a choice anyway, will agree and try to implement the connections between applications that they need most and that can be built in the quickest time. They will start to look for solutions on how to integrate the relevant applications in the easiest way. Let's say that in our present example not all applications have been developed within the company. Some of them are commercial applications, while some of them have been outsourced.

The IT department is therefore not familiar with the finer details of all the applications. To apply changes to the applications, the IT department in our scenario would again have to contract external companies, resulting in additional costs and an extended schedule. This option should therefore be dismissed.

So, the IT department will search for ways in which to integrate their applications without modifying them (or at least minimize the amount of modifications). The most obvious potential solution is to use data-level integration. The IT department could choose to simply move the data between the databases of different applications. As we will see later in this chapter, and in Chapter 5, data-level integration is in most cases the first step – and often the easiest one. The integration of databases is well understood and relatively simple to implement. In most cases it does not require any changes to the code of the involved applications. The challenge thus becomes how to bridge different databases.

Note that in this chapter we will not discuss all the specific solutions, we will simply provide an overview of some of the possibilities; in later chapters we will go into more details about the different levels of integration.

Let us look at a possible outcome of this potential solution. The IT department would probably first implement the data transfer from the customer management application to the invoice printing application. Then they might implement the data transfer from the domestic and international call accounting applications to the tariff and cost management application. The data transfer that had previously been done manually would simply port this data to the tariff and cost management application, which would then return the actual consumption in currency. The same approach would then be applied to other connections.

After implementing all necessary data transfer connections between the applications, it might seem like the problems have been solved. However, the success will only be true on the surface, and new problems will soon emerge. If the IT department follows this pattern of implementing partial solutions, it will soon lead to a system of applications that will have several hidden dependencies. In the proposed scenario almost every application would have to be connected to all the others. This might not seem a lot when connecting two or three applications, but if we consider (more typically) twenty, fifty, or even more applications, it clearly leads to an exponential increase in complexity.

To get a feeling of the number of connections necessary, let us presume that each application will have to be connected with every other, where we will count unidirectional connections (application A has to be connected to B and B to A – these are two connections). The following graph shows the number of necessary connections in relation to number of applications that have to be integrated:

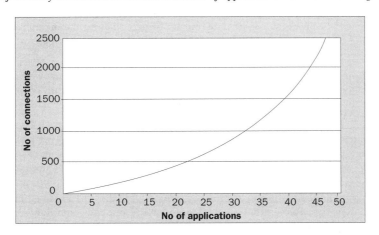

We can see that if we integrate fifty applications on a point-to-point basis we would need around 2500 connections! In practice, in the real world we will probably not need to connect each and every application with all the others. But this does not change the fact that we will have to manage and maintain a large number of individual connections.

The next diagram shows the possible connections of the databases of five applications from our main example:

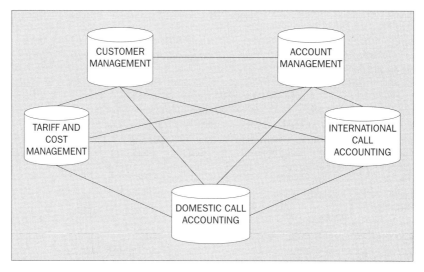

Small changes to one application could require modifications to all the data transfer bridges to other applications. In fact, the maintenance of that integrated system in this case will be more time consuming and costly than the maintenance of the applications themselves, which will make the benefits of integration less obvious.

This approach to integration also soon limits how far we can go, and has several other disadvantages. Here we will consider just two:

❑   We access the databases directly, bypassing the business logic. This makes it necessary to duplicate any business logic in all data transfer bridges, making the maintenance even more difficult. Accessing the database directly is risky because it is easy to break the business rules (and therefore the overall integrity).

❑   Integration based on data exchange between applications requires that we run a process that transfers data from time to time. We can do this every day, every hour, or even every few minutes, but we can hardly implement it immediately, because this would require too many resources. We will discuss this in more detail in Chapter 5.

Numerous examples for similar integration attempts can be found. Let us consider the demand for web-based customer front-ends, which are very popular when updating systems. This is basically a project involving the integration of the newly developed front-end with existing back-end applications. More explicitly, the integration between existing systems is the foundation for implementing this kind of application. However, in the past, some companies assumed that they didn't have time to wait for the integration to be done first. Rather, they needed a web-based front-end "overnight". Companies that were late identifying this need were in a particularly bad position.

Given that most companies did not have the integration solved in time, they again searched for fast solutions that were not based on solid foundations. Most likely, such web-based front-end systems were implemented with point-to-point links to each existing application without a global understanding of the problem. Again, this solution looked successful for a short period of time, but a second look tells us otherwise. Remember, a point-to-point solution requires a lot of maintenance.

In Chapter 1 we identified that the need for integration is primarily a consequence of the lack of global architecture and planning in the past. Thus, implementing the integration without planning is a choice only the most optimistic people would select – or people who are given little choice, because management has already made a decision. Management sometimes sees the purpose of the IT department as to provide a solution in the minimum of time that is cost effective in the short term. Such a management department usually does not want to hear that a total integration solution (with a longer development time) would provide much better results in long term.

The complicated thing is that the company will probably not realize this early enough and will continue to support the other projects in the same way. Soon the point of no return will be reached when additional layers are patched on top. The system will reach an unmanageable level of complexity where it will be impossible to modify because a small modification will provoke the need for changes in so many tightly-coupled parts.

This is why the bottom-up approach to integration will most likely bring the company a step forward at first, but soon the company will have regrets by needing to go two or three steps backward.

> **An information strategy that focuses on individual, uncoordinated integration projects will, over time, introduce even more problems into the company's information infrastructure.**

Thus, attempting to perform integration from the bottom-up approach is highly discouraged. In the following section we'll see why the top-down approach is much better.

The Top-Down Approach

Lack of planning and architecting is one of the principal reasons why many of today's companies have different applications running on different system that are not interoperable in any practical way. As such, it is unreasonable to expect that we can achieve an efficient level of integration without a precise strategy.

Information system building is essentially an engineering discipline. Therefore, let's consider taking a hint from civil engineering – defining the architecture before we begin. To use an analogy, we wouldn't start to build a house without plans, except for, say, a dog kennel! Indeed, there is no real damage done if a dog kennel falls down, it is not even a major problem if the dog does not like the kennel.

Extending our analogy further, let's consider the construction of a whole community of houses. When we start building a house in civilized surroundings, like in a city or a town, we cannot simply build the house anywhere we would like to. We have to position it according to environmental plans and designs. We also cannot build connecting roads to other houses in any random way we like. This would result in one-to-one communications between houses that would be unmanageable, it would be almost impossible to oversee their construction and navigate between them. Rather, we again have to stick to a global design where it has been chosen how the roads will be positioned and interconnected.

This is comparable to application integration. We cannot simply start to connect the existing applications without a good plan and architecture. This would almost certainly result in a large number of point-to-point connections that are very difficult to manage and maintain. Rather, we have to define the architecture of the integrated system first, and only then start to look at the existing applications and decide how they can fit into our integration architecture. This approach has several advantages and will enable us to build the architecture into which the existing applications will fit as good as a new generation system. It will also enable us to replace and re-engineer existing systems with new developments. This way of thinking is what is know as the **top-down** approach to integration.

> **The top-down approach is essentially a defined integration strategy.**

An integration strategy should, by definition, be as comprehensive as possible and should define all foreseeable aspects of the business problems that can occur, be they on a macro- or micro-scale. This effectively strengthens the integrity and consistency of integration through the whole company. The integration strategy should also recognize the dependencies between applications and the application development. It should provide guidelines and priorities by which management will plan and schedule the tasks and requirements addressed to the IT department and the information system. It is unfeasible, for example, to start to build a business-to-business integration before we have realized an adequate level of integration between our existing applications.

> **The top-down approach focuses on integration as a global activity. It identifies a comprehensive integration strategy that defines all foreseeable aspects of the business problems related to integration, analyzes existing dependencies, sets guidelines, and defines priorities. It manages integration as a large coordinated project and gathers efforts from all parties involved.**

Although it sounds reasonable that the integration strategy should be comprehensive, this is a very difficult task to achieve in the real world. Just imagine how many different people have to take part and on how many different levels. The business units have to coordinate the integration efforts, and define the information exchange and technical baselines. The information provided by each business unit should also be consistent. Redundancies in the data model have to be identified and removed to a company-wide level. Physical and electronic supply chains should be based on the same data views and all business units should follow a common pattern, giving the same answers to the same questions. As there are so many parties involved, in the next section we will discuss how and why the centrally managed integration project can be helpful.

A Centrally Managed Integration Project

It should be clear that integration is not only a technical problem. Rather, it also requires a good level of organization and management in order to be successful. Ultimately, it requires the support from senior management. Senior managers have to recognize the need for integration, and that this integration must take place on an enterprise-wide scale.

> **For successful integration, it is crucial that the company initiates the integration project with sufficient resources, priorities, and authorization to be able to achieve the coordination of all parties involved.**

To achieve this there are several possibilities. If a company has a centralized IT department then it can take over the responsibility for integration too. However, we have to be careful to ensure that there are actually enough staff members available for the task at hand. Two or three employees with part-time responsibilities are not enough to make the integration project take off. Obviously, this will depend on the size of a company and the number of application domains, but often this is another area where management and reality do not agree. It will also depend on the planned schedule. Although integration today is one of the main priorities of companies, it is still worth mentioning that planning a very long schedule for integration will probably result in a lack of success. The business and its requirements are prone to rapid changes, and an integration architecture that is defined over a long period of time will be unable to incorporate such changes.

Of course, a centralized IT department is not always the case. Often, companies will have IT departments (or similar structures) distributed all over the company. This can be a consequence of merging or even a consequence of the past needs because of the size of the company. Still, we have to identify somebody that will be responsible for the integration and who will be able to coordinate all the disparate parties. Assigning the responsibility to one of the IT departments would be unwise because it places this IT department above the others. This can lead to the other IT departments being unwilling to fully cooperate – and this can be enough to make integration unsuccessful.

It is a much better idea to introduce and organize a new central body that we will call an integration service, responsible for integration. The integration service should have three major responsibilities:

❑ **Definition** of integration architecture

❑ **Selection** of integration infrastructure and technologies

❑ **Development** and **maintenance** of integration documentation

Definition of Integration Architecture

The first job of an integration service is the operational responsibility of defining the integration architecture. This includes the identification of architectural and semantic questions regarding the integration.

> **The major responsibility of the integration service is to define a logical, high-level integration architecture.**

As we have mentioned previously, the top-down approach has to provide a sort of 'city plan', which will show us the available 'roads' and allow us to place individual 'houses'. The city plan represents a high-level integration architecture. We will discuss this in greater detail later, specifically in Chapter 4. It would be best if the integration architecture would model the integrated information system as it should be, that is, as we would like it to be. Such architecture also needs to enable at least some of the existing application to be reused, while minimizing the dependencies between applications. This last requirement will enable us to replace existing applications with new systems.

The integration service should also resolve the important semantic issues that have to be centrally implemented. This includes unification of the data model, issues regarding the interfaces between applications, the format of messages sent between applications, and so on.

Selection of Integration Infrastructure and Technologies

Another important responsibility is to identify, select, deploy, and maintain a consistent integration infrastructure, based on a set of interoperable technologies. Particularly, the identification and selection of integration infrastructure should be a coordinated effort and the integration service must take into account all aspects for existing applications and try to find an optimal solution. The consistent technology for integration is important.

> **Unification of the technology infrastructure is one of the prerequisites for starting with application integration. It is especially important that the integration infrastructure is defined for the whole enterprise.**

It is not necessary that the integration service selects only one technology for integration. In fact, it may well be that there is no single technology that would be able to incorporate all of the applications. If we select more than one technology we should, however, provide instructions about how to achieve interoperability between them and make these instructions available to all parties involved. We will discuss the integration infrastructure a little later in this chapter and will focus on technologies in Chapter 3.

Development and Maintenance of Integration Documentation

The third responsibility of the integration service is the development and maintenance of the integration documentation. Typically, the documentation consists of a set of interface models that describe the communication between the application domains and applications. These models will be realized from the integration design. The technology selection will also influence how these interfaces are implemented.

The integration service will have to take care that the project teams follow the integration guidelines and that they modify their applications to accommodate the interfaces and technology necessary for integration. They should also include support for any new software that they develop.

Furthermore, the integration service should connect the application vendors that have developed and supplied applications used in the company. They should find out how to incorporate the necessary solutions and technology into their applications and should also define the schedules.

We have to be aware that for successful integration the answers to the technology-related questions alone are not sufficient. Today, there are practically no technological barriers for integration; it is actually quite difficult to find platforms, operating systems, or applications that are impossible to integrate. However, we may experience significant difficulties when integrating two applications on a single operating system, written in the same programming language, and using the same database management system, because we have to solve numerous semantic differences between them. Integration is subordinated to the application architecture and to the interoperability interfaces, particularly their availability. A technology cannot avoid the organizational problems. From this perspective, a solid organizational structure for existing systems integration is a key success factor.

In the next sections we will take a closer look at integration infrastructure and the associated technologies.

Integration Infrastructure and Technologies

> The integration infrastructure consists of a set of middleware technologies that provide the interoperability services necessary to establish communication between applications. This provides the foundation on which we define the integration architecture.

Effective integration infrastructure should address all relevant middleware services that are required by EAI. When the integration infrastructure provides these services it frees the developers from these tasks and they can focus on the actual integration itself.

In Chapter 1 we identified and described the following middleware technologies:

- ❏ Database access technologies
- ❏ Message-oriented middleware
- ❏ Remote procedure calls
- ❏ Transaction processing monitors
- ❏ Object request brokers
- ❏ Application servers
- ❏ Several hybrid and proprietary products

We also identified that we will often have to use more than a single middleware technology to fulfill the needs of integration infrastructure. Therefore we will first define the integration infrastructure requirements. More specifically, we'll try to identify the necessary services and the possible technologies that could fulfill these needs. Then we will introduce the concept of integration broker. Note that a more specific discussion of the middleware products and technologies is reserved for the next chapter. There we will identify the middleware services and technologies offered by the Java 2 Platform, Enterprise Edition.

Infrastructure Services

To make a better selection of technologies that we will use for integration let us first focus on the required infrastructure services. We will try to identify the services from a high-level perspective and separate them into the horizontal and vertical layers. The services in horizontal layers will provide basic infrastructure services useful for the majority of existing and new generation applications. The vertical layer services will provide functionalities related to a specific task within an infrastructure that can span through several horizontal layer services.

The services on the horizontal layer include:

- ❏ Communication
- ❏ Brokering and routing
- ❏ Business intelligence

The vertical layers are:

- ❑ Transactions
- ❑ Security
- ❑ Life cycle
- ❑ Naming
- ❑ Scalability
- ❑ Management
- ❑ Rules

The relations between the services are shown on the next figure:

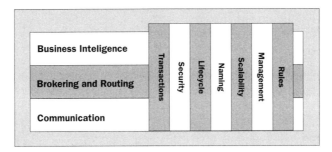

Horizontal Services

Let's now examine these services in finer detail, starting with the three horizontal layers that we've mentioned above.

Communication

The primary responsibility of the communication service is to provide the abstraction for communication details. It provides the transparency for accessing different remote system and unifies the view of them. This insures that developers do not have to deal with low-level communication details. As the communication layer does not execute business logic, it enables the separation of business logic and communication services, while allowing communication between them.

Different types of middleware provide different communication layer services. The most commonly used types for application integration are the database access technologies, like JDBC, that provide data layer abstraction to access different databases through a unified view. Message-oriented middleware (MOM) provides asynchronous communication by sending and receiving messages through a message queue or a message channel. The remote procedure call provides communication services for synchronous, procedural-oriented communication. Somewhat similar are the object request brokers, which provide an object-oriented view on the distributed entities. Middleware typically uses certain standard (or custom) protocols to achieve communication, including Internet Inter-ORB Protocol (IIOP), Simple Object Access Protocol (SOAP), HTTP, TCP/IP, and also proprietary protocols.

The communication layer can also provide the location transparency. This means that the actual location is managed separately from the application logic. This enables flexibility with the deployment and configuration. The location transparency functionality is often connected with the introduction of the naming and directory services which are then used as a repository for storing such information.

Brokering and Routing

The brokering and routing layer takes care of implementing the technical side of integration. No matter what type of integration we use, this layer should adapt the communication between applications in such a way that all participating applications will be able to interoperate. Brokering and routing are essential for integration and actually have a number of responsibilities.

First, this layer has to provide the way to gather the required data from multiple sources, most likely existing and new generation applications and/or data stores. This responsibility is called aggregation, because data is gathered from different sources to represent a business concept, like an invoice or order.

Then this data will have to be processed. Again we will use a mix of existing and new generation systems. Each of these applications will probably have their own interfaces and message syntax. Therefore the brokering and routing layer will have to transform the data and messages into suitable parts that can be processed by individual applications.

Finally, this layer will have to gather the results of all applications and present them consistently. This achieves synthesis of the results into a meaningful business notion.

To achieve these three steps automatically the brokering and routing layer will need meta-data information that will define the participating applications, methods, messages, and interfaces, and the sequence of operations involved. This layer also has to provide a means of handling events, making it appropriate for a declarative environment. Usually it will associate events with certain operations that have to be performed.

There is no single standardized middleware technology that could provide all the specified requirements for brokering and routing, so we will typically use a set of different technologies, including MOM, RPC, ORBs, and application servers.

Business Intelligence

The business intelligence layer is responsible for presenting a high-level interface that allows access to business information for other applications and to the users. This layer presents data to users in an understandable form. With the growth of e-commerce the business intelligence layer also takes some responsibilities for B2B integration.

Today, the business intelligence layer is supported by a flexible, unified presentation tier – most likely in the form of personalized portals. Personalized portals enable the delivery of valuable personalized business data and content directly to employees, business partners, and customers.

In addition to data and content delivery, the business intelligence layer is often connected with data processing technologies like Online Analytical Processing (OLAP), data mining, decision support systems, and executive information systems. These sources analyze enterprise data and provide information like estimation, forecasting, time-series analysis, and modeling.

Vertical Services

Next we'll turn our attention to the vertical service layers that define the integration infrastructure.

Transactions

The integration infrastructure has to provide the means for carrying out the business operations in a transactional manner. Therefore it has to be able to invoke several operations on different existing and new-generation systems as an atomic operation that has to comply with the ACID properties of **atomicity, consistency, isolation** and **durability**.

So, adherence to the ACID properties means that any operation performed on one or more applications that causes a state change, or changes to permanent data, has to be performed as an atomic operation that guarantees that the consistency of the system is preserved. It also has to isolate the operation from other operations and guarantee that the outcomes of operations are written on the persistent storage.

Security

The integration infrastructure has to provide ways to constrain access to the system. The security should include all three horizontal layers. It should be able to reuse the existing application security, and base the security on roles that are defined with a single user login. The security system should not be based on different passwords for different applications or even parts of applications. It should relate to all the important aspects, like communication channel encryption, authentication, authorization, and auditing.

Lifecycle

The integration infrastructure should provide ways to control the life cycle of all applications involved. It should enable existing applications to be replaced one by one, without influencing the other applications in the integrated system. We should emphasize that this replacement should be possible step-by-step, when business needs dictate it and when enough resources are available. It should also provide ways to do the replacement while the system stays online. This functionality is often achieved by minimizing the dependencies between applications and specifying ways for the applications to interoperate.

Naming

A unified naming service will allow for the implementation of location transparency and will enable the replacement of one resource with another if this is required. The naming service is usually implemented with a naming and directory product that enables storing and looking for name-related information. Ideally, the naming service is unified and provides one logical picture of the enterprise although it is physically implemented using replication and distribution to avoid a single point of failure.

Scalability

The integration infrastructure should be designed with scalability in mind. It has to access information about clients and provide concurrent access to the applications. It must incorporate solutions that will enable enough room for extending the load demands on the system. Achieving scalability in an integrated system can be a difficult problem because we have to take into account existing applications that probably have not been designed for the kind of scalability that we would like to achieve. Particularly, the requirements for the number of concurrent clients have probably not been so strict in the past. Therefore, we should implement some prototypes to test what levels of performance we can expect. We should also use load-testing tools that will enable us to simulate high loads and assess the relevant performance criteria.

The integration infrastructure cannot, however, fully compensate for bad application architecture and design. Therefore, we will have to assess the architecture of existing applications to realize how good they scale. We will talk about analyzing existing applications in Chapter 4. With newly developed applications, on the other hand, we should follow sound design and performance related practices to achieve the best possible scalability.

Management

We also have to provide ways to manage the integration infrastructure. Many solutions, particularly custom applications, leave this out, which results in difficulties at the maintenance stage. The management layer should provide methods and tools to manage horizontal and vertical services. It should provide easy configuration and version management. Declarative management enables access for changing and updating the parameters without needing to modify the source code and re-deploy the solutions. Remote management enables the infrastructure management to be carried out from remote locations, minimizing the need for trained personnel on site.

Rules

The horizontal services require specific rules for performing communication, brokering, routing, and business intelligence tasks. These rules should not be hard-coded into applications, but should rather be declaratively specified inside the integration infrastructure. This includes the definitions, data formats, data transformations and flows, events, information processing, and information representation. Often these rules are stored in a repository, which provides a centralized storage to avoid duplication and inconsistencies.

Next, based on the identified infrastructure services, we will discuss the possible technologies that are suitable to implement it.

Infrastructure Technologies

Infrastructure services can be realized by different middleware technologies.

During the previous discussions we have identified some possible technologies and have seen that it is unusual to find a single technology for all the specified needs. In other words, for building a comprehensive enterprise-wide integration infrastructure we will need to use more than one middleware technology.

When selecting and mixing different technologies we have to focus on their interoperability. Achieving interoperability between technologies can be difficult even for those based on open standards; for proprietary solutions interoperability is even more difficult.

It is not only a question of whether we can achieve interoperability but also of how much effort we have to put in to achieve it. Therefore, companies lean more and more towards software platforms that gather compatible technologies. Using a software platform usually saves a lot of additional work. We will mention here three important platforms:

- ❑ Java 2 Platform, Enterprise Edition (J2EE)

- ❑ CORBA

- ❑ Microsoft .NET

J2EE and CORBA both have associated specifications, and different vendors offer products that comply with these specs. In this sense they are open platforms, J2EE controlled by Sun and the Java Community Process, CORBA by the Object Management Group (OMG). In fact, the J2EE and CORBA specs have been converging in the last few years. On the other hand, Microsoft .NET is proprietary and directed specifically towards a Windows platform. All three platforms provide a large set of technologies, and are more or less appropriate for integration.

> *A comparison of these platforms is beyond the scope of this book, which is obviously focused on the J2EE platform. In the next chapter we'll provide an overview of all the technologies that the J2EE platform provides.*

In this chapter we will not focus on a specific technology. Instead, in the next section we will introduce the concept of the integration broker, which will abstract the technologies necessary to build the integration infrastructure.

The Integration Broker

An **integration broker** is an abstraction for the technologies through which we realize the integration infrastructure. The broker provides the horizontal and vertical services that we identified earlier.

We will use the concept of an integration broker throughout the rest of this chapter when we refer to the various integration architectures and services, but we won't occupy ourselves with technologies that have been selected to implement the integration. Rather, we will assume that the integration broker provides a high-level access to the infrastructure.

The integration broker will be used by both existing and newly developed applications to achieve integration on different levels. Applications will access the integration broker transparently through interfaces in either programmatic or declarative ways. A programmatic way means that applications will have to implement code to use the infrastructure services; the declarative way, on the other hand, enables us to just mark specific applications and declare which services they should use – the infrastructure then takes care of the details of invoking a service. How we achieve this will depend on the selected technologies, which we will become familiar with in the next chapter.

The transparency of the provided services will also depend on the choice of technology. Communication, brokering, and routing services can, for example, be implemented transparently with the use of ORBs, which mask remote method invocations to the level that they look like local method invocation to the developers. MOM, on the other hand, will require that the application creates a message, parses incoming messages, and reacts to them accordingly. Declarative transaction and security services can provide services to applications without adding any code to the application, and so on.

> **An integration broker abstracts a set of technologies that should provide an efficient infrastructure for integration. It effectively presents the infrastructure technologies through a technology abstraction layer.**

The integration broker is used on all integration levels, which we will discuss in detail shortly. It opens up the path to build the integration layers step-by-step and reuse the previous results, avoiding any reliance on point-to-point communication between applications.

Remember, point-to-point integration has the following disadvantages:

❏ The number of connections between applications can become very high

❏ A large number of dependencies between applications requires a lot of effort for maintenance

❏ Maintenance of links between applications can become more costly than the maintenance of the applications themselves, which will make the benefits of integration less obvious

The integration broker solves the point-to-point problem. It provides a common mediator, to which all applications connect, thus reducing the n-to-n multiplicity to 1-to-n:

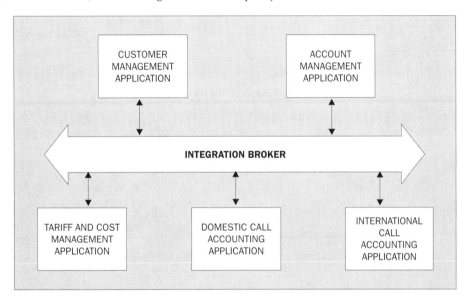

When we compare this diagram to that shown earlier in the chapter which illustrated the point-to-point linking of five application databases from our cell phone operator case study, we can clearly see that the complexity has been greatly reduced.

> **The integration broker does not only connect the applications, but bases the integration on contracts between applications. These contracts are usually expressed as interoperability interfaces. The interoperability interfaces define what services the client applications can request from server applications.**

Interoperability interfaces define relations between applications on which applications depend. Interfaces are effectively long living contracts that define the coupling between integrated applications. They provide a façade through which client applications access the interoperability services and encapsulate the applications. As long as the interfaces stay unchanged we can replace parts or whole server applications without influencing any client application. Therefore great effort has to be put into the definition of interoperability interfaces. We will discuss this topic further in the section on *Business Method Level Integration* later in this chapter, and also in Chapters 4 and 9.

The diagram that follows shows the role of interoperability interfaces when integrating through an integration broker:

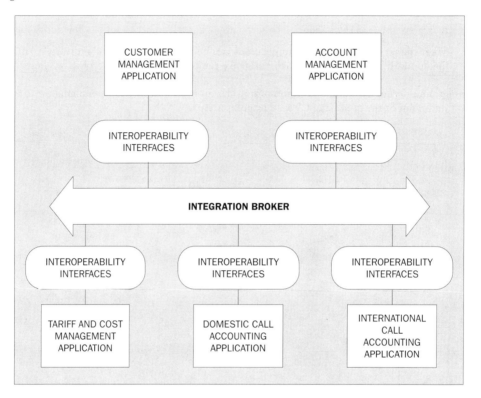

Compared to point-to-point integration the integration broker offers the following advantages:

- ❏ The number of connections between applications is reduced, thus reducing the level of coupling between integrated applications

- ❏ The dependencies between applications are defined as contracts in the form of interoperability interfaces

- ❏ Maintenance effort and costs are reduced to an acceptable level

- ❏ If the interfaces are carefully designed we can replace parts of or whole applications without influencing other involved applications

After we have become familiar with the integration broker as the concept of abstracting the integration infrastructure we can proceed to the actual integration architecture, where we will use the integration broker as the main tool.

Integration Architecture

> Integration architecture specifies the overall structure, logical components and logical relationships between all the different applications that we want to integrate.

We will define the integration architecture as lying on top of the integration infrastructure and we will follow the top-down approach to show how to build the integration architecture through the four integration levels:

❏ Data-level integration

❏ Application interface level integration

❏ Business method level integration

❏ Presentation integration

First, however, we need to define the two primary goals that the architecture has to satisfy. Then we can introduce the approach that results in a multi-tier composite information system architecture, and the concept of virtual components, before looking at how EAI relates to each individual integration level mentioned above.

Primary Goals

The two essential goals for integrated information systems, which must be supported by the integration infrastructure and architecture to ease the development, are:

❏ Single data input

❏ Low latency information access

Single Data Input

> Single data input ensures that data is entered into the information system only once.

Although this sounds like an obvious goal it is very difficult to achieve it 100% in the real world. Entering the data only once means that we have to provide a level of integration where the user does not have to re-enter the same data again for any purpose. This might not be so difficult to achieve for main, or primary applications. But don't forget that the users often use many subsidiary applications as well, which provide solutions to some everyday problems, as we have seen earlier in this chapter.

Clearly, a single data input guarantees data consistency and minimizes the mistakes that are provoked by data retyping and managing local stores of enterprise data.

Low Latency Information Access

The other important goal is data access with low latency, sometimes also called "zero-latency" data access.

> **Low-latency information access assures that the changes made in one part of the information system become visible in all related parts immediately (or in the shortest possible time).**

Achieving this can be a very complex task even in a small information system. If we imagine a distributed information system this can get considerably more complicated.

On the other hand, is achieving near zero-latency very important for today's online systems? Imagine an information system that enables users to book coach tickets over the phone. The clerk on the phone will enter the destination and the dates that the customer wants to travel on. Using a near zero-latency information system the clerk will be able to answer the question of whether the seats are available to a given destination at a given time. Otherwise, this information will have to be mailed to the customer, complicating the process and making it more costly. Introducing latency also means that the company will not be able to sell all the seats, as they will always need a certain number of seats reserved in case of double-bookings. We could find many similar examples, so a general answer is that achieving near zero-latency is indeed very important for today's information systems.

Ultimately, it is only a small step from the scenario mentioned above to the e-business example where the customers access the information system themselves through a web-based interface.

Achieving low latency in front-end systems requires there to be a low-latency strategy implemented in the back-end systems, and therefore also in the integrated enterprise information system. The main reason why low latency is difficult to achieve is because the functionality required to perform business tasks is dispersed across different applications, both conceptually and physically.

Solving the problem of dispersion amongst applications can be achieved in a number of different ways. Historically, this problem has been addressed at the data-level only, where typical solutions include building consolidated databases and data warehousing. These techniques involve taking snapshots of the data from time to time and storing it in the central data storage in a format that is suitable to do the analysis and other ways of validating and analyzing it. This approach was, however, rather poor at achieving near zero latency, because in the real world the data transfers can be run only a few times a day. To be fair we should mention that data warehouses were never intended to solve near zero-latency problems.

Direct access to data in real time is much harder to implement, particularly if we have to deal with many distributed data sources. Real-time access has several performance and scalability limitations.

The most efficient way to access data is actually through application logic. Thus, in the next section we will look at multi-tier integration architecture and the composite information system that enable us to fulfill the stated goals.

The Composite Information System and Multi-tier Architecture

To achieve the integration goals and the other objectives mentioned so far, the architecture of the integrated information system will focus on the concept of **virtual components**.

> **An integrated information system based on virtual components is a system that *looks* like a newly developed information system, whereas in fact it actually reuses the functionality of existing applications.**

In simple terms, we can think of a composite information system as a replacement for all existing applications, which does not have the disadvantages connected with replacement. Since it reuses existing applications it is not as costly and does not require as much time as classic replacement of applications.

The composite information system is the ultimate objective of EAI and should fulfill the two stated goals. It enables access to all information and the use of any functionality through virtual components, which allow us to get information with low latency and guarantee that we need enter the same information into the information system only once.

To implement the composite information system we will follow the run time reusability of the business logic implemented in the existing applications. For this we will define virtual components that will represent business logic and implement it through the delegation of operations to one or more existing applications.

> **Virtual components are the building blocks on which we will base the integration.**

We will achieve interoperability among virtual components through the use of the integration broker. The virtual components will have to define the contracts, or the interoperability interfaces, through which they will provide the functionality to other components.

The interfaces will introduce a service-oriented approach to reusing the functionality, and they will expose a set of normalized services that will differ in their complexity and abstraction. Note that in each integration level we will build more complex and abstract virtual components:

❑ Data-level integration – virtual components will provide the access to data only.

❑ Application interface level – virtual components will enable to reuse not only the data, but also the functionality of existing applications. However, the reuse of functionality will take place at a low abstraction level, and will basically resemble the application programming interfaces built into existing applications.

❑ Business method level integration – will raise the abstraction level of virtual components to the level where the interfaces will provide high-level business functions. The business method level integration will fulfill the composite information system requirements.

❑ Presentation-level integration – will add a newly developed presentation tier on top and make the integrated composite information system look like a newly developed information system.

As we have already mentioned, virtual components will implement the business functions through reuse of existing applications. However, if a certain function cannot be implemented solely by existing systems there is no obstacle to adding some newly developed code.

Indeed, virtual components do not differ from newly developed components from the perspective of the clients. Both provide the functionality through the interfaces. The concept of virtual components will therefore allow us to mix existing and new applications in all and any possible way.

The composite information system is based on the **multi-tier architecture**, which separates the roles and defines the following tiers:

❑ User interface

❑ Business logic

75

❑   Data persistence

We will enforce the divisions between the tiers and the strong encapsulation of virtual components. Existing applications will be located on the data persistence tier. In the first three integration levels (data, application interface, and business method) we will build the virtual components that will provide interfaces to the existing applications. These virtual components will be deployed on the business logic tier, which we'll look at in greater depth shortly.

In the presentation-level integration we will add the newly developed presentation layer and deploy it on the user interface tier. For the communication between the tiers and inside the tiers we will use the integration infrastructure abstracted as the integration broker. This will lead to the multi-tier architecture of the integrated information system that is presented in the following figure:

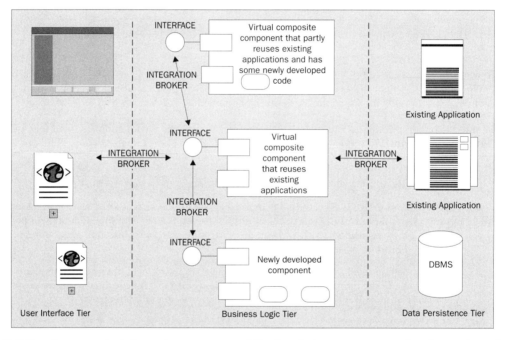

Building the composite information systems is a difficult task that requires a good understanding of requirements for the integrated information system and methods to develop the integrated solution, including familiarity with existing technologies, selecting the infrastructure, defining the new architecture, and good architectural skills.

If organized the right way, the composite information system approach can lead to a highly successful project. Without good organization, however, such efforts are likely to fail; those who have failed will try to convince you that the composite information system is a dream that cannot be implemented in the real world – at least not yet with the current technologies. In this and in the next chapter we will present the methods, techniques, and patterns that will help to make a composite information system a reality.

To develop the virtual components, the main building blocks of the composite information system, we will use a technique called **component wrapping**. Before we continue with a description of the various integration levels, we will have a look at the concept of component wrapping.

Virtual Components and Component Wrapping

> **Virtual components encapsulate the details and methods that existing applications use to satisfy requests.**

On one side, the virtual component presents the existing application through abstract interoperability interfaces, and on the other side, it communicates with the existing application using their existing facilities. Virtual components together with abstract interoperability interfaces present an application view that is implementation-independent. If we keep the abstract interface constant, the other applications are not aware of any changes that are done on the original application. Thus, there is no need for modifying other applications that depend on the original application when a change is made. In other words, client virtual components are unable to determine how the server virtual components are implemented. How the virtual component works is illustrated in the following diagram:

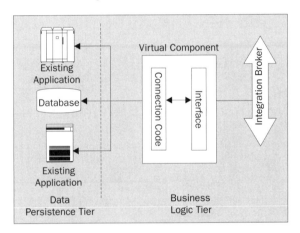

Component wrapping is a relatively simple technique that allows us to build the virtual components and reuse functionality of existing applications in our newly defined composite information system architecture. Component wrapping enables us to implement the functionality of virtual components with the use of existing applications.

The integration broker technology that we choose depends on exactly how a virtual component will be implemented. In each case the virtual component masks the complexity of the existing applications that implement the high-level business functionality in the background. Today there are several tools available for different technologies that allow us to speed up the wrapping process and to automate the development of virtual components and their code.

As stated previously, virtual components are deployed on the business logic tier. They are built in several stages during integration, and different virtual components will expose interfaces offering different abstraction levels to access the functionality. Therefore we will organize the virtual components into several sub tiers within the business logic tier.

We will build the three types of virtual-tier components:

❑   Lower-level virtual components to access:

□ Existing databases (developed in data-level integration)

□ Functionality of existing applications (developed in application interface level integration)

□ Higher-level virtual components to expose high-level business methods (developed in business method level integration)

The virtual components on a lower level will take care of technology adoption, while those on higher levels will transform the high-level business request into a series of lower-level calls to different low-level virtual components for existing applications. High-level virtual components will also do some data conversions and adoptions to finally achieve the goal of implementing the functionality through reuse of existing applications.

The organization of virtual components into multiple sub tiers inside the business logic tier can be more easily understood visually, as shown in the following diagram:

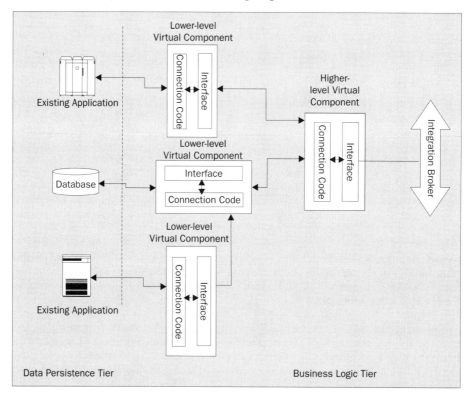

If done the right way, the virtual components are not very difficult to implement. In particular, if applications already provide some APIs through which we can access the required functionality, then for virtual component wrapping we do not even have to change existing applications.

If the application does not provide any application-level interfaces, or if the application interfaces provided by the existing application do not meet our requirements, then we will have to define and build them. For this we will modify the existing application and add the necessary interfaces. We will call the added application interface a **wrapper** and the modified existing application will be referred to as a **wrapped existing application**.

Adding wrappers can be quite straightforward, especially in solutions that have been developed in house and where source code and documentation is available. However, with applications where we do not have the source code and where the documentation is limited, changing the application can be difficult.

When faced with such a situation, we can consider using direct database access, or even using the user interface to access the functionality. Techniques like screen scraping, where wrappers access the application functionality through the user interface, can help us to get the necessary information without modifying the applications.

Wrappers result in the following architecture:

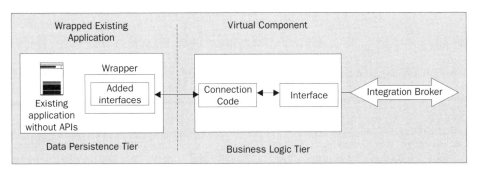

The way in which we implement wrappers will depend, as ever, on the selected technologies, and there are a variety of technology choices – we will discuss these in Chapter 3. Usually we will use the integration broker to obtain the communication between the virtual component and the wrapper. The communication between the wrapper and the existing application will, on the other hand, use proprietary solutions. Sometimes we will integrate the wrapper with the existing application through source code, or we will use some inter-process communication. A third possibility is to use terminal emulation or screen scraping to simulate user interface. With this technique, like terminal emulation, we simulate user typing to enter the data into the application, and read the screens to obtain the results.

As we will see, CORBA is a widely used technology for building wrappers – we will cover this topic at length in Chapter 10.

> **Component wrapping is a powerful technique to address the problem of existing systems that have often been constructed from low-level statements that have nothing to do with the business and its processes.**

The higher-level virtual components raise the level of abstraction to the level of business components. All accesses, including direct and indirect access to state variables, are performed through the interface methods. Wrappers finally add the application programming interfaces to existing applications that did not provide them originally.

The integration broker encapsulates virtual components, which hide differences in programming languages, systems locations, operating systems, algorithms, and data structures. Most integration broker architectures today support such encapsulations, as we will see later.

We are now ready to look at the various integration levels. As such, in the next few sections of this chapter we will focus on building the composite information system on multi-tier architecture. We will examine data-level integration, application interface level integration, defining the abstract business tier through business method level integration, and finally presentation integration. Let's start with the data-level integration.

Data-Level Integration

> **Data-level integration focuses on moving data between applications with the objective of sharing the same data among these different applications.**

This is often the starting point when a company starts to work on integration. From a technical perspective, data-level integration is a relatively simple approach that is well understood by most developers. Accessing databases is relatively easy and there are several tools available that make the data sharing easier and faster. Note that data-level integration does not require changes to the applications.

Although the technology for accessing databases is not too difficult, the whole task of implementing data-level integration is not easy at all. The problem usually lies in the complexity of the databases and in their number. To move the data between databases it is not enough to be familiar with the technology. We also have to understand what data is stored in which database and in what form. We have to know when and how we can extract the data. Even more important is to be familiar with the type and structure of the destination database. Only then will we be able to store data in the database in a format that is understood by all the applications that use this database and that doesn't break the consistency of the database.

The semantics of the databases is the most difficult part of data-level integration. We may have to deal with several hundred different databases over the course of a few integration projects. Some of them will belong to legacy applications, some of them to newer applications. In some cases we will not be familiar with all the applications, meaning that we will also not be familiar with the structure of all of the data involved and the way in which it is stored.

Sometimes we will have limited access to the databases because of contract restrictions. Then we will have to find other possibilities to access the data, for example using APIs, which we will discuss in the next section. If this is not applicable, we might be able to access flat files containing exported data and to add information using flat files again that are imported by the target application. This adds another layer of complexity to data-level integration.

Data-level integration is achieved by following the sequence of tasks shown below:

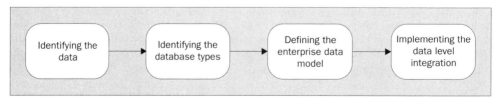

So our first task is to become familiar with the way data is stored in all the applications. We will have to understand what data is stored where, and what the important data flows are.

Identifying the Data

The first step in data-level integration, as shown in the previous schematic, is to become familiar with the data that already exists in the company.

We will have to go from application to application and create data models of each application. This is a difficult and time-consuming job, but in order for the integration to be successful we have to go through it. We should also determine who owns the databases, and how they are deployed. Remember, we can use existing documentation if it is available.

Often, high-level database diagrams, like entity relationships (ER), are available – making it easier for us to become familiar with the data representation. However, low-level details, in the documentation in particular, are often out of date. Therefore, we recommend looking at the actual implementation (even if there is documentation available). Identifying the differences in attributes and fields now will save us a lot of trouble later.

The database schemas and the models will give us insights how the databases are structured, but we will still not understand in detail how this data is managed by applications. We can get the additional information from data dictionaries, if they exist. If they do exist we will again have to check that they reflect the real world situation (and that they are up to date). Otherwise we will have to build them, at least to the extent where we understand how the applications manage the data.

The important point to make here is that we have to really understand the way the data is managed. A common mistake is to stop too early, when we think we understand it. Sooner or later we will realize that we did not fully understand the semantics, and the later we realize this, the harder it will be to correct the mistakes and it will require even more work to fix.

Identifying the Database Types

After identifying the logical structure of the databases we have to become familiar with the physical implementation – the data model and the way in which we can actually access the database. This is the second step in data-level integration.

Today, most data is stored using the relational model, and many developers are comfortable with relational models and most tools support them. Using the relational model only makes the data-level integration easier from the technical perspective. Typically we will have to deal with at least the following types of databases:

- ❑ Relational
- ❑ Object-oriented
- ❑ Universal
- ❑ Multidimensional
- ❑ Hierarchical and Network

We should be aware that legacy systems might also use some other database formats. Most of these will be proprietary file structures, although some other structures have gained popularity and have been widely used. These include:

- ❏ ISAM – a hardware-dependent file structure for sequential and direct access to records in large files

- ❏ VSAM – an improved, hardware-independent version of ISAM

- ❏ CODASYL – a standardized format to store data and access them from COBOL

Defining the Enterprise Data Model

After we have analyzed the databases and are familiar with their logical and physical structure, we have to define the enterprise data model. This is the third step in the data-level integration process.

> **The enterprise data model is a high-level representation of all relevant data used by an organization.**

This model presents the enterprise data in a consistent way, focusing on relations between the data in the enterprise. It also defines which datasets support which business areas throughout the enterprise and how. The enterprise data model is crucial for planning the data-level integration. It may not contain all of the details of the data, but should focus on integration points.

The situation before integration can have the following characteristics:

- ❏ Some data may be redundant

- ❏ Applications are independent, unconnected, and have separated processes

- ❏ Many steps are required for data transfers

- ❏ Transfers are packet based

- ❏ Systems are physically and logically independent

The first step in building the enterprise data model is to go through the data dictionaries and identify the redundant entities. Then we have to identify which application should be responsible for certain redundant data in the integration architecture. We also solve other anomalies that we identify through the analysis of partial data models and dictionaries. If a company has many different databases this task will be time consuming and difficult. We will come back to this in more details in the next few chapters.

Once we have resolved as many problems as possible, we can focus on the enterprise data model. To construct the model appropriately it is a good idea to first define the meta-model. The meta-model will define the rules for designing the model. In particular, for large enterprises the meta-model will provide a way to verify the enterprise data model and will also define the way in which applications should interact to achieve data-level integration.

First, we will create the logical enterprise data model. Although this model in theory can use any database type, the most obvious choice is the relational type, in which case we will need to define the architecture for all data stores and all relations between them.

To do this we will use the entity relationship model and the corresponding ER diagrams. ER diagrams represent the concepts of relational databases in a visual form. Note that different versions of ER diagrams are used for a variety of database design methods and these versions consist of slightly different constructs and employ different diagrammatic notations.

The logical data model that we build should be an integrated view business data through the enterprise. The difference between an enterprise-wide logical model, developed from scratch, and the one constructed for EAI is that the latter is based from existing databases.

Prior to finishing the logical model we should also normalize it. During normalization we will decompose complex structures into simpler relations for which we will use a set of normalization rules.

After we have defined the logical data model, we have to map the logical definitions back to the existing databases and assign the responsibilities for parts of the data model to existing applications. We will do this in the physical model.

Only after we have defined the physical model can we start implementing the relations between applications – in other words we can start to implement the data-level integration. With this top-down approach to data-level integration we have a much better understanding of what we are supposed to achieve.

Implementing Data-Level Integration

The actual implementation of the data-level integration is the final step. Remember, we should always try to avoid point-to-point integration – we are already familiar with the associated disadvantages. This technique results in many connections that become very difficult to manage and maintain as the number of databases increases over time.

Another problem with point-to-point database transfers is the problem of controlling the integrity. To guarantee integrity we have to be familiar with the rules of individual databases. How integrity rules are described actually depends on the database model that is used. In the relational model, for example, the integrity rules can be expressed using formal methods or with database-provided constructs.

Problems of integrity arise because in data-level integration we access the database directly, bypassing the business logic (which usually takes care of integrity checks and is where the business rules are implemented). On the other hand, accessing the database directly is simpler than accessing it through application interfaces, although we will have to reimplement the business rules, which, in the long term, negates this simplicity because of the need for additional maintenance.

The lack of integrity control in data-level integration can result in several problems with existing applications that will fail to work correctly and will produce errors that will be difficult to track down. Unfortunately, most of middleware products do not provide ways to incorporate integrity rules.

> **The solution to implement data-level integration more efficiently is to use the integration broker. Instead of implementing point-to-point connection between the applications, we implement one or more virtual components for each application database.**

The introduction of the integration broker also gives us the opportunity to build the integration layers step-by-step and reuse the previous results.

The virtual components provide interfaces for unified access to the data that is handled by the integration broker. They act like a façade to access the database. In addition to implementing a way to access the data they can also contain the logic necessary to guarantee the consistency of data. Data-level integration achieved using virtual components and an integration broker is illustrated in the diagram overleaf:

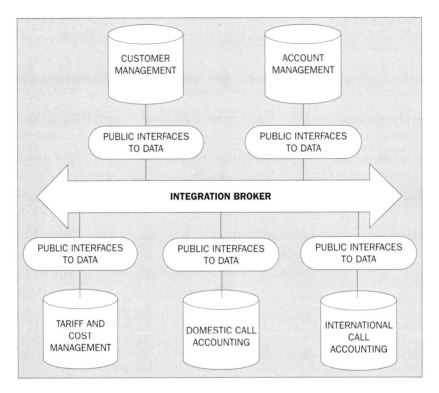

The major benefits of the interface definitions to the data are that they decouple the communication between applications and reduce many-to-many relationships to one-to-many, which is much easier to maintain. By using the integration broker, the communication can be asynchronous, synchronous, or deferred synchronous. The low-latency data access strategy can be partially enabled when using an event or notification service.

We can now summarize the key advantages of defining virtual components with public interfaces for data synchronization as follows:

- ❏   The architecture for application integration is given a solid starting point
- ❏   Reduced maintenance effort because of the simplified relationships
- ❏   Communication can be event driven

The following picture presents the role of virtual components in terms of multi-tier integration architecture. It shows the business logic tier where the virtual components are deployed and the data persistence tier on which the databases of existing applications are located:

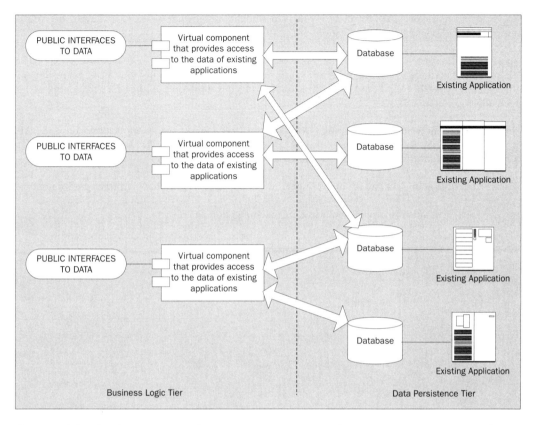

Successful data-level integration is the prerequisite to continue the integration efforts with application interface level integration, which we will discuss in the next section.

Application Interface Level Integration

Application interface level integration is one of the two parts of business-level integration. The other part is business method level integration that we will discuss later in this chapter.

> **Application interface level integration and business method level integration focus on sharing functionality and data, and not only pure data as in data-level integration.**

Application interface level integration is achieved through the use of APIs. Applications that expose their functionality through APIs enable access to the functionality in a programmatic way, without using the user interface.

In the past, developers did not realize the usefulness of APIs, therefore most older applications do not have them. Since then newer applications have accepted the idea that an application can provide services to other applications. Thus, we are more likely to find APIs in newer applications.

So, through the use of APIs we can access the functionality of existing systems. However, the APIs exposed by different existing applications will differ in the way in which we can access them.

Again, we will represent the functionality of existing applications through virtual components that expose the operations of existing applications through their interoperability interfaces, accessible through the integration broker. The application interface level integration therefore masks the technology differences.

Fortunately, application-level integration does not require that the existing applications have the API implemented. If it does not implement the API, we will have to wrap it. We will build wrappers that will add the required interfaces to existing applications.

To use the application-level integration we need to satisfy one of the following three requirements:

❑ That the APIs are already built into the existing application

❑ That we add a wrapper through the modification of existing application source code

❑ That we add a wrapper by accessing the functionality of the existing application through the simulation of user interaction

We will proceed with the application interface level integration by following the steps shown in the diagram below:

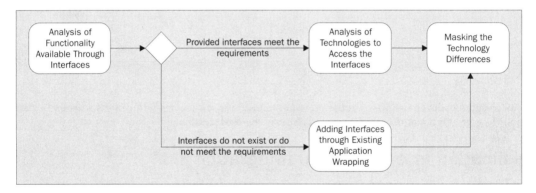

Analysis of Functionality Available Through Interfaces

The analysis of functionality available through interfaces of existing applications is the first step in application interface level integration. The functions that are accessible through the application programming interface can vary from application to application. Some provide access only to limited functionality while others allow access to all functions. Some provide APIs to access the data only, through business rules.

> **There are many differences in APIs in existing applications because they have rarely been designed as part of the original application.**

Older applications, in particular, have been designed on the fly, without putting too much effort towards providing interfaces that would provide all the application functionality in a consistent, easy-to-use way. There are important differences in application interfaces from application to application, it is necessary to analyze each application to figure what interfaces the application provides, and what functions they provide.

The functions that the application interfaces provide are also distinguished in terms of their abstraction. Typically, application interfaces will provide rather low-level, technical (rather than business-oriented) operations. To use them we have to become familiar with the way in which the application works. It is a fact that most of these application interfaces have not been designed with integration in mind. The integration architecture has also not been available, so the best they could do was to provide the technical interfaces to the application functionality.

Application interfaces are a part of most modern applications and most commercial systems. All major ERP systems have, in the last few years, added support for APIs that allow access to their functionality through application-level interfaces. Unfortunately there are no standards to indicate how the application interfaces should be defined.

So, it depends on how well the ERP system providers have designed the interfaces. This will influence how easy we will be able to use them. Often ERP and other large commercial applications have been developed over several years. Rarely has their design included APIs from the ground up. More often, the application interfaces have been added later and usually in several stages. First, some low-level interfaces have provided the support for a limited set of functionality, often through proprietary mechanisms. Then more functions have been added, but the old interfaces have been preserved.

This has resulted in large complexity in the interfaces and often we will have to study them carefully to be able to select the right interfaces and right method for what we want to do. Often we can access the same functionality in different ways, because more than one interface offers it. Then we will have an even harder choice selecting the right one.

> **The analysis of functionalities available through interfaces of existing applications will answer the question whether the existing application provides the required interfaces and if these interfaces are adequate to access the required functionalities.**

If the answer is positive we will continue with the analysis of technologies used to access the interfaces. If the answer is negative we will have to add the required interfaces.

We will look at both scenarios, but before we proceed with the analysis of technologies, it is worth mentioning that the analysis of functionalities provided by existing systems is related to analysis of existing applications, which is addressed in Chapter 4.

Analysis of Technologies To Access the Interfaces

The application interfaces also differ in the technology that they use to implement the interfaces. Thus, in the second step we will analyze the technologies that we use to access the interfaces of existing applications.

In the past, interfaces were implemented in proprietary technologies, but now several different standards have emerged. Interfaces can provide synchronous or asynchronous means of communication, and applications that use standardized interfaces will often utilize middleware to provide this communication. Possible middleware solutions that are appropriate for implementing application interfaces include:

- ❏ MOM

- ❏ RPC

- ❏ ORBs

- ❏ Communication protocols (SOAP, HTTP, TCP/IP)

The choice of technology used for implementation also depends on how we will use these interfaces, what effort we will have to put in, and how well those interfaces align with the selected integration architecture.

The architecture of existing applications is not the deciding factor that would influence the possibility of using APIs. It does not matter whether the application is developed as a monolithic piece, if it facilitates the client/server architecture, or if it is multi-tier architecture. In all cases, if an application offers an API that allows access to the operations we need, we will be able to use it.

Finally, we should note that most commercial applications, and particularly ERP systems, have started to add support for application interfaces based on commonly accepted standard technologies, like CORBA and DCOM.

Adding Interfaces Through Existing Application Wrapping

We have already identified that some existing applications, particularly older legacy applications, will not provide application interfaces. Or perhaps the existing application interfaces don't provide access to all the functionality that we need.

In either case, we will have to add the interfaces to existing applications. For this we will use the existing application wrapping, which is the third step in application interface level integration.

> **Application interfaces can be added to any application, even if it currently does not provide them.**

However, we have to consider whether it is worth the invested effort of adding the application interfaces. After an assessment of costs we might find out that a better solution is to replace the existing application.

If we find out that it is more economical to add the application interfaces we will define the interfaces and connect them with the existing application. Remember, this is called wrapping, and the modified existing application is called wrapped existing application.

To add the application interfaces to an existing application we will first have to analyze the existing application functionality and identify how the application works. A particularly important question that we will have to answer is whether we have the source code that reflects the actual version of the existing application and if we have all the necessary tools to build the existing application.

If we have the source code and the necessary tools, then we can modify the existing application directly and build in the wrapper. Otherwise we can still access the functionality of existing applications using terminal emulation or screen scraping.

We'll discuss building CORBA wrappers in Chapter 10.

Masking the Technology Differences

The final step of application interface level integration is the task of masking the technology differences. We have now either identified the existing application interfaces or developed new ones to the existing applications. However, we cannot use these APIs directly.

The problem with using APIs directly is that, most likely, not all applications will use the same technology to access the interfaces. Some applications will offer some proprietary ways to access the APIs, some will provide access through TCP, others will use middleware solutions, like CORBA, and some will use Microsoft DCOM.

> **We can solve the problem by building virtual components that will mask the differences between the technologies.**

If we follow the integration broker pattern this will be a relatively easy task, similar to developing virtual components for data-level integration.

We have already identified the operations in the existing applications that we would like to access over APIs. Now we will define the same (or slightly modified) interfaces for the virtual components. We will use the integration broker technology to achieve interoperability, and we will simply delegate the requests from the virtual components to the application-specific interfaces of existing applications.

This will provide access to APIs that is based on a single technology and will mask the differences between the protocols and technologies used for APIs by existing applications. It will also put the whole code that takes care of adapting the technologies (the bridge code) in one place – in the virtual component – where it can be used by all clients. There will be no need for each client to bother with the conversion of protocols, and this will simplify the maintenance considerably.

Such virtual components will still present relatively low-level interfaces; therefore we will refer to them as lower-level application interface level virtual components. The architecture of application interface integration with virtual components is shown schematically in the following figure:

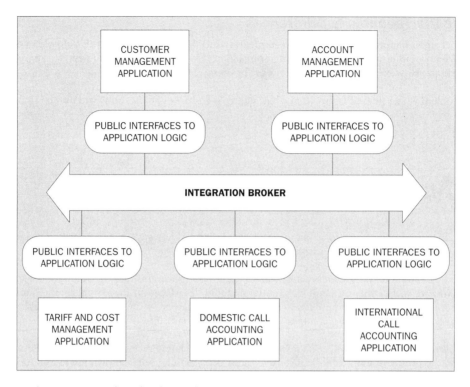

The next figure presents the role of virtual components in terms of multi-tier integration architecture. It shows the business logic tier where the virtual components are deployed and the data persistence tier on which the existing applications are located. Notice the one-to-one connections between the virtual components and APIs of existing applications:

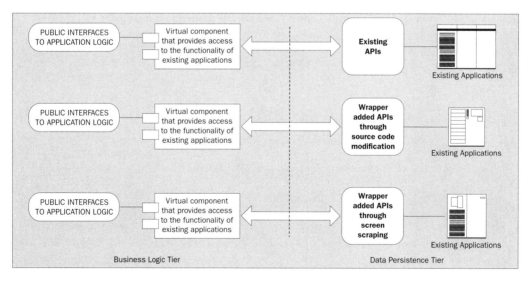

Application interface level integration can be an alternative to the data-level integration if we decide to use the APIs of existing applications instead of accessing the database directly. The access to data of existing applications via built-in APIs is favorable over the direct database access because it does not bypass the business logic. The risk of damaging the database integrity is therefore much lower.

The application level integration is a prerequisite to do the next logical step – business method level integration.

Business Method Level Integration

Method level integration also focuses on integrating the enterprise information system through the sharing of business logic. However, the name implies that the functionality through business method integration will be shared on a much higher level.

> **The goal of business level integration is to develop virtual components that will provide interfaces with high-level business methods that can be considered as business services.**

These higher-level virtual components will provide interfaces based on business requirements. In contrast to the application interface level integration, the interfaces here do not reflect the application design and technology, but high-level business methods. Such interfaces cannot be defined ad hoc, but only after carefully designing the enterprise integration architecture. Consequently, the design of the business logic tier integration architecture will be an important part of business method level integration.

Note that the interfaces provide a contract between the virtual components and the user interface tier. As long as the interfaces stay unchanged this means that the contracts have not been changed. But it also means that the interfaces are the entities that tie different parts of the information system together. Nobody cares how the virtual components that realize these interfaces are implemented, or what applications actually execute in the background. We can change the applications that implement a certain interface without influencing the whole information system or partial applications – as long the interface stays unchanged. This fact will enable us to replace existing applications step-by-step in the future.

On one side, the components expose the high-level business methods, and on the other side they will use the lower level virtual components developed in application interface level integration and data-level integration.

> **A single business method level virtual component will typically call several lower level application interface level components to fulfill a task.**

In general we will probably introduce more than just two levels of virtual components. Rather we will go step-by-step from low-level to high-level virtual components, introducing a hierarchy of virtual components on the business logic tier – we will group them into several sub tiers.

Virtual components developed as a part of business method level integration will use the integration broker to achieve interoperability and will be developed according to the technological requirements of the integration broker and the underlying infrastructure.

91

To achieve business method level integration we will therefore proceed in three steps:

Let's start with the definition of high-level business interfaces.

Defining the High-level Business Interfaces

The definition of high-level business interfaces is the first step in business method level integration. Although the idea for business method level integration sounds good in principle, it is difficult to achieve in practice. One of the most tricky parts is to define high-level business interfaces that are flexible enough to survive for the coming years. The high-level business interface should adhere to the following general guidelines:

❑ Support all the requirements of the integrated information system

❑ Exhibit a high-level of abstraction

❑ Fit into the information architecture of the enterprise

❑ Be designed with future development in mind

Obviously the definition of these interfaces will not be an easy task. It will also not be an ad hoc job, but will rather require the coordinated effort of analysts, designers, and architects.

> **To define the high-level business interfaces we have to build the global design model of the entire integrated information system on a high level of abstraction.**

In simple terms, what we have to do (actually what the analysts, designers, and architects have to do) is to define a global design of the information system as we would like to have it as if we were to build it from scratch.

This is not an easy task and requires a lot of knowledge and effort. Some people might argue that the idea of method-level integration requires too much effort and that the results are too far downstream to be worth doing. Some will even argue that it is impossible to define the stable global enterprise information design in reality. The fact is that this is indeed not so easy and we need experienced people that will take care of it. However, if we cannot define the enterprise design this means that we actually cannot set the fundamental requirements, goals and objectives. This will make the integration project a likely candidate to fail even before it has started.

Since the definition of the global design model is a difficult task we will address it in more detail in Chapter 4, and return to it in Chapter 9. For the moment we will give an overview of the main activities that have to be performed.

To define the global enterprise wide information system design model we have to start with the requirement analysis. Then we have to do the use case analysis and define the analysis model. At the same time we have to investigate existing systems and identify their functionality.

Both the analysis model and the study of existing application functionality are the prerequisites for creating the global design model. It is necessary to ensure that all required functionality is reflected in the new design model. The model should also be designed so that future extensions will be possible without too much pain. Thus, the design model should offer a common architecture baseline for the integrated system.

The following diagram shows the necessary sequence of activities, including the next two steps –mapping the operations and the implementation of virtual components – that we will discuss shortly:

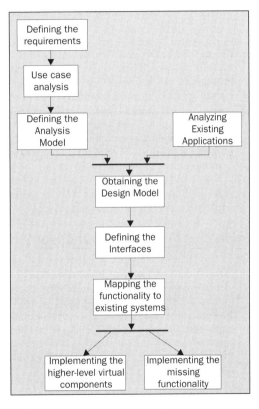

If we use iterative and incremental development we can obtain the global design model through several iterations, which simplifies the task considerably. With this procedure we can partition different tasks and disperse them in time as our needs dictate. We will discuss the integration development process in more depth in Chapter 4.

The global design model is then used for the definition of the high-level interfaces through which we will access the services provided by the system. These high-level interfaces will be implemented by the virtual components that we build in this integration level. However, before we can start developing the virtual components we have to define how each operation from each interface will be implemented. We will discuss this in the following subsection.

Mapping the Business Operations

In the second step we have to map the business operations to the lower-level virtual components that represent the existing applications. After defining the high-level business interfaces we have to figure out how to implement each operation from the interface.

> **We try to reuse as much functionality of the existing systems as possible.**

Therefore, we will first define mappings for each high-level businesses operation to the existing applications.

More precisely, we will not map the operations directly to the existing applications. Rather we will map them to the lower level virtual components that we have developed in the application interface level integration stage. There we have analyzed the existing applications and masked the technology differences. We will use the knowledge that we have obtained there and try to find the best mapping from high-level business methods to the operations provided by existing systems.

Such mapping will exactly define the sequence of operations on lower-level virtual components that each high-level business operation has to perform. The mapping will also define the necessary transformations that have to be done between the calls to lower-level virtual components, and all other constraints, such as timing and syntax.

After we have completed the mapping we have to implement these high-level virtual components and deploy them on the business logic tier.

Implementing the Higher-Level Virtual Components

The implementation of the higher-level virtual components is the last step in business method level integration. Typically, a single high-level business method will use several operations from lower-level virtual components that represent existing applications.

The high-level method will also have to do some processing, adapt the results, transform the data types, and so on, in order to perform the whole operation.

With the mapping of high-level business operation from the interfaces we have been faced with three possible scenarios:

- ❑   We could map a high-level business method entirely to a set of lower-level virtual component operations
- ❑   We could map them partially
- ❑   We could not map them at all

In the first scenario the implementation of the virtual component is the most straightforward. Often however, we will not be able to implement the high-level business method through reuse of existing application functionality only. In this case, we will have to implement the missing code. Sometimes the existing systems will not provide the functionality that we require at all. Then we will have to develop the missing parts ourselves, outsource the development, or buy commercial off-the-shelf components.

The newly developed components and the virtual components share the same technology. Thus, for the client components there is no distinction between virtual components that reuse the functionality of existing systems and newly developed components. Clients access both through the interfaces.

> **The result of the method level integration is the virtual components that expose high-level business interfaces.**

It is important to realize that the higher-level virtual components use lower-level virtual components that we developed with application interface level and data-level integration. This is shown schematically in the next figure:

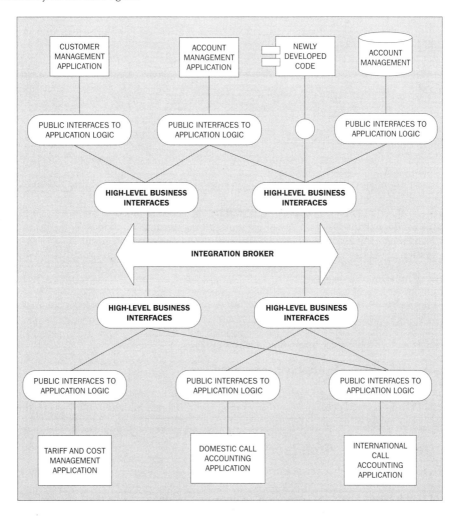

The next figure presents the role of virtual components in terms of multi-tier integration architecture and shows the sub-tiers within the business logic tier:

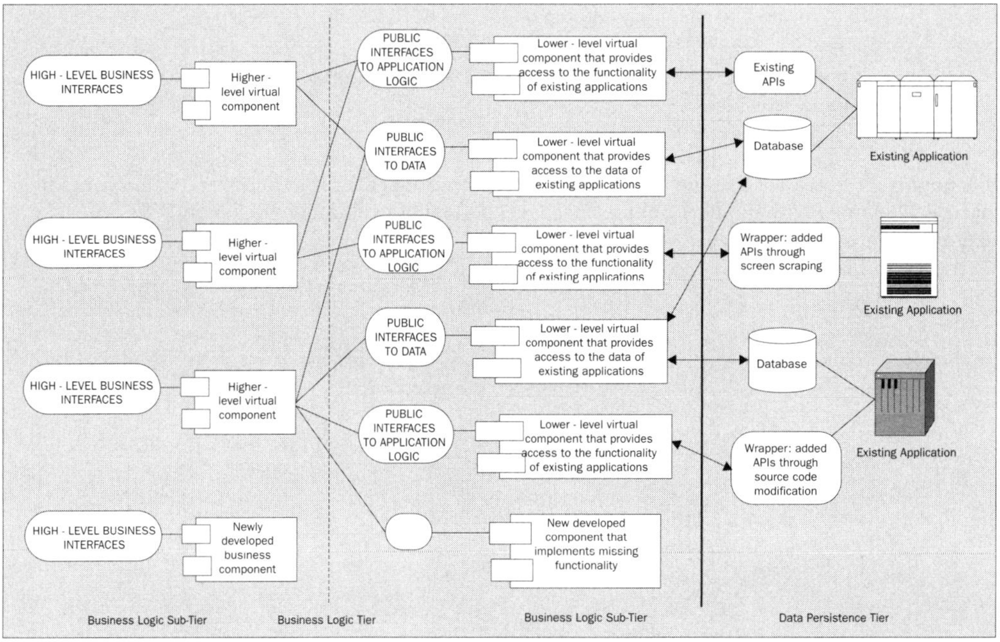

Business method level integration enables applications to share the business logic. Existing and new applications can invoke the functionality of each other in a way that is independent of technology and location. Remember, the technology infrastructure is provided by the integration broker. The method-level integration offers the following important advantages over data integration:

❑   Unified business process

❑   Two-way communication

❑   Immediate operation invocations

❑   Physically and logically interconnected systems

We'll return to the concept of virtual components in Chapter 9.

Before we continue with our overview of the various integration levels, we will have a brief look at the standardized business architectures that address the most difficult problem of business method level integration – definition of the global design model.

Standardized Business Architectures

When defining the business-tier service-oriented interfaces for a company, a common question that can arise is this: why should we reinvent the wheel? Why do we not just use some standardized interfaces? The use of standardized architecture for a given domain provides many benefits, most of all it offers the interoperability of solutions between companies.

In this context, we're not talking about simple interfaces, such as those that enable document and data exchange between companies, which are currently very popular. What we are referring to are the business-domain architectures defined in interfaces that would standardize the business domain – similar to the standardization that takes place in any technical field.

Although the idea sounds reasonable, we are not yet ready to implement it. Seen from the current perspective, there are too many complications involved, too many differences between the companies, and too much complexity to be able to standardize the interfaces. Also, it will take a long time before a consensus can be achieved between the companies. Even simple interfaces between the companies are a long way from being widely accepted.

Still, several organizations try to define standards for vertical domains. The most notable is the effort by the OMG (http://www.omg.org/), which has already successfully defined interfaces for some domains, like medicine and telecommunications. Others will soon follow.

In the next section we will have a look at presentation-level integration.

Presentation Level Integration

We should be aware that business method level integration does not solve all the problems. Although the business logic can be shared, the existing applications are still used in the same way as before. This means that the user is fully aware that several different existing applications are used and a manual switch between them is required. The user interface is not unified and users need to make several steps to perform a certain business operation and have to switch between different applications. Although we have mentioned that the integration architecture will be multi-tier, we have not addressed the user interface tier yet.

Presentation-level integration will solve these problems – this can be considered as the final step in EAI.

> **We will treat presentation integration as a step in which we define and implement a common user interface for the business method level integrated information system.**

Such a user interface will provide the illusion of a new system, and add the missing piece to the multi-tier integration architecture.

We should not look at presentation integration as simple user interface integration, adding web or graphical user interfaces, which we may have covered by application extension. Nor should we consider presentation integration merely a way to extract the data from existing applications through the user interfaces (often referred to as screen scraping). In fact, we have to cover screen scraping as one of the possibilities for component wrapping.

After we have successfully implemented the business method level integration we have a system with a fully functional business logic tier. The functionality of business components has been implemented partially by existing systems, and partially with newly developed components. We also have a functional data persistence tier.

What is missing is the new user interface. In order to define it, we will follow the basic principle of separation of user interface, business logic, and data persistence tiers, as shown in the next figure:

97

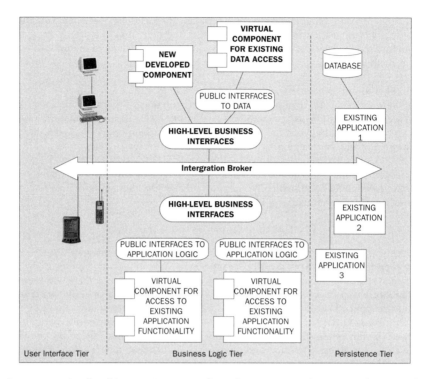

During the presentation-level integration we perform the sequence of activities shown in the figure below, and described in the bullet points that follow:

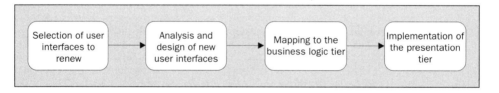

1. We will have to select which user interfaces we need in the integrated information system. We have to be pragmatic and select first those parts that are in greatest need of the user interfaces. Sometimes, particularly if we use some large existing applications, like ERP systems, we will not even renew the whole user interface. Users of ERP systems only, for example, will continue using their existing user interfaces.

2. The major activity in presentation level integration is the analysis and design of a unified user interface for the integrated information system. The integrated information system will look like a completely new system to the end users. The end users will not be able to recognize that existing applications are used behind the scenes, and they will have no direct contact with the existing applications, which are now serving as virtual business components on the middle-tier layer.

When designing the new presentation tier we will have to focus on the requirements of the integrated information system and base the interfaces on the business scenarios. We also have to follow sound design principles for user interfaces, like user friendliness, simplicity, navigability, consistency, visual feedback, clarity, and so on.

3. We will have to map the user interface operations to business methods on the business logic tier. This mapping will be quite straightforward, because all the required functionality already exists on the middle tier.

4. Finally, we will have to implement the new presentation tier. For user interface implementation we can choose different approaches, including:

❑ Graphical user interface clients

❑ Web clients or thin clients

❑ Universal clients for several different types of client technology (web-based, mobile, and so on)

Current practice shows that the thin clients are the most desirable way to implement it. Furthermore, we will try to make the user interface as independent from the device used for presentation as is possible.

When implementing the presentation integration we also have to face the problems of transactional integrity and various security issues. Let's take a quick look at transactions first. From the new presentation tier the users will typically access different systems, both existing and new, through the high-level virtual components. Often we will want such access to be transactional and we therefore have to become familiar with distributed transactions. We need to learn how to integrate existing transactional solutions with the new architecture and how to propagate transactional context. In other words, we will have to ensure that the business logic tier will take the responsibility for transactions. Transaction management for enterprise integration will be covered in depth in Chapter 15.

Turning our attention to the issues surrounding security, with the introduction of the unified presentation tier the users will want to have a single point of authentication – they will want to sign in at the beginning. Our responsibility will be to do the authorization and other security services. Since some functionality is implemented by existing systems we will have to find ways in which to integrate different security domains and how to propagate the security context between existing and new applications inside the information system. In Chapter 16 we will take a specific look at security management in EAI.

We will discuss the presentation tier development in more detail in Chapter 17. There we will cover the technology choices for presentation integration, addressing technologies like JSP pages, servlets, XML, XSLT, and SOAP.

Successful implementation of the presentation tier integration will result in the full multi-tier architecture, as shown in the following diagram:

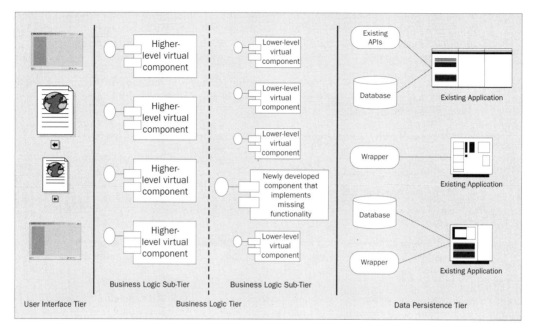

The foremost benefits of the presentation level integration can be summarized as the following:

❏ Unified business process

❏ Entire application integration

❏ Unified user interface

❏ Two-way synchronous communication

❏ Immediate and individual operation invocations and data transfers

❏ Physically and logically interconnected systems

❏ Fully enabled information access with no latency

❏ Fully enabled single data input

> **Implementing the presentation-level integration is the final stage towards an integrated information system.**

In the rest of this chapter we will discuss the options that we have relating to the re-engineering and replacement of existing applications in the proposed integration architecture, and how can we extend the integration architecture to support business-to-business (B2B) collaborations.

Re-engineering and Replacement

The proposed multi-layer integration approach ultimately leads to a multi-tier architecture where we have cleanly separated tiers. The user interface tier is almost completely newly developed and uses the high-level interfaces provided by the business logic tier. Some of the business logic tier is implemented with reuse of existing applications. The other functionality has been freshly developed.

Although this approach provides an efficient and relatively straightforward technique for integrating existing applications, we should not forget that legacy applications will ultimately reach a point when it is no longer reasonable to maintain them. The decision regarding when this might take place will depend on many factors and this process is usually referred to as **legacy applications health assessment**.

As mentioned earlier in the chapter, generally a legacy application is not appropriate anymore when the cost of maintaining it is higher than the benefits it provides. Although this is obvious, some companies have avoided replacing legacy applications even then because such a replacement might introduce many problems to other applications that are tightly connected with the legacy application. Historically, legacy replacement has always been considered as a difficult task.

> **The proposed integration architecture gives us a possibility to replace and re-engineer legacy applications relatively easy.**

As only the dependencies between the tiers, and within the business logic tier, are defined with interfaces, we can again use the fact that everything is hidden behind the interface of virtual components. As we have emphasized, this allows us to replace the implementation of the virtual components without other parts of the system noticing anything.

To replace and re-engineer parts of existing applications we simply provide new implementations for the functionality of virtual components as shown on the next diagram:

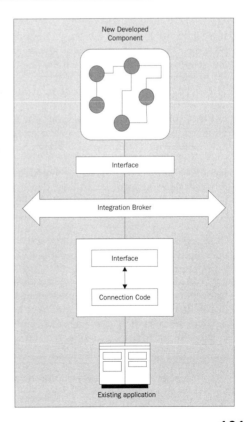

101

How much granulation is allowed in the replacement depends on the implementation of the virtual components and the number of tiers that these components are implemented on. Over time we can replace all existing applications step-by-step until the original applications are redundant and the same functionality is implemented in a more modern way.

This approach reduces cost, enhances maintainability, increases performance, and increases congruency between the system's model and the information architecture. It provides a relatively effortless path to replacing and re-engineering of existing applications.

In the next section we will take a look at how we can extend the integration architecture to support the B2B integration.

B2B Integration and Web Services

Traditionally, there have been many barriers for business partners to collaborate in an electronic form. Systems that were constructed using different technologies, with security loopholes and incompatible data formats, have made large-scale B2B integration only feasible to large businesses and their large partners. In fact, there are two major obstacles to achieving B2B integration:

❑   The information system of a company is not integrated

❑   Technical barriers exist that make B2B integration difficult

If we have implemented EAI as we have discussed in this chapter, then we have solved the first problem. As will become evident in Chapter 3, the advent of new technologies focused on B2B integration, under the name **Web Services**, presents a potential solution to the second problem too.

The architecture of our composite integrated information system provides a good foundation for B2B integration. The functionality is accessed over high-level business interfaces, provided by virtual business components. But remember, the functionality provided by virtual components has not been designed for B2B integration, so we cannot enable direct access to it for business partners. Such functionality offers too much information and we would not want our partners to have access to all of it.

Hence, we can add another tier – **the Web Services tier** – to our architecture that will provide some of those services to business partners. These B2B Web Services will be modeled similar to the business methods for the EAI integration. However, their purpose and meaning will be different, in accordance with the needs and goals of B2B integration.

Web Services are a set of technologies that enable us to define interfaces, which describe a collection of operations that are network accessible through standardized XML messaging, using standardized Internet protocols.

Conceptually, Web Services represent an architecture where tasks within B2B processes can be distributed among the partners that have access to them through the Internet. Technically, Web Services are a set of technologies and standards that enable the service-oriented and component-based architecture of B2B applications.

> **Web services are loosely-coupled components that encapsulate functionality targeted at B2B collaborations.**

Web Services are important because they are built on top of standardized industry specifications. This standardization, which we touched upon briefly earlier, allows Web Service component wrappers to be created and components dynamically mixed and matched at runtime to uniquely fulfill a client's request with B2B collaboration. Also, the use of standardized Web Service interfaces decouples the programming language, operating system, and software deployment platform from each other. Developers can reuse existing solutions to build a complete and fully interoperable Web Service.

The technology of Web Services exploits the openness of specific Internet technologies to address many of the interoperability issues. Specifically, Web Services use HTTP to be firewall-friendly and payload-agnostic, they employ XML as an encoding schema, use the pervasive Internet concept of URLs to address object identification, and offer more than a promise of interoperability.

We will address the concepts of B2B integration and Web Services at length in Chapter 3, and demonstrate a working example in Chapter 18. For now, however, we can summarize with the idea that Web Services allow us to build B2B collaborations on top of the integration architecture. This is seen more clearly in the following diagram:

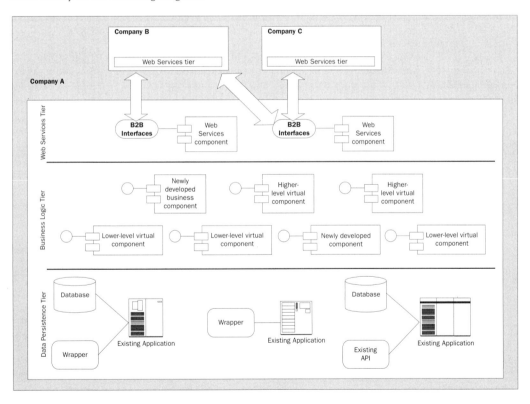

As technologies mature, Web Services will be extended with additional functionality, which will enable smart multipart B2B collaborations to be performed. Web Services are evolving into "smart Web Services" and beginning to operate in an intelligent and dynamic way. The goal is that smart Web Services would understand the context of the requests and produce results that would take into account all specific situations and the context in which the request is processed.

The services should also adapt their processes based on different criteria like preferences, request type, reason, and location. Multiple services should be able to combine their work and provide unique solutions that fit the needs of individual businesses. The technology should be as transparent as possible. Although this is not yet possible today, the technology evolves very quickly in this field.

After we have become familiar with EAI and B2B, and before we summarize the chapter, we will give a quick synopsis of the key integration principles.

Integration Principles

The ideas presented in this chapter can be summarized into some basic integration principles that represent the best practices that we should try to follow:

❑ **Design for the future**
When designing applications and integration architecture we should think of future use and build the architecture so that it will be adaptable and scalable.

❑ **Interface design integrity**
When building integration interfaces we should carefully consider the design and plan of the interfaces and connectivity. The interfaces represent a contract between applications; as long as they stay the same, the changes are limited to a single application.

❑ **Interface abstraction**
We should use the highest possible level interfaces to access existing systems. This makes the link more abstract, which helps to keep it the same even after modifying the applications. Moreover, it will ensure the integrity questions that could arise when using lower-level approaches.

❑ **Multiple entry points**
Some applications might have multiple entry points to access the same functionality. We should use those that best suit our application needs.

❑ **Performance**
We should consider performance issues carefully. When reusing existing systems, we might put them into a situation that they were not designed for. For example, we might enable access to too many simultaneous clients or we might enter too much data.

❑ **Security**
We should consider the security issues even more carefully. In particular, many legacy systems have not been planned with security in mind because they have been limited to closed and trusted environments. When integrating them they might be open to the global network making them vulnerable. Even new applications are not immune to security problems.

Summary

In this chapter we have identified and explained the choices and strategies that are important when defining the integration project. We have seen that the bottom-up approach to integration does not work because it is based on the same presumptions that caused the heterogeneity and lack of integration that we are faced with today. We have also seen that the bottom-up approach can introduce even more chaos into the company information architecture, because it is uncoordinated and based on individual actions.

We considered application replacement as the alternative to integration, but soon realized that this technique is not an ideal option in most cases because it is often more costly and takes longer than planned.

The other solution a lot of companies consider is application extension. This indirect form of integration extends the functionality of existing systems, but again without taking into account the needs of the whole enterprise. Most common cases are extending existing systems with web-based or graphical front-ends. Extension, although a fast and low cost approach, cannot be seen as a step towards global integration.

Thus, the only serious choice for achieving integration on an enterprise-wide level is the top-down approach. This method takes carefully planned steps in order to realize the objectives of integration. It should be supported by senior management, and is a well-coordinated effort. We have also seen why a centrally managed project is crucial for integration and what happens if integration is dispersed over many departments.

Furthermore, we have defined the integration infrastructure and have defined the horizontal and vertical layers. We have become familiar with the communication layer, with the brokering and routing layer and with the business intelligence layer. We have also realized the importance of services like transactions, security, life cycle, naming, scalability, and management.

Next, we defined two important goals: single data input and low-latency information access, and we modeled further steps according to those strategies.

Then we have discussed the composite information system pattern. We have introduced the concept of an integration broker and explained how to use virtual components and component wrapping to reuse the functionality of existing applications.

We covered the four different steps to building the integration architecture that finally bring us to the desired goal of a fully integrated system:

- ❑ **Data-level integration**
  We noted the challenges of building a unified enterprise data model; looked at different models for storing persistent data; showed why we should use the integration broker pattern and virtual components which solve the multiplicity problems and decouple the communications.

- ❑ **Application interface level integration**
  We identified what functionalities are offered by APIs, the types of APIs existing applications provide, which technologies they use, and how we can access them; we have put the application interface level integration in the context of the integration broker; we have shown how to build virtual components and how to add APIs to existing application, through wrapping; we have seen how to map the functionality of existing applications to virtual components and reuse their functionality using component wrapping; we have seen why API access to data is more favorable than direct database access; we have also seen how to mask the technology differences between the applications.

105

❑ **Business method level integration**

We have seen that we should define the service-oriented business interfaces that are at a high abstraction layer. To do this we have to define the architecture of the new, integrated information system and analyze the existing applications. Only then we will be able to define high-level virtual components with interfaces that provide quality business methods that will be able to survive over the years. We have also seen that the interface is the main contract between, and within, the tiers.

❑ **Presentation level integration**

We have seen that this level of integration provides a unified presentation layer on top of multi-tier integration architecture. It gives us the illusion of using a newly developed system, whereas in reality the existing applications are doing the work behind the scenes.

To conclude, we have seen that the composite information system pattern provides ways to re-engineer the functionality of an integrated information system step-by-step until the existing systems become redundant. This architecture enables easy extension to B2B integration projects and enables the definition of Web Services.

In the next chapter we'll start to look at aspects of application integration specific to the J2EE platform.

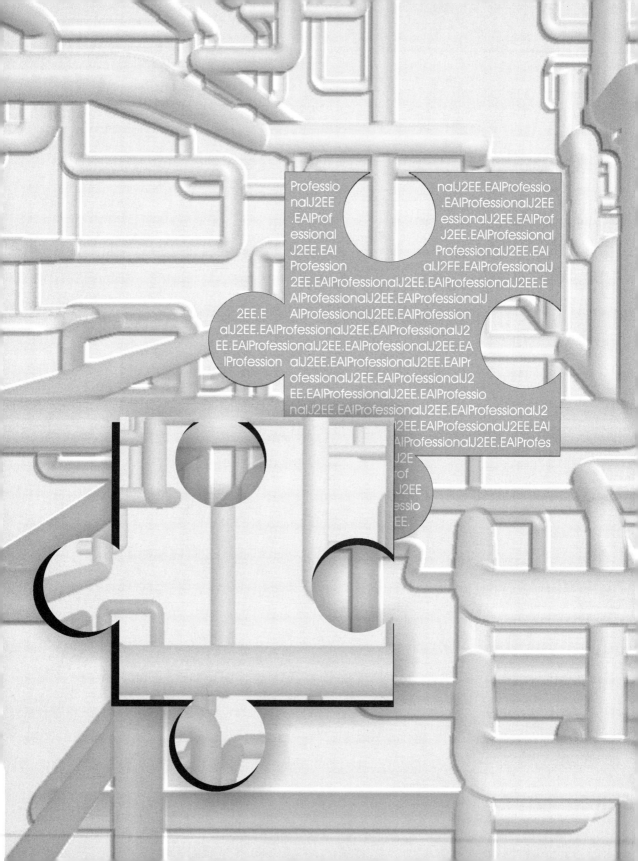

3

The J2EE Platform for EAI

The Java platform was introduced in 1995, bringing with it a revolutionary way of developing, executing, and deploying applications. Four years later, Java gained new functionality dedicated to enterprise computing which became what we now know as the **Java 2 Platform, Enterprise Edition (J2EE)**. Since its release it has opened new opportunities for many companies and today it is one of the most important modern enterprise platforms.

At first, it was not obvious how the J2EE platform could enable interoperability and integration with existing systems and solutions. In fact, when J2EE was first released the concept of EAI had not even been considered. It was only with the development of technologies such as the J2EE Connector Architecture (JCA) that integration issues were introduced.

In this chapter we will look at the J2EE platform from the perspective of application integration. We will present an overview of the various integration technologies, and surrounding issues, in the context of J2EE. This chapter will not, however, describe how to design and achieve specific integrations – such detailed examinations are reserved for later in this book. Here we will concentrate on the following:

❑　How to select the platform for integration

❑　J2EE as an integration platform

❑　Communication between component tiers

❑　Extended J2EE integration architecture

❑　XML support, and support for different types of clients

❑　Virtual components and component wrappers

❑　Transaction support

- ❏ Security considerations
- ❏ Performance and scalability
- ❏ Naming and directory services
- ❏ Support for B2B integration
- ❏ J2EE application servers

Selecting the Platform

In the previous chapter we defined a general integration strategy. We compared the top-down and bottom-up approaches to integration and introduced the concept of the composite information system and the integration broker. To build an integrated information system we have to define a high-level information system architecture and reuse the functionality of existing applications.

In order to reuse the functionality of existing applications we have several distinct possibilities:

- ❏ To acquire data we can access the existing databases directly
- ❏ To access the functionality of existing applications we can use built-in application interfaces
- ❏ We can wrap the existing applications and build interoperability interfaces into them
- ❏ We can even use the user interface to access the functions through techniques such as screen scraping or terminal emulation, where we simulate user interaction with special programs

Accessing the functionality of existing applications is only part of the problem. We also have to present this functionality and data in a common, uniform way according to our global integration architecture. To achieve this we need to build virtual components using component wrapping.

To implement the proposed strategy we have to select the technology base, that is, the enterprise software platform on which we will build the integration architecture.

Selecting the software platform is a very difficult job, which will influence the way software will be developed in the company for many years to come. Obviously for the context of this book, the selection of J2EE has been pre-made, however, we'll briefly cover some of the potential options and provide guidelines on possible selection criteria.

When looking for a modern platform that supports state-of-the-art methods for information system development we have a relatively limited choice:

- ❏ Sun's J2EE platform
- ❏ OMG's CORBA platform
- ❏ Microsoft's .NET platform

All these platforms provide support for multi-tier application architecture, for component-based development, for modern programming languages, and they also provide a large set of enterprise services, such as transactions, security, persistence, naming, resource management, and so on. Still there are several important differences between them.

The J2EE platform is based on Java technology. This makes the platform independent from the operating system and hardware platform on which it runs. However, it limits developers to a single programming language. J2EE is a specification, initially developed by Sun, but today it's controlled by the Java Community Process (JCP) – which makes J2EE a relatively open platform. Different vendors provide implementations that are conformant with the specification.

CORBA is also a specification for a set of technologies, supervised by the OMG (Object Management Group), which is a non-profit consortium. CORBA is an open architecture controlled by the OMG members. CORBA specifies several important technologies, including the ORB (Object Request Broker) and IIOP (Internet Inter-ORB Protocol), CORBA Services, CORBA Facilities, CORBA Component Model (CCM), and others. It has been designed independent of a programming language, operating system, and hardware platform. The first versions date back to 1991 and since then CORBA has established itself as an important integration architecture. Several vendors provide CORBA-compliant products. However, in the last few years it has lost momentum and has increasingly merged with the J2EE platform, which has adopted some of its important technologies, including IIOP and the transaction service, as we will see later.

The .NET platform is Microsoft's latest solution for enterprise computing. Although it is the successor to DNA (Distributed interNet Architecture) it is a completely new product. .NET is implemented by Microsoft and is tightly bound to the Windows operating system. Although rumors exist that Microsoft will standardize .NET and make it an open platform, nothing has been done in that way at the time of writing. .NET is in many ways similar to the J2EE platform. It shares a concept, akin to the JVM, called the Common Language Runtime. It introduces the Intermediate Language (IL), which is conceptually similar to Java byte-code. However .NET can translate different languages to IL (including Java) and will therefore provide support for more than one language. On the other hand, applications built with existing languages have to be considerably modified to fit into the .NET architecture.

> **J2EE and .NET will become competitors in the future. Currently J2EE has an advantage, because it is already an established platform.**

The decision for which architecture to choose should be based on several criteria, including:

- ❏ Support for integration with existing systems and applications
- ❏ Support for open standards and technologies
- ❏ Support for B2B technologies
- ❏ Support for programming languages
- ❏ Support for middleware
- ❏ Robustness, performance and scalability
- ❏ Portability and interoperability
- ❏ Cost and vendor support
- ❏ Existing knowledge and learning curve
- ❏ Maturity

From a J2EE perspective, its main advantages are:

- ❏ It is a specification-based platform, supported by a variety of vendors
- ❏ It is not limited to a certain operating system, hardware platform, or vendor
- ❏ It supports interoperability with existing systems
- ❏ It supports a large set of middleware technologies
- ❏ It is relatively mature
- ❏ It has demonstrated that it can support large enterprise information systems and provide acceptable performance and scalability
- ❏ Several excellent integrated development environments ease development considerably

However, the major disadvantages of the J2EE platform are:

- ❏ Standardized support for B2B technologies is currently poor, although things are improving rapidly
- ❏ Portability between application server vendors is not 100% yet
- ❏ It is limited to the Java programming language, although it provides support for other languages through middleware technologies, such as CORBA and JMS

With this short analysis we will conclude our comparison of the different platforms, and start to look solely at the J2EE platform from the perspective of integration.

J2EE As an Integration Platform

To be able to judge how appropriate the J2EE platform is for integration let us first have a look what J2EE actually is. J2EE is essentially a set of technologies that enable the development and deployment of enterprise applications and enterprise information systems. J2EE addresses the key technologies needed to develop modern solutions. It is designed through the Java Community Process (JCP), which guarantees the direction in which the platform moves and reflects real world needs, as companies can influence the development of the platform.

The J2EE platform is built upon the multi-tier application model. It introduces the following tiers:

- ❏ The client or user interface tier
- ❏ The web component tier
- ❏ The business logic tier, sometimes also called the EJB tier
- ❏ The Enterprise Information System (EIS) tier

The building blocks of each tier are components. Components in J2EE are encapsulated pieces of functionality that are self-contained and expose their functionality through interfaces. The following types of components can be used:

❑   The components for the client tier are **application clients** and **applets**. On the client tier we find application clients, which are typically clients with a rich GUI that execute on desktop computers. They might be written in Java, although this is not strictly necessary, as we will see soon.

❑   The web component tier components are **servlets** and **JSP pages**, which provide the ability to service thin clients. They are deployed in the web component tier and respond to HTTP requests. They generate thin client user interfaces, like HTML, XML, and others.

❑   The components for the business logic tier are **Enterprise JavaBeans (EJB)**. These provide an environment that supports services such as, transactions, security, and persistence, which the EJB components can use, allowing for a high degree of scalability.

Components in each tier execute inside of **containers**. Containers provide the environment in which the components can execute in a controlled and managed way. They also provide an abstraction layer through which the components see the underlying services and the whole architecture. Containers provide services that the components can use, either in a programmatic or a declarative way.

The only tier that does not consist of components is the EIS tier. In this tier we find the existing enterprise infrastructure, like ERP systems, TP monitors, database management systems, and other existing systems.

The described architecture is presented in the following diagram:

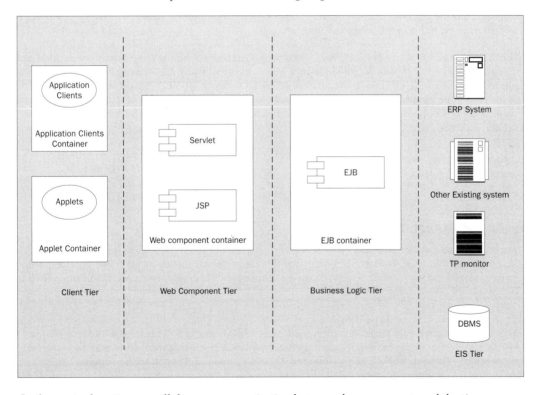

In the next subsection we will discuss communication between the components and the tiers.

Communication Between Components

Components on different tiers need a way in which to communicate. The client-tier components have to communicate with the web components and EJB components, the web components with EJB components, and so on. Furthermore, the components need a specific means to access the EIS tier.

In Chapter 2 we introduced the integration broker that handles communication, which we defined as a set of middleware technologies. The J2EE platform uses a number of protocols and specifications for these purposes.

HTTP(S)

HTTP (Hyper Text Transfer Protocol) is responsible for transferring markup pages to the client, while HTTPS is the secure version. Both protocols are commonly used for communication between the client tier and the web component tier. They can also be used to communicate with other tiers, particularly the EIS tier, if there is an application that supports this protocol.

RMI-IIOP

Client components can also use other ways to communicate with the business logic and EIS tiers, such as Remote Method Invocation (RMI). This is a Java-specific technique for invoking methods on remote objects and components. As it was designed for Java, it fits very well into the architecture of the Java language and the platform as a whole. RMI can be used for communication between the client tier or web component tier and the business logic tier.

For the actual communication, RMI uses a protocol. Originally RMI used the Java Remote Method Protocol (JRMP), which was designed for Java-only communication. RMI has since adopted the Internet Inter-ORB Protocol (IIOP), the protocol defined by CORBA. RMI-IIOP provides the Java-centric way of programming remote method invocations, but transfers them using IIOP. RMI-IIOP addresses the same communication requirements and capabilities as RMI, but also allows for the communication between CORBA and Java components.

> *For the sake of clarity, we will avoid any further discussion of the now deprecated JRMP protocol for communication with the business logic tier. Instead we will focus on the RMI-IIOP protocol only. The IIOP protocols has many advantages over JRMP, amongst which is that it can transmit the context information, which will be important for transaction demarcation and security.*

The Java Message Service

Another way to communicate between tiers is through the use of the Java Message Service (JMS). JMS enables us to use message-oriented middleware (MOM) products through a standard interface. JMS thus enables asynchronous communication based on sending and receiving messages. JMS can be used to communicate between any of the tiers.

Through JMS we can use any JMS-compliant MOM product. JMS provides the abstraction layer and makes applications easily portable between different MOM products. This is very important because MOM middleware has traditionally been used in companies to enable partial integration between applications. Through JMS we can easily reuse this integration and attach to the communication pathways of existing applications on the EIS tier.

JDBC

One system that will almost definitely be found on the EIS tier is a Database Management System (DBMS), and often there will be more than one DBMS deployed. To access data from a DBMS we can use the JDBC API which provides a unified interface to access different relational DBMS products through a common interface. JDBC can be used to access the DBMS on the EIS tier for any of the other tiers: client, web component, or business logic tier.

The Java Connector Architecture

Thus far we have seen that almost all communication technologies and protocols can be used to access the EIS tier too. In addition to standardized protocols there are also several proprietary protocols that we will have to use to access EIS tier systems.

The Java Connector Architecture (JCA) is trying to solve the problem of the custom solutions required today to access different EIS systems. JCA defines system-level contracts for connection management, security and transactions between an application server and a connector. The connector for each EIS system implements these contracts in EIS specific way. J2EE components access the EIS through a standard API, called the Common Client Interface (CCI). The CCI hides the differences of EIS systems. In other words, the JCA is for EIS systems what JDBC is for databases.

Adding the communication technologies to our J2EE architecture diagram, we get the following:

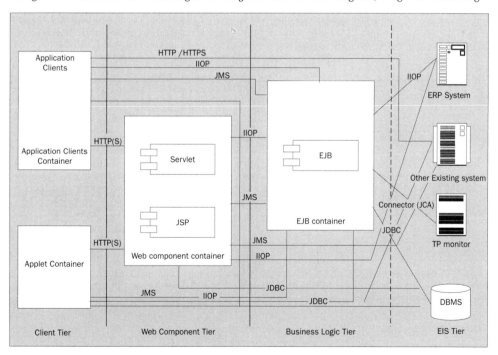

We can see that different technologies can be used for communication between the tiers. We can also see that sometimes the same technology can be used for communication between different tiers. JMS for example can be used to access business logic components or existing systems. To limit the number of choices we have to look at the rules for tier separation.

Tier Separation Rules

From the previous diagram it is obvious that there are plenty of choices for communication and they all complicate the architecture considerably. However, there are also reasons why we do not want to communicate between the tiers without any level of control. For example, we don't want the client tier to access the database directly, for instance. Doing so would result in the need to go back to the client/server technology with this piece of the system. It would also influence security and introduce a lot of complexity in its maintenance. The same goes for the other tiers.

> **Tiers are introduced to reduce application complexity and to separate roles and responsibilities between the different types of component.**

Sound design rules suggest the following communication paths between the tiers:

❑ The client tier should access only the web component and the business logic tiers, depending on if the client is web-based or GUI-based, respectively

❑ The web component tier should only access the business logic tier

❑ The business logic tier should only access the EIS tier

Allowing only these connections between the tiers simplifies the architecture and makes it easier to maintain, because it reduces the complexity and the dependencies between the tiers. The following diagram shows the simplified architecture:

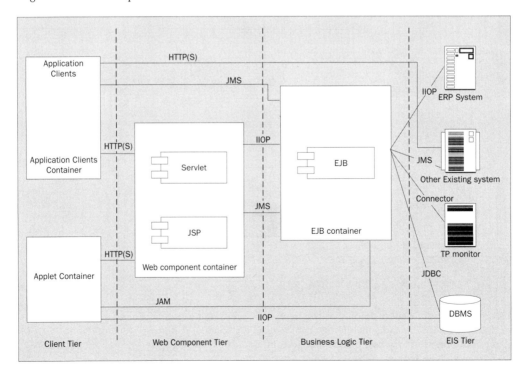

In the next section we will extend the basic J2EE architecture with additional components that will better support our integration needs. We will call such architecture the **extended J2EE integration architecture**.

The Extended J2EE Integration Architecture

From what we have learned about the technologies and protocols that J2EE supports for inter-tier communication, we can see that support for open interoperability standards allows us to include components that have not been developed in Java on practically any of the tiers.

On the business logic tier we can deploy components that have not been developed in Java, such as RMI-IIOP or CORBA distributed objects for example. There can also be components communicating through a JMS-compliant MOM. This is one of the most important facts for integration, and we will use this for building virtual components.

> *Note that these non-Java components do not reside inside a container, and as such they cannot use take advantage of the managed environment provided by containers (including declarative support for services, instance and resource management, performance optimizations, and so on). Rather, they have to use the corresponding APIs. We will come to this a little later.*

On the web component tier we can also deploy other, non-Java components, too. These can include any components that can use one of the afore-mentioned communication mechanisms. Again we cannot execute them into the J2EE application server provided web container. However, we will not be accessing existing systems directly from the web component tier, but rather via the business logic tier.

Similar is true for the client tier – the application clients are not necessarily Java applications. They can be developed in other languages and use the identified protocols to communicate with the other tiers. Examples include web browsers, CORBA clients, etc.

All this brings us to the extended J2EE integration architecture that we will use to achieve J2EE EAI. It is conceptually shown in the following diagram:

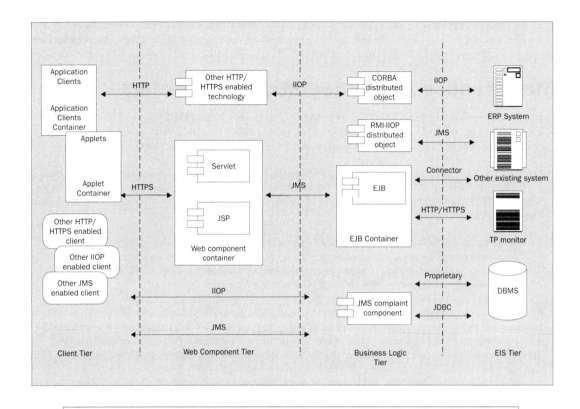

We can see that the extended J2EE integration architecture cleanly separates the tiers and places a limited set of protocols that can be used for communication between the tiers.

The business logic tier separates the web component and the client tier from the EIS tier. The client and web component tier should not access the EIS tier.

The only way to access the EIS tier is therefore from the business logic tier. Here the EJB, CORBA, RMI-IIOP, JMS-compliant components, and the distributed objects use a variety of protocols and technologies to access the EIS tier. Only here are we faced with the heterogeneity of the existing applications that are located in the EIS tier. The business logic tier thus implements the Façade pattern for the web component and client tiers. Through this façade, the business logic tier provides access to business functionality through clearly defined interfaces.

Such architecture directly implements both the composite information system and the Integration Broker pattern. The composite information system is achieved by providing high-level functionality through component interfaces on business logic tier. The components on this tier implement component wrapping to provide high-level interfaces on the one hand, and reuse the functionality of existing system on the other.

The integration broker, as we defined in the previous chapter, is implemented by a combination of middleware, including ORBs and MOMs. More specifically, RMI-IIOP- and CORBA-compliant ORBs provide ORB functionality, and one or more JMS-compliant MOM products provide MOM services. Whilst the interoperability between RMI-IIOP and CORBA is achieved "out-of-the-box", as long as version 2.3.1 or higher of the CORBA architecture is used, the interoperability between different JMS-compliant products sometimes has to be implemented by developing full or half bridges.

XML Support

The previous diagram clearly identified the different tiers, and the various communication protocols and technologies between the tiers. However, this architecture says nothing about the formats that can be used for exchanging data between applications. It is true that to exchange data several different formats can be used, but in the last few years the **eXtensible Markup Language (XML)** has established itself as the de facto standard for data exchange.

> **Due to its simplicity, XML is a commonly accepted way to format and store data between applications.**

In simple terms, XML allows us to describe the content of data using tags that are inserted between data. The power of XML lies in the possibility that we can define the tags ourselves. This allows us to describe any data in any structure (although XML is perhaps best suited to hierarchical data structures). However, freely defined tags can cause semantic problems by the data exchange. It is impossible for a computer to 'guess' the meaning of the data from the tags – a vocabulary agreement must be achieved between the parties, where each party has to support the same set of tags, in the form of a clearly defined DTD or Schema. This can be particularly problematic when data is exchanged between different companies. Today, great effort is put into the definition of standardized vocabularies for different industries.

J2EE version 1.3 provides support for XML through the **Java API for XML Processing (JAXP)**. JAXP provides the ability to verify, create, access, and manipulate XML documents from Java components. To manipulate an XML document, it first has to be parsed. In the process of parsing, the document is often validated. Then the content of the document has to be made available through an API. Currently, two important APIs are supported – the Document Object Model (DOM) and the Simple API for XML (SAX). Both models are supported by JAXP. JAXP 1.1 also includes an XSLT framework based on the Transformation API for XML (TrAX). More on the differences between DOM and SAX will be covered in Chapters 6 and 7 of this book.

Sun's Java Community program is currently defining many XML-related specifications. The following technologies are currently being considered under the Java Specification Requests (JSR):

- ❑ **JAXP (JSR 5) – Java API for XML Processing**
  Allows us to easily use XML parsers in their applications via the industry standard SAX and DOM APIs.

- ❑ **JAXB (JSR 31) – Java API for XML Binding**
  Allows us to compile an XML Schema into one or more Java classes that can parse, generate, and validate documents that follow the Schema.

❏ **JAXM (JSR 67) – Java API for XML Messaging**
Provides an API for packaging and transporting business transactions using on-the-wire protocols being defined by ebXML.org, Oasis, W3C and IETF.

❏ **JAX/RPC (JSR 101) – Java API for XML-based Remote Procedure Calls**
Supports XML-based RPC standards.

❏ **JAXR (JSR 93) – Java API for XML Registries**
Provides an API for a set of distributed registry services that enables business-to-business integration between business enterprises, using the protocols being defined by ebXML.org.

❏ **JWSDL (JSR 110) – Java Web Service Definition Language**
Provides a standard set of APIs for representing and manipulating services described by WSDL (Web Services Description Language) documents. These APIs will define a way to construct and manipulate models of service description.

We'll return to discuss some of these technologies in greater detail later in this chapter when we take a look at B2B integration. Now we will look at the different types of clients.

Different Types of Clients

Another important concern of the integration architecture is to provide a means to support different types of clients. In fact, the integration architecture already supports different types of clients. These clients can implement a rich graphical user interface – for instance, Java applications, applets, or applications in other programming languages. A client may also be a programmatic agent that acts on behalf of a user.

More important are the thin clients that use the web-based user interface – or so called web clients. Web clients use the web component tier, which generates the presentation for the client tier on the fly and sends it to the client. The web component tier has to generate the presentation format that is acceptable by the client. Today the most common approach is to generate HTML pages in the web component tier and display them inside a browser on the client tier.

However, this technique cannot fulfill the increasing requirements to support other types of clients, such as palm top computers, mobile phones, or any other device that enables client access. While there is no hindrance in developing different web components that would generate different presentation format, this solution is costly because it requires additional development of web components for each distinct client type. These web components also contain very similar logic – they differ only in the way they present the data, which introduces maintenance problems.

> **Consequently, the right answer is to separate the content from the presentation format.**

This means that we should generate content in a universal way only once, and then enrich it with the appropriate presentation information, in order to present it to the client.

Unfortunately version 1.3 of the J2EE platform does not provide a technology that would make this procedure automatic, but we can still reach a high level of automatism with its built-in support for XML. Rather than generating HTML pages on the web component tier, we can generate XML. HTML pages contain information on how to represent data on the web browser. XML, on the other hand, simply describes the semantics of the data – it does not say anything about the presentation.

Such XML then has to be transformed to a presentation appropriate for the client tier. This can be HTML for web browsers, WML for WAP devices, or any other appropriate format:

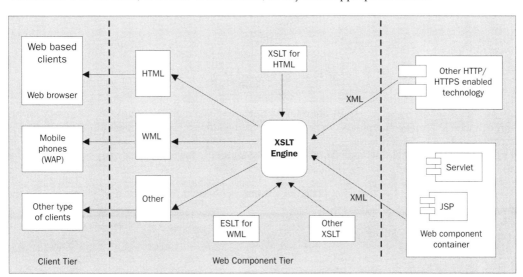

The transformations between these formats can be done with another XML-related technology – **eXtensible Stylesheet Language (XSL)**. In addition to XML, the **XSL for Transformations (XSLT)** engine (supported by JAXP) requires a stylesheet that defines how different parts of the document will be represented on the client. The XSLT engine then performs the transformation. We will address the XSLT, together with different engines, that can considerably vary in performance, in Chapter 7.

In the next section we will look at how we can implement virtual components and wrappers in the extended J2EE integration architecture.

Component Wrapping and Virtual Components

Now that we have defined the extended J2EE integration architecture, we will look at how to represent existing applications. In Chapter 2, we described component wrapping, which we will use to present the existing applications in a consistent, J2EE-compliant manner through components and interfaces. Component wrapping uses two constructs:

❑   Virtual components

❑   Wrappers

Virtual components present the functionality of existing applications on the business logic tier. On one side they expose J2EE-compliant interfaces, whilst on their other side they connect to existing applications through the APIs that the existing applications provide. Virtual components mask the technology differences between different existing systems, because clients access the existing systems through virtual components. To build virtual components in the J2EE integration architecture we can use the following technologies:

- ❑ EJB
- ❑ CORBA
- ❑ RMI-IIOP
- ❑ JMS

All these technologies will be covered in detail in later chapters.

Existing applications sometimes do not provide APIs, or these APIs may not suit our needs. In this case, we have to extend the existing application through wrappers. Wrappers provide the necessary interfaces through which virtual components can access the existing application. Wrappers can use proprietary technologies to provide APIs for existing applications, or they can use standard technologies. Important technologies to wrap existing applications are CORBA and the Java Connector Architecture, which we will cover in Chapters 10 and 13, respectively.

Virtual components and wrappers in J2EE integration architecture are schematically presented in the next figure:

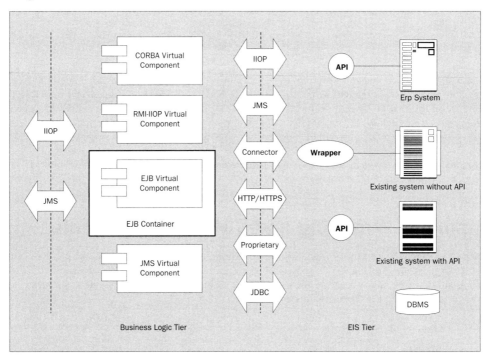

We will typically use component wrapping for one or a combination of following functions:

- ❑ Encapsulate interfaces of EIS systems and present them in the same or rearranged way.
- ❑ Provide a different, higher-level interface and thus mask the way EIS systems implement their APIs.
- ❑ Encapsulate and/or abstract persistent data. For this purpose the wrappers can access EIS databases directly or through provided protocols.

❑   Provide unified access to several EIS databases and handle different combinations of databases in the background.

❑   Map technical differences, such as protocols, implementations, platforms, and so on.

Virtual components will often be layered. High-level virtual components will aggregate the behaviors of lower-level virtual components and provide a higher abstraction level of functionality of existing applications. High-level virtual components will expose high-level business methods to the clients.

High-level virtual components will translate high-level methods into a series of lower-level calls to low level virtual components. Low-level virtual components will:

❑   Provide access to existing applications through APIs

❑   Provide access to existing applications through wrappers

❑   Provide data access

Low-level virtual components will often have to perform parameter and data type transformations, and so on. In simple terms, they will act as an adapter between the clients and the existing systems.

In the J2EE architecture, low-level virtual components will typically be implemented in CORBA, RMI-IIOP, or JMS. High-level virtual components will typically be implemented as EJBs:

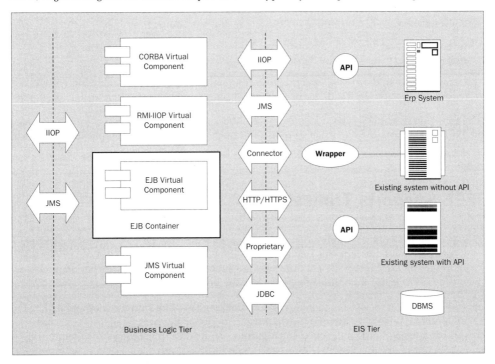

However, providing access to the functionality of existing applications is not the whole story of integration. We will at least have to consider support for transactions and security, and for performance and scalability. In the next sections we will discuss those topics, starting with the support for transactions.

Transaction Support

Transactions ensure the data integrity of the whole information system. Building transactional systems is a key requirement for every enterprise platform and will be a key requirement for integration too.

Transactions are sequences of operations on resources. The typical operations include read, write and update operations. Typical resources in a transaction are components, databases, and existing systems. A transaction guarantees that the sequence of operations performs completely if everything went OK. Otherwise, the whole sequence of operations is rolled back. The system returns to the state it was before the transaction was initiated. Transactions are required to adhere to the ACID properties, which determine their Atomic, Consistent, Isolated, and Durable characteristics.

When we are concerned with integration, we should familiarize ourselves with the most common integration-transactional scenarios. This means that we will have to support transactions that span existing applications, databases and newly developed application components.

In general, the most frequently seen scenarios are as follows:

❑ A component wrapper in the business component tier accesses several different databases (on the EIS tier) within a single transaction.

❑ Several virtual components are included inside a transaction and access several different databases inside a single transaction.

❑ A virtual component calls different EIS systems inside a transaction.

❑ Several virtual components deployed in different containers call different EIS systems inside a transaction.

❑ A combination of the above. Several virtual components may call a combination of EIS systems and access several different databases inside a single transaction.

For each individual scenario it is necessary to figure out if and how the transactions can be propagated from the J2EE integration to the existing systems and back. Things get more complicated because some of the existing database and some of the existing applications we are accessing might already provide transactional support.

How J2EE Supports Transactions

In J2EE, transactions are supported on the web component tier, the business logic tier, and the EIS tier. The J2EE specification does not require that transactions be supported on the client tier, although an application provider might include this as a value-added feature. Although transactions on the web component tier in the J2EE integration architecture are supported, they are not recommended. It is a much better idea to delegate the transactional work to the business logic tier.

To access the transaction service functionality, J2EE provides **JTA (the Java Transaction API)**. JTA provides an abstraction layer on top of **JTS (the Java Transaction Service)**. JTA specifies standard interfaces through which different resources that participate inside a transaction can communicate. The J2EE application server facilitates these resources, which include transactional components and the transaction manager. The transaction manager controls the transaction and the access to shared resources used in the transaction. A JTS transaction manager provides functions to support transaction demarcation, synchronization, transactional context propagation, and resource management:

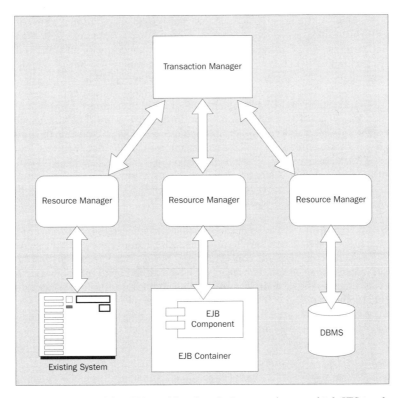

The abstraction layer provided by JTA enables the platform to choose which JTS implementation it will use. The implementation, which is typically provided by the application server, is transparent to the application components because the application components do not interact with JTS directly. Rather, they should go through JTA.

A transaction can span across several different J2EE components and include EIS resources too (if the J2EE application supports distributed transactions). Such a transaction is a distributed transaction and often called a **JTA transaction**. In a JTA transaction, the transaction manager is external and handles the different resource managers involved. A JTA transaction, for example, can include a servlet and a JSP page and several enterprise beans. These beans can access data in existing databases on the EIS tier.

A JTA transaction can be started explicitly in a programmatic way, or they can be started automatically (that is, declaratively). At present, only the EJB container allows declarative transaction management. If we use JTA transactions, and if each tier is running within the same application server, we can access different components from different tiers inside a single transaction without much effort. We do not have to program transaction context propagation manually between components.

When we include other non-compliant resources (particularly existing systems), we will have to find ways to propagate transaction context to those systems and back. This fact becomes more complicated because the J2EE architecture currently does not support nested transactions, which are a welcome way to wrap existing transactions with wider, integration-level transactions. Consequently, we will have to live with the flat transaction model supported by the J2EE.

The type of connectivity with the existing databases and systems depends upon how much effort we put into the transactional context propagation and other transaction-related questions. Fortunately, we can rely on automatic transaction propagation for transaction interaction with all systems that conform to the X/Open DTP standard, which is an established standard among vendors providing transactional systems. An example is the use of several existing DBMS through JDBC.

Also fortunate is the fact that the majority of existing applications support this standard. This includes all the major DBMS, CICS, ERP systems, and so on. In this case, we will be able to rely on the J2EE architecture to take care most of low-level transactional details and still be able to communicate with existing systems on a transactional basis. This will guarantee that the data will stay consistent and integral. Using JTA transactions also allows us to group the work performed by several components (that access several EIS systems) as atomic units. We can even group the work performed by several existing EIS systems as atomic units, as long as the J2EE application server supports distributed transaction together with two-phase commit (2PC).

If, however, we use a proprietary way to access existing systems, we also have to care about transaction demarcation. Careful planning is advised because this can become a very complicated task. Sometimes we will want to propagate transactional context manually; sometimes we simply start a transaction in the existing EIS transactional system. However, we have to implement reliable ways to report the outcome of this transaction to the main JTA transaction. With this technique we can mimic the nested transaction model somewhat. We will address these questions in Chapter 15.

In the next section we will consider the security questions related to integration.

Security

Security is a very important service that we have to provide in an integrated information system. From the perspective of integration we have to address security in connection with existing systems that may or may not implement some security mechanisms of their own.

Generally, security mechanisms fall into the following categories:

❑ **Authentication**
A mechanism where the parties involved in an interaction prove that they are the ones they claim to be

❑ **Authorization**
A mechanism to control the access and limit it to the resources a party is allowed to

❑ **Communication channel protection**
Uses mechanisms to protect communication ways between parties, for example with encryption

❑ **Auditing**
A mechanism for capturing and storing the information about related events that are significant for security

Security mechanisms can be performed programmatically or declaratively. When performed programmatically the application components have to provide the necessary code. With the declarative approach, we mark the application components by the deployment and specify the required security mechanisms that have to be performed. The responsibility for performing security mechanisms is then taken over by the container and/or application server. J2EE application servers provide security functionality completely outside of the application components.

Existing systems will also often have some security mechanisms. Often existing systems will perform authentication and authorization on different levels and in different ways. For example, an existing DBMS system may perform authentication when acquiring a connection to the database. It might then perform the authorization on database tables, columns and rows. An ERP system might provide some authentication mechanisms for accessing their functionality through APIs. Most existing systems will, however, provide some user interface security mechanisms, requiring the user to authenticate when accessing the applications through the user interfaces provided by the EIS system.

After integration, existing systems will be used in a different way. They will most likely be wrapped and used through virtual components on the business logic tier. Then we have to solve different problems. One of them is that users will not be willing to supply different usernames and passwords for different functionalities, now reused as components, for the purpose of authentication. When finishing the presentation level integration we will want to provide a single sign-in to authenticate users and then to authorize them for different usage scenarios.

Therefore, a crucial question relates to how we should reuse the existing security mechanisms and integrate them with the new mechanisms seamlessly. Fortunately, the J2EE platform builds and leverages existing security services, rather than requiring totally new mechanisms to be implemented. This fact is particularly important when we require smooth integration of security mechanisms between existing systems and newly developed applications.

Authentication

The authentication in J2EE is based on users, realms and groups. Users represent people that use the information system. A realm is a collection of users that are authenticated in the same way. J2EE supports two realm types: default and certificate. Default realm is used to authenticate all clients except web clients. Web clients have to use the certificate realm. Users of the default realm can belong to a group. A group is a category of users that share a certain role, for example customers, employees, etc.

In the J2EE architecture a client typically has to go through the container boundaries to gain access to web components or EJB components. In this case the container performs the authorization. The container can do it in different ways.

The J2EE web container can support four authentication mechanisms:

❑ **HTTP basic authentication**
  The web container authenticates based on the username and password obtained from the client. The problem is that the username and password are sent over the wire as plain text, which is not very secure.

❑ **Form-based authentication**
  Similar to HTTP basic authentication. However it enables developers to customize the user interface for authentication presented by web browsers. It shares the same disadvantages as basic authentication.

❏ **HTTPS mutual authentication**
Bases the authentication on X.509 certificates that the client and the server exchange to establish their identities. For certificate exchange a SSL protected channel is used.

❏ **HTTP digest authentication**
Similar to HTTP basic authentication. However the client does not send the username and password to the server, but rather sends a message digest along with its HTTP request. The client calculates the digest with a one-way hash algorithm which it applies to the HTTP request and the password. The web container performs the same algorithm and compares both digests. This way the password is not sent over the wire.

Note that the first three mechanisms are required, whereas the fourth is optional. Hybrid mechanisms that feature HTTP basic, form-based, or digest authentication over SSL can also be supported.

Mainly when integrating J2EE platform with existing EIS systems, we will be faced with different protection and security domains than those used by existing systems. In this case, the container can manage authentication, which is called container-managed resource manager sign-on. On the other hand, the J2EE architecture also supports application-managed resource manager sign-on. The application-managed resource manager sign-on is used with components that want to manage the authentication details themselves.

Authorization

After entities have been authenticated, they will access components and resources in the information system. Authorization mechanisms control the access and limit the interactions of clients with the resources to enforce integrity, confidentiality, and availability constraints.

The containers in J2EE architecture are the authorization boundaries. Authorization boundaries exist inside the authentication boundaries. Authorization is always performed after successful authentication. For incoming calls the container checks the security attributes against the authorization permissions. Authorization can be implemented at different levels of granularity. It can specify the authorization permissions on a component level or on a method level. The J2EE platform supports method-level granularity that enables fine-grained control over who is allowed to invoke certain methods and who is not. Authorization permissions are usually specified as access control lists for each component.

There are two possibilities of how to specify authorization permissions – programmatic and declarative. With declarative authorization, the access control lists in J2EE are defined in terms of permissions, where the actual component deployer has to specify who can do what. Declarative authorization can be specified for EJB and for web components. A component can also utilize programmatic authorization and perform additional controls before it actually executes the request.

When designing the authorization rules and selecting the protected resources, we have to be sure to be consistent. We have to assure that authorization is performed on all entry-points where a component might be accessed.

In existing EIS systems authorization is done in several different ways. In most cases, it is programmatic. Ways have to be found how to connect existing authorization with the roles defined in the global integration architecture. A possible solution is to make the necessary transformations in the existing application wrappers.

Communication Channel Protection

Communication channel protection is particularly significant in distributed environments where data is transferred over the wire using different protocols. In particular, when the data is transferred between the client tier and the rest of the information system the messages are exposed to security risks. Clients almost always execute in untrusted environments and need to be protected. The most vulnerable are the clients executing beyond the local network boundaries, often using the Internet connections.

There are three main types of attacks on messages:

❑ Messages can be monitored to acquire confidential information

❑ Messages can be captured and reused as they are, for the benefit of the attacker

❑ Messages can be intercepted and modified to change their purpose and then forwarded to the recipients

Communication channel protection ensures that communication between parties is not intercepted, modified, or tampered in any other way, and that the communication is kept confidential. A common way to achieve this is through the use of the Secure Sockets Layer (SSL) protocol. SSL was originally developed by Netscape, but has since been universally accepted for authenticated and encrypted communication between clients and servers.

Communication channel protection is particularly important for communication with the client tier, particularly when the clients are located outside the company network. Existing systems are typically deployed inside the company network, on the EIS layer and accessed by EJB and web component tiers. Therefore, the communication will most likely be limited to the local network environments that have a higher level of trust than external networks. Still, communication channel security can be important.

For securing the communication with existing systems we can use SSL as well. However, we have to find ways to integrate it with existing applications. Sometimes existing applications will already implement some communication channel protection. Otherwise, we will have to consider adding this support when wrapping them.

Auditing

Auditing is a procedure where we capture and store the information about related events that are significant for security. With this information we can identify users and systems that are responsible for their actions. Although it can also be used when we need to track what users do over the course of a session, auditing is particularly useful after security breaches, when we want to identify what exactly has happened and who was allowed to use the system.

Auditing should be performed by the component deployers or system administrators and should be powerful enough to provide different auditing options, such as auditing events where some constraints have or have not been satisfied, auditing of all events, and so on. Auditing should not require that the developers or integrators develop additional code. Rather it should be provided by the infrastructure that can be configured by system administrators.

The J2EE specification currently does not require, but only recommends, that the J2EE application servers provide support for auditing. Existing EIS might implement auditing and we have to get a clear understanding regarding what, how, and when it has been audited. Only then can this information be useful to solve security-related questions.

Performance and Scalability

Performance is an important topic for an integrated information system, because its architecture is quite complex and the client requests travel through several tiers and layers before finally getting serviced – by existing or newly developed applications.

When we think of performance, our first thought often relates to **response time** from the perspective of a client. Response time for a client is important and a rule of thumb is that it should not be longer than three seconds. But response time is by far not the only important metric.

To generalize, response time is inversely related to the **throughput**, where throughput refers to the amount of work (number of operations, for example) a component can perform in a measured period of time. The response time and throughput definitely are very important, although too often they are used as the only judge of an application's performance.

Enterprise information systems are designed to serve numerous clients, and at least some of them will use an application simultaneously. In modern information systems the number of simultaneous clients can get very high. Often we cannot foresee the exact number of simultaneous clients in advance. Even if the information system could stand a high load, it is still very important that it offers acceptable response times for each client. In other words, the information system should be able to scale.

> **Response time, throughput, and scalability are not the same, but they are all interrelated.**

Scalability is the metric that refers to the change in response time due to an increase or decrease in the number of simultaneous clients. The ideal is to find an optimum balance between acceptable response time and scalability. In other words, scalability also tells us the ability of our system to grow – it tells us how much the throughput will improve if we add a certain amount of new processing power.

All three measures are important to the integration of existing systems. Wrapped, existing systems are placed in a different environment and used in ways they have not been designed for. Accordingly, it is very important to test existing systems for performance and scalability before we decide on how we will reuse them in the integration architecture. When wrapped, those systems will also be accessed remotely. In this sense, we will want to minimize the number of remote invocations and the number of layers through which calls are passed. Although we have recommended building the integration architecture in tiers, we have to carefully select particular implementation techniques to minimize the communication overhead.

To achieve good performance using the J2EE integration architecture we should focus on many different elements. We should:

- ❏ Define the performance objectives
- ❏ Assess the performance of existing applications
- ❏ Design a sound integration architecture
- ❏ Start assessing the performance in the design phase
- ❏ Implement the integration architecture using performance optimal techniques
- ❏ Tune the integration infrastructure for performance
- ❏ Providing an adequate hardware platform

Defining the Performance Objectives

The first step is the specification of performance objectives and goals. Without clearly stated goals it will be difficult to answer the question whether the achieved performance is acceptable. Such goals can be relatively simple, specifying the maximum response times and the maximum number of simultaneous clients; or they can be more precise and specify several performance metrics for different parts of the information system.

Assessing the Performance of Existing Applications

Of similar, if not greater, importance is that we assess the performance of existing applications.

> **If existing applications do not provide acceptable performance initially, we cannot expect that the performance of the integrated system will be acceptable.**

Therefore, we have to choose in the beginning, which existing applications meet our criteria and which do not. For those that do not, we have to find ways to improve their performance, for example through hardware upgrades, software upgrades, tuning, clustering, etc. The other option is to simply replace them.

Designing a Sound Integration Architecture

In the third step, we should pay great attention to the design of the integration architecture. We should follow sound design practices and patterns, the correct application of which will result in a sound architecture that will most likely provide acceptable performance. Some of these guidelines include:

- ❏ Minimization of communication overhead through lowering of the number of connections between components, coarse-grained interfaces, etc.

- ❏ Minimization of communication between tiers using responsibility-driven design, and the Façade pattern.

- ❏ Making correct decisions on where to store client-dependent state.

- ❏ Using value objects in coarse-grained interfaces that also enable input validation on the web component and client tiers.

- ❏ Minimizing interaction with persistent storage.

- ❏ Decide for synchronous or asynchronous communication models and use the latter for long lasting interactions where no immediate answer is needed.

- ❏ Designing transactions with corresponding isolation and avoiding deadlocks.

- ❏ Setting up protection domains to minimize the security overhead.

- ❏ Understand the resource and instance management algorithms.

Through this book we will explain these and give other guidelines for designing sound integration architecture. However the reader might want to refer to several design books, such as:

❑ *Object-Oriented Analysis and Design with Applications* (Addison-Wesley Object Technology Series) by Grady Booch, Addison-Wesley; ISBN: 0-805353-40-2

❑ *Object-Oriented Modeling and Design* by James Rumbaugh, Michael Blaha, William Premerlani, Frederick Eddy, William Lorenson, Prentice Hall; ISBN: 0-136298-41-9

❑ *Design Patterns* by Erich Gamma, Richard Helm, Ralph Johnson, John Vlissides, Addison-Wesley; ISBN: 0-201633-61-2.

Assessing the Performance Soon Enough

We should also not forget to assess the performance of the integration architecture soon enough. If we wait until the implementation phase and start to assess the performance only then, it will likely be too late or very expensive, if we figure out that the performance is not acceptable. Therefore, we should start to assess the performance in the design phase, through the construction of prototypes for example.

Using Performance Optimal Implementation Techniques

The next very important step is to implement the integration architecture using performance optimal techniques. This is a very broad topic that we won't discuss in detail here. However, we will mention the most important points. In the context of the J2EE, the first question might be the Java programming language, which is still sometimes considered as slow. With the development of the latest just-in-time compilers and new JVMs, Java performance has increased significantly. On the other hand, in enterprise applications the performance of the language is not the deciding factor. The more important factor is communication overhead, particularly network communication and communication with persistent storage. In this sense Java is competitive.

We should also use the implementation techniques in Java known as performance optimal. Some of these include:

❑ Avoid creating garbage, which results in less garbage collection. We can achieve that by reusing existing objects and avoiding creating unnecessary temporary objects.

❑ Avoid memory leaks, that is, referenced unused objects, which cannot be garbage collected.

❑ Avoid using finalizers for regular Java objects

❑ Use performance-optimized classes where possible, like `StringBuffer` instead of `String`, etc.

❑ Use class preloading to avoid sending the class files over the wire.

❑ Use `static` and `final` keywords wherever possible.

When implementing the components on the web component and business logic tiers, we should think about the underlying mechanisms and use them to improve performance. We can for example:

❑ Activate the components that are used rarely on an as-needed basis, while pre-activating important components.

❑ Lazy load business logic components that are related to a certain component.

❑ Use smart stubs and skeletons to accelerate remote method invocations.

❑ Think about threading in web components. We should avoid thread synchronization and limit it to the necessary parts only.

❑ Use local interfaces instead of remote if possible.

Tuning the Integration Infrastructure

The penultimate step is to tune the integration infrastructure for optimal performance. In the context of J2EE, this means primarily tuning the application server and the operating system/platform. First of all, we should identify the appropriate number of physical tiers. From a performance standpoint it is desirable to combine the middle tier with the data persistence tier to form a single physical tier. We should collocate the components that have high affinities into the same container, possibly one that optimizes method invocations.

The next important option is considering load balancing and clustering as a means to improve performance. These techniques might provide results when applied to existing systems too.

We have to pay attention to the selection of components in the integration infrastructure, particularly the J2EE application server and the DBMS, but also other middleware products, such as MOM products, transaction managers, ORBs, naming and directory products, etc. Application servers, DBMS, middleware, and operating system cannot compensate for bad design. However, they all can have a large influence on performance. It is particularly important that the application server provides a capable ORB on one hand, and efficient communication to the persistent storage on the other. The application server is responsible for instance and resource management, transaction, concurrency, and security management. All these factors influence performance.

The problem is that it is very difficult to obtain reliable performance metrics for application servers. ECperf (http://java.sun.com/j2ee/ecperf/) has defined the standard performance load for benchmarking application servers. However, at the time of writing, no performance results have been available for any application server. We will have to wait and see if the ECperf will objectively represent the actual performance of application servers. We should still watch out for ECperf-focused performance optimizations that will allow application servers to achieve better results on the benchmarks. In the meantime, we can develop application prototypes that imitate the final application design and test the performance ourselves. Only then will we know exactly which application server is best suited for us. Obviously, measuring performance requires time and resources.

We can influence the performance through the selection of the underlying technologies as well, which includes the selection of the JVMs and the operation system/platform. When we select the Java SDK, it is safe to assume that newer versions offer better performance. Java 2 SDK version 1.3 performs in almost all cases better than 1.2, which in turn performs better than version 1.1. Different implementations of the JVM offer different performance. Some performance tests have shown that the IBM JVM performs better than the others (take a look at http://www.volano.com/benchmarks.html). Just-in-time (JIT) compilers enormously speed the execution of Java programs. Also consider using the HotSpot Server JVM (see http://developer.java.sun.com/developer/technicalArticles/Programming/JVMPerf/). However, make sure that your application server provider supports it.

JVM execution parameters influence performance too. If we can choose, we should select native threads, which offer much better performance than green threads.

Green threads refer to lightweight threads managed by the JVM itself, and not mapped onto multiple operating-system threads.

We can tune the heap size, which can result in performance improvements. Heap size indirectly determines how often the garbage collection will be performed. With Java 2, larger heap sizes often perform better because of the improved garbage collector algorithms. The heap size should, however, not be so large as to force the operating system virtual memory management into doing memory swapping.

Whatever operating system and platform we choose, we will always have to tune the configuration and set several parameters regarding the network communication, ports, sockets, hard disk and other persistent storage parameters, etc.

Providing Adequate Hardware

Last but not least, we should not forget to provide adequate hardware for the integration architecture. In enterprise computing it is also very important to use the most powerful computers in the middle and the data persistence tier. If we have architected our system well enough, we will also be able to increase the scalability and performance through adding or upgrading the hardware.

Although we have not mentioned all possible performance- and scalability-related topics, we have identified the most important. For more information the readers should refer to related books, such as:

❑   *Professional Java Programming* by *Brett Spell*, from Wrox Press, ISBN 1-861003-82-X.

❑   *Java Platform Performance: Strategies and Tactics* by Steve Wilson, Jeff Kesselman, from Addison-Wesley, ISBN 0-201-70969-4.

❑   *High-Performance Java Platform Computing: Multithreaded and Networked Programming* by George K. Thiruvathukal, Thomas W. Christopher, from Prentice Hall, ISBN 0-130161-614-0.

❑   *Java Performance and Scalability, Volume 1: Server-Side Programming Techniques* by Dov Bulka, from Addison-Wesley, ISBN 0-201-70429-3.

❑   *Java Performance Tuning* by Jack Shirazi, from O'Reilly, ISBN 0-596-00015-4 (or see http://www.javaperformancetuning.com/).

❑   *Enterprise Java Performance* by Steven L. Halter and Steven J. Munroe, from Prentice Hall, ISBN 0-13-017296-0.

Support for Naming and Directory Services

With an integrated information system it becomes an important concern to have a place where we can store environment-specific information in an application-independent way. This provides opportunities to adapt the applications to a specific environment and separate the bookkeeping information from the information system's source code.

Naming and directory services are widely used by many companies for storing information on any (directory) object in a computing environment, such as components, computers, printers, persons, networks, etc. These services provide operations for creating, adding, removing, searching and modifying these directory objects. The most important functionality is the association of names with directory objects and the ability to resolve these names to gain references to the directory objects.

The ubiquity of naming and directory services makes the selection of these services for integration a difficult task. Examples of naming and directory services and protocols include:

- ❑ Lightweight Directory Access Protocol (LDAP)
- ❑ Network Information System (NIS)
- ❑ Network Directory System (NDS)
- ❑ Domain Name System (DNS)
- ❑ CORBA Naming Service
- ❑ Service Location Protocol (SLP)
- ❑ RMI Registry
- ❑ Microsoft Active Directory

Different naming and directory services offer different interfaces through which they provide their services. Although the J2EE platform does not introduce a proprietary naming and directory services, it provides an abstraction interface, called the **Java Naming and Directory Interface (JNDI) API** that can be used to access practically any of the naming and directory services in use.

To provide support for pluggable implementation, JNDI specifies, in addition to the API, also the service provider interface (SPI). The SPI specifies the interfaces that the provider of a naming and directory product has to implement in order for it to be used via JNDI. The following figure shows the described architecture of JNDI:

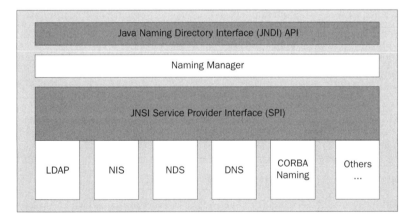

More importantly, with the use of the JNDI we can access and integrate all naming and directory services that already exist in our information system. The prerequisite however, is that the naming and directory products provide support for JNDI – which is true for the majority of important products.

Support for B2B Integration

Thus far we have learnt that the extended J2EE integration architecture provides a good foundation for EAI. We have also identified that companies today cannot afford to stop at EAI, but have to provide support for B2B integration as well.

> **Sometimes the major reason for EAI is the ability to provide online, low-latency B2B solutions.**

EAI architecture, as proposed in this book, is already suitable for extension into the B2B field. Once EAI is finalized we have a multi-tier integrated information system that provides high-level abstract interfaces to access their services. Although these services are implemented with existing systems, these are not visible to any clients.

The business interfaces are implemented on the business logic tier with component wrapping, which hides the existing systems and provides access to them either through IIOP-enabled components (EJB, RMI-IIOP, and CORBA objects) or JMS-enabled components (message-driven beans, and other JMS solutions).

We are probably not comfortable letting business partners access our business logic tier directly. Rather, we would prefer to provide an additional layer of abstraction, where we define the only methods that should be accessed by partners directly and that make sense to them – methods that have been designed especially for B2B integration.

On the other hand, to access the functionality of the business logic tier, we have to use one or both of the communication technologies – IIOP or JMS. B2B integration, however, focuses on accessing services from outside, but IIOP and JMS have been designed for intra-enterprise access. Thus, neither of these technologies are especially appropriate for accessing services from a global network.

The problem is that the IIOP protocol and protocols used by JMS (often proprietary) have been designed as relatively heavyweight protocols that require reliable communication and are built on top of TCP/IP or other transport protocols. Due to this, they will most likely be blocked by most security solutions that separate local networks and the Internet, such as a firewall. This is the most important reason why we have to seek other ways to enable B2B integration.

Connectivity Through the Web Component Tier

A possible solution is to allow access using lightweight Internet protocols, which mainly means HTTP or HTTPS, through the web component layer. Here we can use a combination of JSP pages and servlets to deliver data to the business partner and to acquire data from them.

Web components can generate XML directly, so there is no obstacle to sending this XML directly to the business partner. Conversely, a business partner can submit input, formatted in XML, to be accepted by a web component. The component then transforms the XML data and forwards it to an EJB and finally to the EIS tier (through the business logic tier):

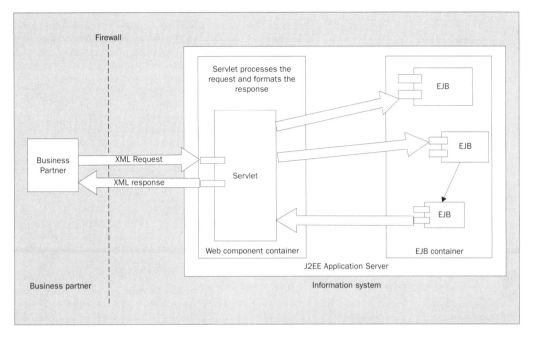

This approach does, however, have a few disadvantages. In particular, it requires that web components are developed for each request made by a business partner. These requests then have to be transformed into a series of requests compatible with the business logic tier. Although this can be done in the web component, it means putting logic on the web component tier, introducing maintenance problems. A better approach is to define a business logic component that will act as a façade between the web components on one side and the business logic components on the other.

For this purpose, we will introduce a new logical tier into the integration architecture. We will call it the **B2B integration tier**. The logical B2B tier sits between the web component and business logic tier and can be thought of as a web component sub tier because it uses similar technologies as the web component tier, including servlets and JSPs.

The responsibility of the B2B tier is to provide the functionality required by business partners, with the addition of extra verification and information filtering. It can achieve this through the translation of B2B requests into a series of requests that can be performed by the business logic tier. Alternatively, it can also implement some functionality on this tier.

The main reason to introduce a new logical tier is to separate the functionality required to build a client presentation tier and the functionality required to provide interfaces for B2B collaborations. As the objectives of both tiers differ, it is reasonable to separate them into two different logical tiers. However, in terms of physical deployment, these two tiers will typically be deployed into a single physical tier.

The logical architecture is shown in the diagram below:

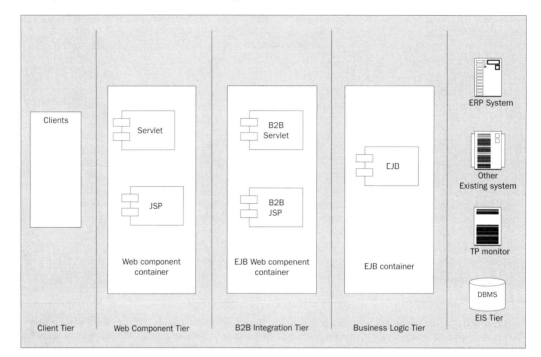

The business partner in B2B collaborations will most likely be a machine, which will access the B2B integration tier directly. Therefore, we need to define a protocol with which a business partner will be able to work with the components on the B2B tier.

To avoid the problems of TCP/IP-based protocols (such as IIOP) with firewalls, which we identified earlier, we will favor HTTP-based protocols, possibly those that format their requests and responses using XML. Such protocols already exist and the most important of them is SOAP.

SOAP

The **Simple Object Access Protocol (SOAP)** – currently in version 1.1 – allows us to invoke methods on objects and components, and return the results. In this sense it is similar to other protocols, such as IIOP. However, SOAP encodes its messages using XML – so transferring a SOAP request or response is no different from transferring any other XML data. SOAP uses the HTTP protocol for transferring requests, although other protocols can be used too (like SMTP or TCP/IP, for instance). This is different to binary protocols, such as IIOP, which encode messages as binary and use TCP/IP as the transport protocol.

> **SOAP is an XML-based protocol for invoking methods on objects and components. It is language- and platform-neutral and easy to understand and work with.**

Due to its simplicity SOAP is widely used in industry. Also, because it is most likely transferred using HTTP, it can go through firewalls without any reconfiguration. SOAP provides exactly the functionality that we're looking for: namely, it allows business clients to access the B2B tier directly.

SOAP is a protocol that can be used for classic synchronous method invocation, where the client waits for the response. For synchronous method invocation the server has to be online and prepared to process the requests when the client needs them. This is very similar to the remote method invocation provided by RMI-IIOP, or CORBA. However, with our EAI integration architecture, we identified that synchronous method invocation is not always what we would like to have (although in most cases it is preferable).

The same goes for B2B integration – sometimes we would prefer to use asynchronous communication, similar to that provided by MOM and JMS. Achieving message style communication is possible using XML-based protocols, including SOAP. Since SOAP is a protocol only, the applications that are using it can decide what style of invocation they will use.

Unfortunately SOAP is currently not natively supported by the J2EE platform, but we can use SOAP manually, implementing SOAP messages using XML tools, such as JAXP. This is however a rather low-level approach. To enable a higher level of abstraction, two new APIs are in preparation:

❑   **JAX/RPC (The Java API for XML Remote Procedure Calls)**

❑   **JAXM (The Java API for XML Messaging)**

JAX/RPC provides an abstraction layer through which developers can invoke remote methods in a synchronous way, similar to RMI. This API is not limited to SOAP, but can use any XML-based protocol for communication. In addition to SOAP it will support other XML-based protocols, such as the XML Protocol (XMLP). JAX/RPC will provide a complete abstraction and mapping to Java methods, which will include marshaling and dispatching.

> *JAX/RPC is currently under the development in the JCP and is not a standard part of the J2EE version 1.3. However, JAX/RPC is an important technology that will be particularly useful for defining B2B integration architecture.*

JAXM provides an abstract interface for asynchronous message-oriented communication using XML protocols. JAXM, similar to JAX/RPC, supports different messaging protocols. By default JAXM provides a high level support for SOAP 1.1 with attachments for messaging.

JAXM also supports the notion of profiles. Profiles enable us to specify different high-level messaging protocols. These high-level protocols extend the functionality of the basic SOAP protocol for messaging. Through profiles we will be able to use JAXM for communication with any high-level XML-based massaging protocol. Examples of such protocols are ebXML Transportation, Routing, and Packaging Message Handling Service or XMLP.

> *JAXM is also currently under the development of the JCP and will most likely be included in future versions of J2SE. It will also be an optional package of the J2SE.*

Adding JAX/PRC and JAXM to the B2B integration architecture simplifies the design somewhat, as shown in the diagram below:

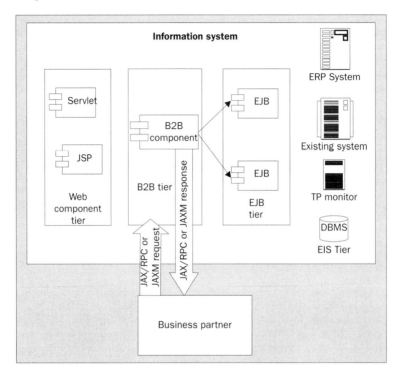

J2EE Application Servers

J2EE application servers are products that have been developed to comply with the J2EE specification. They provide the infrastructure necessary to deploy and run applications based on the J2EE platform. Selecting a J2EE-compliant application server is necessary to deploy the proposed integration architecture. Application servers influence the deployment of logical tiers and define the physical architecture of our information system. A possible physical architecture is presented on the following diagram:

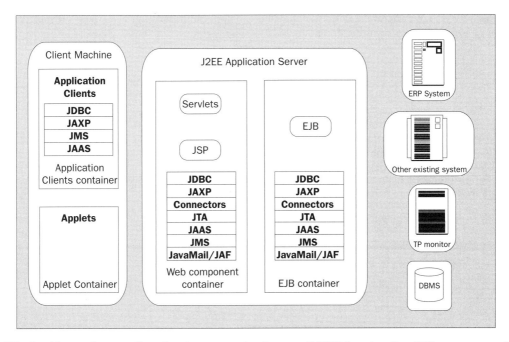

We should note that not all application servers implement all J2EE functionality. Different servers also comply with different versions of the J2EE platform specification. At the time of writing this book there were more than 37 different J2EE application servers, differing in several important factors – which parts of specification they implement, how up to date are they with the latest specification, price, performance, scalability, and reliability.

Some of the important commercial application servers include:

- ❏ Allaire/Macromedia JRun Server (http://www.allaire.com/Products/JRun/)

- ❏ BEA WebLogic Server (http://www.bea.com/)

- ❏ Borland/Inprise AppServer (http://www.inprise.com/appserver/)

- ❏ Fujitsu Software Interstage (http://www.interstage.com/)

- ❏ GemStone GemStone/J (http://www.gemstone.com/)

- ❏ HP Bluestone Total-e-Server (http://www.bluestone.com/)

- ❏ IBM WebSphere (http://www-4.ibm.com/software/webservers/appserv/)

- ❏ IONA iPortal (http://www.iona.com/)

- ❏ Sun iPlanet (http://www.iplanet.com/products/iplanet_application/)

- ❏ Oracle 9i AS (http://www.oracle.com/ip/deploy/ias/)

- ❏ Persistence Power Tier for J2EE (http://www.persistence.com/powertier/)

- ❏ SilverStream Application Server (http://www.silverstream.com/)

- ❏ Sybase Enterprise Application Server (http://www.sybase.com/products/easerver/)

Those who do not want, or cannot afford, commercial application servers might want to consider free open source products, including these:

- ❑ JBoss JBoss (http://www.jboss.org/)
- ❑ Evidian JOnAS (http://www.evidian.com/jonas/)

> *Please notice that some commercial application server vendors provide stripped down free versions of their application servers. The majority of them also provide free time-limited demo versions. A useful link for application server comparison matrix is* http://www.flashline.com/components/appservermatrix.jsp

Choosing among these application servers is the hard part. Therefore, the decision should be based on a large set of criteria, including:

- ❑ J2EE standards compliance and version support
- ❑ Value added features (particularly for integration and B2B)
- ❑ Performance, scalability and availability
- ❑ Support for development tools and environments (like VisualAge, JBuilder, and so on)
- ❑ Cost and licensing
- ❑ Platform support
- ❑ Technical support and vendor reputation

A more detailed discussion of how to choose an application server is out of the scope of this chapter and will ultimately be based on the preferences of each individual company. For up-to-date comparison of features of application servers please refer to their web pages.

However, because all J2EE application servers comply with the J2EE specification, it is *theoretically* possible to port the code developed for one application server to another server. Ideally, no changes to the code are needed.

Back in the real world, this 100% portability goal has yet to be achieved, although it is possible. To achieve portability it is very important that we are familiar with the specification – we should use only standard services in a standard way. As long as we do not use any value-added features, we can count on good portability. Even if we need to make some modifications, these are usually only minor syntax changes. Porting applications between application servers should therefore be possible and can be done in a relatively short period of time. It is certainly easier than porting the solution to some other architecture.

Value-added features can simplify the developers' job considerably. We also have to be aware that application servers can provide value-added functionality that requires the use of specialist APIs. But they can also provide value-added features that work on a declarative basis and do not require that we use specialist APIs in our code.

Value-added features that require the use of specialist APIs include, for example, support for B2B technologies, including XML, SOAP, UDDI, WSDL, and ebXML. Most applications servers that today support these features do no use the JAX* interfaces (such as JAX/RPC, JAXM), but provide their own APIs. When these features are added to the J2EE specification we would have to modify our code to use the JAX interfaces instead.

Unfortunately, we aren't likely to have the luxury of being able to wait for standard implementations, rather we will have to go with what's provided "as is". In this case, it is a good idea to isolate the specialist functionality so that we will know exactly where we have to make modifications, should we have to port the application.

The most important value-added features that do not require us to use specialist APIs from our code, but are based on declarative configurations include:

- ❑ Support for distributed transactions and two-phase commit
- ❑ Load balancing
- ❑ Replication and fail-over
- ❑ Clustering
- ❑ Performance optimizations
- ❑ Connectors for integration with EIS systems (SAP R/3, PeopleSoft, etc.)
- ❑ Connectors for management systems (SNMP, CA-Unicenter, IBM Tivoli, etc.)
- ❑ Support for pluggable middleware, including JMS, JNDI, and ORB implementations, pluggable authentication modules (PAM), etc.
- ❑ Support for automatic logging
- ❑ Support for wireless clients
- ❑ Support for hot deployment of web and business logic components
- ❑ Support for third-party object-relational mapping tools

> **For integration the most important features will be support for distributed transactions and two-phase commit, support for B2B technologies, and those that enable connection with existing EIS systems.**

Integration Servers

Some vendors have already recognized the role of application servers for integration projects and have supplemented their J2EE application servers and focused them directly on integration. Many of them even name them specifically integration servers. For example:

- ❑ BEA WebLogic Integration
- ❑ Iona Enterprise Integrator and B2B Integrator

Such integration servers provide more tools to access existing systems and often provide "out of the box" support for technologies necessary for EAI and B2B integration, which includes adapters for different existing systems and middleware products and support for B2B technologies, such as SOAP.

The Iona Enterprise Integrator, for example, provides adapters for different ERP systems, including SAP R/3 RFC and IDOC interfaces, PeopleSoft, Siebel, JD Edwards, and Baan. It provides support for CICS, support for IBM MQSeries MOM, support for the following DBMS: Oracle, Microsoft SQL Server, Sybase, Informix, and DB/2. It even provides adapters to Microsoft COM+ and .NET architectures and the whole set of B2B technologies. Furthermore, it provides an integrated business process automation engine, which helps manage long-lived process flows, real-time process monitoring, and reporting. It also provides GUI development tools for data mapping, transformation and message routing.

BEA WebLogic Integration provides a similar set of features, including a large set of adapters for existing systems, including ERP systems. It provides an adapter development kit that enables us to develop adapters for existing systems ourselves. Furthermore, it provides a tool for workflow process integration and components to simplify the development of e-business applications, together with extensive support for XML and XML-related standards.

For now integration servers often provide a better solution than to simply collect these technologies piece by piece from third-party developers and integrate them together. However, we have to be aware of the portability traps when we use some custom extensions and value-added features. Too extensive a use of custom features limits portability considerably and we will loose one of the more important J2EE capabilities – vendor independence.

Summary

In this chapter we discussed the J2EE architecture in the context of application integration. For the purposes of integration it is simply not enough that the architecture provides technologies for building next generation systems. It also has to provide ways to integrate new solutions with existing systems. We have identified that J2EE provides support for integration with existing systems. In particular, it is an open platform that builds on open and generally accepted standards, architectures and protocols. Examples include HTTP, IIOP, support for MOM and different databases, and the J2EE Connector Architecture.

Based on the technologies provided by the J2EE platform, we defined the extended J2EE integration architecture. This architecture conforms to the requirements that we outlined in the earlier chapters, using a multi-tier concept. Furthermore, our integration architecture allows us to deploy non-Java components on the different tiers. These non-Java technologies open the door to existing systems that, in most cases, were not developed in Java.

We identified that particularly important components are CORBA distributed objects, RMI-IIOP distributed objects, JMS compliant components. HTTP(S)-enabled technologies also play an important role. We have identified ways how to connect the business logic tier with the EIS tier.

To present the existing systems in a uniform, J2EE-compliant way we have to build virtual components that will mask the technology and semantic differences and present all services on the business logic tier in a consistent way. We identified the role of XML and the need to support different types of clients. We also looked at some possible scenarios that modify the proposed integration architecture, particularly in a client-centric and web-centric scenario.

We identified why component wrappers are important and what type of wrappers we will use. We discussed transaction and security support and concentrated on how to integrate existing transaction and security services with the J2EE platform. We also discussed the performance and scalability questions and the need to have a unified naming and directory scheme.

Then we extended the J2EE integration architecture into the B2B integration architecture. In order to enable B2B collaboration, it is crucial that we have a well-integrated EIS. However, the J2EE integration architecture does not include technologies that directly enable B2B collaborations.

Finally, we identified the most important J2EE application servers – products that implement the J2EE platform specification and that provide the infrastructure to deploy and execute applications. We saw that certain technologies, particularly for B2B integration, are not yet supported by the standard J2EE specification. Several application servers have, however, added these technologies as value added features and targeted those products towards integration – which can be seen from their names.

This concludes our overview of the specific J2EE application integration technologies. In the next chapter we'll be looking at EAI at a more fundamental level and discussing some general integration principles and patterns from the software development perspective.

4

The Integration Process

EAI is not only about developing code. Rather, successful EAI can only be accomplished with a clear understanding of the problem domain, accurately specified requirements, and a strong vision of the desired integrated system. Even with this knowledge, EAI is very difficult to achieve in practice. Indeed, it is probably one of the most difficult software projects that we, as developers, can face.

Many integration projects are unsuccessful for the simple reason that they are not carefully architected, planned and managed. In a lot of cases, managers don't have the necessary insight into the information technology and they are unaware of the exact problems – they just want the results as soon as possible.

> *Of course, there is nothing wrong with delivering results quickly. However, no matter how efficient the technology tools are, we still need to allow sufficient time to think the project through completely, prior to actually coding anything.*

With integration, it is crucial that we perform all the necessary steps: the requirements specification, then the analysis and design, and only after that will we be prepared to actually develop the code and provide working solutions. We should not skip over the early phases of an integration project in order to deliver the results quickly. This will almost certainly result in an unsuccessful integration project, such as the partial solutions and point-to-point integration that we discussed in the Chapter 2.

In this chapter we will focus on the integration process. We will look at an integration project from the software development perspective, covering the main phases and activities. We will also consider some modern development techniques that adhere to a sound approach to software development and enable us to deliver the first versions quickly.

In this chapter we will cover the following major areas:

❑   The integration project

❑   An outline of the integration architecture development process

❑   Overview of activities and phases

❑   An example integration scenario

❑   Detailed discussion of requirements gathering for an integrated information system

❑   Detailed discussion of analysis of existing applications

An Integration Project

> The quality of sophisticated software is only as good as the architecture that underlies it. The investment our enterprise makes in software development will have a much greater long-term payback when we consider the needs of a family of problems rather than just the problem du jour.

An integration project is nothing but a software development project, but it is also a rather special project, because a lot of attention needs to be paid to existing applications. Unfortunately, it is neither a simple nor a small project, but usually a large project that will take a relatively long time to complete. During its course, it will consume a lot of resources (developer time and money), so it is important that integration is done and managed in a defined and consistent way. In other words, an integration project should be started and managed in the same way as a large software development project, and follow sound software development practices.

In this chapter we will focus on the activities unique to integration projects, and show how to incorporate these activities into a software development project. We will assume that a company which is responsible for developing an integrated information system, uses modern software development processes, such as the Rational Unified Process (http://www.rational.com/products/rup/index.jsp). The Unified Process however is not the *only* process that would lead to a successful integration. Rather, it should be treated as a set of general guidelines to follow – modifying this process, or an existing software development process in your company, adding the necessary steps for integration could also be used.

Before we continue our discussion of an integration project, let's consider what possible roles we will most likely find ourselves in:

❑   We might be employed in the IT department of a large company that needs to integrate their existing systems into a global, integrated information system. In this case, the major responsibility will fall on the IT department, which will be responsible for realizing the integration project.

❑   We might be part of a software company that is hired to do the integration for another company. The responsibility for successfully realizing the integration will then fall on the software company completely.

❑ The third possibility is that we will be hired to modify some existing application for the purposes of integration. In this case, we will not be responsible for the whole integration, but only for the application that we have to modify.

From these three roles, the third scenario is obviously the easiest. If we are responsible for a single application only, then we will only partially be involved in the integration. Setting up the integration project, defining the integration architecture, infrastructure and most other difficult tasks will be performed by the company that hired us. We simple have to follow the specifications that we receive to modify the existing application in order for it to fit into the predefined integration architecture.

The first scenario, where the IT department takes over the integration project for its company, is more difficult. The responsibilities of the IT department will be many and include setting up the integration project, designing the integration architecture, selecting the infrastructure, analyzing the existing applications, developing the integrated information system, and so on. However, to its advantage, the IT department will usually be familiar with any existing applications, and it will also have direct contact with employees, which will simplify finding out the requirements. On the other hand, for the IT department this may well be their first integration project, therefore experience may be minimal.

The second scenario is the most difficult. If we are a software company that takes over the integration project, we will have similar responsibilities to the IT department. However, we will be unfamiliar with existing applications, with their functionality, and their finer details. Getting this information might be difficult if the employees are uncooperative in the company for which we perform the integration. On the plus side, we'll probably have a lot of experience from previous integration projects, and experience with many different middleware technologies.

To provide a more formal approach to integration in the next sections, we will define the integration process, where we will focus on the activities that are specific to integration.

This integration process will be based on current software development processes, but since this chapter is not a complete guide to software development methodology, it's probably worth looking into some other books:

❑ *The Rational Unified Process, An Introduction (The Addison-Wesley Object Technology Series)* by Philippe Kruchten, Addison-Wesley; ISBN 0-201707-10-1

❑ *The Unified Software Development Process (The Addison-Wesley Object Technology Series)* by Ivar Jacobson, Grady Booch, James Rumbaugh, Addison-Wesley; ISBN 0-201571-69-2

❑ *Enterprise Modelling with UML: Designing Successful Software through Business Analysis (The Addison-Wesley Object Technology Series)* by Chris Marshall, Addison-Wesley; ISBN 0-201433-13-3

❑ *Managing the Software Process (The SEI Series)* by Watts S. Humphrey, Addison-Wesley; ISBN 0-201180-95-2

❑ *Process Patterns : Building Large-Scale Systems using Object Technology (Managing Object Technology Series, No 16)* by Scott W. Ambler, Cambridge University Press; ISBN 0-521645-68-9

❑ *Extreme Programming Explained: Embrace Change (The XP Series)* by Kent Beck, Addison-Wesley; ISBN 0-201616-41-6.

The Integration Process

> **The integration process defines the sequence of activities to be done in a disciplined manner in order to successfully develop an integrated information system.**

The goal of the integration process is to guarantee the quality of the integrated solution that will satisfy the customer, will be completed on schedule, and will be within the allocated financial resources. An integration project is based on an integration process. A well-managed integration project, based on the proposed integration process, will provide the basis for us to plan, implement, and complete the integration successfully.

The integration process is tightly connected to the software development process, with which it shares several activities. Each company that develops software, has defined a software development process. The quality and maturity of the software development process (as assessed by the Capability Maturity Model (http://www.sei.cmu.edu/cmm/cmm.html), for example) will have an impact on our ability to accomplish integration successfully. A better-defined development process will reach a higher maturity level, and consequently there will be higher odds that the integration will be successful.

> *For more information refer to related literature, for example to the books: The Capability Maturity Model: Guidelines for Improving the Software Process (The SEI Series) by Mark C. Paulk, Charles V. Weber (Contributor), Bill Curtis (Contributor), Addison-Wesley; ISBN 0-201546-64-7; and Successful Software Process Improvement by Robert B. Grady, Prentice Hall PTR; ISBN 0-136266-23-1.*

Software development processes and their quality differ considerably between companies. Modifying an existing development process takes time and requires the cooperation of all involved parties. Likewise, changing a development process overnight is impossible. This is the reason why we will focus here only on the activities unique to integration. Incorporating these activities into your existing software development process is much easier than changing the complete development process.

Before we look into the details of integration process activities, let's first look at some sound development practices that are particularly important for integration.

Sound Practices

There are four important practices that should be considered in each integration project:

- ❑ **Iterative development**
  We have already identified that an integration project will be a very large project that requires a lot of time and resources. On the other hand, it is unlikely that a company will be willing to wait too long (for example a year or more) from the initiation of the integration project until the usable integrated solutions are deployed. Iterative development solves this problem

- ❑ **Incremental development**
  With iterative development we partition the integration into several smaller tasks that will deliver some usable products. However, it is unlikely that we will solve each task in our first attempt adequately. Usually we learn by our own mistakes and improve on ourselves.

❑ **Prototyping**
With prototyping we can build pilot solutions to integration challenges and assess whether they can be developed in the way that we would like and with the technologies we prefer. Prototyping is commonly used to assess, verify, and validate chosen architectures and solutions for integration. Often it is also used to verify the requirements, performance and scalability.

❑ **Reuse**
Reuse is the ability to develop new applications through the use of existing solutions – this is also the exact goal of EAI. The problem is that to achieve reuse we must have software components that have been developed specifically for this purpose. The majority of existing systems are not designed with this in mind, so we have to search for solutions that will make existing systems reusable. When discussing the practice of reuse we should also think about reuse at a higher level of abstraction – the reuse of ideas and sound solutions in the form of pattern reuse.

Although incremental and iterative development strategies are commonly used together, they are actually two different strategies. Iterative development partitions the problem into subproblems, while incremental development supplements and improves partial solutions step-by-step. Iterative and incremental development strategies are important to integration and enable us to partition the integration into several subproblems, allowing us to manage the changing requirements. If possible they should be used in combination with integration projects.

Following these practices will enable us to achieve integration successfully and deliver partial results quickly. This is an important point, as companies that start EAI are not able to wait a long time (it can take a few years in a large company) to gain the whole integrated system. They need partial results that solve their most urgent needs for integration. These most urgent needs will influence the decision of what to prioritize and how to partition the integration into smaller tasks. However, a disciplined development path is still needed to effectively solve even partial needs. Ad hoc solutions, although faster at first sight, will not fulfill long-term integration goals.

Integration Process Activities and Phases

In previous chapters, we saw that integration requires that we analyze existing applications, design the integration architecture, select the integration infrastructure, design the solution, implement the integration, and so on. All these are **activities** of an integration process and they have to be performed step-by-step. Here we will classify these activities and more strictly define the sequence in which they should be performed. In general, we can partition the activities into technical and supporting activities. Technical activities include:

❑ Requirements gathering

❑ Analysis of existing applications

❑ Selection of the integration infrastructure

❑ Problem domain analysis

❑ Design

❑ Implementation

❑ Testing

❑ Deployment

151

In addition to technical activities we also need support activities. The important support activities are:

- ❏ Project management
- ❏ Configuration and change management
- ❏ Communication with the environment

Technical activities will be performed by analysts, architects, designers, developers, programmers, and testers. Support activities will be performed by support staff.

In Chapter 2, we also identified that integration is usually achieved in four phases:

- ❏ Data-level integration
- ❏ Application interface level integration
- ❏ Business-method-level integration
- ❏ Presentation integration

These four integration phases are usually done sequentially, although not always. Sometimes we can skip a phase. For example, we could skip data-level integration and proceed with application interface level.

The question is how to connect the activities and the phases of an integration process. The answer is that we will perform these activities for each of the integration phases.

> **Some activities will differ from phase to phase, some will not.**

The technical activities that will not differ from phase to phase are the first three activities:

- ❏ Requirements gathering
- ❏ Analysis of existing applications
- ❏ Selection of the integration infrastructure

We have to perform these activities before a distinction between the four integration phases will be made. We also perform all support activities equally for all phases.

The rest of technical activities will differ in data-level integration, in application interface and business-method-level and in presentation-level integration.

The next figure presents the relationship between the phases and the activities:

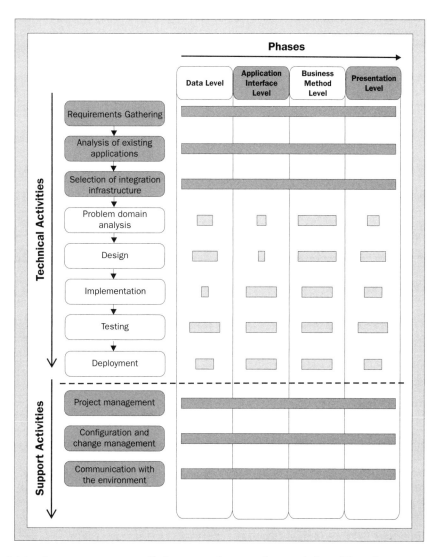

The activities that are common to all phases are shown with a single box. The other activities are shown with separate boxes. The size of the boxes represents the approximate duration of each activity in a certain phase. For example, problem domain analysis and the design activities require the most effort in business-method-level integration, where we have to define the global design model of the integrated information system. The least implementation effort is usually in data-level integration because it rarely requires changes to existing applications.

In the next sections we will look at the different phases and activities and we will finally focus on the requirements gathering and analysis of existing applications. Let's start with the discussion of phases.

Phases

In Chapter 2 we defined the goals and objectives of each integration phase. Here we will look how to partition each phase into smaller units.

Each integration phase requires a lot of effort and time. Therefore, it has to be considered as a sub-project that has to go through several activities. To support iterative incremental development, each phase is usually broken into several iterations. Iterations enable a finer-grained control over the integration phase. Usually there are at least four iterations for each integration phase. These main iterations can however have further sub-iterations, depending on the project size and the schedule.

The four main iterations for each integration phase should be:

❑ **Inception**
Defines the integration phase from the business perspective and estimates its size. We have to specify the requirements, identify all entities our system will cooperate with, and define how it will cooperate. We also have to define the criteria for assessing the success of the integration phase, analyze the risks, and select the resources. Finally, we prepare the plan, which defines the iterations and the milestones.

❑ **Elaboration**
Here we analyze the existing applications and get a clear understanding of what applications we have to deal with. We also analyze the problem domain, define the project plan, the basic architecture, and solve the most hazardous parts of the integration project. We also specify the requirements for the integrated information system. As we have to make architectural choices, it is very useful for us to build architectural prototypes to validate the chosen architecture. At the end of this phase we evaluate the goals, the size of the project, and the architecture decisions, and we should once again assess the risks.

❑ **Construction**
The goal of construction is that we actually implement the integration that will result in completing a certain integration phase. This part is the most time-intensive and will have the largest number of iterations. When constructing the integrated system, we obtain a clear understanding of the integrated information system that we are building. We also need to know how the existing applications map to the newly defined integration architecture and which functionality we will be able to reuse. Then we build the design model, write the implementation code, and perform testing and verification. At the end of the construction phase we verify whether the developed integration satisfies the requirements.

❑ **Transition**
In transition we deploy the integrated information system into the production environment. Upon deployment there are often additional problems and complications that arise, which we have to solve. We also fix any bugs and implement any omitted functionality (deliberately or accidentally). The transition usually begins when we have a beta version of the integrated system ready. Transition finishes when we are satisfied with the functionality of a certain integration phase. After transition we usually proceed to the next integration phase (from data-level to application interface level for example).

Each phase finishes by the fulfillment of the requirements for that phase. The requirements are defined for each iteration by milestones. These milestones influence the project schedule and require decisions be made after each phase is completed.

Although we have already identified the activities we will have a closer look at them in the next section.

Activities

We have seen that activities of an integration process can be classified as technical and support activities and that some technical and all support activities are performed for all phases equally, whilst other activities differ from phase to phase.

We can also see that a lot of integration process activities are similar to regular software development activities. An integration project differs mainly in that it has to take existing applications into account and that it has to select the integration infrastructure relatively early. There are also some differences in requirements gathering, which together with the analysis of existing applications and the selection of infrastructure defines which requirements will be fulfilled in which integration phase. Therefore, we will now take a closer look at the technical and support activities.

Requirements Gathering

Requirements gathering is the first activity of the integration process:

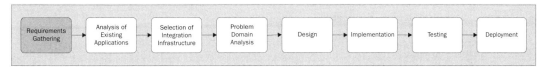

Through integration we attempt to achieve business needs that cannot be realized through partial or unconnected applications. This is, however, far too general a definition to start integration. We need to know exactly which business requirements should be realized through integration.

> *Quite often companies start integration projects simply because they want an integrated information system. Upon asking specifically what they expect from EAI, they do not have an answer. As a consequence of EAI becoming a buzzword over the last few years, companies often believe that EAI is necessary for its own sake.*

> **To achieve successful integration it is very important to define the requirements of the integrated system.**

A clear definition of the requirements at the beginning allows us to:

- ❑   Specify what the organization expects from the integrated information system
- ❑   Determine the current situation at any stage during the integration project
- ❑   Assess the costs and the schedules
- ❑   Identify the integration phases in which we will fulfill the requirements
- ❑   Be highly focused to achieve our desired goals
- ❑   Assess the success of the integration

Requirements gathering is a unified activity for all phases. Actually during requirements gathering we do not partition the process into different phases. Rather the requirements specification enables us to identify which requirements should be fulfilled in which phase. The requirements related to unified databases will, for example, be performed in data-level phase, those on sharing the functionality in the application interface and business-method-level phases, and so on.

Defining the requirements is a difficult task and requires a lot of knowledge and experience. Having precisely determined requirements is a big step towards the final solution. However, in order to define the requirements in a consistent and systematic manner, we have to specify them accurately, concisely, and unambiguously. Specifying requirements should not take too long. As a rule of thumb, the maximum time should be 10% of the total project time.

This does not mean that we have to define all the requirements at the beginning and they can't be changed or added to later. It is practically impossible to define all the requirements initially, mainly because they change as and when the company reacts to market changes. This means that we have to accommodate new, or deal with changed requirements. This requires a lot of flexibility, particularly in the integration architecture.

Due to its importance and because this activity has to be performed for all phases equally we will discuss it later in this chapter. For the moment we only need to realize that the outcomes of this stage are the use case model, the description of scenarios, the non-functional requirements, and the software requirements specification.

Additional reading on requirement gathering include:

❑   *Mastering the Requirements Process* by Suzanne Robertson, James Robertson, Addison-Wesley; ISBN 0-201360-46-2

❑   *Managing Software Requirements: A Unified Approach (The Addison-Wesley Object Technology Series)* by Dean Leffingwell, Don Widrig, Edward Yourdon, Addison-Wesley; ISBN 0-201615-93-2

❑   *Use Cases: Requirements in Context* by Daryl Kulak, Eamonn Guiney, Erin Lavkulich, Addison-Wesley; ISBN 0-201657-67-8

Analysis of Existing Applications

Analysis of existing applications is the second activity and one of the activities that is unique to integration:

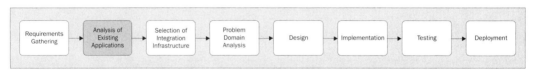

> **To be able to reuse existing applications we have to gain some insight into them.**

Before we start analyzing existing applications we have to select the applications to be integrated. This should include all the major primary "backbone" applications. But we should also not forget subsidiary applications, often self-made or locally developed solutions that users use on a daily basis.

In the analysis of existing applications, we identify and specify the functionality of each application that will be included in the integrated information system. We identify the data models, perform the functional analysis, identify the architecture of existing applications, identify ways to access this functionality, and so on. We also have to answer several other questions, such as:

❑   Are the system interfaces and communication protocols documented?

❑   Is the software architecture and software design well documented?

- ❏ Does the application have a system configuration diagram or design documentation?
- ❏ Does the documentation reflect the real-world situation?
- ❏ What are the dependencies on external interfaces?
- ❏ Do we have the documentation for data and message formats?
- ❏ Which are the critical algorithms? Have we identified them all?
- ❏ Have all the user interfaces been identified?
- ❏ What are the performance characteristics of a system?
- ❏ Which programming languages and tools are used?
- ❏ Is the source code and the environment to build the applications available?
- ❏ Have we identified the dependencies between the systems?
- ❏ What are the undocumented features and have we identified them?
- ❏ Do we understand the application in all of its complexity?
- ❏ How will the integrity of the system be affected by integration attempts?

In the analysis of existing applications we also need to identify redundancy and other semantic problems, where the functionality of several applications may be overlapping. Usually in this phase we will look at the applications in two ways:

- ❏ First, we'll study the data that is stored in applications
- ❏ Second, we'll identify the functionality that is provided and the ways in which to access it – we will extract the business rules that are embedded in the existing applications

The outcome is the data- and functionality-level analysis models of existing applications.

The analysis of existing application will be covered in more detail later in this chapter.

Selection of Integration Infrastructure

Selection of integration infrastructure is the third activity in the integration process:

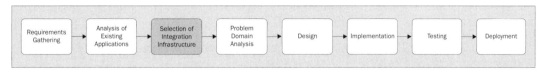

In Chapter 2 we saw that an effective integration infrastructure should address all relevant middleware services that are required by EAI. When the integration infrastructure provides these services, this frees the developers from these tasks so that they can focus on the content of integration. We also saw that the integration infrastructure can be abstracted through the use of the integration broker concept.

Selecting an integration infrastructure and related middleware technologies relatively early in the integration process guarantees that we set up a common technology basis on which we can build the integration architecture. It also assures that the same infrastructure and technologies will be used in the whole enterprise.

We discussed the selection of infrastructure and technologies in Chapter 3. There we compared three possible software platforms. As we have already addressed this activity, through the selection of J2EE, we will not discuss it further.

Problem Domain Analysis

The problem domain analysis is the fourth activity in the integration process:

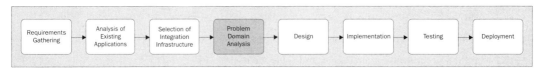

Problem domain analysis and the other technical activities that we will discuss from now on are specific to the integration phase. In other words, they are performed differently if we are dealing with data-level, application interface, business-method-level, or presentation-level integration.

Therefore, we will discuss these activities just briefly here, and in more detail in the corresponding chapters later in the book. The data-level integration phase will be addressed in Chapter 5, the application-interface-level and business-method-level in Chapter 9 and the presentation integration in Chapter 17. These activities are also very similar to regular software development activities, therefore the reader may refer to general software development references.

> **The problem domain analysis activity focuses on the elaboration of the integration solution to the requirements, identified in the requirements gathering activity.**

Problem domain analysis focuses on the integration domain problem and identifies the operations and components that should be a part of the solution. In this stage we only identify functionality, and not any implementation details. This is an important point, which requires analysts with enough skill to differentiate functionality from implementation-related issues.

The products of this activity differ for each integration phase. In the data-level phase they include the logical enterprise data model and the data dictionary; in the application-interface-level and business-method-level phases they include the analysis-level class diagram, the component diagram and the specification of interfaces; in the presentation integration they include a specification of the presentation-tier functionality.

A useful reference for domain analysis is the following book: Analysis Patterns: Reusable Object Models (Addison-Wesley Object Technology: Addison-Wesley Object Technology Series) by Martin Fowler, Addison-Wesley; ISBN 0-201895-42-0.

Design

Design is the fifth activity in the integration process:

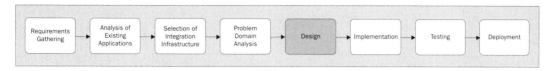

> **The design activity defines the structure and architecture of the integrated information system.**

The design activity is again dependent on the integration phase:

❑ In the data-level phase, the design activity defines the architecture in terms of physical enterprise data models and the connections to existing databases.

❑ In the application-interface-level phase, the design activity specifies the existing application wrappers and the low-level component wrappers. It defines how they should be implemented and how they should be connected to existing applications.

❑ In the business-method-level phase, the design activity defines the high-level business integration architecture, which includes the high-level component wrappers, their interfaces and the business methods that they should provide. Further, this phase defines how the high-level business methods should map to lower-level component wrappers. With this mapping the business-method-level phase design specifies how existing applications will be reused and which functionality will be reused. We also have to make important decisions about visibility, relations, security, transactions, access protocols, concurrency, synchronization, scalability, and performance.

❑ In the presentation-level phase, the design activity defines the new, integrated presentation tier. This includes the definition of user interfaces, identification of client-tier technologies, mapping of user interfaces to the high-level virtual components on the business logic tier, and related security, transaction, and performance considerations.

The design activity is a highly important activity. Getting the design wrong will result in the failure of the whole integration project. Of course the quality of the results in the design activity is dependent on the quality of the inputs from previous activities. Still we should be aware of the importance of this activity. The risk of mistakes can be greatly reduced with iterative and incremental development.

The design activity will, in the same way as other phase-specific activities, be addressed in more detail in later chapters, particularly Chapters 5, 9, and 17. The majority of chapters in this book that are related to particular technologies will also present several design guidelines.

Implementation

The implementation activity is the sixth activity in the integration process:

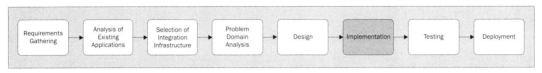

> **The implementation activity requires that we implement the design, defined in the previous activity.**

In the design activity we decided on the technologies we will use. Therefore, in this activity we simply have to follow the design from the previous activity and implement it.

The major difference between developing an application from scratch and integration is that we reuse as many applications as possible. We also have to implement all the interoperability code. Note that we should not include the development of new functionality into an integration project. This does not mean that we cannot extend the functionality of the integrated system. On the contrary, we should provide ways to extend the functionality, but new development should be managed as a separate project.

This is why the implementation activity will usually not be as complicated as in traditional software development. If the design has been done correctly, then no serious performance issues should arise because of implementation decisions. Still the implementation of interoperability with existing applications is not easy and should not be underestimated.

The outcome of the implementation activity is the implementation model, which includes code and documentation. The implementation is addressed in this book in several chapters that address different technologies. In addition to implementation, these chapters provide also valuable design information, therefore they should be considered in both activities. The most important chapters are:

- ❑ Chapter 5, which covers integration through data using JDBC
- ❑ Chapter 6, for using XML for data exchange
- ❑ Chapter 7, for transforming XML
- ❑ Chapter 8, for message brokers
- ❑ Chapter 10, for CORBA
- ❑ Chapter 11, for RMI-IIOP
- ❑ Chapter 12, for EJB
- ❑ Chapter 13, for the J2EE Connector Architecture
- ❑ Chapter 14, for COM bridges for Microsoft integration
- ❑ Chapter 15, for transaction management
- ❑ Chapter 16, for security management
- ❑ Chapter 17, for presentation integration, including JSP and servlets
- ❑ Chapter 18, for Web Services

Testing

Testing is the seventh activity in the integration process:

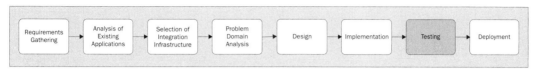

This activity is probably the most obvious, and includes component testing, integration testing, and the testing of existing applications.

> **Since we are likely to be making modifications to existing applications it is very important to retest them.**

Existing applications hide many irregularities which we do not understand and it's therefore quite easy to break their integrity, especially with old systems that do not, perhaps, use OO or modular designs (such as COBOL, APL, or ADA).

Testing multiple integrated applications can be extremely difficult because one must account-for/test multiple interaction sequences. Also, due to the multi-platform nature of EAI, a testing framework must itself be very flexible to support such multi-application testing. The goals of testing include:

❑ Verification of interactions between the components and existing applications

❑ Verification of proper integration of components with existing applications

❑ Verification of those existing applications' functionality that have been modified

❑ Verification that all requirements have been fulfilled

❑ Identification of defects prior to deployment

Many integration projects have failed because they delivered solutions that were not well tested and influenced not only new functionality, but also the working of existing applications.

Testing is not covered in this book, because it does not differ significantly from regular software development testing.

Refer to related books for more information:

❑ *Software Testing in the Real World: Improving the Process (Acm Press Books)* by Edward Kit, Susannah Finzi (Editor), Addison-Wesley; ISBN 0-201877-56-2

❑ *Testing It: An Off-The-Shelf Software Testing Process* by John Watkins, Cambridge Univ Pr (Trd); ISBN 0-521795-46-X

❑ *Testing Computer Software, 2nd Edition* by Cem Kaner, Hung Quoc Nguyen, Jack Falk, John Wiley & Sons; ISBN 0-471358-46-0

❑ *Effective Methods for Software Testing, 2nd Edition* by William E. Perry, John Wiley & Sons; ISBN: 0-471354-18-X

Successful testing is the prerequisite for the final technical activity, deployment.

Deployment

Deployment is the eighth and final activity in the integration process:

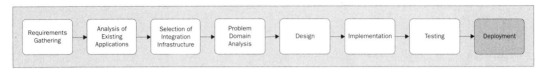

The deployment activity produces software product releases and delivers them to the end users.

Deployment includes packaging, releasing, installing, configuring, updating, and uninstalling a software product, but also providing help and assistance to end users. As a part of the integration process, deployment will have to fulfill the integration requirements. This will mean that the new software products have to be integrated with existing applications to reuse their functionality.

Deployment might be difficult because it will include the definition of several deployment time parameters. These parameters will adapt the software products to the target environment. In the J2EE platform a lot of deployment parameters are specified through deployment descriptors, some of which are specific to the application server that is used. Successful deployment will guarantee that the integrated software will work.

Deployment is specific to a particular technology. Therefore, it will be addressed in the technology chapters of this book, as listed earlier.

Support Activities

In the integration process there will be another group of activities known as support activities. These are intended to support the technical activities and to manage the project. The most important support activities are:

❑ **Project Management**
This is one of the most difficult activities. It takes care of planning the costs, schedules and people, managing risks, balancing the goals of customers and developers, and so on, to finally deliver the integrated information system that satisfies the customers, end users, and the vendor. The success of a software development project, and particularly integration projects, has not been high in the last years. Therefore, careful project management is even more important.

We will not address project management is this book, but we highly recommend readers to refer to related literature, for example *Software Project Management: A Unified Framework (The Addison-Wesley Object Technology Series)* by Walker Royce, Addison-Wesley; ISBN 0-201309-58-0.

❑ **Configuration and Change Management**
This activity addresses the problems of many people working on the same integration project. Configuration and change management on one side helps maintaining different versions of the same product, which is a result of iterative incremental development. It also addresses the problem of several people who work on the same artifacts. Therefore, it is necessary to control and supervise the work to prevent confusion. Configuration and change management should also address parallel development, development at multiple sites, traceability of changes, change request management, and ways to automate code build processes.

We will not address this activity further in this book, therefore refer to related literature, such as *A Guide to Software Configuration Management* (Artech House Computer Library) by Alexis Leon, Artech House; ISBN 1-580530-72-9; and *Anti-Patterns and Patterns in Software Configuration Management* by William J. Brown, Hays W., Iii McCormick, Scott W. Thomas, John Wiley & Sons; ISBN 0-471329-29-0.

❑ **Communication with the Environment**
This activity focuses on the configuration of the integration process in the context of an integration project on the target environment. It also focuses on the guidelines to customize each integration project. For these tasks it should provide an integrated software environment that will simplify this activity.

Communication with the environment will not be covered in this book. Refer to *The Unified Software Development Process (The Addison-Wesley Object Technology Series)* by Ivar Jacobson, Grady Booch, James Rumbaugh, Addison-Wesley; ISBN 0-201571-69-2.

In the rest of this chapter we will focus on the requirements gathering and the analysis of existing applications activities. The selection of integration infrastructure has been covered in Chapter 3. Other technical activities, related to specific integration phases, will be covered in later chapters. Support activities will not be covered in this book.

An Example Scenario for Integration

To provide examples on how to perform several activities of the integration process, we'll introduce an example scenario for integration. We'll use this example in the rest of this chapter and in the Chapters 9 to 12. The example integration scenario is based on a hypothetical cell phone operator company.

Please note, this example is simplified for the needs of this book and focuses only on the relevant aspects. Also because this example is written from a Euro-perspective there may be some inadvertent differences with the operation of cell phone operators from other regions of the world.

The cell phone operator, Two-2-Yellow, provides services for digital (GMS) cell telephony. It started its business many years ago with analog services and over the years has consequently expanded. Today it offers digital telephony only. The main services are two types of cell account:

❑ A **subscriber account** is an account where the customer receives an invoice each month and has to pay it later

❑ The **prepaid account** is an account where the customer has to put money on the account in advance and cannot call more than the current balance

Both accounts support voice communication and a set of related services, usual for GSM networks. The exact details of the services are not relevant for this example.

Unfortunately, the architecture of the information system did not follow the evolution of the company. Two-2-Yellow does not have an integrated information system and uses a set of unconnected or partially connected applications (existing applications in our terminology). The primary applications that the operator uses are the following:

❏ Customer information application
Enables the management of customers. This includes entering new customers, updating existing customers and adding data about the cell phone account that they have.

❏ Application that manages the account balance for users
Manages both types of accounts. It allows data to be entered regarding the consumption of money and about deposits on the accounts (they can be either the payments of the invoices or the advance deposits, depending on the account type). It also enables searching of accounts that have a negative balance (for the subscribers). For prepaid accounts it allows a search of the accounts that have had zero balance for a specified period of time. This is because those accounts are then automatically disconnected. Finally, it allows searching for money deposits on those accounts based on age.

❏ Application that prints the invoices each month
This is a simple one that goes through the subscriber accounts and prints the invoices for the consumptions of the specified month.

❏ Application that evaluates domestic cell phone calls
Calculates the consumption for each account based on the data transferred from the cell phone exchange, but only for domestic calls.

❏ Application that calculates international cell phone calls
Has a similar function to the domestic application. However, it does not have a direct connection with the cell phone exchange. Rather, it receives input data formatted from each roaming partner.

❏ Application that manages cell phone call tariff information
Includes functions to enter and display the tariff information. This includes tariff policies, tariff classes, and costs per minute for voice and data communication.

In addition to the primary application the operator uses a set of individual, subsidiary applications. Although important in real-world integration, we will not discuss these subsidiary applications, because they will not be important for this simplified example and would complicate it too much.

Some of the primary applications are not integrated at all. Therefore, users have to manually enter the data several times in different applications. However, some other primary applications facilitate simple data exchange based on the sharing of files with data, formatted in proprietary format.

We can easily see that such a set of applications cannot fulfill several needs and does not provide the efficiency that could be achieved with an integrated information system.

In the next section we will look at the requirements gathering activity of the integration process, where we will try to identify the new requirements for the integrated system. Later in this chapter we will make a more detailed analysis of these existing applications, where we will become more familiar with the existing application analysis activity and with the situation at our hypothetical cell operator company.

Requirements Gathering

Requirements gathering is an essential first step in EAI, as well as in software development in general, and many other areas of work. When defining the requirements, we have to specify functionality as precisely and completely as possible. We have to include functional and non-functional requirements. Functional requirements are those that describe the behavior of the system, while non-functional requirements describe the attributes of the system that do not directly influence the behavior.

> **Unfortunately, there is no easy pattern to identify all the requirements. Rather, it is a creative process, often done in cooperation with users and customers.**

Creative processes seldom follow a predictable path. Every new idea leads people to notice new, previously unanticipated possibilities. Keeping this in mind, we will try to present the necessary steps for a requirements specification.

> **The requirements specification is a contract between the developers, end users, and customers, which defines what the software will do.**

The requirements specification will be important to customers, who will use it to figure out whether the integrated system meets their needs. It will also be used by analysts, designers, and architects, who will see what they have to do, and testers, who will use it as a basis for defining functional tests.

The requirements specification will consist of a set of documents and diagrams that describe the functionality of the system. Before we can start to gather the requirements for an integrated information system, we need a clear vision of the system. We should be aware what kind of system we would like to have, its goals and the benefits the company is expecting.

In the beginning, it's likely that we will not have a clear understanding of the requirements, and our task will therefore be to gather and understand them. To do this effectively, we have to find the people who understand the existing system and who know what they want. We try to understand the system from their perspective. Typically, they will be the end users and domain experts, as they have the most knowledge of the integrated system we are building. They will also focus only on the problem domain and not on the technical details, of which they may know nothing at all. This allows us to answer the technical questions by ourselves. However, we might consider obtaining the opinion of independent experts as well. Finally, we have to formalize, specify, and describe the requirements. The process of gathering requirements is iterative and interactive so this will not be a once-only operation.

Now imagine that we start defining the requirements for an integration project, let's say for the cell phone operator. We could start defining the specification so that we would describe how the screens of the integrated system's user interface should look, how the user should navigate to the existing applications, which input fields from which applications should be on the screen, the look-and-feel of the solution, and so on. Bear in mind, however, that these are *not* the requirements, as such.

> **Requirements define the problem that the software, in our case the integrated system, should solve. They specify *what* software should do, rather than *how* it should be done.**

In fact, even this definition is a little misleading – sometimes the requirements do dictate an implementation or a direction for design. More accurately, the requirements should not go too much into the technical (implementation) details. Rather, they should specify the problem as precisely as possible but leave the freedom of how to solve the problem to the designers and developers.

This is also exactly the way the customers (and/or the end users) think about software. They will most likely tell us that the integrated information system should, for example, provide the information about a cell phone user's account balance at any time and that the information should be accurate and include all domestic and international calls, as well as any discounts.

So, when defining the requirements, we have to describe the problem domain of the integrated information system that we are developing. Requirements are the effects produced by the application systems and defining what the customers want to achieve with the integrated system.

To define the requirements of an integrated information system consistently, we recommend going through several steps:

❏   Requirements specification

❏   Modeling the requirements with use cases

❏   Revising the use cases

❏   Setting the priorities of use cases

❏   Obtaining the requirements model

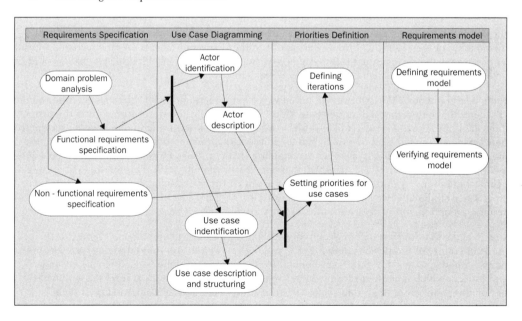

Requirements Specification

Requirements specification is the first step in the requirements gathering activity:

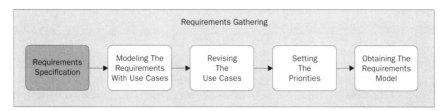

In the requirements specification we have to specify the functional and non-functional requirements with a high level of abstraction, based on the business perspectives of the integrated system. We often do this in an informal manner, using our natural language (English for example). Although we will build the system in several iterations, we should try to include the requirements for the first iteration, as well as for later iterations. To get an overview of the requirements we have to take into account the whole lifecyle of the information system. Usually we will specify the requirements in three steps:

❑ Identification of participants and roles

❑ Specifying the functional requirements

❑ Specifying the non-functional requirements

First we have to **identify the participants and the roles** they play in the system development for each phase and iteration. Participants are those persons involved who care about the success of the project. Based on the participants, we make a list of functional and non-functional requirements, use the appropriate naming, and briefly describe them. We should focus on the business needs and on the expected usage scenarios. We don't yet describe the internal technical behavior of the system, but we should start to write the technical documentation. The most important documents from this activity are the list of involved persons, the list of information sources, and the terminology dictionary.

Then we **specify the functional requirements**. This specification should be based on the business process. We should include as many requirements as possible. Looking at our example integration scenario of the cell phone operator, we will identify two functional requirements that are not fulfilled by the non-integrated applications. The list of complete functional requirements for our example would be out of the scope of this chapter:

❑ Cell phone users should be able to check their account balance at any time online, using a cell phone (WAP or SMS), or a PC (Internet browser). The information provided should be accurate and include all domestic and international calls, as well as any discounts.

❑ Cell phone users should be able to deposit money on the cell phone account using the cell phone (WAP or SMS), or a PC (Internet browser) charged to the credit card, which the user enters. The money deposit should be performed only if the credit card authorization is successful.

Sometimes the functionality specification is based on real needs. Sometimes it is based on the functionality of competing products. For example, allowing customers to check their account balance could only be a real need for some customers, but will become a required function if it is offered by a competing operator.

The functional requirements can also be based on the functionality of existing systems. In particular, in the context of integration, we may think that users will not want to lose functionality that has been offered in previous systems. Obviously, only if the functionality of existing systems has been useful should it be included in the newly integrated system. Sometimes including the functionality of existing applications prevents us from thinking of new solutions and being constructive. In practice, we should only include the functionality that is useful for end users.

> *This is analogous to moving to a new apartment. We might choose to put all our belongings into boxes, move them in, then allow six months during which we only take the things that we really need out of the boxes. All the rest we should throw away. Although this approach is unrealistic in life, applying it to software development will create an information system with a lower number of functions, and thus a reduced level of complexity. But it will still provide the same functionality that the users need. So, we should not include the functionality of existing systems by default. Rather we should include only the functionality that is actually needed.*

After functional requirements we have to **specify non-functional requirements**. These are all the requirements that are not directly connected with the functions of the software. They include quality requirements, time constraints, technical constraints (such as using a certain software platform for integration), and compatibility with existing software or hardware. Quality attributes include performance, reliability, security, usability, extendibility, interoperability, and so on.

The non-functional requirements for our example integration scenario could be:

- ❏ The maximum response time for the cell phone account balance check is three seconds.

- ❏ The maximum response time for the money deposit transaction is five seconds, which includes the credit card authorization.

- ❏ Both functions should provide adequate security for all types of clients, including authentication, authorization and communication channel protection. The probability of security breach should be lower than 0.000001. The exact technology solution should be identified in the design activity.

- ❏ Both functions should be available 99.9999% of time, 24 hours per day, 365/366 days per year.

In the next subsection we will look at use cases, a technique for modeling requirements.

Modeling the Requirements with Use Cases

Modeling the requirements with use cases is the second step in the requirements gathering activity:

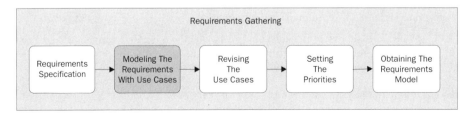

For a long time in software development people used informal techniques to model requirements. This changed when Ivar Jacobson introduced the concept of **use cases**.

> **A use case is an interaction between the user and the application system.**

Use cases capture the functionally of the system and show the relations between the functionalities and the users. They are represented by use case diagrams, which are part of UML notation. With use case diagrams we can easily model the influences of the environment on the system.

For more information on use case diagrams please refer to the book: Applying Use Cases: A Practical Guide *by Geri Schneider, Jason P. Winters, Ivar Jacobson, Addison-Wesley; ISBN 0-201309-81-5.*

We build use case diagrams (and thus gather the requirements) in several steps:

First we have to determine the **system boundary** to find out what is inside the system that we build and what is outside.

Then we can **identify the actors**. As the basis we use the list of involved persons. Remember that not only humans are modeled as actors. Actors can also be other systems that interact with our system. Actors represent roles, so to qualify as an actor the human or some other system has to use our system in a distinctive way. It can happen that a single person can have more than one role and will thus be represented by more than one actor. We can identify additional actors with help of the users and domain specialists. A typical actor for our example integration scenario is the cell phone user.

After identifying actors, we have to **describe the actors**. We describe each actor based on the role it has in the information domain. We have to focus on the role of the actor and not on the physical person or system that plays the actor.

Based on the actors, we should then **identify the use cases**. We should try to identify the fundamentally different ways in which the actors use the system. Each of these ways represents a use case. The user effort is not the standard on which we would select the use cases. Rather, a use case should be focused on a certain purpose. This will be important later when we employ the use cases for determining the schedules and for preparing the test scenarios. The use case should have a measurable value when considered in isolation. This does not mean that the use case cannot be related to other use cases. It just means that it should provide some value when considered alone.

Use cases should never be thought of as computer-related constructs. It would be a mistake to consider user input, input validation, storing data in the database, and so on, as separate use cases. Mapping between the processes and use cases is not one-to-one. A single use case can be related to several processes and a single process can be described by several use cases.

Significant use cases for our Two-2-Yellow operator's integrated information system from the perspective of the cell phone user would be: checking the account balance, getting the history of the calls made, placing money on the phone account, receiving notification when the account is empty, and so on.

Here's an example use case for Checking the Account Balance:

1. The cell phone user is asked for username and password.

2. The user enters their username and password

3. The username and password are successfully validated

4. The accounts are presented (a user can have more than one account)

5. The user selects the account

6. The current balance is presented

This description corresponds to the normal flow of events. There are, however, at least two alternative flows, for example if the user enters a wrong username and password, in which case, for simplicity, we'll only show the normal flow but you would normally model the alternative flows as well.

The description for the normal flow for the use case for Placing Money on the Account would look as follows:

1. The cell phone user is asked for username and password

2. The user enters their username and password

3. The username and password are successfully validated

4. The accounts are presented (a user can have more than one mobile phone account)

5. The user selects the account

6. The user enters the amount of money they wants to place on the account

7. The user enters the credit card information to make the payment

8. The credit card information is checked successfully

9. The user confirms the payment

10. The system performs the money transfer

11. The system displays a confirmation of the payment

After identifying actors and use cases we should combine them into the **use case diagram**. Here we show relationships between actors and use cases. opposite we show a simple use case diagram for our example. The cell phone user is an actor for the application system because it uses it directly (over the phone, WAP, or over the Internet, for example). For simplicity, we show only two use cases here, and they represent distinctive functionalities that make sense when looking at them in isolation:

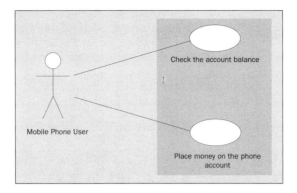

Just identifying actors and use cases, and drawing the use case diagram is not enough. We also have to **describe each use case**. There are two ways of describing the requirements for a use case: either we use our natural language or we can use a UML diagramming technique. Most appropriate are activity and sequence diagrams. Sometimes it is also worth considering using a textual description combined with one or more diagrams.

The use case description should provide the overview of a use case. It should also include the goals of the use case, the prerequisites, the actors involved, the sequence of operations between the actor and the system, and the non-functional requirements. It should include the condition when the use case ends.

The use case description should include the sequence of interactions that the actor has to do in order to complete the use case. Often, particularly with the more complex use cases, there are several possible sequences, which should all be described. Typically, we will describe the common, normal flow, and all of the possible alternative flows. The normal flow describes the use case assuming that everything goes to plan. Alternative flows include the variations in interaction produced by actors and the system. For example, the actor might change their mind and abort the session, or the communication could be interrupted. The description of details on the use cases should be kept to a similar level of abstraction.

Revising the Use Cases

Revising the use cases is the third step in the requirements gathering activity:

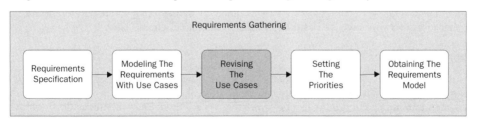

After describing the use cases, we need to try to improve them. First of all, we look at the focus of the use cases, where we try to identify use cases that are too complex, which have to be split into several smaller ones. We also identify use cases that are too simple. Furthermore, we'll identify any functionality that is duplicated and consider separating this behavior into a separate use case.

An examination of our example use cases might indicate that they both perform authorization and selection of the account. These functionalities could be separated and connected with the source use cases using the <<include>> relation. This simplifies the design, making the description of use cases shorter and easier to read, and promotes reuse of the code. The revised use case diagram will then look like this:

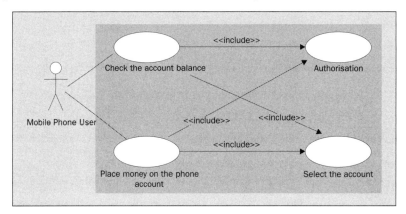

After drawing all the use case diagrams, specifying the descriptions and supplementing them with the other activity diagrams, we can gather them into a use case model. When defining the use cases for an integrated system, we will most likely be faced with a large number of them.

The majority will be more complex than the examples presented in this chapter, so it is useful to structure them by functionality. UML package diagrams can be helpful for this.

It is also important that we do not give up too early and don't get scared due to the large number of use cases. We should try to create high quality use cases and to supplement them with any necessary descriptions and diagrams. Only then will we be able to fully understand the whole system. For a good understanding we need time, which requires a lot of commitment from those involved.

On the other hand, we are gathering requirements to build an integrated information system, so we should concentrate on realistic requirements and not get carried away. Specifying too many requirements would make the results unusable. The requirements must be good enough to form a solid basis for the rest of the system. We won't be able to achieve perfection, therefore, we have to know when to stop and proceed with the rest of the development – thus clear milestones should be defined. In iterative development this is a little easier, because we always have the possibility to improve the requirements later.

Common Pitfalls

When defining the use cases, the most common mistake is not defining the system boundaries. As we are modeling an integrated enterprise information system, the boundary is obvious, but nevertheless we should keep it in mind. We should also be aware that we are modeling the information system and not the business domain. If we don't think about the system boundary, we will most likely end up with too many use cases, mixed relationships between actors and use cases, and confusing use case specifications that will try to tell too much. As a result, we'll not get a clear understanding of the global integrated information system. A poorly defined use case model has knock-on effects at later stages in the software development process; without explicit goals it is difficult to focus on the project and even finish it. The system boundary problem is relevant also because some of the leading modeling tools do not include it. Still, we should be aware that it exists.

When specified, the use cases should be reviewed and improved after each iteration of the integration project. Particularly useful are peer reviews, which help to avoid many common mistakes.

Setting the Priorities

Setting the priorities of the use cases is the fourth step in the requirements gathering activity:

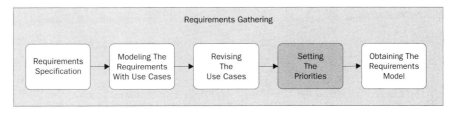

When dealing with a large number of use cases, we have to prioritize which requirements are the most important. Then we can structure the use cases based on priorities into several groups. We should also consider non-functional requirements. Sometimes, after going through them, we'll identify new use cases or have to add additional steps to the use case descriptions.

> **Using priorities we can make a plan of which use cases should be included in which iteration of integration.**

We should include the most important use cases and those with higher risks in the initial iterations and leave the less important ones for later iterations. Planning the integration project this way will enable better risk management and allow us to identify the factors critical for success earlier.

For this purpose we can use the MoSCoW rules, where we separate the use cases into various priorities:

- ❏ **Must** have – fundamental to the success of the project and we should therefore implement them as soon as possible
- ❏ **Should** have – should implement sooner rather than later
- ❏ **Could** have – could be implemented if the possibilities exist, but can wait until the end of the project
- ❏ **Would** have – might have been implemented if time and budget resources allowed

Obtaining the Requirements Model

Obtaining the requirements model is the fifth and final step in the requirements gathering activity:

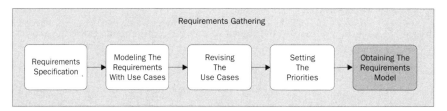

Having defined the use cases, we have to gather all the use cases and connected diagrams, together with the descriptions of scenarios and iterations. All this and the non-functional requirements we should gather into a requirements model. We don't want to reinvent the wheel here, so define the requirements model according to the software requirement specification (SRS) standards. Several organizations have defined their reference SRS documents. One of the most important is the SRS model given in ANSI/IEEE Std 830-1993, Recommended Practice for Software Requirements Specifications (http://standards.ieee.org/reading/ieee/std_public/description/se/830-1993_desc.html).

After we have specified the requirements for the integrated information system we can proceed with the analysis of existing applications.

Analysis of Existing Applications

After defining the requirements of the integrated information system, the next activity in the integration process is to analyze the current situation to gain some insight into all the existing applications that will be integrated. This includes legacy applications and next generation solutions that have either not been designed with integration in mind, or their architecture does not fit into that of EAI. In our case, the EAI architecture is the J2EE platform.

Before the analysis, we have to identify the applications for integration. Typically we will first think of the major (so-called primary) applications that form the backbone of the enterprise. Although we might have a good overview of the major applications, we will probably still need some more details.

Especially in large companies, users often use small, self-made, or locally developed solutions, on a daily basis. These includes small applications for analysis and other work enhancements, most often implemented in productivity tools, such as spreadsheets and word processors. It would be very unwise to omit these subsidiary applications because users need them to do their work effectively. We should seriously consider including their functionality, otherwise employees could continue to use these un-integrated solutions.

After identifying the possible applications, we have to make the final selection of primary and subsidiary applications that will take part in the integration. We have to choose which existing applications are valuable enough to be included in the integration, and which applications do not meet the requirements anymore and will have to be replaced. Generally, the assessment of existing applications will include their functionality and the way they can be changed and modified. In particular, the effort needed to modify the functionality is important and influences the decision.

For the selected existing applications that will be integrated, we have to perform a comprehensive analysis. We have to analyze the selected existing applications one-by-one, and specify the properties that are important for integration. The major objective is to gain a comprehensive understanding of the existing applications, including their functionalities, technical aspects, existing integration, and overlapping functionality with other applications.

Particularly with legacy applications, the chances are high that after years of use, upgrades, and maintenance, the documentation and user manuals will be out of date and will not reflect the current situation. Sometimes just finding the source code can be difficult.

As a single person rarely performs the integration, we have to produce some documentation and perform the analysis in a controlled and disciplined manner. Therefore, we will follow the following steps in order to analyze each existing application selected for integration:

- ❏ Functional analysis
- ❏ Technical analysis
- ❏ Analysis of functional overlapping
- ❏ Analysis of existing integration

The following diagram shows the main steps and their refinement into substeps. We'll discuss the finer details of these steps in the sections that follow:

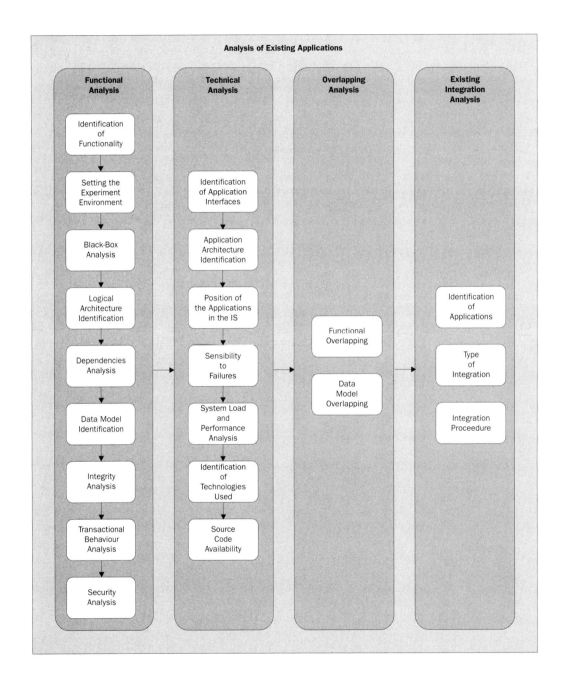

Functional Analysis

First we have to become familiar with the functionality the existing application provides. We start by specifying a list of functions. Therefore, we first locate the documentation for the application, if it exists. From the documentation we can get some idea of the existing applications – but this is not the complete picture. It is vital to talk with users and query them on how they use the application. We also have to test the application and try it for ourselves, to get a feel for it and to identify some of the hidden functionality. Yet another problem is the fact that end users and people in IT departments are somewhat reluctant to change. They may not provide the information that we need.

Identification of Functionality

Identification of functionality is the first step in the functional analysis of existing applications:

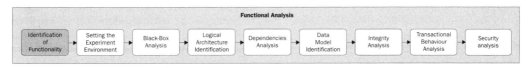

> **In order to reuse as much functionality as possible, it is important to identify all the functions the existing applications possess.**

In addition, we also have to identify how often a function is used. This is important because the existing application could even have some functions that have never been used. There may be no guarantee that these functions actually work correctly. To avoid unpleasant surprises, it is recommended that we consider only the functions that are actually used and which we know work correctly.

The documentation that will be interesting for the identification of functionality includes:

- ❑ Requirements specifications
- ❑ Analysis and design documentation
- ❑ Testing documentation
- ❑ User documentation

For commercial applications, we'll probably have up-to-date documentation, or at least the user documentation (user manual) that will explain how to use the application. With the user documentation it is possible to identify functions, but if the documentation is not very thorough we may miss some important, infrequently used functions. This is why it is always useful to have access to other forms of documentation.

For applications developed in-house we probably won't have up-to-date documentation, but we may be able to find the requirements specification. The requirements specification is often the basis for getting a software development project approved. This can be a good start, but we still have to check how each function is implemented. If the application is not too old, we may be in luck and the original developers may still be around. They will have the best understanding of the application and it is well worth talking to them about the functions that their application implements.

If we cannot talk with the original developers we have to talk with system administrators and users. System administrators will have an overview of how often the application has been used and where the problems have been. Users will be familiar with the functions. Although this is not the time to start developing code, we may take this opportunity to check whether the source code actually exists, and if so – is it in-synch with the executable versions?

> **Many existing applications do not have adequate documentation. For some, even the source code does not exist. Even if the source code does exist we have to check if it is in-synch with the executable versions.**

For outsourced applications we are faced with similar problems as with in-house developments. If the outsourced projects have been managed efficiently then there should be documentation available that will be comprehensive and up-to-date. However, many projects have not been well managed and we will not have the documentation. On the plus side, for almost every outsourced project the requirements specification should exist – indeed, it usually forms the basis for the contract and for assessing the value of the software development project. Software development companies are also more aware of the importance of documentation.

However, for an outsourced application it might be even more difficult to get in touch with the original developers. They are probably not employed by the same company. Even if they are, they are not likely to want to talk with us for free. This problem is exacerbated when we find out that the consulting company does not exist anymore and it has delivered the executable application without source code.

Setting the Experimental Environment

Setting the experimental environment is the second step in the functional analysis of existing applications:

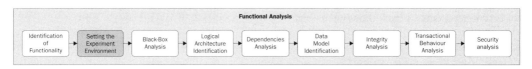

After we have prepared the list of functions with their frequency of use, we have to check each function to get an idea how it works. We do this in an **experimental environment** that we have to set up. This will basically be a copy of the production environment, which will enable us to experiment with existing applications without disturbing their everyday operation. Setting the experiment environment is important only for the analysis phase, but is very useful later when we apply modifications to the existing applications. Without an experimental environment it would be absolutely impossible to safely test and validate the integration solutions.

Setting it up can vary in complexity. It is easy in cases where we have the necessary hardware, and where we can simply copy the applications, with or without the persistent data. The more complicated the application architecture, the more work we have to set up the environment. Becoming comfortable in the environment of the existing applications is crucial to achieving integration.

This will be the most difficult for legacy applications. For them, there will be the problem of obtaining the necessary hardware, and we probably won't be familiar with the environment and the tools, which may present the biggest obstacle. A big problem can be setting up experimental databases. Again it depends on the architecture of the application: if it uses some standard way to access the database it will be easier.

Only with commercial applications do we expect to have some form of installation procedure. However, we have to be sure that the actual product is identical to the application that is used in production. Otherwise it is a better idea to use the production version.

For applications where performance workload is not limited, we are able to use the same hardware for the production and experimental configurations. If we make this decision, we have to be very careful not to interfere with the production data. This approach will not be applicable if the application has a high workload and/or is mission critical. In this case we have to set up a fully isolated experimental environment.

If we are unable to set up an experimental environment for an application we want to integrate, we have to be very careful with the tests that we do. We have to consider what time to perform the tests, for example, when the application is not in use (during nights, weekends, or holidays). This will influence our flexibility considerably.

Black-box Analysis

Black-box analysis is the third step in the functional analysis of existing applications:

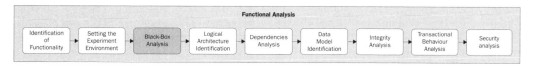

We then have to check each function that we have listed in the functional specification. Note that we're not only talking about the functions accessible from the user interface, we have to include all functions, even those that the application provides through APIs.

When we check the functions we are already starting to make a black-box analysis. We enter the input parameters and then perform some function to obtain the results. Therefore, with black-box analysis, we detail the list of functions with the input and output data that is required to perform each function.

> **We call this activity black-box analysis because we don't care about how the function is performed by the existing application. We are interested solely in the output that we get and what input parameters we have to provide to get the desired output.**

When specifying the input and output behavior we should pay particular attention to the boundary conditions. This means we should consider the allowed intervals for input parameters. We should specify this in the form of preconditions for the input parameters. This will become important later when we reuse the functionality.

To describe the functions of existing application we can use a textual form, where we produce a table and description of the functions. The proposed table should include the following columns:

179

❑ **Function** – name of the function that the application provides.

❑ **Description** – description of the functionality.

❑ **Access via user interface or via API** – we should identify how we can access the functionality.

❑ **Frequency of use** – we should identify if the function is used at all and, if so, how frequently it is used. If possible we should use an objective metric, for example number of times per week.

❑ **Required inputs** – we should clearly identify the input parameters and their allowed ranges.

❑ **Outputs** – we should identify the outputs that we get.

To demonstrate how to describe the functions of existing applications, we will refer to our example integration scenario and demonstrate black-box analysis for the six existing applications of the Two-2-Yellow operator. Let's recall the six applications that the operator has:

❑ Cell phone customer information application

❑ Application that manages the account balance for cell phone users

❑ Application that prints the invoices each month

❑ Application that evaluates domestic phone calls

❑ Application that calculates international phone calls

❑ Application that manages phone call tariff information

We will not show all possible functions of these applications; rather, we'll consider just a selection of them. After specifying the functions and doing the black-box analysis, we can produce the tables for each application. For simplicity, we will specify the frequency of use simply as "never, rarely, occasionally, or frequently". We'll also not show the API operation names, because this would complicate our tables too much.

Cell Phone Customer Information Application

The cell phone customer information application enables the management of phone customers. This includes entering new customers, updating existing customers and adding data about the phone account that they have. We have identified that the application is used frequently and that it provides both user interface and API access to all functions. The corresponding table is shown opposite:

Function	Description	Access via UI	Access via API	Frequency of use	Required inputs	Outputs
Getting the data of each customer	Provides data for each customer, including name, address, number of phone accounts, and status.	Y	Y	Frequently	customer ID	first name, last name, address, number of phone accounts, status
Storing and modifying the personal data for each customer	Stores the data about customer.	Y	Y	Frequently	first name, last name, address	customer ID, confirmation
Entering a new mobile account	Adds a new account to existing user.	Y	Y	Frequently	phone number, start date, type of account (subscriber/ pre-paid/...)	confirmation
Deleting a phone account	Deletes an existing phone account.	Y	Y	Occasionally	phone number	confirmation

Application that Manages the Account Balance for Cell Phone Users

The application that manages the account balance for cell phone users manages both types of accounts, prepaid and subscriber. It allows data to be entered regarding the consumption of money and about the deposits on the accounts. It also enables the searching of accounts that have a negative balance (for the subscribers). For the prepaid accounts it allows a search of the accounts that have had zero balance for a specified period of time. Finally, it allows searching for money deposits on those accounts based on the age. Here's what the relevant table looks like:

Function	Description	Access via UI	Access via API	Frequency of use	Required inputs	Outputs
Gets the account balance	Calculates the account balance. Taken into account are all transactions that are written in this application. This does not include the current monthly consumption that is written each month.	Y	Y	Frequently	account number	account balance
Enter the data about consumption	Enables entering data about phone consumption rate	Y	Y	Frequently	account number, dateFrom, dateTo, dateOf Transaction, sum	confirmation
Enter the data about money deposit	Enables entering the data about advance deposits.	Y	Y	Frequently	account number, dateOf Transaction, sum	confirmation
Search for negative balance	Search subscriber accounts for negative balance.	Y	Y	Occasionally		list of account numbers
Search for accounts with empty balance	Search for the prepaid accounts with zero balance to disconnect them after a specific time.	Y	Y	Occasionally	time period in days	list of: account numbers, days of continuous zero balance
Search for money deposits based on dates	Search for the prepaid accounts for money deposits that have been done before a specific date to null them.	Y	Y	Occasionally	date	list of: account numbers, within account numbers list of deposits that are older that the date

Application That Prints the Invoices

The application that prints invoices each month is a simple one that goes through the subscriber accounts and prints the invoices for the consumptions of the specified month. The table looks like this:

Function	Description	Access via UI	Access via API	Frequency of use	Required inputs	Outputs
Prints the invoices	Prints the invoices for a specified period.	Yes	No	Occasionally	month	invoices (paper output only)

Application that Evaluates Domestic Phone Calls

The application that evaluates domestic cell phone calls calculates the consumption for each account based on the data transferred from the mobile phone exchange, but only for domestic calls. It requires the following information:

❑ What time basis the phone calls are evaluated (every second, ten seconds, first minute then every second, and so on)

❑ What tariff classes there are (high tariffs, low tariffs, for example)

Here's the table relating to this application:

Function	Description	Access via UI	Access via API	Frequency of use	Required inputs	Outputs
Calculates the domestic consumption	Calculates the consumption for each account.	Y	N	Frequently	tariff information, connection with the mobile phone exchange	List of phone number, domestic consumption in minutes sorted per tariff classes

Application that Calculates International Phone Calls

The application that calculates international cell phone calls has a similar function to the domestic application. However, it does not have a direct connection with the cell phone exchange. Rather, it receives input data formatted from each roaming partner, as seen in the following table:

Function	Description	Access via UI	Access via API	Frequency of use	Required inputs	Outputs
Calculates the international consumption	Calculates the consumptio n for each account.	Y	N	Occasionally	tariff information , data from roaming partners	list: phone number, international consumption in minutes (incoming/outgoi ng) sorted per tariff classes

Application that Manages Phone Call Tariff Information

Finally, the application that manages cell phone call tariff information includes functions to enter and display the tariff information. This includes tariff polices, tariff classes, and costs per minute, as show below:

Function	Description	Access via UI	Access via API	Frequency of use	Required inputs	Outputs
Defines the tariff policy for domestic calls	Enables defining the tariff policy for domestic calls.	Y	N	Rarely	length of the talk duration that account is based on (second, minute), date and times of validity	confirmation
Showsthe tariff policy for domestic calls		Y	N	Rarely		length of the talk duration that account is based on (second, minute), date of validity

184

Function	Description	Access via UI	Access via API	Frequency of use	Required inputs	Outputs
Defines the tariff policy for international calls	Enables defining the tariff policy for international calls.	Y	N	Rarely	length of the talk duration that account is based on (second, minute), date of validity, additional costs	confirmation
Shows the tariff policy for international calls		Y	N	Rarely		length of the talk duration that account is based on (second, minute), date of validity, additional costs
Defines the tariff classes	Enables defining the tariff class for domestic and international calls.	Y	N	Rarely	from hour, to hour, class, date of validity	confirmation
List of tariff classes		Y	N	Rarely		list of: from hour, to hour, class, date of validity
Defines the cost per minute	Enables defining the cost of domestic and international mobile phone calls.	Y	N	Occasionally	tariff class, cost per minute, date of validity	confirmation
Lists the cost per minute		Y	N	Occasionally		list of: tariff class, cost per minute, date of validity

Table continued on following page

Function	Description	Access via UI	Access via API	Frequency of use	Required inputs	Outputs
Calculates the cost of a call	Enables calculating the cost of a call based on the type, date, time and length information.	N	Y	Never	type of call, date of start, time of start, date of end, time of end	cost of the call in currency

Logical Architecture Identification

Logical architecture identification is the fourth step in the functional analysis of existing applications:

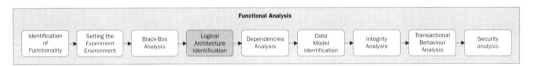

After we have identified the functionality of the existing applications, we have to recognize its logical structure. Here we first have to identify if the application is monolithic, client/server, or multi-tier. Then we try to categorize how it is constituted – if there are several modules or components, where the business logic is, and so on.

To represent the logical architecture we can use UML component diagrams. Components represent all kind of building blocks of applications. A component is represented by the following symbol:

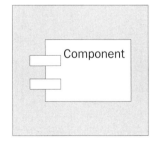

For our example, we will first identify the type of existing applications:

❏ The cell phone customer information application is client/server (fat client with database back end)

❏ The application that manages the account balance for cell phone users is client/server (fat client with database back end)

❏ The application that prints the invoices each month is client/server (fat client with database back end and some stored procedures in the database)

❏ The application that evaluates domestic phone calls is monolithic

- ❑ The application that calculates international phone calls is monolithic

- ❑ The application that manages phone call tariff information is client/server (fat client with database back end), and consists of two applications: policy management and cost and tariff management

Then we represent them as components. We will not yet display the databases. We have also decided to present the phone call tariff application as a large application that constitutes of two applications. We will show this with nested components:

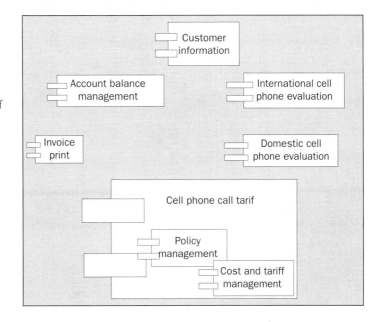

Dependencies Analysis

Dependencies analysis is the fifth step in the functional analysis of existing applications:

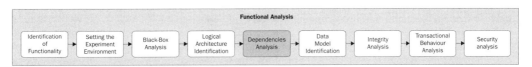

After we have identified the logical architecture we have to classify the dependencies between the applications. Here we should identify all the dependencies.

> **Two applications can have logical dependencies that can be implemented either automatically or manually.**

If implemented automatically then there is a sort of interoperability between the applications – these applications share data or functionality. Often, particularly with legacy systems, such connections are implemented through data exchange, very often via shared files or tables. This will be important later when we come to identify the existing integration between applications. Then we will consider how the integration is implemented from a technical perspective.

More frequently, we will see dependencies that are carried out manually. This means that the users will have to re-enter the same data, leading to possible inconsistencies. An application can provide a summary of some data it processes that the users then enter into some other application. There is obviously a dependency between them that we should identify and show on a diagram. If possible, we can, we can also document these dependencies. This information will be useful later in the analysis.

For our example we can identify the following dependencies:

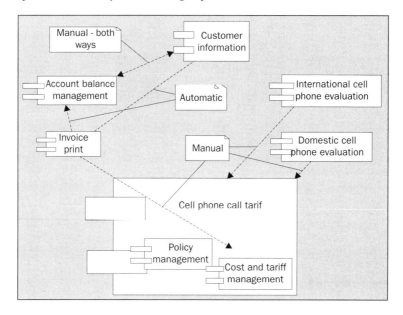

We can see that the invoice print application is dependent on the customer information and the account balance management and that both dependencies are implemented automatically. However, the bidirectional dependency between account balance management and the customer information application is manual, requiring manual data re-entry. The dependencies between invoice print and the cost and tariff management, international and domestic phone evaluation applications and phone call tariff application also require manual data re-entry.

Data Model Identification

Data model identification is the sixth step in the functional analysis of existing applications:

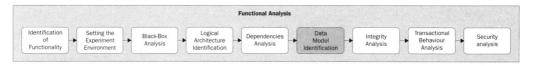

Another very important activity in functional analysis is the identification of the data models used by each application. This is important because we have to understand how data is stored. Data model identification is a time consuming process, where we have to analyze the persistence storage of each application. We will be faced with one ore more of the following types of databases:

- ❏ Relational databases
- ❏ Object-oriented databases
- ❏ Universal databases
- ❏ Multidimensional databases
- ❏ Hierarchical and network databases
- ❏ Other formats, such as flat files

What we have to do is draw the database model for each existing application. This will be the basis for data-level integration. Often it is possible to generate database models automatically with the tools provided by the database. The majority of relational databases, for example, have tools to generate entity-relational (ER) schemas out of existing databases. This is usually better that depending on possibly out-of date documentation. We will go more into the details in the *Data-level Integration* chapters of this book – Chapters 5 to 8.

For our example let us consider that all identified applications use the relational model and that the E-R diagrams were provided in the documentation. For the purposes of our example we will not need to study the database diagrams in detail, therefore we will not show them here.

Integrity Analysis

Integrity analysis is the seventh step in the functional analysis of existing applications:

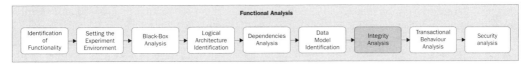

Here we identify how the integrity of databases is achieved and which party is responsible for it. Most likely each application will be responsible for assuring the integrity of their own databases. In this activity we should identify the integrity rules for each database that the system uses. Identifying the integrity rules will be particularly important for data-level integration when we exchange data between applications based on direct database transfers. Since we will most likely omit the business rules at this stage, we have to be aware what the integrity rules are.

The integrity rules are sometimes described in the documentation. Sometimes they are incorporated within the database, if the database allows this. More often these rules are coded within existing applications. Database administrators can be very helpful with the identification of integrity rules.

The problem with the identification of these rules is that it is very difficult to be sure that we have identified all of them. Not identifying them on the other hand can lead to breaking the integrity of databases. Identifying this problem is a difficult task, and tracking down failures to database integrity problems is very time consuming.

Transactional Behavior Analysis

Transactional behavior analysis is the eighth step of functional analysis for existing applications:

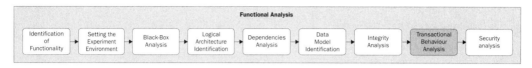

After identifying the database design and the integrity rules we have to analyze transactions:

❑   Does the application use transactions?

❑   If yes, what types of transactions are used?

Transactions play an important role in all non-trivial applications. Their management is known as transactional processing, which can be very complex. The software that is responsible for transaction management is called the transaction manager. Transaction managers can be a DBMS or some dedicated middleware software like TP (transaction processing) monitors. Examples of TP monitors include IBM's CICS, BEA's Tuxedo, and Transarc Encina.

Transactions can work with a single resource – these are the simplest and most commonly used. However, in large systems the transaction might need to be invoked over several systems. This is when distributed transactions come into play. A distributed transaction spans more than one resource. Their context can be propagated or shared by more than one component; they require the cooperation of several different transaction managers. Therefore the distributed transaction manager takes control over the transaction and then coordinates all other transaction managers.

Our goal will be to identify the transactional model (flat, nested, chained or saga) and become familiar with how it works together with the existing application. We have to familiarize ourselves with transactional properties of the existing application, identify how the existing application uses transactions, and how critical the failures are. Transaction management will be discussed in detail in Chapter 15.

Security Analysis

Security analysis is the ninth and final step in the functional analysis of existing applications:

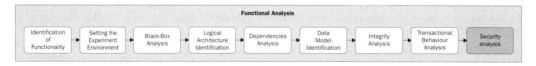

In security analysis we have to examine the way that security is utilized by the existing applications. Generally we need to answer two questions:

❑   Does the application implement security?

 ❑   If yes, how is the security implemented?

 ❑   If no, should we add security now?

190

As we saw in the previous chapter there are four possible security mechanisms:

❏ **Authentication**
The process of verifying that a client is who they claim to be. It can be performed on the client before it interacts with the server. It can also be performed on the server.

❏ **Authorization**
Checks whether the client application is allowed to perform a certain operation. Authorization can be defined programmatically or declaratively, depending on the implementation. Typically it is defined in terms of security roles and Access Control Lists (ACLs). Extracting info on how authorization is performed from existing applications can be complicated because the logic may be in the application code.

❏ **Communication channel security**
Newer applications will typically use Secure Socket Layer (SSL) and Transport Layer Security (TLS), but this can differ significantly with older legacy systems.

❏ **Auditing**
Some systems also perform auditing, which lets us see an exact history of operations performed on the system and is useful for analysis of past events.

The fact is that a lot of existing applications do not have much security implemented. Therefore a lot of attention will have to be paid to how to introduce security to existing applications. Security management will be discussed in more depth in Chapter 16.

Technical Analysis

After we have become familiar with the functionality an existing application provides, it is time to do the technical analysis where we get to grips with the technologies used and other important technical aspects. We need to:

❏ Identify how the interfaces (APIs) are implemented

❏ Identify the application architecture

❏ Identify the position of the application in the existing information system

❏ Do the performance analysis

❏ Identify the system load

❏ Identify the technology used, including programming language and middleware

❏ Check the source code availability

Identification of Application Interfaces

The identification of application interfaces is the first step in the technical analysis of existing applications:

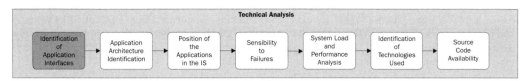

We have already identified the components and their dependencies. We have also identified the functions that existing applications provide. For each function we have identified if it is accessible through a user interface or through an API, or maybe even both.

In this activity we focus on the application interfaces. Our goal will be to specify the interfaces that an existing application provides to other applications. First of all, we have to identify how many interfaces there are and which operations they provide. Then we have to identify which technology is used to access them.

To identify the number of application interfaces we will have to go through the documentation, talk with the developers, and even analyze the source code.

We might also consider using tools for analyzing existing applications. Such tools sometimes can identify application interfaces even if no source code is available. We should mention that we could consider every form of communication between two applications as an application interface. For now it's not important if those interfaces are implemented in a proprietary technology, if they are procedural or functional, even on protocol level (although we will identify technology a little later).

We can specify the interfaces on the UML component diagrams using the interface stereotype, shown as a circle. We can also identify the operations of each interface and show their signatures. This means that we have to identify the names and the syntax of operations, the necessary parameters and the return value. These can be specified using the interfaces in the component diagram.

Sometimes we have a situation in which the applications are tightly coupled, so there will have to be some preconditions fulfilled before an operation can be called or invoked. We then need to identify these preconditions (and maybe post-conditions). We also try to identify if there are some restrictions in the order in which the operations have to be invoked. Another important thing is to recognize the way that the application signals errors or other exceptional conditions. We can use the documentation and describe these constraints with our natural language, or we can use an appropriate diagramming technique. For representing the sequence of operation calls we could use, for example, sequence diagrams.

Identifying the interfaces is very important, particularly for application-to-application integration, but sometimes also for data-level integration. If we identify that there are operations available via APIs that allow access to the business logic, we can use this in application-to-application integration. If we identify operations that allow access to the persistent data, this will be useful for data-level integration. Accessing data through operations is better than going directly to the database because we avoid circumventing the business logic. This makes it easier for us to maintain database integrity.

Therefore, it is important that we are as precise as possible. Identifying the interfaces precisely and correctly now will pay off later when we come to implement the integration. If we identify that interfaces have to be used in another way than proposed at a late stage then we will have to make large modifications to the integration architecture.

For the example that we are examining in this chapter, we will build on the component model. We should not forget that we have already identified the functions of the existing applications as shown in the earlier tables, and which of them are accessible via APIs. So now we have to identify these interfaces and the signatures of their functions, and represent them on the component diagram. For our example we have identified three application interfaces: CustomerInt, AccountInt, and CostTariffInt, which are shown on the diagram:

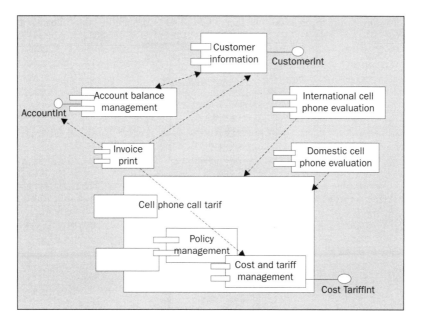

Please notice that in the dependency analysis that we did before, we identified that there are only two automatic dependencies between the applications – between the invoice print application, customer information application and account balance management application.

Here we have identified that these dependencies are implemented through the application interfaces `CustomerInt` and `AccountInt`. This is why the dependency arrows between applications are now shown on the interfaces. All other dependencies are carried out manually, that is with manual data re-entry from one application into the other. Therefore the other (manual) dependencies still exist on the diagram. From the diagram we can also see that the third application interface, `CostTariffInt`, is not currently used by any existing application.

Let's now look into the three identified interfaces. For the sake of simplicity, we'll show only the operation names without parameters and return values. In a real-world scenario you would want to add the parameters and return values too. The interface to the account balance management application, `AccountInt`, specifies the following operations:

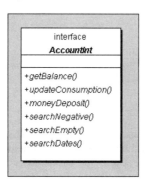

The customer information application interface, `CustomerInt`, specifies the following operations:

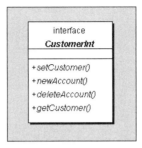

The third interface is `CostTariffInt`, for the cost and tariff management application, that specifies only a single method:

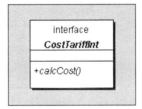

Then we have to identify which technology is used for each interface and how we can access it from the outside. This means we should identify the middleware that is used to access the APIs and other technical details. For our example we will introduce the technology details for these interfaces in later chapters when we demonstrate how to use different technologies (such as CORBA) to wrap existing applications and how to develop virtual components. The reader should refer to Chapters 10, 11, and 12 for more information.

Application Architecture Identification

Application architecture identification is the second step in the technical analysis of existing applications:

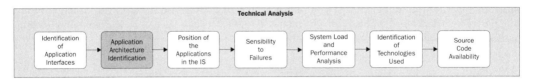

Having identified the logical architecture and the interfaces, we should now consider the physical architecture. We need to become familiar with the environment in which the production application is deployed, so we identify the computers on which the application parts are deployed and the type of connection between them. This step should be done for each application separately, although applications will frequently share resources.

To represent the architecture we can use UML deployment diagrams. They show the runtime configuration of hardware devices and the software components that execute on them. The basic building blocks are nodes, which are represented with a cuboid:

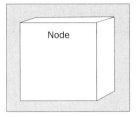

Nodes can contain component instances, which show that the instances execute on a certain node. Typically there will be several component instances on a single node; however this depends on the granularity of the application. Monolithic and client/server applications will be typically represented by a few components only. It can happen that an existing legacy application is represented as a single component, if it is actually packed as a single executable and does not have the possibility to separate the executable into several parts.

It is also very useful to show the dependencies between the component instances using a dependency relationship. If the components provide interfaces that their communication relies on, then we should show the dependencies using the interfaces that we have already identified. For example, an existing application can provide a custom API for communication with clients, and clients can use a remote procedure call or message-oriented middleware to call the procedures and functions in the API. This can be seen as an interface although it is not an interface in the sense of component/OO-based development. If there are no interfaces that we can identify, then we should just show the dependencies between the components. Sometimes we can specify the communication protocol for each dependency too.

With all these points in mind, it's obvious that deployment diagrams can range from simple to rather complicated, depending on the types of existing applications.

For our example integration scenario we will present two simplified deployment diagrams, where we will not show the communication protocols on the dependencies. For the account balance management application, a deployment diagram looks like this:

We have already identified that the application is implemented in a client/server architecture, with a fat client that executes on PCs. It has a database management system, such as DB2, running on the AIX platform.

And here's the architecture for our phone call tariff application:

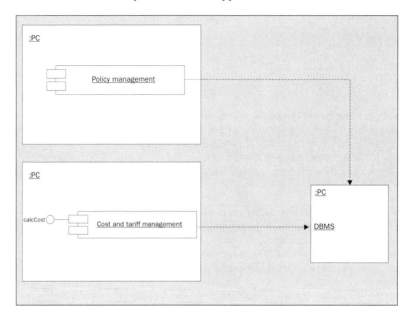

Position of the Applications in the Information System

Position of the applications in the information system is the third step in the technical analysis of existing applications:

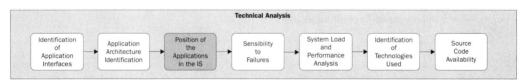

After we have identified the architecture of each application separately we should build the diagram of the whole existing information system. This basically means that we gather together the deployment diagrams that we drew in the previous step. We also need to identify which resources the application share and denote the dependencies (already identified previously) on this diagram.

We should extend this diagram with the other existing applications that are present in the current information system, but have not been selected for integration. We should mark them clearly with the <<external>> stereotype, and note whether there are some dependencies between the external applications (those not selected for integration) and the applications that we are integrating.

Presenting the whole architecture in one diagram is a nice way to show the complete architecture and dependencies:

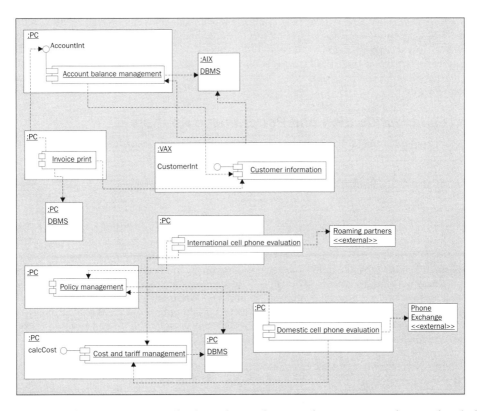

In the previous diagram we can see the dependencies between the components that we identified earlier. Additionally, we can see the position of components on the actual nodes (computers), and the relations to services that we have not identified yet, such as DBMS systems. From here we can identify that there are three different DBMS systems, one of them is shared between two applications (customer information and account balance management). We can also see that both the phone evaluation applications are dependent on external resources that will not be considered for integration. For the international call evaluation application these are the roaming partners that send data, for the domestic calls there is a dependency on (direct connection to) the phone exchanges.

On this diagram we can also represent other middleware services that exist in the current information system, including message-oriented middleware, object request brokers, and TP monitors. We should also include directory services if they exist. We should mark all these with stereotypes. For more information on stereotypes refer to UML literature or the following URL: http://www.uml.org/.

Sensibility to Failures

Sensibility to failures analysis is the fourth step in the technical analysis of existing applications:

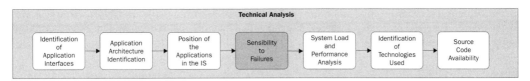

Here we have to identify how critical each application is for the company. We have to see if the company has alternative scenarios regarding what to do if an application fails. If it does not (and most do not have such scenarios), we must develop them. Note that when altering an existing application we will considerably increase the risk of failing, so we have to take every measure possible to minimize the risk. This includes efficient backup systems, which include application data as well as the executable application files.

System Load Identification and Performance Analysis

System load identification and performance analysis is the fifth step in the technical analysis of existing applications:

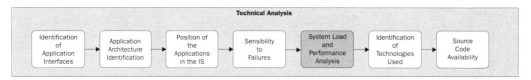

Here we should clarify what the performance considerations of applications are. In the requirements gathering phase we should have already identified the performance expectations for the integrated system. Here we have to see how the existing applications perform. When integrating applications, one of the goals is to provide instant access to information. The technical implications are that after integration there will be a larger number of clients that will simultaneously use the application. Sometimes, for example when making applications accessible online, this number can be considerably higher.

> **It would be wrong not to consider the performance limitations now.**

We will look at the system from two perspectives: the **client load**, that is, the number of concurrent clients, and the **data load**, that is, the quantity of persistent data.

Client Load

To identify the client load we should look at:

❏ The predicted average and maximum number of concurrent clients

❏ The response time by average and maximum number of clients

❏ The highest acceptable response time

❏ How much we increase the number of clients to fulfill the response time limit in the current configuration

❏ The possibilities there are to increase scalability (hardware and software solutions)

If we identify that the application currently offers acceptable response times (and it should, because this is a production application, although in real-world it often does not), we will try to identify how much potential there exists in the application for raising the number of simultaneous clients. From this, we will try to infer the highest possible number of concurrent clients that the existing system can support in its current configuration.

Assessing this will not be an easy task. Although there are several methods for performance assessment, they are out of the scope of this book. The most pragmatic is to test the response times. We can use the experiment configuration that we have set up earlier, together with load test tools to simulate the real-world scenario. However, we have to use the same hardware configuration; otherwise we will not get correct results.

It will then depend on the requirements for the integrated system what to do next. If we are lucky, the existing system will be scalable enough to support the increased requirements, but this will be unlikely. Otherwise we have to consider possibilities to improve scalability.

The most straightforward approach is to upgrade the hardware. To do this we have to identify the hardware bottlenecks. Usual hardware bottlenecks include:

❏   Network and I/O usage

❏   CPU usage

❏   Memory usage

> **Hence, it makes no sense upgrading the processor if the real bottleneck is in the network I/O.**

If a hardware upgrade does not solve the problem, we have to consider software changes. These include changes to the operating system and middleware. Maybe an upgrade to the latest versions will solve the problems. Otherwise we have to think about source code modifications, which will introduce a number of problems. First of all we have to be aware that making changes to the existing application is difficult and error prone. So, if the application is mission critical we should be really careful. The same goes for operating system and other software upgrades.

The alternative is to develop a new system as a replacement instead of integrating the existing system. This was discussed in Chapter 2, and we should note that this decision is not just a technical one.

Data Load

Here we will first assess the current persistent data size. Then we try to identify if the integration will increase the data size. The reasons can be different. For example, it is possible that pre-integration the data between applications is transferred only once per month and only summary values are recorded. Upon integration we may require this transfer several times per day or even instantly. This will also mean that the integrated system will record each transaction separately, thus increasing the persistent data dramatically.

We need to go through similar steps as before. In the experiment configuration we should test the performance with the increased data load, and if the performance is unacceptable we will have to find solutions, first with faster hardware, if applicable. If the system uses a separate DBMS then we can try to upgrade it. We can think of clustering the DBMS server or using distributed DBMS. Otherwise, we can consider modifications of the existing application or ultimately even replacement.

Identification of Technologies Used

Identification of technologies used is the sixth step in the technical analysis of existing applications:

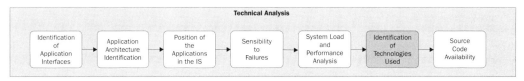

In this step we have to familiarize ourselves with the technology used in each existing application. If this is a commercial application we have to check the exact version that is being used. If it is a custom-developed application we have the following points to check:

❑   Programming language, compiler, IDE, linker

❑   Operating system version

❑   DBMS versions

❑   Middleware and versions

❑   All other related software

We also have to look if those versions of software still exist, and if not, how we can obtain them. This will be important for making decisions on rebuilding the system using the source code.

Source Code Availability

Source code availability analysis is the seventh and final step in the technical analysis of existing applications:

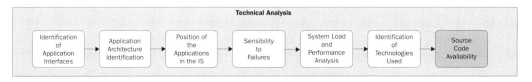

After we have defined the technology we have to see if the source code is available for the existing application. There are a large number of systems (particularly legacy) where source code is not available. Source code will also probably not be available for commercial applications.

For custom-built applications, we will most likely have access to the source code, unless they are old or the source code has been lost, be it accidentally or intentionally. But even if we find the source code we have to check that:

❑   We have all the necessary tools to rebuild the application

❑   The source code version corresponds to the actual version used in production

Often it happens that a single missing library or configuration file prevents us from rebuilding the application. Then it depends on how familiar we are with the application and for us to decide if it is reasonable to try to make the application compile or to dismiss it.

To check whether the production version is identical to the source code we can use a simple procedure. We build the application from the source code and compare it to the production version using a file compare utility. We have to be sure that we compare the executable files only, without any data. If this simple procedure does not work then we will have to compare applications, which can be very difficult for small changes.

Sometimes source code will be managed by configuration management software, such as Rational ClearCase, Concurrent Versions System CVS, Revision Control System RCS, or similar. Such configuration management software can simplify our work considerably, if we are familiar with their function.

Overlapping Analysis

After we have analyzed the existing applications from functional and technical perspectives, we are familiar enough with them to perform an overlapping analysis. The objective here is to identify which parts of the applications overlap – which functionality and data is redundant. We also select which application is responsible for which overlapping functionality.

Overlapping analysis consists of just two steps:

❑   Functional overlapping

❑   Data model overlapping

Functional Overlapping

Functional overlapping analysis is the first step in the overlapping analysis of existing applications:

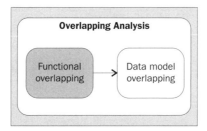

As existing applications are not usually integrated, an application can often contain certain functionality that has already been implemented by some other application. This is essentially due to a lack of architecting.

So, we are often faced with two or more applications that implement the same functionality. Often one application implements it in the detail, while another implements only the parts that they need. Typically these applications will introduce a slightly modified view of the functionality, which will complicate the situation even more.

We would like to identify which functionality is overlapping in the applications that we have selected for integration.

> **Now we identify which functions of which existing application we will use later, when we reuse some existing functionality for the integrated information system.**

For example, there could be two applications that have a list of customers. We now have to select which application does this better (regarding the requirements that we have) and will then reuse the functionality of this selected application.

To identify the overlapping functions it is a good start to have a look at the dependency analysis that we performed as part of the functional analysis. We should look at the dependencies; particularly those that are implemented manually are suspicious. Implementing a dependency manually means that the user has to re-enter some data that has been processed from one application into another. This will almost always mean that the applications had to overlap a part of their functionality. We also have to check the dependencies that are implemented automatically. If there is only data exchange between applications it can still mean that the functionality is overlapping.

To describe the functionalities that are overlapping we first have to identify the function, then all the applications where the function is implemented and finally select the application that will be responsible for that function (the application that we will use when reusing this function for integration).

In our example, we can see that there are several dependencies that we have identified, and five of them are performed manually. We'll start our search here. Let's first look at the invoice print application. We can see that the application needs to perform the call cost calculation. It does not use the function provided by the cost and tariff management part of the phone call application. Rather, it needs the tariff data to be manually re-entered into the invoice print application. There is also a function that calculates the call cost. It is more natural that the cost of a call is determined by the phone call tariff application; therefore we will mark this application as being responsible for this function.

The account balance management application and the customer information application are dependent in both directions. The account balance management application needs a subset of data about customers and the customer information application needs the number and the IDs of accounts held by the customers. Again the dependency is manual. In this case, this means that the users have to re-enter parts of data. We will mark the account balance management as responsible for account management and the customer information application for customer information management.

The international and domestic phone evaluation applications are dependent on the cell phone call application, because they need the policy management information and tariff information. This is again achieved with manual data transfer. It is clear that the responsible application for managing that information should be the phone call tariff application.

Analysis of dependencies that are implemented automatically in our example, shows that the invoice print application already reuses some of the functions of the account balance management and customer information applications. Therefore, there is no redundancy in functionality between these applications.

The functional overlapping analysis for our example is gathered in the following table, where a tick denotes an application responsible for a certain function and a cross the application that is not responsible for the function in the integrated information system:

Function	Applications that implement it	Responsible application when reusing the function in the integrated information system (✓)
Call cost calculation	Cost and tariff management	✓
	Invoice print	✗
Customer information management	Customer information	✓
	Account balance management	✗
Account management	Customer information	✗
	Account balance management	✓
Call policy and tariff management	International phone evaluation	✗
	Domestic phone evaluation	✗
	Cell phone call tariff	✓

Data Model Overlapping

Data model overlapping analysis is the second step of overlapping analysis for existing applications:

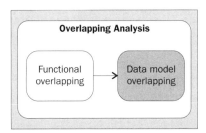

After we have analyzed the functions, we also have to identify the data that might be overlapping in the databases of different applications. Dependency and functional overlapping analysis can be useful here. Functional overlapping almost always means that there is data overlapping under it. But note that there might be data overlapping somewhere else, too.

To identify it, we should again focus on identified dependencies between applications and evaluate first those implemented manually and then those implemented automatically. For data model overlapping analysis, it is very helpful if we have the schemas of all the databases. Then we can identify the data that is overlapping. Similarly, as in functional overlapping, we should select the databases that will be responsible for certain data. These databases will then be used in the integrated information system.

If we are lucky we will only have to deal with one database model, probably relational. Then we have to identify the entities that are overlapping. If we build the data dictionary is very useful to supplement the information that each entity name represents. This point it is also a good opportunity to resolve the name conflicts and to explain the cryptic names for entities and attributes. The most difficult task will however be to resolve semantic issues.

If we have to deal with other database models, like hierarchical, or even flat files, this will make our task a little more difficult. We will discuss these problems in greater detail in Chapter 5.

Existing Integration Analysis

There is one last activity that we have to do before finishing the existing application analysis. We have to identify any existing integration solutions. It is very likely that we will be faced with some form of already implemented integration. The most common ways are data exchange using shared databases or flat files, or the use of message-oriented middleware to enable point-to-point communication between applications. We have to be aware of existing solutions when planning our integration, although it is often simpler if we don't have any integration at all and can start from scratch.

Identification of Applications

Identification of applications is the first step in the existing integration analysis of existing applications:

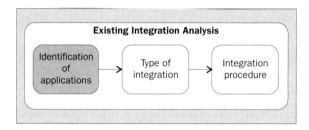

Here we identify all the applications that each application is integrated with. As we have already done the dependency analysis this will not be very difficult. We pay attention to all automatic dependencies, and focus on some specific details that we need to identify:

❑   Type of integration

❑   Exact procedure of how integration is implemented and performed

For our example, we can identify that the invoice print application is already integrated with the account management balance and customer information application.

Type of Integration

The type of integration identification is the second step in the existing integration analysis of existing applications:

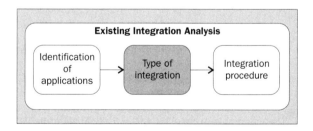

We will identify what integration level the existing integrated applications have been implemented on:

❑   Data-level

❑   Application interface level

❑ Business process level

❑ Presentation integration

In our example scenario, we have application interface level integration, because the RPC mechanism is used to invoke the functions defined in the interface.

Integration Procedure

Integration procedure identification is the third and last step in the existing integration analysis of existing applications:

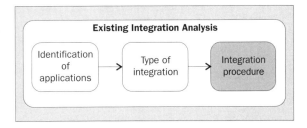

Next we have to identify how the integration is actually performed. Typically there are two possibilities:

❑ Asynchronous (batch)

❑ Synchronous

These two approaches refer to all levels of integration. For example, data can be transferred between applications and this can be done asynchronously (once a day, every five minutes, and so on). For asynchronous integration it is important to identify the frequency and the initiator. Usually the initiator is an application scheduled to execute at specific times. Human intervention is also frequently required.

On the other hand, data can also be transferred at the time when it is entered, that is, synchronous. The same is true for application interface level and business process level integration where operations and methods can be invoked synchronously or asynchronously.

Summary

In this chapter we discussed the systematic approach to software integration. We presented the process for application integration that presents a disciplined approach to top-down integration. The integration process first introduces sound practices, like iterative and incremental development, prototyping and reuse. Then it specifies the activities and phases that we should follow. The integration process separates the four integration phases – into data-level integration phase, application interface level integration phase, business-method-level integration phase, and presentation-level integration phase.

For each phase the integration process defines several activities that have to be performed in order to obtain results. Some of these activities are equal for all phases, some depend on the phases. They can be classified into technical and support activities. The technical activities include:

❑ Requirements gathering

❑ Analysis of existing applications

❑ Selection of integration infrastructure

❑ Problem domain analysis

❑ Design

❑ Implementation

❑ Testing

❑ Deployment

The support activities include:

❑ Project management

❑ Configuration and change management

❑ Communication with the environment

Particularly the requirements gathering and the analysis of existing applications are highly important activities for integration projects. For the requirements gathering activity we defined the necessary steps, including the specification of functional and non-functional requirements, representation of the requirements with the use case diagrams, and definition of priorities.

Even more important is the analysis of existing applications. We have to get a clear understanding of the existing situation in order to be able to later map this functionality to the newly integrated system. We went through four steps. First we have covered the functional analysis, where we have discussed steps, such as identification of functions, setting the experimental environment, black-box analysis, logical architecture identification, dependencies analysis, data model identification, integrity analysis, transactional, and security analysis. Second, we have discussed the technical analysis, where we have identified application interfaces, the architecture of applications, and their position in the information system. We performed a sensibility analysis, identified system load characteristics, performance, and scalability. We also identified the technologies, and located source code. Third we addressed the identification of functionality overlapping, where we showed how to identify functional and data model overlapping. Fourth and finally we addressed the already existing partial integrations between existing applications. Therefore we have looked at applications that already implement a form of integration, identified what type of integration they use, and identified the exact procedure to perform it.

This chapter defined the integration process and addressed the two important activities, the requirements gathering and analysis of existing applications. From here the book goes in three directions that have a logical continuation. Each direction covers a different integration phase and the connected activities. First the data-level integration phase is covered (Chapters 5 – 8). Then application-to-application integration is covered, which includes application interface level and business-method-level integration phases (Chapters 9 – 16). Finally the presentation integration phase and the possibilities for B2B integration are covered (Chapters 17 – 18).

In the next chapter we will start with a detailed overview of the data-level integration phase and the connected activities.

5

Integration Through Data

In many instances, the easiest way to integrate two applications is to simply allow them to share their data. This can be done in a number of ways: by opening access permissions on an application's database, by copying data from one application's database to another, or through vendor-supplied database replication services. Data sharing is also one of the easiest ways to bridge widely different hardware platforms, data models, or legacy applications.

This chapter will examine the many issues and techniques surrounding data integration:

- ❏   What is data integration and when is it appropriate?
- ❏   Data integration design strategies
- ❏   Identifying data
- ❏   Developing an integrated data model
- ❏   Bridging data models
- ❏   Managing redundancy
- ❏   Building the integration plan
- ❏   Implementing a data integration project

What is Data Integration?

Data integration is the process of sharing or merging data from two or more distinct software applications to create a more highly functional enterprise application. Traditional business applications are highly data oriented – that is, they rely on persistent data structures to model business entities and processes. When this is the case, the logical approach is to integrate the applications by sharing or merging data. Often, this is as simple as peeking "under the hood" of the other application to grab the information it needs. In other cases, data from one application may be restructured to match the data structure of another application, and is then written directly into another database.

Data integration can take many different forms. As such, to set the scene at this early stage we'll present a few examples of how to include data integration within an EAI project:

❏   **Data Sharing**
    In a financial service business, a customer service application will often retrieve data directly from the loan-processing database to provide account balance information or payment history.

❏   **Data Migration**
    When migrating a legacy application into an ERP installation, data will be extracted from the legacy application, and then written into the ERP database.

❏   **Data Transformations**
    When sending orders to a vendor using Electronic Data Interchange (EDI), data retrieved from the purchasing application will be transformed into a vendor-specific data format (either traditional flat file or XML), and then written to a disk file for transmission to the vendor.

❏   **Replication**
    When order processing occurs at several locations, it may be more cost-effective to keep copies of the database at each location, and then use the replication service of the DBMS to periodically synchronize them (note that replication will be covered in more detail later in this chapter).

When is Data Integration Appropriate?

Data integration is often the simplest and most straightforward approach for EAI solutions. It can usually be implemented using basic file I/O or standard database calls and it does not require distributed APIs or complex middleware. Almost any programmer fresh out of school will have the skills necessary to create such software so implementation cost is lower and scheduling is easier. Additionally, there are several tools out there in the market, often produced by database vendors, which support simple data migration and replication techniques.

However, data integration is not always the best solution. Direct data access opens up new opportunities for data corruption and security breaches. Integrity checks built into user applications may be bypassed resulting in bad data that may generate program exceptions (and crashes). Changes in access controls may open new security loopholes and data imports and exports may release sensitive data onto public networks. We should think long and hard before choosing data integration as our primary strategy.

Applications that are not appropriate for data integration include:

- ❑ Applications that have little persistent data

- ❑ Applications with complex business rules

- ❑ Large commercial applications (such as ERP) that have many complex data structures

- ❑ Applications with undocumented data structures, such as commercial or legacy applications

- ❑ Applications where data integrity is critical

- ❑ Transaction-oriented applications (such as banking or accounting)

- ❑ Applications that store sensitive personal data, trade secrets, or other business-critical data

Data Integration Strategies

If data integration *is* an appropriate solution, the next step is to begin a detailed analysis and design process. As stated above, programming for data integration is often straightforward and does not always require great technical skill. But putting the right data in the right place must be done flawlessly. There is no room for error since data integration problems are usually not discovered until it is too late. By then, errors are likely to have been compounded and it can be difficult (and sometimes impossible) to recover the corrupted data.

The best way to make sure this does not happen is to plan, research, and analyze. All applications and data structures that will be accessed or impacted within the scope of the integration project must be documented. We must collect any documentation available, locate developers who have experience with the applications, discuss the data flow with users, and learn everything about the data that is physically possible.

Once this is done, we need to develop a comprehensive data model, identifying the location of the entities, data storage models, their contents, origins, uses, constraints and business rules, and data transformations. Along the way, we verify this model by physically inspecting the data, and we can write short programs to verify that constraints and business rules are followed. If the documentation says that a column will have, say, one of four specific values, we can run a short query to verify this. Again, we need to know the data inside and out so there will be minimal unwanted surprises.

> To illustrate this, one of my worst nightmares was a data migration project done back during the heyday of mainframes and minicomputers. Our team was migrating data into a new healthcare billing system and we were going to shift from the organization's self-defined ID numbers to social security numbers (SSNs) as the primary identifier. While we ran short tests to verify the migration software, the staff contacted patients to verify the SSNs and cleaned up the data. We thought that we were ready to go but, unfortunately, there were about 30 duplicate SSNs scattered through the data. This oversight came back to bite us many times during the following weeks. If we had only written one short program to verify that there were no duplicate SSNs, we would have saved ourselves so much grief.

In this section we will briefly examine some of the techniques that can be used to analyze the data and help identify the issues that need to be addressed to develop a successful data integration plan. Naturally, we'll start with the identification of the data.

Identifying the Data

Identifying the data is often the most difficult task in enterprise data integration. Data is spread throughout the organization in many forms, on different platforms. Even if the data can be found, it will have different names in different applications, it may be coded using different standards and may have to be translated before it can be used in other applications.

So how do we go about finding the data that we need for our integration project? What do we look for? What data is relevant to our project and what can we ignore?

What Data Do We Need?

Before we can go searching for data, we need to determine the scope of our search. Often the best place to start is at the end. What data will the new integrated system generate or store? If specifications have been developed for the newly integrated application, we can examine the outputs (reports, screens, export files, and so on) to determine what data will be needed. If appropriate, examine the database schemas to see what data is stored. If there are no formal specifications, then we begin a more traditional analysis by interviewing potential users, collecting requirements, identifying report and screen contents, and doing all the other activities that we learned in those systems analysis and design courses.

Finding the Data

Once the requirements for the new application are gathered, it's time to play detective. Let's call this the Kinsey Millhone analysis pattern (or substitute your favorite mystery novel hero here!). In each book, Kinsey goes from character to character asking a series of questions to gather clues. In most books, she also goes to the library or public records to research information that she has gathered during an interview.

Now let's apply our Kinsey Millhone pattern to track down the data for our integration project. In most cases, data will describe entities or processes, so we should start by going to the people who are responsible for these business functions. Find out how the data is currently managed, locate the data entry or retrieval screens, and these will lead to the programs that manage the data, then research the program code (if it's available) to locate the data stores.

But don't stop there. Get out of the IT department and talk to the managers and end users who work with this data. Determine the administrative processes and rules that support the data. Find out where the data comes from, what procedures the staff use to validate and correct each data item, and what do they do with the paper once they have completed their work. Just as Kinsey gets leads from her interviews, use the information about data flow to follow up leads in your data investigation.

Understanding the Data

Finally, once all the clues are collected, they have to be merged and correlated before developing an integrated data model. Organize your information by processes and entities then validate every assumption to correct erroneous information. Quantify data volumes and determine the meaning of coded values. Fields with names like status, code, or type often represent categorization or process flow information that will have relevance to the data integration project.

There are many techniques for organizing data and, most likely, you already have some favorite methods. Desktop databases and spreadsheets or even index cards work well for collecting and correlating data, while requirements documents, data dictionaries, data mapping, Entity Relationship (ER) diagrams, and other techniques form good frameworks for organizing all of the information.

In addition to collecting and organizing the information, it is imperative that the data itself be examined to ensure that it conforms to the assumptions documented above. Locate the physical data, examine its structure, count the number of entries, check that it conforms to documented constraints and, for legacy data, determine its physical format. Then we should write short programs or use SQL query tools to inspect and validate the data. Let's now consider some techniques to help us understand the data.

Physically Locate the Data

Enterprise data is usually spread across many computers throughout large geographic areas, so finding the physical location of the data can often be a challenge of its own. Once the data is found, document its location, including physical location, network address, URL, machine directory structure, file name or any other information that may assist someone in finding the data. Often it is helpful to register this information into a directory service such as LDAP or NDS using JNDI (this will be discussed in more detail later in this chapter).

Count Everything

This will be a recurring theme throughout this chapter. The only way to know if the data was transformed correctly is through counting and summary totals. From the beginning, determine how many items need to be processed. Operations on large data sets can take considerable time, especially over wide area networks. Find these bottlenecks early and things will go much easier.

Verify Data Structures

Documentation rarely keeps up with changes made in data structures so it is important to verify the structure of each table or data file. Run database utilities to examine each table definition and physically inspect data files to ensure that they match the specs. When discrepancies occur, check the source code to determine what changes have been made.

Check Constraints

Documented constraints and business rules often do not match the real world. Legacy data may have been migrated into a database, program bugs may have gone unnoticed long enough to corrupt data, procedures may be ignored, or the documentation may just be wrong. In any case, the only way to ensure that the constraints are correct is to create scripts or programs to validate the data. Expecting data to conform to unverified assumptions almost guarantees that your integration programs will crash and burn.

Check Ranges

In addition to constraints, minimum and maximum values should be known for numeric values and maximum string lengths should be catalogued. Are there negative values or zeros? Are there empty or null strings? We can expect null pointer exceptions or data truncation losses if these issues are ignored.

Catalog Values

Fields with names like type, status, or code are often application specific and will need to be translated into common nomenclature. Check lookup tables or application pull-down boxes to determine the meaning of each possible value, and then query the data to ensure that the values stored in the data tables match the assumptions gathered from the software. When multiple applications are merged or data is migrated, develop translation tables either within the integration database or in property files that map equivalent codes from one application to the other.

Define Legacy Data Formats

One of the more ugly tasks in data integration is converting data representations from one platform to another. Characters may have to be translated between EBCDIC, ASCII, and Unicode. Numeric data will often be stored in different formats, sometimes with decimal points and sometimes without. Numbers can be represented in binary, ASCII, packed decimal, or any number of different floating-point standards. Positive and negative numbers can be represented by high-order bits, low-order bits, overstrikes (logical representation of numeric value and sign character), or separate fields. Often, the only way to verify these formats is to look at the physical data.

Designing the Integrated Data Model

Once you thoroughly understand the data, the next step is to develop an **integrated data model**. This will often include a requirements list, an architectural diagram, some type of data dictionary, a high-level ER diagram, or other detailed specifications. No matter what form this model takes, the goal is to map the existing data, then define new links and data structures to support the integrated enterprise application.

The structure and detail of this data model will greatly depend on the type of integration that needs to take place. The model for a data migration project will typically describe the old and new data structures in limited detail, then offer a comprehensive data mapping that lists the source and destination of each data element. In contrast, a new enterprise information system (EIS) data model will begin with a comprehensive architectural diagram showing the location of each data source as well as a high-level ER diagram linking a large number of existing entities to new data warehouse structures.

Later in this chapter we will examine the design of an integrated data model for our sample EAI application. First though, there are several issues that are unique to data integration modeling that we should introduce. These include:

- ❑ Data mapping
- ❑ Bridging data models
- ❑ How to manage redundancy

Data Mapping

In traditional relational data modeling, data is stored using consistent naming conventions; redundancy is avoided at all costs. However, with data integration we must deal with data that is scattered throughout the enterprise, in many different forms, stored under many different names, in different databases, and different locations. So one of the most critical tasks is to determine how the data in each application corresponds to data in other applications. A customer list in the marketing database may contain much of the same data as that found in the billing application, but in the marketing database, a customer's name may be stored in the table under the column NAME and the company may be stored as COMPANY, while in the billing database, the customer's name may be stored under CONTACT and the company name stored under NAME. Data mapping simply documents these equivalencies.

In addition to data structure and item location mapping, differences in data representations must also be documented. These can include how to translate numeric formats between items, date and time formats, and character encoding. Translation between data representations such as internally defined codes or competing industry coding standards (such as medical procedure codes, for instance) must also be described in detail, listing equivalents for each code value. Processing requirements for null values, empty strings, missing data, and data errors must also be determined.

Once these data maps are completed, they become the road maps for the developers. Without this information it is impossible to build effective data models or define the integration tasks. It also becomes the primary source of information for detailed design and programming specifications.

Bridging Data Models

Another distinguishing characteristic of EAI is the need to bridge different data models. Most enterprise data grows and evolves over time, but there are always a few applications that time forgot and others that took on bleeding edge technologies that seemed promising at the time (what ever happened to Turbo Prolog?), without considering that data would some day have to be shared. Here are the most common data models that will be encountered during data integration:

- Relational
- Object
- Hierarchical
- Multidimensional
- Commercial Applications
- Legacy

Relational

Relational database management systems (RDBMS) are the most prevalent storage medium for enterprise data. Since most data modeling techniques are based on some form of relational data theory, there is little difficulty understanding or modeling these data structures.

But difficulties can arise when extending traditional modeling techniques across the enterprise. Differences in naming and data representations often complicate logical relationships. For example, for integration a simple foreign key in a standard application may require intermediate links to data value maps or require transformation functions. If a marketing database uses a ten digit customer ID and the order entry system uses a different twelve digit identifier, an additional translation table will need to be placed between the two databases before a marketing exec can determine what happened to the customer's order.

Accessing relational data is also quite trivial (although knowing where it is and configuring access may not be so simple). In Java, data can be accessed through JDBC, JDO, SQLJ, or other data access technologies. Data can easily be translated to other formats using the vendor's bulk copy or interactive SQL utilities, and there is a wealth of data access technologies available for almost any programming language.

Object

Object database management systems (ODBMS) are designed to store program objects encapsulating behavior (instead of data) into easily accessible persistent data stores. While relational modeling is based on table-to-table relationships such as one-to-one and one-to-many, objects can be related by association, containment, and inheritance. Often, a hybrid modeling notation, using a combination of ER and object modeling symbols will be sufficient to communicate the basic concepts.

Accessing data that is stored in an ODBMS is typically done using either vendor-supplied language extensions or through an interface like Java Data Objects (JDO). Once the objects are instantiated, their attributes can be copied into other data forms such as relational tables or disk files.

Hierarchical

Although hierarchical data structures bring to mind memories of Information Management Systems or legacy disk and tape file structures, the industry has recently adopted a number of important standards that rely heavily on this data model. The most prevalent is XML, but directory services and the Windows registry all use the same hierarchical model. The best way to model these structures is through a hierarchy of linked entities and this will be illustrated later in this chapter.

The Data Object Model (DOM) is often the best approach for accessing hierarchical data structures. DOM works well with XML, directories and, as we will see in Chapter 7, even for legacy data. DOM offers standardized APIs that are available in a number of different languages and, although the learning curve is somewhat steep, it is a powerful model that makes hierarchical data access much easier to manage. In addition to DOM, hierarchical data access can also be performed using the Simple API for XML (SAX), JDO, or even the standard file I/O.

Multidimensional

Online analytical processing (OLAP) tools (such as Cognos's PowerPlay – http://www.cognos.com/products/powerplay/index.html) offer proprietary data structures that optimize analytical reporting. These are often referred to as multidimensional databases and are found in data warehousing and EIS applications. They allow quick access and summaries of large volumes of data for analysis and reporting. These structures can be modeled as if they were relational data, concentrating only on the source data, not on the internal data structures. For example, a multidimensional database to support marketing may contain sales by customer, city, region, and state. In this case, your data model would list these items along with measurement data such as number of sales, dollar sales by product, and so on.

Multidimensional database vendors provide their own proprietary utilities for loading and extracting data and a discussion of these utilities and APIs are far beyond the scope of this chapter.

Commercial Applications

Commercial applications such as financial packages, ERP, or CRM offer their own data modeling mechanisms. Quite often, they must be treated as "black boxes" since the internal data structures are complex, undocumented, and unknown. Many products offer data import (loading) and export (unloading) facilities that provide all of the data access that will be needed. But, as we will see in the example later in this chapter, the import and export capabilities often leave a lot to be desired.

If the import and export facilities are not adequate, the next step is to contact the vendor for technical support. Depending on the vendor, they may offer additional documentation or consulting services to help us access the data directly in a manner that will avoid any problems. Vendors do not usually provide these services without a price, but the additional cost can often save later grief if your mission critical finance system comes crashing down.

When modeling commercial applications, we should use the import and export files as our data entities. Furthermore, we need to run test extracts to obtain plenty of data to examine, and then carefully map the data to the destinations where they will be sent. Since the data is usually processed as disk files, standard Java file I/O will usually be all that is needed to access the data.

Legacy

Legacy data models, other than hierarchical (discussed above), will each have to be modeled in their own way, based on their organization and the technology used. Data may be in flat files, indexed structures such as ISAM, hierarchical or network databases, or other forms. In most cases, this data can be copied into flat files that can be read using standard Java file I/O, although additional translation and decoding will often be necessary. We will discuss this in more detail later in this chapter, and in Chapter 7.

Other Data Formats

As new technologies are introduced, new data structures and formats may appear that do not conform to those listed above. The Internet allows us to access data from e-mail servers, online data entry from JSP pages and servlets, messaging, and other new data streams. In most cases, these are operational data sources that are processed through local applications, and eventually stored in enterprise databases. But occasionally data may need to be retrieved from directory systems or data files that support these functions (such as the list of users from a mail server or the list of remote servers from a directory service). This data can often be accessed using DOM, directory service APIs like JNDI or other special purpose APIs. The data structures can be modeled either as relational (tables or lists) or hierarchical data (as in the case of directories).

How To Manage Redundancy

Another critical issue in enterprise data modeling is how to manage redundancy throughout the enterprise. In each case, the consideration is whether to go out across the network to retrieve data or to keep a copy of the data on a local computer to speed access time. Each case will have its own tradeoffs but, in most cases, it comes down to the volume of data involved, performance needs, and the volatility of the data.

Like the saying goes, "you can pay me now, or you can pay me later". If data has to come across the network at some time, the choice is to grab a small amount of data in real time or to periodically copy larger data sets. If all that is needed is a quick look-up such as a customer service person looking up an account balance, it will be acceptable to go across the network and grab the data. But if the billing system has to constantly merge data from three or four databases throughout the country, it makes more sense to copy all of the relevant data to the local system before beginning the merge.

In addition to data volume, another consideration is the volatility of the data – that is, how much has the data changed on the remote machine since it was copied. Some data, like the tables that populate pull-down boxes, changes little and can be copied to other machines in a deliberate, controlled manner. Most operational data, on the other hand, changes quickly so real-time access is an absolute necessity.

So the questions we must ask now are: when should we access the data, and how much should we move? The goals are to optimize performance while maintaining the integrity of the data. Here are a number of techniques that can be used to achieve these goals:

❏ Shared data access

❏ Batch file transfers

❏ Replication

❏ Transformations

❏ Establish ownership

Let's take a closer look at each of these methods.

Shared Data Access

The simplest way to manage redundancy is to not have redundant data. When data is needed, the program simply sends a database request across the network and gets the data it needs. This alleviates the need to copy and synchronize data in multiple places and ensures that the data is not corrupted.

Unfortunately, when used in online applications, direct data access can severely degrade the response time and bring down applications when data is not available. It also generates a large volume of random, unpredictable traffic that may overload the network or force your organization to buy much more bandwidth than necessary, just to handle peak traffic.

Data sharing is appropriate when:

❏ The network will always be available

❏ The network can accommodate the additional load or upgrades will be cost-effective

❏ Small amounts of data are sent or retrieved

❏ The data is relatively static (few changes occur)

❏ The number of accesses are kept to a minimum

❏ Static data can be stored in memory during the life of the application

❏ Data access volume does not impact network bandwidth

Batch File Transfers

When larger data volumes are needed, it makes sense to copy the data across the network during off-peak times. This may be overnight or over the weekend. Once copied, the data can be stored in local databases for quick access throughout the day, eliminating network traffic and speeding up performance. But unless some form of replication can be implemented (as described below), it can no longer be maintained in real time. The data must either be static, that is, few changes occur in the data, or is such that recent changes will not impact the needs of those accessing the local data.

There are several ways that batch transfers can be implemented and each has its own tradeoffs with regard to performance and complexity. The simplest is to erase the data from the destination machine, then copy all of the data. This will ensure accuracy but may not be practical when large data volumes are involved. Another choice is to track changes, then only copy the changes to the destination machine. This will speed transfers, but adds significant complexity to the transfer programs. It also raises the chance for differences to occur between the source and destination data when program errors or network drops occur. Often a combination of the two works best, copying all of the data periodically (such as on holiday weekends), then processing adds and changes nightly.

Batch transfers are appropriate when:

❑   Large data volumes are involved

❑   Adds and changes are isolated to a single source location

❑   Changes made to the data will not impact its use at the destination site

❑   Off-peak network bandwidth can support the data transfer volume

Replication

Replication is a feature of most database management systems that maintains and synchronizes a number of copies of the database from a central location. This is a feature designed for mobile computing, but also works well in some data integration models. For example, a traveling sales rep may carry a copy of the sales database on their notebook computer. During the day, they will take orders and update customer information. When they get back to their hotel that evening, they dial up to the central sales system and the database replication service copies these changes to the central database, adding orders and updating customers. Once this is done, the replication service sends back changes received from other sales reps so that, when the service finishes, the copy of the database on the notebook computer exactly matches that of the central database. In the same way, large-scale order entry applications or centralized warehouse applications may be good candidates for replication as long as the data can be segregated by location.

This sounds like the perfect solution for all data integration needs but there are a number of drawbacks. First, data must be segregated in a manner that prevents multiple remote changes to the same data. If our sales rep changes the address for customer Jones and another sales rep also changes the address for customer Jones (maybe the wrong Jones), one of the changes will be lost. Also, new data must be stored under unique identifiers so that duplicate key violations do not occur. If our sales rep adds a new order number 10052 and another sales rep adds an order under the same identifier 10052, one of the two orders will be lost or a duplicate key violation may occur.

Replication is restricted to a single database platform since the DBMS is responsible for the replication service. Replicating between Oracle and MS SQL Server databases cannot be done without writing the replication code by hand (often a daunting task). Also, depending on the vendor, replication can be difficult to set up and performance is often not satisfactory for large databases. It is useful to spend some time experimenting with the replication service before adding it to our data integration model.

Replication is a good integration choice when:

❑   Source and destination databases are from the same vendor

❑   Databases can be segregated by some distinct identifier (such as region, sales rep, and so on)

❑   Changes in the data are small and isolated

❑   Replication processes can run without degrading online performance

Transformations

So far the data integration techniques we have discussed have all assumed that the data will be copied in the same form, from one location to another. However, often the data must be transformed to match various structure, format, or coding standards before it can be used. Additionally, only summary statistics or small subsets of the data need to be extracted so it makes little sense to copy all of the data in its existing form. In these cases, the above techniques will have to be augmented to perform the necessary translations. This is why data mapping is critical – so that data can be delivered in a consistent form and that it is not corrupted and applications do not crash.

In Chapter 7, we'll take a closer look at the XML standards for transformations.

Establish Ownership

No matter how the data is passed throughout the enterprise, it is imperative that someone be assigned the responsibility for maintaining the integrity of the data. Some organizations call this person a data owner or data administrator (not the same as a database administrator). Often each table will have its owner and, in some cases, the ownership may be distributed to a number of owners based on some vertical differentiation of the data such as accounts, region, or other business-related identifiers. Instead of allowing anyone in the organization to grab an item and change it, the changes are routed to the data administrator who makes the changes and ensures that the data remains correct.

This is especially true when data is stored in more than one place. If two people make changes to the same data item on the same day, one of the changes will be lost when the data is copied. By isolating the changes to one person or location, changes will be managed consistently and data corruption will be avoided.

Completing the Integrated Data Model

After all of the data has been located and mapped, and techniques have been selected to bridge data models and manage redundancy, it needs to be organized in a manner that can be used by the developers. Starting with a high-level map showing the locations of the data sources, we should drill down to the lower levels of detail until all data sources and relationships have been documented. Once this is done, an integration plan can be designed to create any new entities and connect the relationships.

In addition to an integrated data model, there needs to be an **implementation plan** describing how the data will be connected. This plan must include database specifications for any new entities that are needed to complete the data model, program specifications for the functions that manage relations and perform transformations, specifications of new network connections, middleware or third-party software, and an implementation schedule. In the next section, we will examine a simplified data integration project that will illustrate how this is constructed.

Grocery Point-of-Sales Integration

Now it's time to put all of this information to work. The project will be to integrate a number of different grocery store point-of-sales (PoS) applications. Our fictitious grocery chain has grown from a small regional chain into a national powerhouse through expansion and acquisitions. But, like most companies, this growth has resulted in a number of different systems running in different regions that all perform the same basic task. Replacing these systems would be far too costly, so it is our job to integrate these systems to meet the following objectives as stated in the initial project request:

- ❑ **Combine reporting**
  Merge sales data into one common database to allow both store-level, regional, and combined reporting.

- ❑ **Consolidate purchasing**
  Once sales trends can be established using the new consolidated reports, much of the purchasing can be done from a central location, allowing better discounts on larger quantity purchases.

- ❑ **Unify pricing**
  Other than limited regional products or in-store specials, most pricing decisions will be managed from company headquarters so this data must be communicated back to the stores.

- ❑ **Replace obsolete equipment**
  One of the regions is running a very old PoS system that needs to be replaced, so in addition to integrating the other systems, we will be migrating data from this legacy system to one of the other PoS systems.

> It should be noted that this is only a sample application, designed to examine the issues and difficulties that arise in data integration. As such, many details have been ignored and data structures have been simplified for clarity.

In this chapter, we will begin with the analysis and design as discussed above, and then we will implement a few of the data integration processes. In the next two chapters we will continue working on this project, enhancing some of the data integration processes using XML, and completing the legacy conversion.

Designing the Point-of-Sales Integration

Given the objectives we outlined above, we now must design and implement our EAI project. As with any development project, the first step is to gather more information. So, it's time to start our detective work.

Current Architecture

After meeting with a number of people in both technical and user departments, we have gathered enough preliminary information to determine the following:

Business Structure

The business is divided into twelve regions, each running independently, managing their own warehouses and stores. The diagram below shows a block diagram of the first three regions:

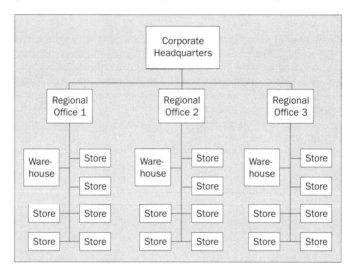

Overall Application Architecture

Each region also maintains their own point-of-sales system but, fortunately (and to simplify the example), there are really only three distinct systems. These are:

❑   **The Original In-House System**
    This was the original system purchased by the parent company and has evolved over time; we'll refer to this as Application 1. Each store has a number of scanners and registers as well as a small database server connected by a local area network. Each store's server communicates daily with a regional database server (MS SQL Server 2000) using dial-up lines to send sales information and receive product and pricing data. Product and pricing is maintained at the regional office using PCs connected to the database server. The following diagram shows the overall architectural view for a single region:

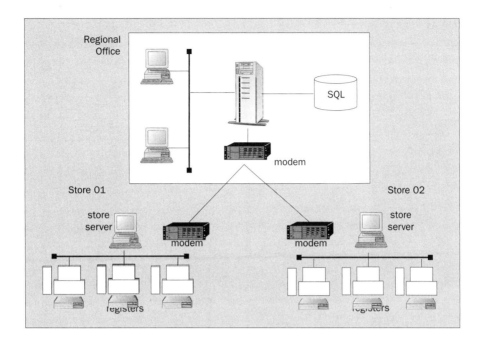

- ❑ **The Commercial Turn-Key System**
  Many of the regions acquired by the chain run a commercial system that runs similarly to Application 1 (this will be called Application 2). The major difference is that data cannot be accessed directly from the regional server, but must be entered or extracted using vendor-defined flat file imports and exports. These will be discussed below.

- ❑ **The Legacy System**
  One of the first regions acquired ran a primitive legacy system (we'll call this Application 3). Each store runs independently, manually entering pricing information while transaction data is written to a shared tape cartridge machine. Tapes are shipped to the regional office, where they are read into an IBM mini-computer. Due to the cost of maintenance and the difficulty in obtaining scanners and spare parts, it was decided that this system should be scrapped and replaced with Application 1. If possible, the legacy data should be carried over into the new system.

Identifying the Data Structures

Further detective work has helped us to discover the data accessible for each application. Let's take a look at what we've found.

Application 1

Data in App1 is stored in a relational database on each regional server. The diagram below shows the ER diagram for this database:

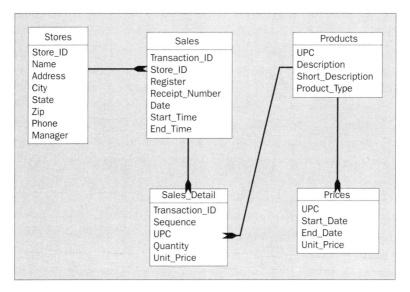

The database uses the following tables:

- ❑   Stores – holds basic information about each of the store locations

- ❑   Products – contains descriptions for each product sold in the stores

- ❑   Prices – holds prices for each UPC, aged by date (Start_Date and End_Date)

- ❑   Sales – contains one entry per customer transaction

- ❑   Sales_Detail – for each sale, detailed information is kept listing each product sold, along with the quantity and unit price

Application 2

App2 is a commercial system used by several of the acquired regions. The vendor does not publish their internal data structures, but they do offer functions in their administrative program to import and export data into disk files. As can be seen from the file descriptions below, there is little data available, but the data retrieved should be sufficient for integration:

- ❑   **Pricing File**
  The pricing file is a simple flat file listing each product UPC, description, and unit price.

- ❑   **Sales File**
  The sales file is also a flat file containing transaction details for any range of time or search criteria keyed into the administrative program. The file includes one entry per item sold, including the store ID, register, number, date, time, UPC, quantity and total price.

Detailed specifications can be found within this chapter's source code files, as App2_File_Specs.doc.

Application 3

App3 is an old legacy system with no central reporting other than a few simple RPG programs that read the tape files generated by each store, then consolidates them into a series of combined reports. Due to a lack of disk space on the regional minicomputer, the data has never been stored on a central machine. But there are many boxes of tapes, going back anywhere from six to twelve months that should allow us to collect some history, so we will do what we can to extract the data.

The tape files can be copied onto the minicomputer, and then moved to a PC where they can be written to CD-ROM. According to the vendor documentation, the tape data is stored in a hierarchical format with a number of different record types. The diagram below shows the basic organization of the data:

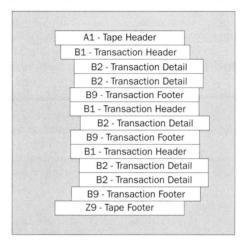

As can be seen from the diagram, each tape file contains an initial header record (type A1) that gives the store number and the date when the tape was loaded. Each sale is written to a set of transaction records with record types beginning with the letter B. Record B1 is written at the beginning of each new transaction, B2 records are written for each item (or group of items sold) and record B9 is written at the end of the transaction. When the tape is closed, a Z9 record is written that totals all transactions on the tape. Note that other record types are also written, storing administration and diagnostic information, but are not needed for our integration project. Also, on the tape file itself transactions can be interspersed, since each activity that occurs on a register is immediately written to tape. Our mini-computer program that writes the tape to CD-ROM, also sorts the file by the first 18 characters so transactions will be grouped together.

It's useful to summarize all of the relevant record types:

❏ **Tape Header (A1)**
A tape header record is written at the beginning of each tape. The only fields of concern to us are the store number and name.

❏ **Transaction Header (B1)**
A transaction header is written at the start of each sale (listed below). Other than triggering a new transaction, the only information of interest is the transaction number.

❏ **Transaction Detail (B2)**
Transaction detail records are written for each item purchased. We will need to extract the UPC, quantity, and price of each item sold.

❑ **Transaction Footer (B9)**
At the end of each transaction, a footer record is written (footer is an old mainframe term for the totals in a file or report). The record contains the sales tax collected as well as totals for the transaction. Since media problems were much more prevalent in older technologies, space was usually reserved for check totals to ensure that data was transferred correctly. When we process this data, we will also want to check these totals, to make sure all data was read accurately.

❑ **Tape Footer (Z9)**
Finally, at the end of each tape, a tape footer record is written summarizing all of the data. As with the transaction footer, we need to verify the totals to ensure that all records have been read.

Since we have little need to examine the specific data formats at this time, detailed specifications for the tape files can be found in the file `App3_File_Specs.doc` (again, this file is located within the source code directory). We will examine these data structures in more detail when we get to Chapter 7.

Designing the Integrated Data Model

Given the data specifications mentioned above, it is now time to begin developing an integrated data model. Given the requirements that data must be consolidated for reporting, we can quickly determine that a new centralized database (we'll call Headquarters) is needed. We also know that sales data from each of the applications will have to be sent to the centralized database. Another requirement is that pricing will be centralized at corporate headquarters, so we know that product and pricing data will have to be sent to each regional application. Finally, we also know that App3 will be phased out and replaced by a new installation of App1 so we can immediately add this to the model. Given these requirements, we derive the following preliminary model:

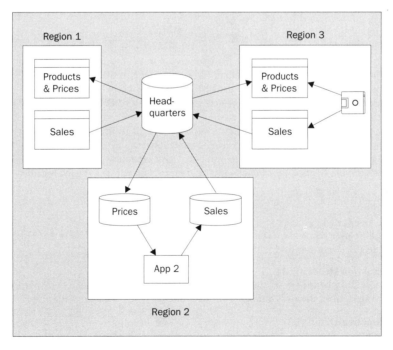

Here are the relationships that will need to be created to bridge the applications of each region:

❑ Region 1 uses a relational database so data can easily be transferred over a network from this database to headquarters.

❑ Region 2 may be a little more difficult to manage, but pricing data can be written to a disk file then imported to the application, and sales data can be exported into a disk file then read into the Headquarters database.

❑ Region 3 will install their own server and purchase new scanners and other equipment, and install their own copy of App1 onto their new server; a one-time data migration will be run to move existing tape data onto the regional server.

The next task in our integrated data model is to create a centralized Headquarters database. As can be seen from the preliminary model, the database must contain product and pricing information that can be sent to each region and store sales information that can be consolidated for reporting. In addition to these tables, centralized reporting will require other new structures for regional information and to administer data transfers.

Centralized Product and Pricing Information

Each application will receive product and pricing information from the centralized database, so let's begin with these data structures. The table below is a mapping that shows how the three applications product and pricing information relate to each other:

Item	Application 1	Application 2	Application 3	Headquarters
1	UPC	UPC	UPC	UPC
2	Description	NAME	n/a	Description
3	Short_ Description	n/a	n/a	Short_ Description
4	Product_Type: P – Product, C – Coupon, R – Refund, T - Tax	Not used (only send type P items)	TX_TYPE: 00 – Sale, 10 – Credit,(and so on), 90 – Sales Tax	Product_Type: P – Product, C – Coupon, (others not stored)
5	Start_Date (note 1)	n/a	n/a	Start_Date
6	End_Date (note 1)	n/a	n/a	n/a
7	Unit_Price	UNIT_PRICE	UNIT_PRICE	Unit_Price

In this case, data mapping is rather simple. There are only 7 elements and their associated mapping is straightforward. In App1, product and pricing information will be stored in the Products table (items 1-4) and the Prices table (5-7). App2 uses an import table that can only receive UPC, name, and unit price. Since App3 data will be transferred to a new instance of App1, pricing data must be derived from the transaction history, and will come from the transaction detail records (B2 in the notation used above).

The only mapping issue that may cause minor difficulties is item 4. This is a type code that describes special handling for coupons, sales tax and refunds. In App1, non-standard company-defined UPC codes are used to track these activities so an additional type code is needed to categorize these transactions, otherwise all of these special codes would have to be hard coded into each program. App3 uses transaction type codes in the B2 record to aid in processing. These map closely to the App1 type codes and can easily be translated in the migration programs.

With the mapping complete, we can begin to define the `Products` and `Pricing` tables for the Headquarters database. Since App1 was developed in-house and the programmers are already familiar with these data structures, it makes sense to pattern the Headquarters database closely to App1. The new `Products` table must contain all of the items in the App1 `Product` table and the new `Prices` table must contain all items in the App1 Pricing table other than the dates. In addition to the items matched in the mapping, we must add new items to manage the transfer process. Since it is not practical to send the entire file every night, it makes much more sense to use a replication process, sending only enough data to synchronize them with Headquarters. Instead of getting into all the gory details here, we will cover these when we get into the program implementation.

Mapping Sales Data Between Applications

Developing the sales data integration again involves comparing the data elements from each of the three applications, then deriving a new data structure that combines all of these items. Once this is completed, we can determine our data migration mapping, as shown below:

Item	Application 1	Application 2	Application 3	Headquarters
1	Transaction_ID (concatenate region and transaction ID)	Concatenate region with a program-generated sequence	B1-TX_NUMBER	Transaction_ID
2	Store_ID	STORE	A1-STORE_NUMBER	Store_ID
3	Register	REGISTER	B1-REGISTER	Register
4	Receipt_Number	n/a	n/a	n/a
5	Date	DATE	B2-DATE	Sale_Date
6	Start_Time	TIME		Sale_Time
7	End_Time		B2-TIME	
8	Sequence	counter	counter	Sequence
9	UPC	UPC	B2-UPC	UPC
10	Quantity	QTY	B2-QUANTITY	Quantity

Item	Application 1	Application 2	Application 3	Headquarters
11	Unit_Price	PRICE (calculate unit price from this price and quantity)	B2-UNIT_PRICE	Unit_Price
12			B9-TAX (create new Sales Detail for tax entry)	

Data from App1 is retrieved by joining `Sales` (items 1-8) and `Sales_Detail` (items 9-11). App2 data comes from the sales export file. App3 data is extracted by reading data from the CD-ROMs generated from the tape cartridges.

Again, the new Headquarters database will closely match the App1 `Sales` and `Sales_Detail` tables. Since times are not critical for corporate reporting, only the start time will be kept.

Designing the Headquarters Database

Using the data mappings above and the App1 database as a baseline, we can now complete design of the Headquarters database. The ER diagram is shown below.

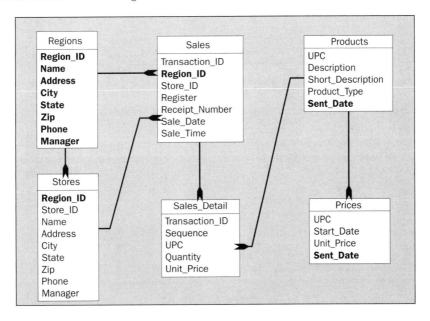

Note the addition of the `Regions` table – this is included to store information about each region. Additional columns (marked in bold) are added to the `Sales` table to track the region where the sale occurred and the `Sent_Date` columns are added as discussed above.

With the Headquarters database in place, our integrated data model is complete. To recap, here are the steps we used to design the model:

1. We located and identified the data for the three applications.

2. We developed a preliminary data model showing the relationships between the data stores. These relationships included locations of redundant data and how data will flow from each source to the destination.

3. We built data mappings for each major data structure.

4. We used the mapping to determine the new integration database requirements.

5. We completed the design for the new integration database.

Developing the Integration Plan

Given the data integration model shown above, we can now begin to develop an integration plan. This plan will list all of the steps necessary to integrate these applications and will become the baseline for our project plan. First, let's update the architectural diagram that we used for our data model:

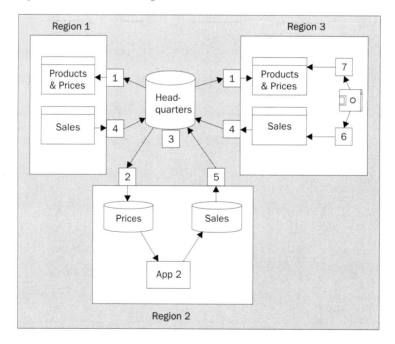

The main changes made to this diagram are the generalization of the databases and the addition of small numbered boxes between the applications, which represent the programs that we will need to create in order to implement the data integration:

1. Transfer products and prices to App1

2. Transfer products and prices to App2

3. Complete prices transfer

4. Transfer sales from App1

5. Transfer sales from App2

We also have the following one-time-only operations to perform:

6. Transfer sales from App3 tape cartridges to new Region 2 instance of App1

7. Transfer prices from App3 tape cartridges to new Region 2 instance of App1.

Final Integration Plan

Once all of the tasks are specified, a detailed design document should be drawn up that can be used to create a final project plan. The plan will include detailed task lists specifying programming assignments, hardware purchases and upgrades, resource allocations, and all those other things needed to keep the project running. Once this is in place, implementation can begin.

Implementing the Product and Pricing Integration

Using the integration plan listed above, we're ready to start writing the code. As stated before, data integration programming is not that difficult if the analysis and design are performed correctly. All of the programming can be done with the basic JDBC API so we will keep the programs as simple as possible. Once we have completed the basic implementation, we will go back and discuss some other enhancements that could make administration easier.

Since the integration plan lists quite a few programs, we will limit our implementation in this chapter to transferring products and pricing. These will give a good sample of the techniques needed to implement data integration. We will continue this example through the next two chapters, covering the warehouse interfaces (not discussed in this chapter) using XML, and then we will implement the legacy tape migration as well as some additional XML transformations in Chapter 7.

In this section we will examine the following tasks:

❑ Setting up the development environment

❑ Creating the databases

❑ Transferring products to App1

❑ Transferring prices to App1

❏ Transferring products and prices to App2

❏ Marking products and prices as sent

❏ Testing and deploying the pricing integration

Setting Up the Development Environment

Before we can start programming, we will need at least one computer that can run Java and several software development tools. Due to the number of choices and options available, specific installation instructions will not be given; you should consult the documentation provided with each package for detailed instructions. Let's consider the tools we will need:

❏ **Java Development Tools**
Choose your favorite Java 2-compliant development tool or IDE. The code in this chapter was developed using the Java SDK 1.3 and a popular text editor (for example, EditPlus – http://www.editplus.com/).

❏ **Relational Database**
Again, choose your favorite relational database (as long as JDBC drivers are available for it). My database of choice is Sybase SQL Anywhere because of its small footprint, multi-platform capabilities and Java support. A trial can be downloaded from http://www.sybase.com. To make things interesting, we will also use Microsoft SQL Server 2000 for the App1 databases (Region 1), and a trial of this database can be obtained from http://www.microsoft.com/sql/evaluation/default.asp.

❏ **JDBC Drivers**
You will also need JDBC drivers for your database of choice. The code in this chapter was tested using jConnect 5.5 (http://www.sybase.com) and Microsoft's SQL 2000 JDBC Driver (http://www.microsoft.com/SQL/downloads/2000/jdbc.asp). Drivers for other databases are available from i-net Software at (http://www.inetsoftware.de). Follow the directions given by the vendor to install and use these drivers.

Setting Up the Databases

The example will use two databases, the new Headquarters database and the App1 database of Region 1. Since data integration often involves working with data from a number of locations, stored in databases from different vendors, we will use Microsoft SQL Server 2000 for the App1 database and Sybase SQL Server Anywhere for the Headquarters database. In this section we will describe how to set these up on these platforms, but you may have to change your procedures if you choose a different vendor's DBMS.

Setting Up the Headquarters Database

The Headquarters database is implemented on Sybase. Use Sybase Central to create a new database (I called mine IntegratedPOS). Once this is done, start the new database server then start ISQL and execute the file HQ.sql (listed below). This will create the database:

```
CREATE TABLE Regions
(
    Region_ID     CHAR(4)       NOT NULL,
    Name          VARCHAR(30)   NOT NULL,
    Address       VARCHAR(30)   NULL,
```

```
      City            VARCHAR(25)    NULL,
      State           CHAR(2)        NULL,
      Zip             CHAR(10)       NULL,
      Phone           VARCHAR(20)    NULL,
      Manager         VARCHAR(30)    NULL,

      PRIMARY KEY (Region_ID)
)
go

CREATE TABLE Stores
(
      Region_ID       CHAR(4)        NOT NULL,
      Store_ID        CHAR(4)        NOT NULL,
      Name            VARCHAR(30)    NOT NULL,
      Address         VARCHAR(30)    NULL,
      City            VARCHAR(25)    NULL,
      State           CHAR(2)        NULL,
      Zip             CHAR(10)       NULL,
      Phone           VARCHAR(20)    NULL,
      Manager         VARCHAR(30)    NULL,

      PRIMARY KEY (Region_ID, Store_ID),
      FOREIGN KEY Region_ID REFERENCES Regions
)
go

CREATE TABLE Products
(
      UPC                 CHAR(12)      NOT NULL,
      Description         VARCHAR(30)   NOT NULL,
      Short_Description   CHAR(10)      NULL,
      Product_Type        CHAR(2)       NOT NULL,
      Sent_Date           DATE          NULL,

      PRIMARY KEY (UPC)
)
go

CREATE INDEX Products_Sent ON Products (Sent_Date)
go

CREATE TABLE Prices
(
      UPC               CHAR(12)      NOT NULL,
      Start_Date        DATE          NOT NULL,
      Unit_Price        NUMERIC(5,2)  NOT NULL,
      Sent_Date         DATE          NULL,

      PRIMARY KEY (UPC, Start_Date),
      FOREIGN KEY UPC REFERENCES Products,
)
go
```

```
CREATE INDEX Prices_Sent ON Prices (Sent_Date)
go

CREATE TABLE Sales
(
    Transaction_ID      CHAR(10)      NOT NULL,
    Region_ID           CHAR(4)       NOT NULL,
    Store_ID            CHAR(4)       NOT NULL,
    Receipt_Number      CHAR(10)      NULL,
    Register_Number     CHAR(3)       NULL,
    Sale_Date           DATE          NULL,
    Sale_Time           TIME          NULL,

    PRIMARY KEY (Transaction_ID),
    FOREIGN KEY Region_ID REFERENCES Regions,
    FOREIGN KEY (Region_ID, Store_ID) REFERENCES Stores
)
go

CREATE TABLE Sales_Detail
(
    Transaction_ID      CHAR(10)      NOT NULL,
    Sequence            SMALLINT      NOT NULL,
    UPC                 CHAR(12)      NOT NULL,
    Quantity            NUMERIC(5,2)  NOT NULL,
    Unit_Price          NUMERIC(5,2)  NOT NULL,

    PRIMARY KEY (Transaction_ID, Sequence),
    FOREIGN KEY Transaction_ID REFERENCES Sales,
    FOREIGN KEY UPC REFERENCES Products
)
go
```

Each of the tables match the ER diagram shown earlier and there is little to explain here. Once this is complete, run the script HQData.sql to load the initial test data.

Setting Up the Region 1 Database

The Region 1 database (App1) will be run from within Microsoft SQL Server 2000. Open up the Enterprise Manager, create a new database (for instance, I called mine PointOfSales), then run the script Reg01.sql, as shown below, to create the tables:

```
/*  Reg01.sql - Schema for Region 1 database  */

CREATE TABLE Stores
(
    Store_ID      CHAR(4)       NOT NULL,
    Name          VARCHAR(30)   NOT NULL,
    Address       VARCHAR(30)   NULL,
    City          VARCHAR(25)   NULL,
    State         CHAR(2)       NULL,
    Zip           CHAR(10)      NULL,
    Phone         VARCHAR(20)   NULL,
```

```
    Manager         VARCHAR(30)  NULL,

    PRIMARY KEY (Store_ID)
)
go

CREATE TABLE Products
(
    UPC                 CHAR(12)     NOT NULL,
    Description         VARCHAR(30)  NOT NULL,
    Short_Description   CHAR(10)     NULL,
    Product_Type        CHAR(2)      NOT NULL,

    PRIMARY KEY (UPC)
)
go

CREATE TABLE Prices
(
    UPC                 CHAR(12)       NOT NULL REFERENCES Products (UPC),
    Start_Date          DATETIME       NOT NULL,
    End_Date            DATETIME       NULL,
    Unit_Price          NUMERIC(5,2)   NOT NULL,

    PRIMARY KEY (UPC, Start_Date),
)
go


CREATE TABLE Sales
(
    Transaction_ID      CHAR(8)      NOT NULL,
    Store_ID            CHAR(4)      NOT NULL REFERENCES Stores(Store_ID),
    Receipt_Number      CHAR(10)     NULL,
    Register_Number     CHAR(3)      NULL,
    Start_Date          DATETIME     NULL,
    Start_Time          DATETIME     NULL,
    End_Time            DATETIME     NULL,

    PRIMARY KEY (Transaction_ID),
)
go


CREATE TABLE Sales_Detail
(
    Transaction_ID      CHAR(8)        NOT NULL REFERENCES Sales(Transaction_ID),
    Sequence            SMALLINT       NOT NULL,
    UPC                 CHAR(12)       NOT NULL REFERENCES Products (UPC),
    Quantity            NUMERIC(5,2)   NOT NULL,
    Unit_Price          NUMERIC(5,2)   NOT NULL,

    PRIMARY KEY (Transaction_ID, Sequence),
)
go
```

235

Other than the format of the comments and the manner in which referential integrity is declared, the script is almost identical to the Headquarters database. Once this has been created, run the `Reg01Data.sql` script (available in the code download for the book) to load the test data.

Transferring Products To App1

The first program example will examine how we send products from the Headquarters database to App1. As we described earlier, most product and pricing information is managed from a central pricing department. As the pricing administrator makes changes, the data entry application marks the product and price changes so we can send them to each region. Note that in this example, prices are never deleted, so we do not need to concern ourselves with this problem.

Since this program will have to be run once for each region, we will accept the URL of the destination database as a command-line parameter. At some point, these URLs can be added to an administration database so the entire process can be automated, but at this point we will use a command script to run each region individually. This script will be described at the end of this section.

Here is the program code for the `App1Products` program:

```
import java.io.*;
import java.sql.*;

public class App1Products {

    private String dbName;
```

The program imports only two packages: `java.io` for console messages and `java.sql` for all of the basic JDBC functionality. Although we could list the individual packages here instead of using wild cards, there is little reason to be so detailed and we will be using several of the JDBC packages anyway.

Once we've imported the packages, we begin the class definition, and declare a single instance variable `dbName`. This will hold the URL of the destination database when it is received by the constructor:

```
public App1Products (String nm) {
    dbName = nm;
}

public void copy () {
    System.out.println ("Processing " + dbName);
    try {
```

The `copy()` method performs most of the work of this class. It begins by printing the URL to the console, then it opens the connections, selects and copies the data, closes connections, and handles errors. This could be split into several granular methods, performing each individual task separately, but since the code is not that long, it is easier to read if kept in straight-line form.

Since many of the method calls generate exceptions, we'll wrap the entire method in a `try/catch` block. Normally this would again be done in a more granular manner, but for this example we'll keep it simple.

```
// Initialize the database connections
Class.forName("com.sybase.jdbc2.jdbc.SybDriver");
String hqUrl = "jdbc:sybase:Tds:localhost:2638";
Connection connHQ = DriverManager.getConnection (hqUrl, "HQ", "hq");
```

The first task is to get Connection objects for each of the databases. Here we will use the traditional JDBC 1.0 approach using the `Class.forName()` method to declare the JDBC driver for Sybase. Although we are using a JDBC 2.0-compliant driver, we will not need any of the JDBC 2.0 functionality. Since this is a batch program running at off-peak times, there is no reason to implement connection pooling and we do not need scrollable cursors or extensive locking capabilities.

Once the driver is declared, we create a string containing the URL of the Headquarters database, then we use the `DriverManager`'s `getConnection()` method, passing the URL, user ID and password, to obtain the `Connection` object.

Then we repeat the process for the remote database, declaring the MS SQL Server JDBC driver, and then we get the `Connection` object. Note that we do not pass the user ID and password here, since they will change for each destination database. Unfortunately, they must be embedded in the URL. This could present a security risk – we'll discuss this in more detail at the end of the chapter.

```
Class.forName("com.microsoft.jdbc.sqlserver.SQLServerDriver");
Connection connApp1 = DriverManager.getConnection (dbName);
```

The next step is to create a number of SQL commands. The first command is used to access only new products from the Headquarters database. When a new product is added or changed, the administration program sets the Sent_Date column to null, so this SQL command selects only those products with null Sent_Dates. After this data is copied to all regions, a separate program (shown below) will set the Sent_Date fields to today's date:

```
// Define SQL commands
String sqlRead = "SELECT UPC, Description, "
            + " Short_Description, Product_Type "
            + "FROM Products "
            + "WHERE Sent_Date IS NULL "
            + "ORDER BY UPC";
```

The next SQL command is used to add new products to the destination database. Note the question marks in the value list. This command will be used to create a prepared statement and the parameters (question marks) will be filled in before each execution of the statement:

```
String sqlAdd = "INSERT INTO Products "
            + " (UPC, Description, Short_Description, "
            + " Product_Type) "
            + "VALUES (?, ?, ?, ?)";
```

237

The final SQL command is used to update existing data. It will also be used to create a prepared statement that can be run for each new product:

```
String sqlUpd = "UPDATE Products "
              + "SET Description = ?, "
              + "Short_Description = ?, "
              + "Product_Type = ? "
              + "WHERE UPC = ?";
```

Using the first SQL command, we create a `Statement` and use it to generate a new resultset (`rs`) containing all new products from the Headquarters database:

```
// Locate new products in HQ database (sent date = null)
Statement stmt = connHQ.createStatement();
ResultSet rs = stmt.executeQuery(sqlRead);
```

We also use the SQL `ADD` and `UPDATE` commands in `PreparedStatement psAdd` and `psUpd`, with the destination connection:

```
// Now create prepared statement to add or update App1 data
PreparedStatement psAdd = connApp1.prepareStatement(sqlAdd);
PreparedStatement psUpd = connApp1.prepareStatement(sqlUpd);
```

Now we can finally set up our `while` loop to read and process the new prices found in the Headquarters database. First we set up some counters (remember, we need to count everything), and then set up our `while` loop, moving through the result set `rs`. As we loop, we count the number of entries read:

```
// Now loop through the data and add/update new products
int nRead   = 0;
int nAdd    = 0;
int nUpdate = 0;

while (rs.next()) {
  nRead++;
```

Here's where things start to get interesting. Using the prepared statement, we load each of the data items retrieved from the new pricing entry into its corresponding parameter in the prepared statement for the SQL `UPDATE` command. Once all the parameters are loaded, we use the `executeUpdate()` method to run the command. If an entry is found and updated in the destination database, the method returns the number of rows affected (hopefully one), but if the entry does not exist, the method returns -1. If this is the case, we know that we need to create a new product entry:

```
// First try to update
psUpd.clearParameters();
psUpd.setString (1, rs.getString("Description"));
psUpd.setString (2, rs.getString("Short_Description"));
psUpd.setString (3, rs.getString("Product_Type"));
psUpd.setString (4, rs.getString("UPC"));
if (psUpd.executeUpdate() <= 0) {
```

238

```
// If update count is zero, need to add new record
psAdd.clearParameters();
psAdd.setString (1, rs.getString("UPC"));
psAdd.setString (2, rs.getString("Description"));
psAdd.setString (3, rs.getString("Short_Description"));
psAdd.setString (4, rs.getString("Product_Type"));
psAdd.executeUpdate();
nAdd++;
}
```

So if we need to add a new product entry, we go through the same steps using the prepared statement for the other SQL command. We also count the number of entries added:

```
else {
nUpdate++;
}
```

If the return from the first `executeUpdate()` method is greater than zero, we count the number of products updated. We then close the loop and either start over, or quit if there are no more products in the resultset `rs`.

Now, before anything else can go wrong, we display the counters. Hopefully the number of products read will match the sum of the products added and updated. If not, we've got a program problem. After everything is done, we close out all of the resources and catch any exceptions:

```
// Now display number of products copies
System.out.println ("Copy complete");
System.out.println ();
System.out.println (" Products read =    " + nRead);
System.out.println (" Products added =   " + nAdd);
System.out.println (" Products updated = " + nUpdate);

// Close the statements and resultsets s
stmt.close();
rs.close();
psAdd.close();
psUpd.close();

// Finally close the connections
connHQ.close();
connApp1.close();

// Catch any errors
catch (Exception e) {
System.out.println ("Exception occurred during copy");
e.printStackTrace();
}
}
```

The main() method checks that a single command-line parameter was entered. If there was no parameter (args.length != 1), a gentle reminder is printed; otherwise, we create a new instance of the App1Products class, passing the parameter name to the constructor, then call the copy() method to start copying the products:

```
public static void main(String args[]) {
   if (args.length != 1) {
      System.out.println ();
      System.out.println ("Usage: java App1Products url");
      System.out.println ();
      System.out.println ("  url is url of regional database");
      return;
   }

   App1Products app = new App1Products (args[0]);
   app.copy();
}
```

If all runs well, the program will send all new products to the App1 database. To compile the program, make sure that all JDBC drivers have been included in your CLASSPATH environment variable, and then compile it with javac (or from within your favorite IDE). Note that if you are using the Microsoft JDBC driver, all three classes must be included in the classpath (why didn't they put all of these into a single .jar file?). We will wait to test and deploy all of the integration programs at the end of this section.

Transferring Prices to App1

The next task is to copy prices to the App1 databases. As we discussed above, most products and prices are maintained at a central location, then periodically sent to each of the regions where they can be routed to each store using their own regional point-of-sale applications. Here we transfer prices to the regions running App1.

When we transfer products to App1, we actually insert new products into the database if they were not on file, or modify them if they already exist. In transferring prices, we will take a slightly different approach. All prices will be inserted as new entries after aging any previous prices for the same product. For example, when a new price of $1.89 is sent on March 15 for a carton of milk, the existing price of $1.79 will be marked as effective through March 14, and then a new price entry of $1.89 will be inserted, effective on March 15.

This may seem like a lot of extra work but by aging this data like this, we more accurately reflect business rules within the database, allowing us to send price changes out in advance and correctly price refunds. We also maintain a historical view of the prices over time for trend analysis and regional decision-making.

Let's examine this in more detail. Here is the Prices entry in the Region 1 database as it appears before the update:

Product	Start Date	End Date	Price	End Date
Milk	01/01/2001	(null)	$1.79	(null)

Before we can insert an entry for the new price, we must first set back the end date of the old price by one day prior to the effective date of the new price:

Product	Start Date	End Date	Price	End Date
Milk	01/01/2001	03/14/2001	$1.79	(null)

Now we can add the new price effective March 15:

Product	Start Date	End Date	Price	End Date
Milk	01/01/2001	03/14/2001	$1.79	
Milk	03/15/2001	(null)	$1.89	(null)

This is repeated for each new price received from the Headquarters database.

The code to implement the transfer (`App1Prices.java`) closely matches that of `App1Products` above so only the critical portions of the code are examined below. Since all of this code is identical to the previous program we will not discuss it in detail. Again we import the packages then declare the class and the instance variable. The constructor then saves the command-line parameter in the instance variable:

```
import java.io.*;
import java.sql.*;

public class App1Prices {
  private String dbName;

  public App1Prices (String nm) {
    dbName = nm;
  }
```

As before, the `copy()` method begins by printing the destination database URL, then it opens up the JDBC connections:

```
public void copy () {
  System.out.println ("Processing " + dbName);
  try {

    // Initialize the data sources and connections
    Class.forName("com.sybase.jdbc2.jdbc.SybDriver").newInstance();
    String hqUrl = "jdbc:sybase:Tds:localhost:2638";
    Connection connHQ = DriverManager.getConnection (hqUrl, "HQ", "hq");

    Class.forName("com.microsoft.jdbc.sqlserver.SQLServerDriver");
    Connection connApp1 = DriverManager.getConnection (dbName);
```

241

The SQL command that follows extracts the new pricing data from the Headquarters database. Again, only entries with `Sent_Date` set to `null` are selected. Also, to ensure that the aging process works correctly, the data is sorted in ascending order by `UPC` and `Start_Date`:

```
// Define SQL commands
String sqlRead = "SELECT UPC, Unit_Price, Start_Date "
          + "FROM Prices "
          + "WHERE Sent_Date IS NULL "
          + "ORDER BY UPC, Start_Date";
```

The next SQL command ages the existing data. Each existing entry found that is not effective at the new start date will have its end date set to one day prior to the new start date. Note that the SQL date function `DATEADD()` is used to subtract one day (by adding –1) from the parameter date:

```
String sqlAge = "UPDATE Prices "
          + "SET End_Date = DATEADD(day, -1, ?) "
          + "WHERE UPC = ? "
          + " AND (End_Date IS NULL "
          + " OR  End_Date > DATEADD(day, -1, ?))";
```

There is one flaw with the aging command that occurs when a future price is already in effect (this could happen if someone runs the update more than once). Suppose an existing price's start date is set to June 1, 2001. If a new price is received that starts on March 16, we will set the existing price's end date to March 15. Now we have a price entry with start date of June 1 and an end date of March 15 so the start date is after the end date – clearly, this doesn't make much sense! To prevent this from happening, we add an SQL delete command to remove these items:

```
String sqlDel = "DELETE FROM Prices "
          + "WHERE UPC = ? "
          + " AND Start_Date > End_Date";
```

Finally, we need a SQL command to insert the new pricing entry:

```
String sqlAdd = "INSERT INTO Prices "
          + " (UPC, Unit_Price, Start_Date, End_Date) "
          + "VALUES (?, ?, ?, NULL)";
```

Now we can run the query that selects the new prices from the database at the headquarters, and create the prepared statements for each of the other SQL commands:

```
// Locate new prices in HQ database (sent date = null)
Statement stmt = connHQ.createStatement();
ResultSet rs = stmt.executeQuery(sqlRead);

// Now create prepared statement to add or update App1 data
PreparedStatement psAge = connApp1.prepareStatement(sqlAge);
PreparedStatement psDel = connApp1.prepareStatement(sqlDel);
PreparedStatement psAdd = connApp1.prepareStatement(sqlAdd);
```

Just as before, we initialize some counters and begin reading the Headquarters data:

```
// Now loop through the data and add/update new products
int n     = 0;
int nRead = 0;
int nAge  = 0;
int nDel  = 0;
int nAdd  = 0;

while (rs.next()) {
  nRead++;
```

Then we start the aging process:

```
// Age any old records
psAge.clearParameters();
psAge.setDate    (1, rs.getDate("Start_Date"));
psAge.setString  (2, rs.getString("UPC"));
psAge.setDate    (3, rs.getDate("Start_Date"));
n = psAge.executeUpdate();
if (n > 0) {
  nAge += n;
}
```

First, we clear and load the parameters for the `PreparedStatement` that ages the existing prices matching the new UPC code, and then check the number of items updated (n) and if this is greater than zero, we add it to the counter. Note that if no entries are found, the `executeUpdate()` method returns -1, which would corrupt our counter. Hence, we only count when the returned value is greater than zero.

Next, we run the DELETE query to remove any future prices as discussed above:

```
// Delete any over-aged records
psDel.clearParameters();
psDel.setString (1, rs.getString("UPC"));
n = psDel.executeUpdate();
if (n > 0) {
  nDel += n;
}
```

Finally, we clear and set the `PreparedStatement` to insert the new pricing record, and then complete the loop:

```
// Finally, add the new entry
psAdd.clearParameters();
psAdd.setString (1, rs.getString("UPC"));
psAdd.setString (2, rs.getString("Unit_Price"));
psAdd.setDate   (3, rs.getDate("Start_Date"));
psAdd.executeUpdate();
nAdd++;
}
```

```
        // Now display number of products copies
        System.out.println ("Copy complete");
        System.out.println ();
        System.out.println ("   Prices read =      " + nRead);
        System.out.println ("   Prices added =     " + nAdd);
        System.out.println ("   Prices aged =      " + nAge);
        System.out.println ("   Prices removed  = " + nDel);

        // Close the statements and recordsets
        stmt.close();
        rs.close();
        psAdd.close();
        psAge.close();
        psDcl.close();

        // Finally close the connections
        connHQ.close();
        connApp1.close();
    }

    // Catch any errors
    catch (Exception e) {
        System.out.println ("Exception occurred during copy");
        e.printStackTrace();
    }
}
```

As with the products program, we complete the copy() method by displaying the counters, closing the JDBC resources, and catching any exceptions.

The main() method also looks like that of the App1Products program:

```
public static void main(String args[]) {
    if (args.length != 1) {
        System.out.println ();
        System.out.println ("Usage:  java App1Prices url");
        System.out.println ();
        System.out.println ("  url is url of regional database");
        return;
    }

    App1Prices app = new App1Prices (args[0]);
    app.copy();
}
```

We will discuss compiling and testing these programs shortly.

Transferring Products and Prices to App2

Now that products and prices have been sent to the in-house application (App1), it is time to move on to the commercial application (App2). As we saw during our analysis, the only access point to this application's data is through simple import and export files. Although the next version will certainly need to support a more comprehensive XML format, we need to get the price transfer working now so we will go ahead and get the flat file transfer programming running.

Products and prices are transferred to App2 through a simple column-oriented disk file. As we will see, Java does not support this data format well, but there are several work-around techniques that we can use to reformat the data as required by the application.

Since our `App2Prices` program uses some different techniques than the others, we should examine the entire program here. The program begins with the same imports as the others and uses the standard class declaration. In addition, we declare an instance variable to hold the name of the new file that will receive the product and pricing data:

```
import java.io.*;
import java.sql.*;

public class App2Prices {
  private String fName;
```

Instead of accepting the destination database URL, this program accepts the destination file name and saves it as an instance variable:

```
public App2Prices (String fn) {
  fName = fn;
}
```

The `copy()` method is declared, then a number of instance variables are defined to hold strings containing each data item that will be written to the file. We also initialize the counter here and print the name of the destination file:

```
public void copy () {
  String upc, desc, prc;
  int nRead = 0;

  System.out.println ("Processing " + fName);
```

Next we open the `try/catch` block and get the JDBC `Connection` object for the Headquarters database:

```
try {

  // Initialize the data source and connection
  Class.forName("com.sybase.jdbc2.jdbc.SybDriver").newInstance();

  String hqUrl = "jdbc:sybase:Tds:localhost:2638";
  Connection connHQ = DriverManager.getConnection (hqUrl, "HQ", "hq");
```

245

In addition to the connection, we also need to create objects to write the destination disk file. A `FileOutputStream` object is created using the file name received from the command line, and then we can use this object to create a `PrintWriter` object. `PrintWriter` allows us to use the `print()` and `println()` methods to write character data with line delimiters as required by the import specs of Application 2:

```
// Initial file
FileOutputStream os = new FileOutputStream (fName);
PrintWriter pr = new PrintWriter (os);
```

Since only one file is used to pass both products and prices, we need to create an SQL command that joins the two tables. Data is joined by matching UPC from each table, and then the appropriate columns are selected and sorted. Note that the query assumes that each product will have an associated price (that is, no outer joins are used), but this should be a valid assumption:

```
// Define SQL commands
String sqlRead = "SELECT Products.UPC, Description, "
               + " Unit_Price * 100 "
               + "FROM Products, Prices "
               + "WHERE Products.UPC = Prices.UPC "
               + " AND (Products.Sent_Date IS NULL "
               + " OR Prices.Sent_Date IS NULL) "
               + "ORDER BY Products.UPC, Start_Date";
```

Also note that the unit price is multiplied by 100 – this converts the amount to cents and allows us to retrieve the data as an integer without any decimal point.

As with the other programs, we create a result set then loop through the data, as shown below:

```
// Locate new prices in HQ database then loop through data
Statement stmt = connHQ.createStatement();
ResultSet rs = stmt.executeQuery(sqlRead);

while (rs.next()) {
  nRead++;
```

Next we reformat the columns to match the requirements (these methods will be discussed in more detail below). Then we write the data to the disk file using the `PrintWriter`'s `println()` method and complete the loop:

```
upc  = sizeString(rs.getString(1), 12);
desc = sizeString(rs.getString(2), 30);
prc  = sizeNumber(rs.getInt(3), 6);

pr.println(upc + desc + prc);
}
```

The rest of the `copy()` method matches the earlier programs. We display the counters, close out the resources (including the `FileOutputStream` and `PrintWriter`), and catch any exceptions:

```
    // Now display number of products copies

    System.out.println ("Copy complete");
    System.out.println ();
    System.out.println ("  Prices copied = " + nRead);

    // Close the statements and resultsets
    stmt.close();
    rs.close();
    pr.close();
    os.close();
    connHQ.close();
  }

  // Catch any errors
  catch (Exception e) {
    System.out.println ("Exception occurred during copy");
    e.printStackTrace();
  }
}
```

One of the difficulties of writing out column-delimited data is to ensure that the items returned by JDBC match the formats required by the data file. Although these are not elegant solutions, they do the job.

In this first method, string data is resized to match a specific column width. The method receives the string and column width, and copies it to a new string. First it checks to see if the string exceeds this width and, if so, it truncates it down to the correct width. If it is shorter than the required width, it uses a `while` loop to pad spaces to the back of the string:

```
  // Format string
  private String sizeString (String s, int n) {
    String sWork = s;
    if (sWork.length() > n) {
      return sWork.substring(1, n);
    }
    while (sWork.length() < n) {
      sWork += " ";
    }
    return sWork;
  }
```

The following method formats numbers into zero-filled strings of a given length. Remember, our SQL command told the database to multiply the number by 100, so that the program retrieves the number as an integer. Once received by this method, it is appended to an empty string to convert it into its string representation. After that, a `while` loop is used to pad leading zeros until it matches the required length. Again, this isn't so elegant, but it does get the job done:

```
    // Format number
    private String sizeNumber (int s, int n) {
      String sWork = "";
      sWork += s;
      while (sWork.length() < n) {
        sWork = "0" + sWork;
      }
      return sWork;
    }
```

Finally, the `main()` method retrieves the file name from the first command-line parameter, creates a new instance of the `App2Prices` object and calls its `copy()` method:

```
    public static void main(String args[]) {
      if (args.length != 1) {
        System.out.println ();
        System.out.println ("Usage:  java App2Prices filename");
        System.out.println ();
        System.out.println ("  filename is destination file name");
        return;
      }

      App2Prices app = new App2Prices (args[0]);
      app.copy();
    }
  }
```

If all runs correctly, a new disk file will be created listing UPCs, product descriptions, and prices. We will see the output when we run all of the code at the end of the chapter.

Marking Products and Prices as Sent

The previous programs determined which products and prices to send, based on the absence of a sent date (set to `null`). But none of the programs had any way to set the sent date once the data was successfully transferred. So our final programming task is to mark the data as sent by setting the sent date to today's date. This program can be placed at the end of the command script after all other programs complete.

This is done by a simple Java program, which runs two SQL commands that set the `Sent_Date` to the current date. Below is the listing of the program `MarkPrices.java` that performs this task:

```
  import java.io.*;
  import java.sql.*;

  public class MarkPrices {

    public static void main(String args[]) {
      System.out.println("Setting sent date");

      try {

        // Initialize the data sources and connections
```

```
      Class.forName("com.sybase.jdbc2.jdbc.SybDriver").newInstance();

      String hqUrl = "jdbc:sybase:Tds:localhost:2638";
      Connection connHQ = DriverManager.getConnection(hqUrl, "HQ", "hq");

      // Define SQL commands
      String sqlProd = "UPDATE Products " + "SET Sent_Date = GETDATE() "
                  + "WHERE Sent_Date IS NULL";

      String sqlPrice = "UPDATE Prices " + "SET Sent_Date = GETDATE() "
                  + "WHERE Sent_Date IS NULL";

      // Run the queries
      Statement stmt = connHQ.createStatement();
      int nProd = stmt.executeUpdate(sqlProd);
      int nPrice = stmt.executeUpdate(sqlPrice);

      // Print the results
      System.out.println("   Products updated = " + nProd);
      System.out.println("   Prices update =    " + nPrice);

      // Close the statements and record sets
      stmt.close();
      connHQ.close();
    }

    // Catch any errors
    catch (Exception e) {
      System.out.println("Exception occurred during copy");
      e.printStackTrace();
    }
  }
}
```

Other than the SQL commands, the program is very similar to all of the others shown in this chapter. The only new features are the update queries, which we repeat here for clarity:

```
      String sqlProd = "UPDATE Products "
                  + "SET Sent_Date = GETDATE() "
                  + "WHERE Sent_Date IS NULL";

      String sqlPrice = "UPDATE Prices "
                  + "SET Sent_Date = GETDATE() "
                  + "WHERE Sent_Date IS NULL";
```

In each case, the SQL commands are simple queries that update the Sent_Date column to the value returned by the SQL function GETDATE() which returns a datetime date type containing the current date and time.

Once these queries are run, the program returns the number of rows updated by each SQL command.

Testing and Deploying the Integration

Now that all of the programs have been presented, it's time to give them a try. Start by compiling each of them with `javac`, or your favorite IDE. Make sure that you include all of your JDBC drivers in your `CLASSPATH` environment variable. If you are using Sybase's jConnect, include `jconn2.jar` in your classpath. Likewise, if you are using the Microsoft SQL Server 2000 JDBC driver, include `mssqlserver.jar`, `msbase.jar`, and `msutil.jar` files. These will also need to be in place before you can run the programs.

To run the programs, launch the `SendPrices.bat` file included with the source code. This batch file is shown below (note that the indented lines should be part of the previous line – here they are too long for the book text – and are shown correctly in the batch file):

```
java App1Products
    jdbc:microsoft:sqlserver://localhost:1433;user=Reg01;password=reg01
java App1Prices
    jdbc:microsoft:sqlserver://localhost:1433;user=Reg01;password=reg01

java App2Prices prices.dat

java MarkPrices
```

Once the programs have run, open the Region 1 database and examine the `Products` and `Prices` tables. In SQL Server, this can be done using the Enterprise Manager; in Sybase you will need to open the Interactive SQL utility and type:`SELECT * FROM Products` to view the Products table, and type:

```
SELECT * FROM Prices
```

to view the `Prices` table. You can also view the Headquarters database `Products` and `Prices` tables to make sure that the `Sent_Date` has indeed been set.

In a production environment, the first two lines would be repeated once for each region running the in-house application and the `App2Prices` program would be run once for each region running the commercial application, with a URL directing the file to each region's server.

Room for Improvement

In this example, we tried to stick to the basics with the emphasis on demonstrating techniques for moving data and managing redundancy. We made quite a few tradeoffs to enhance understanding and readability. In the following subsections we'll now take a brief look at some potential enhancements that could be made to improve this example:

❏   Enhanced exception handling

❏   Administration

❏   Directory services

❏   Transferring sales data

Enhanced Exception Handling

In each of the examples, we simply caught and reported exceptions as they occurred. This is fine for our simple examples, since we are working with a small set of sample data that we know works correctly with the examples. But if this were deployed in a production environment, we would want to check the data to ensure that it conforms to business rules, catch errors related to network and JDBC connections, report them in a more readable manner, and throw them to the calling program so the execution could be halted.

Administration

The batch file shown previously is fine for testing the programs, but could present a couple of serious problems if it were put into production:

❏ Including database passwords directly in the URLs offers a major security breach. Since the programs need write-access to move products and prices into the database, the passwords published would allow anyone with write access to corrupt the database.

❏ If network errors occur, there is no mechanism to stop processing. The final program will mark the data as sent and those regions that did not copy successfully would never see the new data.

Clearly, both of these issues need to be addressed before a production-level application is produced. A good solution would be to include the URLs within the `Regions` table of the Headquarters database, along with which application that is running in each region. We could then create a simple administration program that would read each `Region` record and then instantiate the appropriate class and call its copy method to send the data. With a simple change to the class to throw exceptions back to the calling program, the program could detect errors and prevent the prices from being marked if any errors were to occur.

Directory Services

Another solution to the security issues caused by embedding the passwords in the batch file would be to store JDBC (version 2.0) `DataSource` objects within a JNDI compliant directory service. Once this is done, each program could retrieve these objects by name and then get the connection from the DataSource object.

Although this does simplify and streamline the programming, it does open up a few additional problems. First, all JDBC drivers must be compliant with version 2.0. This can be a problem on some database platforms and may require some additional expense to purchase third-party drivers. It also does not completely resolve the security issue since the passwords will most likely be embedded in the `DataSource` object. Once a programmer knows the JNDI name, they have programmatic access to the database. Finally, JNDI adds an additional level of complexity and administration to the integration process, so unless JNDI is already implemented, there is little reason to complicate the integration.

Transferring Sales Data

So far, we have only implemented the products and prices transfers. We still need to get the sales transfers running. In the next chapter we will implement the App2 sales transfer process, but implementing App1 sales transfers is your job (call it an extra-credit project). The transfer works almost identically to the transfers above, just move the data from Region 1 to the Headquarters database. The data transfers are spelled out in the data-mapping table. Here are a few pointers:

❑   Accept the database URL from a command-line parameter as we did for `App1Products` and `App1Prices`

❑   Since we need to know which region the data is coming from, accept the region code from a second command-line parameter

❑   Create the Headquarters transaction ID by concatenating the two-digit region code with the App1 transaction ID

❑   Remember to copy the region code into the Headquarters' `Sales` table

Security and Performance Considerations

Although these issues have been mentioned throughout the chapter, there are a number of security and performance issues that are unique to data integration. In this final section, we will revisit some of these issues and consider their implications to integration design and implementation.

Security

Data integration is probably the least secure of all the integration solutions. To make data interchange possible, the data sources must be opened to other applications, and often to the outside world. If not implemented correctly, the data sources may also be open to undesirable characters. Here are a few techniques that may make our data integration process a little more secure:

❑   **Keep sensitive data out of data integration solutions**
Personal or company confidential data should not be transferred using data integration techniques.

❑   **Split databases**
When sensitive data resides in the same database as the one that holds shared data, we should create new databases to hold the sensitive data. This will put it out of the reach of anyone who may use the integration programs to gain unauthorized access.

❑   **Use DBMS access control features**
Judicious use of access controls by user and password can limit the vulnerability of the data. Create new user accounts and passwords for the data integration programs, restricting read and write access to those tables that need to be read or written by the integration programs.

❑   **Avoid public networks**
If possible, do not allow data access over public networks such as Internet or dial-up lines. When networks are connected to the Internet, use firewalls to isolate private data.

❏ **Use VPN technology**
The next best thing to isolating the data is to use Virtual Private Network (VPN) technology to encrypt the data and limit access to other authorized VPN users.

❏ **Use encryption**
If data must be exposed on public networks, use secure Internet technologies such as SSL or secure FTP. For file transfers, encrypt data using PGP or password-protected zip files.

❏ **Hide passwords**
As we've mentioned, one of the flaws of the implementation shown above is that the user IDs and passwords are included in the command lines. Using JDBC 2.0 `DataSource` objects is a little better, but also opens up programmatic access to anyone who can obtain the directory name of the data source. As we described above, these could be stored in a database table that could drive an administration program.

❏ **Log all data access**
Generate log files listing who has sent or requested data. Although it does not directly protect the data, it gives you the opportunity to see who is using it and enforces accountability.

Performance

The other issue that we will revisit is performance. Data integration can require the movement and synchronization of large quantities of data. Choosing the right strategy can make or break the project and often solutions that work when they are first implemented, soon sag under the weight of new business. Here are some issues to consider that will optimize performance:

❏ **Limit data movement**
The more data that has to be sent, the longer the processes will run. Only move data items that are needed for the other application and limit the data to only the entries needed at the remote site.

❏ **Anticipate future growth**
Business applications always seem to grow, either through normal growth, new lines of business, or through acquisitions. Remember that the initial volume of data will almost always be a small fraction of its future capacity, so anticipate growth and build in extra capacity.

❏ **Monitor replication**
In the same way, replication may work well in the beginning, but as data volumes grow, transfer times may suddenly increase. Unanticipated data collisions may also begin to occur with increasing frequency as new business functions are implemented. Monitor replication times frequently and start developing alternative solutions if times start to lag.

❏ **Limit transformations**
Any processing that must be done during data migration will impact the transfer time, so try to limit this kind of processing. When possible, force the client programs to use the data in its current form, or transform the data only when it is accessed.

❑ **Use separate servers**
   Several years ago, one of my clients came up with a novel approach for running batch processing. He had an Electronic Document Interchange (EDI) process that was eating up server time, so he went to the storeroom and grabbed an old computer, added some memory, loaded up SQL Server, and moved the batch process onto this old machine. Even though the process ran about four times slower, it wasn't tying up the production server and there was no longer any pressure to get it running faster. He segregated the production server database so the transferred data was in a separate database. Then, once the process was done, he simply restored the new data onto the production server.

❑ **Choose security options wisely**
   Security is always a trade-off with performance, so choose solutions that support business needs but do not adversely affect performance.

Summary

In this chapter we have examined data integration and how to develop an integrated data model. We also looked at a sample data integration project and implemented the first part of the application.

Some of the things to remember when approaching data integration include:

❑ Make sure that data integration is the appropriate solution. It should only be used when a limited amount of data must be accessed and when data can be managed in a controlled manner.

❑ Start by identifying and locating the relevant data, then learn everything you can about it. Understand its structure, contents, data volumes, business rules, sources, and destinations.

❑ Develop an integrated data model that maps the location and content of all of the data structures.

❑ Use the techniques described in this chapter to bridge different data platforms and models. Determine relationships between data structures and add them to your integration model.

❑ The data integration model must also manage redundancy throughout the enterprise. Ensure that duplicated data remains synchronized and that discrepancies cannot occur.

❑ Build an integration plan, based on the data model, that specifies all of the tasks needed to create the relationships.

In the next chapter we will continue to examine data integration, turning our attention to using XML. We will see how XML can simplify data integration and how it can be used to expand our grocery chain example.

6

Using XML for Data Exchange

Although XML is usually thought of in the context of an Internet technology or document presentation, it is also an excellent medium for data exchange. With its ability to store structured, self-describing data in a platform-independent way, it makes sense that the industry has embraced XML technology for electronic data interchange. This chapter will examine how XML can simplify data exchange both within an organization and between organizations.

In this chapter, we will explore the following XML issues and technologies as they apply to data exchange:

❑   Why should we use XML for data exchange?

❑   How to transfer data using XML

❑   Standardizing data exchange using DTDs and XML schemas

❑   Java support for XML

❑   Using SAX and DOM to read XML

❑   Using standard file I/O to write XML

Let's start off by looking more closely at why XML is a great format for data exchange.

Why Choose XML for Data Exchange?

Traditional data exchange required programmers to either develop their own proprietary data formats or conform to complex industry standards. These formats were often tightly bound to specific programming languages (COBOL or RPG) and were difficult to read without some low-level programming tricks. Writing data to these exchange formats was a very detailed, precise task and the only way to verify that they were generated correctly, was to send them to the vendor or customer. After waiting several days, they would send back a cryptic computer-generated edit report stating that one or two fields were out of place by a single character or that the control totals were calculated incorrectly. This would have to be repeated many times over several weeks until everything was perfect.

Applying the **Extensible Markup Language** (**XML**) to data exchange eliminates much of this frustration. XML is platform independent, requiring nothing more than standard text, so it can be read or written by almost any programming language. With its use of start and end tags, there is no need to precisely place data items in specific locations, and its self-describing nature eliminates the need to wade through complex specifications. Also, with the addition of Document Type Definitions (DTDs) and XML Schemas, general purpose parsing programs can be used to validate and locate inconsistencies before they are sent to the customer or vendor.

But XML does not solve every data exchange problem. Data format standards, including tag names and data hierarchies, must still be negotiated between sender and receiver, and programs must still be written to move XML data streams to and from corporate databases (although most relational database vendors are starting to provide XML translation facilities). Nevertheless, XML does make data exchange much easier.

Transferring Data Between Databases

Data integration using XML works in the same manner as we described in the last chapter. The only difference is that data is encapsulated into an XML structure before it is sent to the destination machine. But XML offers us some additional benefits over traditional file transfers. Since XML data is coded in a structured manner, it can be easily processed, reformatted, segmented by vendor, then routed to the appropriate destination. Traditional data transfers may have required several complex programs, each selecting a small subset of data for a single vendor or customer, formatted to their specific needs. If we use XML, a single program can select and write the data for all customers, and small programs can be written to select and reformat the data according to each business partner's needs.

In this section, we will examine how XML can assist in data integration. The issues we will discuss include:

❑   XML data exchange architectures

❑   Defining a common vocabulary for communication

❑   Transferring data

Let's begin by examining the architectures used for XML-enabled data exchange.

XML Data Exchange Architectures

XML data exchange can be as simple as extracting data from one database then loading it into another, or it can involve multiple customers and vendors exchanging data over the Internet through third-party EDI (Electronic Data Interchange) vendors. Here we will look at two typical data exchange architectures. The first will be an internal process, sending data from one database into a number of others (a process we will examine in more depth later via the grocery chain example we developed in the previous chapter). Then we will examine an electronic commerce architecture based on the model proposed by the XML/EDI Group.

Internal Data Exchange Architecture

The first example illustrates architecture for data exchange within a single organization. Suppose our grocery chain wants to distribute employee data to each region. Using XML, we can generate a single file containing all employee information. Next, we can write a number of small XSLT scripts which segregate the data by region and restructure it to match each region's human resource applications (since they are running different point-of-sales systems, they are probably running different HR programs as well).

> **XSLT, the Extensible Stylesheet Language for Transformations, is a scripting language used for reformatting and transforming XML data files. It will be discussed in greater depth in the next chapter.**

Once we've created these files, we can send them via FTP to each region so they can load them into their HR applications. The diagram below illustrates this process:

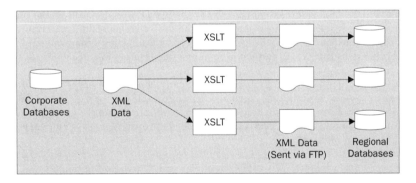

As can be seen in the diagram, the process is not much different than any other traditional data exchange. The only difference is that data is written into XML instead of another format. All data is written to a single XML file, then is programmatically split and reformatted using XSLT scripts. These files are then sent via FTP to the regional offices where they are loaded into local databases.

Electronic Commerce Exchange Architecture

Business-to-Business (B2B) electronic commerce often spans multiple customers and vendors, exchanging business documents such as purchase orders, invoices, payment transfers and other documents. In an effort to streamline this process, the XML/EDI Group (http://www.xmledigroup.org) has proposed an integrated architecture to support business partners and EDI organizations. Although still a work in progress, it offers an interesting example of how to create a large-scale XML data exchange architecture and allows us to see the potential that XML offers. This architecture is illustrated in the figure below:

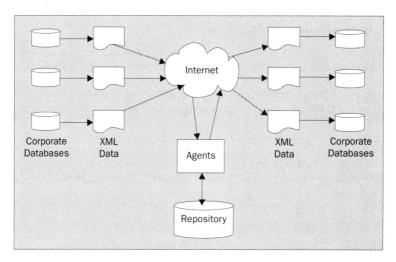

As an example, suppose that your company needs to order new raw materials from the production system. The production manager selects the items that need to be ordered, chooses the preferred vendor for each product, and then places the order. At the end of the day, the production system gathers all of these order documents, formats them into XML, and sends them over the Internet to an EDI service company.

Once the orders are received by the EDI service company, a purchase order agent program sorts these documents by vendor, and then reformats them into each vendor's preferred data format. They are then either sent directly to the vendor, or stored in a repository until the vendor requests them. When the vendor receives the data, they import it into their order entry system where it is processed and the raw material is shipped.

Although this is a very brief overview of the architecture, it is easy to see the potential that XML offers. In this system, customers don't have to concern themselves with managing data transfers to multiple vendors: all activities can be written to one common data stream. As agent technology improves, customers may develop their own agents to perform price comparisons and reroute orders to different vendors depending on price and availability. At the same time, vendors can route orders to regional warehouses to minimize shipping costs and optimize order turnaround.

Every XML data exchange will require its own architecture, depending on business requirements and the complexity of the problem. You should approach the analysis and design using the same processes that were discussed in the last chapter for data integration.

Defining the Vocabulary

Before data can be exchanged between two organizations (or applications), a common vocabulary must exist to allow them to communicate. If one application calls an item a `Product` and the other is expecting a `Product_Number`, neither will understand the other's messages. Just as with other data exchange formats, the organizations must first agree on a common language. This still involves some negotiation between the two organizations, but XML does eliminate many possible points of contention such as file structures, field widths, numeric representations and other platform-specific standards. The only issues that must be agreed on when using XML are data item names (tag names) and logical structure.

To facilitate communication of these issues, the XML standards group (http://www.w3.org/XML) has proposed standards for describing XML data formats. For simple declarations of structures and relations, the Document Type Definition (DTD) is often sufficient. When more extensive definitions are needed, including data types, complex relationships, key values and other specifics, the XML Schema definition may be a better choice. Both of these declarative languages simplify communication of XML standards and, with the use of validating parsers, allow developers to verify data formats and speed EDI development.

In many cases, organizations no longer need to design and negotiate common definitions for XML data exchange because industry standards already exist. Go to http://www.xml.org/xml and click on the XML in Industry button for a list of standards for more than sixty different industries. These are developed by panels of subject domain experts and reflect years of experience in electronic data interchange. Although the standards may be broader than necessary, they can often be used as a starting point for a comprehensive XML data exchange format.

Java Support for XML

Given the fact that XML was intended to be platform independent, it seems logical that a platform-independent language like Java would be the best choice for XML development (my bias may be showing, but it makes sense to me). Fortunately, this is true – the Java language provides strong support for XML, offering a number of APIs and technologies to support XML development. Those relevant to data exchange include:

- ❏ JAXP – Java API for XML Processing
- ❏ TrAX – Transformation API for XML
- ❏ JDOM – Java Data Object Model
- ❏ JAXB – Java Architecture for XML Binding
- ❏ Java XML parsers

Let's take a closer look at each of these.

JAXP

As a wrapper for many of the XML API's, the **Java API for XML Processing (JAXP)** (previously known as the Java API for XML Parsing) offers the highest level interfaces. JAXP-compliant parsers are available from many different sources (these will be listed at the end of this section), and each supports SAX, DOM and an XSLT API such as TrAX.

SAX

SAX, the **Simple API for XML**, is an event-driven parser interface. SAX allows a programmer to read an XML data stream, then break it apart into its individual elements. Versions of this API are available for C, C++, Visual BASIC, PERL and other languages in addition to Java (for more information, see http://www.megginson.com/SAX/). The programming model is based on **events**, a model familiar to those who write user interface screens. Each event (start element tag, end element tag, character or other event) can be bound to a program function or method that is called when the event occurs. It is up to the programmer to interpret these events in a way that processes the data stream. While SAX can be a little more difficult to program than the DOM model we will discuss in a moment, it works well when large volumes of data must be processed and the data stream has consistent structure. We will see how to import data using SAX programming later in this chapter.

DOM

The Document Object Model (DOM) is a somewhat more programmer-friendly API that represents the XML data stream as a tree structure. DOM, like SAX, is available for many different programming languages (see http://www.w3.org/DOM/ for more details). The DOM parser loads the entire data stream into a tree that can easily be navigated in an object-oriented manner. The top node of the data structure represents the root element. This node contains lists representing its elements and attributes. Each item in a list can reference another node object (also containing element and attribute lists) or a text string. DOM also offers API methods to add, modify or delete objects within this structure and write the new document to disk. DOM is somewhat easier to program than SAX, but becomes difficult to use when large data volumes need to be processed, since the entire data stream must be loaded into memory. An example of DOM programming will be included later in this chapter.

TrAX

TrAX, the **Transformation API for XML,** is a standard API for processing XSLT scripts. We will be covering this in detail in the next chapter.

JDOM

JDOM extends the standard document object model to use Java objects. DOM translates everything into text strings, forcing developers to translate the data into appropriate data formats; using XML Schemas, JDOM translates the elements directly into its associated Java objects. JDOM is still an early access technology, so we will not be covering it in detail in this chapter. Also, since most data exchange processes move data directly from XML into relational databases, the DBMS can manage the data type transformations from text string to native objects.

JAXB

One final Java XML technology is the **Java Architecture for Data Binding (JAXB)**. Its approach is somewhat like JDO (Java Data Objects), allowing Java objects to store and retrieve persistent attributes directly into an XML data stream. At the time of writing, this is still early access technology so no examples are offered in this chapter. But the technology is promising, and will greatly streamline development for programs that must go beyond simply copying XML data into databases. By automatically creating Java classes that represent XML nodes, there will be no need to traverse DOM trees or write SAX parsers, instead the data will automatically be bound to data objects, just like relational data can now be bound to EJB entity beans.

Java XML Parsers

Both open source and commercial parsers are available that support some, or all, of these APIs. Below is a list of vendors and products:

Vendor	Product	Open Source	URL
Apache	Xerces	Yes	http://xml.apache.org/xerces-j/index.html
JDOM.org	JDOM Beta	Yes	http://www.jdom.org/downloads/index.html
Oracle	XML Developers kit for Java	No	http://otn.oracle.com/software/content.html
Sun	JAXP Reference Implementation	Yes	http://java.sun.com/xml/download.html

In addition to these packages, many of the application server vendors include an XML parser (often a version of Xerces) within their products. Check your application server documentation for more information.

XML at the Grocery Chain

It's time to get back to our grocery chain integration project, and make it XML-enabled. In the last chapter we began to write code to consolidate the data from the regions using the in-house application (App1) into a centralized database. In this chapter, we will continue to consolidate data and begin to look at the data warehouse.

As with most projects, things change along the way and, as developers, we need to be able to react and adapt to these changes. In the last chapter, we noted that the export files from the commercial application (App2) were very minimal. Fortunately, we were not the only ones who had difficulty with this format. In the latest release, the vendor has added XML support for both their Point-of-Sales and purchasing systems (how convenient). As good, flexible developers, we will change our implementation plan to exploit this feature for the following tasks:

1. Import sales data from the commercial application into our consolidated database.

2. Export data from our consolidated database into a form that can be used for data warehouse and purchasing systems.

3. Import data from the consolidated database into the data warehouse.

Our New App2 XML-Based Data Model

Based on the vendor's documentation and the sample files obtained from the upgrade team, we can begin to repeat the mapping exercise that we did in the last chapter. We will begin by examining the general structure of the data, then walk through the Document Type Definition and Schema provided by the vendor. Once this data has been collected and understood, we can create a new data mapping.

263

A Sample XML Data File

Since XML offers both data and structure in a single file, much of it can be understood by just looking at the data. Below is a short, condensed version of a sample file (you can find this file in the source code download under `Sales01.xml`):

```
<?xml version="1.0"?>
<!DOCTYPE Sales SYSTEM "Sales01.dtd">

<Sales>
  <Store>
    <Store_ID>01</Store_ID>
    <Sale>
      <Register>01</Register>
      <Receipt>10005</Receipt>
      <Date>09/01/2001</Date>
      <Time>09:00:00.0</Time>
      <Item>
        <UPC>051000000115</UPC>
        <Quantity>5</Quantity>
        <Price>1.29</Price>
      </Item>
    </Sale>
  </Store>
</Sales>
```

Given this sample, we can see that the structure consists of a number of nested objects. We can show this graphically using the figure below:

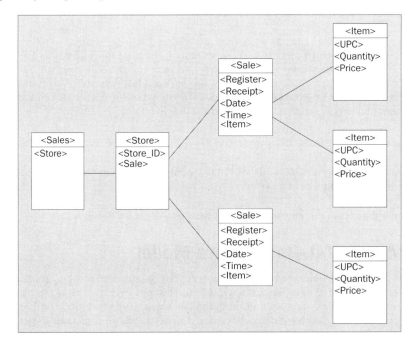

In this structure, the root element <Sales> contains any number of <Store> elements, each containing one or more <Sale> elements, which in turn contain any number of <Item> elements. Since XML is represented in hierarchical form, there is no need to store key values in lower-level data structures. Since all elements within the <Store> element for store 01 are logically associated with this store, there is no reason to repeat the <Store_ID> element in any lower-level elements.

The XML Data File DTD

In addition to the sample file, the commercial system vendor also provided the following DTD in their documentation. Since the file is available, and we will reference it in our sample program, the file Sales.dtd is listed below:

```
<!ELEMENT Sales (Store+)>

<!ELEMENT Store (Store_ID, Store_Name?, Sale+)>
<!ELEMENT Store_ID (#PCDATA)>
<!ELEMENT Store_Name (#PCDATA)>

<!ELEMENT Sale (Register, Receipt, Date, Time, Item+)>
<!ELEMENT Register (#PCDATA)>
<!ELEMENT Receipt (#PCDATA)>
<!ELEMENT Date (#PCDATA)>
<!ELEMENT Time (#PCDATA)>

<!ELEMENT Item (UPC, Quantity, Price)>
<!ELEMENT UPC (#PCDATA)>
<!ELEMENT Quantity (#PCDATA)>
<!ELEMENT Price (#PCDATA)>
```

New Data Mappings

With our new understanding of the App2 Sales XML data structure, we can now determine how to map the data between this new data source and the Headquarters database. Here is the new mapping:

Item	App2 Sales XML	Headquarters Database
	Sales/Stores element	**Sales Table**
1	Programmatically generated sequence	Transaction_ID
2	Receive from program	Region_ID
3	Store_ID	Store_ID
4	Store_Name	Not used
	Sales/Stores/Sale element	
5	Register	Register_Number
6	Receipt	Receipt_Number
7	Date	Sale_Date

Table continued on following page

Item	App2 Sales XML	Headquarters Database
8	Time	Sale_Time
	Sales/Stores/Sale/Item element	**Sales_Detail Table**
10	Copy from Sales	Transaction_ID
11	Programmatic counter	Sequence
12	UPC	UPC
13	Quantity	Quantity
14	Price	Unit_Price

The mapping closely matches those we saw in the last chapter. Since the source data is arranged in the XML file in a hierarchical manner, we can use standard path notation. The root path is `Sales`, followed by the `Store` element (`Sales/Store`), to `Sale` and `Item` (`Sales/Store/Sale/Item`). Data elements within each node are listed below the path names. These paths have been marked as bold. On the destination side, we marked the two table names as bold also. Under each path or table name, we list individual elements from source to destination. Numbered items are the data elements that must be moved.

Importing App2 Data Using XML

Now that we have a better understanding of the new XML data structure from the commercial application (App2), we can begin to load the data into the Headquarters database. As you may remember from the last chapter, we are consolidating regional data into a centralized database. In the last chapter we centralized pricing, sending product and pricing data from the central database to each of the regional offices. We also discussed how to transfer cash register sales data from the in-house application running at some of the regions into the Headquarters database. Now, in this example we will consolidate cash register sales information from the commercial system into the Headquarters database.

Using the mapping information shown above, we can now develop a Java XML program to load this data. In this first example, we will use the Document Object Model (DOM) programming interface of Apache's Xerces Java parser. Since DOM parses the entire data stream into memory objects, it is not always appropriate for data integration. But in this case, the size of the data files will be small enough to allow us to examine how it can be used to load data.

> On a personal note, between SAX and DOM, my preference is DOM: it is a much richer API, giving detailed information about the data structures, including many different node types, easy access to parameter data and comments and the ability to modify structures in memory and rewrite them to disk.

However, towards the end of this chapter, we will use SAX in a data integration example, because it is much better than DOM at handling large volumes of data.

Setting Up the Development Environment

The Xerces parser can be downloaded from Apache's web site at (http://xml.apache.org/xerces-j/index.html). Download the package, and then follow the installation instructions provided in the package. Once extracted, copy the file `xerces.jar` into the folder where you keep your third party class packages (I keep mine in `java\lib`). Then add it to your classpath and you should be ready to run.

In addition to the Xerces package, you will also need the Headquarters database that was described in the previous chapter. The schema and data files can be found with the source code for that chapter; for more information about getting these databases up and running, refer back to Chapter 5.

A Little More Background on DOM

Since we will be using DOM for our first program example, we need a little more background before we start. The DOM is a complex data structure, relying on many different classes and subclasses. It can get very confusing. Fortunately, most applications only need a small subset of these classes, so in this section we will only survey the classes and terminology that we will need to implement our first example. Let's look at the classes used within the tree structure:

Class	Description
Document	The top-level node, containing a reference pointing to the root element.
Node	A node is a point on the tree. Each node contains a NodeName representing the name of an element or property, and at least one NodeList holding references to other nodes.
NodeName	A String object containing the name of the Node.
NodeList	This structure is a container object that can hold references to other Nodes. It can be accessed either as a linked list or as an indexed array.
Element	A subclass of Node, containing the NodeName and at least one NodeList pointing to its child nodes.
Text	Another subclass of Node that holds the text data found within the lowest level element tags.

Since the Java DOM API may be unfamiliar to some readers, we will now walk through the first few nodes of our sample XML structure. Once the XML file has been parsed by Xerces, we will encounter the objects shown in the following diagram:

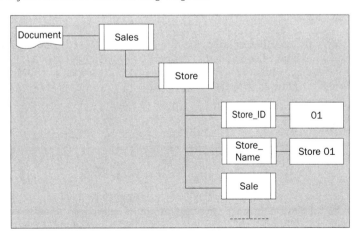

Now let's walk through the diagram one step at a time.

1. At the top of the tree is the `Document` node pointing to the root element `Sales`.

2. The root element `Sales` contains a single node `Store`.

3. The `Store` element contains a `NodeList` (represented by the vertical box) pointing to the elements `Store_ID`, `Store_Name` and `Item`.

4. Since the `Store_ID` element has no child elements, its `NodeList` points to a single item containing a text object. This text object contains a string accessible using the `getData()` method that contains the text found in the file between the start and end tags. This is where we find our data.

5. The same occurs for the `Store_Name` element. Its data can be found in a text object referenced in its `NodeList`. Within this text object, we will find a text string holding the name of the store.

6. Also referenced in the `Store` element's `NodeList` is an object representing the `Sale` node. We can navigate to all of the elements within this node using the same process described above. The `Sale` node will contain a `NodeList` pointing to other nodes containing either text objects or other `NodeLists`.

This process continues recursively through the entire tree. Each node is retrieved from the object's `NodeList`, and then the child element's `NodeList` is traversed to find additional nodes. Note that to safely traverse the tree, we need to either be intimately familiar with the tree structure or inspect node property indicators to interrogate node types (elements, text or other node types). In this example, we will rely on our knowledge of the data structures involved.

Implementing the App2Sales Program

Now we can finally start looking at the code that loads the XML data into the Headquarters database. Using the naming convention from the last chapter, we will call this program `App2Sales`. Since much of the code is the same as that found in the last chapter, we will not spend a lot of time discussing the JDBC portions of the program.

The program begins with a number of imports and most of these are the same as those from the last chapter. Two new imports have been added to support DOM. The first (`java.xml.parsers.*`) provides the JAXP package, while the second (`org.w3c.dom.*`) loads the DOM package. Once all of the imports are listed, the class `App2Sales` is declared:

```
import java.io.*;
import java.sql.*;
import javax.xml.parsers.*;
import org.w3c.dom.*;

public class App2Sales {
```

Next come a number of private instance variables. All but the last are the same as those found in the last chapter to support JNDI and JDBC. The last, `salesDoc`, is the DOM Document object that points to the tree structure:

```
private String            fName, region;
private Connection        connHQ;
private PreparedStatement psSales, psDetail;
private long              nextID;
private int               nSales, nDetail;
private Document          salesDoc;
```

The constructor is much the same as we saw in the last chapter. We save the XML data file name and the region that it came from; these are retrieved from the main() method's parameter list:

```
public App2Sales (String fn, String rg) {
  fName = fn;
  region = rg;
}
```

Next come the copy() method which copies the data:

```
public void copy () {
  System.out.println ("Processing " + fName + " for region " + region);

  initJDBC();
  initXML();

  getFirstID();
  processXML();
  printResults();

  closeJDBC();
}
```

Due to the size of the code, to make it more readable we have split the copy() method up into a number of called methods.

initJDBC()

The first method called by copy() initializes the database connection and sets up the JDBC resources. We begin by obtaining a connection to the Headquarters database:

```
private void initJDBC() {
  try {
    Class.forName("com.sybase.jdbc2.jdbc.SybDriver").newInstance();
    String hqUrl = "jdbc:sybase:Tds:localhost:2638";
    connHQ = DriverManager.getConnection (hqUrl, "HQ", "hq");
```

Next we define SQL commands, and create two PreparedStatements to load data into the Sales and Sales_Detail tables:

```
String sqlSales = "INSERT INTO Sales "
                + " (Transaction_ID, Region_ID, Store_ID, "
                + " Receipt_Number, Register_Number, "
                + " Sale_Date, Sale_Time) "
```

```
                             + "VALUES (?, '" + region +   "', ?, ?, ?, ?, ?)";

          String sqlDetail = "INSERT INTO Sales_Detail "
                           + " (Transaction_ID, Sequence, UPC, "
                           +   " Quantity, Unit_Price) "
                           + "VALUES (?, ?, ?, ?, ?)";

          psSales  = connHQ.prepareStatement (sqlSales);
          psDetail = connHQ.prepareStatement (sqlDetail);
```

We finish the method, as usual, by catching any exceptions that may have occurred:

```
        } catch (Exception e) {
          System.out.println ("Error initializing JDBC connection");
          e.printStackTrace();
        }
      }
```

initXML()

In this method, we parse the XML file and retrieve a `Document` object pointing to the DOM data structures:

```
      private void initXML() {
        try {
          DocumentBuilderFactory docBldrFac
                            = DocumentBuilderFactory.newInstance();
          DocumentBuilder docBldr = docBldrFac.newDocumentBuilder();
          salesDoc = docBldr.parse (fName);
        } catch (Exception e) {
          System.out.println ("Error initializing XML structures");
          e.printStackTrace();
        }
      }
```

Using JAXP, we create a `DocumentBuilderFactory` from the static `DocumentBuilder` object. This is then used to retrieve the default `DocumentBuilder` provided by Xerces. This `DocumentBuilder` provides the functionality to parse the XML document into the DOM tree structure by calling its `parse()` method, passing it the file name of the XML data stream (fname). Once the document is parsed, a new `Document` object is returned into our class instance variable `salesDoc`.

getFirstID()

Next we have the interesting task of programmatically generating `Transaction_ID`'s. The XML file does not provide a transaction ID field so we have to create our own. As stated in the notes of our data mapping, this ID will be created by appending the region code with a sequential number. This offers a unique identifier that is easy to generate and allows us to sort data by region. Although this may not be the most efficient process, it only has to be executed once to get the first ID number. After that, we simply add one to the ID number.

Note that this could be a problem if we try to load two XML files for the same region concurrently, but since data is submitted by each region periodically, the chances of this occurring should be rare.

```
      private void getFirstID() {
        try {
          String sqlFind = "SELECT MAX(Transaction_ID) "
                         + "FROM Sales "
                         + "WHERE Transaction_ID LIKE '"
                         +  region + "%'";
```

As you can see, in the first few lines, we build a SQL command to try to locate the last sequence number on file. The LIKE operator uses a pattern containing the region number and percent sign ('02%' if region were 02) to find all Transaction_ID's that start with the same two digits as the region number. Within the SELECT clause, we use the MAX operator to locate the largest number on file.

Next, we execute the SQL command. If nothing was found, we create our own first transaction number by shifting the region number 8 digits, then adding the number 1 (remember we are using a Long data type, not a String so we have to do this mathematically). If we do find a number, we increment it by one and we're set to go:

```
          Statement stmt = connHQ.createStatement();
          ResultSet rs = stmt.executeQuery(sqlFind);
          if (rs.next()) {
            nextID = rs.getLong(1);
          } else {
            nextID = Integer.parseInt(region) * 100000000;
          }
```

As most implementations of SQL return 0 instead of "not found" when a MAX operator is used, we have to repeat the "not found" logic if the command returns 0:

```
          if (nextID == (long)0) {
            nextID = Integer.parseInt(region) * 100000000 + 1;
          } else {
            nextID++;
          }
```

Once we've got the new ID number, we print it to the screen. We also catch any exceptions if they occur:

```
          System.out.println ("First ID Number is " + formatID(nextID));

          rs.close();
          stmt.close();
        } catch (Exception e) {
          System.out.println ("Error locating next ID number");
          System.out.println (e);
          e.printStackTrace();
        }
      }
```

processXML()

In this method, we start processing the DOM data structure. We begin by locating the first node from the Document object retrieved in the initXML() method, then walk through the tree structure, extracting data and writing it to the database.

We begin by retrieving the root element using the document's `getDocumentElement()` method:

```
private void processXML() {
  try {
    Element root = salesDoc.getDocumentElement();
```

The root element's `getElementsByTagName()` method allows us to retrieve all of the `Store` elements from the data structure and put them into a `NodeList storeNodes`. We then loop through the `NodeList`, casting each `Node` into an `Element` which is passed to the `processStore()` method:

```
    NodeList storeNodes = root.getElementsByTagName("Store");
    for (int i = 0; i < storeNodes.getLength(); i++) {
      processStore ((Element)storeNodes.item(i));
    }
```

Again, we close the method by catching any exceptions:

```
  } catch (Exception e) {
    System.out.println ("Error processing XML data");
    e.printStackTrace();
  }
}
```

The `processStore()` method receives each `Store` element and parses out the `Store_ID` as well as all of the `Sale` elements for the `Store`. We start by setting up a number of local variables including a generic node object, a string to receive the `nodeName` and the current `Store_ID`:

```
void processStore (Element store) {
  Node    node;
  String nodeName;
  String currentStore = "??";
```

In this method, we get all of the child nodes, then loop through them, processing the nodes that are of interest to us. We create a `NodeList` object (`storeItems`) using the `Store` element's `getChildNodes()` method. We then loop through each node using the `NodeList`'s `getLength()` method to determine the number of nodes. For each node, we first retrieve its `nodeName` using the node's `getNodeName()` method, then depending on the name, we decide if we need to do anything with it:

```
  try {
    NodeList storeItems = store.getChildNodes();
    for (int i = 0; i < storeItems.getLength(); i++) {
      node = storeItems.item(i);
      nodeName = node.getNodeName();
```

If the node name is `Store_ID`, we know that the node contains a text node object containing the ID number of the store. We use the local method `getText()` (we will examine this below) to extract the store ID from the node and save it for later use:

```
        if (nodeName.equals("Store_ID")) {
          currentStore = getText(node);
          System.out.println ("Store ID = " + currentStore);
        }
```

If the node name is `Sale`, we know that the node contains a `Sale` element, so we pass it along with the store ID we retrieved above to the `processSale()` method (that we will define in a moment), again casting the node into an `Element` object. After checking the names that we are interested in, we close out the `for` loop with a closing brace.

Note that we are assuming here that the `Store_ID` node will always precede the `Sale` nodes. This is a valid assumption since we know the structure of the XML file:

```
        if (nodeName.equals("Sale")) {
          processSale(currentStore, (Element)node);
        }
      }
    }
```

At the end of the method, we again catch any exceptions:

```
    } catch (Exception e) {
      System.out.println ("Error processing stores");
      e.printStackTrace();
    }
  }
```

Now we use the same approach to process the `Sale` elements. In this method we also need a counter (`seq`) to assign sequence numbers to the `Sales_Detail` entries. This will be passed to the next method, but we need to do the counting here:

```
  private void processSale (String store, Element sale){
    Node    node;
    String nodeName;
    int     seq = 1;

    try {
```

Here we create the next transaction ID using the `formatID()` method to translate the number into a ten-digit string, then we increment the numeric transaction ID:

```
        String tx = formatID(nextID);
        nextID++;
```

Next, we clear the `PreparedStatement` that stores the `Sales` entries, and set the transaction ID and store ID retrieved from the previous method:

```
        psSales.clearParameters();
        psSales.setString (1, tx);
        psSales.setString (2, store);
```

Just as in the last method, we again retrieve the node list, loop through the nodes and retrieve the node name:

```
NodeList saleItems = sale.getChildNodes();
for (int i=0; i<saleItems.getLength(); i++) {
  node = saleItems.item(i);
  nodeName = node.getNodeName();
```

For each node name that contains data, we retrieve the data using our program's getText()method, then load it into one of the prepared statement's parameters. When we retrieve the last of the data elements (Time), we call the PreparedStatement's executeUpdate() method to store the data, then we increment the counter:

```
if (nodeName.equals ("Receipt")) {
  psSales.setString (3, getText(node));
}

if (nodeName.equals ("Register")) {
  psSales.setString (4, getText(node));
}

if (nodeName.equals ("Date")) {
  psSales.setString (5, getText(node));
}

if (nodeName.equals ("Time")) {
  psSales.setString (6, getText(node));
  psSales.executeUpdate();
  nSales++;
}
```

For each Item node encountered, we again cast the node into an Element node object and send it to the processItems() method along with the transaction ID and the sequence counter which is incremented after each occurrence.

Again, since we know the structure of the XML file, we can use this knowledge to optimize the program. If we did not know the specific order of the elements, we would have to perform the loop twice, first to retrieve the data and create a Sales entry in the database, then loop through the nodes a second time to process the Item elements. We must store the Sales entry before the Sales_Details or a relational integrity exception would be thrown by the database:

```
if (nodeName.equals ("Item")) {
  processItems (tx, seq, (Element)node);
  seq++;
}
}
```

As usual, we close out the method by catching any exceptions:

```
} catch (Exception e) {
  System.out.println ("Error processing sale");
  e.printStackTrace();
}
}
```

Next, the `processItems()` method uses the same approach as `processSale()`, extracting the NodeList, looping through the nodes retrieving each of the data items and storing them into the PreparedStatement. In this case, we can wait until the end of the loop to call the PreparedStatement's `executeUpdate()` method since there are no subordinate nodes that contain nested data elements:

```
void processItems (String tx, int seq, Element item) {
  Node    node;
  String nodeName;

  try {
    psDetail.clearParameters();
    psDetail.setString (1, tx);
    psDetail.setInt    (2, seq);

    NodeList itemNodes = item.getChildNodes();
    for (int i = 0; i < itemNodes.getLength(); i++) {
      node = itemNodes.item(i);
      nodeName = node.getNodeName();

      if (nodeName.equals ("UPC")) {
        psDetail.setString (3, getText(node));
      }

      if (nodeName.equals ("Quantity")) {
          psDetail.setString (4, getText(node));
      }

      if (nodeName.equals ("Price")) {
          psDetail.setString (5, getText(node));
      }
    }

    psDetail.executeUpdate();
    nDetail++;
  } catch (Exception e) {
    System.out.println ("Error processing items");
    e.printStackTrace();
  }
}
```

In many of the processing methods above, we called the `getText()` method to extract data from the data elements. Here is the code that does the dirty work. Since the text data is not stored directly in the element node, we have to get the first child node within the element and cast it into a `Text` node object. We can then retrieve the data by calling the text node's `getData()` method:

```
private String getText(Node node) {
  Text txtNode = (Text) node.getFirstChild();
  return txtNode.getData();
}
```

As an alternative, we could retrieve the first child element using the `getElementsByTagName()` method as we did above, then retrieve `item(0)` from the `NodeList`.

Other Private Methods

After the DOM tree has been processed, we need to print the counters and close the JDBC resources. We also have some small formatting methods used by the XML methods above.

As in the last chapter, we count the number of `Sales` and `Sales_Detail` entries written, so when we're done, we have to print the numbers:

```
private void printResults() {
  System.out.println ("Copy complete");
  System.out.println ();
  System.out.println ("  Sales copied =    " + nSales);
  System.out.println ("  Details copied = " + nDetail);
}
```

We also need to close all of the JDBC resources that we used:

```
private void closeJDBC() {
  try {
    psSales.close();
    psDetail.close();
    connHQ.close();
  } catch (Exception e) {
    System.out.println ("Error closing jdbc resources");
    e.printStackTrace();
  }
}
```

In the following method we translate the numeric transaction ID into a ten-digit character string. If the resulting conversion produces only nine digits, we insert a "0" in front of the string to fill it out:

```
private String formatID (long n) {
  String id = "";
  id += n;

  if (id.length() == 9) {
    id = "0" + id;
  }

  return id;
}
```

main()

Finally we include a program `main()` method to instantiate the class and run it:

```
public static void main(String args[]) {
  if (args.length != 2) {
    System.out.println ();
    System.out.println ("Usage:  java App2Sales filename region");
    System.out.println ();
    System.out.println ("  filename is XML data file name");
    System.out.println ("  region   is two digit region code");
    return;
  }
```

```
        App2Sales app = new App2Sales (args[0], args[1]);
        app.copy();
    }
}
```

We check that we've received two parameters (the XML file name and the region code), then we create a new instance of the class and call its `copy()` method.

Compiling and Testing the Program

Compile the program with `javac` or your favorite IDE. Make sure that you include your JDBC drivers and the `xerces.jar` packages in your `CLASSPATH` environment variable. To test the program, make sure that your database server is running, then run the program with the file `Reg02Sales.xml`, assigning the data to Region 02, as follows:

```
java App2Sales Reg02Sales.xml 02
```

This should display several lines describing the status of the load, then it will display the counters showing how many entries were loaded into `Sales` and `Sales_Detail` as shown in the screenshot below:

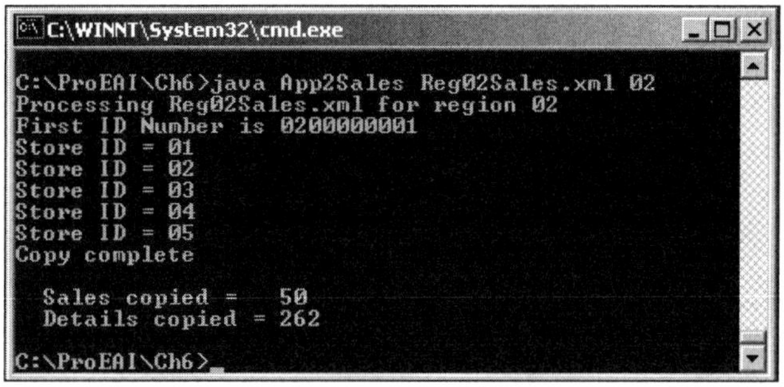

Exporting to the Data Warehouse Using XML

As our integrated point of sales database continues to grow, we may find that we are not able to handle the data volume for any sustained period of time. Also, as management begins to request summary data, we may find that the processing load is too great, and most of the requests summarize the data in the same way. To resolve this difficulty, we will keep 12-18 months of data in our integrated database, then periodically pass older data onto a **data warehouse** where data can be stored in both raw and summarized form. This will have the added benefit that we can collect together old data for reporting and trend analysis.

To extract data from the Headquarters database, we will create an XML data structure that closely resembles the commercial application's XML file, but with additional elements to store regions and transaction IDs. Once we extract the data, we will load it in raw form (with fewer details) into the new data warehouse. We will also summarize it in a number of different ways using XSLT before loading it into our new data warehouse (these processes will be examined in the next chapter).

New Data Structures for the Data Warehouse

Before we can get into the program code, we need to create a new database to represent the data warehouse. Again, use your database of choice, although for the purpose of illustration we will again use Sybase Adaptive Server Anywhere, and we will call the database DataWarehouse. In addition, we also need to design an XML file structure to transfer the data between the Headquarters database and the new data warehouse.

The DataWarehouse History Tables

Although we will develop several new tables in the next chapter, we will begin here with the tables that hold short forms of the original consolidated data. These tables are Sales_History and Sales_History_Detail. These new tables can be found in the file DataWarehouse.sql, available in the download. Create a new database using your favorite DBMS, and then execute this script to create the new tables.

Sales_History contains all of the data from the Headquarter's Sales table. Here are the SQL DDL commands to create the new table:

```
CREATE TABLE Sales_History
(  Transaction_ID    CHAR(10)     NOT NULL,
   Region_ID         CHAR(4)      NOT NULL,
   Store_ID          CHAR(4)      NOT NULL,
   Sale_Date         DATE         NULL,
   Sale_Time         TIME         NULL,

   PRIMARY KEY (Transaction_ID)
)
```

The structure is the same as the Sales table in the Headquarters database, but lacks the foreign key references for region and store (done so that we do not have to fight referential integrity errors, and to speed large data transfers).

The DDL for the Sales_History_Detail table is listed below:

```
CREATE TABLE Sales_History_Detail
(  Transaction_ID    CHAR(10)       NOT NULL,
   Sequence          SMALLINT       NOT NULL,
   UPC               CHAR(12)       NOT NULL,
   Quantity          NUMERIC(5,2)   NOT NULL,
   Unit_Price        NUMERIC(5,2)   NOT NULL,

   PRIMARY KEY (Transaction_ID, Sequence),
   FOREIGN KEY Transaction_ID REFERENCES Sales_History
)
```

Again, the structure matches our Headquarters database but without the Register_Number and Receipt_Number fields, since these items were not deemed relevant for trend analysis. The only foreign key constraint links Transaction_ID to Sales_History.

The New XML Data File Structure

The new XML structure is similar to the one we looked at for the first example, but is enhanced to include `Region` in the `Store` node and `Transaction_ID` in the `Sale` node. Below is the sample we looked at before enhanced with these additional elements highlighted:

```
<?xml version="1.0"?>
<!DOCTYPE Sales SYSTEM "Sales01.dtd">

<Sales>
  <Store>
    <Region>01</Region>
    <Store_ID>01</Store_ID>
    <Sale>
      <Transaction_ID>0200000001</Transaction_ID>
      <Register>01</Register>
      <Receipt>10005</Receipt>
      <Date>09/01/2001</Date>
      <Time>09:00:00.0</Time>
      <Item>
        <UPC>051000000115</UPC>
        <Quantity>5</Quantity>
        <Price>1.29</Price>
      </Item>
    </Sale>
  </Store>
</Sales>
```

Extracting Data from the Headquarters Database

To get the data from the Headquarters database into the XML file, we will keep things really simple. This may seem too trivial an example to bother with, but often the simplest approach is the best. So here we will use the simplest approach possible to create XML from the Headquarters database – plain old Java file I/O. Since all of the data is encoded with XML-safe characters, there is little reason to go through the trouble of using parsers and libraries in the program. In many cases, this is all that is needed to generate XML.

Here is the `HQSales.java` program. It is structured in a similar way to those we saw in the last chapter but, in this case, we will write the data into XML instead of copying it to another database:

```
import java.io.*;
import java.sql.*;

public class HQSales {

  private String      fName;
  private Connection connHQ;
```

Until this point, everything looks familiar. We import the packages we need to use JDBC, and declare the class and some class variables. We also use the same constructor, saving the file name for later use:

```
public HQSales (String fn) {
  fName = fn;
}
```

The `copy()` method begins by declaring several method variables and initializing them with empty strings. We will need these to determine when to start a new `Store` element:

```
public void copy () {
   int nSales   = 0;
   int nDetails = 0;

   String region, store, tx, dt, tm;
   String lastRegion = "";
   String lastStore  = "";

   System.out.println ("Processing " + fName);
```

Next we set up our JDBC connection and initialize our `FileOutputStream` and `PrintWriter`. The `PrintWriter` will allow us to use the `println()` method to output our lines of XML:

```
try {
   Class.forName("com.sybase.jdbc2.jdbc.SybDriver").newInstance();
   String hqUrl = "jdbc:sybase:Tds:localhost:2638";
   connHQ = DriverManager.getConnection (hqUrl, "dba", "sql");
   FileOutputStream os = new FileOutputStream (fName);
   PrintWriter pr = new PrintWriter (os);
```

Now we write out the XML header, DOCTYPE declaration and open element tags for the root element `Sales`:

```
pr.println ("<?xml version=\"1.0\"?>");
pr.println ("<!DOCTYPE Sales SYSTEM \"Sales.dtd\">");
pr.println ();
pr.println ("<Sales>");
pr.println ();
```

Next, we define SQL commands to locate `Sales` and `Sales_Detail` entries. Although we will eventually need an approach to select only new data, at this point we will take everything. We create a `Statement` and `ResultSet` containing all of the `Sales` data, and set up a `PreparedStatement` to allow us to get `Sales_Detail` by `Transaction_ID`. Once these are set up, we begin to loop through the `Sales` entries.

```
String sqlSales = "SELECT * "
               + "FROM Sales "
               + "ORDER BY Region_ID, Store_ID, Transaction_ID";

String sqlDetail = "SELECT * "
                + "FROM Sales_Detail "
                + "WHERE Transaction_ID = ? "
                + "ORDER BY Sequence";

Statement stmt = connHQ.createStatement();
ResultSet rsSales = stmt.executeQuery(sqlSales);
PreparedStatement psDetail = connHQ.prepareStatement (sqlDetail);

while (rsSales.next()) {
   nSales++;
```

As we read the `Sales` data, we need to determine when the region or store changes so we can close or open new `Store` elements. After gathering the sales data, we check to see if a change has occurred. If so, we close out the previous element group if needed, then open a new `Store` element group.

Note that we must truncate the region and store to two digits. This is done because the Sybase DBMS returns a four-character string (the fields were declared as `char(4)`) even though only two characters are stored in the table. Since this was the field size in the original in-house database, we have carried this through the Headquarters and DataWarehouse tables too:

```
tx     = rsSales.getString ("Transaction_ID");
region = rsSales.getString ("Region_ID");
store  = rsSales.getString ("Store_ID");
dt     = rsSales.getString ("Sale_Date");
tm     = rsSales.getString ("Sale_Time");

if (!region.equals (lastRegion) || !store.equals (lastStore)) {
  if (lastRegion.length() != 0) {
    pr.println ("  </Store>");
    pr.println ();
  }

  pr.println ("  <Store>");
  pr.println ("    <Region>"
            + region.substring(0,2)
            + "</Region>");
  pr.println ("    <Store_ID>"
            + store.substring(0,2)
            + "</Store_ID>");

  lastRegion = region;
  lastStore  = store;
}
```

For every sale, we open a new `Sale` element. We get the data from the result set, then write the data into XML format, surrounding each data item with a start and end tag.

Note the reformatting of the date and time fields. In Sybase, both are returned as a date/time pair so for the date, we extract the first 10 characters, and, for the time, we extract all characters after position 11. This gives us only the date string in the date and a time string in the time element. Note that this is most likely a Sybase implementation issue and may need to be changed for your RDBMS:

```
pr.println ("    <Sale>");
pr.println ("      <Transaction>" + tx + "</Transaction>");
pr.println ("      <Register>"
          + rsSales.getString("Register_Number")
          + "</Register>");
pr.println ("      <Receipt>"
          + rsSales.getString("Receipt_Number")
          + "</Receipt>");
pr.println ("      <Date>"
          + dt.substring(0, 10)
          + "</Date>");
pr.println ("      <Time>"
          + tm.substring(11)
          + "</Time>");
```

Next, we use the `PreparedStatement` to locate all `Sales_Detail` entries for the given `Transaction_ID`. We clear the `PreparedStatement`, load the `Transaction_ID` parameter, then use the `PreparedStatement`'s `executeQuery()` method to return a `ResultSet` that contains the data. Once this is returned, we loop through the entries:

```
psDetail.clearParameters();
psDetail.setString(1, tx);
ResultSet rsDetail = psDetail.executeQuery();
while (rsDetail.next()) {
  nDetails++;
```

For each `Sales_Detail` entry, we write a new `item` element containing all of the text entries:

```
pr.println ("       <Item>");
pr.println ("         <UPC>"
         + rsDetail.getString("UPC")
         + "</UPC>");
pr.println ("         <Quantity>"
         + rsDetail.getString("Quantity")
         + "</Quantity>");
pr.println ("         <Price>"
         + rsDetail.getString("Unit_Price")
         + "</Price>");
pr.println ("       </Item>");
}
```

After all `Sales_Detail` entries are read, we close the `ResultSet` and write out the end tag for the `Sale` element:

```
rsDetail.close();

pr.println ("     </Sale>");
pr.println ();
}
```

Now, before anything else can go wrong, we print the counters:

```
System.out.println ("Copy complete");
System.out.println ();
System.out.println ("  Sales copied =   " + nSales);
System.out.println ("  Details copied = " + nDetails);
```

Finally, we write out the final end tags for the `Store` and `Sales` elements:

```
pr.println ("  </Store>");
pr.println ("</Sales>");
```

After all data is written, we close the JDBC resources and close the `PrintWriter` and `FileOutputStream`, and then we catch any exceptions:

```
        stmt.close();
        rsSales.close();
        psDetail.close();
        pr.close();
        os.close();
        connHQ.close();
    } catch (Exception e) {
        System.out.println ("Exception occurred during copy");
        e.printStackTrace();
    }
}
```

We finish the class with our `main()` method:

```
public static void main(String args[]) {
    if (args.length != 1) {
        System.out.println ();
        System.out.println ("Usage:  java HQSales filename");
        System.out.println ();
        System.out.println ("  filename is destination file name");
        return;
    }

    HQSales app = new HQSales (args[0]);
    pp.copy();
  }
}
```

Writing XML using standard file I/O is the easiest way to do the job when you know the content of the data, and are sure that it will conform to the rules of XML. Other than getting the data from JDBC, there is little code involved.

Loading the Data Warehouse

With data extracted from the database in XML form, we can now load the data into the DataWarehouse database using the program DWSales.java that we will walk through shortly. Since the volume of data will be much larger than what we had in the earlier example (HQSales), we will use the SAX API to load the data.

While DOM loads the XML File into memory data structures, SAX processes the file sequentially, using program events to signal start and end tags and return data. In this program we will be intercepting the following events:

❑   startElement
This event is called after a start tag is read and returns the namespace and start tag information.

❑   characters
This event is called after a block of data is read or when the buffer fills up. If a large amount of data is read, the characters event may be called more than once, returning a part of the data on each call.

❑   endElement
    This event is called after an end tag is read. It also returns the namespace and tag name.

❑   error
    This event is called when a parsing error occurs. It passes a SAXException object to the
    error handler.

❑   fatalError
    This event is similar to the error event but is called when a fatal error occurs.

To use the SAX interface, we simply collect the data from each characters event, then process the
start and end tag events as they occur. In this program, we will use the startElement event to clear
the text buffer (a String object). As each characters event occurs, we copy the characters into the
string, then when the endElement event occurs, we copy the data into PreparedStatements and
write the data to the database when the last data item is retrieved.

You should note that processing is tightly bound to the XML data structure. A much more complex data
mapping process could be used, but many database vendors already provide these utilities so there is little
reason to go through so much work. Obviously, we could probably use the same utility to perform the task
we are implementing here, but then you wouldn't learn how to use the SAX interface for data integration.

Now, let's walk through the DWSales.java program:

```
import java.io.*;
import java.sql.*;
import javax.xml.parsers.*;
import org.xml.sax.*;
import org.xml.sax.helpers.*;
```

Among the packages that must be imported into the program, note again the import of the
javax.xml.parsers package and the two new packages, org.xml.sax and
org.xml.sax.helpers. These provide the SAX interfaces we will need to process the XML data.

To process the event callbacks, our class must be subclassed from DefaultHandler. This class
provides a number of event methods that can be overridden so we can handle the events:

```
public class DWSales extends DefaultHandler {
```

Next, we declare a number of local class attributes. Many are familiar from other examples, but there
are a few new ones. The string xmlText will hold character data as it is received by the character's
event handler, while region, store, tx, and seq hold data that will be written to the database:

```
private String            fName;
private Connection        connDW;
private PreparedStatement psSales, psDetail;
private int               nSales, nDetail;
private String            xmlText;
private String            region, store, tx;
private int               seq;
```

Since our class is a descendent of DefaultHandler, we have removed the constructor and placed the code that stores the program parameters into the copy() method. Although this is probably not necessary, we do not want to cause unanticipated problems if the DefaultHandler class ever gets a new constructor method that takes a single String object as its parameter:

```
public void copy (String fn) {
   fName = fn;
   System.out.println ("Processing " + fName);
```

The remainder of the copy() method clears the text buffer and calls each of the methods that copy the data from the XML file to the database. Each of these methods will be presented below:

```
   xmlText = "";
   initJDBC();
   processXML();
   printResults();
   closeJDBC();
}
```

In the first method, initJDBC(), we initialize the database connection and create the PreparedStatements that will store the data. In this application, we open the data warehouse database and change the SQL commands to write the data into the sales history tables:

```
private void initJDBC () {
   try {
      Class.forName("com.sybase.jdbc2.jdbc.SybDriver").newInstance();
      String dwUrl = "jdbc:sybase:Tds:localhost:2640";
      connDW = DriverManager.getConnection (dwUrl, "DW", "dw");

      String sqlSales = "INSERT INTO Sales_History "
                  + " (Transaction_ID, Region_ID, Store_ID, "
                  + " Sale_Date, Sale_Time) "
                  + "VALUES (?, ?, ?, ?, ?)";

      String sqlDetail = "INSERT INTO Sales_History_Detail "
                  + " (Transaction_ID, Sequence, UPC, "
                  + " Quantity, Unit_Price) "
                  + "VALUES (?, ?, ?, ?, ?)";

      psSales  = connDW.prepareStatement (sqlSales);
      psDetail = connDW.prepareStatement (sqlDetail);
   } catch (Exception e) {
      System.out.println ("Error initializing JDBC connection");
      e.printStackTrace();
   }
}
```

In the next method we set up the SAX processor. First, we open an XMLReader object using the name of the Xerces SAX parser. Using this object, we declare that this same class (this) will be used as the content and error handler. This is done by calling the setContentHandler() and setErrorHandler() methods. Finally we pass the XML file name to the parse() method to launch the parser:

```
private void processXML() {
  String DEFAULT_PARSER_NAME = "org.apache.xerces.parsers.SAXParser";

  try {
    XMLReader rdr =
            (XMLReader)Class.forName(DEFAULT_PARSER_NAME).newInstance();
    rdr.setContentHandler (this);
    rdr.setErrorHandler (this);
```

At this point, we pass execution to the parser. The parser reads the XML file and calls the content handler (this same class) event handling methods when events occur. Execution will return to the next statement after the parser completes its task:

```
rdr.parse (fName);
```

Then we close out the class and catch any exceptions:

```
  } catch (SAXException e) {
    System.out.println ("Error initializing XML structures");
    System.out.println (e.getMessage());
    e.printStackTrace();
  } catch (Exception e) {
    System.out.println ("Error initializing XML structures");
    e.printStackTrace();
  }
}
```

As with all of the other programs, we finish up by printing the counters and closing all of the JDBC resources:

```
private void printResults() {
  System.out.println ("Copy complete");
  System.out.println ();
  System.out.println ("  Sales copied =   " + nSales);
  System.out.println ("  Details copied = " + nDetail);
}

private void closeJDBC() {
  try {
    psSales.close();
    psDetail.close();
    connDW.close();
  } catch (Exception e) {
    System.out.println ("Error closing jdbc resources");
    e.printStackTrace();
  }
}
```

As with all of the other programs, we finish up by printing the counters and closing all of the JDBC resources.

Now we start our event handlers. In a SAX program, this is where all of the real work is done. In the `DefaultHandler` implementation, each of these methods are empty, so when an event occurs that we do not handle, the default implementation will do nothing with them. We only need to replace those methods that we are interested in. Consult the documentation provided with the Xerces package for a complete list of these methods:

```
public void startElement (String nameSpace,
                          String localName,
                          String qName) {
  xmlText = "";
}
```

When a new element start tag is encountered, the SAX parser calls the `startElement()` method. Here, all we need to do is clear the text buffer. We could include code to react to start tags, doing things like initializing the `PreparedStatements`, but the code is much more readable if it is all kept together in one place. We will handle all of the processing in the `endElement()` method. If more complex processing were needed, we may want to react to start tags, but for our purposes the code will be more readable if we keep it all in the `endElement()` method.

The `characters()` method below is called by the SAX processor when character strings are encountered, either within an element tag, or anywhere else in the file. Although this method is probably not the most elegant, it illustrates how the data is passed to the method. Data is passed in a character array, with a starting index and length. We simply copy the characters by appending them to the end of the string:

```
public void characters (char[] ch, int start, int len) {
  for (int i = start; i < len; i++) {
    xmlText += ch[i];
  }
}
```

The `endElement()` method is called when an end tag is encountered by the SAX processor. Here is where we start our work. We will use our knowledge of the XML data structure to call JDBC methods to initialize the `PreparedStatements`, load the data, and then execute them when the last data element is received:

```
public void endElement (String nameSpace,
                        String localName,
                        String qName) {
  System.out.println (localName + "/" + xmlText);
  try {
```

Note the commented out `println()` method; just remove the comment marks if you want to see the data as it is received.

Since the region and store number are held in the parent element `Store`, we simply hold on to these values until we need them by copying them into a class variable:

```
if (localName.equals("Region")) {
  region = xmlText;
}
```

```
         if (localName.equals("Store_ID")) {
            store = xmlText;
         }
```

When we receive the `Transaction_ID`, we know that it is time to start processing a new `Sales_History` entry. We clear the parameters of the `PreparedStatement`, set the `Transaction_ID`, region and store parameters, store the `Transaction_ID` into a class variable for later use, then initialize the sequence counter for the `Sales_History_Detail` entries:

```
         if (localName.equals("Transaction")) {
            psSales.clearParameters();
            psSales.setString (1, xmlText);
            psSales.setString (2, region);
            psSales.setString (3, store);
            tx = xmlText;
            seq = 1;
         }
```

When we receive the `Date` element, we enter it into the `PreparedStatement`:

```
         if (localName.equals("Date")) {
            psSales.setString (4, xmlText);
         }
```

When we receive the `Time` parameter, we know that we have all of the data we need to store the `Sales_History` entry. We set the `Time` parameter into the `PreparedStatement`, then execute the statement using its `executeUpdate()` method. As usual, we also count the number of entries written:

```
         if (localName.equals("Time")) {
            psSales.setString (5, xmlText);
            psSales.executeUpdate();
            nSales++;
         }
```

On receipt of the `UPC` element, we clear the `PreparedStatement` that stores the `Sales_History_Detail` entry, and then we initialize it with the `Transaction_ID`, sequence and the UPC code:

```
         if (localName.equals("UPC")) {
            psDetail.clearParameters();
            psDetail.setString (1, tx);
            psDetail.setInt    (2, seq);
            psDetail.setString (3, xmlText);
         }
```

The same process is repeated for the `Quantity` and `Price` elements. We add the parameters into the `PreparedStatement`, execute the query to store the data, and then count the number of entries written. We also increment the sequence counter to get ready for the next `Item` element (containing more `UPC`, `Price` and `Quantity` elements):

```
            if (localName.equals("Quantity")) {
              psDetail.setString (4, xmlText);
            }

            if (localName.equals("Price")) {
              psDetail.setString (5, xmlText);
              psDetail.executeUpdate();
              seq++;
              nDetail++;
            }
```

Finally, no matter what tag we receive (even those we do not handle), we clear out the text buffer. Also, since we are using JDBC calls within the method, we have to catch any exceptions that occur:

```
            xmlText = "";
          } catch (Exception e) {
            System.out.println ("Error writing to the database");
            e.printStackTrace();
          }
        }
```

We also override the exception handlers so we can catch any exceptions that occur while the SAX processor is running. Each of these are handled just as if they were received by a catch block:

```
      public void error (SAXParseException e) {
        System.out.println ("Rrror occured");
        System.out.println (e);
        System.out.println ();
      }

      public void fatalError (SAXParseException e) {
        System.out.println ("Fatal error occured");
        System.out.println (e);
        e.printStackTrace();
      }
```

Finally, we have our usual main() method. As mentioned above, the filename parameter is passed to the copy() method instead of the constructor:

```
      public static void main(String args[]) {
        if (args.length != 1) {
          System.out.println ();
          System.out.println ("Usage:  java DWSales filename");
          System.out.println ();
          System.out.println ("  filename is XML data file name");
          System.out.println ("  region   is two digit region code");
          return;
        }

        DWSales app = new DWSales();
        app.copy (args[0]);
      }
    }
```

Compiling and Testing the Programs

Compile the programs `HQSales.java` and `DWSales.java` using `javac` or your favorite IDE. Make sure that the classpath includes your JDBC package and the `xerces.jar` file.

Before running the programs, make sure that your database server is running and that the file `Sales.dtd` is in the same directory as your compiled class files. Once these are all running, start the `HQSales` program using the following command:

```
java HQSales SalesData.xml
```

This will create a new XML file called `SalesData.xml` containing any sales data currently stored in the Headquarters database. Open the file with your favorite text editor to see the contents of the file. If you ran the `App2Sales` program above, there should be 50 `Sale` elements, containing a little over 260 `Item` elements (this will be a fairly large file!).

Once you have verified that this file was built correctly, you can use it to load the new data warehouse database using the command:

```
java DWSales SalesData.xml
```

This will load the XML file `SalesData.xml` into the data warehouse tables `Sales_History` and `Sales_History_Detail`:

You can then use your database vendor's Interactive SQL utility or Query Analyzer to view the data in the tables.

Summary

In this chapter we examined how XML can be used in data integration. Here are the most important points to remember.

- ❑ XML works well for data exchange since it is self-describing, platform independent, has strong vendor support across the industry, and is easy to read and write using a number of different programming languages.

- ❑ XML data can be transferred easily using any of the standard internet protocols such as FTP, e-mail or HTTP.

- ❑ DTDs and XML schemas offer standardized formats for communicating XML data structure definitions in a form that is readable by both humans and computers.

- ❑ Java offers a number of API's to support XML development, including JAXP, SAX, DOM, JDOM and JAXB.

- ❑ The Document Object Model (DOM) loads the entire XML data stream into a memory tree using a variety of `Node` and `NodeList` objects.

- ❑ XML can often be written using standard Java file I/O.

- ❑ SAX, the Simple API for XML, is an event-driven model that passes element and character events back to event handlers.

During the course of the chapter we illustrated the use of many of these XML technologies for J2EE-enabled data integration, by exchanging data between databases created for our Grocery Point of Sales case study.

In the next chapter, we will examine how to transform our XML data streams for use in a wide variety of applications, using Java and XSLT.

7

Transforming XML for Data Integration

In the last two chapters, we saw how data integration can simplify an EAI project. But so far, the processes have all been limited to copying data from one source to another. We moved data from relational databases in and out of flat files and XML data streams, but in each case there was little change to the data itself.

In this chapter, we will move beyond copying data and discuss ways that data can be transformed using XML technologies as well as other Java techniques. The topics we will cover include:

❑ The role of transformations in data integration

❑ Reasons for transforming data

❑ Java technologies for data transformations

❑ Transformation examples

Let's start by examining why we should need to transform data during integration.

Data Transformation Throughout the Enterprise

Data exchange is not just an internal process. With the growth in electronic commerce, supply chain management, just-in-time inventory and e-business frameworks such as ebXML (http://www.ebxml.org/), data integration encompasses many businesses besides our own. As a result, data must be molded and modified into forms that match a variety of external needs, requiring changes to formats, and coding schemes, filtered to include only relevant data, sorted in different orders, then summarized and presented in different ways.

In the last chapter we discussed an Electronic Commerce Exchange Architecture. Let's begin by revisiting this scenario. As seen from the diagram below, data can come from any number of customers and be sent to any number of suppliers.

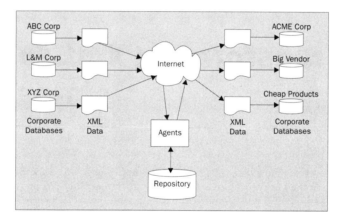

Once the orders are sent, agent programs (usually provided by an EDI vendor) receive them, separate them by vendor, reformat them to the vendor's preferred format, then route them on to their destination or hold them in a repository until the vendors' agent programs download them into their order entry system.

Whether data is moved and integrated across corporate boundaries as described above, or within a single organization, the structure and content of the data will often have to be transformed to meet the requirements of different applications. Although these changes must be tailored to the needs of the applications, most of these changes follow a few distinct patterns. We will begin by looking at these transformation functions and see where they are appropriate. These transformations include:

- ❑   Filtering
- ❑   Routing
- ❑   Sorting
- ❑   Restructuring data
- ❑   Restructuring meta data
- ❑   Translating data
- ❑   Presentation

Filtering

Filtering is the process of selecting and extracting a distinct subset of data. Given a set containing sales information, a regional manager may only want to see the sales occurring within their area of responsibility. This can be accomplished by reading the entire data stream, then copying only the relevant data, or it can be accomplished using pointers or indices (such as that used in relational databases). In either case, a filtering transformation will always result in less data than was present in the original data stream.

Routing

For this discussion, routing involves the selection and movement of data, separating the file into a number of subsets, and then transferring each subset to a different location. In the previous diagram, a customer may write a purchase order file containing orders for several different companies. The EDI vendor then splits the file (using filtering) into separate vendor files, and sends each to the correct vendor based on business rules stored in the repository. Routing can be accomplished using the same techniques as for filtering, and data can be sent using any transport method available. Messaging (discussed in the next chapter) is one of the most effective transport methods for routing these data streams.

Sorting

Sorting is the process of reordering data into a more convenient sequence. A sorting operation does not change the content itself, it just rearranges the sequence of the data. A customer list may be stored in a relational database by an arbitrary identifier such as ID number. This may work fine for the DBMS, since it can quickly scan through the data and locate a specific customer by name. But it may not be as easy for a human reader. When presenting the data on paper, the reader may prefer the list to be presented in, say, alphabetical order. Although the data on the list is the same as in the relational table, the paper list is sorted in a more convenient form. Sorting can be accomplished using sort utilities, DBMS commands or through programmer-defined sort algorithms.

Restructuring Data

When moving data from one application to another, the external interfaces (such as import or export functions) can only read or write data according to the format and structure that it understands. Unless both applications come from the same vendor and were designed to expect data in the same format, restructuring will be required. Restructuring functions includes presenting data elements in different sequences (field1, field2, field3 becomes field1, field3, field2), changing the length of a field or its data representation (for example from an integer to a long) or changing logical groupings (such as a change from relational to hierarchical structure). The data itself remains the same, only the structure and sequence change. Restructuring almost always requires some form of programming to direct the computer to move data into new formats.

Restructuring Meta Data

When using tagged data formats such as XML and PDF, or when working with database management systems, often the data remains the same, but the names used to describe the data change. When this occurs, data mapping is needed to identify the equivalent names, then either the file that contains the meta data can be changed, or data can be moved into the other structure.

Translating Data

Another variation of data restructuring is translation. When coding standards vary from one application to another or when moving data to another organization, the meaning of the data will remain the same, but the codes or identifiers representing this data will have to be changed. Identifiers such as customer or account numbers, product codes, fields with names like type or status, units of measurement and currencies often must be translated using either cross-reference tables or mathematical functions.

Refer back to the earlier EDI example. When XYZ Corporation places an order, they must include their own customer ID number with each vendor request. But, when the EDI service sends the orders on to vendors, they must replace this customer number with the number that matches the vendor's customer database. If an order is sent to Acme, the customer number may be 1234, but when the order is sent to Big Vendor, the customer number will be 10034. In each case, the identifier is different, but it represents the same customer, XYZ Corp.

Presentation

In each of the functions above, data was transformed from one electronic form to another. In addition to these, presentation transformations reformat the data into a form that is easily readable by humans. Presentation often includes all of the above functions, but in a manner that transmits meaning and understanding. Data is sorted for easy navigation and location of specific information. It is often summarized with counters or totals, or it may be presented in graphical form to show relationships between data groups.

XML Standards for Transforming Data

XML offers several approaches for data transformation. Each fits a specific need and will be suited for some tasks better than others. Below are the most frequently used XML technologies:

- ❏ XSLT
- ❏ XPath
- ❏ JAXP
- ❏ XML Query

XSLT

XSLT, the **Extensible Stylesheet Language Transformations**, is a declarative language specifically designed for processing XML transformations. Although most often used to reformat XML data for HTML presentation, it is also extremely useful for XML-to-XML transformations. It will be covered in depth throughout this chapter and more information on XSLT can be found at http://www.w3.org/Style/XSL.

XPath

XPath (**XML Path Language**) is a W3C standard for specifying and navigating XML document paths. It is used heavily in XSLT and offers a clean, simple syntax for locating or operating on XML elements. This subject will also be discussed in this chapter and more information can be found at http://www.w3.org/TR/xpath.

JAXP and Java XML Parsers

Although we covered JAXP in the last chapter, we did not discuss its support for XSLT. While we saw how a Java program can read or write XML using DOM or SAX, we also need to see how JAXP allows us to first process the XML file through an XSLT script before reading or writing the data stream. A Java program could gather data from a relational database, represent it with a simple DOM, then run it through XSLT to transform it into a much more complex document before it was written. Using these technologies together, we can create some very sophisticated data integration processes.

XML Query

Another XML technology, not as well known as XSLT, is the **XML Query** standard. Again supported by the W3C (see http://www.w3.org/XML/Query/), this standard offers a SQL-like syntax for gathering data from an XML document or persistent data store. The focus of XML Query is to develop hierarchical databases that can store and retrieve XML data. To date, this has had limited acceptance since so much of the world's data is already in relational databases, but it does work well for EDI repositories and other applications that need to store and retrieve XML data.

Other Technologies

In addition to the above technologies, Java transformations can be done using standard file I/O, DOM, SAX or other tools. Later in this chapter, we will see how standard Java file I/O can be used to transform our grocery chain's legacy data into XML with a simple filter program, then we will process it with XSLT to transform it into the App2Sales data format used in the last chapter. Often a little creativity can go a long way towards solving a particularly difficult transformation problem.

A Brief Tutorial On XSLT and XPath

Before we get back to the grocery chain example that we have been building up over the previous few chapters, we need to understand the basics of XSLT and XPath. This will be done through a series of simple examples, processing an XML file through a few of the basic transformations. Each of the transformations will be performed on the `HQSales.xml` file using Apache's Xalan XSLT processor.

Setting Up the Development Environment

Before we can begin, we need an XSLT processor and a few changes to our development environment. For our examples, we will be using Apache's Xalan XSLT transformer (version 2.2) since we are already using Apache's Xerces XML parser. But if you are already familiar with another vendor's XML parser and transformer, feel free to use it – any XSLT-compliant processor should work.

Downloading and Installing Xalan

The Xalan transformer can be downloaded from the Apache web site from http://xml.apache.org/xalan-j/. Once the file has been downloaded, make sure that `xalan.jar` and `xerces.jar` are included in your Windows `CLASSPATH` environment variable along with the JDBC driver for your DBMS.

The XSLT Batch File

Xalan can be run as a command-line processor, but the command line is fairly long and tedious. To speed development and minimize typing, here is a single line batch file (`XSLT.bat`) to run the processor:

```
java org.apache.xalan.xslt.Process -in %1 -xsl %2 -out %3
```

To use this to run an XSLT script, simply type the following:

```
XSLT in xslt out
```

Where `in` is the name of the XML file to be processed, `xslt` is the XSLT script file and `out` is the name of the output XML or HTML file. For example, say we used:

```
XSLT HQSales.xml Sample01.xsl output.xml
```

This command will process the file `HQSales.xml` using the XSLT script `Sample01.xsl` to produce a new XML file named `output.xml`.

XSLT Basics

XSLT is a declarative language, like SQL. This means that we do not write out the specific steps describing how to perform a task like we do in Java, instead, we describe the results that we want and let the XSLT processor decide how to get the work done. Since we are already familiar with SQL, using a declarative language should not be a difficult concept to grasp. But while SQL is relatively easy to read, using an English-like command structure, XSLT is written in XML and is a bit more cryptic.

A Simple XSLT Script

Below is our first XSLT script (`Sample01.xsl`). Functionally, all it does is copy an existing XML file whose root is `<Sales>`, but it does illustrate the basic structure of an XSLT program. Let's walk through the file a line at a time.

```
<?xml version="1.0"?>
```

We start off with our standard XML declaration tag: nothing new here.

All XSLT programs have the root element `xsl:stylesheet`. We now declare that the namespace `xmlns:xsl` is defined by the W3.org (world wide web consortium) 1999 standard for XSL transforms.

```
<!-- Copy entire file -->
<xsl:stylesheet
    xmlns:xsl="http://www.w3.org/1999/XSL/Transform"
    version="1.0">
```

Note that the processor will not actually link to this URL, it is just used as a text reference to define the standards for tag names and formats: you do not have to be connected to the Internet while processing XSLT scripts. Note too that there are a number of different XSLT standards, so you should check the documentation that came with your XSLT processor to see which standards are appropriate. The namespace declaration shown before is the one appropriate for Xalan version 2.2.

Our first instruction within the stylesheet is `xsl:output`. Here we define the method as `xml`, meaning that we will be outputting data in XML format. We also want to indent the resulting XML output.

```
<xsl:output method="xml" indent="yes" />
```

> To avoid confusion, we'll use the word "instruction" to refer to an element within an XSLT program and an "element" to refer to the elements within the XML data file being processed.

In addition to XML, we can also write HTML (default) or other formats. Check the specifications for other format options available in your specific XML processor.

The `template` instruction is the basic building block for XSLT transformations. Everything within a template describes how the data is formatted to the output stream. The `match` parameter specifies the starting point within the input stream where formatting begins.

```
<xsl:template match="/">
  <xsl:copy-of select="Sales" />
</xsl:template>
```

Within the template, processing elements (instructions) are all formed with an element name (within the `xsl` namespace) followed by one or more parameters. Here we have the instruction `xsl:copy-of`, followed by the parameter `select="Sales"`. The `xsl:copy-of` instruction tells the XSL processor to copy everything starting at the element specified by the `select` parameters. Since `<Sales>` is the root element, the entire XML structure is copied to the destination file.

Finally, we close out the `xsl:stylesheet` element with its end tag. As stated above, the program conforms to well-formed XML and looks like any other XML file (other than the `xsl:` namespace preceding many of the tags).

```
</xsl:stylesheet>
```

Running the XSLT Script

To run `Sample01.xsl`, enter the XSLT command shown below. This will invoke the `XSLT.bat` file that we built earlier to run Xalan from the command line. Note that the file `HQSales.xml` can be found with the program files for this chapter.

```
XSLT HQSales.xml Sample01.xsl output.xml
```

After a brief wait, the processor will finish. There will be no output (other than an echo of the full command line) unless an error occurs. To see the results, open the file `output.xml` using your text editor. The file will be almost identical to the input file, other than loss of the `DocType` declaration and some additional formatting provided by Xalan.

XPath Basics

As XML technology evolved, and as more tools were introduced, the XML standards group decided that it needed a common notation for referencing nodes within XML data structures. This notation became the XPath standard. Just as we use forward slashes to delimit directories in a file name or a URL (like the one just listed), XPath uses the same notation to traverse XML nodes. The root node is a single forward slash; following this, additional nodes can be listed to arrive at the desired location. In our `<Sales>` example, we could get to the `<Store_ID>` using `/Sales/Stores/Store_ID`. Below are some of the most common notations:

XPath Notation	Description	Example
`/`	Document root	`/`
`/element/child`	Absolute path from root	`/Sales/Store`
`child`	Relative path	`Store`
`..`	Parent element	`../child`
`element[child='value']`	Select a specific element node	`Store[Store_ID='01']`
`child[.='value']`	Select a specific child element	`Store_ID[.='01']`

XPath also offers a wide range of functions to manage nodes, accumulate values, extract partial data and format values and some of these will be covered in the examples below. For a complete list of these functions (as well as a great reference for XSLT), see Wrox Press' *XSLT Programmer's Reference* (ISBN 1-861005-06-7).

Filtering with XSLT

In the rest of this section, we will examine some of the capabilities of XSLT as they relate to XML data transformations. Each example can be run using the same command line as shown above. Simply change the second command-line parameter from `Sample01.xsl` to the name of the file shown.

`Sample02.xsl` works just like the previous script, but it filters the XML file so that it only includes data for store number 02. The script is constructed in the same manner as `Sample01.xsl` shown above, but with a few changes to the template. Let's take a look.

```
<?xml version="1.0"?>

<!-- Sample02.xsl - Filter for Store 02 -->

<xsl:stylesheet
    xmlns:xsl="http://www.w3.org/1999/XSL/Transform"
    version="1.0">

    <xsl:output method="xml" indent="yes" />

    <xsl:template match="Sales">
```

Notice that when we declare the template, we changed the match parameter to `"Sales"`. Each template specifies where to start processing within the XSL stream. Here we select the `Sales` node.

```
<Sales>
```

In XSLT, a template describes how the elements and data that qualify within the `match` parameter should be sent to the output file. In this example, the template begins with the `<Sales>` node, so we are presenting the `<Sales>` node's child elements that include `<Store>` nodes as well as all of the descendants under each `<Store>` node. Within this template, we can include new XML element tags, text or other processing instructions.

Here we start our template with the element tag `<Sales>`. Since any XML tag that is not within the `xsl` name-space will be written by XSLT to the output stream, the `<Sales>` and `</Sales>` tags will be copied directly to the new XML file.

> **Watch out! Since only tags with declared namespaces will perform processing instructions (here we're using `xsl`), all others will be copied to the output stream. So if we accidentaly typed `<xslt:copy-of...>` instead of `<xsl:copy-of...>` it would go to the output stream instead of performing the `copy-of` instruction.**

Since we will be presenting data from the `<Store>` elements and its descendants, we need to surround it with a new root element. Since the original file used the root element `<Sales>`, we'll do the same here.

```
<xsl:copy-of select="Store[Store_ID='02']" />
```

Next, we use the `xsl:copy`-of instruction to copy the store elements and their descendants. By adding the `[Store_ID='02']` to the XPath declaration, we only copy those store elements that contain a `Store_ID` equal to `'02'`. This is how we implement the filtering function.

```
</Sales>
```

Before we finish, we need to add the closing tag for the `<Sales>` element. This line will be sent to the output file after all of the data within the `<Store>` element is copied.

```
    </xsl:template>
</xsl:stylesheet>
```

Finally, we close out our `xsl:template` and `xsl:stylesheet` tags.

Run the script, and then open the file `output.xml` using a web browser that supports XML (such as Internet Explorer version 5.0 or higher) to see the new filtered structure. overleaf is a screenshot of the file `output.xml`:

Sorting and Restructuring with XSLT

Our final example shows how to sort and restructure an XML document. It also illustrates how to use multiple templates to create more complex structures. This example uses two different templates to process the data stream. The first template selects and sorts the data, then the second template formats each selected node. Since this can be somewhat confusing, the figure below shows this process graphically:

Let's walk through this diagram one step at a time.

1. The input file is sent to the first template.

2. This template writes a new root element tag (`<Product_Sales>`) to the output file.

3. Next, the template selects all `<Item>` element nodes (`select="//Item"`), generating a temporary list of item nodes, sorted by UPC. Note the use of the XPath notation `//Item`. The double-slash indicates that all `<Item>` nodes be selected.

4. Now the second template goes into effect. This template processes each `<Item>` node, one at a time.

5. The second template copies the data from each `<Item>` node to the output file.

6. After all `<Item>` nodes are processed, the first template takes over, copying an end tag for the `<Product_Sales>` element.

With this background in mind, let's begin walking through the source code.

```
<?xml version="1.0"?>

<!-- Sample03.xsl - Sort Items by UPC -->

<xsl:stylesheet
    xmlns:xsl="http://www.w3.org/1999/XSL/Transform"
    version="1.0">

    <xsl:output method="xml" indent="yes" />
```

We start this example with the same declarations that we had for our two earlier examples.

```
<xsl:template match="/">
    <Product_Sales>
      <xsl:apply-templates select="//Item">
        <xsl:sort select="UPC" />
      </xsl:apply-templates>
    </Product_Sales>
</xsl:template>
```

The first template looks much like the one used in Sample 2. In this example, we start at the root node (/) and open the new output file with the root element `<Product_Sales>`. Within this element, we use a couple of new instructions. The first, `xsl:apply-templates`, is the mechanism for selecting data and sending it to any other templates defined below this one. In this case, we select all `Item` nodes (XPath `//Items`) so when the second template is invoked, it will see each `Item` node.

Within the `xsl:apply-templates` start and end tag is the qualifier `xsl:sort`. This states that the data selected will be sorted before it is sent on to any lower-level templates. In this case, the data is sorted by the contents of the `UPC` child element.

```
<xsl:template match="Item">
  <Item>
    <UPC><xsl:value-of select="UPC" /></UPC>
    <Quantity><xsl:value-of select="Quantity" /></Quantity>
    <Price><xsl:value-of select="Price" /></Price>
  </Item>
</xsl:template>
```

The second template, above, describes how we will format each Item node. Notice that where in the first template the apply-templates sent all item nodes as a group, the second template sees each Item node individually and all of the instructions within the second template will be executed once for each Item node encountered.

In this template we will format each individual element within the Item node. We begin by wrapping each group of elements with the Item element start tag.

Next, we format each individual element UPC, Quantity and Price. Within each element tag pair, we insert the XSLT instruction xsl:value-of. This writes the data from within the element tags in the input stream to the output stream. Since it is our responsibility to describe the output file format, we have to fill in the names of the start and end tags ourselves.

Finally, we write the Item element closing tag and close out the template.

After we finish the second template, we need to add an end tag to indicate that the stylesheet is complete. The </xsl:stylesheet> tag does this:

```
</xsl:stylesheet>
```

To test this script, run the XSLT command shown below.

```
XSLT HQSales.xml Sample03.xsl output.xml
```

The resulting XML file (output.xml) can again be viewed using your text editor or web browser. Opposite is a screenshot of the beginning of this file as seen through IE 5.0:

With some forethought and planning, we can navigate just about any XML data structure using this same technique. Each template begins at the highest level, then passes lower-level nodes down to other templates using the xsl:apply-templates instruction. When we get to the lowest-level elements, we copy them one at a time as we did with the second template.

Other Capabilities of XSLT

This has been a brief introduction to XSLT and has only scratched the surface of its features and capabilities. Even so, the techniques illustrated above will allow us to perform many complex data transformations. Later in this chapter, we will see how XSLT can restructure fairly complex documents from one form to another.

Transforming the Grocery Transaction Data

With our new-found knowledge of XSLT, we can now take on the final tasks of our grocery chain integration project. As you may remember, we were integrating sales data from each of the grocery chain's regions into a centralized database. So far, we have integrated the data from the regions running the original in-house system and the XML exports from the regions running the commercial system, but we still have not done anything with all those boxes of tapes from the legacy system running in Region 3. This was the application that we called App3. Our first task will be to import this legacy data; once this is complete, we can begin to move the consolidated data into the data warehouse.

Legacy Application Integration

The legacy point-of-sales system ran locally in the Region 3 stores, writing data from the registers and scanners as they occurred directly onto tape cartridges throughout the day. One of the programmers has already copied the tapes onto CD-ROMs, sorting the data by transaction. We now need to load this data into the Headquarters database.

You may notice that we had initially planned on loading this data into the new Region 3 database, but after some additional discussion with management, it was decided that it would not be needed at the regional office, but it would be helpful to have it in the Headquarters database. We also decided that, since the data was in hierarchical form, it could easily be transformed into XML, making it work with our current App2 load programs. Here is the process that we will use for each file:

1. Reformat the file from its hierarchical form into XML

2. Transform this file into the App2Sales XML format using XSLT

3. Load the file into the Headquarters database using the `App2Sales` program from Chapter 5

Why such a simple approach? JAXP gives us the capabilities to combine XSLT with custom parsers that would allow us to directly read the legacy files into XSLT, but this is overkill for this application (if you are interested in this approach, see http://java.sun.com/xml/jaxp-1.1/docs/tutorial/xslt/3_generate.html). This process will only be run once then thrown away, so there is little reason to expend any more effort than necessary. We could also do all of the work in the Java program, including the restructuring and/or load process, but this would make the load program much more complicated.

By using this simple approach, we only need to insert start and end tags within existing data so the Java programming is trivial, then we use a fairly simple XSLT script to shuffle the elements up or down to the proper level. Finally, this solution gives us the ability to use other XSLT scripts to extract other data if it becomes necessary.

Restructuring Hierarchical Data Into XML

Our first task is to reformat the hierarchical data into XML. We will perform this task using nothing more than Java file I/O, reading the data one record at a time, then writing it out to XML, inserting start and end tags where appropriate.

Input File Structure

Reviewing the specs from Chapter 5, we see that the hierarchical data conforms to the following structure. Although the transactions were interspersed as items were scanned, the programmer who copied the tapes to CD-ROM has sorted them so that each transaction is grouped together.

Record Type	Description	Fields
A1	Tape Header	Tape ID, Store number, Store name, Date
B1	Transaction Header	Transaction number, Register number

Record Type	Description	Fields
B2	Transaction Detail	Transaction type, Date, Time, UPC, Quantity, Unit price, Total price
B9	Transaction Footer	Transaction count, Total price, Sales tax, Sale price
Z9	Tape Footer	Transaction count, Total sales tax, Total sales

For complete details of the record formats, see the file `App3_File_Specs.doc` *found with the program listings for this chapter.*

Output Data Structure

From this file, we will create a new XML data structure. At this point we will not worry about the App2 XML format, we will simply insert start and end tags where appropriate. Below is a sample of the anticipated XML structure:

```
<App3Data>
  <TapeID>01090100</TapeID>
  <Store_ID>0002</Store_ID>
  <Store_Name>Store 2</Store_Name>
  <Tape_Date>090101</Tape_Date>
  <Sale>
    <Transaction>00000004</Transaction>
    <Register_Number>16</Register_Number>
    <Item>
      <Transaction_Type>01</Transaction_Type>
      <Date>01-09-01</Date>
      <Time>09:15</Time>
      <UPC>041565141166</UPC>
      <Quantity>03.00</Quantity>
      <Unit_Price>002.59</Unit_Price>
      <Total_Price>007.77</Total_Price>
    </Item>
  </Sale>
</App3Data>
```

Implementing the Filter Program

The filter program, `App3Sales.java` simply reads each line of the hierarchical data file, then inserts start and end tags where appropriate. Let's walk through this program a few lines at a time.

The program begins with the usual imports, class definition and instance variables. In this case, the only imports we need are `java.io` and `java.util`. We also only have one private class variable that saves the file names received by the constructor:

```
import java.io.*;

public class App3Sales {
```

```
      private String fnameIn, fnameOut;
```

As we've seen in the last couple of chapters, the constructor simply copies the input parameters into
class variables then displays a message listing these names:

```
   App3Sales (String fIn, String fOut) {
      fnameIn  = fIn;
      fnameOut = fOut;
   }
```

The `copy()` method copies the data from input to output file. We begin by declaring a string to hold
the record type (`recID`) and counters for each of the record types:

```
   private void copy() {
      String recID;

      int lnCount = 0;
      int A1Count = 0;
      int B1Count = 0;
      int B2Count = 0;
      int B9Count = 0;
      int Z9Count = 0;
      int B9Items = 0;
      int Z9Txs  = 0;


      System.out.println ("Processing " + fnameIn + " into " + fnameOut);
```

Next, we set up our input and output streams and helper classes. We use a `BufferedReader`, created
from a `FileInputStream`, to give us the ability to read the input file one line at a time. Then we
create a `PrintWriter` for the `FileOutputStream` to allow us to write data out one line at a time:

```
      try {
         FileInputStream  inStream = new FileInputStream (fnameIn);
         BufferedReader    rdr = new BufferedReader
                                 (new InputStreamReader(inStream));
         FileOutputStream outStream = new FileOutputStream (fnameOut);
         PrintWriter      pr       = new PrintWriter (outStream);
```

To initialize our new XML file, we need to first write an XML declaration:

```
         pr.println ("<?xml version=\"1.0\"?>");
         pr.println ();
```

Once we have our XML file set up, we can begin to read records from the hierarchical file. The
`readLine()` method of the `BufferedReader` is used to load a line into the string `buff`. The
`readLine()` method returns `null` when the end of file is encountered, so we use this to drive our
`while` loop. We also count each input line:

```
         String buff = rdr.readLine();
         while (buff != null) {
            lnCount++;
            recID = buff.substring(8, 10);
```

We extract the record type using the string's `substring()` method. This method receives two numbers: the first is the beginning position (0 relative – the first character is position 0, second position 1, and so on...); the second is the end position (exclusive). In this case, we copy the ninth and tenth character. Index 8 is the ninth character, and we copy to index 10 exclusive or up to the tenth character. This may seem confusing at first, but as you work with it, it begins to make sense.

Now we start to process each record type. To prevent any index out of bounds exceptions while pulling apart the data, we begin by checking to ensure that the length of the line matches the documented length. For the A1 record type, we are expecting 39 characters. If the length is correct, we copy the data to the output stream; otherwise we print an error message with a copy of the data read:

```
if (recID.equals("A1")) {
  if (buff.length() == 39) {
    pr.println ("<App3Data>");
    pr.println ("  <TapeID>"
                + buff.substring(0, 8)
                + "</TapeID>");
    pr.println ("  <Store_ID>"
                + buff.substring(12, 14)
                + "</Store_ID>");
    pr.println ("  <Store_Name>"
                + buff.substring(14, 33).trim()
                + "</Store_Name>");
    pr.println ("  <Tape_Date>"
                + buff.substring(33, 39)
                + "</Tape_Date>");
  } else {
    System.out.println ("Error at line " + lnCount +
                        " Incorrect record length");
    System.out.println (buff);
  }
  A1Count++;
}
```

Note how for record type A1, we create the root element (`<App3Data>`) and child elements for each of the data elements in the header record. Translating this into XML, we create the following structure (shown here with sample data):

```
<App3Data>
  <TapeID>01090100</TapeID>
  <Store_ID>02</Store_ID>
  <Store_Name>Store 2</Store_Name>
  <Tape_Date>090101</Tape_Date>
```

Note that each element corresponds to a field in the header record. Again, we use the `substring()` method to extract each field.

Next, we do the same with the B1 record:

```
if (recID.equals("B1")) {
  if (buff.length() == 20) {
    pr.println ("  <Sale>");
    pr.println ("    <Transaction>"
```

```
                            + buff.substring(10, 18)
                            + "</Transaction>");
              pr.println ("    <Register_Number>"
                            + buff.substring(18, 20)
                            + "</Register_Number>");
          } else {
            System.out.println ("Error at line " + lnCount +
                                " Incorrect record length");
            System.out.println (buff);
          }
          B1Count++;
      }
```

Each record is translated into a `<Sale>` element as shown below:

```
<Sale>
  <Transaction>00000004</Transaction>
  <Register_Number>16</Register_Number>
```

Then we translate the transaction detail (B2) record into an `Item` element. This takes a little more effort since there are several small data transformations that must take place.

❑   Date – Change sequence from `mmddyy` to `yy-dd-mm`

❑   Time – Insert delimiter to `hh:mm`

❑   Numbers – Insert a decimal point between the dollars and cents

Here's the code:

```
          if (recID.equals("B2")) {
            if (buff.length() == 56) {
              pr.println ("    <Item>");
              pr.println ("      <Transaction_Type>"
                            + buff.substring(18, 20)
                            + "</Transaction_Type>");
              pr.println ("      <Date>"
                            + buff.substring(24, 26) + "-"    // yy
                            + buff.substring(20, 22) + "-"    // mm
                            + buff.substring(22, 24)          // dd
                            + "</Date>");
              pr.println ("      <Time>"
                            + buff.substring(26, 28) + ":"
                            + buff.substring(28, 30)
                            + "</Time>");
              pr.println ("      <UPC>"
                            + buff.substring(30, 42)
                            + "</UPC>");
              pr.println ("      <Quantity>"
                            + buff.substring(42, 44) + "."
                            + buff.substring(44, 46)
                            + "</Quantity>");
              pr.println ("      <Unit_Price>"
                            + buff.substring(46, 49) + "."
                            + buff.substring(49, 51)
```

```
                        + "</Unit_Price>");
        pr.println ("       <Total_Price>"
                        + buff.substring(51, 54) + "."
                        + buff.substring(54, 56)
                        + "</Total_Price>");
        pr.println ("    </Item>");
    } else {
        System.out.println ("Error at line " + lnCount +
                            " Incorrect record length");
        System.out.println (buff);
    }
    B2Count++;
    B9Items++;
}
```

Once we complete the transformations, we output the following structure:

```
<Item>
  <Transaction_Type>01</Transaction_Type>
  <Date>01-09-01</Date>
  <Time>09:15</Time>
  <UPC>041565141166</UPC>
  <Quantity>03.00</Quantity>
  <Unit_Price>002.59</Unit_Price>
  <Total_Price>007.77</Total_Price>
</Item>
```

Notice too that in addition to counting the number of B2 records, we also increment a counter (B9Items) that will be used to verify the control total.

For the B9 record, we write an end tag for the `<Sale>` element, and then check to make sure that the control total that counts the number of items matches our counter. If they are not the same, we display an error. We then zero our item counter (B9Items) then increment the number of transactions read (Z9Txs):

```
if (recID.equals("B9")) {
  if (buff.length() == 35) {
    pr.println ("  </Sale>");

    if (B9Items != Integer.parseInt(buff.substring(18, 21))) {
      System.out.println ("Error at line " + lnCount
                          + " Control total error: expected "
                          + buff.substring(18, 21)
                          + " actual " + B9Items);
      System.out.println (buff);
    }
  } else {
    System.out.println ("Error at line " + lnCount +
                        " Incorrect record length");
    System.out.println (buff);
  }

  B9Count++;
```

```
        B9Items = 0;
        Z9Txs++;
    }
```

The logic to handle the tape footer is similar to the code we used for the transaction footer. In this case, we close the root element with an </App3Sales> tag, then check the control total counting the number of transactions:

```
    if (recID.equals("Z9")) {
      if (buff.length() == 32) {
        pr.println ("</App3Data>");

        if (Z9Txs != Integer.parseInt(buff.substring(10, 14))) {
          System.out.println ("Error at line " + lnCount
                              + " Control total error: expected "
                              + buff.substring(10, 14)
                              + " actual " + Z9Txs);
          System.out.println (buff);
        }
      } else {
        System.out.println ("Error at line " + lnCount +
                            " Incorrect record length");
        System.out.println (buff);
      }
      Z9Count++;
    }
```

At the end of each read loop, we read the next record. The `while` loop will terminate if the `readLine()` method returns `null`:

```
    buff = rdr.readLine();
  }
```

Next we print all of the counters:

```
    System.out.println ("Copy complete");
    System.out.println ();
    System.out.println ("  A1 Records read = " + A1Count);
    System.out.println ("  B1 Records read = " + B1Count);
    System.out.println ("  B2 Records read = " + B2Count);
    System.out.println ("  B9 Records read = " + B9Count);
    System.out.println ("  Z9 Records read = " + Z9Count);
    System.out.println ();
    System.out.println ("  Total Records read = " + lnCount);
```

We finish the `copy()` method by closing the file objects and catching any exceptions. Remember to close out the `PrintWriter` before closing the `FileOutputStream` objects, or data may not be written to the output file:

```
    rdr.close();
    inStream.close();
    pr.close();
    outStream.close();
```

```
    } catch (Exception e) {
      System.out.println ("Error copying file at record # " + lnCount);
      e.printStackTrace();
    }
  }
```

The `main()` method first checks to see that two parameters were received. If not, it prints a friendly reminder. If there are two parameters, it creates a new instance of the `App3Data` class, passing the file names into the constructor, then calls the `copy()` method to start processing:

```
  public static void main(String args[]) {
    if (args.length != 2) {
      System.out.println ();
      System.out.println ("Usage:  java App3Sales fileIn fileOut");
      System.out.println ();
      System.out.println ("  fileIn  - input file name");
      System.out.println ("  fileOut - output file name");
      return;
    }

    App3Sales app = new App3Sales (args[0], args[1]);
    app.copy();
  }
}
```

Compiling and Testing the Program

Compile the program using `javac` or your favorite IDE. This time we don't need to worry about including any third-party packages in our `CLASSPATH` environment variable, since this program only uses Java file I/O.

Once the program compiles, copy the file `App3Sales.dat` from the program files available for this chapter, then run the program using the following command:

```
java App3Sales App3Sales.dat App3Sales.xml
```

The program will print record counters then end:

Open the file `App3Sales.xml` with your text editor or XML-capable web browser to see the results, then save the file for use in the next example. Below is a portion of the new XML file:

Transforming XML Data into the Commercial Format

Now that we have an XML version of our hierarchical data, we can use XSLT to transform it into the commercial (`App2Sales`) format, so it can be loaded into the headquarters database. This will be done using the XSLT script `App3Sales.xsl`.

Data Mapping

As with any other data integration process, it is best to begin by mapping the data structures from source to destination. Below is the mapping from the `App3Sales.xml` data structure described above as it relates to the `App2Sales` structure found in the last chapter.

App3Sales.xml	App2Sales.xml
<App3Sales>	<Sales>
	<Store>
<Tape_ID>	
<Store_ID>	<Store_ID>
<Store_Name>	<Store_Name>
<Tape_Date>	
<Sale>	<Sale>

App3Sales.xml	App2Sales.xml
`<Transaction>`	
`<Register>`	`<Register>`
	`<Receipt>`
`<Item>`	
`<Date>`	`<Date>`
`<Time>`	`<Time>`
	`<Item>`
`<UPC>`	`<UPC>`
`<Quantity>`	`<Quantity>`
`<Unit_Price>`	`<Price>`
`<Total_Price>`	
`<Item>`	`</Item>`
`</Sale>`	`</Sale>`
	`</Store>`
`</App3Sales>`	`</Sales>`

We see from the mapping that there are some structural changes and some meta data translations that will need to be performed. We will highlight these as we get into the program listing.

Creating the XSLT Script

When creating an XSLT script, it is usually best to define one template for each level of the desired output file. So in this example, we will need four templates for the `Sales`, `Store`, `Sale` and `Item` elements. Here is the entire `App3Sales.xsl` script. Notice how each template matches the structure of the `App2Sales.xml` file (the right column in the above mapping). Let's walk through it, looking at each template individually:

```
<?xml version="1.0"?>

<!-- Reformat App3Sales data -->

<xsl:stylesheet
    xmlns:xsl="http://www.w3.org/1999/XSL/Transform"
    version="1.0">

    <xsl:output method="xml" indent="yes" />
```

The first template creates the root element Sales. When we declare the template, we use the match="/" parameter to let the XSLT processor know that we want to start processing from the source root element. We write the <Sales> tag to create the root element for the new file, and then we use the apply-templates instruction to pass all data within the root element to the next template. Once all data is copied, we come back to this template to write the Sales element end tag. Note that this template forces a meta data translation, converting the root element App3Sales to the new root Sales.

```
<xsl:template match="/">
  <Sales>
    <xsl:apply-templates />
  </Sales>
</xsl:template>
```

The second template creates a single Store element. Since the source structure has its store ID and name as children to the root element, we match to the root (App3Data) element. We create an opening <Store> tag, and then copy the Store_ID and Store_Name elements to the output stream. Next, we pass all Sale elements within the root App3Sales to the next template using the apply-templates instruction. Once these templates complete their work, we write the Store element's end tag.

Note here that we are performing a major structural transformation, adding the new level (Sale) where none existed in the input file.

```
<xsl:template match="App3Data">
  <Store>
    <Store_ID><xsl:value-of select="Store_ID" /></Store_ID>
    <Store_Name><xsl:value-of select="Store_Name" /></Store_Name>
    <xsl:apply-templates select="Sale" />
  </Store>
</xsl:template>
```

Our next template copies Sale elements, but with a slight twist. Since the Date and Time elements are stored within the Item elements in the source file, we need to move them up to the Sale level when we write them to the output stream. To do this, we use the value-of instruction selecting elements Item/Date and Item/Time. This copies them from the first Item element found inside each Sale.

```
<xsl:template match="Sale">
  <Sale>
    <Register><xsl:value-of select="Register_Number" /></Register>
    <Receipt>0</Receipt>
    <Date><xsl:value-of select="Item/Date" /></Date>
    <Time><xsl:value-of select="Item/Time" /></Time>
    <xsl:apply-templates select="Item" />
  </Sale>
</xsl:template>
```

The other elements are simply copied from source to destination by writing an opening tag, the data itself using the value-of instruction followed by an end tag. Once these elements are copied, we pass the list of Item elements within this Sale to the last template using the apply-templates instruction. After this template completes its work, we write an end tag for the Sale element.

The final template simply copies the `Item` elements one at a time to the output destination as specified by the mapping above:

```
<xsl:template match="Item">
  <Item>
    <UPC><xsl:value-of select="UPC" /></UPC>
    <Quantity><xsl:value-of select="Quantity" /></Quantity>
    <Price><xsl:value-of select="Unit_Price" /></Price>
  </Item>
</xsl:template>
</xsl:stylesheet>
```

While at first XSLT can look somewhat cryptic and difficult to understand, it is not a difficult language to use. Begin by mapping the input data structure with your output stream, then create templates for each level of elements, copying the data using the `value-of` instruction enclosed within the new start and end tags.

Also make sure to synchronize the list of elements passed to the next template by matching the elements sent in the `select` parameter of the `apply-templates` instruction with the `match` parameter in the next template declaration. Again, this can be confusing at first, so start by developing the first template, then run it to see that the desired data is sent. The `apply-templates` instruction will list all of the data selected without any element tags. When the right data is listed, create the next template and run it again. You should see the XML structure begin to match your desired output. Continue this process, refining and adding templates until the output matches the requirements.

Testing the Script

To run the script, use the `XSLT` command, sending it the file we created from the Java program (`App3Sales.xml`), the script file, and a destination file, as follows:

```
XSLT App3Sales.xml App3Sales.xsl output.xml
```

This will run the XSLT processor, converting this file into the `App2Sales` XML format. Again, view the resulting output with your text editor or your web browser by opening the file `output.xml`. The first portion of the new file is shown overleaf:

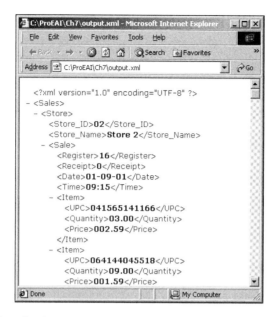

If you want to try loading the data into the Headquarters database, start your database and run the following command:

```
java App2Sales output.xml 03
```

This will load the file `output.xml` and assign the data to Region 03.

Loading Summary Data Into the Data Warehouse

Our final example will summarize the `HQSales.xml` data from the last chapter into a table in the data warehouse to provide quarterly sales totals by store and region. To get these results we will need to perform several transformations including structural changes, computations and grouping.

Grouping is an operation that sorts and merges data by a set of common identifiers. In our example, we will be grouping total sales by store, region, and month. Unfortunately, XSLT does not handle grouping operations well so we will use SQL to perform this task.

> XSLT grouping operations can be performed using more complex coding techniques, or by invoking vendor-specific grouping operations available in some XSLT processor implementations, but both are beyond the scope of this chapter.

We will also use TrAX (the Transformation API for XML, discussed in Chapter 6) so our Java program can read the XML file and transform it into a DOM data structure inside our program.

Storage Structure Design

Before we can start developing the code, we need to back up and perform a little design work. We know the structure of our XML input stream and we have a general description of the output requirements, but we need to determine the data structures and processes involved. Since we know that we need to save store sales by region and quarter, designing a persistent storage structure is probably the best place to start.

The Quarterly Sales Data Structure

Our data warehouse table will be simple, but will contain enough data to provide quarterly sales by region, store year and quarter. Below is the SQL script to create the table (DataWarehouse2.sql):

```
CREATE TABLE Quarterly_Sales
(  Region_ID  CHAR(4)       NOT NULL,
   Store_ID   CHAR(4)       NOT NULL,
   Year       CHAR(4)       NOT NULL,
   Quarter    CHAR(2)       NOT NULL,
   Sales      NUMERIC(8,2)  NULL,
   PRIMARY KEY (Region_ID, Store_ID, Year, Quarter)
)
```

The table is simple and straightforward, containing only the data we need to locate and accumulate totals, but could easily be extended to accumulate other information in the data warehouse. In this example, we will keep it simple to make the processes easier to understand.

The Temporary XML Data Structure

Although we could load the data directly from the HQSales.xml file into the database using SAX or DOM, we can make the Java programming much simpler if we first transform the XML file into a more workable form. To see the difference in complexity, compare the App2Sales.java program in the last chapter with the program below. By flattening out the XML file first, we only have to traverse a single layer of nodes. A little bit of XSLT makes the Java programming much easier.

Ideally, we would like to have a data structure that exactly matches our destination table, because we could then easily copy the data directly into the database. Unfortunately, the HQSales data is generated weekly, not quarterly, so totals will have to be accumulated over time. Also, as we mentioned above, it is much easier to allow SQL to do the grouping operations. So our best route is to create an XML structure that matches the database table, but at a detailed level. Below is the proposed XML structure with some sample data:

```
<Sales_Volume>
  <Item>
    <Region>02</Region>
    <Store_ID>01</Store_ID>
    <Year>2001</Year>
    <Quarter>03</Quarter>
    <UPC>011110816542</UPC>
    <Quantity>4.00</Quantity>
    <Price>0.39</Price>
    <Total_Price>1.56</Total_Price>
  </Item>
</Sales_Volume>
```

Each element corresponds to the database structure, one Item element per HQSales Item element. In addition to the database items, we will also retain the UPC, Quantity and unit Price to verify that the program is working correctly and that all data has migrated from the Headquarters database to the data warehouse.

The Data Mapping

Finally, to make sure that we understand how the data moves through the application, we will create a map starting with the HQSales data, to the temporary XML structure, onto the Quarterly_Sales table. Below is the mapping:

HQSales	Temporary XML	Quarterly Sales
<Sales>	<Sales_Volume>	
<Store>		
	<Item>	
<Region>	<Region>	Region
<Store_ID>	<Store_ID>	Store_ID
<Sale>		
<Date>	<Year> (calculated)	Year
	<Quarter> (calculated)	Quarter
<Item>		
<UPC>	<UPC>	
<Quantity>	<Quantity>	
<Unit_Price>	<Unit_Price>	
	<Total_Price> (calculated)	Sales (Accumulated)

This may seem like a lot of work for something so straightforward, but by mapping out the relationships, we can verify that all of the data migrates correctly and nothing is forgotten.

Creating the XSLT Script

With our map in hand, we can now create the XSLT script that will be plugged into our Java program. Below is the script DWQuarterlySales.xsl. Much of it will be familiar XSLT, but there are a few new instructions and techniques that we need to examine, including variables, calculations, and conditional logic. Let's look at the two templates in detail.

```
<?xml version="1.0"?>

<!-- DWQuarterlySales.xsl - Sort Items by Store and Quarter -->

<xsl:stylesheet
    xmlns:xsl="http://www.w3.org/1999/XSL/Transform"
```

```
    version="1.0">

    <xsl:output method="xml" indent="yes" />
```

The first template is quite similar to the ones we've seen. Since we want to flatten out the HQSales structure, we use the apply-templates instruction to select all Item elements (//Item) throughout the file. These items are then sorted by Region, Store, Date, and UPC. Note the multiple sort instructions placed between the apply-templates start and end tags. The major sort is listed first, followed by additional fields. Note too that since the Region, Store and Date are not contained inside the Item elements, we must use the parent-of notation (../) to navigate back up the tree.

```
    <xsl:template match="/">
      <Sales_Volume>
        <xsl:apply-templates select="//Item">
          <xsl:sort select="../../Region" />
          <xsl:sort select="../../Store" />
          <xsl:sort select="../Date" />
          <xsl:sort select="UPC" />
        </xsl:apply-templates>
      </Sales_Volume>
    </xsl:template>
```

The second template formats each Item element, again navigating up the tree to get Store, Region and Date.

```
    <xsl:template match="Item">
```

There are a few new constructs within this template. Let's look at each of them one at a time.

```
    <xsl:variable name="month" select="substring(../Date, 6, 2)" />
```

The first is a new instruction xsl:variable. This instruction creates a new variable with its name specified by the name parameter and its value specified by the select parameter. In this case, we declare a new variable month that contains a substring of the Date element (found in the parent of the Item element). Unlike the Java substring() method, the XPath substring() function selects characters beginning at the location of the first parameter, and copies the number of characters in the second parameter. In this case, we select the sixth character and copy two characters. If the date were 2001-09-15, the month variable would contain the digits 09.

The next new construct determines the number of the quarter (01, 02, 03 or 04 – don't ask me why we use two digits, just habit I guess). We begin by creating and opening a <Quarter> tag that will contain the quarter number. Next, we compare the contents of the variable month ($month) and test it using the xsl:if instruction. In the first xsl:if, we check to see if the content of the month is less than '04', if so, we write the digits 01 to the output stream to indicate that this is the first quarter. Note that XSL only provides < and > entities for less than and greater than, so we need to test for less than 04 instead of the more readable less than or equal to 03. We repeat this three more times, once for each quarter, then close the Quarter element with the end tag </Quarter>:

```
    <Item>
      <Region><xsl:value-of select="../../Region" /></Region>
      <Store_ID><xsl:value-of select="../../Store_ID" /></Store_ID>
      <Year><xsl:value-of select="substring(../Date, 1, 4)" /></Year>
```

```
    <Quarter>
        <xsl:if test="$month &lt; '04'">01</xsl:if>
        <xsl:if test="$month &gt; '03' and $month &lt; '07'">02</xsl:if>
        <xsl:if test="$month &gt; '06' and $month &lt; '10'">03</xsl:if>
        <xsl:if test="$month &gt; '09'">04</xsl:if>
    </Quarter>
```

Our final new construct is a calculation. Here we simply multiply the element `Quantity` by the element `Price` to give a new `Total_Price` element:

```
        <UPC><xsl:value-of select="UPC" /></UPC>
        <Quantity><xsl:value-of select="Quantity" /></Quantity>
        <Price><xsl:value-of select="Price" /></Price>
        <Total_Price><xsl:value-of select="Quantity * Price" /></Total_Price>
    </Item>
  </xsl:template>
</xsl:stylesheet>
```

Testing the Script

Even though this script will be processed within the Java program, it always makes good sense to test it using the XSLT command line. Unexpected data may create unexpected (and undeterminable) errors, so make sure that the transformation produces the correct results before you plug it into the program. To test this script, run it through the command-line processor as shown below:

```
XSLT HQSales.xml DWQuarterlySales.xsl output.xml
```

Once it runs, open `output.xml` with your web browser or text editor, and make sure that the quarter is being translated correctly and that the total `Price` element is calculated correctly (this is why we included the `Quantity` and unit `Price` elements). The first portion of the output file is shown below. Once this has been verified, we can move on to the Java program.

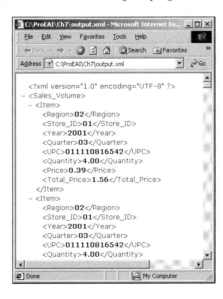

Implementing the Summary Data Load

Our last task is to summarize the data and load it into the `Quarterly_Sales` table of the `DataWarehouse` database. This program will use JAXP and TrAX to perform the transformation programmatically, then load the results into a DOM (Document Object Model) data structure for processing. Below is a brief outline of the program:

1. Use TrAX to load the `HQSales` XML data file.

2. Use TrAX to transform this file using the XSLT script listed above.

3. Retrieve the results from TrAX by fetching the root node of the new DOM data structure.

4. Traverse the DOM structure to retrieve data from the `Item` elements.

5. Accumulate the total sales amount into the `Quarterly_Sales` database table by `Region`, `Store`, `Year` and `Quarter`.

Let's begin our walk-through of the `DWQuarterlySales.java` program.

```
import java.io.*;
import java.sql.*;
import javax.xml.parsers.*;
import org.w3c.dom.*;
import javax.xml.transform.*;
import javax.xml.transform.dom.*;
import javax.xml.transform.stream.*;
```

There are three new packages that are imported to support TrAX, all found in JAXP. These are `javax.xml.transform`, `javax.xml.transform.dom`, and `javax.xml.transform.stream`. The first provides the basic TrAX functionality, the second adds support to transform DOM data structures, and the third to transform streams (data files). Since we plan on reading a stream and writing to DOM, we need both of these packages. We also declare the class name `DWQuarterlySales`:

```
public class DWQuarterlySales {
```

Next we see some private instance variables including the input file name, JDBC resources, `PreparedStatements` and counters. For this program we also have a DOM `Node` object (`rootNode`) that will receive the root of the DOM structure returned by TrAX:

```
private String          fName;
private Node            rootNode;
private Connection      connDW;
private PreparedStatement psInsert, psUpdate;
private int             nInsert, nUpdate;
```

The constructor receives the file name from the command line parameter and stores it in the class attribute `fName`:

```
   public DWQuarterlySales (String fn) {
      fName = fn;
   }
```

The `copy()` method calls private class methods to initialize JDBC, initialize the XML resources, process the XML data, print counters, then close the JDBC resources.

```
   public void copy () {
      System.out.println ("Processing " + fName);

      initJDBC();
      initXML();

      processXML();
      printResults();

      closeJDBC();
   }
```

Each of these methods will be discussed individually below.

To initialize the JDBC resources, we obtain a `Connection` object (connDW) using the same process that we have used in the last two chapters.

```
   private void initJDBC () {
      try {
         Class.forName("com.sybase.jdbc2.jdbc.SybDriver").newInstance();
         String dwUrl = "jdbc:sybase:Tds:localhost:2640";
         connDW = DriverManager.getConnection (dwUrl, "DW", "dw");
```

Next, we create two `PreparedStatements`, the first to create a new entry in the `Quarterly_Sales` table, the second to accumulate sales into the table. Note in the second SQL command (sqlUpdate), that we accumulate into the `Sales` column by computing a new `Sales` amount (= Sales + ?) instead of replacing the value as we have in previous examples:

```
      String sqlInsert = "INSERT INTO Quarterly_Sales "
                     + " (Region_ID, Store_ID, Year, "
                     + " Quarter, Sales) "
                     + "VALUES (?, ?, ?, ?, ?)";

      String sqlUpdate = "UPDATE Quarterly_Sales "
                     + " SET Sales = Sales + ? "
                     + "WHERE Region_ID = ? "
                     + " AND Store_ID = ? "
                     + " AND Year = ?"
                     + " AND Quarter = ?";

      psInsert = connDW.prepareStatement (sqlInsert);
      psUpdate = connDW.prepareStatement (sqlUpdate);
```

Finally, before closing out the method, we catch any exceptions that may have occurred:

```
    } catch (Exception e) {
    System.out.println ("Error initializing JDBC connection");
    e.printStackTrace();
    }
  }
```

Next, we initialize the XML resources. This is where we use TrAX to transform the XML input stream and save it into a DOM data structure. We will examine this process one line at a time:

```
    private void initXML() {
      try {
```

First we create a new instance of `TransformerFactory` by calling the `newInstance()` method of the static instance of the object provided by TrAX:

```
        TransformerFactory tFac = TransformerFactory.newInstance();
```

Next, we create two `StreamSource` objects, one for our input XML file, the other for the file containing the XSL script listed above. `StreamSource` objects come from the `javax.xml.transform.stream` package and represent XML data streams, either from disk files or URL's. They can be used to send or receive XML data streams in or out of the `Transformer` object we will see below:

```
        StreamSource xmlData   = new StreamSource(fName);
        StreamSource xslSource =
        new StreamSource("DWQuarterlySales.xsl");
```

We also need to create a `DOMResult` object that will receive the DOM data structure once the transformation is complete. The `DOMResult` object is a wrapper that comes from the `javax.xml.transform.dom` package. Just like the `StreamSource` object we saw above, it can be used to send or receive DOM data structures into or out from the `Transformer` object we will see next.

```
        DOMResult domResult = new DOMResult();
```

Finally, we create a `Transformer` object from the `TransformerFactory` using the `StreamSource` that contains our XSLT script. This `Transformer` object is then used to transform the `StreamSource` containing our input file to produce the `DomResult` object. This closely mirrors what we do when we use the XSLT command where we invoke `org.apache.xalan.xslt.Process`, giving it the XML input file, XSLT script and an output file. The main difference here is that instead of requesting an output file, we pass it a `DOMResult` object. Once this has executed, we can call the `getNode()` method of the `DOMResult` to get the root node of the DOM data structure which is stored in the class attribute `rootNode`. This will be our starting point when we begin to extract data:

```
        Transformer trans = tFac.newTransformer(xslSource);
        trans.transform (xmlData, domResult);
        rootNode = domResult.getNode();
```

Before we close out the method, we catch any exceptions that may have occurred while transforming our XML data:

```
        } catch (Exception e) {
            System.out.println ("Error initializing XML structures");
            e.printStackTrace();
        }
    }
```

To process the XML data (the DOM structure), we begin by declaring two local variables that will be used later and initialize our counters:

```
    private void processXML() {
        String nodeName;
        Node    node;

        nInsert = 0;
        nUpdate = 0;

        try {
```

Since the `nodeRoot` retrieved from the `DOMResult` object is one level above the root element, we first need to move down one level in the DOM structure. To do this, we use the `getFirstChild()` method to retrieve the first `Node` object under the root. This will move us into the `<SalesVolume>` element.

```
        Node topLevel = rootNode.getFirstChild();
```

Once we have the top-level node `<Sales_Volume>`, we can get all `<Item>` nodes by calling the `getChildNodes()` method. This will return a `NodeList` object containing all of the `Item` nodes plus any other nodes found in this element:

```
        NodeList itemNodes = topLevel.getChildNodes();
```

Once we have the `NodeList` `itemNodes`, we can look through the list looking for `Item` nodes. When we find one, we cast it into an `Element` node and pass it to the `processItem()` method we will see in a moment:

```
            for (int i=0; i<itemNodes.getLength(); i++) {
              node = itemNodes.item(i);

              nodeName = node.getNodeName();
              if (nodeName.equals("Item")) {
                processItem ((Element)itemNodes.item(i));
              }
            }
```

Once the loop is completed, we close out the method by catching any exceptions that may have been thrown:

```
        } catch (Exception e) {
          System.out.println ("Error processing XML data");
          e.printStackTrace();
        }
    }
```

The `processItem()` method begins by declaring some local variables and initializing strings that will hold the data items extracted from the `Item` node.

```
void processItem (Element item) {
   Node    node;
   String nodeName;

   String region  = "";
   String store   = "";
   String year    = "";
   String quarter = "";
   String amount  = "";

   try {
```

We extract a `NodeList` from the `item` object by calling its `getChildNodes()` method. We then loop through these nodes looking for specific node names. Each element could be retrieved explicitly by name, but the only method available to do this is `getElementsByTagName()`. Each call would loop through the current `NodeList`, requiring many iterations to do the same task that can be done by our single `for` loop.

```
NodeList saleItems = item.getChildNodes();
for (int i=0; i<saleItems.getLength(); i++) {
  node = saleItems.item(i);
  nodeName = node.getNodeName();
```

Depending on the node name, we copy the contents of the node to its corresponding `String` object. The `getText()` method that extracts the data from the node will be discussed in a moment.

```
if (nodeName.equals("Region")) {
  region = getText(node);
}

if (nodeName.equals("Store_ID")) {
  store = getText(node);
}

if (nodeName.equals("Year")) {
  year = getText(node);          }

if (nodeName.equals("Quarter")) {
  quarter = getText(node);
}

if (nodeName.equals("Total_Price")) {
  amount = getText(node);
}
```

When the loop completes, we pass the data elements to the `addToQuarter()` method as above (we will encounter the implementation of this method in a moment).

```
   }
   addToQuarter(region, store, year, quarter, amount);
} catch (Exception e) {
   System.out.println ("Error processing stores");
```

327

```
        e.printStackTrace();
    }
}
```

The addToQuarter() method uses SQL to accumulate totals by region, store, year and quarter. While we could do these accumulations programmatically, it is much simpler and the code is much easier to read if we let SQL do the work.

The method is called once for each Item element read. If an entry exists for the region, store, year and quarter, we execute a SQL UPDATE command that adds the total sale amount to the entry, accumulating as we go. If the entry does not exist, we create a new entry.

This may seem terribly inefficient, but actually it's not as bad as it seems. SQL buffers its I/O, so most of the accumulation is done in memory anyway, and since the program will be run at off-peak time, we are not impacting performance. In addition, we save a day or two of programmer time (worth a significant amount at current salary levels).

There is one potential problem with this method. If the program crashes in the middle of execution, the database table will be corrupted and prior totals will be lost. But since this is run as a batch process (most likely with other similar update processes), we can begin the process by backing up all tables that will be put at risk; if an error occurs, we restore the data and start the process over.

```
private void addToQuarter (String region, String store, String year,
                                    String quarter, String amount) {
    try {
```

First we attempt to update the entry. The PreparedStatement psUpdate adds the amount into the record that matches by region, store, year and quarter. The integer n receives the number of records updated, or –1 if no data was found:

```
        psUpdate.clearParameters();
        psUpdate.setString (1, amount);
        psUpdate.setString (2, region);
        psUpdate.setString (3, store);
        psUpdate.setString (4, year);
        psUpdate.setString (5, quarter);
        int n = psUpdate.executeUpdate();
```

If nothing was updated, we need to create a new entry. This entry will begin with the total sales amount set to the amount found in this Item element, then will be increased as each matching item is read from the DOM structure. We also count how many new entries were created:

```
        if (n < 1) {
          psInsert.clearParameters();
          psInsert.setString (1, region);
          psInsert.setString (2, store);
          psInsert.setString (3, year);
          psInsert.setString (4, quarter);
          psInsert.setString (5, amount);
          psInsert.executeUpdate();
          nInsert++;
```

If we did update the entry, we need to count that too:

```
    } else {
      nUpdate++;
    }
```

Finally, we catch any exceptions and close the method:

```
    } catch (Exception e) {
      System.out.println ("Error writing to database");
      e.printStackTrace();
    }
  }
```

Although we discussed the `getText()` method in the last chapter, it bears repeating here. To retrieve the data from the lowest-level elements (often called leaf elements), we must descend one level lower to retrieve its only child element – a text node. The data can then be extracted from the text node using its `getData()` method. This will return a `String` object containing any text data found between the start and end tag:

```
    private String getText(Node node) {
      Text txtNode = (Text) node.getFirstChild();
      return txtNode.getData();
    }
```

The next two methods are called to complete the `copy()` method. They print the counters and close the JDBC resources. Since they are identical to the methods shown in the last two chapters, we will not discuss them here.

```
    private void printResults() {
      System.out.println ("Copy complete");
      System.out.println ();
      System.out.println ("  Inserts = " + nInsert);
      System.out.println ("  Updates = " + nUpdate);
    }

    private void closeJDBC() {
      try {
        psInsert.close();
        psUpdate.close();
        connDW.close();
      } catch (Exception e) {
        System.out.println ("Error closing jdbc resources");
        e.printStackTrace();
      }
    }
```

Finally, here is our `main()` method. It checks to see that a single command-line parameter has been received, then creates an instance of the `DWQuarterlySales` class, passing the parameter to the constructor, then calls the `copy()` method to start processing:

```
    public static void main(String args[]) {
        if (args.length != 1) {
            System.out.println ();
            System.out.println ("Usage:  java DWQuarterlySales filename");
            System.out.println ();
            System.out.println ("  filename is XML data file name");
            return;
        }

        DWQuarterlySales app = new DWQuarterlySales (args[0]);
        app.copy();
    }
}
```

Compiling and Testing the Program

Compile the program using javac or your favorite IDE, making sure that xalan.jar and xerces.jar (both obtained from the Xalan package) and j2ee.jar are included in your classpath along with the JDBC drivers.

To run the program, make sure that the file containing the XSLT script (DWQuarterlySales.xsl) and the data file (HQSales.xml) are both in the current directory. Also make sure that your database server is running, and then type the command:

```
java DWQuarterlySales HQSales.xml
```

This will read the data and the XSLT files, run the transformation, and then accumulate the totals into the Quarterly_Sales table of the DataWarehouse database. You will see the following displayed on your command console:

Once the program completes, use your database vendor's interactive SQL or query analyzer to view the data.

Summary

In this chapter we examined the role of XML data transformations in a data integration project. We catalogued the types of transformations that are used and the technologies that are available to the Java programmer. We then examined XSLT and XPath in detail and applied them to our grocery chain integration project.

Transformations allow us to mold and shape data as it moves from one application to another. We noted that there are various forms of transformation:

- ❑ Filtering – extracting subsets of data
- ❑ Sorting – reordering data groups
- ❑ Routing – moving data to other locations
- ❑ Restructuring data – changing data element locations
- ❑ Restructuring meta data – changing element names when data is stored in self-describing form
- ❑ Translating data – changing data representations
- ❑ Presentation – formatting and summarizing to extract meaningful information

Java technologies for data transformations include XSLT, XPath, JAXP and XML Query. XSLT, the Extensible Stylesheet Language Transformations, is a declarative language for describing XML transformations. XPath is used within XSLT to navigate XML data structures and extract data from elements. In addition, XML transformations can also be performed using standard file I/O, DOM and SAX.

In the next chapter, we will see how messaging can simplify data movement from many locations in a safe, fault-tolerant manner.

Message Brokers and Enterprise Messaging in EAI

In this chapter we will discuss enterprise messaging, an important mechanism for EAI that enables applications to communicate reliably across heterogeneous platforms.

There are two forms of software that we can use to implement messaging. **Message brokers** are used to provide a middleware environment for transporting and managing messages, reconciling network and protocol differences, and also ensuring message delivery across a wide-range of applications and platforms. They support various forms of communication, including:

❑ **Synchronous**
  In this case the message sender requires confirmation that the message was received and processed by the receiving application before it can continue execution.

❑ **Asynchronous**
  Here the sender does not require confirmation.

We will discuss the differences between these two forms of messaging in more depth early in this chapter.

Message-Oriented Middleware (MOM) also enables enterprise messaging. MOM software provides an environment for applications distributed across heterogeneous platforms to communicate asynchronously. By using reliable message queues and providing the directory, security, and administrative services required to support messaging, MOM ensures guaranteed message delivery across applications. Current MOM often supports industry-standard interfaces such as CORBA and J2EE.

Since message brokers often exhibit many of the characteristics of a typical MOM, the terms are often used interchangeably. However, unlike MOM, message brokers do not adhere to industry standards and provide generic interfaces; instead they provide their own proprietary interfaces and mechanisms.

In an enterprise messaging framework, message brokers and MOM enable **loosely-coupled** application integration, where an application communicates with another application by sending a message to a particular destination, and the receiving application retrieves the message from the destination. In this system both the sending and the receiving application need not be available at the same time. Loosely-coupled integration plays a vital role in integrating enterprise information systems, legacy systems, business workflow applications, databases, and data warehouses across the enterprise. Message-based integration can automate complex and time-consuming integration tasks, reducing the cost and effort required to create, deploy, and manage integration solutions.

With the emergence of the J2EE standard, the use of MOM and message brokers in a J2EE-based infrastructure allows easier integration of applications in an open architecture environment via a proven methodology.

This chapter provides an in-depth study of message brokers and enterprise messaging within the context of J2EE. We will particularly focus on the following:

❑   Why messaging is a useful means of performing integration between applications

❑   Message broker architecture and topologies

❑   Commercially-available message brokers

❑   JMS-based messaging within J2EE

❑   Implementing J2EE-based messaging between applications

❑   J2EE-based messaging using message-driven beans

❑   Developing XML-based messaging applications in J2EE

❑   Using the JAXM API for messaging

Why Should We Use Messaging for EAI?

To perform successful EAI, we need heterogeneous applications to communicate in a way that each application involved in the communication can understand. Not only that, we need the communication to be reliable: we do not want data to be lost or corrupted during communication.

Since we often deal with applications running on heterogeneous platforms when we perform EAI, ensuring reliable communication is often a tricky task. The applications may communicate via different protocols and with different data formats. Not all of the applications involved in the communication may be running at the same time, which presents problems if we want to transfer data or make requests directly from application to application via RPC. If the receiving application is not running when the request is made, the request may be lost. While acceptable in some scenarios, losing requests is often unacceptable, for instance if the request results in the processing of work that is a contractual obligation.

Therefore, if we need a reliable communication mechanism for our application integration, we need to look beyond simple RPC. The most common way of ensuring reliable communication within an enterprise is to use **messaging**. Messaging is an event-driven communications layer that allows applications to transfer information securely and reliably. In this context, a message is simply a collection of data sent from one application to another.

Here's a typical real-world scenario, involving a component assembly manufacturer, in which enterprise messaging could be used to integrate applications:

1. A Sales application receives an order from the customer and places a request for delivery. An Inventory application receives the requests and checks for availability.

2. The Inventory application sends a message to a Manufacturing application when the inventory level for a particular assembly of components falls below a certain level, so that the Manufacturing application can create a production plan for the assembly.

3. Then the Manufacturing application sends a message to a Production application, asking it to create the required assembly.

4. The Production application can send messages to its own Inventory application, asking it to place orders for components if necessary.

5. Both Production and Inventory applications can send messages to Finance applications to allocate budgets and generate financial information.

6. Then the Production application sends a message to the Manufacturing application informing it that the component assembly has been completed. The Manufacturing application in turn sends this status message to the Inventory application, so that it can update the availability status.

You can see that messaging is a good choice here, because it is important that manufacturing information is passed through the process reliably.

Advantages of Asynchronous Communication

Perhaps the most important feature of messaging that aids reliable message transfer is that it is based on the **asynchronous** form of communication that we mentioned in the introduction. In asynchronous communication, the messaging clients (the applications involved in messaging) do not need to be session-connected for the message to be transferred successfully – in other words the receiving client does not need to be executing when the message is sent. If the message transfer fails the sending client can continue to execute, because it does not require a confirmation of the transfer from the receiving application. Asynchronous communication systems often also include resend functionality, where a message that failed to be transferred correctly initially can be resent later.

This type of communication should be contrasted with RPC, a form of **synchronous** communication. When an application makes a request via a remote procedure call, the application is blocked (it stops execution) until it receives confirmation that the request has been successful. If the call is not successful, execution will not continue until the problem is resolved, and the request is lost.

Message Brokers and Message-Oriented Middleware

In the previous section we noted that the advantages of asynchronous messaging over other types of communication were that, if the initial transfer fails, we can resend the message later and the sending application will not block execution. This implies that a system using asynchronous communication requires an intermediary between the two applications, to keep track of whether the message transfer succeeded, and resend the message if necessary. Software that acts as an intermediary, managing the transfer of messages between applications is known as a **message broker** or **provider**. Software that is used to provide the infrastructure for messaging between applications, is known as **Message-Oriented Middleware** (**MOM**). Since these roles are closely related, it is not surprising that the terms "message broker" and "MOM" are often used interchangeably.

Message Broker Architecture

The diagram below represents a physical representation of a message broker acting as an intermediary that enables enterprise messaging between applications and services:

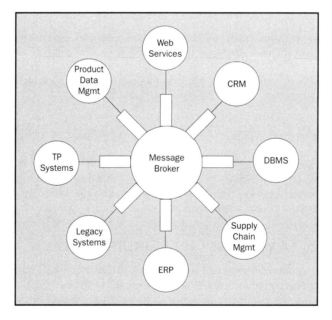

In an enterprise messaging framework, the message broker acts as a "hub", by providing message transformation, transport, and flow control of data, ensuring reliable message delivery across applications, and ensuring that processes can communicate and operate in a distributed applications and network environment. Using the broker means that we can decouple message delivery from both sending and receiving applications. Clients send messages to the broker, which in turn routes the messages to the appropriate receiver.

Message Broker Communication Models

Message brokers support and provide a variety of message communication models (also referred to as messaging domains). In these models, the broker is known as the message **destination**. The most common communications models are as follows:

❏ **Point-To-Point (PTP) Messaging**
In point-to-point messaging, each message is sent by a **producer** synchronously or asynchronously to a specific **queue** established by the consumer to hold its messages. A receiver (called a **consumer**) can have more than one message queue attached to it at once.

❏ **Publish/Subscribe (Pub/Sub) Messaging**
Using Pub/Sub messaging enables an application to send a message to many applications at once. The destination for messages in the Pub/Sub domain is called a **topic**. Consumers **subscribe** to the topic, and when a message is **published** to the topic it is forwarded to all of the subscribers.

❏ **Request and Reply Messaging**
This is typical for a synchronous communication or an RPC application; the producer sends a message and receives a message in return. Most message brokers do not support this messaging domain.

A Closer Look At the Roles of a Message Broker

The following figure represents a typical message broker and the elements that enable inter-application communication:

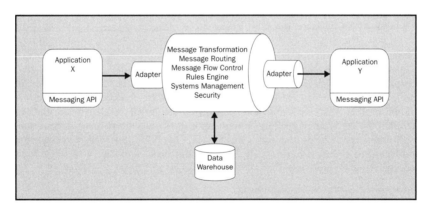

Let's have a closer look at the roles of a message broker that we outlined above:

❏ **Message Transformation**
The message broker transforms data from one application into a form that can be transmitted over the network, and restructures the data to a format that makes sense to another application. It also provides a common dictionary of message formats, including those appropriate for each application, and also industry standard formats such as EDIFACT (http://www.edifact.org), HL7 (http://www.hl7.org) and SWIFT (http://www.swift.com).

❑ **Message Routing and Transport**

The broker sends the message to the correct destination, and implements the communication logic required by the network protocol and the remote application. Message brokers generally implement asynchronous communication and store-and-forward messaging. They interconnect and interact between applications using abstraction techniques. Initiating applications send messages to the message broker, and other applications receive the messages. Both the source of the message and its destinations are not required to be session-connected. To achieve high availability and performance, most message brokers also provide load-balancing support by rerouting messages to balance and respond to outages for uninterrupted service. Brokers allow load-balancing because messages can be retrieved from the queue in any order.

❑ **Message Flow Control**

This is also referred to as intelligent routing. Here the broker identifies messages dynamically from the source application and routes the message to the target application based upon information provided in the message. This process uses a rules engine.

❑ **Rules Engine**

A rules engine allows us to create rules to control message processing and distribution. These rules may be based upon conditional testing, table lookups, mathematical functions, date conversion, character string parsing, data extraction, and so on.

❑ **Message Warehouse**

A message warehouse provides the capability to store and forward messages on request or as required. It is a database facility that can store messages that flow through the broker. Brokers therefore encourage fault tolerance by persisting messages in a database, allowing us to recover messages lost during system or network failures.

❑ **Adapters**

In a typical EAI scenario, the producer sends messages to the message broker via an adapter interface, and it is distributed to the destination application(s) via another adapter interface. Adapters are prebuilt components that enable integration with a wide variety of business applications, middleware, files, databases, mail systems, and so on. Adapters are modular and completely reusable across multiple integration scenarios. The adapter that couples the application and the message broker is usually a CORBA, RPC or SQL-based interface. The adapter performs mostly syntactical transformations (source code transformations that maintain the program algorithms) and using it does not require any modifications to the application source or destination. Most message brokers offer custom **resource adapters** to interface with common business applications, databases and legacy systems (such as SAP, PeopleSoft, CICS and so on).

❑ **Centralized Systems Management**

Centralized Systems Management provides an administration console for enterprise messaging, and a focal point for monitoring exceptions, fine tuning processes, and meta data maintenance.

Message Broker Topologies

From an EAI implementation standpoint, a message broker is a system that is located between application sources and application destinations. It is not important how the application sources and target destinations are represented and accessed from a physical location, because it is possible to configure the message broker according to many different application topologies. The performance and scalability of a message broker topology depends upon its features, the vendor-specific implementation, and the deployment environment.

The choice of message broker topology is usually based on the vendor implementation, number of interconnected applications in the framework, working load, and type of data exchange. Additionally, other factors such as web deployment, communication with other brokers over the Internet, message persistence for guaranteed message delivery, and remote administration support, should also be considered before adopting a topology.

The most common message broker topology configurations are described below.

Hub and Spoke

This is the traditional configuration for a message broker. Here the broker acts as a hub by mediating the interaction between the applications, so that the application sources and destinations can be anonymous. Messages are sent from the source application to a central hub (the message broker), and the hub translates the message as necessary and relays it to the various "spokes" (destination clients):

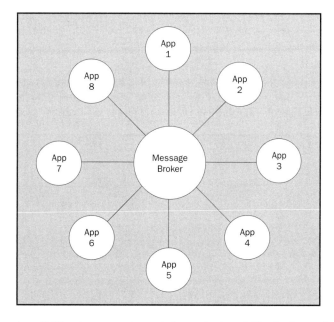

Hub topologies work well if business events are independent, and if a single vendor's message broker solution is deployed.

Bus

In the bus configuration, the message broker is configured on the network, providing interface services to the applications on a logical bus. In this case, the source applications put their messages onto a logical bus, which is accessible to other applications:

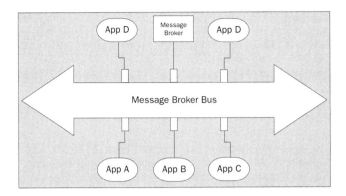

This scenario works quite well for publish-and-subscribe domains, and when message brokers play less of a role in EAI.

Multi-Hub

This topology provides the scalability and clustering of the hub and spoke topology by linking many message brokers with their source and target applications. This topology is a simple extension of the basic hub and spoke topology. It provides the scalability and clustering of the hub and spoke topology by linking many message brokers with their source and target applications, as shown below:

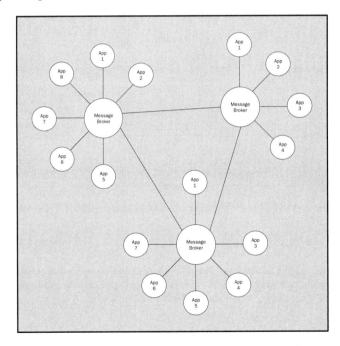

This enables us to integrate any number of source and target applications, because if we need to integrate more applications than one message broker can handle, we simply add more message brokers to the network.

Pipe

This configuration is based on a typical FIFO (first-in first-out) model. This topology works well when there is no need for dynamic configuration. However, this configuration is not supported by most broker implementations.

Network Bus

This topology is the best if there is significant asynchronous activity and independent transactions must coexist with one another. But in this case the broker is tied up to a network bus, which affects the integration scenario because it becomes protocol-dependent. This configuration is also not supported by most broker implementations.

Commercial Message Brokers

On top of the basic architectural features of message brokers outlined in earlier sections, when you choose a message broker you may also be interested in the following features:

- ❑ Business process integration, which provides the ability to execute business processes and integration efficiently using business-specific application interfaces.

- ❑ Industry standard application interface, which allows adherence to an industry standard with minimal complexity (for example the JMS API).

- ❑ Portability and interoperability, so that developers can write their messaging code once and deploy it over a variety of messaging systems, and can also share data, queues and topics with other message brokers over intranet/Internet (for example, using XML data, web services support, and JMS).

- ❑ Central manageability, which gives us the ability to manage and monitor message traffic of connected applications, rules and message routing administration, performance and status of connected systems, and so on.

- ❑ Support for distributed transactions by coordinating transactions across boundaries of applications.

- ❑ Support for content-based filters and routing.

- ❑ Scalability and performance.

- ❑ End to end security.

The industry today has many types of message brokers and MOMs available to solve a variety of problems in EAI and enterprise messaging.

Below is a list of popular message broker products available in the market today. You should note that the following list is not intended to be a recommendation or endorsement for a particular message broker. The choice of broker selected for a particular project depends on the requirements, factors and issues specific to the problem domain.

- ❑ **BusinessWare** (Vitria Technology Inc – http://www.vitria.com)
  BusinessWare provides a common environment to manage the message flow for EAI and B2B-based application solutions. The BusinessWare integration server provides a comprehensive functionality by providing an integrated architecture for Business Process Management (BPM), EAI, B2B integration, Real-time Analysis (RTA) and Common runtime services, for guaranteed, secure execution and scalability of all business processes.

❑ **Connextive Enterprise** (Connextive – http://www.connextive.com)
Connextive Enterprise provides an integration infrastructure using Connextive Broker for providing EAI, B2B, and BPM solutions. The Connextive Enterprise suite has been implemented using Java and it can be deployed on any Java environment.

❑ **eBI** (SeeBeyond Technology Corporation – http://www.stc.com)
The SeeBeyond eBusiness Integration Suite provides an infrastructure solution for EAI, B2B, and BPM. e*Gate Integrator is the Integration platform part of eBI that solves connectivity issues and provides dynamic, guaranteed delivery of information across applications and systems, to partners and customers.

❑ **ENGIN** (Muscato Corporation – http://www.muscato.com)
Enterprise Generic Integrator (ENGIN) provides a message broker infrastructure designed to handle online and batch exchange of electronic data, allowing communication and data transfer between various computer systems with dissimilar native communication protocols and message formats.

❑ **EntireX** (Software AG – http://www.softwareagusa.com)
EntireX provides a message broker infrastructure based on Microsoft DCOM technology. It aids integration of all applications across a variety of platforms, and allows Microsoft Windows systems to integrate their applications with Unix systems and mainframes using the DCOM standard.

❑ **Geneva** (Level8 – http://www.level8.com)
Geneva Integration Broker is a message broker that allows EAI applications and e-business systems to communicate with each other regardless of protocol, transport or format.

❑ **Mercator Enterprise Broker** – (TSISoft – http://www.tsisoft.com)
Mercator Enterprise Broker is part of Mercator Integration Broker suite. It provides a message broker infrastructure for EAI solutions to integrate disparate applications, legacy systems, databases, data warehouses and also for integration across the enterprise.

❑ **MQSeries Integrator** (IBM – http://www.ibm.com/)
MQSeries Integrator is part of the IBM MQSeries product family suite for providing a message broker infrastructure solution for BPM, EAI, and B2B. It allows integration of business applications and processes both within the enterprise and across the Internet.

❑ **NEONet** (Sybase – http://www.sybase.com)
NEONet is a message broker application that enables EAI by providing a multi-platform messaging framework. It provides cross-platform, guaranteed-delivery messaging, and queuing mechanisms.

❑ **TIBCO MessageBroker** (TIBCO – http://www.tibco.com)
TIBCO MessageBroker is part of the TIBCO ActiveEnterprise family of products. MessageBroker facilitates EAI, B2B and BPM solutions. It allows integration of business applications and processes both within the enterprise and across the Internet. It is a Java-based application capable of sending and receiving messages to and from Java and non-Java applications on any platform.

Enterprise Messaging Using J2EE

Today's Internet-based applications and inter-enterprise B2B applications are typically distributed applications from different vendors. These distributed applications support a variety of communication protocols, standards, and exchange information formats. A lack of a standard approach and common platform for distributed computing increases the cost of development and deployment of distributed systems.

Many business organizations and enterprise application vendors currently support and implement the J2EE standard. To take the best advantage of the benefits of J2EE, it is important to have message brokers that support J2EE-based applications.

The Java Message Service (JMS)

To make message broker support possible Sun Microsystems created an API called **JMS (Java Message Service)**. JMS defines a loosely-coupled application communication mechanism that enables J2EE components to send and receive messages asynchronously with enterprise applications and legacy systems. As part of the Java Community Process (JCP), Sun developed JMS working with leading enterprise message broker vendors.

JMS is vendor-independent, defining a generic and consistent messaging API designed to support a wide range of enterprise messaging vendor products. This allows the J2EE developer to write JMS applications with a minimal need to understand the underlying messaging systems and providers. JMS applications written for a JMS provider will work on all JMS-compliant messaging systems, which means that JMS applications are readily portable across J2EE-based architectures hosted by any hardware and operating systems.

JMS also supports both PTP and Pub/Sub styles of messaging. In JMS messages can also be persistent or non-persistent. A persistent message is assured of delivery; if it is not delivered, the JMS broker writes the message to a file or database provided during configuration. Non-persistent messages are not stored in a database and may be lost during a system or communication failure.

Commercial JMS Providers

The J2EE 1.3 Reference Implementation contains a JMS implementation, and the following vendors also provide JMS-compliant product implementations:

Company	Product
BEA Systems, Inc.	BEA Weblogic Server (http://www.beasys.com)
Brokat Technologies (formerly GemStone)	Brokat advanced Server/J version (http://www.brokat.com)
Fiorano software	FioranoMQ (http://www.fiorano.com)
IBM	IBM MQSeries (http://www.ibm.com)
iPlanet (Sun/Netscape Alliance)	iPlanet JMQ (http://www.iplanet.com)
Macromedia	JRun Server (http://www.macromedia.com)

Table continued on following page

Company	Product
Oracle Corporation	Oracle Message Broker (http://www.oracle.com)
SilverStream Software	Silverstream application server (http://www.silverstream.com)
Sonic Software (Progress software)	SonicMQ (http://www.sonicsoftware.com)
SpiritSoft, Inc. (Push Technologies Ltd.)	SpiritWave (www.spirit-soft.com)
Talarian Corp.	Workbench (http://www.talarian.com)

The full list of JMS-compliant vendors is available from http://java.sun.com/products/jms/licensees.html. A list of vendor companies providing JMS implementations that are not fully compliant with J2EE compatibility is available at http://java.sun.com/products/jms/nonlicensedvendors.html.

JMS-Enabled Messaging in J2EE

Since JMS is now an integral part of the J2EE 1.3 platform, messaging has been integrated into the J2EE platform in several ways:

❑ J2EE components can send or synchronously receive a JMS message

❑ Message-driven beans (a recently implemented type of EJB) can receive asynchronous messages from a JMS provider

❑ JMS clients can look up configured JMS server objects using JNDI

❑ JMS messages can also participate in transactions using JTA (the Java Transaction API)

We will look more closely at these issues later in the chapter.

JMS Messaging Domains

The JMS API specification defines and provides the two common messaging domains: PTP and Pub/Sub. Let's look at the implementation of these domains in JMS.

The PTP Domain

Recall from earlier in the chapter that PTP provides the delivery of a message to exactly one recipient via a queue. There is no timing dependency between the producer and consumer, as the consumer application does not have to be running while the producer sends the message.

In a JMS implementation of PTP, the QueueSender (message producer) sends a Message to a Queue. The QueueReceiver (consumer) is ready to receive the Message from the Queue when it's forwarded on:

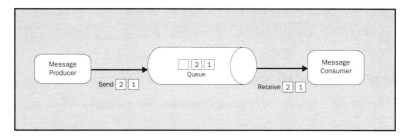

If multiple QueueReceiver(s) are listening for messages on a Queue, the message broker determines the priority of which of the consumers will receive the next message. If no QueueReceiver(s) are listening on the Queue, messages remain active in the Queue until a QueueReceiver connects to the Queue. The PTP model is implemented with javax.jms.Queue.

The Pub/Sub Domain

We saw earlier in the chapter that the Pub/Sub messaging model can deliver a message to many recipients subscribed to a particular topic. There is timing dependency between the producers and consumers, as the consumer clients need to be active to receive the messages produced by the publisher. However, the timing dependency does not apply to durable subscriptions that we discuss in the later part of this chapter.

In JMS, TopicPublishers (producers) send messages to a Topic, and TopicSubscribers (consumers) retrieve messages from a Topic. The Pub/Sub model is implemented with javax.jms.Topic:

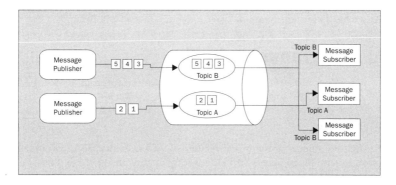

Both PTP and Pub/Sub extend the class javax.jms.Destination.

Message Delivery

Although JMS-compliant message brokers provide only asynchronous communication mechanisms, the JMS specification defines two methods of consuming messages:

❑   Synchronous – Within a specific time limit, a client can fetch and consume a message by calling the receive() method. The receive() method blocks until a message arrives within a definite time or it can time out if a message does not arrive within the specific time limit.

❑ Asynchronous – In a similar way to an event listener mechanism, JMS uses a `MessageListener`. Whenever a message arrives at the destination, the message is delivered by calling an `onMessage()` method.

JMS Application Architecture

A typical JMS application architecture consists of the following elements:

❑ **JMS Service Provider**
The service provider is the JMS-compliant message broker, which implements JMS API interfaces and classes. The service provider also provides an administration console and other adapter features to external applications.

❑ **JMS Clients**
JMS clients are JMS application components, which send and receive JMS messages.

❑ **JMS Messages**
Messages are data and events in a JMS communication.

❑ **JMS Administered Objects**
A JMS-compliant broker provides administered objects, which include connection factories, sessions, and destinations.

❑ Connection factories are a set of preconfigured connections to a broker, which provides connection from a JMS client

❑ Sessions are single-threaded context for sending messages (producers) or receiving them (consumers)

❑ As we have seen, destinations can be either a queue or a topic

The JMS API Programming Model

JMS provides a messaging infrastructure and API – a set of interfaces and classes. Let's take a closer look at these.

Administered Objects

These are preconfigured objects stored in a directory service provider (JNDI provider) by the JMS administrator, for use with JMS clients. JMS clients look up and access these objects using a JNDI interface. JMS administered objects include the following:

Connection Factories

Connection factories contain connection configuration information used for creating connections to a JMS provider. This information includes the host on which the provider is running, and the port on which it is listening. Connection factories also provide for client authentication during the creation of connections.

Connection factories are defined in JMS using the root interface `javax.jms.ConnectionFactory`. As a root interface it specifies `ConnectionFactory` subclasses for JMS messaging domains, which include `javax.jms.QueueConnectionFactory` specific to PTP and `javax.jms.TopicConnectionFactory` specific to Pub/Sub.

The following code snippet shows how to obtain an `InitialContext` object and use it to look up a `QueueConnectionFactory` and `TopicConnectionFactory` by name:

```
Context jndiContext = new InitialContext();

TopicConnectionFactory  topicConnectionFactory =
        (TopicConnectionFactory) jndiContext.lookup("myTopicConnectionFactory");

QueueConnectionFactory  queueConnectionFactory =
        (QueueConnectionFactory) jndiContext.lookup("myQueueConnectionFactory");
```

Destinations

`Destination` objects contain the identity of the message source and identity of the message receiver. They are configured and managed in JNDI namespace. `Destinations` are defined in JMS using the root interface `javax.jms.Destination`. As a root interface it specifies `Destination` subclasses for JMS messaging domains, which include `javax.jms.Queue` and `javax.jms.TemporaryQueue` (specific to the PTP domain) and `javax.jms.Topic` and `javax.jms.TemporaryTopic` (specific to Pub/Sub).

The following code snippet obtains an `InitialContext` object and uses it to look up a `Queue`:

```
InitialContext jndiContext = new InitialContext();
Queue myQueue = (Queue) jndiContext.lookup("myQueue");
```

Connections

`Connections` are created using the methods defined in `ConnectionFactory`. `Connection` objects provide factory methods for creating JMS sessions. Like `ConnectionFactory`, JMS also defines connections specific to the messaging domains: `javax.jms.QueueConnection` for PTP and `javax.jms.TopicConnection` for Pub/Sub. Here's how to create them:

```
TopicConnection myTopicConnection =
            topicConnectionFactory.createTopicConnection();

QueueConnection myQueueConnection =
            queueConnectionFactory.createQueueConnection();
```

Connection States

To start message delivery, the `Connection` needs to be started, using the `start()` method:

```
myTopicConnection.start();
myQueueConnection.start();
```

To temporarily stop message delivery, the `Connection` needs to be stopped using `stop()`:

```
myTopicConnection.stop();
myQueueConnection.stop();
```

After utilizing the connection, it is important to close the connection to the client application. Failure to close the connection results in resources not being released by the JMS provider. Closing a connection also closes all JMS sessions and its message producers and consumers:

```
myTopicConnection.close();
```

Sessions

`Session` defines a serial order for the messages produced and consumed in an active `Connection` with a JMS provider. `Session` is a single-threaded context for sending and receiving messages. It also provides support for sessions, which involve JMS-based transactions. Like `Connection`, JMS also defines `Sessions` specific to the messaging domains: `javax.jms.QueueSession` for PTP and `javax.jms.TopicSession` for Pub/Sub.

To create a `QueueSession`:

```
QueueSession myQueueSession = myQueueConnection.createQueueSession(true, 0);
```

The first argument to the `createQueueSession()` method indicates whether the session is transacted, and the second argument '0' indicates that the message acknowledgement is not specified for the transacted sessions.

To create a `TopicSession`:

```
TopicSession myTopicSession = myTopicConnection.createTopicSession(false,
                                           Session.AUTO_ACKNOWLEDGE);
```

Again the first argument indicates whether the session is transacted, and the second argument specifies automatic acknowledgement of messages. We'll discuss message acknowledgement in more depth later.

Message Processors

Message processors are objects created by a `Session` to send and receive the messages in an active `Connection` with a JMS provider. JMS also defines these message producers and consumers specific to the message domains as `javax.jms.QueueSender` and `javax.jms.QueueReceiver` (for PTP) and `javax.jms.TopicPublisher` and `javax.jms.TopicSubscriber` (for Pub/Sub). A JMS session can have multiple producers and receivers.

Sending Messages

To create a `QueueSender`, the `QueueSession` creates a sender using a `Queue`, as in the following example:

```
QueueSender myQueueSender =
        myQueueSession.createSender(myQueue);
myQueueSender.send(myMessage);  // sends the message
```

Note that we can call the `send()` method on the `QueueSender` object to actually send a message (`myMessage` in this case). Similarly, to create a `TopicPublisher`, the `TopicSession` creates a sender using a `Topic`, and then we can publish the message using the `publish()` method:

```
TopicPublisher myTopicPublisher =
        myTopicSession.createPublisher(myTopic);
myTopicPublisher.publish(myMessage);    // publishes the message
```

Receiving Messages

It follows that to create a `QueueReceiver`, the `QueueSession` creates a receiver using a `Queue`, and to create a `TopicSubscriber`, the `TopicSession` creates a subscriber using a `Topic`:

```
QueueReceiver myQueueReceiver =
               myQueueSession.createReceiver(myQueue);

TopicSubscriber myTopicSubscriber =
               myTopicSession.createSubscriber(myTopic);
```

To receive the messages from the `Queue`, we need to use the `receive()` method. However, before we call this, we need to call the `QueueConnection.start()` method to start the connection:

```
myQueueConnection.start();
Message ms = myQueueReceiver.receive();
```

Similarly, to receive the messages from the `Topic`, we start the connection and then use the `receive()` method:

```
myTopicConnection.start();
Message ms = myTopicSubscriber.receive();
```

Durable Subscriptions

The `TopicSession.createSubscriber()` method we saw above provides only **non-durable** subscriptions. A non-durable subscription only lasts for the lifetime of its subscriber object, meaning that delivery only occurs when the consumer is active. If the consumer is not active, these messages are not published to the subscriber at all. With a consumer registered to a durable subscription, the JMS provider holds the message with a unique identity, and retains the subscription until it expires. This is considered to be the reliable delivery mechanism of JMS.

To create a durable `TopicSubscriber`, we would use the `createDurableSubscriber()` method:

```
TopicSubscriber myTopicSubscriber =
               myTopicSession.createDurableSubscriber(myTopic, UniqueID);
```

Note the two arguments: the `Topic`, and the `String UniqueID` which is a name that identifies the subscription. To delete a durable `TopicSubscriber`, we first `close()` the subscriber then use the `unsubscribe()` method, specifying the subscription:

```
myTopicSubscriber.close();
myTopicSession.unsubscribe(UniqueID);
```

Asynchronous Message Delivery

`MessageListener` defines an object that acts upon messages as an asynchronous event-handler for all messages. It implements the `javax.jms.MessageListener` interface, which contains the `onMessage()` method that defines the actions to be taken upon the arrival of a message.

The following code snippet illustrates how to create and register a MessageListener for a Queue:

```
myQueueReceiver.setMessageListener(
  new MessageListener () {
    public void onMessage(Message msg) {
      try {
        TextMessage tMsg = (TextMessage) msg;
        System.out.println("Message : " + tMsg.getText());
      } catch(Exception ex) {}
      ...
  }
);
```

Here we defined a new MessageListener object and its associated onMessage() callback method. Then we registered the MessageListener using setMessageListener(). During message delivery, the message consumer QueueReceiver or TopicSubscriber calls the MessageListener's onMessage() method to take actions upon the message.

Say we had defined a class called TopicListener that implemented the MessageListener interface for a Topic. To create and register this MessageListener we could use the following code:

```
TopicListener myTopicListener = new TopicListener();
myTopicSubscriber.setMessageListener(myTopicListener);
```

JMS Messages

A JMS javax.jms.Message object defines the information exchanged by applications. JMS messages have a basic, and therefore highly flexible, format, which is obviously well-suited to EAI because it allows us to create messages to match formats used by non-JMS applications in a heterogeneous environment. A JMS message is composed of three basic components:

❑   Header

❑   Properties

❑   Body

Let's take a closer look at each of these.

Message Header

All JMS messages contain a standard set of header fields that are included by default and available to message consumers. The JMS provider and the application developer use the headers to set parameters like the destination, the reply-to destination, the message type and the message expiry time.

The following table describes the header fields in the message header:

JMS Headers	Description	Set by
JMSMessageID	Contains a string value that uniquely identifies each message sent by a JMS Provider. All JMSMessageIDs start with an ID: prefix.	send()
JMSCorrelationID	Used to correlate messages, by specifying the JMSMessageID of the message to correlate to.	Producer
JMSDeliveryMode	Specifies PERSISTENT or NON_PERSISTENT messaging.	send()
JMSDestination	Specifies the destination (queue or topic) of the message.	send()
JMSExpiration	Specifies the expiration time for a message.	send()
JMSPriority	Specifies the priority level. This field is set before a message is sent. JMS defines ten priority levels, 0 to 9, 0 being the lowest priority. Levels 0-4 indicate gradations of normal priority, and levels 5-9 indicate gradations of expedited priority.	Producer
JMSRedelivered	Provider sets this field to True if the message has already been delivered once.	Provider
JMSReplyTo	Specifies a queue or topic to which reply messages should be sent.	Producer
JMSTimeStamp	Contains the time at which the message was sent by the provider.	send()
JMSType	Specifies the message type identifier (a String) set by the sending application.	Producer

Message Properties

The property fields of a JMS message contain header fields added by the application. The JMS specification defines the following types of message properties:

❑ **Application-specific properties**
A mechanism to add application-specific header fields as name/value pairs. JMS provides them primarily for use in message selectors (discussed in the following section).

❑ **Standard properties**
JMS defines some optional header fields, which can be included as standard properties.

❑ **Provider-specific properties**
Defines naming conventions specific to a provider.

Message Body

A JMS message body contains the actual content being delivered from producer to consumer. JMS defines several types of message bodies, covering most message formats used in the industry.

351

The following table describes the different messaging content types supported by JMS:

JMS Message Type	Description
javax.jms.BytesMessage	Contains a stream of uninterpreted bytes that must be understood by the sender and receiver. The access methods are based on java.io.DataInputStream and java.io.DataOutputStream.
javax.jms.MapMessage	A map of name/value pairs in which the names are strings and the values are Java primitive types.
javax.jms.ObjectMessage	A serializable Java object.
javax.jms.StreamMessage	A stream of Java primitive values filled sequentially. It is similar to a BytesMessage, except that only Java primitive types are written to or read from the stream.
javax.jms.TextMessage	A typical string message, which can also contain XML content.

The following code snippet uses a TextMessage format to send a message using JMS:

```
String myText = "Professional J2EE EAI - Wrox";
TextMessage msg = myQueueSession.createTextMessage();
msg.setText(myText);
myQueueSender.send(msg);
```

We created a TextMessage using createTextMessage(), and then used the setText() method to add a string to the message. Finally we sent the message by calling send() on the QueueSender. To receive this TextMessage at the consumer end, we call the receive() method on the QueueReceiver, cast the message to a TextMessage, and then use the getText() method to retrieve the body of the message:

```
Message msg = myQueueReceiver.receive();
if (msg instanceOf TextMessage) {
  TextMessage tmsg = (TextMessage) msg;
  System.out.println("Browsing Message: " + tmsg.getText());
} else {
 // Handle receiving error
 }
```

Basic Programming Steps for Using JMS

According to the JMS specification, the programming steps for implementing a typical JMS domain application are as outlined below.

Publishing or Sending Messages

The following steps are required to implement a JMS Pub/Sub publisher client application:

1. Use JNDI to look up and create a TopicConnectionFactory

2. Use JNDI to look up a `Destination`

3. Create and start a `TopicConnection` using the `TopicConnectionFactory`

4. Use the `TopicConnection` to create a `TopicSession`

5. Use the `TopicSession` to create `TopicPublisher`

6. Create a message using a required `Message` style

7. `publish()` one or more messages to the `Topic`

8. Close the `Connection`, to close the `Session` and the `TopicPublisher`

The steps above can also be followed for a JMS PTP sender, except that we need to use `QueueConnectionFactory`, `QueueConnection`, `QueueSession`, and `QueueSender` (instead of `TopicPublisher`) objects instead, and the `send()` method instead of `publish()`.

Subscribing To or Receiving Messages

To implement a JMS Pub/Sub subscriber client application, we need to do the following:

1. Use JNDI to look up and create a `TopicConnectionFactory`

2. Use JNDI to look up a `Destination`

3. Create and start a `TopicConnection` using the `TopicConnectionFactory`

4. Use the `TopicConnection` to create a `TopicSession`

5. Use the `TopicSession` to create `TopicSubscriber`

6. Create an instance of your own `Listener` and register it as a `MessageListener` for the `TopicSubscriber`, then implement the listener with the `onMessage()` method

7. Start the `Connection`

8. Use the `MessageListener.onMessage()` method to receive messages

9. `onMessage()` method receives messages using the required `Message` style

10. Close the `TopicConnection`

Again, the steps needed to implement a JMS PTP receiver application are similar to those of the Pub/Sub domain, but in this case they diverge significantly at the end. For steps 1-5, just substitute the objects stated above for `QueueConnectionFactory`, `QueueConnection`, `QueueSession`, and `QueueReceiver` (for `TopicSubscriber`). The last five steps are as follows:

1. Start the `Connection`

2. Use `QueueReceiver.receive()` or `QueueReceiver.receiveNoWait()` for receiving messages

3. Optionally use an instance of `MessageListener` and register it for the `QueueReceiver`, then use `MessageListener.onMessage()` method to receive messages

4. Use the required `Message` style and receive messages

5. Close the `QueueConnection`

These processes are summarized diagrammatically below:

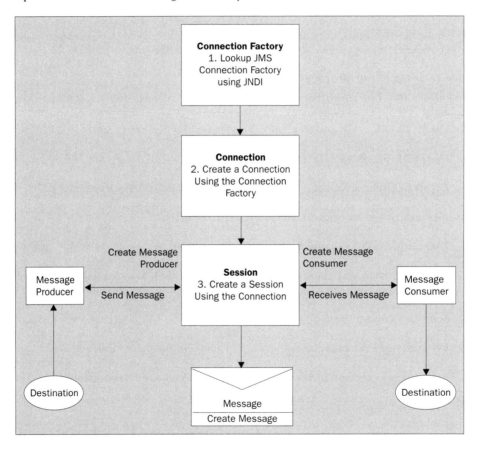

Message Selectors

Messaging applications are required to filter and categorize messages based on defined header properties before routing. This reduces the bandwidth use and also avoids sending unwanted messages to the consumers. JMS sets the filtering criteria using application-specific message properties.

JMS clients specify message selection criteria using the message header and its properties. In JMS, **message selectors** (query strings based on ANSI SQL-92 syntax and expressions) are used by consumers for filtering messages delivered to them.

The following code snippet defines a selector which enables a consumer to filter messages with priority greater than or equal to four:

```
String selector = "JMSPriority >= 4";
    qsession.createReceiver(queue, selector);
```

Note that we have used the `createReceiver()` method to create a queue receiver with a specified message selector. We can also create a topic subscriber in a similar way using `createSubscriber()`.

JMS Reliability Mechanisms

JMS provides mechanisms to achieve high reliability and assured message delivery. JMS specifications categorize these into two types:

- ❑ Basic reliability
- ❑ Advanced reliability

We can further subcategorize basic reliability mechanisms into:

- ❑ Acknowledgement
- ❑ Persistence
- ❑ Priority
- ❑ Expiry

Advanced reliability mechanisms can also be split into:

- ❑ Durable subscriptions
- ❑ Local transactions

We will now discuss each of these mechanisms in turn.

Message Acknowledgement

If we employ the message acknowledgement mechanism, message delivery is considered unsuccessful until a JMS message is acknowledged. Acknowledgement can be initiated either by the JMS provider or by the client applications, based on the acknowledgement mode.

For transacted sessions, acknowledgement happens automatically when a transaction is committed. If a transaction is rolled back, the messages must be redelivered by the JMS provider. In non-transacted sessions, the message acknowledgement depends upon the acknowledgement mode value, which is specified in the arguments of the `createQueueSession()` or `createTopicSession()` methods. The different modes are as follows:

- ❑ `AUTO_ACKNOWLEDGE` – the session automatically acknowledges a message receipt.

355

❑   CLIENT_ACKNOWLEDGE – a client acknowledges a message by calling the message's acknowledge() method.

❑   DUPS_OK_ACKNOWLEDGE – considered as a lazy acknowledgement of the message delivery. It is likely to result in the redelivery of unacknowledged messages if the JMS provider fails.

Message Persistence

In the case of JMS provider failure, the JMS API supports two types of persistence modes for message delivery:

❑   Using PERSISTENT delivery mode makes sure the message is stored in a database or file by the JMS provider when it is sent

❑   Using NON_PERSISTENT delivery mode does not provide a guarantee or message storage

The delivery modes can be set using the setDeliveryMode() method provided by the MessageProducer interface, or via the second argument to the myQueueSender.send() or myTopicPublisher.publish() methods.

Message Priority

This mechanism instructs the JMS provider to deliver the messages based on priority. Priority values are between 0 – 9. It is used as the third argument of the QueueSender.send() or TopicPublisher.publish()methods.

Message Expiry

By default in JMS a message never expires. If a message needs to become obsolete after some time, we must set an expiration time. The expiration time can be set by defining a number of milliseconds for the message to live and passing it to the setTimeToLive() method provided by the MessageProducer interface. Another approach is to pass the time to live as the fourth argument to the QueueSender.send() or TopicPublisher.publish() methods.

Durable Subscriptions

JMS provides durable topic subscriptions, which allow consumers to receive messages while they are not active.

Local Transactions

The Session interface provides commit() and rollback() methods for use in JMS based transactions. A transaction commit occurs when all of the participating consumers acknowledge messages. A transaction rollback occurs when the transaction is incomplete and all messages must be redelivered.

Using Enterprise JavaBeans with JMS

Usually EJB-based applications send and receive messages synchronously but not asynchronously; they cannot spawn threads and asynchronously respond to requests. This becomes a limiting factor in a J2EE-based integration framework involving EJBs.

Message-driven beans, a new feature in the Enterprise JavaBeans 2.0 specification, resolve these issues by extending the EJB component model to support asynchronous messaging. Message-driven beans provide asynchronous messaging behavior for EJB-based applications by acting as a `MessageListener` asynchronously receiving messages, typically as message consumers. Message-driven beans can be tied up with a JMS queue, topic, or durable subscription, to receive messages sent by J2EE applications and also non-J2EE applications.

Like a `MessageListener` for a JMS message consumer, a message-driven bean contains an `onMessage()` method, which is called automatically when a message arrives for the bean in the EJB container. However, from an implementation standpoint, the message-driven bean differs from a JMS message consumer in the following ways:

- ❑ The EJB container associates a message-driven bean with a `Destination` and `ConnectionFactory`

- ❑ The container registers the `MessageListener` (we don't need to call `setMessageListener()`)

- ❑ The EJB container specifies the message acknowledgment mode when distributed transactions are involved

- ❑ The bean class implements the `MessageDrivenBean` and `MessageListener` interfaces

- ❑ In addition to the `onMessage()` method, the bean implements an `ejbCreate()` method for synchronous messages, especially for looking up JNDI connection factories, and so on

- ❑ The bean implements an `ejbRemove()` method too, for closing connections with connection factories, and so on

- ❑ The bean implements the `setMessageDrivenContext()` method to provide additional methods (especially for managing transactions):

```
public void setMessageDrivenContext(MessageDrivenContext mc) {}
```

Unlike entity beans and session beans, message-driven beans do not have home or remote interfaces. They are instantiated by the EJB container directly. Like stateless session beans, message-driven bean instances are short-lived and do not maintain or retain any client-specific state. We can have many interchangeable message-driven bean instances running at the same time, which are managed by the container as a pool. The container creates a new instance of a message-driven bean in three steps:

1. A new instance is created by calling the `newInstance()` method

2. The context object is passed to the instance by calling the `setMessageDrivenContext()` method

3. The instance's `ejbCreate()` method is called

For more information about using message-driven beans, refer to Chapter 12 of this book or Professional EJB, Wrox Press, ISBN 1-861005-08-3.

Managing Distributed Transactions in JMS

We can put together a series of operations into an atomic unit of work, known as a local transaction. We have seen that the `Session` interface provides `commit()` and `rollback()` methods for use in JMS clients when they require transactional support. A client uses the `Session.commit()` method to ensure that all produced messages are sent and then consumed by message consumers. A call to `Session.rollback()` means that, due to a failure, all produced messages are destroyed and all the received messages are recovered and require redelivery.

The JMS specification does not require that users have to support distributed transactions. This is because, even though it is possible for JMS clients to handle transactions directly, it is believed that not many clients will need to do this. However, JMS specifies that if the user were to provide support for distributed transactions, it should be done through the Java Transaction API (JTA). Similarly, if a JMS provider is also a distributed transaction monitor, it should provide control of the transaction through JTA. We'll cover transactions in more detail in Chapter 15.

XML Messaging with JMS

In Chapter 6, we noted that one of the major strengths of XML is its open standard and platform/application-independent data format, which allows us to use it for information exchange between heterogeneous applications. XML can be used to define data covering a wide range of contexts and applications by providing rich functional data structures organized hierarchically rather than in a presentation format. This allows an XML parser to parse and interpret the data accordingly.

In EAI, using XML as an exchange data mechanism between heterogeneous applications environment promotes scalability of the architecture, and provides a standard data format between inter-business application processes. XML is currently backed by many ERP (PeopleSoft, SAP) and database (Oracle, IBM, and Sybase) vendors, who provide XML interfaces and promote data exchange via XML.

JMS offers a standard communication channel across heterogenous platforms, and provides us with a generic API to communicate with a wide range of applications. You may have noticed by now that there is no XML message type that has been provided or is a requirement in the JMS specification and its compliant implementation. XML also does not provide or include a transaction or communication infrastructure.

Combining XML and JMS in a messaging-based application infrastructure results in:

❑ Loose-coupling of applications

❑ Less payload compared to other data formats

❑ Readable data and simplified data exchange

❑ Easier JMS message routing and transformation

❑ The addition of transactional ability to XML messaging

As JMS does not provide XML message type support, in practice XML messages are converted to string-based `TextMessage` messages, and then we can use the JMS provider to send it. At the message consumer end, the `TextMessage` is retrieved, the string is converted to XML, it is validated, and then it is transformed to the required format.

Developing an XML/JMS Messaging Application

In this section we build on the case study scenario we encountered in the previous three chapters, and illustrate how XML messaging can be incorporated in the scenario of loading summary data (HQSales.xml) into the DataWarehouse database.

In this example, XML messaging using JMS is used to transport XML messages between the source application and the destination DataWarehouse application. To achieve this we need to create the following XML-based messaging service classes for sending and receiving messages from the JMS queue:

❑   A QueueSender (SendXMLService) sends the XML data (HQSales.xml) wrapping it as a TextMessage to the JMS Queue.

❑   A QueueReceiver (ReceiveXMLService) receives a TextMessage from the JMS Queue. The TextMessage is unwrapped to retrieve the XML document.

From here, we use the XSLT mechanism described in the previous chapter to transform the XML received using the XSLT script (DWQuarterlySales.xsl), into a temporary XML format. It is then parsed to retrieve the data to insert/update into the Quarterly_Sales table in the DataWarehouse database. This example uses the Apache Xerces parser to parse the XML and the Xalan XSLT processor. The following figure represents the implementation scenario with service components:

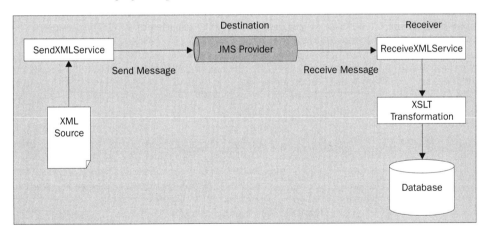

Sending XML Using JMS

The following source code, SendXMLService.java, illustrates sending XML (HQSales.xml) using JMS as a TextMessage:

```
import javax.jms.*;
import org.w3c.dom.*;
import org.apache.xml.serialize.*;
import org.apache.xerces.parsers.DOMParser;
import org.apache.xerces.dom.*;
import org.xml.sax.InputSource;
import java.io.*;
import javax.naming.*;
```

```
public class SendXMLService {
  String             queueName = null;
  Context            jndiContext = null;
  QueueConnectionFactory  queueConnectionFactory = null;
  QueueConnection    queueConnection = null;
  QueueSession       queueSession = null;
  Queue              queue = null;
  QueueSender        queueSender = null;
  TextMessage        message = null;
  String             userName = null;

  final static int MIN_DATA_SIZE = 10;

  public SendXMLService(String queueName, String userName) throws JMSException {
    this.queueName = queueName;
    System.out.println("queueName " + queueName);
    this.userName = userName;
    System.out.println("userName " + userName);
```

In the first method, the constructor `SendXMLService()`, we begin by displaying the name of the queue and the user. Then we create a JNDI `InitialContext` object if none exists yet.

The next three lines of code are specific to readers who are using BEA WebLogic as their application server. We need to create a new `Properties` object, and add to it the initial context factory and the provider URL. If you are not using WebLogic, you should consult your applications server's documentation to find out how to do this:

```
try {
  Properties prop = new Properties();
  prop.put(Context.INITIAL_CONTEXT_FACTORY,
           "weblogic.jndi.T3InitialContextFactory");
  prop.put(Context.PROVIDER_URL, "t3://localhost:7001");
```

We then feed this `Properties` object to the `InitialContext`:

```
  jndiContext = new InitialContext(prop);
} catch (NamingException e) {
  System.out.println("Could not create JNDI " +
                     "context: " + e.toString());
  return;
}
```

We then look up a `QueueConnectionFactory` and a `Queue`, and create a `QueueConnection` and a `QueueSession`:

```
try {
  queueConnectionFactory = (QueueConnectionFactory)
                        jndiContext.lookup("QueueConnectionFactory");
  queue = (Queue) jndiContext.lookup(queueName);
  queueConnection = queueConnectionFactory.createQueueConnection();
  queueSession = queueConnection.createQueueSession(
                            false,Session.AUTO_ACKNOWLEDGE);
  queueSender = queueSession.createSender(queue);
```

Next we start the connection and create a `TextMessage`:

```
queueConnection.start();
TextMessage message = queueSession.createTextMessage();
```

Then we read the XML into a string from `HQSales.xml`, and instantiate a new parser (we'll define the `MyXMLFileReader()` method in a moment):

```
String myXML = MyXMLFileReader("HQSales.xml");
DOMParser parser = new DOMParser();
```

Then we read the XML into an `InputSource`, parse this object, retrieve the contents as a `Document` object, and serialize the contents of this into a string using the `SerializeDoc()` method that we will also define later in the class:

```
org.xml.sax.InputSource is = new org.xml.sax.InputSource(
                          new java.io.StringReader(myXML));
parser.parse(is);
org.w3c.dom.Document doc = parser.getDocument();
String myMessage = SerializeDoc(doc);
```

Next we display the contents of the string, and set the body of the `TextMessage` to the contents of the string. Then we send the message and close the connection:

```
    System.out.println(myMessage);
    message.setText(myMessage);
    queueSender.send( message );
    queueConnection.close();
} catch (Throwable e) {
    System.out.println(e);
}
}
```

The next method, `SerializeDoc()`, serializes a `Document` object into a string:

```
public String SerializeDoc(Document doc) {
    String textMsg = "";
    try {
```

We need to instantiate a `StringWriter` and an `XMLSerializer`:

```
StringWriter sw = new StringWriter ();
XMLSerializer serializer = new XMLSerializer();
```

Then we set the output stream to be serialized into a string, and instantiate an `OutputFormat` object to control the `serializer`:

```
serializer.setOutputCharStream(sw);
OutputFormat fmt = new OutputFormat(doc);
fmt.setIndenting(true);
```

We use the `OutputFormat` object to set the indentation on, and then we finally serialize the `doc` as a string:

```
            serializer.setOutputFormat(fmt);
            serializer.serialize(doc);
            textMsg = sw.toString();
      } catch (Exception e) {
            e.printStackTrace();
      }
```

The method returns the resulting string:

```
      return textMsg;
}
```

The next method reads the XML file:

```
public String MyXMLFileReader (String filename) throws Exception {
      int iBytesRead = 0;
      char[] cBuf = null;
      File filestat = null;
      int iFileSize = 0;
```

The method takes a `String` filename as argument. This is converted into a `File` object, and `FileReader` is instantiated for this object:

```
      filestat = new File (filename);
      cBuf = new char[(int)filestat.length()];
      FileReader fXMLFile = new FileReader (filename);
      iBytesRead = fXMLFile.read(cBuf);
```

If the data in the `File` is less than a minimum number of characters we throw an exception:

```
      if (iBytesRead < MIN_DATA_SIZE) {
          throw new IOException("File less than " + MIN_DATA_SIZE + " bytes.");
      }
      String xml = new String(cBuf);
      return xml;
}
```

We finish the class with the `main()` method that instantiates the `SendXMLService` class:

```
public static void main(String[] args) {
    try {
        String queueName = "XMLQueue";
        String userName = "XMLSender";
        SendXMLService sendXML = new SendXMLService(queueName, userName);
    } catch (Throwable e) {
        System.out.println("Caught exception: " + e );
        e.printStackTrace();
    }
  }
}
```

Receiving XML Using JMS

The following source code, `ReceiveXMLService.java`, shows how to receive XML using JMS as a
TextMessage:

```java
import javax.jms.*;
import org.w3c.dom.*;
import org.apache.xml.serialize.*;
import org.apache.xerces.parsers.DOMParser;
import org.apache.xerces.dom.*;
import org.xml.sax.InputSource;
import java.io.*;
import javax.naming.*;

public class ReceiveXMLService {
    String                  queueName = null;
    String                  userName = null;
    Context                 jndiContext = null;
    QueueConnectionFactory  queueConnectionFactory = null;
    QueueConnection         queueConnection = null;
    QueueSession            queueSession = null;
    Queue                   queue = null;
    QueueReceiver           queueReceiver = null;
    TextMessage             message = null;

    public ReceiveXMLService(String  queueName, String userName)
                                            throws JMSException {
        this.queueName = queueName;
        System.out.println("queueName " + queueName);
        this.userName = userName;
        System.out.println("userName " + userName);
```

In a similar way to the constructor for `SendXMLService`, we start the `ReceiveXMLService()`
constructor by displaying the names of the queue and user. Then we create a JNDI `InitialContext`
object if none exists yet. As with the other client, if we are using WebLogic application server we need
to create a new `Properties` object, and add it to the `InitialContext`:

```java
try {
    Properties prop = new Properties();
    prop.put(Context.INITIAL_CONTEXT_FACTORY,
            "weblogic.jndi.T3InitialContextFactory");
    prop.put(Context.PROVIDER_URL, "t3://localhost:7001");
    jndiContext = new InitialContext(prop);
} catch (NamingException e) {
    System.out.println("Could not create JNDI " + "context: " + e.toString());
    System.exit(1);
}
```

Then we look up the queue connection factory and queue. If either does not exist, we exit:

```
try {
  queueConnectionFactory =
        (QueueConnectionFactory) jndiContext.lookup("QueueConnectionFactory");
  queue = (Queue) jndiContext.lookup(queueName);
} catch (NamingException e) {
  System.out.println("JNDI lookup failed: " + e.toString());
  System.exit(1);
}
```

Next we create a connection, as we did in `SendXMLService()`. Create a session from a connection (the false agreement means that the session is not transacted):

```
try {
  queueConnection =
  queueConnectionFactory.createQueueConnection();
  queueSession =
        queueConnection.createQueueSession(false, Session.AUTO_ACKNOWLEDGE);
  queueReceiver = queueSession.createReceiver(queue);
  queueConnection.start();
  System.out.println("QueueReceiver Started");
```

Our next step is to create a receiver, then start message delivery. We receive all text messages from the queue until a non-text message is received, indicating the end of the message stream (then we close the connection):

```
  Message message = queueReceiver.receive();
  System.out.println("Received Message");

  if(message != null) {
    if (message instanceof TextMessage) {
```

Here we transform the XML using the `DWQuarterlySales` class as discussed in the previous chapter. However, we will modify this to accept a `TextMessage` in a string format, rather than reading from a file:

```
      DWQuarterlySales dwqsTransformer =
        new DWQuarterlySales( ((TextMessage)message).getText() );
      dwqsTransformer.runTransform();
    } else {
      System.out.println(" Non Text message ");
    }
  }
  queueConnection.close();
} catch (JMSException e) {
  System.out.println("JMS Exception occurred: " + e.toString());
  e.printStackTrace();
} catch (Exception ex) {
  System.out.println("Exception occurred: " + ex.toString());
  ex.printStackTrace();
} finally {
  if (queueConnection != null) {
    try {
      queueConnection.close();
```

```
        } catch (JMSException e) {
          System.out.println(e.getMessage());
        }
      }
    }
  }

  public static void main(String[] args) {
    try {
      String queueName = "XMLQueue";
      String userName = "XMLReceiver";
      ReceiveXMLService test = new ReceiveXMLService(queueName, userName);
    } catch (Throwable e) {
      System.out.println("Caught exception: " + e );
      e.printStackTrace();
    }
  }
}
```

Performing the XML Transformation

In the previous chapter, we saw how the DWQuarterlySales program was used to transform and process the XML and store the data in the database. In the XML messaging scenario, we will be using the same class with changes to enable it to receive an XML message in a string format.

To achieve this we reimplement the DWQuarterlySales class used in the previous chapter with following minor changes:

❑   We need to declare a new string object at the beginning of the class:

```
public class DWQuarterlySales {

  private String              xmlMsg;
  private Node                rootNode;
  private Connection          connDW;
  private PreparedStatement   psInsert, psUpdate;
  private int                 nInsert,  nUpdate;
```

❑   The constructor of this class DWQuarterlySales accepts a XML message as string instead of a filename:

```
DWQuarterlySales (String inputXMLMsg) {
  xmlMsg = inputXMLMsg;
}
```

❑   The method name copy() has been renamed to runTransform():

```
public void runTransform () {
  initJDBC();
  initXML();
  processXML();
  printResults();
  closeJDBC();
}
```

❑   The method `initXML()` has been modified to get the XML message from the string:

```
private void initXML() {
  try {
    TransformerFactory tFac = TransformerFactory.newInstance();
    StreamSource xmlData   = new StreamSource(new StringReader(xmlMsg));
    StreamSource xslSource = new StreamSource("DWQuarterlySales.xsl");
    DOMResult domResult = new DOMResult();

    Transformer trans = tFac.newTransformer(xslSource);
    trans.transform (xmlData, domResult);
    rootNode = domResult.getNode();
  } catch (Exception e) {
    System.out.println ("Error initializing XML structures");
    e.printStackTrace();
  }
}
```

❑   We also need to remove the `main()` method from `DWQuarterlysales.java`.

Compiling and Running the XML Messaging Application

When you compile the above classes, make sure you have `xerces.jar`, `xalan.jar`, `j2ee.jar`, and `weblogic.jar` (if you are using BEA WebLogic as your application server) added to your classpath. Remember that both of the `xerces.jar` and `xalan.jar` files are bundled with the Xalan download (obtained from http://xml.apache.org/).

To run the program, make sure that the file containing the XSLT script `DWQuarterlySales.xsl`, the data file `HQSales.xml`, and the DTD file `sales.dtd` are all in the current directory. Change the `<!DOCTYPE>` declaration to the more specific path:

```
<!DOCTYPE Sales SYSTEM "file://localhost:/ProEAI/Ch8/Sales.dtd">
```

or the equivalent path to `Sales.dtd` on your machine.

Then restart your J2EE application server. Create a `Queue` with JNDI name `XMLQueue` and a `QueueConnectionFactory` with JNDI name `QueueConnectionFactory` on the server.

Start the XML message Sender and Receiver clients in separate command windows:

```
java SendXMLService
```

```
java ReceiveXMLService
```

As the programs run, you will see the following in the `SendXMLService` window:

366

```
C:\WINNT\System32\cmd.exe                                    _ □ ×

C:\ProEAI\Ch8>java SendXMLService
queueName XMLQueue
userName XMLSender
<?xml version="1.0" encoding="UTF-8"?>
<!DOCTYPE Sales SYSTEM "file://localhost:/ProEAI/Ch8/Sales.dtd">
<Sales>   <Store>    <Region>02</Region>     <Store_ID>01</Store_ID>
          <Sale>     <Transaction>0200000001</Transaction>
          <Register>05</Register>         <Receipt>1006</Receipt>
          <Date>2001-09-01</Date>         <Time>09:25:00.0</Time>
              <Item>        <UPC>051000000115</UPC>
              <Quantity>5.00</Quantity>         <Price>0.89</Price>
          </Item>       <Item>     <UPC>051000026491</UPC>
              <Quantity>4.00</Quantity>         <Price>0.89</Price>
          </Item>       <Item>     <UPC>051000115522</UPC>
              <Quantity>3.00</Quantity>         <Price>0.99</Price>
          </Item>       <Item>     <UPC>031000109011</UPC>
              <Quantity>6.00</Quantity>         <Price>1.25</Price>
          </Item>       <Item>     <UPC>04991409    </UPC>
              <Quantity>5.00</Quantity>         <Price>2.99</Price>
          </Item>       <Item>     <UPC>020000104195</UPC>
              <Quantity>3.00</Quantity>         <Price>0.89</Price>
          </Item>       <Item>     <UPC>011110816542</UPC>
              <Quantity>4.00</Quantity>         <Price>0.39</Price>
          </Item>    </Sale>     <Sale>
          <Transaction>0200000002</Transaction>
          <Register>24</Register>         <Receipt>1012</Receipt>
          <Date>2001-09-01</Date>         <Time>09:55:00.0</Time>
```

The program displays the name of the queue and the client name (XMLSender). Then, as the program parses the XML file, we see the contents of the file displayed in the window.

In the ReceiveXMLService window, you will see something similar to the following (the number of inserts and updates depends upon whether data already exists in the DataWarehouse database):

```
C:\WINNT\System32\cmd.exe                        _ □ ×

C:\ProEAI\Ch8>java ReceiveXMLService
queueName XMLQueue
userName XMLReceiver
QueueReceiver Started
Received Message
Copy complete

  Inserts = 0
  Updates = 262

C:\ProEAI\Ch8>
```

As you can see, this program also displays the names of the queue and the client. We also get messages informing us that the program has started, and that it has received a message (from SendXMLService). After the XML transformation has been completed, and the data has been placed in the DataWarehouse, we receive a status report on the data transfer.

Some J2EE vendors (such as SonicMQ, Fiorano, iBus, IBM MQSeries, and TIBCO) provide JMS implementation with support for XML messaging to send and receive XML documents in a JMS application, rather than using the TextMessage class. Using those JMS implementations it is possible to use XML-specific message selectors to filter unwanted messages based on the results of a query. This helps to reduce network traffic and improve performance of the JMS application.

Using JAXM for Messaging

A JMS-based messaging infrastructure stands inside the enterprise, or within a firewall, and it lacks a generic message type to provide interoperability between B2B vendor applications over the Internet. This problem has the potential to stifle B2B. To overcome these issues, as part of a Java Community Process (JCP) initiative focusing on B2B messaging, Sun Microsystems released the **JAXM (Java API for XML Messaging)** specification. JAXM uses a common message type (it supports standard XML messaging protocols such as SOAP 1.1 and ebXML), and establishes interoperability via XML messaging.

> **JAXM is a Java-based messaging API, used for development of XML-based messaging applications for use over the Internet.**

At the time of publication, JAXM Version 0.93 has been released for Public Review as Draft. Sun plans to release JAXM 1.0 soon, initially as an optional package for J2SE (SDK) and then with future releases of J2EE, especially targeting J2EE 1.4.

This section discusses JAXM features and implementation limited to the JAXM version 0.93-draft specification and its reference implementation. It is too early to dive into the intricate details of the JAXM specification, as there are many potential JCP requests pending for JAXM 1.0.

For more detailed information about JAXM than we provide here, take a look at http://java.sun.com/xml/jaxm/index.html. The JAXM 0.93 reference implementation bundle is also available to download with simple exercises to try out, which can help you understand its concepts.

Features of JAXM

There are many advantages of using JAXM with your Java applications:

❑   Packaging, routing and transporting of XML-based messages and transactions is performed using common protocols such as HTTP, SMTP, FTP, and so on.

❑   JAXM establishes a foundation for supporting other XML-based messaging protocol standards defined by ebXML.org, SOAP.org, UDDI.org, Oasis.org, W3C.org and IETF. As of the JAXM 0.93 specification, the JAXM vendor implementation provides transport bindings for SOAP messages in compliance with the SOAP 1.1 specification. This enables JAXM providers to support most industry standard messaging and networking protocols such as HTTP, SMTP (IMAP, POP) and so on. JAXM also implements Simple Object Access Protocol (SOAP) 1.1 with Attachments. This allows developers to build messaging applications to send, receive, and decompose messages for their SOAP-based applications without using low-level communications routines.

❑   A JAXM application may be written as a SOAP-based web service, a SOAP service client, or both.

❑   JAXM supports message exchange templates (sometimes referred to as message choreography).

❑   It extends support for a variety of data types in message payloads.

❑ Supports the non-repudiation of messages – especially focusing upon privacy and integrity of communications between message producers and consumers over the Internet.

❑ Enables access control to business-oriented services.

❑ Supports security, audit trails authentication and authorization mechanisms.

❑ In a JAXM-based messaging application, the communication between business applications or partners over an intranet or the Internet can be synchronous (request/reply) or asynchronous.

Typical JAXM Messaging Infrastructure

In this section we will outline a typical JAXM infrastructure (as of the JAXM 0.93 specification).

First, the **JAXM provider** provides the communication infrastructure, implementing message routing and other reliable messaging mechanisms typical to a JMS provider. **JAXM clients** are JAXM applications that provide a client view in a request-response service, or a service view in a messaging service. In a peer-to-peer communication model, a JAXM client can also play a client role or a server role. The `javax.xml.messaging.SyncListener` interface allows JAXM clients to work in a HTTP request/response style with JAXM services. HTTP is the basic transport mechanism for JAXM and it supports security protocols such as SSL and the use of digital signature technologies to sign application-level XML fragments.

Similar to JMS `MessageListener`, the `javax.xml.messaging.AsyncListener` and `javax.xml.messaging.JAXMServlet` interfaces provide message listener interfaces that allow JAXM clients to deliver messages to message-driven beans and web components. In EJB containers, the `AsyncListener` interface may be implemented using message-driven beans. Similarly JAXM clients may extend the `JAXMServlet` interface and implement the `onMessage()` method.

JAXM profiles provides the information contract, which uniquely identifies a particular industry standard of messaging. JAXM applications use profiles for enabling agreements to exchange business messages with peer services. For example, the JAXM profile for ebXML Transport, Routing and Packaging 1.0 could be identified by the following URI:
http://www.ebxml.org/project_teams/transport/messageHeader.xsd.

JAXM API Programming Model

JAXM specification version 0.93 defines two major packages: `javax.xml.messaging` and `javax.xml.soap`.

javax.xml.messaging

JAXM clients intending to support asynchronous one-way messaging use an implementation of this messaging package. The package includes several interfaces:

❑ `AsyncListener` – An asynchronous messaging listener interface for client components intended to be consumers of JAXM messages

❑ `SyncListener` – A synchronous messaging listener interface for client components intended to be consumers of JAXM messages

❑ `ProviderConnection` – A client's active connection to its JAXM provider

❑ `ProviderConnectionFactory` – A connection factory for creating connections to a JAXM provider

❑ `ProviderMetaData` – Details of the JAXM provider to which the client has a connection

It also includes the following classes:

❑ `Endpoint` – Represents an application endpoint, typically a destination of messages

❑ `JAXMServlet` – This is the superclass for servlet components residing in a web container that receives JAXM messages

❑ `URLEndpoint` – This represents an URL as a special `Endpoint` class, used by a simple JAXM application that communicates directly with another SOAP-based application without using a JAXM provider

javax.xml.soap

This package provides the SOAP package for handling SOAP messages and its MIME attachments. Additionally, it provides a client view of a request-response style of interaction with a `SOAPService`.

There are several interfaces in this package, including:

❑ `SOAPBody` – An object that represents the contents of the SOAP body element in a SOAP message

❑ `SOAPBodyElement` – Represents the contents of a `SOAPBody` object

❑ `SOAPElement` – Represents the contents of a `SOAPBody` object, the contents of a `SOAPHeader` object, and the content that can follow the `SOAPBody` object in a `SOAPEnvelope` object

❑ `SOAPEnvelope` – The container for the `SOAPHeader` and `SOAPBody` portions of a `SOAPPart` object

❑ `SOAPHeader` – An object representing the contents of the SOAP `HeaderElement`

❑ `SOAPHeaderElement` – An object representing the contents of the SOAP header part of the SOAP envelope

❑ `Name` – A representation of an XML name

There are also several classes in the package:

❑ `AttachmentPart` – An attachment to a `SOAPMessage` object

❑ `MessageFactory` – Provides a factory for creating `SOAPMessage` objects

❑ `MimeHeader` – An object which stores a MIME header name and its value

❑ `MimeHeaders` – A container for `MimeHeader` objects representing the MIME headers present in a MIME part of a message

We will encounter many of these interfaces and classes in the next sections, when we show how to use the JAXM API for SOAP messaging.

Programming Steps for Using the JAXM API

The JAXM specification defines two scenarios where we would use the JAXM API for creating and sending messages. The one we choose depends upon whether we use a JAXM provider or not.

Scenario: No JAXM Messaging Provider

Let's walk through the programming steps required when developing applications using JAXM without a messaging provider.

The first step is to create a SOAPConnection object for sending messages directly to a remote partner represented by a URL:

```
SOAPConnection soapCon = SOAPConnection.newInstance();
```

To create a new message, we then obtain an instance of the MessageFactory class, from which you can create SOAPMessage objects:

```
MessageFactory mf = MessageFactory.newInstance();
SOAPMessage message = mf.createMessage();
```

All messages are created with a SOAP part that contains a SOAP envelope, that in turn contains a SOAP body. The SOAP part of a message, including its headers and content, can contain only data formatted using XML, whereas an attachment can contain any kind of data, including XML or non-XML data and image files.

Next we get the message's SOAPPart object, then get its SOAPEnvelope object:

```
SOAPPart sp = message.getSOAPPart();
SOAPEnvelope envelope = sp.getSOAPEnvelope(true);
```

SOAPPart.getSOAPEnvelope(true) creates a new SOAPHeader object and sets it on the SOAPEnvelope object. We use the SOAPEnvelope object to obtain both the SOAPHeader object and also the envelope's SOAPBody object used for setting the contents of the SOAP part of the message:

```
SOAPHeader header = envelope.getSOAPHeader();
SOAPBody body = envelope.getSOAPBody();
```

Then we add content to the header using a SOAPHeader object to contain SOAPHeaderElement objects, so a new SOAPHeaderElement object is created and added to the header. The new SOAPHeaderElement object is initialized with the specified Name object.

```
SOAPHeaderElement headerElement = header.addHeaderElement(
    envelope.createName("GetBookPrice","WROX","http://www.amazonbooks.org/buyer")
);
headerElement.addTextNode("EAI");
```

Next, we add content to the SOAPBody using SOAPBodyElement objects, so a new SOAPBodyElement object is created and initialized with a new Name object:

```
SOAPBodyElement bodyElement = body.addBodyElement(
    envelope.createName("Text","jaxm","http://java.sun.com/jaxm")
);
bodyElement.addTextNode("Java Rules");
```

Our next step is to create and add an attachment part `AttachmentPart` to the message using the JavaBeans Activation Framework (JAF) API:

```
URL url = new URL("http://java.sun.com/duke.jpg");

AttachmentPart atp1 = message.createAttachmentPart(new DataHandler(url));
message.addAttachmentPart(ap1);

AttachmentPart atp2 =
    message.createAttachmentPart("sun","text/plain; charset=ISO-8859-1");
message.addAttachmentPart(ap2);
```

Then we update the `SOAPMessage` object with all the changes that have been made to it by calling the method `saveChanges()`:

```
message.saveChanges();
```

Now the message is ready to be sent. We create a `URLEndpoint` object with the URL of the endpoint to which the message is to be sent:

```
URLEndpoint endPoint = new URLEndpoint("sunfire:8000");
```

Then we send the message as a synchronous call to the above endpoint using the `connection`, and the reply message is also received back on the same `connection`:

```
SOAPMessage reply = connection.call(message, endPoint);
```

Finally we close the `SOAPConnection` object:

```
connection.close();
```

Scenario: Using a JAXM Messaging Provider

If a messaging provider is used when a client sends a message, the message goes to the messaging provider and it is then forwarded to its recipient. It is important to note that, to run a JAXM application using a messaging provider, we must configure the JAXM client and the messaging provider. Refer to the Configuration and Deployment guide of the JAXM Reference Implementation available at http://java.sun.com/xml/jaxm/index.html.

The programming steps for developing applications using JAXM with a messaging provider are described opposite.

First we need to instantiate a `ProviderConnection` object to create an active connection to the messaging provider. To create this connection, we use JNDI lookup to obtain an instance of the `ProviderConnectionFactory` class. Once we get an instance of the connection factory then we create a connection to the messaging provider:

```
Context ctx = new InitialContext();
ProviderConnectionFactory pcf = (ProviderConnectionFactory)ctx.lookup(
                                                          providerURI);

ProviderConnection pc = pcf.createConnection();
```

Next we use the `connection` to create a `MessageFactory` object, used to create a message. When you create a `MessageFactory` object, the `MessageFactory` returned will create instances of `SOAPMessage` subclasses appropriate to the given profile. Before creating `MessageFactory`, we first make sure the provider supports the profile we passed. In the following snippet, the profile that matches the ebXML profile is passed as a `String` to the method `createMessageFactory()`:

```
ProviderMetaData metaData = pc.getMetaData();
String[] supportedProfiles = metaData.getSupportedProfiles();
String profile = null;

for(int i=0; i < supportedProfiles.length; i++) {
  if(supportedProfiles[i].equals("ebxml")) {
    profile = supportedProfiles[i];
    break;
  }
}
MessageFactory mf = pc.createMessageFactory(profile);
```

Using the `MessageFactory` object, we now create a `SOAPMessage` object according to a minimal ebXML profile used in the JAXM 1.0 RI:

```
EbXMLMessageImpl message = (EbXMLMessageImpl)mf.createMessage();
message.setFrom(new Endpoint(from));
message.setTo(new Endpoint(to));
```

Next we populate the message, in a similar way to when we populated the message passed without using a messaging provider.

Now that the message has been created and contents added, the message is ready to be sent. The message can be sent asynchronously using the `ProviderConnection` method `send()`:

```
pc.send(message);
```

We finish by calling the `ProviderConnection.close()` method to close the `ProviderConnection`:

```
pc.close();
```

A `JAXMServlet` object or a message-driven bean is registered for the endpoint at deployment time because they have implementations of the method `onMessage()`. When the messaging provider gets a message, it calls the `onMessage()` method of `SyncListener` or `AsyncListener`, passing it the `SOAPMessage` object. The implementation of the `onMessage()` method determines how the message is processed.

Implementing a Standalone JAXM Client

Although we discussed the programming steps associated with different scenarios for using JAXM above, at the time of publication the JAXM 1.0 Reference Implementation is currently available as an early access release. It provides an application-programming model for web-based and stand-alone B2B applications.

The JAXM RI provides client-side libraries to generate SOAP messages using the JAXM API, and a client-side run time library is used to send messages to remote partners using either a local provider or a remote provider. A local provider is a library implementation of the JAXM API that allows us to send SOAP messages directly to a remote partner. The remote provider is similar to a JMS message broker.

To round off this section on using JAXM, we are going to use the JAXM RI to implement a standalone JAXM application client. This client will test communication with a receiver using a local JAXM provider.

To run the example, you will need to install the current JAXM Reference Implementation and its libraries as described in the instructions provided in the bundle. Also install Apache Tomcat in order to run the JAXM RI using the Tomcat servlet engine.

Here's the code for the client:

```
import java.io.*;
import javax.xml.soap.*;
import javax.xml.messaging.*;
import java.net.URL;
import javax.mail.internet.*;
import javax.xml.transform.*;
import javax.xml.transform.stream.*;

import org.dom4j.*;

public class TestJaxmClient {
```

The following URL represents the receiver JAXM application bundled with the RI. You should make sure this application is running while testing this client:

```
static final String SIMPLE_SAMPLE_URI ="http://localhost:8080/simple/receiver";

public static void main(String args[]) {
  try {
    URLEndpoint endpoint = null;
    if( args.length > 0 ) {
      endpoint=new URLEndpoint( args[0] );
    } else {
      endpoint=new URLEndpoint(SIMPLE_SAMPLE_URI);
    }
```

In the main() method, our first step is to create the URLEndpoint object that contains the URL of the endpoint to which the SOAP message will be sent. We have two choices here: we can supply the endpoint as an argument to the program at run time, or we can use the default URL. Then we create a SOAPConnection:

```
SOAPConnection connection = SOAPConnection.newInstance();
```

Next we get an instance of MessageFactory for creating messages, and use this to create a SOAPMessage:

```
MessageFactory mf = MessageFactory.newInstance();
SOAPMessage msg = mf.createMessage();
```

Our next step is to populate the message. Again we have two choices here: we can supply the content of the message as an argument to the program at run time, or we can let the program create a dummy message for us:

```
SOAPPart soapPart=msg.getSOAPPart();
SOAPEnvelope envelope = soapPart.getEnvelope(true);

if( args.length > 1 ) {
  StreamSource ssrc=new StreamSource( args[1] );
  soapPart.setContent( ssrc );
} else {
  SOAPBody body = envelope.getBody();
  body.addChildElement(
```

Now we create a Name object, initialized with the local name GetReply, the namespace prefix jaxm, and the URI of the namespace (http://java.sun.com/jaxm/jaxmrules/). We then add this to the body of the SOAP message, along with a string object "name", and a Text object "jaxrules":

```
    envelope.createName("GetReply",
                        "jaxm",
                        "http://java.sun.com/jaxm/jaxmrules/")
  ).addChildElement("name").addTextNode("jaxrules");
}
```

Next we update the contents in the Message:

```
msg.saveChanges();
System.out.println("Sending message to URL: "+ endpoint.getURL());
```

Then we send the message msg to the endpoint using the call() method. The reply message is received back on the same connection:

```
SOAPMessage reply = connection.call(msg, endpoint);
System.out.println("Sent message is logged in \"sent.msg\"");
```

Next we define a file output stream to write to the file sent.msg, and we write our SOAP message to this file. When we have done this we close the stream, and display a message stating that we received a reply:

```
FileOutputStream sentFile = new FileOutputStream("sent.msg");
msg.writeTo(sentFile);
sentFile.close();
System.out.println("Received reply from: " + endpoint);
```

Then we display the results:

```
boolean displayResult = true;
if( displayResult ) {
```

We then perform a transform on the contents of the reply message:

```
System.out.println("Result:");
TransformerFactory tFact = TransformerFactory.newInstance();
Transformer transformer = tFact.newTransformer();
Source src=reply.getSOAPPart().getContent();
StreamResult result = new StreamResult( System.out );
transformer.transform(src, result);
System.out.println();
}
```

We finish by closing the connection:

```
connection.close();
} catch(Throwable e) {
e.printStackTrace();
}
}
}
```

Compiling and Running the JAXM Example

Compile this TestJaxmClient, setting your CLASSPATH to include tools.jar, log4j.jar (which comes with the Tomcat download) and client.jar (this jar file comes with the JAXM download). Then run the program with default parameters using the following command:

```
java TestJaxmClient
```

You should see the following:

The program sends the SOAP message to the URL shown; the message is then logged in the file sent.msg. If you open this file you will see the following XML:

```
<Envelope xmlns="http://schemas.xmlsoap.org/soap/envelope/">
  <Header/>
  <Body>
    <jaxm:GetReply xmlns:jaxm="http://java.sun.com/jaxm/jaxmrules/">
      <name>jaxrules</name>
    </jaxm:GetReply>
  </Body>
</Envelope>
```

A reply is then posted back via the same connection, which contains the response `This is a response`. This SOAP message is displayed in the command window.

Summary

In this chapter, we have discussed how to employ messaging-based solutions for J2EE-enabled EAI. We noted that messaging provides a reliable means of communication between applications running on heterogeneous platforms. We have covered the following messaging topics:

❑ The role of enterprise messaging, message brokers, and Message-Oriented Middleware (MOM) in EAI

❑ Message broker infrastructure and components

❑ The role of the Java Message Service (JMS) as a message broker

❑ Implementing applications that use enterprise messaging applications, using J2EE

❑ How to develop XML-based messaging applications using J2EE

❑ Using JAXM for messaging-enabled EAI between businesses

In the next chapter we will move away from looking at data integration, and discuss ways that we might implement business process integration.

Business-level integration

In the previous four chapters we investigated data-level integration, so now we'll move on to focus on reusing more than just the data for integration. Business-level integration focuses on reusing the functionality of existing applications. However, business-level integration is a collective name for two integration phases:

❑ **Application-interface-level integration** solves technical aspects connected with reusing the functionality of existing applications. Usually it is achieved through the use of APIs, exposed by existing applications, or added later. Application interfaces enable access to the functionality on a programmatic level without using a user interface. However, application interfaces provided by existing applications usually provide only low-level functions that don't fit directly into a high-level integration architecture.

❑ **Business-method-level integration** raises the abstraction level of the application interfaces. Instead of low-level functions, these interfaces expose high-level business methods (business interfaces). The goal of business-method-level integration is to develop the business interfaces that can be considered as business services. To achieve this, the business interfaces have to be based on a newly designed integration architecture, which presents the integrated information system with clear requirements and support for modern technologies. These high-level business interfaces, however, reuse the functionality of the lower-level application interfaces, defined in application-interface-level integration.

Instead of getting into the technologies and implementation details immediately, in this chapter we will focus on the important concepts that enable us to design and later implement business-level integration. We will discuss approaches that we introduced in Chapter 2, such as virtual components and component wrapping. We will show how to use them to hide the technical and semantic differences of existing applications to achieve application-interface-level integration. We will also show how to present the functionality of existing applications at different levels of abstraction to achieve business-method-level integration. For the latter we will have to design the high-level integration architecture of the integrated information system. We will build on top on the integration process that we introduced in Chapter 4 and will base our architecture on the extended J2EE integration architecture that we introduced in Chapter 3.

In the following seven chapters (Chapters 10 – 16) we will look at relevant technologies for business-level integration and provide code examples. We will look at CORBA, RMI-IIOP, EJBs, the Connector Architecture, COM bridges for Windows integration, transaction management, and security management.

In this chapter we will cover the following topics:

- ❑ Objectives of business-level integration

- ❑ Application-interface-level integration

- ❑ Reusing the functionality of existing applications with existing application wrapping

- ❑ Masking the differences through virtual components

- ❑ Business-method-level integration

The Objectives of Business-level integration

Business-level integration has three important objectives to fulfill:

- ❑ To reuse the functionality of existing applications

- ❑ To mask technology differences by representing the functionality of existing applications as components of the J2EE integration architecture

- ❑ To provide high-level business-oriented interfaces on top of existing applications

We will fulfill the first two objectives in the application-interface-level integration phase and the third objective in the business-method-level integration phase.

Application-interface-level Integration

Application-interface-level integration fulfills the first two goals of business-level integration. We will look at both, starting with reusing the functionality of existing applications.

Reusing the Functionality of Existing Applications

The first objective of business-level integration is to reuse not only the data stored in the databases of existing applications, but also the code – the functionality that resides inside these applications. Reusing the functionality of existing applications is not possible without first becoming familiar with their functionality and without performing a technical analysis. We discussed this in Chapter 4.

Once we know the functionality we would like to reuse, we have to solve the technical challenges. Often existing applications provide an API. Sometimes however, as API won't be available, so we will have to attach a wrapper to reuse existing applications' functionality. One approach would be to modify existing applications and add to them the missing APIs. Another would be to simulate interaction through user interfaces – using screen scraping or terminal emulation. We will discuss existing application wrapping a little later.

In Chapter 4 we described the procedure of how to analyze existing applications. There we also introduced an example integration scenario of a cell phone operator company (Two-2-Yellow) and showed how to identify the functionality that existing applications provide through APIs. We will come back to this topic later in this chapter.

Masking Technology Differences

The second objective of business-level integration is to mask the technology differences when reusing existing applications. APIs and wrappers that we use to reuse the functionality of existing applications differ in the way we access them and which technology we use. If every client that accesses existing applications had to use a different technology and know the exact details of how to access the API or the wrapper, then clients would be difficult to develop and tightly coupled to the existing applications.

We want to present the functionality of existing applications in the business logic tier of J2EE integration architecture (defined in Chapter 3) and use common J2EE technologies to access the functionality. Therefore, we need to mask any technology differences between the J2EE platform and existing applications.

To achieve this we will use **virtual components**.

> **On one side virtual components present the functionality of existing applications through J2EE-compliant interfaces, while on the other side they connect to existing applications through the APIs that existing applications provide.**

The virtual components will have interfaces that provide the same operations as the APIs or wrappers of existing applications. These operations will often be rather low-level; therefore we will call these virtual components **lower-level virtual components**. To build lower-level virtual components in the J2EE integration architecture, we can use the following technologies:

- ❏ EJB
- ❏ CORBA
- ❏ RMI-IIOP
- ❏ J2EE Connector Architecture
- ❏ JMS

Virtual components are deployed in the business logic tier, from where they communicate with existing applications on the EIS tier. For this communication they use a variety of protocols, including IIOP, HTTP(S), protocols used by the J2EE Connector Architecture and MOM products, and proprietary protocols. The selection of protocols will depend on the APIs and wrappers provided by existing applications.

The next figure shows the lower-level virtual components that mask the technology differences and are deployed on the business logic tier. It also shows the existing applications on the EIS tier and the choice of protocols for communication between the tiers:

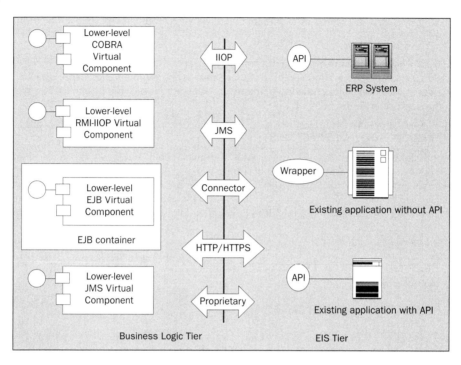

Lower-level virtual components for the cell phone operator example could have interfaces for operations such as calculating the domestic and international consumption based on the total consumption in minutes in a month, or getting the account balance for the last month, etc.

Business-method-level Integration

The business-method-level integration fulfills the third objective of the business-level integration – that is to provide **high-level business-oriented interfaces** on top of existing applications.

With the lower-level virtual components built in the application-interface-level integration, we present the operations of each existing application in the way that they are defined by the application. The problem is that using these low-level operations provided by existing applications will require that clients are familiar with how the existing applications work – they will usually have to invoke several low-level operations in a certain order etc. In other words, clients will be fully aware that they are using existing applications. This will make the clients tightly coupled with the existing applications (although separated by lower-level virtual components).

> **What we would like to achieve is to provide a loose coupling between the new integrated information system and existing applications.**

New clients should not only have access to the functionality of existing applications in a technically uniform way, but the interfaces should also provide semantically uniform business-oriented operations. Interface operations should be logically structured, fit the business requirements, and model the interaction in the same pattern. But most of all, they should present the clients with a high-level view of system functionality.

To achieve this, business-method-level integration introduces **higher-level virtual components**. Higher-level virtual components will aggregate the behaviors of lower-level virtual components and provide a higher abstraction of the existing applications. Higher-level virtual components will on one side expose high-level business methods to the clients, and on the other side translate high-level methods into a series of calls to lower-level virtual components.

In the J2EE architecture, higher-level virtual components will most likely be implemented as EJBs, although other technologies, such as RMI-IIOP, CORBA, JMS, and the J2EE Connector Architecture could be used too:

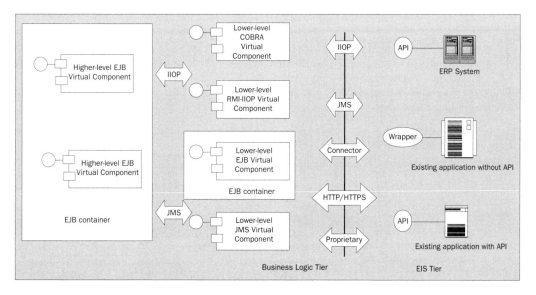

Through higher-level virtual components, business-method-level integration provides several benefits over application-interface-level integration. First of all clients are unfamiliar with the details of existing applications – they don't care how exactly they should invoke low-level operations on existing applications in order to get the results.

The fact that the clients are decoupled from the details of existing applications, will give us the freedom to replace existing applications with newly developed solutions without influencing other applications (clients) that use this application through the higher-level virtual components, thereby making the whole system more flexible and manageable. To replace existing applications, we develop a new component on the business logic tier that will replace the higher-level virtual component, but provides the same interface. Instead of calling existing applications, this newly developed component will implement the operations itself.

To fulfill this goal, it is important that we keep the interface declarations constant. As long as the interfaces of higher-level virtual components stay the same, clients will be unaware when we replace the existing applications. Modifying the interfaces, especially changing the signature of existing operations, would depreciate our objectives and would mean having to update all the clients of that interface, which can be a lengthy process.

> **These high-level interfaces will enable us to not only replace existing applications but also enable our information system to grow and be modified for many years to come.**

Defining the interfaces therefore cannot be done in an ad hoc fashion, but requires serious thought. Let us recapitulate the requirements that we set for the interfaces of higher-level virtual components:

- ❏   Interfaces should be at a high abstraction level

- ❏   Methods should be related to business processes

- ❏   Interfaces should fit into the information architecture of the enterprise

- ❏   Interfaces should be designed with the future in mind – they should be adaptable to future requests

Actually the definition of these interfaces is nothing else but the definition of the global design model of the integrated information system at a high abstraction level. Therefore, later in this chapter, we will address the necessary activities to define such a design model and other necessary activities to perform business-method-level integration.

Here's how we structure the development of business-level integration:

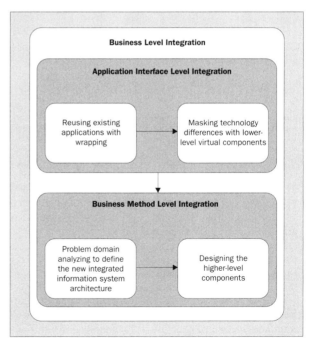

Let's discuss the wrapping of existing applications in more detail first.

Wrapping Existing Applications

It's obvious that if we want to reuse the functionality of existing applications, we have to access them somehow. The most obvious possibility is to access them through a provided API. Sometimes however, existing applications do not provide any APIs, not even proprietary ones. Or they will provide only a subset of functionality through their APIs, but we need access to other functions too. In these cases, we have to add our own interfaces to the existing application, which we will call **wrappers**. There are two possibilities on how to add wrappers to existing applications:

- ❏ We can modify existing applications and provide the missing access functionality

- ❏ We can use screen scraping or terminal emulation to access the functionality though user interfaces

One criterion that influences the decision is the availability of source code and required tools. We have to make sure that the versions of source code are complete and that they reflect the current executable code. If we do not have the source code and all the tools and libraries necessary to build the working executable of the existing application, our only choice will be to utilize user interface wrapping (discussed a little later).

Even if we have the source code and all the required tools, we might still choose not to modify existing applications and use screen scraping or terminal emulation instead. This could be because we may not want to risk introducing bugs into existing applications, when we may not be familiar with the technology etc.

> *Even before we select one of these choices we have to analyze the existing applications to determine which operations will be reused. In Chapter 4 we covered how to perform this analysis to identify the functionality that an existing application provides and how to identify which functions are available through APIs and which are not.*

Modifying Existing Applications

After we have identified the operations of an existing application that we need, but where no existing API is provided, we have to figure out how to modify the application to implement an interface with these operations. In other words, how to go about implementing the wrapper. In this instance, it is obvious that we need to be somewhat familiar with the programming language of the existing application.

An examination of the source code will allow us to focus on the particular functions that we are looking to wrap. A good idea is to start with the user interface and follow which parts of the code (functions, procedures, objects, and so on) are called to implement the functionality. With the analysis of user interface code, we can also become familiar with the required input parameters, the validation of those input parameters, and the sequence of interactions.

The goal here is to identify all the necessary operations we have to perform from the wrapper. In most cases, we have to deal with procedural applications, where we have to call a single or a sequence of functions and procedures. As with many problems, this will depend on the architecture of the existing application. If the application has been developed with sound practices, it may be that we only have to call a few functions.

On the other hand, it can happen that the logic will be interlaced with user interface code and no single set of functions will be responsible for the operation we are trying to wrap. In such a scenario, we have to follow the user interface code and extract the necessary operations. We will also have to care about pre- and post conditions for each function, as expressed through the state of public or global variables.

We then gather the identified code to access the functionality and try to execute it in the experimental environment we set up during our existing application analysis (as described in Chapter 4). We have to be sure that we can invoke the desired functionality inside the application programmatically before we start to add the wrapper code.

Changing the entry points considerably in the existing application is not recommended. This would be too much effort in an unfamiliar environment and programming language. We should keep the amount of change that we apply to a minimum, thus reducing the possibility of introducing bugs. Rather, we should provide higher-level operations within the J2EE business logic tier using virtual components.

Accordingly, testing the modified application is crucial for detecting bugs and errors. A bad experience with the modification of existing applications can ruin the information strategy and the whole integration project. Although it is not an easy task, with careful planning and analysis changes to existing applications can be kept under control.

Screen Scraping and Terminal Emulation

It is not uncommon that we will, sooner or later, experience an integration project in which the source code of the existing applications will be unavailable, or the versions will be incorrect, and so on. Indeed, research from consulting companies, such as Forester, indicate that for more than 40% of legacy applications the source code is not available anymore. It may have been lost or destroyed over the years, but companies have continued to use these applications.

In such a scenario, we have to find a means to access the functionality of these systems in other ways. Unfortunately, there are not many choices. If we deal with character-based or terminal-based applications we can use screen scraping or terminal emulation. Fortunately, many older applications are in fact character-based. Terminal emulation is limited to legacy mainframe solutions, but screen scraping is not very successful for GUI-based applications.

> Although it may be strange at first sight, screen scraping and terminal emulation have been successfully used to integrate a lot of existing applications.

A screen scraper or terminal emulator is a wrapper component that emulates a user interacting with the system. It reads the screen to access the information stored inside the system. To perform operations and enter data it emulates typing. If the system uses any of the standard terminal types we can emulate the control (escape) sequences of those terminals. With character-based applications we can read the screen memory directly.

More difficult to implement is the appropriate handling of exceptions. If something goes wrong we have to be prepared to recognize the errors that the application signals on screen and delegate those mistakes to the client. Such mistakes are not always the fault of the user – there could be bugs or system errors as well. A multitude of errors and exceptional cases have to be catered for in order to design a robust system. If we fail to implement proper error monitoring our wrappers will lock up without reporting the reason, which is far from ideal. For such cases we might consider implementing a recovery mechanism.

When using these techniques we have to pay special attention to performance. With integration, we will open access to existing systems to a much larger number of users than initially planned. In addition, reading the screen and emulating data entry adds additional overhead and process time. Wrappers implemented in this way can be relatively slow and will not scale very well to a larger number of simultaneous clients. We should be aware of these facts when we use this technique. However, several legacy applications have been successfully integrated using this technique. If we figure out that screen scraping or terminal emulation do not provide adequate performance, we have several choices:

❑ We can try to improve the performance of existing applications with hardware upgrades, clustering, replication and other techniques

❑ We can consider modifying existing applications directly (if applicable)

❑ Otherwise we will have to replace the existing application or limit the number of simultaneous clients

For implementing wrappers with screen scraping or terminal emulation, we can use several different technologies that we will discuss in the next section.

Choosing the Technology

The decision of which technology to use to build the wrappers will obviously depend on the technology that the existing system was developed in. In general we can choose from the following:

❑ ORB-style communication, using CORBA or COM+

❑ MOM communication using a product, such as IBM MQSeries (one that support JMS mapping)

❑ Implement communication at a protocol level (SOAP, HTTP, TCP/IP, and so on)

❑ RPC-style communication using a distributed computing environment (DCE)

The type of communication also implies the communication model: synchronous or asynchronous. Again, which we choose is dependent on the existing application architecture.

We also have to check which of the mentioned technologies are applicable to the existing application. For newer existing applications, we can probably implement any of them. However, legacy applications could be implemented in programming languages and technologies that are no longer supported.

Nevertheless, with a little luck we will be able to find at least one technology that we can use. If possible, it is wise to choose either of the first two options in the list above – the ORB or MOM solutions align well with the J2EE integration architecture.

CORBA-compliant products are traditionally available for the majority of platforms, operating systems, and programming languages, so it should not be difficult to find an appropriate product. Note that we should also check which version of the CORBA specification is supported to know which features we can use and what concerns we will have in achieving interoperability with RMI-IIOP.

For integration on a Windows platform, we might consider COM-based solutions and look at using DCOM or COM+ to provide interoperability interfaces for existing applications. There are several ways in which the J2EE platform can communicate with the COM architecture. We can either build custom bridges between the two architectures or we can use a third-party product. We will address this topic in Chapter 14.

For MOM products it is also very common to support both old and not so old platforms relatively well. Most of the serious MOM providers offer support for the JMS specification in their newer versions, therefore it is not too difficult to integrate them.

For most applications it is possible to implement protocol-level communication. Instead of defining our own protocols it is a good idea to stick with one of the standard protocols. Particularly interesting is the SOAP protocol, because it is important for B2B integration, as we will see in the final two chapters of this book. Since SOAP is an XML-based protocol it is not very difficult to program even if we have to do it completely manually. However, for older legacy platforms we will probably not be able to find support libraries for SOAP, so we will have to choose other protocols – popular choices include HTTP and TCP/IP.

If none of these options are applicable we can look towards an RPC solution, such as OSF DCE (Open Software Foundation Distributed Computing Environment). Otherwise, we will have to find a proprietary way in which to achieve communication between the existing application and the J2EE business logic tier. This is not a big disadvantage because the wrapper together with the virtual component will mask the technology.

Implementing Wrappers

After we have selected the technology, we have to implement the necessary interfaces and connection code. These two elements are the most important elements of a wrapper and are presented in the following diagram:

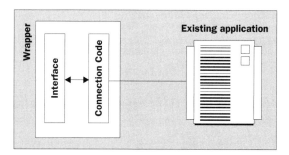

We won't actually explore implementation any further here, as we will be looking at it in detail over next few chapters.

After we've become familiar with how to wrap existing applications that do not provide access to their functionality by default, we have to take a look at how to present existing applications on the business logic tier of the J2EE integration architecture. As we already know we will use virtual components for this.

Virtual Components

In the first section of this chapter we became familiar with the basic idea of virtual components. Now let's discuss them a little more. We discussed lower-level virtual components, defined within application-interface-level integration, and higher-level virtual components, defined within business-method-level integration.

> **From the technical perspective, there is not much difference between lower-level and higher-level virtual components.**

In both cases they present existing applications' functionality in a uniform way, recognized by new developments, and are compatible with the way modern user interfaces are defined. Virtual components on one side expose J2EE-compliant interfaces through which clients can access the functionality of existing applications, while on the other side, they communicate with existing applications or with other virtual components:

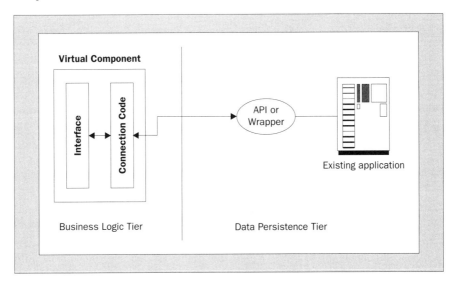

> **The major difference is in the abstraction level of the operations provided through the interface.**

Business-method-level integration exposes higher-level, business-oriented interfaces that are a consequence of detailed analysis and design of the business domain. Therefore, the virtual components for the higher level will be more complicated and will invoke a larger set of underlying existing applications. Often, business-method-level virtual components will be based on top of application-level virtual components, which will result in the chaining of virtual components. This approach also allows us to separate functionality and to build on top of previous results – to upgrade one integration level to the next.

Technical Aspects

We will now look at the technical aspects of building virtual components that are applicable for business-level integration. We will typically use virtual components for one or a combination of following functions:

❑ Virtual components encapsulate the functionality of existing applications and present them in the same way, or some rearranged way. Virtual components can, for example, present exactly the same functionality that can be found in the existing application APIs. In this case they just mask the technology differences and are called lower-level virtual components.

❑ Lower-level virtual components implement code that translates method invocations into one or more calls to APIs of existing applications and database access. This code will often have to do parameter transformations, alignment of data types, and other transformations to mask the technology differences between the J2EE technologies and the technologies used by existing applications. In more simple terms, the lower-level virtual components will act as adapters between the new and the existing applications.

❑ Virtual components can provide a different, higher-level interface and thus mask the way existing applications implement their APIs, too. Such virtual components are called higher-level virtual components and their interfaces should be defined based on a global design model, which we will discuss later in this chapter.

❑ Virtual components can encapsulate several existing applications and help in maintaining transaction integrity and security.

❑ Virtual components are also useful to encapsulate or abstract persistent data. For this purpose, virtual components can access EIS databases directly or through provided protocols. In this case, they will often also implement the validation logic. This is an extra level of security, which might not have been handled by the old application that will keep the database in a consistent state.

❑ Virtual components can provide a unified access to several EIS databases and can handle different combinations of databases in the background. Alternatively they can use APIs to access data, if those APIs are provided by existing applications.

❑ Virtual components will often be layered, thus higher-level virtual components will aggregate the behaviors of lower-level virtual components and provide the higher-level of abstraction required for multiple levels of abstraction of EIS application functionality.

❑ Virtual components can also be used to map technical differences. A particularly useful scenario is to adapt synchronous and asynchronous communication models. Through J2EE technologies, particularly JMS, they will be able to adapt different MOM products. Adapting ORB products will, in most cases, not be difficult because they are all based on the IIOP protocol (and are therefore interoperable).

Technology Choices

We have also already identified that virtual components will be deployed in the business logic tier. In the J2EE integration architecture, we can use the following appropriate technologies: EJB, RMI-IIOP, CORBA, JMS, JCA, JAX/RPC (including SOAP), and JAXM. The latter two technologies are still under development, and therefore currently not very common, but this might change in the future.

Selecting the appropriate technology will not be a particularly difficult task. The first three technologies – EJB, RMI-IIOP, and CORBA – are based on the IIOP protocol, making the choice rather simple. They provide synchronous, ORB-like communication interfaces. Virtual components built in any of these three technologies look similar, exposing their functionality for remote method invocation to Java-based and other IIOP-compliant clients. Due to this similarity, we can effectively exchange the implementations in any of these technologies without the need to alter the clients (clients would not even notice the difference).

CORBA and RMI-IIOP

We will use CORBA and RMI-IIOP particularly for lower-level virtual components that will often have to communicate with existing applications in other programming languages. We will use CORBA virtual components when they will have to use proprietary mechanisms to access existing applications APIs that cannot be invoked from Java. For this purpose, we'll consider using CORBA together with the programming language of the existing application. To access these CORBA virtual components we will often use RMI-IIOP.

Lower-level virtual components will often communicate directly with existing applications on the EIS tier. They will use any or a combination of protocols and technologies to access the EIS tier. This includes the use of JMS, Connectors, IIOP, HTTP, JDBC, or proprietary mechanisms to access the APIs or databases of existing applications. CORBA will be covered in detail in Chapter 10 and RMI-IIOP in Chapter 11.

JMS

We'll use JMS particularly for lower-level virtual components when we have to achieve asynchronous message-oriented communication, through one or a combination of MOM products. Often, we will use MOM on one side through JMS, and on the other side we will usually use the MOM product natively. MOM and JMS were covered in Chapter 8.

EJB

We will use EJBs particularly for developing higher-level virtual components. These virtual components will often communicate with lower-level virtual components, developed in other technologies.

If we need to provide synchronous access over RMI-IIOP to APIs or wrappers we will use session beans to implement virtual components. They will often have to call more than several methods and will also have to transform and adapt the results. If the virtual component does not need to store any client-dependent data between method invocations (from the client and web component tier) we will select stateless session beans; otherwise, we will implement them as stateful session beans.

If we would like to provide asynchronous access to APIs or wrappers then we can use message-driven beans. We implement the connection with the existing systems in a similar way to session beans. The fact that message beans are stateless does not create any problems – with asynchronous requests it is highly unlikely that the bean would need to memorize client-dependent information.

To represent persistent data we can use entity beans. If we implement direct access to the database using JDBC we can use container-managed persistence. If we access data over proprietary protocols or over APIs or wrappers we will have to use bean-managed persistence. We will discuss access to existing databases over virtual components a little later in this chapter. EJBs are covered in detail in Chapter 12.

The J2EE Connector Architecture

The J2EE Connector Architecture (JCA) solves the problem of custom solutions for accessing commercial EIS systems. JCA defines system-level contracts for connection management, security, and transactions between an application server and a connector. The connector for each EIS system implements these contracts in an EIS-specific way. J2EE components access the EIS through a standard API, called the Common Client Interface (CCI).

391

SOAP, JAX/RPC, and JAXM

Sometimes, particularly when integrating newer systems or even next generation systems developed on other enterprise architectures, we will consider using modern XML-based protocols, such as SOAP. For this purpose we will use the same architecture for wrapping different existing systems. The only difference will be that we will use JAX/RPC or JAXM interfaces to access those systems through XML-based interfaces. Using XML-based protocols moves the integration towards B2B integration. This will be covered in Chapter 18.

Developing Virtual Components

When developing virtual components we should follow these guidelines:

❏   We should design virtual components such that they can be used in different situations. High-level virtual components should support different combinations of low-level virtual components. Low-level virtual components should be easily adjustable to different EIS systems.

❏   A higher-level virtual component should not rely on the environment in which it is executing, and should also not make assumptions about the environment. This will make replacement with a newly developed component easier.

❏   A virtual component should be capable of cooperating in the transaction and security models used by the J2EE integration architecture. Furthermore, it should be capable of mapping those transaction and security models to existing applications, if they support transactions and/or security. If they do not, the virtual component will have to provide this functionality, depending on the particular requirements of the project at hand.

Virtual components can be used for a number of several different scenarios. In the following sections we will discuss developing virtual components for:

❏   Accessing existing applications through APIs or wrappers

❏   Accessing large commercial systems

❏   Accessing existing databases

❏   Chaining higher-level virtual components with lower-level virtual components

Accessing Existing Applications Through APIs or Wrappers

Using an API or wrapper directly from J2EE clients (from the client tier, web component tier or business logic tier) would make clients aware of the fact that they are using existing applications. Clients would also need to use a variety of different technologies, which would make them too complicated. As clients use low-level methods, provided by APIs or wrappers, they would be tightly coupled with existing applications, which would make replacing the existing applications later very difficult.

Instead, we will use lower-level virtual components to abstract access to existing applications. The virtual components through which we access the functionality of existing applications are deployed on the business logic tier.

The following figure presents different virtual components implemented in different technologies, together with corresponding APIs and wrappers. Lower-level virtual components implement a one-to-one mapping with existing applications. We can see three different virtual components, using JMS, CORBA, and RMI-IIOP technologies:

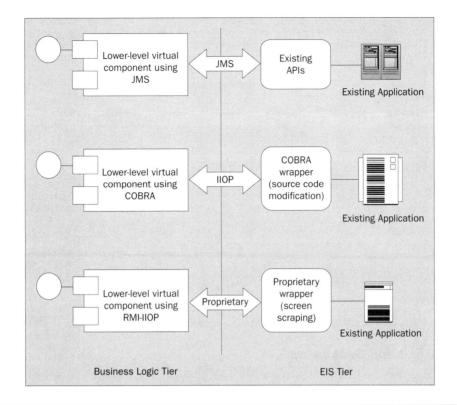

Sometimes a single physical component can take over both roles, the role of the lower-level virtual component and the role of the wrapper.

Accessing Large Commercial Systems

For accessing particularly large commercial systems, such as ERP (Enterprise Resource Planning) and CRM (Customer Relation Management) systems, we will often use the J2EE Connector Architecture (JCA). The J2EE Connector Architecture addresses the problem of providing a standard architecture to integrate application servers with large and commercial EIS systems. With JCA, EIS vendors can provide a single solution (an adapter) to integrate their product with any J2EE 1.3-compliant application server.

Consequently, application server vendors do not need to implement custom interfaces to connect to different business EIS systems, and equally EIS vendors do not need to customize their products for each individual application server.

To access the functionality of commercial EIS systems, the Connector Architecture defines a standard API, the Common Client Interface (CCI). The next figure schematically shows the CCI interface, and two different resource adapters:

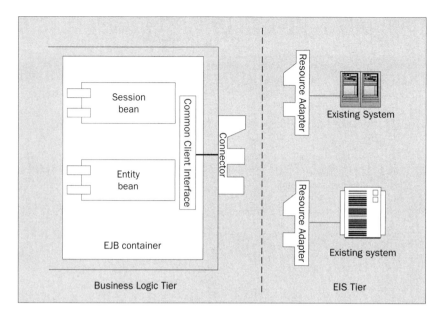

We'll return for an in-depth discussion on JCA with working examples in Chapter 13.

Accessing Existing Databases

Virtual components can be used for accessing existing databases too. This will enable us to add some functionality to the virtual components for manipulating data. Manipulating data can take several forms: incorporating additional database rules, integrity checks, semantic transformations, and so on.

To access a database on the EIS tier we have to select the technology with which we will implement the wrapper. To do this we have to answer questions on how we would like to access the virtual component. If we would like to access it synchronously over an ORB we will choose EJB entity beans.

Entity beans provide both high-level interfaces to the client and web component tiers, as well as access to a database. To access the database from entity beans we need to select how to implement the code for retrieving and storing the data, either manually (bean managed persistence – BMP), or using automatically generated code (container-managed persistence – CMP). The main advantage of CMP over BMP is that we do not have to develop code, which saves time and effort.

CMP however, will only be applicable in simpler scenarios where the existing database is in a relational format and we can access it using a JDBC driver. There are considerable differences between CMP in EJB version 1.1 and version 2.0. The EJB 1.1 persistence model was less flexible and allowed only simple mappings of attributes to database columns, whereas CMP 2.0 provides more flexible object-to-relational mapping. Still, we will have to check whether the mapping supports access to our existing databases.

BMP requires that we implement the code for interacting with the database manually, which requires a lot of effort and is error-prone. Manually developed code will however give us a greater degree of flexibility, as we will be able to use database types other than relational. We will also be able to implement complicated mapping schemas between component attributes and database columns (or other database constructs).

Databases from entity beans are typically accessed using JDBC. If we use a database that provides JDBC support, this approach is applicable. Also, if the database we access provides at least ODBC support we will be able to use JBDC-OBDC bridge drivers. Alternatives to JDBC are SQL/J and Java Data Objects (JDO).

However, in some cases we will have to access other types of databases. From BMP entity beans we can access data in a variety of formats, but sometimes we will not be able to access the data from entity beans directly. For example, let us consider a scenario where the entity bean is deployed on the application server, but we would like to access data stored in a legacy system. In this case, we will have to implement a wrapper for the database. We will provide a single, or several, wrapper objects (for example CORBA or RMI-IIOP objects) on the EIS tier. These objects will provide a bridge that will then be used by entity beans. The wrapper object will provide methods through which the entity bean will be able to access the data. The actual access will be implemented in the wrapper object:

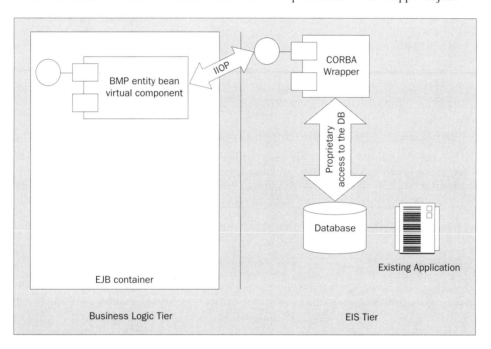

This approach is favorable and offers distinct advantages over the direct access from web component or client tier to the wrapper on the EIS tier. Although the access is transparent to the client, it would complicate the process of replacement of the existing databases. Adding the entity bean in the communication makes the architecture more flexible to change. This approach, however, influences the performance, therefore we have to assess the performance before making a final decision, which is only wise after considering the specific priorities of the project – there will clearly be some compromise between performance and flexibility.

> **Virtual components for accessing existing databases will often implement the database validation logic necessary to keep the database in a consistent state.**

In addition, directly accessing the database bypasses the rules that the existing application has defined regarding the database structure. If we implement those rules in virtual components like entity beans, then we will be able to control the consistency of the database.

Chaining Virtual Components

Often, we have to combine several virtual components to produce the functionality of existing applications with a high-level interface. This can be because we are likely to implement the integration in several steps. We may start by implementing data-levelintegration and provide virtual components to access the database. Then we may proceed with application level integration and continue on to business-method-level integration. In each step, we may reuse the lower level virtual components from previous steps.

This leads to a **multi-layer virtual component architecture**, where higher-level virtual components will be chained to lower-level virtual components. Higher-level virtual components will typically be implemented as EJBs, while lower-level components will use other technologies. The higher-level virtual components will implement a façade to the system.

> **Virtual components will be connected with the Chain of Responsibility pattern.**

The combination of virtual components can also adapt to communication needs. For example, a suitable combination could enable asynchronous access to synchronous interfaces.

This architecture provides the most flexible design and allows us to change or modify the applications easily. However, this approach also introduces a lot of communication between virtual components, and this can influence performance. So, we must find ways to optimize communication when implementing multi-layer virtual component architecture. The chaining of virtual components is shown on the next diagram:

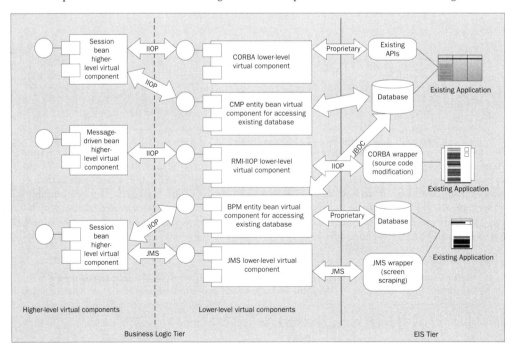

Now that we have become familiar with two of the most important approaches to application-interface-level integration, with the wrapping of existing applications and virtual components, we will look at an example integration scenario.

Example Cell Phone Operator Scenario

Before we start discussing business-method-level integration, we will have a look at an example integration scenario that will help us to demonstrate how to use the concepts of wrapping and virtual components. Based on this example we will also provide solutions with different technologies that we will discuss in the next chapters.

Recap of the Example Scenario from Chapter 4

In Chapter 4 we introduced the example of a cell phone operator company Two-2-Yellow. To refresh our memory, here's a quick recap:

Two-2-Yellow provides services for digital (GMS) cell telephony. The main services are two types of cell accounts: the subscriber account is an account where the customer receives an invoice each month and has to pay it later. The prepaid account is an account where the customer has to put money on the account in advance and cannot call more that the current balance.

The company does not have an integrated information system and uses a set of unconnected or partially connected existing applications. The primary applications that the operator uses are the following:

Customer information application
Enables the management of customers. This includes entering new customers, updating existing customers and adding data about the cell phone account that they have.

Application that manages the account balance for users
Manages both types of accounts. It allows data to be entered regarding the consumption of money and about deposits on the accounts (they can be either the payments of the invoices or the advance deposits, depending on the account type). It also enables searching of accounts that have a negative balance (for the subscribers). For prepaid accounts it allows a search of the accounts that have had zero balance for a specified period of time. Finally, it allows searching for money deposits on those accounts based on age.

Application that prints the invoices each month
This is a simple one that goes through the subscriber accounts and prints the invoices for the consumptions of the specified month.

Application that evaluates domestic phone calls
Calculates the consumption for each account based on the data transferred from the cell phone exchange, but only for domestic calls.

Application that calculates international phone calls
Has a similar function to the domestic application. However, it does not have a direct connection with the cell phone exchange. Rather, it receives input data formatted from each roaming partner.

Application that manages phone call tariff information
Includes functions to enter and display the tariff information. This includes tariff polices, tariff classes, and costs per minute for voice and data communication.

Virtual Components for Existing Applications with APIs

In Chapter 4 we discussed the necessary activities for existing application analysis. In the functional analysis of existing applications we used black box analysis to identify the functions that are provided by the existing applications. For each function, we also identified how it can be accessed – whether the application provides API access or only user interface access.

We identified that the cell phone customer information application, account balance management, and cost and tariff management applications provide their functions through APIs. Moreover, we identified these APIs in more detail and became familiar with the signatures of the operations. We identified that the cell phone customer information application provides an API with the name `CustomerInt`, the account balance management application provides an API with the name `AccountInt` and the cost and tariff management application an API with the name `CostTarifInt`:

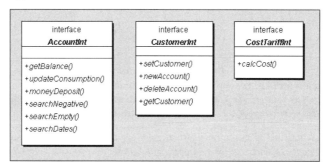

For these three applications we will use the provided APIs. For the purpose of application-interface-level integration, we will define lower-level virtual components on the business logic tier so that they can be accessed from J2EE clients in a consistent way. At this point we won't try to abstract the API methods with higher-level methods yet. On the next figure we can see three virtual components on the business logic tier and three existing applications on the EIS tier. Virtual components access the APIs of existing applications using proprietary protocols:

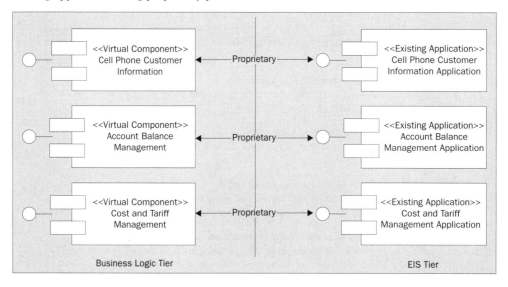

Wrapping Existing Applications Without APIs

We also identified that four of the existing applications do not provide APIs. For these applications we will have to implement our own wrappers, either through source code modification or through terminal emulation or screen scraping. Let's go through the interfaces that the added wrappers will have to provide.

The interface of the invoice print application wrapper is relatively simple and provides a single method to print the invoices only:

Similarly simple are the interfaces of the wrappers for the domestic and international phone evaluation applications. Both provide methods to calculate the domestic and international consumption, respectively:

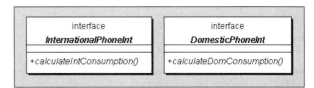

The interface for the policy management application wrapper is, however, a little more complicated. It provides methods for managing the domestic and international tariff policies, for managing tariff classes and costs per minute:

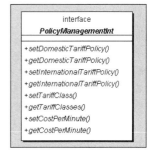

These wrappers will be added to the existing applications to provide programmatic access to the functionality, described in the interfaces. To represent the functionality on the business logic tier, we will also define lower-level virtual components for these applications. We will use JMS for one wrapper and CORBA IIOP for the other three wrappers. Implementing wrappers for our example scenario will bring us to the following architecture:

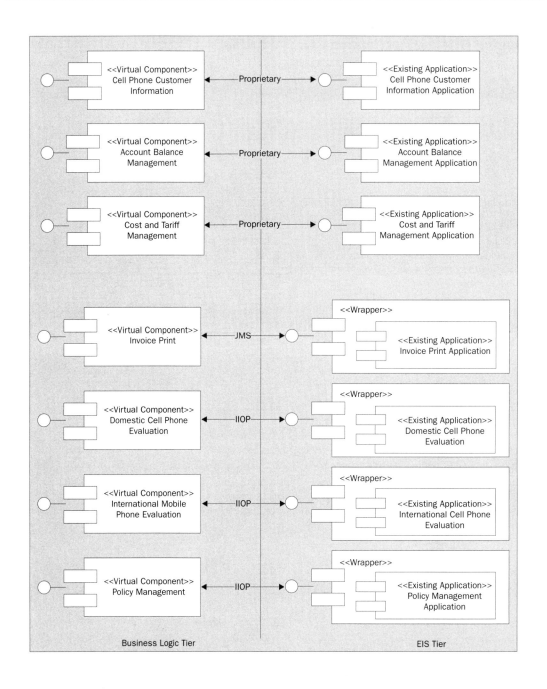

Please notice that sometimes, particularly when using CORBA, RMI-IIOP, or JMS, we will implement the wrapper and the lower-level virtual component as one physical component. At a logical level however, we will think of them as of two separate components.

In the following chapters we will look more closely at how to implement virtual components and wrappers with technologies such as CORBA, RMI-IIOP, EJB, J2EE Connector Architecture, etc.

Achieving Business-method-level Integration

Application-interface-level integration forms the basis for proceeding with business-level integration. After finishing application-interface-level integration we have all the relevant APIs of the existing applications represented as business logic tier virtual components in the J2EE integration architecture.

> **Our goal is to build an integrated information system using a top-down approach. Therefore, the integrated system should expose high-level business-oriented interfaces rather than the low-level application-oriented interfaces that have been directly mapped from existing applications' APIs and wrappers.**

The major challenge of business-method-level integration is how to define the high-level business methods. Interfaces of high-level virtual components should namely be at a high abstraction level, they should be related to business processes, they should fit into the information architecture of the enterprise, and they should be designed with the future in mind and be resistant to change.

The definition of these interfaces is nothing else but the definition of the global design model of the integrated information system. This definition of the global design model is a part of the integration process, as defined in Chapter 4.

The integration process in Chapter 4 defined eight technical activities. Three technical activities do not differ between the integration phases. These are:

❏ Requirements gathering

❏ Analysis of existing applications

❏ Selection of integration infrastructure

These three activities have been covered in Chapter 3 and Chapter 4. The rest of the technical activities are bound with the integration phase:

❏ Problem domain analysis

❏ Design

❏ Implementation

❏ Testing

❏ Deployment

In this chapter we will focus on the **problem domain analysis** and the **design** activities. Implementation, testing and deployment will be addressed in the following chapters for all relevant technologies.

Problem Domain Analysis

Problem domain analysis is the first important activity in defining the global design model for business-method-level integration. In the context of the integration process it is the fourth step:

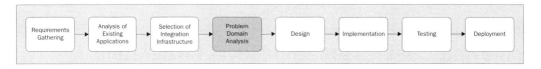

> **In the problem domain analysis activity, we examine and understand the requirements in order to explore their implications and solve any inconsistencies. Most importantly, we identify the high-level components from which the integrated informant system will be composed, their responsibilities, and their relationships.**

We do not, however, consider any implementation questions yet. This means that we don't need to think about the architecture, programming language, or development tools used for actual development.

In the problem domain analysis, and later in the design activity, we want to design the integrated information system so that it reflects our current needs and provides a modern architecture without paying too much attention to the existing/legacy applications. This architecture will then be implemented with higher-level virtual components and mapped to the functionality of existing applications.

The prerequisite for starting the problem domain analysis is the finished requirements gathering activity. Each use case forms the basis for a class diagram in which all components that participate in the use case are identified.

Please notice that components will in this activity be modeled as analysis classes in UML class diagrams.

Components from all class diagrams are then gathered and presented together in a number of smaller diagrams. Concentrating on each use case separately helps reduce the complexity. Finding all components in a reasonably large information system cannot be done in a single step. Rather, it requires building the model step-by-step through numerous iterations. To accomplish the problem domain analysis there are nine major steps we should go through:

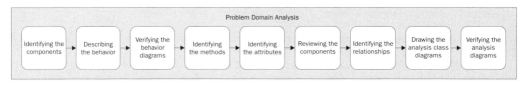

> **Although the steps are shown as a sequence, they do not necessarily need to be performed one-by-one.**

If we facilitate an iterative development approach, we will usually need to go over these steps several times and not always in a sequential order.

The problem domain analysis for business-method-level integration does not differ significantly from problem domain analysis in regular software development processes. Therefore, we will just provide an overview and show the examples connected with our cell phone operator integration scenario. For more detailed information about analysis and software development processes refer to related literature, such as the following books:

❑ *The Rational Unified Process, An Introduction (The Addison-Wesley Object Technology Series)* by Philippe Kruchten, Addison-Wesley; ISBN 0-201707-10-1

❑ *The Unified Software Development Process (The Addison-Wesley Object Technology Series)* by Ivar Jacobson, Grady Booch, James Rumbaugh, Addison-Wesley; ISBN 0-201571-69-2

As our problem domain analysis will be based on the cell phone operator from Chapter 4, it is important that we keep in mind the use case diagram:

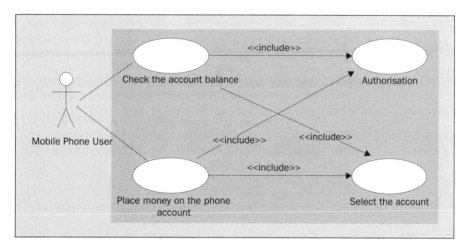

Identifying the Components

Identifying the components is the first step in the problem domain analysis activity:

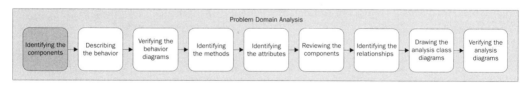

Our goal here is to define the **analysis-level class diagram** of the integration domain. We have to include the concepts found in our problem domain, which includes classes, operations and their relations. To be able to define the class diagram we have to go through several substeps.

First, we have to identify the **components**, on which we will build our functionality. This is probably the most difficult task of the analysis. Indeed, it is one of the most difficult tasks of EAI. Again, there is no simple procedure we can follow that would guarantee the identification of all components. Instead, this will be a creative process usually done in several iterations.

We will use the requirements specification model to identify the components. We should try to keep them simple, use a consistent naming scheme, and be sure about the responsibilities each component represents. A good way to identify the components is to perform a lexical analysis of the requirements specification. The components should be named with nouns so we can look for nouns in the requirements descriptions. Typically we will identify three types of components:

❑   Entity

❑   Boundary

❑   Control

Entity Components

> **Entity components represent the data and business operations in a system.**

Luckily, of the three types of component, entity components are the easiest to identify. The previously proposed method of identifying the nouns works very well for entity components. Another possibility is to focus on the data and the operations on that data, as a means to identify the entity components. Of these, the first approach is preferable, because it is closer to an OO way of thinking. In addition to being nouns, entity components should solve some problems of the system and therefore include some logic and operations. Entity components should also make sense to the domain experts.

For example, we could identify the following entity components after doing the analysis of requirements specifications for our cell phone operator system:

Boundary Components

In the second step, we identify the boundary components. They are used for communication between the system and the actors in the outside world. We identify them through relationships between actors and use cases.

> **Boundary components will represent interfaces with the outside world. If the actor is human, the interface will be a user interface; otherwise it will be a system interface.**

Boundary components should not process the data. They have only two tasks to fulfill: they should present the data to the actor and they should get the input from the actor and transfer it to the system. Business data and operations do not belong to the boundary components.

In our example we can identify four boundary components. Note that we have added an Int suffix to the names to denote that they represent interfaces:

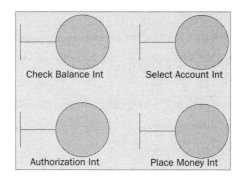

Check Balance Int   Select Account Int

Authorization Int   Place Money Int

Control Components

The last step is to identify the control components, which model the workflow.

> **Control components accept a high-level request from the boundary component and translate it into several requests for entity components, representing a sort of façade to the system.**

This allows the boundary and entity components to concentrate on their functions and decouple the complexity. As a rule, each use case has one type of control component in the analysis model.

> *This may lead you to start thinking of mapping control components to session beans. But control components do not map directly to implementation components, such as session beans. Mapping each control component to a separate session bean is not considered a sound design practice.*

As shown in the following diagram, in our example, we can identify four control components:

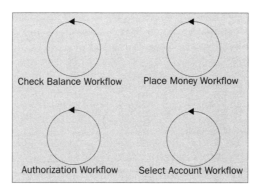

Check Balance Workflow   Place Money Workflow

Authorization Workflow   Select Account Workflow

Describing the Behavior

Describing the behavior is the second step in the problem domain analysis activity:

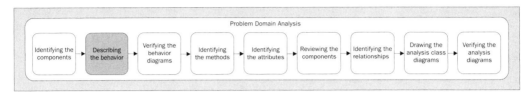

After identifying the components we should describe their behavior.

> **We will study the behavior based on the interactions between the components.**

We will look at each use case and model the interactions between the components in order to fulfill the use case. To describe the interaction we can use UML interaction diagrams: sequence or collaboration diagrams. Sequence diagrams show the explicit sequence of interactions between the components based on a time perspective. Collaboration diagrams show the relations, but the sequence of interactions is organized around roles rather than with a time perspective. Although we'll focus on sequence diagrams here, we should at least note that collaboration diagrams can be used as well.

Let's describe the four uses cases for our cell phone operator example. Please note that, for simplicity, we will describe the normal flows only, that is, we won't consider the alternative flow. Let's start with the Authorization use case that is included in the Checking the Account Balance and Placing Money on the Account use cases. The sequence diagrams for the normal scenario looks like this:

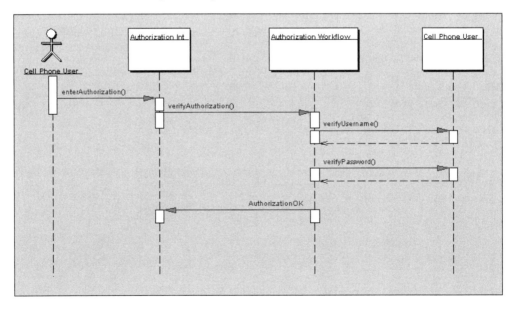

The sequence starts when the actor enters the username and password to the boundary component. The boundary component forwards these details to the control component. The control component forwards the request to validate the username and password to the Cell Phone User entity component. The latter is responsible for validating the username and password and for returning the result. The result is forwarded to the boundary component. In our case we show the sequence for the positive scenario in which we assume that the authorization was successful.

Then we will describe the Select Account use case. As with the previous use case, this too will be included in the two other use cases and will therefore not be used alone:

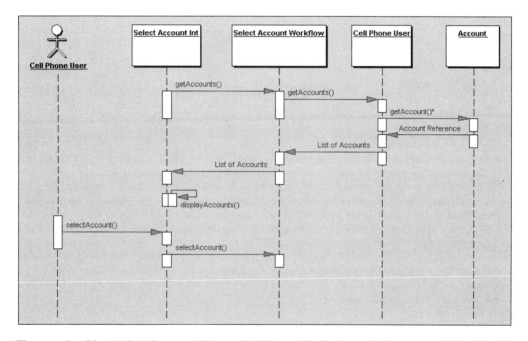

The user should get a list of accounts from which they will select a particular account. Therefore the boundary component has to acquire the list of accounts for which it asks the control component. The control component will ask the Cell Phone User entity component – this knows which accounts belong to the user. It will ask each Account to get a reference and return a list of references over the control component to the boundary component. After that, the boundary component will display a list of accounts and the actor will have to select the account. Again please notice that this is the sequence for the normal flow of events, assuming no problems occur.

Then we have to develop the sequence for Checking the Account Balance use case. As already mentioned this use case will include both use cases described previously. Therefore it will be rather simple:

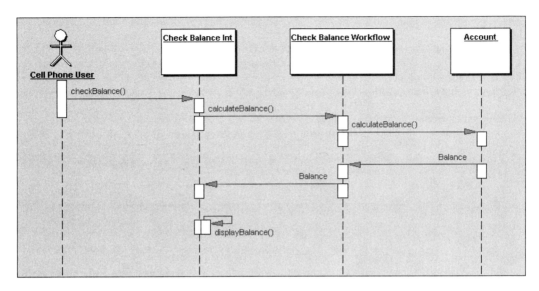

In this use case the actor will invoke the interaction with the `checkBalance()` message to the boundary component. The boundary component will then forward the request to the control component. The control component already knows which account the actor selected (from the previous use case). Therefore the control component will ask the Account entity component to calculate the balance. Then the boundary component will display the balance. Although the sequence is quite simple, we will see later that even a simple scenario in the analysis phase can present a complicated task when attempting to integrate it with existing applications.

In the next example of the Placing Money on the Account use case, we can see that the control component can be very useful for interpreting a high-level request in terms of several smaller requests. In that sense it represents a façade:

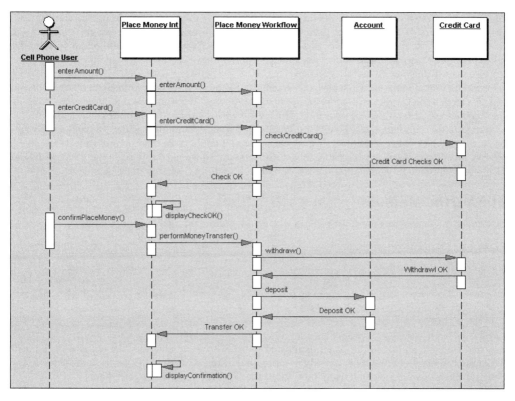

In this case, after the actor selects the account (as shown in the previous use case) they have to enter the amount of money that it wants to put on the account. The actor also has to enter their credit card information from where the money will be withdrawn and put on the cell phone account. After they enter the credit card information, the details have to be checked, so the request is forwarded to the control component, which asks the Credit Card entity component to do the check. We presume that the check is OK; therefore the boundary component displays a confirmation and asks the actor to confirm the money transfer. After the actor enters a positive confirmation, the boundary component asks the control component to perform the money transfer. Now the control component has more work to do. First it has to do the withdrawal from the credit card, for which it sends a message to the Credit Card entity component. Then it has to deposit the amount on the Account entity component. Here we can see how a control component acts as a dispatcher – a façade for underlying entity components. The sequence ends when the boundary component displays a confirmation.

Verifying the Behavior Diagrams

Verifying the behavior diagrams is the third step in the problem domain analysis activity:

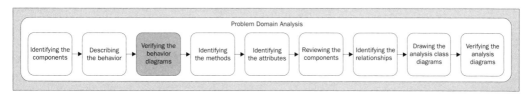

After we have drawn the sequence diagrams we should verify them. We can do this by starting backwards and follow the messages from the end to the beginning. For each message we should ask if the component that is responsible for performing the method (the receiving component) is actually able to do the required tasks. For instance, does the component have all the necessary information?

Returning to the previous example we can see that the Account entity component can do the money deposit and that the Credit Card entity component can do both the withdrawal and the credit card check. The Account can also return this reference. The reason why the request to acquire the account is forwarded to the Cell Phone User entity component is that this component will most likely keep a list of all the accounts a user has and will then just ask each Account entity component to return its reference. If we find any inconsistencies or problems we have to solve them, so we need to look at the use case diagram, clarify the requirements again, and then incorporate the findings back into the sequence diagrams.

Identifying the Methods

Identifying the methods is the fourth step in the problem domain analysis activity:

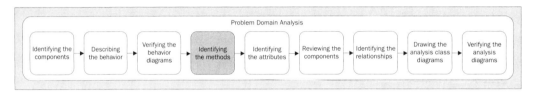

Now that we have identified the components and their associated behaviors, we are in a good position to identify the methods. We have already mentioned that the messages that we have modeled in the sequence diagrams are executed as method invocations by the receiving components.

> **Keeping this in mind we can identify the methods of each component by looking at the sequence of method invocations.**

Remember that the analysis model does not have to be a perfectly complete picture of the system, but rather a more or less accurate sketch of the problem domain we are analyzing, outlining the general flow of information.

To identify the methods in the first step we should consider all the incoming messages for a certain component. We do the same for boundary, control, and entity components. We can already define the visibility of the methods, namely private and public – public methods are all that are called from outside, and private are those that the component calls on itself.

To represent the methods we will use the UML class diagrams, where we will model the components as classes. For our example we get the following results:

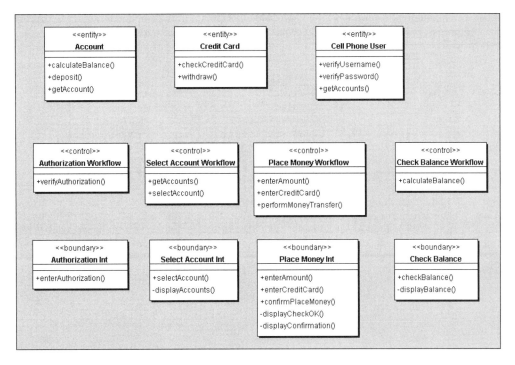

Identifying the Attributes

Identifying the attributes is the fifth step in the problem domain analysis activity:

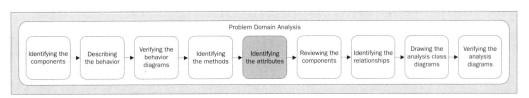

After we have identified the methods we should identify the attributes – but only those that are sufficient for the implementation of the identified operations. Note that we're not yet focusing on the implementation details.

> **It is best to identify the operations first and then the attributes.**

Although it is also possible to go the other way around, if we start by identifying the attributes, our model can easily become too data-related. Sometimes if the architects lack experience, it can also mimic the persistence (database or entity-relationship) model. This is definitely not what we would like to have. Identifying operations first enables us to think about responsibilities rather than data, especially in the case of the control components that actually implement the business rules.

Often we will identify the attributes for entity components first. Entity components are those that hold the state – important persistent information. For our example the important attributes would be the following:

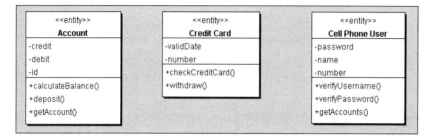

Control and boundary components can store state too. In our example, this can be seen by the Place Money Workflow control component, which remembers the amount to be placed on the account, and the credit card number from which to make the withdrawal. This means that the Place Money Workflow component will have to store client dependent state. To realize this we have to declare two attributes:

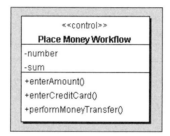

Reviewing the Components

Reviewing the components is the sixth step in the problem domain analysis activity:

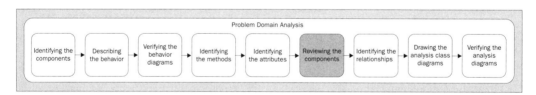

When defining the methods we must be accurate. We have to be sure that every message has a corresponding method assigned in the appropriate component. We should also try not to introduce too much complexity at this point, as we are still only in the analysis stage where we can afford to keep things simple.

To identify possible problems, we should look out for methods that perform the same operations that could be gathered into a single method. We should also look for overly complex methods that could be separated. We can also try to identify simple generalizations between classes. However, we should be careful not to invest too much time looking for inheritance structures where they do not exist. The tradeoff between inheriting behavior and implementing it is a subtle one. In the past, inheritance tended to be over-emphasized, but on the other hand, total reliance on implementation may mean replicated code, which is clearly bad.

Then we should see if the components are still focused on their responsibility – which should be clear from the methods. If they are not, we should either change the method signatures or reconsider the previous steps, and whether we have identified the correct components.

Identifying the Relationships

Identifying the relationships is the seventh step in the problem domain analysis activity:

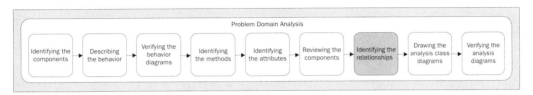

Components are related to other components. In order for two components to be able to communicate, they must have a relationship. Relationships have directions: they can be one way or both ways. It is important to determine the directions of relationships because this will simplify analyzing the dependencies between the components.

In UML notation there are three different types of relationships:

- ❑ Dependency
- ❑ Generalization
- ❑ Association, which has the following two special forms:
    - ❑ Aggregation
    - ❑ Composition

Returning to our example, we can identify several relationships. Keeping in mind the sequence diagrams that we have looked at, it is clear that there are relationships between boundary components and control components: Authorization Int is related to Authorization Workflow, Select Account Int is related to Select Account Workflow and the same for the Place Money Workflow and Check Balance components. For now these relationships can be unidirectional. We have not identified any message that would be sent from the control component to the boundary component. We have decided to use associations for these relationships because it is reasonable that the boundary component (the user interface) keeps a permanent reference to the control (workflow) component.

The Authorization, Select Account, and Check Balance control components do not hold any state that would be client dependent. But the Place Money Workflow control component does. This is reflected by the multiplicity. With a stateless control component, all clients could be connected with the same component (thus a multiplicity of one), but we will need a separate component for the stateful Place Money Workflow control component (thus a multiplicity of many). As we are in the analysis phase we need not consider questions like how the boundary components will obtain a reference to the control components.

The relationships between control and entity components are modeled as dependencies because it is unlikely that the control components would need permanent references to all entity components. For example, the Place Money Workflow component will not keep the references to all Account and Credit Card entity components. Rather, it will locate these components (using a location service) that it needs in a certain interaction and use them for a certain amount of time. However, there is a permanent relationship between the Cell Phone User and Account entity components. This should be modeled as an association, where each Cell Phone User component permanently keeps the references to all related Account components and each Account component knows exactly which Cell Phone User it belongs to.

Drawing the Analysis Class Diagram

Drawing the analysis class diagram is the eighth step in the problem domain analysis activity:

From the identified components with methods and attributes and the relationships we can draw the analysis class diagram. The proposed analysis class diagram for our example is shown below:

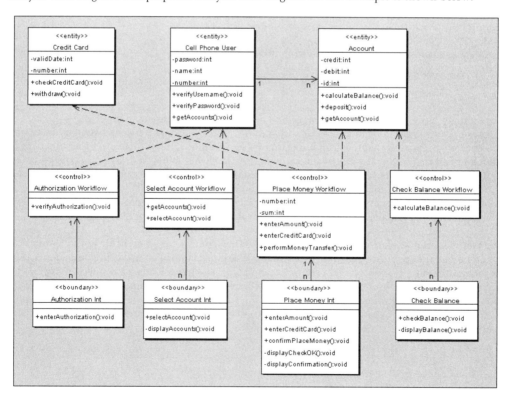

Verifying the Analysis Diagrams

Verifying the analysis diagrams is the last step in the problem domain analysis activity:

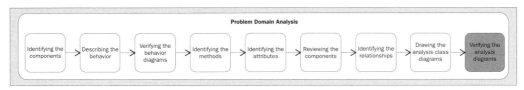

> **The review of the analysis diagrams has to answer whether we have realized the use cases appropriately, and whether we have identified system operations according to the specifications.**

To assess the validity of our analysis diagrams we have to check:

❑ The accordance between the use case diagrams and the analysis diagrams.

❑ The accordance between the operations specification and the analysis class diagrams. All components, relationships, and parameters mentioned in the specifications have to be represented in the analysis class diagrams.

Remember, that to achieve integration we have to do the analysis on a global, enterprise-wide level and devote enough time to the requirements and analysis phase. An ad hoc approach to integration will probably provide some partial results quicker than the approach proposed here, but will later demonstrate an inability to provide a comprehensive solution due to the lack of a strategic plan.

The proposed approach brings us to a well-structured class diagram that will provide the basis for the next steps in the integration, particularly for the design, which we will cover next. An important observation is that they provide solutions that already have the notion of tiers. In the previous class diagram we can easily see the tier boundaries, which will be very helpful in obtaining the final integration architecture. In real-world scenarios the diagrams will no doubt be more complex, larger, and include a greater number of components than our limited example. As such, we would probably need to go through several iterations that we do not cover explicitly in our example. However, the actual process of identifying and building the diagram remains the same.

> *Note that the proposed method is not the only possible way to build the analysis class diagrams; it simply demonstrates the general techniques in which the problem domain analysis should work, based on the concept of responsibility-driven design.*

Design

Design is the second important activity to define the global design model for business-method-level integration. In the context of the integration process it is the fifth step:

In this activity we focus on the global architectural design model, where we represent the integrated information system as a set of components (identified in the problem domain analysis activity) that have well defined interfaces through which they communicate. Instead of focusing on how to implement each component from scratch, we focus on how to reuse existing applications to provide implementations for the components.

We approach architectural design from a high-level perspective. Due to the size and complexity of the problem domain, it is practically impossible to design the integration architecture down to the finest detail. This would also be unreasonable because a lot of functionality is implemented by existing applications. Accordingly, we approach the architectural design in a more high-level way, where we define the global architecture in the sense of components and their interfaces. This is somewhat analogous to the planning of a city's architecture compared to designing a house.

Several key steps of this activity characterize the architectural design process. Firstly, we cope with the global situation, and then we focus on information system-specific-functions. Here we start to solve the use cases that influence the architectural decisions and, as a result, we produce a set of subsystems. Each of the subsystems realizes a use case. After iterating though the subsystems we start building the global architecture step-by-step and finally define a stable architecture.

The main tasks of the design activity can be organized into three groups with the following steps:

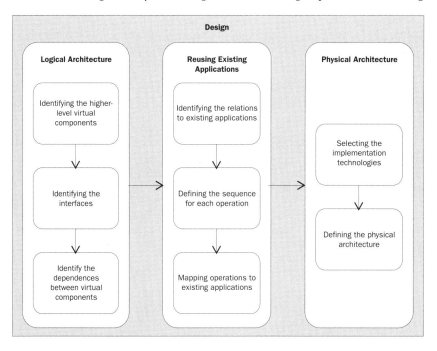

Although the steps are shown as a sequence they do not necessarily need to be performed one-by-one.

Those familiar with software development processes will notice that this activity is focused on integration and therefore introduces steps related to mapping the functionality to existing applications. Although specific to integration, readers might still want to look into the related literature on OO design as previously listed earlier in the book.

Before We Begin

Before we can start identifying the high-level virtual components we have to clearly understand the problem we are trying to solve with each component. This information is included in the requirements specification, use case diagrams, and other related diagrams. We also have to consider the analysis model because it influences this step considerably.

As well as being familiar with the problem domain, we also have to understand the technology – the J2EE integration platform. As previously emphasized, without a good understanding of technologies at hand (which we have already discussed in Chapter 3), we will not be able to make the correct choices. Therefore, we have to become familiar with the strengths and weaknesses of each of the J2EE technologies. Furthermore, to become familiar with the technologies, we must also consider the knowledge of the developers. Rather than introduce a new technology, we sometimes must select a solution because it is less effort to allow developers to continue to work with a technology they are already familiar with. Each new technology introduces the need for training and introduces a certain risk, because many developers will not be able to use it optimally at first.

Without a good understanding of the problem domain and the technologies involved, we will not be able to build a sound architecture. As architects, we also have to realize that a sound architecture is a tradeoff between different orthogonal goals and objectives. Realizing one goal fully might result in not being able to realize another one.

Most integration projects have the following goals:

❑ **Reusability**
   This is a top-level priority when designing an integration architecture. Reusing as much of existing systems' functionality as possible will be a key decision criterion for integration.

❑ **Expandability**
   Also important because it allow us to use this architecture over time and adapt it to the new and changed requirements. This includes adding new functionality and modifying existing functionality. A well-designed system will allow modifications and expansions without influencing the other parts of the system.

❑ **Maintainability**
   Addresses the problem of maintaining the information system over the years by different people. In most cases, the original designers of the integration architecture will leave and new people will take over their role. This is why the architecture must be easily understandable, and the major decisions should be well documented. The architecture should stay as clear and as simple as possible.

❑ **Reliability**
   A common sense requirement that we have to fulfill. The non-functional requirements (sometimes known as "quality attributes") in the requirements specification tell us what level of reliability we should design for. If the required reliability of the integrated system is considerably larger than the one provided by existing systems, we need to search for ways to guarantee the necessary reliability with the reuse of existing systems.

❏ **Performance and Scalability**
We have already mentioned that we have to study the performance and scalability of existing applications. However, we also have to design the new integrated system with scalability in mind. Poor architectural choices can reduce the scalability considerably, and we will not always be able to blame the existing applications.

❏ **Testability**
Testability expresses a measure of the ability of the integrated system to be made to demonstrate its faults through testing.

Identifying the Higher-level Virtual Components

Identifying the higher-level virtual components is the first step in the design activity:

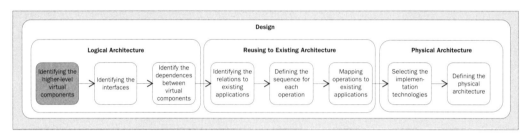

We need to identify the higher-level virtual components that constitute the integrated system. The problem is that although this task sounds easy, in reality it is not.

> **Selecting the correct higher-level virtual components will have a long-lasting influence on the information system as a whole.**

The selection also determines how suitable the integration architecture is to re-engineering existing applications and replacing them with newly developed solutions.

To identify the high-level virtual components, we focus on the analysis model class diagram that we constructed in the previous section of this chapter. The analysis-level entity and control components that we identified will map to virtual components on the business logic tier, so we will focus on them. The analysis-level boundary components represent user interface constructs. These will be realized in the client and web component tiers.

To identify the virtual components we go through the control and entity components from the problem domain analysis activity. We try to group them into virtual components based on their functionality. Components encapsulate their internal implementation and represent their functionality through the interface. To identify the higher-level virtual components we can follow these guidelines:

❏ Start with the analysis class diagram that we've defined in the previous section

❏ Gather the analysis components that are logically connected because they implement a part of a larger functionality

❏ Try to make the virtual components as independent of other components as possible

❑ Often we will have to add other specific components that will implement non-functional requirements, for example, or model some implementation-related concepts

Our example of the cell phone operator, introduced in Chapter 4, is relatively simple. Therefore the identification of virtual components will also be simple. For our example, we can identify the following higher-level virtual components:

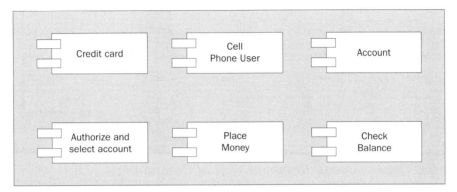

Identifying the Interfaces

Identifying the interfaces is the second step in the design activity:

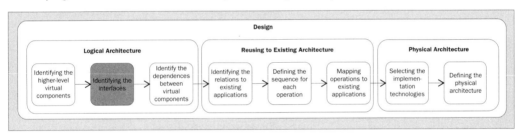

After we have identified the higher-level virtual components, we define the interfaces through which we access the functionality of these components – we simply provide the necessary operation signatures.

> **We should ensure that the interfaces are high-level and that they focus on business processes and not on implementation details.**

The interfaces act as the contracts between the components. The interfaces represent a part of the integration architecture that we should not change – each change will influence all dependent components.

Keep in mind, however, that we can still add operations to existing interfaces without creating problems on related components. Therefore we will often introduce modified methods as new methods with a slightly different signature. This protects us from having to change all related components. However, doing this too many times will make the interfaces very hard to use because we will have to cope with the redundancy of methods – we will not know exactly which to use and when. So we have to be very cautious with the interfaces that we define.

Returning to our example, we can identify the following interfaces for our virtual components:

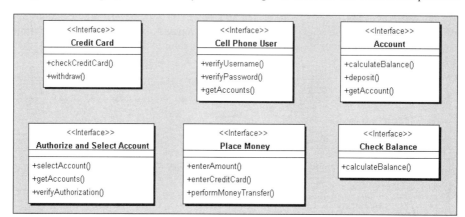

Identify the Dependences Between Virtual Components

Identifying the dependencies between virtual components is the third step in the design activity:

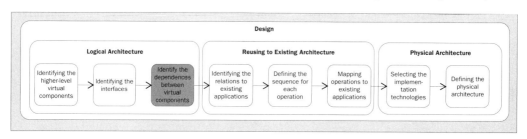

> **Identifying the dependencies is important because they show how the changes to one part of the system will influence other parts.**

Dependencies between parts of the system can be direct, in which case a change in one part will require a modification to another part. For example, if part A is directly dependent on part B, this means that if we change something in B we also need to update A.

Dependencies can also go through interfaces, which will decouple the direct connection between the two parts of a system. This will obviously be the preferred way and we will model the integration architecture through interfaces, as we have already stressed several times over. Making components dependent only on component interfaces simplifies their management considerably. As long as we do not modify the interfaces we can change the implementation of the component.

Still, we have to be aware which dependencies exist between virtual components, so we will identify them and show them on the diagram. This enables us to efficiently track and measure the complexity. As we apply changes to the architecture, we should also update these diagrams, otherwise they are effectively useless.

In our example the dependencies between higher-level virtual components looks like the following:

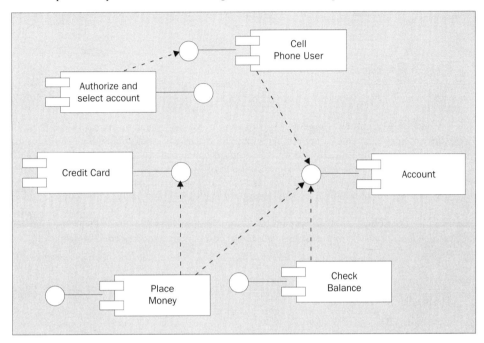

The degree of coupling between components can be used to identify and describe the dependencies. Weak coupling shows that the groups are relatively independent, and fewer dependencies between components show that we have gathered the classes correspondingly and that the system will be relatively easy to understand, maintain, and extend.

Strong coupling, on the other hand, indicates that there are many dependencies between components. This suggests that changes to one part of the system (to an interface, for example) will require modifications in many other parts. It also makes the structure of the system less easy to understand. Sometimes strong coupling is a consequence of incorrectly gathered classes and poorly identified components, and in such cases, it might be a good idea to rethink the architecture. Indeed, such re-evaluations can be a normal part of the whole process – a rethink in the strategy might mean more delays, but it should still be regarded as a viable option.

Identifying the Relations To Existing Applications

Identifying the relations to existing applications is the fourth step in the design activity:

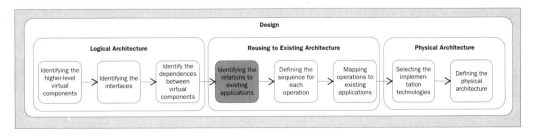

After we have defined the component architecture of the integrated system, we have to identify the relations to existing applications. As a first step, we identify which existing applications have the required functionality. It is recommended to show the relations for each component, because this will make it easier to follow later steps.

> *This stage is dependent on the existing applications that we have. To be able to identify the relations to existing applications we have to be familiar with their functionality, and to achieve this we have to do the analysis of existing applications. We have described how to do this in Chapter 4.*

Let us consider the Account component of our example. We will focus on the operation that allows checking the account balance of a certain account. The existing applications will certainly support this functionality; however, the functionality is not gathered inside a single existing application. Therefore, this component will have to depend on more than one existing system. More precisely, we will not use the existing applications directly. Rather, we will use the lower-level virtual components that present the functions of existing applications in a J2EE-compliant manner on the business logic tier.

To calculate the current balance of an account, the component will have to interact with the following existing applications: that is, with the lower-level virtual components that represent these existing applications:

❑ Account balance management

❑ Domestic phone evaluation

❑ International phone evaluation

❑ Cost and tariff management

Please notice that we have defined these lower-level virtual components in the application-interface-level integration phase earlier in this chapter. The dependencies are shown on the following diagram:

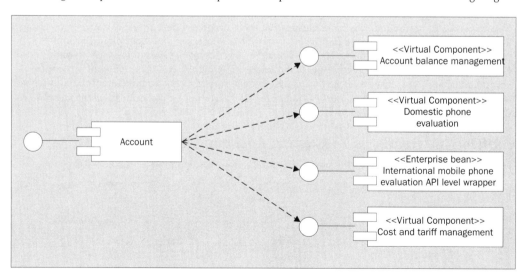

Defining the Sequence for Each Operation

Defining the sequence for each operation is the fifth step in the design activity:

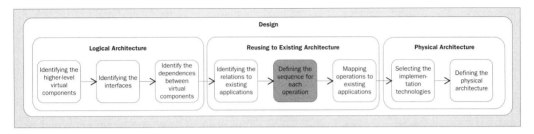

When we have identified the existing applications that the higher-level virtual component has to interact with, we identify the exact sequence of operations that the higher-level virtual component has to invoke in order to get the desired result.

> **To identify the operations and the sequence that needs to be invoked we study the interfaces of existing applications lower-level virtual components and map the desired functionality in the best possible way.**

In real-world examples we will frequently be overwhelmed with the complexity of the interfaces that existing applications provide. We will often also be confused about which operations to actually use, because often there will be more than one way to achieve the same result. As ever, the more familiar we are with the functionality of the existing applications, the easier it will be to decide.

To model the sequence of operations that have to be invoked we can use UML sequence diagrams to show exactly what we have to do. For our example we can produce a sequence diagram representing the process for calculating the account balance. Note that we have set the requirement that the account balance should reflect "real time" balance. Included in this balance should be all domestic and international calls up to the last minute.

Unfortunately, the existing applications do not provide this information. Although the account balance management application can calculate the account balance (as its name suggests), it does not take into account the calls made in the last month. In fact, this application requires that data regarding monthly consumption be entered into it to take it into account.

So, to calculate the "real time" account balance we will first have to access the account balance management existing application (that is the lower-level virtual component), get the current balance, evaluate domestic and international calls, then calculate the cost for the duration of domestic and international calls, and finally calculate the account balance:

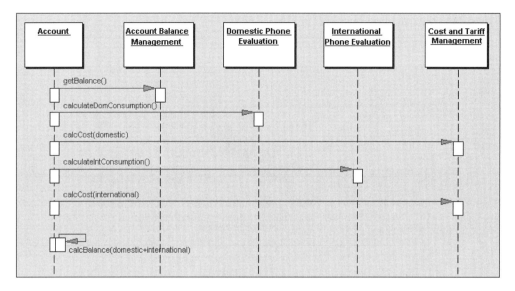

It is very important that we model *all possible* sequences of operations, including the normal flow of events and any alternative flows in which something could go wrong. In this way we can define how to handle all exceptional situations, how and to whom we should propagate the exceptions, and we will ultimately make our components highly robust.

Mapping Operations To Existing Applications

Mapping operations to existing applications is the sixth step in the design activity:

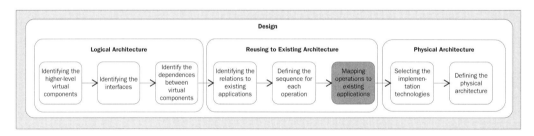

The sequence of operations sometimes is not enough and the component has to do some calculation, and perform other operations to get the desired result. As such, in this step we must identify what exactly has to be done.

> **The goal is to identify the interaction with the existing application to such a level that we will be able to write code directly from the specification.**

It will vary from operation to operation how complex a mapping we will have to use. With a highly complex mapping we might consider representing the whole procedure with an activity diagram too; sometimes we could even use "pseudo code".

We have to map each operation of the newly defined higher-level virtual component to lower-level virtual components that represent existing applications. In the example we have provided the mapping for one method only. Sometimes we will not be able to find the corresponding methods in the existing applications. This means that the functionality we require is not supported by existing applications, in which case we have to implement it from scratch. Or we might be able to reuse only a part of the whole functionality. Following the proposed integration process we will be able to add the missing functionality in a relatively painless manner.

Selecting the Implementation Technologies

Selecting the implementation technologies is the seventh step in the design activity:

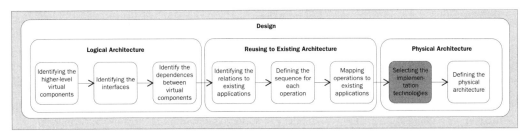

After we have defined the components we will have to select which J2EE technologies we will use to implement the higher-level virtual components. Earlier in this chapter we discussed possible technologies for developing virtual components. There we concluded that for higher-level virtual components we would in most cases select EJBs. The EJB technology provides four different types of beans (or components):

❑   Stateless session beans

❑   Stateful session beans

❑   Message-driven beans

❑   Entity beans

Entity beans represent persistent transaction data that is shared between clients of the information systems. The other types of beans represent the processes that do not have to preserve state or that hold a conversational state between client method invocations.

Having said that, it becomes quite straightforward to choose which type of beans we should use for which type of higher-level virtual component. Entity beans represent virtual components that, from the analysis activity, have their roots in entity components. For other components we will use session beans for synchronous communication, and message-driven beans for asynchronous communication.

425

Defining the Physical Architecture

Defining the physical architecture is the last step in the design activity:

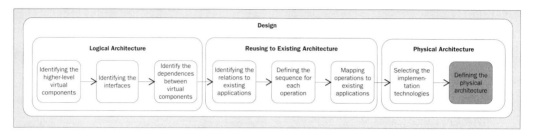

After selecting the implementation technologies we have to consider the physical architecture too. Here, we first of all have to consider the non-functional requirements. We have to take into account the requirements regarding performance and reliability. This will then influence the deployment scenarios that we select.

To achieve acceptable performance we consider locating tightly-coupled components inside a single container and use local access to components to optimize the method invocation performance. To achieve higher reliability we might consider clustering or replication.

To identify the most suitable physical architecture we would probably select a few different candidate architectures first. Then we build prototypes that help us to validate these candidate architectures by the criteria that we have to meet. Only then will we select the final appropriate architecture and do the implementation.

Although defining the physical architecture is an important step we will not discuss it here in any more detail. Refer to Chapter 3 and the technology-related chapters for more information.

Summary

In this chapter we covered the processes involved with business-level integration. Initially, we discussed the objectives of business-level integration, and saw that business-level integration is performed in two phases.

First we described application-interface-level integration. We discussed how to reuse the functionality of existing applications. For existing applications that do not provide APIs we have to add them.

Then we covered virtual components. We saw that lower-level virtual components abstract the technology differences between existing applications and provide the functionalities through J2EE-compliant interfaces on the business logic tier.

Lower-level virtual components can be used to abstract the access to the functionality of existing applications through APIs or wrappers. They can also be used to abstract the access to existing databases and commercial EIS systems.

Business-method-level integration then raises the abstraction level further. It introduces higher-level virtual components that provide a higher-level of abstraction and reuse the lower-level virtual components. Higher-level and lower-level virtual components are connected in layers to form a chain of responsibility.

The difficult part however, is to define the high-level business-oriented interfaces for the higher-level virtual components. To achieve this, business-method-level integration requires that we model the global architecture of the integrated systems – as we would like to have it if we built it from scratch. We have to continue the integration development process, as defined and initiated in Chapter 4. We explained how to perform a problem domain analysis and how to identify the components and interfaces that an integrated system consists of on a high abstraction level.

In the next few chapters we will focus on technologies, and show how to use different J2EE technologies to implement both the application-interface-level and the business-method-level integration. We'll start by looking at CORBA.

10

Reusing Existing Applications with CORBA

An important part of business level integration is reusing the functionality of existing applications. This is achieved by wrapping existing applications and exposing their functionality through virtual components on the business logic tier, as we discovered in the previous chapter. In this chapter we will look at the Common Object Request Broker Architecture (CORBA) for wrapping existing applications and exposing their functionality through virtual components.

In many cases, existing applications are not written in Java. Rather, they use other programming languages, like C, C++, or even older ones like COBOL or PL/I. One way to achieve interoperability between Java and other programming languages is with CORBA.

CORBA is a distributed object architecture that was initially designed to allow interoperability between different programming languages, operating systems and platforms. Not only is CORBA supported by the J2EE platform, it is also tightly integrated with other technologies, like RMI-IIOP and the Java Transaction Service. This level of support allows us to use CORBA to enable high-level interoperability between the J2EE integration platform and existing applications.

In this chapter, by examining the theory and through use of examples, we will cover the following main topics:

❑   The role of CORBA in EAI

❑   An overview of CORBA architecture

❏ How to build a CORBA component wrapper

❏ Multi-threading

❏ The Factory pattern

❏ Using the any data type

❏ Implementing the component wrapper in C++ and using a Java client for the C++ wrapper

The Role of CORBA in EAI

In previous chapters we emphasized that EAI can be achieved in four phases. We usually begin with the data level integration phase, where we focus on sharing and reusing the data. We continue with the application interface integration phase and then the business method integration phase. Remember – these two are sometimes referred to as business level integration. In both phases the objective is to reuse the functionality of existing applications. The fourth, and final, phase is the presentation level integration phase, where we provide a new presentation layer on top of the integrated information system.

In this part of the book we focus on business level integration. In Chapter 9 we discussed the ideas behind this integration stage and provided an overview of the necessary activities and steps that we should perform. We evaluated the possibilities of reusing the functionality of existing applications and presented these in the form of the J2EE integration architecture.

To reuse the functionality of existing applications for an integrated information system we have to answer two important questions:

❏ How can we access the functionality of existing applications in a programmatic way?

❏ How do we present the functions in the J2EE architecture in a common way, and thus mask the technology differences of existing applications?

We answered these questions in Chapter 9, but let's make a quick synopsis of what we determined, and relate the results to the CORBA architecture.

Accessing the Functionality of Existing Applications in a Programmatic Way

As we saw in the last chapter, there are two ways to provide a wrapper to programmatically access an existing application:

❏ By modification of source code

❏ With techniques like screen scraping or terminal emulation

Modification of Source Code

With source code modification we define one or more APIs with operations that we need to access externally and then connect these operations with the existing code.

> **CORBA is a perfect technology for wrapping existing applications via the modification of source code.**

As we will see later in this chapter, CORBA supports many different programming languages, operating systems, and platforms. As such, it is very likely that our existing applications will be written in a language and will use an operating system and platform that is supported by CORBA. Accordingly, we'll be able to use the same programming language, which will simplify the development of the wrapper considerably, and minimize the risk of introducing errors into the existing application.

For each interface that we want to add to the existing application, we will define a new CORBA distributed object. We will then declare the operations of the interface. Finally, we'll connect each operation to the source code of existing applications.

Later in this chapter we will return to our customer information application from the cell phone operator example that we introduced in Chapter 4 and used in Chapter 9. We'll look more closely at how to develop a CORBA wrapper that provides two main operations through the interface: `getCustomer()` for getting information about a customer and `setCustomer()` for modifying/updating information, and we'll study the mapping to the existing procedures.

Screen Scraping and Terminal Emulation

If source code is not available, if we do not have all the tools necessary to rebuild the existing application from the source code, or if we simply don't want to modify the source code, we can develop wrappers with **screen scraping** or **terminal emulation**. With these techniques, which are appropriate mainly for character-based applications, the wrappers simulate user typing to perform the functions of existing applications and read the screen to extract the results.

> **CORBA is highly appropriate for developing wrappers through screen scraping or terminal emulation.**

To perform these tasks most effectively it is beneficial to develop the wrappers on the same platform that the existing application is executing. CORBA is therefore an ideal choice because of its support for different operating systems. Although later in this chapter we will demonstrate how to develop CORBA wrappers, we will not demonstrate screen scraping or terminal emulation explicitly; these techniques are often very specific to the existing application and their platform.

In the next section we will answer the second question that we posed earlier: how to present the functions of existing applications in the J2EE integration architecture in a common way.

Masking the Technology Differences of Existing Applications

As we have stated, the second problem with reusing the functionality of existing applications is how to present the interfaces through which we access these functions in a common way in the J2EE integration architecture. The goal here is to present these interfaces on the business logic tier. As we identified in Chapter 9, we will use **lower-level virtual components** to achieve this.

Let's investigate the role of CORBA in virtual components. In the previous section we saw that to reuse the functions of existing applications in a programmatic way there are basically two possibilities:

❑   Existing application already provides an API

❑   We add a wrapper that provides an interface, which can be achieved in two ways:

❑   By modifying the source code and adding a CORBA wrapper

❑   By implementing the CORBA wrapper using screen scraping or terminal emulation

In the first case, where the application already provides APIs it can happen that we will have to use some proprietary mechanisms to access them. To mask these differences we can effectively use CORBA to implement lower-level virtual components. As we have identified in Chapter 3, we can deploy CORBA-distributed objects on the business logic tier of the J2EE integration architecture. CORBA uses IIOP for remote method invocations, as we will discuss in depth shortly, so clients can invoke methods on CORBA-distributed objects in J2EE-compliant way, using RMI-IIOP.

To demonstrate using CORBA for developing lower-level virtual components let's look at an example with our customer information application. Let's assume that the customer information application already provides a proprietary API, through which it exposes two methods: `newAccount()` and `deleteAccount()`. We'll also assume that a proprietary mechanism is necessary to access them. To mask this mechanism, we can develop a CORBA lower-level virtual component that will expose these methods through CORBA interfaces on one side, and on the other side, it will use the proprietary mechanism to invoke the existing application API. The important (and rather obvious) point is that clients will be able to access these two methods using RMI-IIOP rather than the proprietary mechanism.

We will deploy the CORBA virtual component on the business logic tier, as shown schematically in the diagram below:

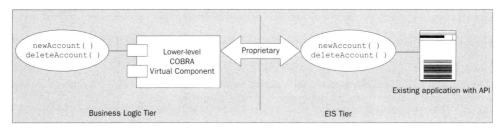

In the second case, we have already added a CORBA wrapper. For invoking operations exposed by CORBA interfaces, we can use RMI-IIOP or CORBA clients. This means that CORBA wrappers already provide the operations in a J2EE-compliant way; hence, we do not have to develop additional lower-level virtual components for them. CORBA provides location transparency (which we'll also discuss shortly), therefore CORBA wrappers can be deployed on the EIS tier and expose the interfaces on the business logic tier (note that we are talking about logical architecture here).

> **CORBA wrappers fulfill both the role of the wrapper, and the role of the lower-level virtual component.**

Implementing Wrappers and Virtual Components in CORBA

We have seen that there is minimal difference in using CORBA technology to implement wrappers or lower-level virtual components. When implementing CORBA wrappers we will either directly connect the interface operations to the source code, or will make the connection through the user interface (using screen scraping or terminal emulation). When implementing lower-level virtual components in CORBA, we will connect the interface operations with the APIs already exposed by existing applications, through a proprietary mechanism, which is required to access that API.

> **Due to this similarity, we will discuss CORBA wrappers and lower-level virtual components in this chapter together, referring to them both as component wrappers.**

In the following sections of this chapter we will first introduce the CORBA architecture in order to familiarize ourselves with CORBA technology. Then we will present examples on how to develop CORBA component wrappers.

A Brief Introduction to CORBA

CORBA consists of a specification for a programming language, platform, and an operating system-independent distributed object model. CORBA is developed by the Object Management Group (OMG – see http://www.omg.com/) and is considered to be the first major distributed object architecture. The first version of the specification dates back to 1991. Since then, other distributed object architectures have borrowed concepts from CORBA. As will soon become clear, the J2EE platform supports CORBA technology, making the integration between them easier.

The main part of the CORBA specification is the core, or the **object request broker (ORB)**. The ORB provides the necessary infrastructure for communication in that it takes over all the details of the communication between distributed objects. This part will be the most interesting for integration.

CORBA also specifies the interoperability – this was added with version 2 of CORBA, adopted in 1995. The interoperability specification introduced the General Inter-ORB Protocol (GIOP), which is the standard protocol that all CORBA products use to communicate with each other. The GIOP has to be mapped to a specific transport protocol. For instance, when mapped to TCP/IP it is called the **Internet Inter-ORB Protocol (IIOP)**. Mappings of GIOP to other protocols have never played an important role and have been used mainly for connectivity with older distributed systems, such as the Distributed Computing Environment (DCE).

Use of the IIOP protocol guarantees interoperability between different CORBA implementations. It's worth noting that CORBA is not the only product to use IIOP – the Java platform adopted IIOP for RMI and EJBs, making both interoperable with CORBA.

CORBA also specifies the interworking architecture, which details how to achieve interoperability with other models, particularly with the Microsoft COM model.

Also very important to CORBA are the **language mapping specifications**. These define how the CORBA concepts can be used from different programming languages. Mapping the concepts to the programming language enables us to use the CORBA functionality through a mechanism that fits well with the programming language. CORBA has been designed in a language-neutral way – this means that there are no obstacles to supporting almost any programming language. Still, some of the language mappings are standardized by OMG, such as C, C++, Java, Smalltalk, Ada, COBOL, PL/I, Python, Lisp, CORBA Scripting Language, and XML.

The standardization of language mapping is, however, not essential. It simply guarantees that if we use the tools from different CORBA-compliant products, all the tools will produce the same results. If we have existing applications that are written in other languages, we can consider non-standardized language mappings. This is not such a big obstacle because we will rarely port the wrapper code from one CORBA product to another.

The CORBA specification also defines **CORBA services**, which are additional functionalities offered through standard interfaces. They include naming, trader, life cycle, transaction, security, persistence, and several others. Not all CORBA services have been used extensively in real-world information systems. In terms of integration two services are important: naming and transaction services. The naming service is important to obtain initial object references – this is conceptually similar to JNDI. The transaction service is important for achieving distributed transactions (that is, transactions that span multiple systems). In fact, CORBA's Object Transaction Service (OTS) forms the basis for the Java Transaction API (JTA).

> *For more information on CORBA services, have a look at some more specific literature, for example, the book* Enterprise CORBA *by Dirk Slama, Jason Garbis, and Perry Russell, from Prentice Hall PTR, ISBN 0-13-083963-9. The OMG web site is also a valuable resource:*
> http://www.omg.org/technology/documents/spec_catalog.htm#CORBAservices.

CORBA Implementations

To use the CORBA architecture we need a product that is compliant with the CORBA specification. In the "CORBA vocabulary" such products are called CORBA implementations. Today, CORBA implementations from several different vendors exist. The foremost CORBA vendors include:

❑   IBM Component Broker – http://www-4.ibm.com/software/ad/cb/

❑ Inprise/Borland Visibroker – http://www.inprise.com/visibroker/

❑ Iona ORBacus – http://www.iona.com/products/orbacus_home.htm

❑ Iona Orbix – http://www.iona.com/products/orbhome.htm

❑ PrismTech OpenFusion – http://www.prismtechnologies.com/

❑ Vertel eORB – http://www.vertel.com/products/eorb.asp

There are also several free or open-source CORBA implementations available. For more information see http://www.corba.org/vc.htm.

The interoperability between them is achieved using the IIOP protocol. CORBA is also integrated in some other products, like application servers (such as Iona iPortal or Inprise/Borland AppServer) and DBMSs (Oracle 9i, for example). Last and by no means least, CORBA has been a part of the Java SDK since version 1.2 and thus, it is also a part of J2EE.

Obviously, different vendors provide products that can differ considerably in quality and in the number of supported options.

> **The major differences in products relates to the number of supported programming languages, operating systems, platforms, and CORBA services.**

For instance, most vendors provide support for Java and C++, but not so many provide support for other programming languages. For the purposes of integration we need to pay particular attention to which languages are supported, and this will clearly depend on the existing applications that we have. So, although almost all vendors will support the major operating systems, we will probably have to search a little for support for exotic or outdated operating systems.

There are also major differences in which CORBA services are supported. Most vendors' products support naming service, majority support transaction, security, and trading. For other services we will again have to search a little, although these are not so important for integration.

An important question also relates to which CORBA implementation we should choose – particularly if we do not have one yet. This choice is of comparable difficulty to choosing a J2EE application server (discussed in Chapter 3), and we will have to take certain criteria into account. These include:

❑ CORBA standards compliance and version support

❑ Programming languages support

❑ Operating systems and platform support

❑ Performance, scalability, and availability

❑ Support for CORBA services

❑ Support for development tools and environments (like VisualAge, JBuilder, and so on)

❑ Cost and licensing

❑ Technical support and vendor reputation

❑ Value-added features

Most companies will, however, already have a CORBA implementation and, as such, we will have to use it. Note that the source code is nearly 100% portable between different CORBA implementations, which are also interoperable among each other because they use the GIOP/IIOP protocol. This means that we can mix different CORBA implementations in the same environment.

Sometimes, particularly with older implementations, we might experience problems in achieving interoperability between these products and J2EE. Older implementations support older versions of CORBA specification, which do not support all the new functions required for interoperability with J2EE. Furthermore, the CORBA architecture does not provide any rules for compliance checking, or a reference implementation. As a result, it is very difficult to check how well a particular implementation supports the standard specification. Older implementations often did not perform these checks very precisely, whereas newer versions comply with the standard much more strictly and the interoperability is not as problematic anymore, as we will demonstrate in this and the next two chapters.

How CORBA Objects Communicate

CORBA objects are, by nature, distributed. This means that we can deploy one object on a certain machine, and another object on a second machine. As long as these machines are network connected (with the appropriate protocol, like TCP/IP) they can communicate with each other. Conceptually, CORBA hides all the details of remote communication. The developer (or the user) can barely differentiate between local and remote objects.

To provide access to operations a CORBA object defines an interface. In the interface it lists all the operations that can be accessed from outside. The CORBA object then has to implement these operations. As mentioned earlier, the CORBA object can do this in practically any supported programming language. Then a client can connect to this CORBA object and invoke the operations. The client can be written in any supported programming language and can in fact be distributed over the network using a totally different operating system, platform, or even programming language. The roles of client and server objects are not fixed, however, and an object that has been a client in one method invocation can become a server for another invocation.

When a client invokes a method on a server object it sends some data as parameters and receives the result. Clients and server can be written in different programming languages so we have to find a way in which to avoid the differences in programming languages, especially the differences in supported data types and their lengths. For this purpose, the CORBA architecture introduces the **Interface Definition Language (IDL)**, which is used to define the interfaces that objects provide to their clients. The IDL definitions are then mapped to different programming languages.

Stubs and Skeletons

As we have already said, the CORBA architecture then hides the details of communication to the developers and they invoke the methods on distributed CORBA objects in the same way as they access local language objects. To achieve this in any programming language (without any modifications to the programming language), CORBA uses the concept of proxies.

To achieve transparent remote method invocation CORBA generates two proxies. The proxy for the client side is called the **stub**. This is deployed in the client process and is a local object, implemented in the programming language of the client. There it mimics the server object by providing the same interface as the server object. It does not, however, implement the operations locally. Rather, it forwards them to the server side.

On the server side, a CORBA-distributed object does not actually receive the requests directly. Instead, a proxy, called a **skeleton,** is generated. A skeleton is a local object implemented in the programming language of the server object, and deployed in the server process. The skeleton receives the forwarded request from the stub and invokes a corresponding method on the server object. In this way the server object thinks that the client is local. The result is returned in the same way. For sending the request between the client and the server over the network the IIOP protocol is used.

The whole process is presented graphically in the diagram below:

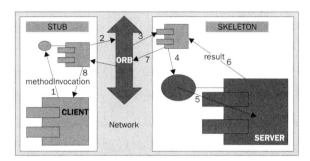

Fortunately, the stub and skeleton do not have to be implemented manually.

They are generated when the IDL interface definitions are mapped to the programming language. Different languages can be used for the client and server; the stubs and skeletons are generated by mapping the IDL to the client and server language, respectively. All the developer has to do is to include this generated code with the application it develops.

As the name already implies, the CORBA architecture is object oriented and therefore aligns very well with OO programming languages, where we can access the distributed objects in a 'natural' way. But what about non-OO languages? In this case, we communicate at a lower level and we will probably have to cope with the stubs and skeletons directly.

Dynamic Invocation and Skeleton Interfaces

The process of invoking methods on distributed objects that we described above is called the **static invocation interface**. This is because the clients need to know ahead of time which interfaces and operations a server provides. In other words, the clients need access to the IDL definition of a server object in order to access the methods. The stub code for each object the client accesses has to be bound with the client at the time of compiling the source code.

CORBA provides another alternative that is called the **dynamic invocation interface (DII)**, which allows the client to build the request at run time. To provide the possibility to dynamically acquire the operations that a CORBA object offers, the CORBA architecture has introduced the interface repository, which stores the details of CORBA object interfaces, including operation names, parameters, and return values. Using dynamic invocation with the interface repository, the client can first query for the operations of an interface, then discover the operation signature, and finally construct the method invocation, all at run time.

The dynamic invocation interface is important in situations where we have to access CORBA interfaces but do not have the appropriate IDL. For example, several commercial applications, such as ERP systems (such as SAP R/3), provide their APIs in a CORBA-compliant manner, but sometimes the IDL files are not included.

Even if the interface operations are not stored in the interface repository, it is sometimes easier to use DII than to reconstruct the IDL. We should, however, be aware that DII adds overhead to remote method invocation, making it less appropriate if performance is critical.

In the same manner as developing dynamic clients, it is also possible to develop a dynamic server – using the **dynamic skeleton interface (DSI)**. With the DSI we can develop a server object that dynamically reacts to the server request. The server request is a special object that holds the information about what the operation client requested. DSI servers are useful to integration when we have to bridge different distributed object models, or if we have to bridge different CORBA implementations (like connecting older implementations with newer).

Interoperable Object Reference

We are now familiar with how client and server CORBA objects communicate. However, before they can start communicating they have to obtain initial references – the client has to acquire a reference to the server CORBA object.

The information that the ORB needs to locate a CORBA object is called the **Interoperable Object Reference (IOR)**. The client has to obtain the server's IOR, which holds important information including the host name, port number, and object unique identification key. Once the client has the IOR it can use it to communicate with the server without paying attention to where the server object is actually located.

Server objects can obtain IORs in two different ways. The server objects can be **transient**, meaning that the IOR is generated by the instantiation of the object. In other words, if we destroy the object and instantiate once again, the IOR will be different. On the other hand, the server object can be **permanent**, which means that it will have a permanent IOR. This way, once a client has the IOR it will be able to locate the server even if we shut it down and reinstantiate it on another location in the network. Permanent IORs are useful for CORBA objects that provide services to several clients. On the other hand, CORBA objects that will be instantiated on the client request will not need a persistent IOR.

Ways for Clients To Obtain IORs

The client can obtain the IOR in several different ways, the most common of which are as follows:

❑   Using a naming and directory service

❑   Exchanging the IOR converted to a string

❑   Using an IOR as a result from method invocations

❑   Proprietary ways

The naming and directory service is probably the most common way to obtain initial references.

> **CORBA defines the Naming Service as a standard way for storing and retrieving name bindings.**

A name binding is nothing more than a human-readable name with the IOR. The Naming Service provides the functionality, through CORBA interfaces, allowing us to store naming bindings and retrieve IORs based on the names of objects.

For the purposes of integration with J2EE, the CORBA Naming Service is not the most appropriate – it actually introduces the same functionality that is provided by JNDI. Therefore, for the purposes of integration, we will concentrate on how to use JNDI to store and obtain the IOR instead.

Another possibility is to convert IORs to strings. IORs are complex data structures, which we cannot, for example, write to a database or a file. Converting them to strings makes this possible because it serializes the object references. The ORB provides the methods to do this: `object_to_string()` and `string_to_object()`. Once we have converted the reference to a string we can exchange it as any other data. The receiver simply converts the string back to the IOR and gains access to the object. Although simple, this method will not be very usable for real-world integration, because storing IOR strings in files or databases to exchange them is quite primitive.

The third possibility is to return the IOR as a result of method invocation. Once we have obtained a reference to one CORBA object, this object can provide methods to create or find other objects and return the references directly. This approach is suitable for implementing factory objects, for example. These are objects that create new CORBA objects (similar to home objects in EJBs) – we will talk about them later in this chapter. In fact, the CORBA Naming Service uses returning IORs as a result of method invocation too, because it provides general methods to resolve name bindings that return the CORBA object as a result. All we have to do is to narrow the reference to the actual object.

Finally, the clients and servers can use some proprietary way to exchange IORs. The majority of commercial ORBs implement the `bind()` method that allows the easy location of objects. However, this method of acquiring IORs is not compliant with the specification. Actually the CORBA specification does not even mention this possibility. If we use proprietary extensions we will not be able to achieve interoperability with other CORBA implementations.

> Using the `bind()` method is a common mistake that can seriously hinder the interoperability between different CORBA implementations.

The described IOR mechanisms guarantee location independence and enable clients to use the server objects without concern about where they are located. Furthermore, they can be moved without influencing the client.

Implementation Repository and Server Activation

Until now we have presumed that the server objects are active all the time. In other words, we need to start the server objects manually before we can start the client(s). In most cases this will be enough, but sometimes we might need server-side objects to be started automatically when a request is submitted. For example, this could enable rarely used existing applications to have wrappers that could instantiate on-demand, rather than being instantiated all the time and wasting resources.

The CORBA architecture provides an **implementation repository**, which stores the information about executables that implement certain CORBA objects. When a client invokes a method, the server activator can look into the implementation repository and start the corresponding server executable automatically. Furthermore, after a certain period of inactivity it can destroy the server process automatically. However, not all CORBA implementations provide this functionality.

Object Adapters

We've now covered many of the concepts associated with the way in which CORBA objects communicate, but we have not yet clarified *where* the server objects are instantiated. CORBA objects need a process whereby we can instantiate them and make them available to the clients. We also have to register them with the ORB (which handles the communication), and provide ways for the ORB to access server-side CORBA objects.

Unfortunately, the CORBA architecture does not provide a specific container in which the CORBA object might execute, like the EJB architecture for example; therefore we have to provide a process manually. We'll have to create a server application that will instantiate the objects and register them.

The ORB provides a special interface for that purpose – the **Object Adapter**. The object adapter is based on the adapter pattern, and it guarantees that the ORB core stays relatively small. The major tasks of the object adapter are:

❑   Creation of requests

❑   Dispatching the requests to objects

❑   Activation and deactivation

❑   Generation of IORs

Although the architecture has been defined flexibly, in practice only two object adapters have been used:

❑   **Basic Object Adapter (BOA)**

❑   **Portable Object Adapter (POA)**

The BOA provides very limited support for CORBA server objects and does not define some important things from the start, such as how the connection between the skeletons and object implementations should be achieved, or how the servers should register. Nor does the BOA say anything about multi-threading, or what a server should do to wait for client requests. Different CORBA vendors have solved these problems in their own ways with the result that code has not been 100% portable between different CORBA implementations.

The solution arrived in the form of the POA, which introduced important changes in the way server objects are developed and registered. It also brings in a much more powerful model to control the behavior of server objects, based on policies. However, this also introduces the necessary changes to existing applications if they want to use the POA. We will examine the POA at length a little later in this chapter.

The problem, however, is that not all CORBA implementations currently support POA. Older or more exotic implementations and operating systems have not yet been upgraded. POA is connected with some other modifications in the CORBA specification, so it might become a challenge to achieve true interoperability between BOA-based and POA-based versions.

440

Value Types

Another important new technology added to the CORBA specification is the **value types**. Until now we have only considered scenarios where the client locates the server-side object, then sends the request (or invoke methods) to the remote computer, and gets the result delivered as the returns from method invocations.

Sometimes, however, it might be a good idea if we could send the object from the server computer to the client where it would execute locally; to optimize performance, for example. Instead of invoking several remote methods on a remote object it might be more effective to transfer the object to the client side and execute the methods locally; for input validation for example.

Sending objects by value became popular with the introduction of the Java platform. The problem was that if we serialized the state of the object and sent it to the client computer we would need the implementation (the behavior) of the object there too. With Java it is possible to send the code too; this has not been possible with other programming languages because we could never know what operating system and platform is on the other side of the wire.

The value types are the CORBA constructs that enable us to send objects by value in a CORBA environment using any supported programming language. They have been added to CORBA mostly because of the integration with Java RMI-IIOP, which needs to support this feature. We will say more on this in Chapter 11.

CORBA Versions

As with every other technology, CORBA has evolved over time. We have already identified that the POA and value types have been added in the latest versions. Some other additions include interceptors, CORBA messaging for asynchronous communication, Minimum CORBA for embedded systems, Real-Time CORBA, and Fault-Tolerant CORBA. For more information refer to the CORBA specification: http://www.omg.org/technology/documents/formal/corba_iiop.htm.

With regard to different versions, even small additions can be important. For example, data types wchar and wstring have been added to support character strings, including Unicode characters, longer than 8-bits. Support for these data types is important for interoperability with J2EE where we use Unicode characters by default.

To support these features, changes to the underlying GIOP and IIOP have had to be done too. Therefore today, we have three different versions of GIOP – 1.0, 1.1, and 1.2. CORBA implementations that use higher protocol versions will not interoperate smoothly with older versions. More specifically, the older CORBA implementations will not be able to access new concepts and will not be able to interpret them.

Using older CORBA implementations will also prevent interoperability with RMI-IIOP. So, wherever possible, try to use the most recent version of the CORBA specification available for the target platform. But not all CORBA products have been upgraded to support the latest version and sometimes we will be forced to stick with older versions.

CORBA Implementations Used in This Chapter

CORBA has been a part of Java since JDK 1.2. It hides under the name Java IDL, which we will use for the examples in this chapter. We should note, however, that Java IDL supports the Java language only. So, because we will show some examples with C++, we will also use Inprise/Borland Visibroker version 4.5. Let's now take a closer look at Java IDL.

Java IDL

The Java IDL ORB is the CORBA-compliant ORB bundled with Java SDK Standard Edition since version 1.2. As J2EE version 1.3 actually requires J2SE 1.3, Java IDL is included too. Note that Java IDL is a Java-only ORB – it does not enable us to build the CORBA objects in other programming languages. For this we will need other CORBA implementations. Java IDL does, however, provide an IDL compiler and the Naming Service.

Unfortunately, Java IDL in version 1.3 does not support the latest CORBA specification. It is based on the CORBA 2.1 specification and therefore does not support POA, value types, and other new features. Likewise, it does not support some other parts of the CORBA specification, like Interface and Implementation Repositories and the DII. In fact, the support for the BOA is not even complete. The biggest disadvantage of Java IDL in version 1.3 has proved to be that it supports transient servers only. Indeed, the naming service, `tnameserv`, is only a transient implementation, meaning that once shut down it loses all information about registered objects.

Java IDL is, however, much improved in JDK 1.4. This version will be CORBA 2.3.1-compliant, which means that it will implement the POA and value types, it will provide support for persistent servers and persistent naming (through the CORBA Naming Service), and it will implement the GIOP version 1.2 and portable interceptors. With all these additions, Java IDL will become a fully capable Java-based ORB. As a comparison, in this chapter we will present examples using both the BOA-based Java IDL 1.3, and the POA-based Java IDL 1.4.

Inprise Visibroker

To build wrappers and virtual components around existing applications we will have to select some other CORBA product that supports programming languages other than Java. For our examples with C++ wrappers we will use the Inprise/Borland Visibroker for C++ version 4.5. We will also show clients using Visibroker for Java version 4.5. Visibroker in version 4.5 supports the CORBA specification 2.3.1 with all major functions and provides some advanced features, such as fault tolerance and bi-directional communication.

To run the examples in this chapter we will need a CORBA implementation that is compliant with version 2.3.1 or higher and supports Java and C++ programming languages. We will also need Java and C++ compilers. The examples have been tested with the following products, which can be downloaded from the corresponding web sites (except Microsoft Visual C++):

❑ Inprise/Borland Visibroker for C++ version 4.5 – http://www.inprise.com/visibroker/download/

❑ Inprise/Borland Visibroker for Java version 4.5 – http://www.inprise.com/visibroker/download/

❑ Java 2 SDK version 1.3 – http://java.sun.com/j2se/1.3/

❑   Java 2 SDK version 1.4, beta2 or higher – http://java.sun.com/j2se/1.4/

❑   Microsoft Visual C++ 5.0 (or higher) – http://msdn.microsoft.com/visualc/

Building a CORBA Component Wrapper

We explained the role of CORBA component wrappers in the first section of this chapter. Now we will look a little closer at how to actually implement them. Building a CORBA component wrapper is similar to building a general purpose CORBA distributed object. The procedure we have to follow is:

1. Define the interface that the component wrapper should expose in CORBA IDL

2. Compile the IDL interface to generate stubs and skeletons

3. Connect the operations from the interface with the existing application

4. Implement the server process

5. Implement the client to test the component wrapper

The whole procedure for developing wrappers in CORBA is visually summarized in the following diagram:

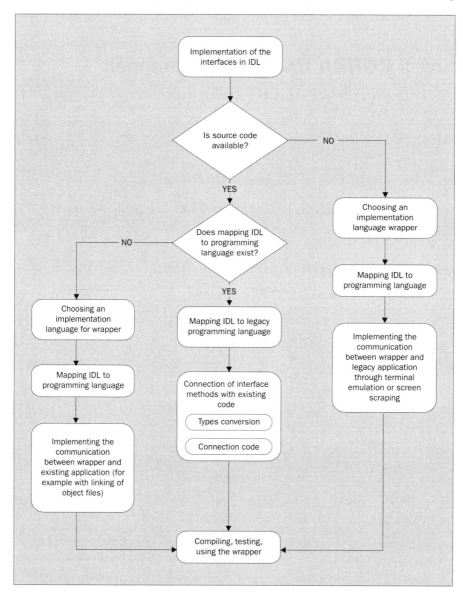

In order to demonstrate this process, we will build a simple component wrapper for the customer information application from our cell phone operator integration example.

We will not, however, be able to show exactly how to connect the operation from the component wrapper interface to the 'existing application' because readers will clearly not have such an application installed. Nevertheless, we will highlight the places in the code where we would do the connection. The fact of the matter is that connection with an existing application is rather specific for each application.

Thus, the examples presented in this chapter will be universal. We can use them to access a proprietary API, already provided by an existing application. Or we can use them to wrap existing applications, either through source code modification, or through screen scraping or terminal emulation.

In the first attempt we will build a simple component wrapper using the Java IDL bundled with the JDK 1.3. This will mean that we will use the CORBA 2.1-compliant ORB and the BOA.

Defining the Interface

In the previous chapter we identified the CustomerInt interface that our customer information application provides. We will build a low-level component wrapper, so we'll simply use the same API as provided by the existing application. The API that the Customer Information application provides is shown in the following UML diagram:

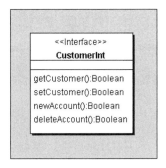

The operation signatures are not completely defined by the previous figure, so let's have a closer look at those provided by the existing application:

❏   The getCustomer() method requires the customerId as an input parameter. It returns the following data: firstName, lastName, address, numberOfPhoneAccounts, status. This method returns the actual data through parameters (by reference). As a method result it returns a Boolean value that indicates if the customer with the supplied ID has been found.

❏   The setCustomer() method requires the following input parameters: firstName, lastName, address, numberOfPhoneAccounts, status. It returns the customerId through a parameter by reference. It uses a Boolean as the return value to indicate whether or not adding the customer was successful.

❏   The newAccount() method requires the following input parameters: phoneNumber, startDate, typeOfAccount. The typeOfAccount uses a numeric representation, where 1 means the subscriber and 2 a prepaid account. The return value is Boolean, which indicates if the operation has been successful.

❏   The deleteAccount() method requires the phoneNumber input parameter. It also returns a Boolean, which indicates if the account has been deleted successfully.

Now we will define the CORBA IDL that will represent the operations exactly as provided by the existing application. The IDL looks like this:

445

```
module CustomerManagement {

  interface Customer {

    Boolean getCustomer (in long customerId,
                         out string firstName,
                         out string lastName,
                         out string address,
                         out short numberOfPhoneAccounts,
                         out char status);

    Boolean setCustomer (in string firstName,
                         in string lastName,
                         in string address,
                         in short numberOfPhoneAccounts,
                         in char status,
                         out long customerId);

    Boolean newAccount (in string phoneNumber,
                        in string startDate,
                        in short typeOfAccount);

    Boolean deleteAccount (in string phoneNumber);

  };
};
```

First of all we defined a module `CustomerManagement` to provide a namespace. Then we defined the interface. To model returning the data through parameters we have used the `out` type of parameters that have been designed exactly for this purpose. We have also modeled the interface exactly after the existing application API.

Although the IDL looks OK at first sight, a closer examination reveals several shortcomings. First of all, we have used primitive data types to model the data attributes, like the `typeOfAccount` or `status`. We have also used a simple string to model the `startDate`. It is true that this is the way the API provides the functionality. However, a component wrapper is a good location to provide more "developer-friendly" interfaces that will fit more naturally with Java components. Therefore, we will introduce user-defined data types. We will use the `enum` for account types and status and a `struct` for the date.

We have also used the data type `string`. In CORBA IDL a `string` is a set of 8-bit characters. Using this data type in the component wrapper will prevent us from sending Unicode characters that are natively used by Java to the wrapper. This might not be a big problem for the United States, but for other countries that use additional characters, using the `string` data type in the component wrapper will either prevent us from using other characters or will require that we do the mapping between the Unicode used by Java and the old 8-bit data representations on the client (on the client of the wrapper, which might be an EJB for example).

The solution here will be to use the `wstring` data type and to provide a mapping between different characters in the wrapper. The component wrapper is a good place to do the mapping between the Unicode and such old character schemas.

The modified, more appropriate IDL then looks as follows:

```
module CustomerManagement {

  interface Customer {

    enum statusType {normal, silver, gold};

    enum typeOfAccounts {subscription, prepaid};

    struct dateType {
      short date;
      short month;
      short year;
    };

    Boolean getCustomer (in long customerId,
                         out wstring firstName,
                         out wstring lastName,
                         out wstring address,
                         out short numberOfPhoneAccounts,
                         out statusType status);

    Boolean setCustomer (in wstring firstName,
                         in wstring lastName,
                         in wstring address,
                         in short numberOfPhoneAccounts,
                         in statusType status,
                         out long customerId);

    Boolean newAccount (in wstring phoneNumber,
                        in wstring startDate,
                        in typeOfAccounts typeOfAccount);

    Boolean deleteAccount (in wstring phoneNumber);

  };
};
```

Such an interface for the wrapper is more appropriate and will be easier to use from Java components. Note that we will explain how all the different IDL data types (enum, struct) map to Java a little later. When defining the interfaces of wrappers in IDL we should think about providing as clean an interface as possible. Hence, we should use the built-in IDL data types and associated mechanisms for defining our user-defined data types. These include:

❑ The any data type – which can hold any other primitive or user-defined data type, including an object reference (comparable to java.lang.Object)

❑ struct keyword – for user-defined structures

❑ union keyword – for discriminated unions

❑ enum keyword – for enumerators

❑ sequence – for variable or fixed-length sequences

❑ We can even use fixed-length arrays and a `native` type that is not managed by the ORB

With Java it is a particularly good idea to use `valuetypes`, which define the objects that are transferred by value; `valuetypes` are somewhere between the structures and CORBA objects and map relatively cleanly to Java serializable objects. We will look more precisely at how to handle `valuetypes` a little later.

The next improvement to the IDL is to avoid using a `Boolean` return value to signalize the success of an operation, and instead use the CORBA exception mechanism, with which we will be able to more precisely signalize exceptional events, such as "customer not found". What we can do is declare user-defined exceptions and raise them in case of failures. For that we will use the IDL `exception` keyword. We will also have to modify the operations signatures and declare that they can raise these exceptions – using the IDL `raises` keyword. We can also modify the `setCustomer()` operation that can now return the `customerID` as a normal return value rather than through the `out` parameter. The IDL is thus as follows:

```
module CustomerManagement {

  interface Customer {

    enum statusType {normal, silver, gold};

    enum typeOfAccounts {subscription, prepaid};

    struct dateType {
       short date;
       short month;
       short year;
    };

    exception customerNotFound {
       string reason;
       short errorCode;
    };

    exception customerNotUpdated {
       string reason;
       short errorCode;
    };

    exception accountNotAdded {
       string reason;
       short errorCode;
    };

    exception accountNotDeleted  {
       string reason;
       short errorCode;
    };

    void getCustomer (in long customerId,
                      out wstring firstName,
```

```
                        out wstring lastName,
                        out wstring address,
                        out short numberOfPhoneAccounts,
                        out statusType status)
            raises (customerNotFound);

    long setCustomer (in wstring firstName,
                        in wstring lastName,
                        in wstring address,
                        in short numberOfPhoneAccounts,
                        in statusType status)
            raises (customerNotUpdated);

    void newAccount (in wstring phoneNumber,
                        in wstring startDate,
                        in typeOfAccounts typeOfAccount)
            raises (accountNotAdded);

    void deleteAccount (in wstring phoneNumber)
            raises (accountNotDeleted);

    };
};
```

Compiling the IDL Interfaces

When we compile the IDL interfaces we do two things:

- ❑ We map the IDL to a specific programming language in which we will implement the component wrapper

- ❑ We generate stubs and skeletons that enable remote communication

The IDL compiler does the mapping of the IDL to the programming language. This is part of every CORBA implementation. For the language mappings that are standardized by the OMG, the IDL compilers from different vendors should produce exactly the same results. To achieve this in practice we often need to use some switches that will require strict mappings. Some IDL compilers do not conform 100% to the mapping specification, and this can sometimes limit their interoperability.

It is worth noting that this mapping is done separately for the server and client side. For the server side the IDL compiler generates the skeleton, for the client side it generates the stub. The power of CORBA is in the language independency. This means that we can implement the clients in one language, and the server object in another. Then we will have to generate the mappings separately for the client and the server objects and use the appropriate IDL compilers.

For now we will stay with Java IDL, and first look at how to implement the wrapper in Java completely. We will assume that we can access the existing application API for Java. To compile the IDL interface that we have defined we will use the `idlj` compiler, which is a part of JDK 1.3 (and also higher versions). To generate both mappings, for the client and the server side, we have to use the `-fall` option, which generates *all* the bindings:

```
C:\WINNT\System32\cmd.exe                                          _ □ x
C:\ProEAI\Ch10\CustomerInformation1>idlj -fall CustomerInt.idl
C:\ProEAI\Ch10\CustomerInformation1>_
```

The other options for the −f parameter are:

❏   client – to generate client-side bindings only

❏   server – to generate server-side binding only

❏   serverTIE and allTIE – to generate the tie bindings, which we will discuss later

The IDL compiler has generated a set of Java interfaces and classes that we will use to implement the wrapper. Note that we have defined a module so it has placed everything it has generated into the CustomerManagement folder. This is because the IDL module maps to the Java package. This and all other details of IDL-to-Java mapping are defined by the specification. To use the CORBA architecture effectively it is useful to familiarize ourselves with language mapping.

Another subfolder has been generated, nested under the CustomerManagement folder, with the name CustomerPackage. Inside are the user-defined data types dateType, statusType, and typeOfAccounts. If we take a look into these files we will see that the enum as well as the struct have been mapped to Java final classes. Java does not support these data types natively so they have to be simulated with these classes.

In addition to user-defined data types, this folder contains the declarations for user-defined exceptions too. We can find the accountNotAdded, accountNotDeleted, customerNotFound, and customerNotUpdated exceptions. These exceptions map to Java final classes that extend the org.omg.CORBA.UserException. They contain all the attributes that we have declared. In the attributes, additional information about the exception is carried. Also, two constructors are declared, one without parameters and one for setting the initial attribute values by the creation. For example, the accountNotAdded exception is declared as follows:

```
package CustomerManagement.CustomerPackage;

/**
 * CustomerManagement/CustomerPackage/accountNotAdded.java
 * Generated by the IDL-to-Java compiler (portable), version "3.0"
 */

public final class accountNotAdded extends org.omg.CORBA.UserException
  implements org.omg.CORBA.portable.IDLEntity {
  public String reason = null;
  public short errorCode = (short) 0;

  public accountNotAdded() {}   // ctor

  public accountNotAdded(String _reason, short _errorCode) {
    reason = _reason;
    errorCode = _errorCode;
  }   // ctor
}     // class accountNotAdded
```

We can also see that, in addition to the Java classes with the same names as the original data types and exceptions, additional classes have been generated. First are the helper classes, like `dataTypeHelper` or `accountNotAddedHelper`. Helper classes provide support operations to manipulate the data type. For example, they provide methods to insert and extract a user-defined data type to `any`, to return the data type ID, and to write/read them to/from a stream. We will see a little later how to use helper classes.

The others are the holder classes like the `dataTypeHolder` or `accountNotAddedHolder`. The holder classes are responsible for returning the data type instance as the `out` parameter from an operation invocation. In the interface that we defined, we have used a lot of `out` parameters, which should be transferred by reference and used to return the result to the client. Java does not provide support for this, but other programming languages like C++ do (which will be familiar to all who have experience with older languages).

To achieve returning results through parameters, the Java to IDL mapping specification defines special holder classes that hold a value of the data type. With the use of such classes the data can be transferred back via parameters because classes are transferred by reference in method invocations (be sure not to confuse this with passing parameters by value in RMI – here we're talking about local invocation, the stub and skeleton will ensure that the value is propagated accordingly).

Understanding the holder classes is relatively simple. Let us first have a look at the `dateTypeHolder`, generated by the `idlj`:

```
package CustomerManagement.CustomerPackage;

/**
 * CustomerManagement/CustomerPackage/dateTypeHolder.java
 * Generated by the IDL-to-Java compiler (portable), version "3.0"
 * from CustomerInt2.idl
 */

public final class dateTypeHolder
  implements org.omg.CORBA.portable.Streamable {
  public CustomerManagement.CustomerPackage.dateType value = null;

  public dateTypeHolder() {}

  public dateTypeHolder(CustomerManagement.CustomerPackage.dateType
                                                    initialValue) {
    value = initialValue;
  }

  public void _read(org.omg.CORBA.portable.InputStream i) {
    value = CustomerManagement.CustomerPackage.dateTypeHelper.read(i);
  }

  public void _write(org.omg.CORBA.portable.OutputStream o) {
    CustomerManagement.CustomerPackage.dateTypeHelper.write(o, value);
  }

  public org.omg.CORBA.TypeCode _type() {
    return CustomerManagement.CustomerPackage.dateTypeHelper.type();
  }

}
```

We can see that the holder is a final Java class that declares a public attribute value of the type dateType. There are also two constructors, the default one without parameters, and a constructor that takes this data type as a parameter and sets the attribute. There are some other service methods defined, but we're not so interested in them at the moment. For primitive data types the holder classes are already defined, which we will see a little later.

Client-Side Mapping

In addition to the CustomerPackage folder, the following files are of interest to the client side:

- ❑   Customer.java
- ❑   CustomerHelper.java
- ❑   CustomerHolder.java
- ❑   CustomerOperations.java
- ❑   _CustomerStub.java

The Customer.java file defines the Java interface for the IDL defined Customer interface. It achieves this with inheritance from the CustomerOperations, org.omg.CORBA.Object, and org.omg.CORBA.portable.IDLEntity. The CORBA.Object defines the necessary support operations, while the IDLEntity is a marker interface that eases the work to the ORB by marshaling and provides information related to the Java to IDL mapping, which we will address in Chapter 11.

The client will use the interface, defined in Customer.java, to access the functionality of the component wrapper. Customer.java looks like this:

```
package CustomerManagement;

/**
 * CustomerManagement/Customer.java
 * Generated by the IDL-to-Java compiler (portable), version "3.0"
 */
public interface Customer
  extends CustomerOperations, org.omg.CORBA.Object,
          org.omg.CORBA.portable.IDLEntity {}   // interface Customer
```

The CustomerOperations.java file defines the interface and the methods we are looking for. It is interesting (and useful) to look into this file to become familiar with IDL-to-Java mapping:

```
package CustomerManagement;

/**
 * CustomerManagement/CustomerOperations.java
 * Generated by the IDL-to-Java compiler (portable), version "3.0"
 */

public interface CustomerOperations {
  void getCustomer(int customerId, org.omg.CORBA.StringHolder firstName, org
          .omg.CORBA.StringHolder lastName, org.omg.CORBA
            .StringHolder address, org.omg.CORBA
```

```
                .ShortHolder numberOfPhoneAccounts, CustomerManagement
              .CustomerPackage.statusTypeHolder status)
                  throws CustomerManagement.CustomerPackage
                      .customerNotFound;

      int setCustomer(String firstName, String lastName, String address,
            short numberOfPhoneAccounts, CustomerManagement
              .CustomerPackage.statusType status)
                  throws CustomerManagement.CustomerPackage.customerNotUpdated;

      void newAccount(String phoneNumber, String startDate, CustomerManagement
              .CustomerPackage.typeOfAccounts typeOfAccount)
                  throws CustomerManagement.CustomerPackage.accountNotAdded;

      void deleteAccount(String phoneNumber)
              throws CustomerManagement.CustomerPackage.accountNotDeleted;
  }    // interface CustomerOperations
```

First, we should notice how the data types have mapped from IDL-to-Java. We are already familiar with the mapping of user-defined types. The basic data type mappings are shown in the following table:

IDL	Java
Boolean	Boolean
char and wchar	char
octet (unsigned)	byte (signed)
short and unsigned short	short
long and unsigned long	int
long long and unsigned long long	long
float	float
double	double
long double	No support in Java
fixed	java.math.BigDecimal
string and wstring	java.lang.String

We should also notice how out parameters map to the Java language. For each out parameter a corresponding Holder class is used. For built-in primitive data types the holder classes are defined in the org.omg.CORBA package, like the org.omg.CORBA.StingHolder for example. For user-defined types the holder classes are generated, as we have seen before.

The other generated files, relevant for the client-side are the CustomerHelper.java, which provides service methods, similar to the helper classes generated for user-defined classes. The CustomerHolder.java is the holder class for the Customer object reference. The last file is the _CustomerStub.java, which implements the functionality of the stub on the client side. Knowing what's hidden in the different Java classes is useful later, at the implementation stage.

453

Server-Side Mapping

We already know that the server-side requires the skeleton. In addition to this, the ORB also defines how to connect our implementation with the skeleton. The server-side mapping depends on the object adapter we use, and we have already mentioned that there are two possible adapters – the older BOA and the newer POA.

The server-side mapping also depends on whether we choose the inheritance model to implement the operations or whether we choose the delegation model. The inheritance model is called the `ImplBase` and our CORBA object has to inherit from a specific predefined class. The delegation approach on the other hand enables us to define a class that will then be invoked through delegation rather than inheritance. This can be of advantage, particularly in Java, where we cannot use multiple inheritance for classes.

First, let's take a look at the `ImplBase` inheritance approach. The files that the IDL compiler generated which are of interest to the server side are as follows:

- ❑ `Customer.java`
- ❑ `CustomerOperations.java`
- ❑ `_CustomerImplBase.java`

In addition to these files, the server-side also requires the `CustomerPackage`, where the user-defined data types are declared.

We are already familiar with the `Customer.java` and `CustomerOperations.java`. In both files the object interface is defined. The third file is `_CustomerImplBase.java`, which is the skeleton. We connect to the skeleton through the use of inheritance.

After we have become familiar with the IDL interface, its compilation, and the client- and server-side mapping, we have enough knowledge to start developing the wrapper. The main task here will be to connect the interface operations with the existing applications.

Connecting the Interface Operations with the Existing Application

Once we have become familiar with the IDL-to-Java mapping we are ready to continue with the development of the component wrapper. Now we have to connect the operations that we defined in the interface with those of the existing application. The same example is suitable for accessing the existing application through a proprietary API, or by source code modification, screen scraping, or terminal emulation.

We will first look at how we do this using the inheritance (`ImplBase`) approach. Later we will look at how to implement the wrapper in another programming languages (C++).

To implement the component wrapper we have to define a class that will implement the functionality of the IDL interface. We will name this class `CustomerImpl`. As already mentioned we will use the inheritance approach, so we have to inherit (extend) the `_CustomerImplBase` class, provided by the IDL compiler. We just have to implement the operations. In the next code example we show the general idea of how to implement two wrapper methods:

```
package CustomerManagement;

public class CustomerImpl extends _CustomerImplBase {

  public void getCustomer(int customerId, org.omg.CORBA
          .StringHolder firstName, org.omg.CORBA.StringHolder lastName,
            org.omg.CORBA.StringHolder address,
              org.omg.CORBA.ShortHolder numberOfPhoneAccounts,
                CustomerManagement.CustomerPackage.statusTypeHolder status)
      throws CustomerManagement.CustomerPackage.customerNotFound {

    // Connect to the existing application
    // Locate the customer and retrieve the data
    Boolean successful = true;    // Determined from existing application

    if (successful) {

      // Fill in the data
      firstName.value = "Jack";
      lastName.value = "B. Good";
      address.value = "Warwick Road";
      numberOfPhoneAccounts.value = 2;
      status.value = CustomerManagement.CustomerPackage.statusType.silver;
    } else {
      throw new CustomerManagement.CustomerPackage
        .customerNotFound("Bad customerID", (short) 1);
    }
  }
  public int setCustomer(String firstName, String lastName, String address,
      short numberOfPhoneAccounts, CustomerManagement
          .CustomerPackage.statusType status)
            throws CustomerManagement.CustomerPackage.customerNotUpdated {

    // Connect to the existing application
    // Generate the customerID
    // Add the customer data
    int customerId = 1;
    Boolean successful = true;

    if (successful) {
      return customerId;
    } else {
      throw new CustomerManagement.CustomerPackage
        .customerNotUpdated("DB error", (short) 1);
    }
  }

  public void newAccount(String phoneNumber, String startDate,
    CustomerManagement.CustomerPackage.typeOfAccounts typeOfAccount)
      throws CustomerManagement.CustomerPackage.accountNotAdded {

    // Similar to above example
  }
```

```
    public void deleteAccount(String phoneNumber)
          throws CustomerManagement.CustomerPackage.accountNotDeleted {

      // Similar to above example
    }
  }
```

Implementing the Server Process

At this stage, we have *almost* implemented the component wrapper. However, we still have to implement the process where the CORBA distributed object will execute; and we have to create at least one instance of the object. Note that the CORBA architecture does not provide the container-managed environment in which we could deploy the components. Furthermore, it does not provide instance management algorithms that would create and destroy instances – as does the EJB architecture. Consequently, we have to define the server process ourselves and also create the instance or instances and register them with the ORB.

We will define a class with the name Server. We have to do the following:

- ❑ Obtain the reference to the ORB
- ❑ Create a new instance of the Customer wrapper
- ❑ Connect the instance with the ORB

This is quite straightforward and the code to achieve this looks like this:

```
package CustomerManagement;

import org.omg.CosNaming.*;
import org.omg.CosNaming.NamingContextPackage.*;
import org.omg.CORBA.*;

public class Server {

  public static void main(String[] args) {

    try {
      ORB orb = ORB.init(args,null);

      Customer c = new CustomerImpl();

      orb.connect(c);
```

This is still not enough; we have to provide a way for the client to obtain the initial reference. The client cannot communicate with the server-side component unless it can get the IOR. We have mentioned that there are several ways to exchange the IOR. The most commonly used technique is with the help of the Naming Service.

The Naming Service allows us to define name bindings – a readable name for a specific IOR. Name bindings are stored in naming contexts, where they are resolved, and we can build a hierarchy of these naming contexts, preventing naming collisions. The names in the Naming Service are stored using the NameComponent structure that is defined by the CORBA Naming Service specification:

```
typedef string Istring;

struct NameComponent {
   Istring id;
   Istring kind;
};
```

The important part of the `NameComponent` is the `id`, which we use to name the component. The `kind` can be used for any purpose. The name is then finally defined as:

```
typedef sequence<NameComponent> Name;
```

To bind a name with a CORBA object, we have to create a `NameComponent` and define the name we would like to use. For our example we will register the name in the root context. Therefore, the path to the name will be simple. Finally, we have to use the `rebind()` method to bind the name with the component IOR. Note that we have used the `rebind()` method instead of `bind()` to prevent the `AlreadyBound` exception if a component under the same name is already registered.

However, before we can use the Naming Service, we have to obtain a reference to it. We have already mentioned that the Naming Service is nothing more than a standard CORBA object, so we'll use the standard mechanism to bind to it. The code continues as follows:

```
org.omg.CORBA.Object objRef =
   orb.resolve_initial_references("NameService");
NamingContext ncRef = NamingContextHelper.narrow(objRef);

NameComponent nc;
NameComponent path[] = {
  Null
};

nc = new NameComponent("CustomerWrapper", "");
path[0] = nc;
ncRef.rebind(path, c);

System.out.println("Server is ready...");
```

That's almost everything, but we should remember not to allow the server process to end. This would destroy the distributed object instance that we have just created. So we have to persuade the process to stay alive. One of the ways to do this is as follows:

```
java.lang.Object sync = new java.lang.Object();
synchronized (sync) {
  sync.wait();
}
```

Finally, we have to catch any possible exceptions:

```
} catch (Exception e) {
    System.out.println(e);
  }
 }
}
```

Implementing a Client to Test the Component Wrapper

Although we have finished the development of the component wrapper, obviously it is still a good idea to test it. For this purpose we can develop a small CORBA client that will invoke some of the methods. The client has to do the following:

❏   Obtain a reference to the ORB

❏   Obtain a reference to the Naming Service

❏   Resolve the name binding

❏   Narrow the reference to the Customer interface

❏   Invoke the methods on the wrapper

The client also has to catch the corresponding exceptions. In production applications it would catch each CORBA user-defined exception separately. In the example that we present here we catch CORBA user exceptions, CORBA systems exceptions, and all other exceptions:

```
package CustomerManagement;

import org.omg.CosNaming.*;
import org.omg.CORBA.*;

public class Client {
  public static void main(String args[]) {
    try {

      // Connect to the wrapper
      ORB orb = ORB.init(args, null);

      org.omg.CORBA.Object objRef =
        orb.resolve_initial_references("NameService");
      NamingContext ncRef = NamingContextHelper.narrow(objRef);

      NameComponent nc = new NameComponent("CustomerWrapper", "");
      NameComponent path[] = {
        nc
      };
      Customer c = CustomerHelper.narrow(ncRef.resolve(path));

      // test the functionality
      StringHolder firstName = new StringHolder();
      StringHolder lastName = new StringHolder();
      StringHolder address = new StringHolder();
      ShortHolder numberOfPhoneAccounts = new ShortHolder();
      CustomerManagement.CustomerPackage.statusTypeHolder status =
        new CustomerManagement.CustomerPackage.statusTypeHolder();

      c.getCustomer((int) 1, firstName, lastName, address,
                numberOfPhoneAccounts, status);
      System.out.println("First name: " + firstName.value);
      System.out.println("Last name:  " + lastName.value);
      System.out.println("Address:    " + address.value);
```

```
            System.out.println("No. of phone accounts: "
                              + numberOfPhoneAccounts.value);

            int customerId =
              c.setCustomer("Jack", "B. Good", "Birmingham", (short) 1,
                         CustomerManagement.CustomerPackage.statusType.gold);
            System.out.println("Setting new customer... id: " + customerId);

        } catch (UserException e) {
          System.out.println("User exception: " + e);

        } catch (SystemException e) {
          System.out.println("System exception: " + e);

        } catch (Exception e) {
          System.out.println("Exception: " + e);
        }
      }
    }
```

Compiling and Testing the Wrapper

Now we have to compile the Java code and run the example. To compile the Java code we simply use the following command line:

```
javac CustomerManagement/*.java
```

To run the example we first have to start the Naming Service. JDK 1.3 provides a transient name service, called the tnameserv. Then, after setting the appropriate classpath, we simply start the Server and Client classes, each in their own process, as shown below:

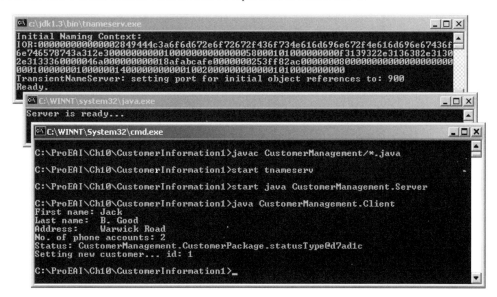

If we decide to start the client and the server on different machines, we have to provide the address of the naming service using the -ORBIntialHost switch. We can also select the port manually, using the -ORBInitialPort switch.

The Portable Object Adapter

The Portable Object Adapter (POA) provides several distinct advantages over the basic version (BOA). It enables greater control over the server-side object life cycle and provides portability of the server-side code. Ultimately, BOA does not define all the necessary concepts in the specification, whereas POA provides an extensive specification.

In addition to portability, POA provides support for objects with persistent identity. It allows control over the activation of objects. POA also introduces a new terminology: often the word **servant** is used to refer to the code that implements the methods of a CORBA object. POA provides control over how objects should be managed and how they behave through policies.

POA sits between the servant and the ORB, and routes the requests. While there is only one BOA, there can be more than one POA instance in a single server. In fact, each servant can have its own POA instance. Alternatively, a single POA can manage several servants, but at least one POA has to be present in each server – the root POA. Other POAs are created from the root POA and they build a hierarchy from the root POA. We define the characteristics of a POA through POA policies, which are in turn defined when we create a new POA. We can either use the default policies or define our own.

So, POA should successfully replace BOA for building server-side CORBA objects. However, at present there are still several CORBA implementations that have not been upgraded yet. In particular, implementations for less prevalent platforms will use BOA for a while.

POA also changes the language mappings a little, meaning that the POA code is somewhat different from the BOA example. Also, language mappings for some less common programming languages have not been updated yet. The discrepancy between the two different versions of the object adapter is the reason why we have first looked at an example featuring BOA.

Now we will look at how to implement the same example using POA. To do this we will need a CORBA implementation that supports POA. The Java IDL included in JDK version 1.4 will support POA. Visibroker for Java 4.5 supports POA as well. So, for the next example we will use JDK 1.4.

Required Changes To BOA Implementation

POA affects only the server-side mappings, hence there are no changes required on the client side. There are also no changes in the mapping of the user-defined data types and exceptions in CustomerPackage.

The difference on the server side is that instead of _CustomerImplBase.java, the CustomerPOA.java file is generated. When using the inheritance approach the implementation class (the servant) has to inherit from the CustomerPOA class instead. The implementation of the methods remains unchanged, therefore the only change necessary is as shown opposite:

```
...
public class CustomerImpl extends CustomerPOA {
...
```

There will, however, be more changes required to the implementation of the server process, where the component wrapper is instantiated. Instead of using BOA, we will have to use POA. Remember, with BOA we just had to initialize it. Now, with POA we have to perform the following general steps:

❑ Initialize the ORB and obtain a reference

❑ Create the servant

❑ Obtain a reference to the root POA

❑ Define the policies we want to use

❑ Create a child POA with the specified policies

❑ Activate the servant with the POA

❑ Activate the POA through the POA manager

If we want to build simple transient servers we can stick with the policies that are defined with the root POA. Therefore it is not needed to define extra policies and to create a child POA. For the moment we'll concentrate on the simple example.

The Server class for the example looks like this:

```
package CustomerManagement;

import org.omg.CosNaming.*;
import org.omg.CosNaming.NamingContextPackage.*;
import org.omg.CORBA.*;
import org.omg.PortableServer.*;

public class Server {

  public static void main(String[] args) {

    try {
      ORB orb = ORB.init(args, null);

      CustomerImpl c = new CustomerImpl();

      POA rPOA = (POA) orb.resolve_initial_references("RootPOA");

      rPOA.the_POAManager().activate();

      rPOA.activate_object(c);

      org.omg.CORBA.Object objRef =
        orb.resolve_initial_references("NameService");
      NamingContext ncRef = NamingContextHelper.narrow(objRef);

      NameComponent nc;
```

```
        NameComponent path[] = {
          null
        };

        nc = new NameComponent("CustomerWrapper", "");
        path[0] = nc;
        ncRef.rebind(path, rPOA.servant_to_reference(c));

        System.out.println("Server is ready...");

        orb.run();

      } catch (Exception e) {
        System.out.println(e);
      }
    }
  }
```

To compile and run this example under JDK 1.4 we first have to amend the relevant environment variable (usually %JAVA_HOME%) to look under the SDK 1.4 directories. Then we have to compile the IDL (using idlj, same as in the previous example). We also have to compile the Java code (using javac, again the same as in the previous example).

In addition to the transient CORBA Naming Service implementation, tnameserv, which we used in the previous example, JDK 1.4 provides a persistent implementation, called the orbd. To start the orbd, we have to specify the initial port that the ORB will use (-ORBInitialPort). We can choose any free TCP/IP port, 1050 for example. We also have to specify the initial ORB host URL (-ORBInitialHost). For this we will use the localhost. The following screenshot shows the commands that we should enter:

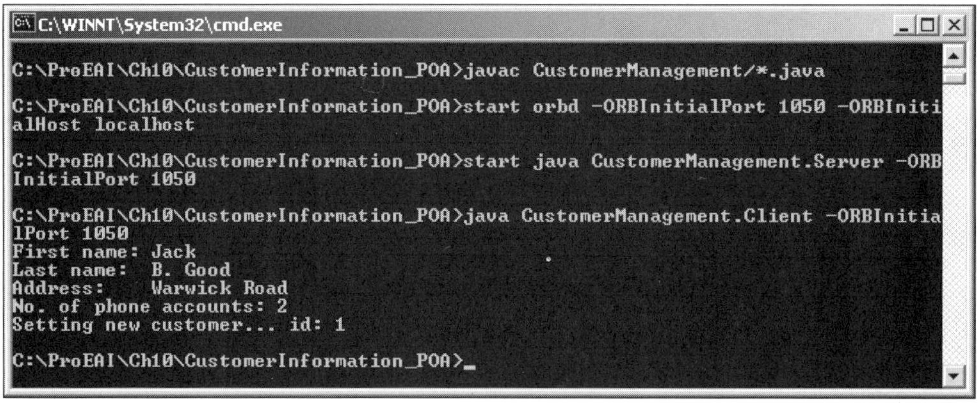

With this simple modification we have not even come close to exploiting the full potential of POA, but we won't delve much further into POA in this chapter. Refer to the CORBA documentation for more information.

The Tie Approach

When we implement the component wrapper classes that connect the interface operations with the existing code, we have to inherit from the generated `CustomerPOA` class. Sometimes this is not very useful – either we cannot use the inheritance from the POA generated class because we already have an inheritance structure, or we are wrapping an application when we just need to associate each operation with a certain class that implements it.

In both cases we can use the **tie approach**. Instead of using inheritance the tie approach connects the ORB and the implementation classes using delegation. The delegation class simply forwards the request to the actual implementation class and returns the results the same way. Thus, the implementation class does not have to inherit from the POA class. However, the tie approach requires that we have two objects instantiated in memory – the delegation object and the actual implementation object.

To use the tie approach the IDL compiler has to generate the corresponding classes. If we use the Java IDL (`idlj`) compiler from JDK 1.4, we have to use the `-fserverTIE` switch to tell the IDL compiler to generate POA support. The command line that we have to use is shown on the next screenshot:

```
Select C:\WINNT\System32\cmd.exe                          _ □ x

C:\ProEAI\Ch10\CustomerInformation_POA_tie>idlj -fserverTIE CustomerInt.idl

C:\ProEAI\Ch10\CustomerInformation_POA_tie>_
```

Note that we could also use the `-fallTIE` switch, which would generate both the server-side TIE mapping *and* the client-side mapping in one step. If we use Visibroker for Java 4.5 we do not have to specify any switches. The Visibroker IDL-to-Java compiler (`java2idl`) generates the POA support by default.

Instead of `CustomerPOA.java`, the IDL compiler will generate `CustomerPOATie.java`. In the implementation class `CustomerImpl` we do not have to inherit from any class. However, to guarantee the semantic of the interface, the `CustomerImpl` class has to implement the `CustomerOperations` interface. There are only two changes necessary. The first is in the signature of the class:

```
...
    public class CustomerImpl implements CustomerOperations {
    ...
```

Secondly, we must also subtly modify the `Server` class. Instead of creating the `CustomerImpl` directly we have to wrap it with the `CustomerPOATie` class like the code shows:

```
...
        CustomerPOATie c = new CustomerPOATie(new CustomerImpl());
...
```

Running this example is similar to the previous examples and there is not much difference to see from the perspective of client output. This time we will show how to build and run the example with JDK 1.4 (using Java IDL).

First we have to set the PATH and CLASSPATH variables to point to the JDK 1.4 directory. Then we have to compile the example using javac, start the orbd and specify the initial port and initial host, and run the Server. Finally, on running the Client, we get the result that we are probably rather familiar with by now:

Multi-threading

If we try to run any of the previous examples with multiple simultaneous clients we will see that the component wrapper services all clients concurrently. This is because the ORB supports the multi-threading model. In a multi-threading model the ORB processes each client request in a separate thread, thus giving the illusion that the code executes simultaneously.

There are several different multi-threading models implemented by different ORBs. These models differ in the way ORB manages the threads. They include:

❑ **Thread per client**
Allows only one thread per client, as its name suggests. This means that invocation made in different threads on a multi-threaded client will be serialized.

❑ **Thread per connection**
Simultaneous requests (made in multiple threads on the client) to the same object and executed in sequence, one-by-one (serialized).

❑ **Thread per request**
Creates a thread for every request a client makes, therefore guaranteeing multi-threading support on the server-side no matter how many requests and from what type of clients they come.

❑ **Thread pooling**
Creating threads can invoke a certain amount of overhead; therefore the thread pooling provides a number of pre created threads that are then assigned to the clients. With this method the server also does not allow too many threads to be created. There are two types of thread pool:

    ❑ Working thread pool

    ❑ Leader/follower thread pool

Serving the client requests in multiple threads is different from serving it in different processes. When using multi-threading we have to write so-called thread-safe code. This means that we have to put locks on shared resources. In the component wrappers we might not have many shared resources, maybe some attributes. Particularly in Java we can synchronize the threads easily, using the `synchronized` keyword. Nevertheless, writing thread-safe code can be difficult.

However, component wrappers will not be the major concern for multi-threaded code. We will have to be very careful how the existing application supports simultaneous clients and how we are allowed to invoke the operations on the existing application. In particular, if we wrap applications directly through source code integration, we have to consider multi-threading carefully.

To prevent multi-threaded execution we can use the thread POA policy `SINGLE_THREAD_MODEL`. This will force the serialization of the client requests. In Java we define this policy like this:

```
myPolicy[0] = rPOA.create_thread_policy(
                     ThreadPolicyValue.SINGLE_THREAD_MODEL);
```

Sometimes ORBs provide command-line switches through which we can influence the threading model used. For example, we can choose between different threading models implemented by the ORB and we can control the number of threads.

Note that JDK version 1.4 does not implement the single-threaded model according to the documentation available at the time of writing this book. It only provides the multi-threaded model. To run this example we will have to use another CORBA implementation, like Visibroker for Java 4.5.

When using BOA instead of POA we do not have a possibility to restrict the threading model from the server class. Rather, we have to use the command-line switches to force the single-threaded model if the ORB provides this option – the majority of commercial ORBs do. Sometimes we can even limit the number of threads in a thread pool to one and achieve serialization of requests that way.

The Factory Pattern

When we restrict the threading to the single-threaded model the requests from clients get serialized. This means that we limit the interaction to one client at a time (for each component wrapper). In a busy environment clients will have to wait a long time, which is clearly not the most favorable solution. Existing applications will also often support more than one simultaneous client (but not too many). A better solution would be to set the upper limit for the number of simultaneous clients. We can achieve this by instantiating several instances of the same component wrapper. Each client would then connect to a certain instance and the clients would not share a single instance.

However, if we need to instantiate a fixed number of component wrapper instances in advance, this wouldn't be a pretty solution. In non-peak times these instances would be unused. A better way would be to allow clients to create the component wrapper instances themselves, but to limit the maximum number of them. To achieve this we can use the Factory pattern. We will generate a CORBA factory object that will provide an interface for creating new instances of the component wrapper. The client will first connect to the factory object and create a new instance that it will use alone.

The additional factory interface in IDL is very simple:

```
interface CustomerFactory {
  Customer create();
};
```

However we might want to add a user-defined exception to notify the client that the maximum number of component wrapper instances has been reached:

```
interface CustomerFactory {
  exception limitReached {
  };

  Customer create() raises (limitReached);
};
```

Now we have to implement the `CustomerFactory` interface. The code to do this looks like this:

```
package CustomerManagement;

import org.omg.PortableServer.*;

public class CustomerFactoryImpl extends CustomerFactoryPOA {

  private POA poa;
  private static int noOfInstances = 0;
  private static final int MAX_NO_OF_INSTANCES = 10;

  public CustomerFactoryImpl(POA poa) {
    this.poa = poa;
  }

  synchronized public Customer create() throws
                  CustomerManagement.CustomerFactoryPackage.limitReached {
    if (noOfInstances<MAX_NO_OF_INSTANCES) {
      Customer c = null;
      CustomerImpl cs = new CustomerImpl();
      try {
        c = CustomerHelper.narrow(poa.servant_to_reference(cs));
        noOfInstances++;
      }
      catch (Exception e) {
        e.printStackTrace();
      }
      System.out.println("Wrapper created..."+c);
      return c;
    } else {
      throw new CustomerManagement.CustomerFactoryPackage.limitReached();
    }
  }
}
```

To implement the `create()` method we have to narrow the `CustomerImpl` method to the `Customer` interface. To do this we need the reference to the POA because we have to invoke the `servant_to_reference()` method on it. This is why in the `CustomerFactory` we will store the reference to the POA that we will obtain by the creation of the constructor.

Note that we have to change `Server.java` too. The server class now has to create an instance of the factory object, which is the `CustomerFactory`:

```
package CustomerManagement;

import org.omg.CosNaming.*;
import org.omg.CosNaming.NamingContextPackage.*;
import org.omg.CORBA.*;
import org.omg.PortableServer.*;

public class Server {

  public static void main(String[] args) {

    try {
      ORB orb = ORB.init(args, null);

      POA cPOA = (POA) orb.resolve_initial_references("RootPOA");

      cPOA.the_POAManager().activate();

      CustomerFactoryImpl cf = new CustomerFactoryImpl(cPOA);

      cPOA.activate_object(cf);

      org.omg.CORBA.Object objRef =
        orb.resolve_initial_references("NameService");
      NamingContext ncRef = NamingContextHelper.narrow(objRef);

      NameComponent nc;
      NameComponent path[] = {
        null
      };

      nc = new NameComponent("CustomerFactory", "");
      path[0] = nc;
      ncRef.rebind(path, cPOA.servant_to_reference(cf));

      System.out.println("Server is ready...");

      orb.run();

    } catch (Exception e) {
      System.out.println(e);
    }
  }
}
```

Finally, we have to change the client so that it obtains the reference to the factory first and then use the `create()` method to create one or more wrapper instances. The client should also catch the user-defined exception to figure out when the maximum number of clients is reached:

```
package CustomerManagement;

import org.omg.CosNaming.*;
import org.omg.CORBA.*;

public class Client {
  public static void main(String args[]) {
    try {

      // Connect to the wrapper
      ORB orb = ORB.init(args, null);

      org.omg.CORBA.Object objRef =
        orb.resolve_initial_references("NameService");
      NamingContext ncRef = NamingContextHelper.narrow(objRef);

      NameComponent nc = new NameComponent("CustomerFactory", "");
      NameComponent path[] = {
        nc
      };
      CustomerFactory cf =
        CustomerFactoryHelper.narrow(ncRef.resolve(path));

      // Create a Customer Wrapper
      Customer c = cf.create();

      // Test the functionality
      // ...

    } catch (CustomerManagement.CustomerFactoryPackage.limitReached e) {
      System.out.println("Maximum limit of component wrapper reached: "
                                                             + e) ;

    } catch (UserException e) {
      System.out.println("User exception: " + e);

    } catch (SystemException e) {
      System.out.println("System exception: " + e);

    } catch (Exception e) {
      System.out.println("Exception: " + e);
    }
  }
}
```

To run this example we can use either JDK 1.4 or Visibroker for Java 4.5 (with JDK 1.3). Here, we will demonstrate building and running the example with JDK 1.4.

First, we have to remember to change the PATH and CLASSPATH variables again to point to the JDK 1.4 directory. Then we have to compile the IDL interfaces (more specifically, we have added a new interface) using the idlj compiler. Next we have to compile the source code using javac, start the orbd and specify the initial port and host, and run the Server. Finally, on running the Client, we will get the usual well-known result:

```
C:\WINNT\System32\cmd.exe                                        _ □ ×

C:\ProEAI\Ch10\CustomerInformation_POA_factory>idlj -fall CustomerInt.idl

C:\ProEAI\Ch10\CustomerInformation_POA_factory>javac CustomerManagement/*.java

C:\ProEAI\Ch10\CustomerInformation_POA_factory>start orbd -ORBInitialPort 1050 -
ORBInitialHost localhost

C:\ProEAI\Ch10\CustomerInformation_POA_factory>server

C:\ProEAI\Ch10\CustomerInformation_POA_factory>start java CustomerManagement.Ser
ver -ORBInitialPort 1050
C:\ProEAI\Ch10\CustomerInformation_POA_factory>client

C:\ProEAI\Ch10\CustomerInformation_POA_factory>java CustomerManagement.Client -O
RBInitialPort 1050
First name: Jack
Last name:  B. Good
Address:    Warwick Road
No. of phone accounts: 2
Setting new customer... id: 1
C:\ProEAI\Ch10\CustomerInformation_POA_factory>_
```

We can also look into the server process window, where we see the following:

```
C:\WINNT\system32\java.exe                                      _ □ ×
Server is ready...
Wrapper created...CustomerManagement._CustomerStub:IOR:000000000000002449444c3a4
37573746f6d65724d616e6167656d656e742f437573746f6d65723a312e30000000000001000000000
000007000010200000000f3139322e3136382e31302e313336000043a000000000021afabcb000
000002001ac12b200000001000000000000000000400000010a000000000001000000010
000002000000000000010001000000205010001000100200001010900000001000101100
```

Keeping in mind that we have set the limit of simultaneous clients to ten in the code, if we start ten simultaneous clients, we will get the following output on attempting to start the eleventh client:

```
C:\WINNT\System32\cmd.exe                                        _ □ ×

C:\ProEAI\Ch10\CustomerInformation_POA_factory>java CustomerManagement.Client -O
RBInitialPort 1050
Maximum limit of component wrapper reached: CustomerManagement.CustomerFactoryPa
ckage.limitReached: IDL:CustomerManagement/CustomerFactory/limitReached:1.0

C:\ProEAI\Ch10\CustomerInformation_POA_factory>_
```

Using the any Data Type

Sometimes it is useful if we can avoid the need to specify the types of parameters and return values. Some existing applications might return different data types from the same operation. If we cannot foresee all the possible combinations it can be useful to use the CORBA IDL data type any.

As its name implies, the any data type can hold any other primitive or complex IDL data type. For built-in data types the operations to insert and extract to and from any data type are provided on the any instance. For user-defined data types the corresponding insert and extract methods are generated as a part of the helper class.

To demonstrate how to use the any data type we will build a simple example with the following IDL:

```
module CustomerManagement {

  interface Customer {

    any getCustomer (in long customerId);

  };
};
```

The implementation class CustomerImpl will insert a string into the any data type and return this to the client side:

```
package CustomerManagement;

public class CustomerImpl extends CustomerPOA {

  public org.omg.CORBA.Any getCustomer (int customerId)
  {
    // Connect to the existing application
    // Locate the customer
    // Retrieve the data

    // Fill in the data
    org.omg.CORBA.Any myAny=org.omg.CORBA.ORB.init().create_any();
    java.lang.String name="Wrox Press";
    myAny.insert_string(name);
    return myAny;
  }
}
```

The server process is identical to the ones we implemented earlier in this chapter, so we will not show it here. The client is also very similar, however it has to accept the any value and interpret it accordingly. In the example we will assume that we know that there will be a string inside the any data type. However, it would be possible to interpret the any dynamically, for which we will have to test for all possible data types. To construct the any without any static knowledge we could also use the dynamic any. For more information on dynamic any values take a look into the CORBA specification at http://www.omg.org/technology/documents/formal/corba_iiop.htm.

Our simple client code looks like this:

```
package CustomerManagement;

import org.omg.CosNaming.*;
import org.omg.CORBA.*;
```

```
public class Client {
  public static void main(String args[]) {
    try {

      // Connect to the wrapper
      ORB orb = ORB.init(args, null);

      org.omg.CORBA.Object objRef =
        orb.resolve_initial_references("NameService");
      NamingContext ncRef = NamingContextHelper.narrow(objRef);

      NameComponent nc = new NameComponent("CustomerWrapper", "");
      NameComponent path[] = {
        nc
      };
      Customer c = CustomerHelper.narrow(ncRef.resolve(path));

      // Test the functionality
      org.omg.CORBA.Any a = c.getCustomer((int) 1);

      System.out.println(a.extract_string());

    } catch (UserException e) {
      System.out.println("User exception: " + e);
    } catch (SystemException e) {
      System.out.println("System exception: " + e);

    } catch (Exception e) {
      System.out.println("Exception: " + e);
    }
  }
}
```

Run this example using JDK 1.4 in the usual way. First, compile the IDL interfaces (we have changed the method declaration) using the `idlj` compiler, then compile the source code using `javac`. Next, start the `orbd` and specify the initial port and host, and then run the `Server`. Finally, we have to run the `Client`, at which point we will get a slightly different output this time:

Implementing the Component Wrapper in C++

In many cases we will not be able to develop the component wrapper in Java. For example, we will have to connect the server side of the component wrapper to existing applications written in different programming languages. Or we will have to use proprietary ways to access the APIs of existing applications, which we cannot use from Java because we have support libraries for C/C++ only (for example). We have already established that CORBA supports different languages and platforms. In most cases we will be able to find a CORBA-compliant product for the operating system and language we are using.

The procedure for developing the component wrapper in other programming languages is similar to that of using Java. We have to become familiar with the IDL mapping to the language we are using. Here we will demonstrate how to build the component wrapper in C++, which can include directly connecting the operations to the source code or the use of different proprietary mechanisms to connect to existing applications. For most proprietary mechanisms C/C++ is likely to be supported.

To build the wrapper in C++ and to build the client in Java we will use:

❑ Inprise/Borland Visibroker for C++ version 4.5

❑ Inprise/Borland Visibroker for Java version 4.5

❑ Microsoft Visual C++ 5.0 (or higher) to compile the examples

❑ JDK version 1.3 to compile the Java client

Compiling the IDL

Developing the wrapper in C++ starts with the definition of the IDL. We will use the same IDL definitions including the factory interface for this example, repeated below for completeness:

```
module CustomerManagement {

  interface Customer {

    enum statusType {normal, silver, gold};

    enum typeOfAccounts {subscription, prepaid};

    struct dateType {
       short date;
       short month;
       short year;
    };

    exception customerNotFound {
       string reason;
       short errorCode;
    };

    exception customerNotUpdated {
       string reason;
       short errorCode;
    };
```

```
      exception accountNotAdded {
         string reason;
         short errorCode;
      };

      exception accountNotDeleted  {
         string reason;
         short errorCode;
      };

      void getCustomer (in long customerId,
                        out wstring firstName,
                        out wstring lastName,
                        out wstring address,
                        out short numberOfPhoneAccounts,
                        out statusType status)
            raises (customerNotFound);

      long setCustomer (in wstring firstName,
                        in wstring lastName,
                        in wstring address,
                        in short numberOfPhoneAccounts,
                        in statusType status)
            raises (customerNotUpdated);

      void newAccount (in wstring phoneNumber,
                       in wstring startDate,
                       in typeOfAccounts typeOfAccount)
            raises (accountNotAdded);

      void deleteAccount (in wstring phoneNumber)
            raises (accountNotDeleted);

   };

   interface CustomerFactory {
      Customer create();
   };
};
```

To compile the IDL interfaces we will use the IDL compiler included with Visibroker for C++, the idl2cpp. We will use the -src_suffix switch to define the file extension of the generated files. The following command line builds the example:

```
C:\ProEAI\Ch10\CustomerInformation_cppwrapper>idl2cpp -src_suffix cpp Customer.i
dl

C:\ProEAI\Ch10\CustomerInformation_cppwrapper>_
```

473

The IDL compiler generates the stubs and skeletons, including the following files:

❑ `Customer_c.cpp` – contains the client-side stub

❑ `Customer_c.hh` – in which we can find the definitions of the `Customer` and `CustomerFactory` classes

❑ `Customer_s.cpp` – contains the server-side skeleton and other server-side support utilities

❑ `Customer_s.hh` – in which we can find the definitions of the `POA_CustomerManagement::Customer` and `POA_CustomerManagement::CustomerFactory` classes that we will use to implement the server-side operations (to actually connect them with the existing application)

Mapping from IDL to the C++ programming language is, in some respects, similar to Java mapping. With certain concepts, like data types, the IDL maps cleaner to C++ (primarily because it was defined with C++ in mind). However, C++ does not support concepts like interfaces so classes are used instead. A major difference is also in the data type mappings. In contrast to Java, the C++ built-in data types are not of fixed length. In fact, the length of certain C++ numeric data types depends on the underlying platform. This is unacceptable for interoperability, so the C++ mapping defines corresponding data types for each built-in primitive IDL data type. These mappings are shown in the following table:

IDL	C++	IDL out C++
short	CORBA::Short	CORBA::Short_out
long	CORBA::Long	CORBA::Long_out
long long	CORBA::LongLong	CORBA::LongLong_out
unsigned short	CORBA::UShort	CORBA::UShort_out
unsigned long	CORBA::ULong	CORBA::ULong_out
unsigned long long	CORBA::ULongLong	CORBA::ULongLong_out
float	CORBA::Float	CORBA::Float_out
double	CORBA::Double	CORBA::Double_out
long double	CORBA::LongDouble	CORBA::LongDouble_out
char	CORBA::Char	CORBA::Char_out
wchar	CORBA::WChar	CORBA::WChar_out
Boolean	CORBA::Boolean	CORBA::Boolean_out
octet	CORBA::Octet	CORBA::Octet_out

Existing applications will typically use native C++ data types, so we will have to convert them to the CORBA C++ data types. For more information regarding IDL to C++, refer to the OMG C++ Language Mapping Specification available from
http://www.omg.org/technology/documents/formal/corba_language_mapping_specs.htm.

Developing the Component Wrapper

To implement the server side we will use the `Customer_s.hh` and the `Customer_s.cc` files generated by the IDL complier. We will follow the identical procedure as when we used Java. We will have to implement the functionality of the interface operations, and then implement the server process, which will instantiate the factory object and register it with the Naming Service and the ORB.

First we will implement the class that will connect the interface operations with the existing application. We will name this class `CustomerImpl`, and it will inherit from the `POA_CustomerManagement::Customer` class that is defined in the `Customer_s.hh`, generated by the IDL compiler. The example code, in which we have not shown how to connect to the existing application, looks like this:

```
#include "Customer_s.hh"

USE_STD_NS

class CustomerImpl : public virtual POA_CustomerManagement::Customer,
                     public virtual PortableServer::RefCountServantBase
{
  public:
    CustomerImpl() {}

    void getCustomer(CORBA::Long customerId,
                     CORBA::WString_out firstName,
                     CORBA::WString_out lastName,
                     CORBA::WString_out address,
                     CORBA::Short_out numberOfPhoneAccounts,
                     CustomerManagement::Customer::statusType_out status) {

      // connect the operation with the existing application
    }

    CORBA::Long setCustomer(const CORBA::WChar* firstName,
                     const CORBA::WChar* lastName,
                     const CORBA::WChar* address,
                     CORBA::Short numberOfPhoneAccounts,
                     CustomerManagement::Customer::statusType status) {

      // connect the operation with the existing application
      return (CORBA::Long)1;
    }

    void newAccount(const CORBA::WChar* phoneNumber,
                     const CORBA::WChar* startDate,
                     CustomerManagement::Customer::typeOfAccounts
                     typeOfAccount) {

      // connect the operation with the existing application
    }

    void deleteAccount(const CORBA::WChar* phoneNumber) {

      // connect the operation with the existing application
    }
};
```

Then we have to implement the factory interface, for which we will build the `CustomerFactoryImpl` class that inherits from `POA_CustomerManagement::CustomerFactory`. This interface has only one operation, the `create()` method, which creates the `Customer` CORBA object and returns it to the client. To do this it needs to invoke the `servant_to_reference()` method of POA to convert the servant to the CORBA reference. We have only obtained the default POA in this example, but we could also obtain the reference to POA through the constructor:

```
class CustomerFactoryImpl : public POA_CustomerManagement::CustomerFactory
{
  public:
    CustomerFactoryImpl() {}

    CustomerManagement::Customer_ptr create() {
      // Create a new wrapper instance servant
      PortableServer::ServantBase_var servant = new CustomerImpl();

      try {
        // Get the reference to the default POA
        PortableServer::POA_var default_poa = _default_POA();

        // Activate the servant and get the reference
        CORBA::Object_var ref = default_poa->servant_to_reference(servant);

        // Narrow the reference
        CustomerManagement::Customer_var c =
                        CustomerManagement::Customer::_narrow(ref);

        cout << "Wrapper created: " << c << endl;

        return CustomerManagement::Customer::_duplicate(c);
      } catch(const CORBA::Exception& e) {
        cerr << "Exception: " << e << endl;
      }
    }
};
```

Implementing the Server

Next, we have to implement the server process in which we will instantiate the factory object and register it. We have to do the following:

❑ Initialize the ORB and get a reference

❑ Obtain a reference to the root POA

❑ Define the policies

❑ Obtain the reference to the POA manager

❑ Create a child POA with the corresponding policies

❑ Create an instance of `CustomerFactory`

❑ Activate the CORBA object and the POA manager

❏   Obtain a reference to the Naming Service

❏   Register the object with the Naming Service

❏   Wait for client requests

The C++ code for the server side looks like this:

```cpp
#include "CosNaming_c.hh"
#include "CustomerImpl.h"

USE_STD_NS

int main(int argc, char* const* argv)
{
  try {
    // Initializing the ORB and obtaining the reference
    CORBA::ORB_var orb = CORBA::ORB_init(argc, argv);
    // Obtaining a reference to the root POA
    PortableServer::POA_var rPOA = PortableServer::POA::_narrow(
      orb->resolve_initial_references("RootPOA"));

    // Specifying the policies
    CORBA::PolicyList policies;
    policies.length(1);

    policies[(CORBA::ULong)0] =
      rPOA->create_lifespan_policy(PortableServer::PERSISTENT);

    // Getting a reference to the default POA manager
    PortableServer::POAManager_var poa_manager = rPOA->the_POAManager();

    // Creating the child POA with the policies and the default POA manager
    PortableServer::POA_var cPOA =
      rPOA->create_POA("customer_poa", poa_manager, policies);

    // Activating the Customer Factory
    CustomerFactoryImpl cf;

    PortableServer::ObjectId_var cfId =
      PortableServer::string_to_ObjectId("CustomerFactory");

    cPOA->activate_object_with_id(cfId, &cf);

    // Activating the POA manager
    poa_manager->activate();

    CORBA::Object_var cf_ref = cPOA->servant_to_reference(&cf);

    // Storing the name binding for Customer Factors into the Name Service
    CosNaming::NamingContext_var rootContext =
      CosNaming::NamingContext::_narrow(
        orb->resolve_initial_references("NameService"));

    CosNaming::Name name;
```

477

```
        name.length(1);
        name[0].id = (const char *) "CustomerFactory";
        name[0].kind = (const char *) "";
        rootContext->rebind(name, cf_ref);

        cout << cf_ref << " is ready" << endl;

        // Waiting for client requests
        orb->run();
    }
    catch(const CORBA::Exception& e) {
      cerr << e << endl;
      return 1;
    }

    return 0;
}
```

Implementing the Client

To test the functionality of the wrapper we will develop a simple C++ CORBA client. The client will have to do the following:

❑   Initialize the ORB and get a reference

❑   Obtain a reference to the Naming Service

❑   Resolve the name to get the IOR of the `CustomerFactory`

❑   Create one or more instances of the wrapper

❑   Invoke methods on the wrapper

The example code for the client is shown here:

```
#include "CosNaming_c.hh"
#include "Customer_c.hh"

USE_STD_NS

int main(int argc, char* const* argv)
{
  try {
    // Initializing the ORB and obtaining the reference
    CORBA::ORB_var orb = CORBA::ORB_init(argc, argv);

    // Obtaining a reference to the Naming Service
    CosNaming::NamingContext_var rootContext =
      CosNaming::NamingContext::_narrow(
        orb->resolve_initial_references("NameService"));

    // Resolving the name to CustomerFactory in the Name Service
    CosNaming::Name name;
    name.length(1);
    name[0].id = (const char *) "CustomerFactory";
```

```
      name[0].kind = (const char *) "";
      CustomerManagement::CustomerFactory_var cf =
        CustomerManagement::CustomerFactory::
                                    _narrow(rootContext->resolve(name));

      // Create a wrapper
      CustomerManagement::Customer_var c = cf->create();
      cout << "Component wrapper created..." << endl;

      // Invoke methods on the wrapper
    }
  catch(const CORBA::Exception& e) {
    cerr << e << endl;
    return 1;
  }
  return 0;
}
```

Running the Example

To build the example we first have to compile and link the source code files. We will use Microsoft Visual C++ 5.0 command-line tools. First we have to set the environment variables for the Visual C++. The easiest way is to use the vcvars32.bat batch file, which you can find in the Visual C++ installation bin subdirectory. Most likely this directory will be C:\Program Files\DevStudio\VC\bin.

We have already compiled the IDL interfaces using the Visibroker IDL to C++ compiler (idl2cpp). Now we have to compile the C++ source code. We assume that the Visibroker is installed in the C:\Inprise\vbroker folder. Obviously, if your installation differs you will have to adapt the command line. For clarity, we will compile server and client separately.

To compile and link the server-side component wrapper we will use the command shown in the following screenshot that will produce the Server.exe executable file (note that this command is also runnable from the batch file compile.bat, available in the downloadable source code package):

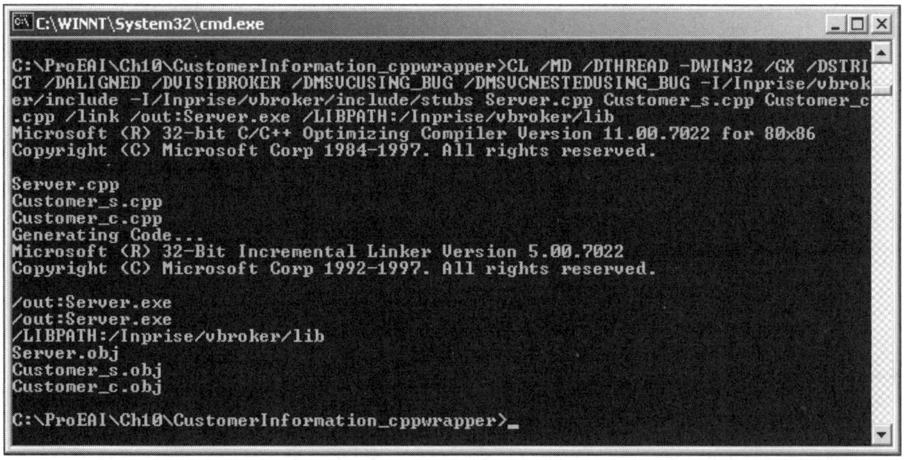

To compile and link the client we will use the following command that will produce the `Client.exe` executable file:

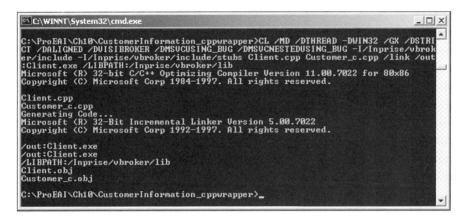

Then we have to start the following:

- ❑ The ORB daemon `osagent`
- ❑ The Naming Service
- ❑ The server application
- ❑ The client application

The following screenshot shows all the necessary commands to start this example:

If we look into the server process window we will see the following:

Using the Java Client

To access the C++ component wrapper shown in this example we can use the same Java client that we have developed at the beginning of this chapter:

```java
package CustomerManagement;

import org.omg.CosNaming.*;
import org.omg.CORBA.*;

public class Client {
  public static void main(String args[]) {
    try {

      // Connect to the wrapper
      ORB orb = ORB.init(args, null);

      org.omg.CORBA.Object objRef =
        orb.resolve_initial_references("NameService");
      NamingContext ncRef = NamingContextHelper.narrow(objRef);

      NameComponent nc = new NameComponent("CustomerFactory", "");
      NameComponent path[] = {
        nc
      };
      CustomerFactory cf =
        CustomerFactoryHelper.narrow(ncRef.resolve(path));

      // Create a Customer Wrapper
      Customer c = cf.create();
      System.out.println("Component wrapper created...");

      // Test the functionality
      // ...

    } catch (UserException e) {
      System.out.println("User exception: " + e);

    } catch (SystemException e) {
      System.out.println("System exception: " + e);

    } catch (Exception e) {
      System.out.println("Exception: " + e);
    }
  }
}
```

To run the server and the client on the same machine we can compile the client using Visibroker for Java version 4.5. First we have to generate the client-side mapping using the idl2java IDL compiler that is included with Visibroker, then we need to compile the client-side code and run the Java client. Again, the C++ server, the Naming Server and the osagent must be running before we can run the client. The following screenshot shows the relevant commands:

```
C:\WINNT\System32\cmd.exe                                         _ □ ×

C:\ProEAI\Ch10\CustomerInformation_cppwrapper>idl2java -no_servant Customer.idl

C:\ProEAI\Ch10\CustomerInformation_cppwrapper>javac CustomerManagement/*.java

C:\ProEAI\Ch10\CustomerInformation_cppwrapper>osagent

C:\ProEAI\Ch10\CustomerInformation_cppwrapper>start nameserv -J-Dvbroker.se.iiop
_tp.scm.iiop_tp.listener.port=1234

C:\ProEAI\Ch10\CustomerInformation_cppwrapper>start server -ORBInitRef NameServi
ce=iioploc://localhost:1234/NameService

C:\ProEAI\Ch10\CustomerInformation_cppwrapper>vbj -DSVCnameroot=NameService Cust
omerManagement.Client
Component wrapper created...

C:\ProEAI\Ch10\CustomerInformation_cppwrapper>_
```

Summary

In this chapter we discussed the role of CORBA in EAI. We demonstrated how to build a component wrapper using the CORBA architecture and familiarized ourselves with the CORBA specification, identifying the important points for selecting an appropriate CORBA implementation.

We demonstrated how to build IDL interfaces for CORBA wrapper components and what to look for when defining the interfaces for existing applications. We showed how to change the signatures of existing APIs to make them more usable by Java and other clients.

Next, we investigated the IDL language mappings for the server- and client-side. We saw that the language mappings depend on the programming model and object adapter that we use. Accordingly, we demonstrated the possibilities for inheritance and delegation approaches and for the basic (BOA) and portable (POA) object adapters. More specifically, we discussed the differences between these two approaches and we saw how to build component wrappers using both object adapters.

We then covered the scenarios in which multiple clients simultaneously access a CORBA component wrapper. We discussed the multi-threading models and identified the aspects of thread-safe programming. We also demonstrated how to serialize the requests and the use of single-threaded models. In connection with multi-threading, we have shown how to use the Factory pattern to build component wrappers on-demand to limit the maximum number of simultaneous clients. These component wrappers must then not be shared between clients, which simplifies the development.

We demonstrated how to use the IDL data type any to provide methods that are not strictly typed. This can be of benefit when accessing existing applications developed in programming languages that are not well defined or that, for whatever reason, return different types from the same method invocation.

Finally, we saw how to build a component wrapper in C++, for which we have to use a CORBA-compliant ORB product that specifically supports C++. We also demonstrated how to access the C++ component wrapper from Java.

CORBA component wrappers are important for reusing existing applications. With custom-developed applications, in particular, they are the most effective choice to access the required functionality. In the J2EE integration architecture the CORBA component wrappers will, in most cases, be accessed from J2EE clients (which will usually be EJB components). For this purpose the clients will use the RMI-IIOP.

In the next chapter we will look at the role of RMI-IIOP in integration and demonstrate how to access CORBA component wrappers with RMI-IIOP.

RMI-IIOP for CORBA Integration

Remote Method Invocation (RMI) is the distributed object networking protocol developed specifically for the Java platform. It is the communication mechanism used for other Java technologies, particularly EJBs and Jini. RMI offers a programming interface for Java developers, which is tightly integrated with the Java platform and is therefore relatively easy to use. Since RMI has adopted to use the CORBA-compliant IIOP protocol instead of the Java Remote Method Protocol (JRMP), it is now known as RMI over IIOP (RMI-IIOP).

RMI-IIOP has an important role in J2EE integration because it allows seamless interoperability with CORBA on either side. This means that CORBA clients can access RMI-IIOP server objects, and that RMI-IIOP clients can access CORBA server objects. RMI-IIOP is also used by EJBs, meaning that they too can access CORBA server objects, and CORBA clients can access EJBs (which we will discuss in Chapter 12). RMI-IIOP is also important for developing virtual components that expose the functionality of existing applications of the J2EE business logic tier.

In this chapter we will take a look at the role of RMI-IIOP in EAI and focus on the areas particularly important to integration. Over the course of this chapter we'll cover the following areas:

❑ The role of RMI-IIOP in EAI

❑ A short overview of RMI-IIOP to find out how it works

❑ Developing a virtual component in RMI-IIOP

❑ CORBA for interoperability

❑ How to handle multiple simultaneous clients

❑ How to implement virtual components with callbacks using RMI-IIOP

❑   Interoperability with RMI

❑   IIOP and firewall issues

The Role of RMI-IIOP in EAI

RMI-IIOP plays an important role in the application interface and business method integration phases. These phases, sometimes referred to by the common name of business level integration, focus on sharing and reusing the functionality of existing applications. In Chapter 9 we discussed these two phases at length and suggested the necessary activities and steps that we should perform.

To reuse the functionality of existing applications for the integrated information system, we have to answer two important questions:

❑   How can we access the functionality of existing applications in a programmatic way?

❑   How do we present these functions in the J2EE architecture in a common way (and thus mask the technology differences of existing applications)?

Let us briefly highlight what we found out in Chapter 9, and then discuss the role of RMI-IIOP for both.

Accessing the Functionality of Existing Applications Programmatically

As we know, there are two ways to wrap existing applications:

❑   Modification of source code

❑   Screen scraping or terminal emulation

With **source code modification** we define one or more interfaces (APIs) with operations that we need to access from outside, and then connect these operations to the existing code. Usually we define these interfaces in the same programming language that has been used for the existing application.

> **RMI-IIOP is not appropriate for wrapping existing applications with source code modification.**

RMI-IIOP distributed objects have to be implemented in the Java programming language. However, existing applications will probably not be implemented in Java. Although Java provides the Java Native Interface (JNI), through which we can access source code written in other programming languages (particularly C/C++), this approach is quite complicated – and therefore not very well suited for developing wrappers.

If source code is not available, if we do not have all the tools necessary to rebuild the existing application from the source code, or if we simply don't want to modify the source code, we can wrap existing applications using **screen scraping** or **terminal emulation**. With these techniques, which are appropriate mainly for character-based applications, the wrappers simulate user typing to perform the functions of existing applications and read the screen to extract the results.

> **RMI-IIOP is completely inappropriate for developing wrappers with screen scraping and not very appropriate for terminal emulation too.**

To perform these tasks most effectively it is beneficial if we can develop the wrappers on the same platform that the existing application is executing. For screen scraping we will usually have to access the video memory directly. RMI-IIOP distributed objects have to be implemented in Java, therefore they are inappropriate for such wrappers. Java, which executes inside a JVM and is platform independent, does not provide a means to access video memory (or other screen-related resources) directly. Although it could be achieved using JNI, this would be too complicated compared with using CORBA for this task, for example.

For developing wrappers with terminal emulation we could use Java RMI-IIOP objects. From Java we can program network communication at the socket level, using TCP/IP. However, not many legacy terminal applications will use this protocol. More often they will have other, even proprietary protocols, for communication between the terminal and the main computer (mostly mainframe). This will make developing wrappers with terminal emulation in RMI-IIOP inappropriate and much more difficult compared to using CORBA.

We can see that CORBA is a much better technology for wrapping existing applications, which we covered in detail in Chapter 10. Therefore the interoperability between RMI-IIOP and CORBA is very important for EAI, as we will see shortly.

In the next section we will answer the second question: How to present these functions of existing applications in the J2EE integration architecture in a common way using RMI-IIOP.

Presenting Functionality of Existing Applications

Here we are concerned with presenting interfaces through which we can access certain functions in a standardized way in the J2EE integration architecture. Our goal is thus to present these interfaces on the business logic tier. As we identified in Chapter 9 we will use:

- ❑ **Lower-level virtual components** to expose lower-level APIs, provided by existing applications, and to mask the technology differences

- ❑ **Higher-level virtual components** to expose high-level business-oriented interfaces

Lower-level virtual components mask the technology differences between the J2EE integration architecture and the existing applications. On one side they present the functionality of existing applications through J2EE-compliant interfaces. On the other side they connect to existing applications through the APIs that the existing applications provide. Higher-level virtual components raise the abstraction of the methods to the level of business operations. Therefore, we say that higher-level virtual components expose business-oriented interfaces. To implement the business operations, higher-level virtual components use lower-level virtual components.

> **RMI-IIOP is appropriate for developing virtual components, particularly for lower-level virtual components.**

RMI-IIOP for Lower-level Virtual Components

Existing applications that already provide APIs use a variety of different technologies to allow access to their APIs, including:

- ❏ Message-Oriented Middleware (MOM)
- ❏ Remote Procedure Call (RPC)
- ❏ Protocols, such as TCP/IP, or HTTP
- ❏ CORBA
- ❏ J2EE Connector Architecture
- ❏ Various proprietary mechanisms

Using MOM (such as IBM MQSeries) is a very popular mechanism, particularly with legacy applications. Legacy applications also use RPC or require use of network protocols directly. Some legacy applications provide proprietary mechanisms. Newer existing applications might use CORBA, or protocols like TCP/IP and HTTP.

RMI-IIOP is appropriate for developing lower-level virtual components. These will hide the variety of technology from J2EE clients (including clients on the client tier, web component tier, and business logic tier). RMI-IIOP virtual components will expose this functionality in a J2EE standard way for synchronous remote method invocation. Notice that RMI-IIOP virtual components are deployed on the business logic tier.

In this chapter we will show how to develop RMI-IIOP virtual components and will base the example on the cell phone operator integration example. We will show how to develop a virtual component that will represent the functionality of the cost and tariff management application, which is one of the existing applications that the cell phone operator has.

We will name this virtual component `CostTariff`. It will expose a single method, `calcCost()`, which will calculate the cost of a cell phone connection, based on the duration and the tariff used. We will, however, not address exactly how the `CostTariff` virtual component will access the existing application. Rather, we will explicitly point to the places in the code where the connection should be established. For the connection we can use any of the previously mentioned mechanisms:

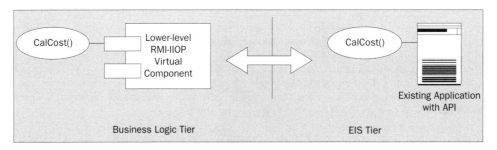

RMI-IIOP for Higher-level Virtual Components

Higher-level virtual components will aggregate the behaviors of lower-level virtual components and enable the abstraction of functionality of existing applications to a higher degree. Higher-level virtual components, on one side, expose high-level business methods to the clients, while on the other side, they translate high-level methods into a series of calls to lower-level virtual components.

RMI-IIOP is also appropriate for developing higher-level virtual components. However, it is more common to develop higher-level virtual components using EJBs, which we'll address in Chapter 12. This does not lower the role of RMI-IIOP in higher-level virtual components. Higher-level virtual components, regardless of whether they are implemented as RMI-IIOP distributed objects or EJBs, will use RMI-IIOP to access lower-level virtual components.

Let's present the situation visually. We have existing applications on the EIS tier, some of which provide APIs. The other APIs have to be added with wrapping (remember, we should be familiar with CORBA wrapping after Chapter 10). On the business logic tier we have lower-level virtual components developed in RMI-IIOP or CORBA. On this tier we also have higher-level virtual components, developed in RMI-IIOP or EJBs (not all possibilities are shown in this diagram):

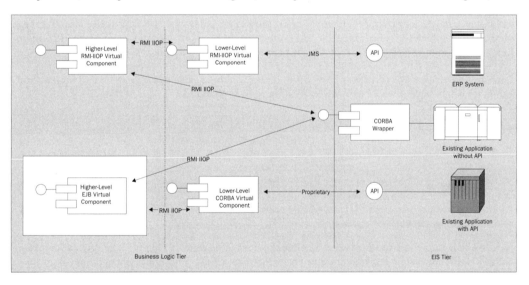

Now we can see that all higher-level virtual components use RMI-IIOP to access lower-level virtual components (including CORBA component wrappers). In this case, higher-level virtual components are RMI-IIOP clients for lower-level virtual components, which are either RMI-IIOP server objects or CORBA server objects. The first scenario is nothing special, the second, however, deserves a little more consideration.

In this chapter we will show how an RMI-IIOP client can access a CORBA server object. We will use the same cell phone operator integration scenario and the associated cost and tariff management application. We will show how to develop a lower-level virtual component, called `CostTariff` in CORBA using C++. Then we will show how to access it using an RMI-IIOP client, as shown in the next figure:

489

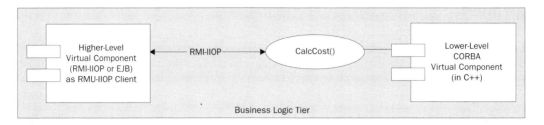

Implementing Callback

In the scenario shown in the previous figure, a higher-level virtual component invokes a method on a lower-level virtual component. Using synchronous RMI-IIOP-style invocation, the higher-level virtual component (which is now a client for the lower-level components) will be blocked for the duration of the method call. That means that higher-level component will be unable to do anything else while it waits for the lower-level component to finish.

Sometimes, this is not an ideal situation. Occasionally it might take a really long time for the lower-level components to finish. For example, it might take a long time to calculate the cost of a call in our example. A much better approach would be, if the higher-level virtual component could invoke a method on the lower-level component and then continue its work. When the lower-level component finishes, it should call back the higher-level component and report the result.

Later in this chapter we will show how to implement callback scenarios. First we will look at how to achieve callback when we have RMI-IIOP objects on both sides:

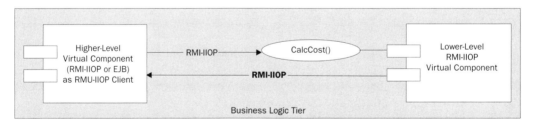

Next we will show how to implement a callback when an RMI-IIOP higher-level virtual component calls CORBA lower-level virtual component, written in a programming language other than Java (C++ in our example). Here it is important to understand the interoperability – first, how an RMI-IIOP client calls a CORBA server object and second, how a CORBA client calls an RMI-IIOP server object, as shown in the next figure:

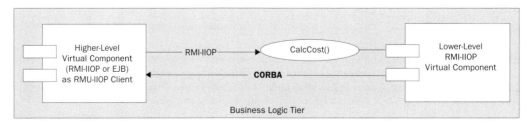

Other Advanced Concepts

In addition to this we will also address the problem of a large number of clients that will access the existing application. Sometimes existing applications cannot stand the load of a large number of simultaneous clients, because they have not been designed for such a large number of them. We identified as early as in Chapter 2 that integrated systems often require support for many more simultaneous clients than before the applications were integrated.

To solve this problem we will first look at multi-threading. Then we will show how each client can create its own virtual component. For this we will use the Factory pattern. Then we will show how we can limit the maximum number of simultaneous clients using this pattern.

Then we will address interoperability with existing applications using RMI with the Java Remote Method Protocol (JRMP, before it was updated to the IIOP protocol). We will show how to develop virtual components that can be accessed by RMI-IIOP and RMI-JRMP clients simultaneously.

Finally, we will discuss the problems, and possible solutions, that clients outside the company's firewall might experience when trying to use IIOP to access components inside the company intranet.

Overview of RMI-IIOP

Way back in version 1.1, Java introduced its own distributed object model under the name RMI. It is worth noting that because RMI was developed exclusively for Java, it integrates very well with the Java programming language. When Sun introduced RMI there already existed CORBA support for Java, and several CORBA implementations for Java had been around for a while. However, RMI provided a cleaner integration with Java and also supported some features that CORBA did not support at that time. These included passing objects by value, dynamic code downloading, URL-based object naming, and distributed garbage collection. Since then, RMI has become the distributed Java model on which other technologies have been built, particularly Enterprise JavaBeans (EJB).

Sticking with the proprietary RMI however had several disadvantages. Instead of using a more general protocol, RMI used the **JRMP (Java Remote Method Protocol)** to communicate between distributed objects. This prevented RMI objects from communicating with objects written in other programming languages. In particular, it prevented communication with CORBA. CORBA established itself as an important distributed technology, which Sun supported through the Object Management Group (OMG). Nevertheless, the lack of interoperability of RMI with other programming languages represented a distinct disadvantage when using Java as an enterprise platform, because it was not very easy to achieve interoperability with existing applications.

Sun realized the problem relating to how to get CORBA clients and servers to communicate with RMI very early on, and by 1997 plans existed to make RMI and CORBA compatible, that is, to move RMI to the CORBA standardized IIOP protocol. However, at that time CORBA did not support passing objects by value and dynamic class downloading. Furthermore, a Java-to-IDL mapping had not been defined. Thus, CORBA was extended with two additional specifications that made RMI-IIOP possible:

❑ **Objects by Value** specification – later integrated into the CORBA specification and can be found under the *Value Type Semantics* chapter in the CORBA 2.5 specification.

491

❏ **Java Language to IDL Mapping** specification – defined how the Java interfaces could be mapped to an Interface Definition Language (IDL). This is important to allow CORBA objects to access RMI-IIOP objects that originally did not have CORBA IDL, as we will see later.

It took until 1999 for the release of the CORBA-compatible RMI-IIOP, which is now a part of Java SDK Standard Edition and is the required communication mechanism between clients and EJBs in the J2EE platform.

How RMI-IIOP Works

RMI-IIOP provides the functionality of an object request broker. It hides the communication details between distributed objects that are deployed in different JVMs and on different computers. Conceptually, RMI-IIOP is very similar to CORBA, hence the reason why interoperability between them is relatively easy.

To achieve communication, RMI-IIOP uses the same concepts of stubs and skeletons as CORBA does. Since JDK 1.2, RMI-IIOP has used generic skeletons on the server side, so what effectively gets generated are stubs only. However, skeletons are still present and it is correct to think about them when explaining the remote communication between two distributed objects. Nonetheless, it's true to say that skeletons are no longer explicitly generated by the compiler (the compiler, in this context, is actually the `rmic` compiler, which we will describe later).

RMI-IIOP (as well as RMI) is implemented in three layers:

❏ The **stub/skeleton layer** connects the application objects and the rest of the RMI system. A stub on the client side forwards the requests to the server-side remote object. A skeleton dispatches the remote calls to the actual object implementation. As already mentioned, since Java 2 generic code is provided for skeletons.

❏ The **remote reference layer** is responsible for the semantics of the communication between distributed objects. It connects the stubs and skeletons with the low-level transport layer.

❏ The **transport layer** is responsible for the communication management and for dispatching the messages. For transport over the network, RMI-IIOP uses the IIOP protocol (obviously).

The RMI-IIOP architecture is shown schematically in the diagram opposite:

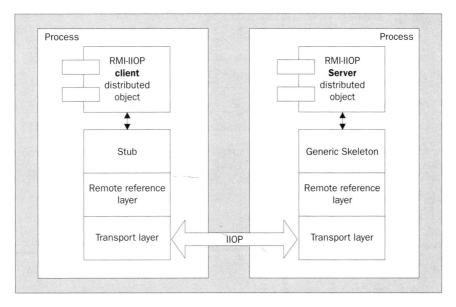

The major difference between RMI and RMI-IIOP is in the wire protocol they use for communication. RMI uses JRMP, which makes use of Java **object serialization**, which is used for call marshaling and returning results. Usually the RMI transport layer opens direct sockets to hosts through which it transports IIOP requests. To bypass firewalls, which usually block IIOP, an alternative HTTP-based mechanism is also available. It wraps IIOP requests with HTTP POST requests before entering the firewall and unwraps them when inside. Such wrapped IIOP requests look to firewalls like regular HTTP requests, which they do not block. Encapsulation with HTTP POST however requires additional time, so HTTP connections are therefore at least an order of magnitude slower than those sent through direct sockets.

As with CORBA objects, RMI-IIOP objects define the interfaces through which they expose their functionality. As we have emphasized, RMI-IIOP was derived from RMI, which was originally designed specifically for Java-to-Java usage and therefore it was not necessary to introduce a separate IDL. RMI interfaces are defined in Java. RMI-IIOP has adapted the RMI programming model as much as possible, therefore RMI-IIOP interfaces are also defined in Java.

Developing a Virtual Component in RMI-IIOP

As we have identified in the first section of the chapter, RMI-IIOP is particularly appropriate for developing virtual components. Therefore, now that we've become familiar with how RMI-IIOP works, we will show how to develop a simple virtual component.

We will base the example on our ongoing cell phone operator integration example, introduced in Chapter 4. We will develop a virtual component that will represent the functionality of the cost and tariff management application. The virtual component, which we will name CostTariff, will expose a single method, the calcCost(), that calculates the cost of a cell phone connection, based on the duration and the tariff used. More accurately, the CostTariff virtual component will not actually perform the calculation, but will reuse the existing application to do this.

The `CostTariff` interface is shown on the next figure:

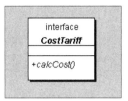

The virtual component is, in RMI-IIOP vocabulary, an RMI-IIOP server object and we will sometimes use this term to refer to the virtual component.

Defining the Interface

First, we have to define the corresponding RMI-IIOP interface. We do this in Java directly and do not have to use a separate IDL (like we had to do with CORBA in Chapter 10). To make a Java interface accessible from remote clients, the interface has to inherit from the `java.rmi.Remote` interface.

In a distributed environment the virtual component (server object) also has to be able to pass exceptions back to the client side. On top of this, we have to be prepared to deal with a larger number of possible exceptions. To support remote exceptions each method in remote interface also has to be able to throw the `java.rmi.RemoteException` that we have to declare explicitly. With this knowledge we can define our simple interface:

```
import java.rmi.Remote;
import java.rmi.RemoteException;

public interface CostTariff extends Remote {

  double calcCost (long durationInSeconds,
                   short tariffUsed) throws RemoteException;

}
```

Connecting the Interface with Existing Applications

The next step is to implement the functionality for the interface – that is, to connect the interface methods to the existing application. To do this, we will declare a class that will implement the previously defined `CostTariff` interface. To make this class an RMI-IIOP class (to connect it with the RMI-IIOP object request broker) the implementation class has to inherit from `javax.rmi.PortableRemoteObject` and implement the interface, `CostTariff` in our case. The implementation class looks like this:

```
import java.rmi.RemoteException;
import javax.rmi.PortableRemoteObject;

public class CostTariffImpl extends PortableRemoteObject implements CostTariff  {
```

```
public CostTariffImpl() throws RemoteException {}

public double calcCost (long durationInSeconds, short tariffUsed)
                                            throws RemoteException {

    double cost = 0;
    // connect to the existing application
    // calculate the cost
    return cost;
  }
}
```

When using this virtual component in the real world, we would have to add the code that actually connects it with the existing application. This will differ from existing application to existing application. But we have not finished the development yet. Next we have to make instances of this component and register them so that clients will be able to locate them.

Creating Instances and Registering Them

In contrast to EJBs, RMI-IIOP virtual components are not deployed in a container. Clearly, the RMI-IIOP virtual components need a process by which they can execute. Therefore we have to provide a server application that will create a server process in which we instantiate an instance (or several) of the RMI-IIOP virtual component implementation class.

Clients will be able to connect to these instances if they can obtain the **Interoperable Object Reference (IOR)**. Obtaining the IOR can be done in the following ways:

❑   A central storage (naming service) for IORs is used, comparable to the CORBA Naming Service or a naming and directory service product, compliant with Java Naming and Directory Interface (JNDI).

❑   An IOR can be exchanged as a return value from a method invocation. However, in this case we still need a way to get the initial reference, for which in most cases the naming service is used.

❑   An IOR can also be exchanged in other ways, for example by writing it into the file or similar.

For our example we will use the first possibility – the server will instantiate a single RMI-IIOP virtual component instance and register the instance with the naming service. We will do this in a few lines of Java code, shown below. First we will obtain a reference to the initial naming context from the naming service (for which we will have to start a naming service provider, as we will see shortly). Then we create a new instance of the CostTariff RMI-IIOP instance and bind it with the naming service (under the name CostTariff, obviously). The code looks like this:

```
import java.rmi.RemoteException;
import javax.rmi.PortableRemoteObject;
import javax.naming.*;

public class Server {

  public static void main(String[] args) {
```

```
    try {

      // Obtain the initial reference to the naming service
      Context iNamingContext = new InitialContext();

      // Create a new instance of CostTariff
      CostTariff ct = new CostTariffImpl();

      // Associate it with the CostTariff name in naming service
      iNamingContext.rebind("CostTariff", ct);

      System.out.println("Server ready...");

    } catch (Exception e) {
      System.out.println(e);
      e.printStackTrace(System.out);
    }
  }
}
```

This is almost everything we have to implement. If we compare this example to the CORBA component wrapper from Chapter 10 we can see that the RMI-IIOP code is shorter, and more transparent and well integrated with the Java language. However, we still have to develop a simple client to test the functionality of the RMI-IIOP virtual component.

Developing the Client

To test the functionality of the virtual component we have to develop a simple RMI-IIOP client. The client will connect to the Naming Service, resolve the name, and invoke the remote operation. The code for the client is as follows:

```
import java.util.*;
import javax.naming.*;
import javax.rmi.PortableRemoteObject;

public class Client {

  public static void main(String[] args) {

    CostTariff ct = null;

    try {
      // Obtain a reference to the naming service initial context
      Context inc = new InitialContext();

      // Resolve the name and bind to the RMI-IIOP object
      ct = (CostTariff)PortableRemoteObject.narrow(
                        inc.lookup("CostTariff"), CostTariff.class);

    } catch (Exception e) {
      System.out.println(e);
```

```
    }

    try {

      // Invoke the method to calculate the call cost
      double r = ct.calcCost((long)4, (short)2);

      // Print the result to console
      System.out.println(r);

    } catch (Exception e) {
      System.out.println(e);
    }
  }
}
```

Building and Running the Virtual Component

The example, `CostTariffApp` in the source code package available for download from http://www.wrox.com/, can be run under JDK versions 1.3 or 1.4. To run the example, we first have to compile the source code using the `javac` compiler.

Then we have to generate the stubs and skeletons using the Java RMI Compiler, or `rmic`. The `rmic` generates them for both RMI protocols, for IIOP (where the skeletons are named ties and stored in files with a _Tie suffix to the name), and for JRMP (Java Remote Method Protocol). It generates them from compiled classes. That's why we had to compile the Java source files first. The `rmic` takes several switches, the most important of which for our purposes are described below:

❏   `-iiop` – generates IIOP stubs and skeletons (ties). This switch is needed to achieve interoperability with CORBA.

❏   `-poa` – has to be used together with `-iiop` and suggests use of the Portable Object Adapter (POA) instead of Basic Object Adapter (BOA).

❏   `-idl` – generates CORBA IDL from Java interfaces. We'll use this to achieve interoperability with CORBA.

❏   `-keep` – does not delete intermediate-generated Java source files for stubs and skeletons. We can look into them, but we're not allowed to modify them.

For more information about `rmic`, look into the JDK documentation. For our example we will use the `-iiop` switch. We can also use the `-keep` switch to look into the generated source code. The following commands should be used to build the example:

```
Select C:\WINNT\System32\cmd.exe

C:\ProEAI\Ch11\CostTariffApp>javac *.java

C:\ProEAI\Ch11\CostTariffApp>rmic -iiop -keep CostTariffImpl

C:\ProEAI\Ch11\CostTariffApp>_
```

Before starting the server object and the client, we have to activate the naming service provider. For this we can use the transient CORBA Naming Service, `tnameserv`, which is provided by the JDK, as we did in the previous chapter. We should start it with this command:

```
Select C:\WINNT\System32\cmd.exe - tnameserv                    _ □ x
C:\ProEAI\Ch11\CostTariffApp>tnameserv
Initial Naming Context:
IOR:000000000000002849444c3a6f6d672e6f72672f436f734e616d696e672f4e616d696e67436f
6e746578743a312e3000000000010000000000000005800010100000000f3139322e3136382e3130
2e31333600000580000000000018afabcafe0000000255817bc9000000080000000000000000000
0001000000001000000140000000000010020000000000001010000000000
TransientNameServer: setting port for initial object references to: 900
Ready.
```

Finally, we are ready to start the server class that instantiates the RMI-IIOP virtual component. We have to specify the initial naming factory and the naming provider URL. This instructs the naming service to use the `tnameserv`. The command should read like this:

```
C:\WINNT\System32\cmd.exe - java -Djava.naming.factory.initial=com.sun.jndi.cosnaming.CNCtxFact...   _ □ x
C:\ProEAI\Ch11\CostTariffApp>java -Djava.naming.factory.initial=com.sun.jndi.cos
naming.CNCtxFactory -Djava.naming.provider.url=iiop://localhost:900 Server
Server ready...
```

To start the client we also have to provide the initial naming factory and the naming provider URL (note that to run the example on different computers we have to modify this URL accordingly), which gives the following *amazing* result:

```
C:\WINNT\System32\cmd.exe                                        _ □ x
C:\ProEAI\Ch11\CostTariffApp>java -Djava.naming.factory.initial=com.sun.jndi.cos
naming.CNCtxFactory -Djava.naming.provider.url=iiop://localhost:900 Client
8.0

C:\ProEAI\Ch11\CostTariffApp>_
```

JDK 1.4 provides the CORBA ORB that implements the POA instead of BOA, as discussed in Chapter 10. To use the POA approach we can generate the stubs for the RMI-IIOP using the –poa switch with `rmic` compiler. Without the switch the generated classes inherit from `org.omg.CORBA_2_3.portable.ObjectImpl`, whereas the –poa switch changes this inheritance to `org.omg.PortableServer.Servant`. This fact will become important when using CORBA on the other side.

Furthermore, with JDK 1.4 we can use the persistent naming service instead of the transient. The transient naming service (`tnameserv`) preserves the name bindings in memory. That means that once we shut it down, it looses all bindings. Conversely, the persistent naming service is implemented inside the ORB daemon, and we can start this service by starting the `orbd` instead of the `tnameserv`. Note, however, that in this case we have to specify the ORB initial port and the initial host name:

```
C:\WINNT\System32\cmd.exe - orbd -ORBInitialPort 900 -ORBInitialHost localhost   _ □ x
C:\ProEAI\Ch11\CostTariffApp>orbd -ORBInitialPort 900 -ORBInitialHost localhost
_
```

Achieving Interoperability with CORBA

The fact that RMI-IIOP interfaces are defined in Java is all right as long as we implement the virtual components in Java only. In the first section of this chapter we saw that RMI-IIOP virtual components will often have to communicate with CORBA virtual components or CORBA wrappers. Examples include:

❏ RMI-IIOP virtual component accessing existing application through a CORBA wrapper

❏ RMI-IIOP virtual component accessing existing application through an already provided API that uses CORBA (which is quite common with larger commercial existing applications)

❏ RMI-IIOP higher-level virtual components accessing CORBA lower-level virtual component

These examples are also shown in the next figure:

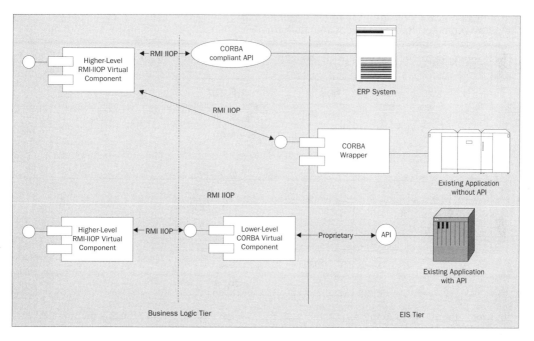

However, Java interfaces are insufficient when we need to achieve interoperability between RMI-IIOP virtual components and CORBA virtual components written in other programming languages, like C++, COBOL, PL/I, Smalltalk, and so on. Then we will need the CORBA IDL interface definitions instead. We have to find a way in which to map the Java interfaces into IDL. This is what the Java Language to IDL mapping specification defines. Let us have a look at the Java-to-IDL mapping first, because this will ease our understanding of how to achieve the interoperability between CORBA and RMI-IIOP.

RMI/IDL

RMI/IDL defines a subset of Java RMI that can be mapped to IDL for which IIOP (or, more generally speaking, GIOP) can be used as the underlying protocol for communication. RMI/IDL data types include the following:

❑   Primitive Java data types

❑   Java remote interfaces

❑   Java objects transferred by value (vale types)

❑   Arrays of conforming types

❑   Appropriate exceptions

❑   Object references (IORs)

❑   IDL entity types (classes that implement `org.omg.CORBA.portable.IDLEntity` – those that have been generated from IDL)

Many of the mentioned data types have to conform to certain restrictions. For more information the curious reader is encouraged to look into the OMG Java Language to IDL Mapping Specification, available from the following link:
http://www.omg.org/technology/documents/formal/java_language_mapping_to_omg_idl.htm.

The mapping of primitive data types is straightforward and is similar to the mapping from IDL to Java:

Java	OMG IDL
void	void
boolean	boolean
char	wchar
byte	octet
short	short
int	long
long	long long
float	float
double	double

So, when attempting to map `java.lang.String`, we have to be aware how this mapping takes place. If defined as a constant (`final static`) then it maps to IDL `wstring`. In all other cases, including method parameters and return values, it is mapped to the `CORBA::WStringValue` value type. This value type is defined as a part of CORBA module and the definition is as follows:

```
valuetype WStringValue wstring;
```

This is equivalent to the following longer definition, however the first definition maps more cleanly to Java:

```
valuetype WStringValue {
    public wstring data;
};
```

The other important mappings include the special case mappings for Java classes. The following table shows the special case mappings:

Java	OMG IDL
java.lang.Object	::java::lang::_Object
java.lang.String	::CORBA::WStringValue or wstring
java.lang.Class	::javax::rmi::CORBA::ClassDesc
java.io.Serializable	::java::io::Serializable
java.io.Externalizable	::java::io::Externalizable
java.rmi.Remote	::java::rmi::Remote
org.omg.CORBA.Object	Object

Discussion of Interoperability

Accessing a CORBA virtual component or wrapper (in CORBA terminology these are CORBA server objects, or CORBA servers) from an RMI-IIOP virtual component (RMI-IIOP client) is possible only for the subset of data types and classes defined by RMI/IDL. This can introduce problems if we use RMI-IIOP clients to access existing CORBA server objects that have been developed in other programming languages and did not take into account the RMI/IDL restrictions. To guarantee that RMI-IIOP clients can access CORBA server objects, the best way to develop CORBA server objects in other programming languages is to use the following sequence of steps:

1. Define the interfaces in Java

2. Map the Java interfaces into IDL

3. Develop the server in any programming language using these IDL interfaces

4. Develop the client in RMI-IIOP from Java interfaces

We will identify the problems specific to the case in which a CORBA server cannot be accessed by RMI-IIOP clients shortly. For the moment this fact is not very important because we can always use the Java IDL supplied by the JDK to access CORBA servers directly.

The other possibility is to develop virtual components in RMI-IIOP and access them from CORBA clients. This possibility should work in all cases, because we will always first define the interface in Java and then map this interface to IDL. However, this will include a lot of value types that have to be implemented by the CORBA implementation. Currently, not many CORBA implementations implement these value types. Therefore, we have to modify the interface manually or try to stick with the RMI/IDL primitive data types to simplify the communication.

Although sticking with primitive data types is not possible in real-world examples, we should not forget that here we are talking about connecting to existing applications. Many existing applications, particularly procedural legacy applications will very rarely implement complex data structures in their APIs. If existing applications do not provide APIs, then we'll have to add wrappers – and we always have the choice of how we implement such wrappers.

However, when mixing RMI-IIOP and CORBA servers and clients we also have to use the appropriate CORBA versions.

> **To access the RMI-IIOP or CORBA objects from RMI-IIOP we have to use an ORB compliant with CORBA version 2.3.1 (or higher).**

We also have to pay attention to the object adapter we use – BOA or POA (clearly, if we have the choice, the preference should always be POA), and generate the stubs for RMI-IIOP accordingly. To demonstrate the interoperability let us examine this process for the previous example.

Generating IDL Interfaces

To generate IDL from the `CostTariff` interface definition in Java we have to use a tool that implements the Java-to-IDL mapping – the `rmic` compiler, for example. Some CORBA implementations also provide such tools (Visibroker for Java, for instance, provides the `java2idl` tool).

To use the `rmic` for Java-to-IDL mapping we have to use the `-idl` switch:

This generates `CostTariff.idl`. As we can see below, an interface `CostTariff` is generated, which has a single method, `calcCost()`. This method returns a result of a data type `double`. It accepts two parameters, the first of type `long long` and the second `short`. Note that the IDL data types have been mapped from Java data types according to the Java to IDL Mapping Specification. In the table earlier we showed how the basic data types map. From that we can see that Java data types `double` and `short` map to the IDL data types of the same name, however Java data type `long` maps to IDL data type `long long`.

We can also see that `ord.idl` is included in the generated `CostTariff.idl` file. The `orb.idl` file contains Java-related declarations, such as `StringValue` and `WStringValue` value types, which we discussed earlier. This file can be found in the JDK installation `\lib` subdirectory (for example `\jdk1.4\lib`). Finally a `pragma` directive is generated. This directive defines the repository ID name of the generated interface, that is, the name under which this interface will be stored in the CORBA Interface Repository. Interfaces generated from Java get an RMI prefix in contrast to interfaces that are defined directly in IDL, which get an `IDL` prefix.

> *For more information about the Interface Repository, refer to the CORBA specification:*
> *http://www.omg.org/technology/documents/formal/corba_iiop.htm.*

Returning to the example, we can see that the generated `CostTariff.idl` (discussed above) has the following contents:

```
/**
 * CostTariff.idl
 * Generated by rmic -idl. Do not edit
 */

#include "orb.idl"

#ifndef __CostTariff__
#define __CostTariff__

    interface CostTariff {

        double calcCost(
            in long long arg0,
            in short arg1);

    };

#pragma ID CostTariff "RMI:CostTariff:0000000000000000"
#endif
```

The generated IDL is relatively clean and contains the interface and the operation as we expect. This is mainly because we have used primitive data types only. User-defined data types can complicate the IDL considerably, as we will see later.

To develop a CORBA client, we have to generate CORBA stubs from the IDL definitions. To develop a CORBA server we have to generate CORBA skeletons. In all cases we have to use a CORBA implementation for some other programming language, for example C++.

Virtual Component in C++ with a Java Client

To develop the virtual component (the server object) in CORBA using C++, we first have to compile the IDL with the compiler. We will use Inprise/Borland Visibroker for C++ version 4.5, which provides the idl2cpp compiler, along with the JDK 1.3. We will use the –src_suffix switch to define the file extension of the generated files. The relevant command is shown in the next screenshot:

```
C:\WINNT\System32\cmd.exe                                      _ □ ×

C:\ProEAI\Ch11\CostTariffApp_CORBA>idl2cpp -src_suffix cpp CostTariff.idl

C:\ProEAI\Ch11\CostTariffApp_CORBA>_
```

We have to be sure that the ord.idl and the related ir.idl files are accessible to the idl2cpp compiler (in this case, we have simply copied them into the current directory – %BOOK_HOME%\Ch11\CostTariffApp_CORBA). As noted above, these files can be found in the \lib subdirectory of your JDK installation.

Connecting the Interface with Existing Applications

Next we have to implement the interface in C++. Here, we have to connect the virtual component with the existing application. For more information on how to implement the CORBA server object in C++, take a look at Chapter 10. In the code that is shown below we can see that all we have to do is to declare the `CostTariffImpl` implementation class and implement the `calcCost` method. Notice that we have to use CORBA data types (such as `CORBA::Double`, `CORBA::LongLong`, or `CORBA::Short`), which have been mapped from the IDL interface definition to C++:

```
#include "CostTariff_s.hh"

USE_STD_NS

// Declare the implementation class
class CostTariffImpl : public virtual POA_CostTariff,
                       public virtual PortableServer::RefCountServantBase
{
  public:
    CostTariffImpl() {}        // Constructor

    // Declare the method
    CORBA::Double calcCost(CORBA::LongLong durationInSeconds,
                                    CORBA::Short tarifUsed) {

      CORBA::Double callCost = 0;

      // Connect to the existing application
      // Calculate the call cost

      return callCost;
    }
};
```

Creating Instances and Registering Them

Then we have to implement the server process that will instantiate the `CostTariffImpl` class and register it with ORB, POA, and Naming Service. More precisely, we have to do the following:

❏ Obtain a reference and initialize the ORB

❏ Obtain a reference to the root POA

❏ Obtain a reference to the Naming Service

❏ Define the policies

❏ Obtain a reference to the POA manager

❏ Create a child POA with the policies

❏ Create an instance of `CostTariffImpl`

❏ Activate the object and the POA manager

❏ Register the object with the Naming Service

The commented code shown below, `Server.cpp`, performs these steps (for more information refer to Chapter 10):

```cpp
#include "CosNaming_c.hh"
#include "CostTariffImpl.h"

int main(int argc, char* const* argv)
{
  try {
    // Obtain a reference and initialize the ORB
    CORBA::ORB_var orb = CORBA::ORB_init(argc, argv);

    // Get a reference to the root POA
    PortableServer::POA_var rPOA = PortableServer::POA::_narrow(
      orb->resolve_initial_references("RootPOA"));

    // Get a reference to the root naming context
    CosNaming::NamingContext_var rootContext =
                                    CosNaming::NamingContext::_narrow(
        orb->resolve_initial_references("NameService"));

    // Define POA policies
    CORBA::PolicyList policies;
    policies.length(1);

    policies[(CORBA::ULong)0] =
      rPOA->create_lifespan_policy(PortableServer::PERSISTENT);

    // Get a reference to the POA manager
    PortableServer::POAManager_var poa_manager = rPOA->the_POAManager();

    // Create child POA with policies and default POA manager
    PortableServer::POA_var cPOA =
      rPOA->create_POA("customer_poa", poa_manager, policies);

    // Activate the CORBA virtual component
    CostTariffImpl ct;

    PortableServer::ObjectId_var ctId =
      PortableServer::string_to_ObjectId("CostTariff");

    cPOA->activate_object_with_id(ctId, &ct);

    // Activate the POA manager
    poa_manager->activate();

    CORBA::Object_var ct_ref = cPOA->servant_to_reference(&ct);

    // Bind the virtual component in the naming service with the name CostTariff
    CosNaming::Name name;
    name.length(1);
    name[0].id = (const char *) "CostTariff";
    name[0].kind = (const char *) "";
    rootContext->rebind(name, ct_ref);
```

```
    cout << ct_ref << " is ready" << endl;

    // Wait for requests
    orb->run();
  }
  catch(const CORBA::Exception& e) {
    cerr << e << endl;
    return 1;
  }

  return 0;
}
```

Building and Running the Example

To build the example we first have to compile and link the source code files. We will use Microsoft Visual C++ 5.0 command-line tools (but obviously you can use any other C++ compiler that you are familiar with). First we have to set the environment variables for Visual C++. The simplest way to do this, as we did in the previous chapter, is by running the vcvars32.bat batch file (which you can find in the Visual C++ installation bin subdirectory, usually C:\Program Files\DevStudio\VC\bin).

We have already compiled the IDL interfaces using the Visibroker IDL to C++ (idl2cpp) compiler. Next we have to compile the C++ source code. Here we assume that Visibroker is installed in the C:\Inprise\vbroker folder (obviously, if your installation differs you will have to adapt the following command line). To compile and link the server-side CORBA virtual component we will use the command shown on the following screenshot that will produce the Server.exe executable file (note that here we are using the batch file compile_server.bat included with the code download):

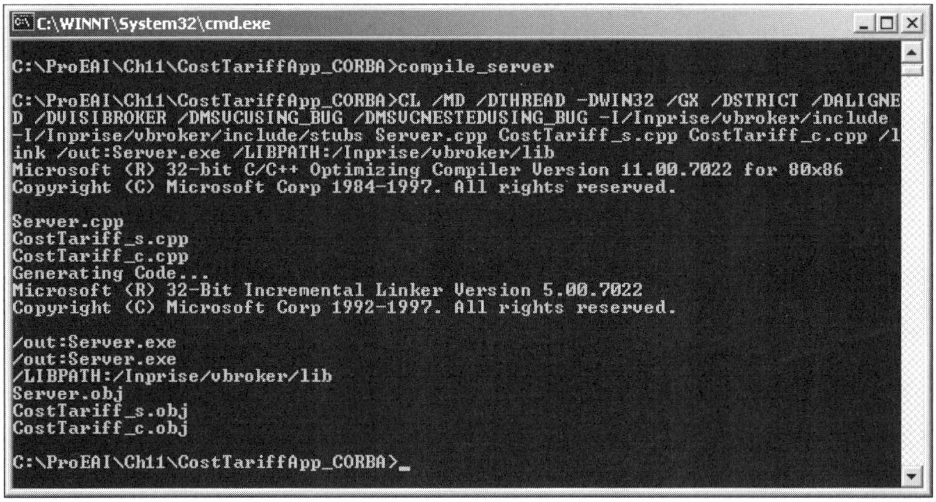

Next, we have to start the CORBA C++ server-side virtual component. To do this we have to start the following components:

❑   First we start the Visibroker ORB daemon "Smart Agent" `osagent`.

❑   Then we start the CORBA Naming Service. Here we will use the `orbd`, part of JDK 1.4, but we could also use the `nameserv` as usual.

❑   Then we have to start the C++ server executable.

❑   Finally, we start the RMI-IIOP Java client.

To start the Visibroker Smart Agent we simply enter `osagent` at the command prompt. We'll see it as a small icon on the right-hand side in the Windows taskbar. To start the Naming Service we should use the following command, where we supply the initial port number and initial host URL to be used:

```
C:\WINNT\System32\cmd.exe - orbd -ORBInitialPort 1234 -ORBInitialHost localhost    _ □ ×

C:\ProEAI\Ch11\CostTariffApp_CORBA>osagent

C:\ProEAI\Ch11\CostTariffApp_CORBA>orbd -ORBInitialPort 1234 -ORBInitialHost loc
alhost
```

To start the C++ server we also have to specify the initial reference for the Naming Service, together with the port used:

```
C:\WINNT\System32\cmd.exe - server -ORBInitRef NameService=iioploc://localhost:1234/NameServi...  _ □ ×

C:\ProEAI\Ch11\CostTariffApp_CORBA>server -ORBInitRef NameService=iioploc://loca
lhost:1234/NameService
Repository ID: RMI:CostTariff:0000000000000000
  Object name: NONE
  is ready
```

Finally, we should start the Java RMI-IIOP client (that we developed in the beginning of this chapter – notice the change in working directory in the following figure). We have to specify the initial naming factory and the naming provider address:

```
C:\WINNT\System32\cmd.exe    _ □ ×

C:\ProEAI\Ch11\CostTariffApp>java -Djava.naming.factory.initial=com.sun.jndi.cos
naming.CNCtxFactory -Djava.naming.provider.url=iiop://localhost:1234 Client
15.0

C:\ProEAI\Ch11\CostTariffApp>_
```

Remember, if we were to use a different Naming Service we would have to specify this accordingly when starting the client.

In this section we have seen that it is possible to achieve interoperability between a CORBA virtual component (for example in C++) and an RMI-IIOP client in Java. Now, let's try it the other way around – we'll develop the client in CORBA (using C++) and attempt to access a virtual component developed in Java RMI-IIOP.

Client in C++ and Virtual Component in Java

In the previous section we demonstrated how to achieve interoperability between an RMI-IIOP client in Java and a CORBA virtual component in C++. In this section we will do things the other way around: we will take the RMI-IIOP virtual component in Java that we developed in the first section of this chapter, and develop a CORBA client in C++ to access this virtual component. It is quite common that, sooner or later, we will need to enable this type of communication as part of an integration project. What we learn from this exercise will also be important for the more advanced concepts, such as implementing callback, which we will discuss a little later.

To develop the client in CORBA we have to generate the CORBA C++ stubs from the IDL. We will use the Visibroker IDL-to-C++ compiler (idl2cpp). This time we will use two switches: the -src_suffix switch defines the file extension of the generated files, and the -no_servant switch, because we only need the client-side mapping. Notice that in the example in the previous section we have already run the idl2cpp compiler. There, we generated mappings from the server and the client side – and can therefore use this mapping in the example here (we had to generate the client-side mapping in the previous example because Visibroker doesn't provide a switch to turn off client-side mapping generation). Essentially, this means that you only need to use the following command if you skipped the previous example:

Then we have to develop the CORBA client in C++. The client has to:

❑   Initialize the ORB and obtain a reference

❑   Obtain a reference to the Naming Service

❑   Resolve the name and bind to the server object

❑   Invoke a method on the server object

These steps will be performed in the code Client.cpp, shown below (again, refer to Chapter 10 for more details on developing CORBA C++ clients):

```cpp
#include "CosNaming_c.hh"
#include "CostTariff_c.hh"

int main(int argc, char* const* argv)
{
  try {
    // Initialize and obtain a reference to the ORB
    CORBA::ORB_var orb = CORBA::ORB_init(argc, argv);

    // Obtain a reference to the root naming context
    CosNaming::NamingContext_var rootContext =
      CosNaming::NamingContext::_narrow(
        orb->resolve_initial_references("NameService"));
```

```
    // Resolve the CostTariff name to get IOR
    CosNaming::Name name;
    name.length(1);
    name[0].id = (const char *) "CostTariff";
    name[0].kind = (const char *) "";
    CostTariff_var ct =
      CostTariff::_narrow(rootContext->resolve(name));

    // Invoke a method and output the result
    cout << ct->calcCost((CORBA::LongLong)10,(CORBA::Short)2) << endl;

  }
  catch(const CORBA::Exception& e) {
    cerr << e << endl;
    return 1;
  }

  return 0;
}
```

To test the client we first have to compile it. Again, we'll use the Microsoft Visual C++ 5.0 command-line tools. To compile and link the CORBA client we will use the command shown in the following screenshot to produce our Client.exe executable file:

After the compilation we have to run the following commands:

1. Start the CORBA Naming Service (note that here we use orbd from JDK 1.4):

```
orbd -ORBInitialPort 1234 -ORBInitialHost localhost
```

2. Start the RMI-IIOP server-side virtual component (developed in the first section of this chapter):

509

```
java -Djava.naming.factory.initial=com.sun.jndi.cosnaming.CNCtxFactory -
Djava.naming.provider.url=iiop://localhost:1234 Server
```

3. Start the C++ CORBA client:

Ultimately, we see that the CORBA client developed in C++ has no problem accessing an RMI-IIOP virtual component developed in Java.

> **Note that we do not need the Visibroker Smart Agent ORB process (osagent) to be active while running this example (remember that osagent was required for the previous example) because Visibroker packs the necessary client-side ORB functionality with the client.**

In this section we have seen how to solve a common problem in EAI – achieving interoperability between RMI-IIOP, which is the communication mechanism of both J2EE and CORBA. CORBA is the main technology for wrapping existing applications (as we have seen in Chapter 10). It is also a popular interoperability technology and is facilitated in many existing applications.

In the next section we will look at how to handle multiple simultaneous clients that access the existing application through virtual components. We'll also examine how to limit the maximum number of simultaneous clients accessing the same existing application.

Handling Simultaneous Clients

Clients will access existing applications through virtual components. Often several clients will access a single virtual component simultaneously. In this section we will discuss what happens when multiple clients simultaneously access a single virtual component instance. We will first look at how RMI-IIOP handles multi-threading and what we should pay attention to when developing multi-threaded virtual components.

RMI-IIOP virtual components can process the requests from clients in different threads. This means that when several clients invoke the methods on the same virtual component, the requests will be processed concurrently in multiple threads.

This means that we have to think about the different scenarios in which the RMI-IIOP virtual components will be used. We have two choices. We can make our code thread-safe and allow multiple threads. Or we can instantiate a new instance for each client.

Developing Thread-safe Virtual Components

Developing thread-safe code is generally not easy, but the Java language simplifies this task considerably by associating each object with a lock. To synchronize parts of code or whole methods we can use the `synchronized` statement. When using this statement the thread will acquire a mutual-exclusion lock, execute the code, and finally release the lock. When a lock is acquired other threads can still access this object. They can, for example, access the attributes and methods that do not require synchronization.

However, we have to be aware how and where we will use this technique. Using `synchronized` all over the code will not ensure thread safety and is likely to provoke deadlocks. It is also quite difficult to debug such code, because errors occur when we have a lot of simultaneous users.

Thread synchronization is also costly from the performance perspective. New Java Virtual Machines and Just-in-time Compilers managed to reduce the cost of synchronization considerably. Still, it is believed that synchronization makes code 10 to 20 times slower when using the HotSpot JVM, or 30 to 60 times with Classic JVM.

Therefore we should synchronize the smallest part of code possible to guarantee thread safety. It is much better to use code like the following:

```
void myMethod() {
    ...
    synchronized(this) {
    ...
    }
    ...
}
```

This executes faster and lets us focus more precisely on what we want to synchronize, rather than if we were to synchronize the whole method, like this:

```
synchronized void myMethod() {
    ...
}
```

It is also possible to synchronize on the data structure we are using. For this purpose we can use fields that we mark with the `volatile` keyword. If a field is declared volatile then the thread has to reconcile the working copy of the field with the master copy each time the variable is accessed. Operations on the master copy of the variable are also performed in the exact order.

Declaring volatile attributes is simple:

```
class myClass {
    static volatile int myAttribute;
    ...
}
```

However, when accessing existing applications we also have to keep track of the existing applications and their support for simultaneous clients. If we open the connection to existing application we should check whether we could use the same connection for different clients or if we need a new one for each client. We should also consider the maximum number of simultaneous clients an existing application would allow. If necessary we should limit this number to prevent the existing application crashing.

Creating Virtual Component Instances

When integrating existing applications, this often involves an increase in the number of simultaneous clients. Often, however, existing applications have not been designed to support such high numbers of simultaneous clients. Under such a high load, in the best-case scenario existing applications will perform very slowly, in the worst case, they will crash. Thus, it is vital that we find ways in which to control and limit the number of simultaneous clients.

A solution is that we create an instance of the virtual component for each client. This will make it possible to control the number of instances created and thus limit the maximum number of simultaneous clients. If each client uses its own instance of the virtual component, it will also ease the development of code, which will consequently not have to be thread-safe.

To provide clients with the ability to create instances of the virtual component, we can implement the Factory pattern. We simply define a new virtual component, a factory component, which provides a method for creating new instances of the CostTariff virtual component that we implemented in our last example. We then only need to instantiate a single factory component in the server process.

The clients will connect to the factory component and create new instances of virtual components, as they need them. This also means that an instance will be used by a single client only, which will simplify thread management.

In the interface of the factory component we can also provide other methods, for example, for deleting instances. We can also limit the maximum number of instances that can be created and thus limit the number of connections to the existing application. With this we can prevent putting too much load on the existing application.

To define the factory interface for the CostTariff interface we need to write a CostTariffFactory interface, like the following:

```
import java.rmi.Remote;
import java.rmi.RemoteException;

public interface CostTariffFactory extends Remote {

  CostTariff create() throws RemoteException;

}
```

Then we have to implement a class that will provide the functionality for the factory. As such, we will create a CostTariffFactoryImpl class that will provide the required functionality:

```
import java.rmi.RemoteException;
import javax.rmi.PortableRemoteObject;

public class CostTariffFactoryImpl extends PortableRemoteObject implements
CostTariffFactory {

  public CostTariffFactoryImpl() throws RemoteException {
  }
```

```
    public CostTariff create () throws RemoteException {

       System.out.println("New virtual component created...");

       return new CostTariffImpl();

    }
}
```

Next we have to modify the server process where we should instantiate a single instance of the factory object and register it with the Naming Service:

```
import java.rmi.RemoteException;
import javax.rmi.PortableRemoteObject;
import javax.naming.*;

public class Server {

  public static void main(String[] args) {

    try {

      Context iNamingContext = new InitialContext();

      CostTariffFactory ct = new CostTariffFactoryImpl();

      iNamingContext.rebind("CostTariffFactory", ct);

      System.out.println("Server ready...");

    } catch (Exception e) {
      System.out.println(e);
      e.printStackTrace(System.out);
    }
  }
}
```

Finally, we should modify the client that has to connect to the factory; it has to invoke the create() method on the factory to obtain a reference to the actual virtual component. Notice that with each create() a new virtual component instance is created on the server side. In real-world examples, in most cases we would also want to provide a remove() method that would delete the instances on the server side. Although we haven't done this in our example for simplicity, it is a fairly trivial procedure. Here's the code for our Client class:

```
import java.util.*;
import javax.naming.*;
import javax.rmi.PortableRemoteObject;

public class Client {

  public static void main(String[] args) {
```

513

```
    CostTariffFactory ctf = null;
    CostTariff ct = null;

    // Connect to the initial naming context
    // and resolve a reference to the CostTariffFactory
    try {
      Context inc = new InitialContext();
      ctf = (CostTariffFactory)PortableRemoteObject.narrow
              (inc.lookup("CostTariffFactory"),CostTariffFactory.class);
    } catch (Exception e) {
      System.out.println(e);
    }

    try {
      // Create a new virtual component instance
      ct = ctf.create();

      // Invoke a method
      double r = ct.calcCost((long)4, (short)2);
      System.out.println(r);

    } catch (Exception e) {
      System.out.println(e);
    }
  }
}
```

It is not especially difficult to limit the maximum number of instances that are allowed. We have to add this functionality to the factory implementation class, the `CostTariffFactoryImpl`:

```
import java.rmi.RemoteException;
import javax.rmi.PortableRemoteObject;

public class CostTariffFactoryImpl extends PortableRemoteObject implements
CostTariffFactory {

  private int noOfInstances = 0;
  private final static int maxNoOfInstances = 10;

  public CostTariffFactoryImpl() throws RemoteException {
  }

  public synchronized CostTariff create () throws RemoteException {

    if (noOfInstances < maxNoOfInstances) {
      noOfInstances++;
      System.out.println("New virtual component created...");
      return new CostTariffImpl();
    } else

    throw new RemoteException();

  }
}
```

To run this example we have to follow the usual procedure:

1. Compile the Java source files

2. Generate the stubs, using the `rmic -iiop command`

3. Start the Naming Service (`tnameserv` or `orbd`)

4. Start the `Server.class`

5. Start one or more `Client.` classes

The full procedure is shown in the following screenshot:

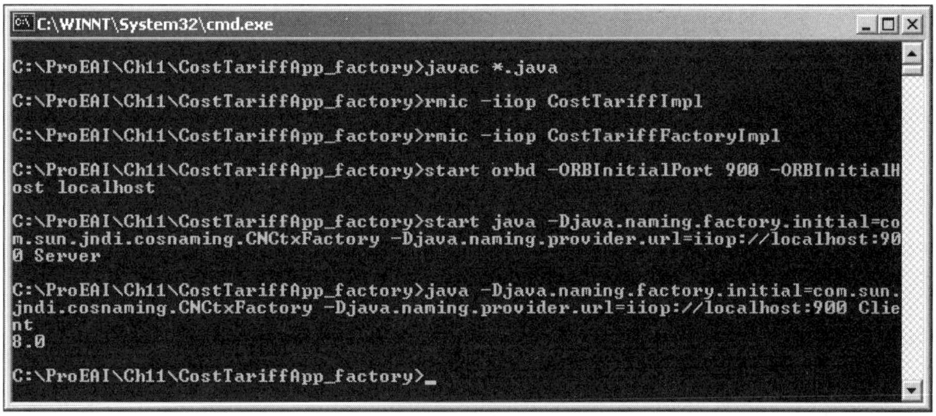

After starting ten simultaneous clients, we will get the following message when trying to start the eleventh:

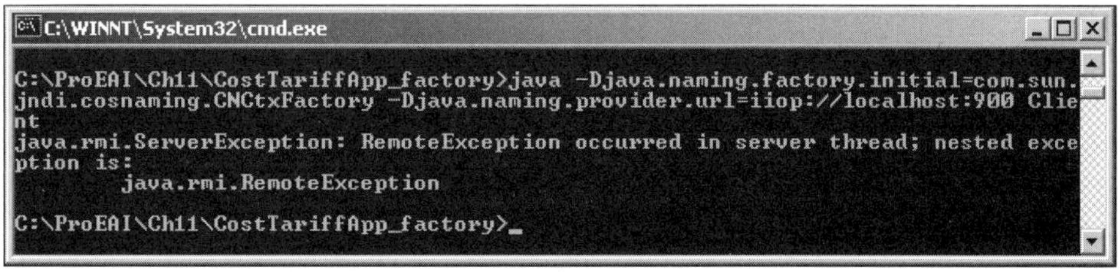

In real-world examples we would probably use a user-defined exception instead of RemoteException to signal that we have reached the maximum number of simultaneous clients. Adding this is not difficult and the readers should do this alone. We have however learned how to effectively limit the number of simultaneous clients.

In the next section we will address another problem. We will look at how virtual components can call back the client and report the results, so the client does not have to wait for the existing application to execute the operation.

Callbacks

Sometimes the operations of existing applications will take a longer time. Using synchronous RMI-IIOP-style method invocation, clients (such as higher-level virtual components, web component tier clients or client tier clients) that access the existing application through lower-level virtual components will be blocked for the duration of method invocation, and will be unable to do anything else, while they will wait for the lower-level component (actually the existing application) to finish.

We might not want to wait. Instead, we'd much rather simply have the client freed after submitting the request for operation invocation to the lower-level virtual component, and have the virtual component then notify the client when the operation is finished.

The scenario is shown in the collaboration diagram below:

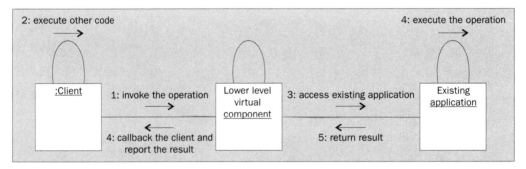

For example, it might be the case that in our cell phone operator integration example, the existing cost and tariff management application requires a lot of time to calculate the cost of a call. Other examples might be situations that require batch tasks, such as printing the invoices every month. Also, different query operations often require a lot of time – for example, finding all phone subscribers that have not paid their bills, or finding all pre-paid accounts that have had zero balance for more than three months (to disconnect them). There are many comparable circumstances in other domains too.

In this section we will show how to develop callback scenarios using RMI-IIOP. First we will look how to achieve callback when we have RMI-IIOP objects on both sides, as shown in the following figure:

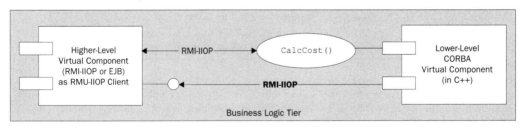

Next we will show how to implement callback when an RMI-IIOP higher-level virtual component (or other RMI-IIOP client) calls a CORBA lower-level virtual component, written in a programming language other than Java (for example, in C++). Here it is important to understand the interoperability, first how an RMI-IIOP client calls a CORBA server object and second, how a CORBA client calls an RMI-IIOP server object, which we have discussed earlier in this chapter. The scenario is shown in the next figure:

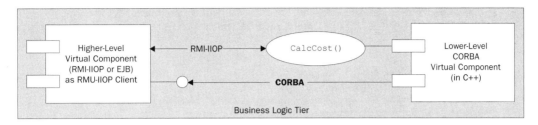

Before we start discussing how to implement these scenarios let us mention that an alternative to this approach is using asynchronous messaging, that is, MOM products through JMS. JMS, covered in Chapter 8, provides a loosely-coupled interaction model that differs considerably from remote method invocations.

Let us now start discussing how to achieve a callback with RMI-IIOP.

Achieving Callback with RMI-IIOP

To realize the callback scenario when we have RMI-IIOP on both ends is not so difficult. We will have to implement two-way communication. The first part when the client calls the virtual component (server object in RMI-IIOP terminology) will not be difficult and will be almost the same as in the previous examples.

After the virtual component finishes processing the client request, it will call the client object. In fact, at this point the roles will be swapped. The virtual components will become the client, and the client the server. The server and client roles are defined for each method invocation, but we will still use the client for the object that made the initial invocation and the server for the virtual component. To achieve this, the client will have to expose an interface through which the virtual component will notify it on completion. Therefore, we will have to make the client a distributed object too.

Defining the Interfaces

Let's first have a look at the interfaces for the virtual component, and for the client object. The interface for the virtual component requires slight modifications. First of all we have to modify the return value from the method `calcCost()`. Namely, the method will not return the result immediately. Rather, it will calculate the cost and return the result later via the callback. Hence, we change the return type to `void`.

The virtual component also has to know which client called it. Actually, there could be many different clients calling the virtual component and it therefore needs to know who to notify about the result of the invocation. The simplest and most effective way is that the client sends its reference together with the method request. Therefore, we add a third parameter to the `calcCost()` method that will hold the client reference:

```
import java.rmi.Remote;
import java.rmi.RemoteException;

public interface CostTariff extends Remote {

  void calcCost (long durationInSeconds,
             short tariffUsed, Client c) throws RemoteException;

}
```

517

We also have to define the interface for the `Client`. We define a method with the name `operationFinished()` that has a parameter through which the virtual component will report the result – the cost of a call:

```
import java.rmi.Remote;
import java.rmi.RemoteException;

public interface Client extends Remote {

  void operationFinished(double result) throws RemoteException;

}
```

Implementing the Interfaces

Now we have to implement both interfaces. On the server side we have to implement the virtual component, where we actually connect to existing application, like we did it in the previous examples. Instead of returning the value through a return statement we invoke the callback method. To demonstrate the callback, instead of connecting directly to the existing application, in the next example we simply wait 10 seconds before calling back the client:

```
import java.rmi.RemoteException;
import javax.rmi.PortableRemoteObject;

public class CostTariffImpl extends PortableRemoteObject implements CostTariff  {

  public CostTariffImpl() throws RemoteException {
  }

  public void calcCost (long durationInSeconds, short tariffUsed,
                          Client c) throws RemoteException {

    double cost = 0;

    // connect to the existing applications and calculate
    System.out.println("Calculating...");
    try{
      Thread.sleep(10000);
    } catch (Exception e) {};

    cost = durationInSeconds * 2;

    System.out.println("Notifying the client...");
    // notify the client
    c.operationFinished(cost);
    System.out.println("Client notified...");
  }
}
```

Next we have to implement the client interface. We do this in the `ClientImpl` class. We first implement the `operationFinished()` method. The method reports the result – in our example it simply writes it to the screen. We also implement the constructor, which starts the callback sequence (we will define this a little later on):

```
import java.util.*;
import javax.naming.*;
import javax.rmi.PortableRemoteObject;
import java.rmi.RemoteException;

public class ClientImpl extends PortableRemoteObject implements Client {

  public ClientImpl() throws RemoteException {
        performOperation();
  }

  public void operationFinished(double r) throws RemoteException
  {
    // Report the result
    System.out.println("");
    System.out.println("The call cost is: "+r);
  }
}
```

Then we implement a private method that actually performs the whole operation. This method has to connect to the virtual component and invoke the method:

```
  private void performOperation() {

    // Connect to the server virtual component
    System.out.print("Connecting to server...");
    CostTariff ct = null;
    try {
      // Accessing the initial naming context
      Context inc = new InitialContext();
      // Resolving the name and binding to the virtual component
      ct = (CostTariff)PortableRemoteObject.narrow
                  (inc.lookup("CostTariff"),CostTariff.class);
    } catch (Exception e) {
      System.out.println(e);
    }

    // Invoke the method
    System.out.print("Invoking the method...");
    try {
      ct.calcCost((long)4, (short)2, (Client)this);
    } catch (Exception e) {
      System.out.println(e);
    }
  }
}
```

The example above looks fine at first glance. However, the problem is that the client is not freed after invoking the calcCost() method. In fact, it waits until the server finishes the callback, which is exactly what we didn't want to achieve, because we would like to have the client freed to do other operations while the server processes the request.

To achieve this we have two options:

❑ We can create a new thread on the client and invoke the method from that thread.

❑ We can modify the virtual component and service the method request in a separate thread while returning the acknowledgement to the client immediately. This will free the client to do other things.

Here we will show the first possibility, which I believe is better. Remember, the virtual components will be accessed by several clients simultaneously and will serve these requests in multiple threads. So the computer on which virtual components will be deployed, will already be under high load (definitely higher than the client computer). Creating additional threads in the virtual components (which the second solution proposes) will put the server computer under even higher load and might influence the scalability. On the other hand, creating an additional thread on the client computer does not make much difference.

Accordingly, we write a class that executes the method invocation in a separate thread:

```
class invokeInNewThread extends Thread {
   private long d = 0;
   private short t = 0;
   private Client c = null;
   private CostTariff ct = null;

   public invokeInNewThread(long d, short t, Client c, CostTariff ct) {
      this.d = d;
      this.t = t;
      this.c = c;
      this.ct = ct;
   }

   public void run() {
      try {

         ct.calcCost(d, t, c);

      } catch (Exception e) {
         System.out.println(e);
      }
   }
}
```

Next, we modify the `performOperation()` method such that it creates a new thread. However, we must not forget that the client will have to do something while the method executes on the existing application. This means that the client must not finish before the virtual component notifies it about the result. For the purposes of our demonstration, we'll add a loop in which the client prints dots on the screen (obviously, an enterprise-scale solution would do something a little more useful at this point):

```
private void performOperation() {

   // Connect to the server virtual component
   System.out.print("Connecting to server...");
```

```
CostTariff ct = null;
try {
  // Accessing the initial naming context
  Context inc = new InitialContext();
  // Resolving the name and binding to the virtual component
  ct = (CostTariff)PortableRemoteObject.narrow
                (inc.lookup("CostTariff"),CostTariff.class);
} catch (Exception e) {
  System.out.println(e);
}

// Invoke the method
System.out.print("Invoking the method...");

new invokeInNewThread((long)4, (short)2, (Client)this, ct).start();

// Do something else while waiting for response
System.out.print("Doing something else while waiting...");
int i=0;
while (i<500) {
  try{
    Thread.sleep(100);
  } catch (Exception e) {};
  System.out.print(".");
  i++;
};
}
```

Writing the Server Processes

We've almost finished the callback example – we just have to write the server processes. We learned that we need to create a process where the RMI-IIOP object is instantiated. Now we have two objects, the client and the virtual component, we have to instantiate both. To instantiate the client object we write the `ClientRun` class. However we do not have to register the `Client` with the Naming Service because we send the reference to the server:

```
import java.util.*;
import javax.naming.*;
import javax.rmi.PortableRemoteObject;
import java.rmi.RemoteException;
import org.omg.PortableServer.*;

public class ClientRun {

  public static void main(String[] args) {
    try{

    Client c = new ClientImpl();

    } catch (Exception e) {
      System.out.println(e);
    }
  }
}
```

To instantiate the server-side `CostTariff` virtual component we define the usual server-side class `Server` in which we create a new instance and register it with the Naming Service that the client will be able to do a lookup on:

```
import java.rmi.RemoteException;
import javax.rmi.PortableRemoteObject;
import javax.naming.*;

public class Server {

  public static void main(String[] args) {

    try {

      Context iNamingContext = new InitialContext();

      CostTariff ct = new CostTariffImpl();

      iNamingContext.rebind("CostTariff", ct);

      System.out.println("Server ready...");

    } catch (Exception e) {
      System.out.println(e);
      e.printStackTrace(System.out);
    }
  }
}
```

Running the Example

To run the example we have to do the following:

1. Compile the source files

2. Generate the stubs

3. Run the Naming Service

4. Run the server object

5. Run the client

The following screenshot shows the necessary commands that will perform the first three of these tasks:

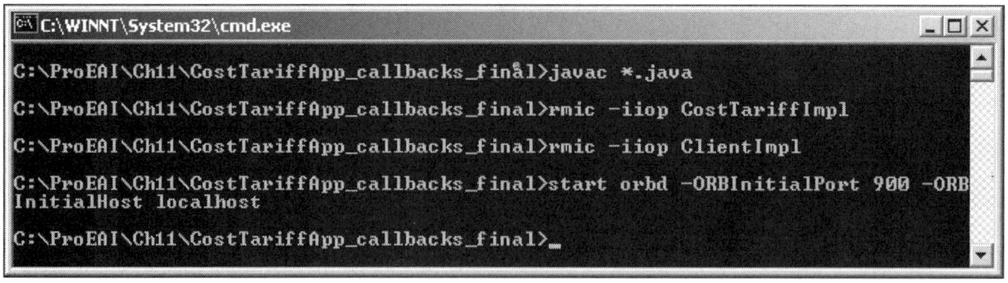

Then we have to start the virtual component. The next screenshot shows the necessary command and the output after the client has invoked the method (see the next step):

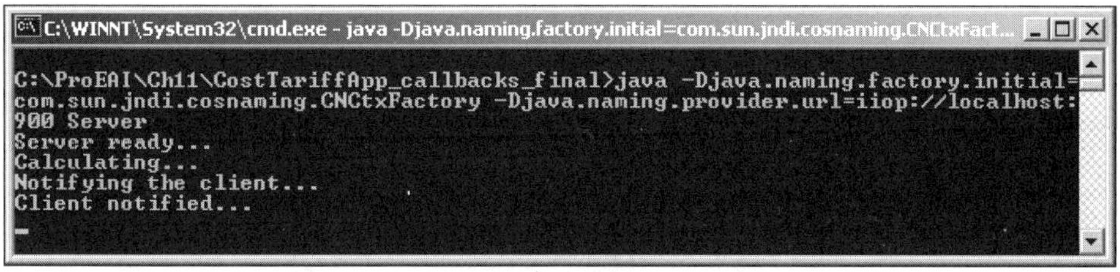

Finally, we can run the client, which should produce the following result:

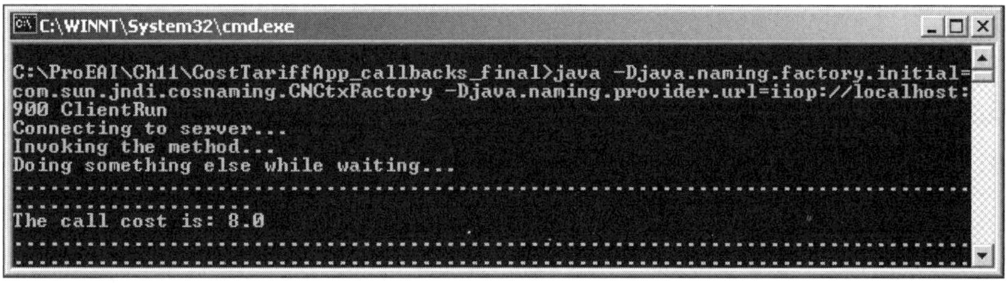

In this example we learned how to implement callback scenarios with RMI-IIOP at both ends, that is, with an RMI-IIOP client and RMI-IIOP virtual component. In the next section we will look at a slightly trickier example: how to implement callback with an RMI-IIOP client and a CORBA virtual component.

Achieving Callback Between RMI-IIOP and CORBA

Strictly speaking, in an integration scenario, the client *and* the virtual component will rarely both be implemented in RMI-IIOP. More commonly, we will have the virtual component (or a component wrapper) implemented in CORBA, and we will use RMI-IIOP to access it. This includes regular RMI-IIOP clients, and also EJBs. For this reason, we will look at how to achieve callback functionality with this combination.

Developing the Virtual Component in CORBA

We are already familiar with how to develop server-side CORBA virtual components and wrappers, so we will reiterate the major stages in this process only:

1. Generate the IDL from the Java interfaces. For this we use the `rmic -idl` tool and generate the IDL for both the `CostTariff` and `Client` interfaces. The `CostTariff` is the server-side virtual component that we implement in CORBA. `CostTariff` calls the `Client`, so we need the `Client` interface too. The commands are shown in the next screenshot:

523

2. Compile the IDL interfaces into the corresponding programming language. For simplicity we develop the CORBA server in Java and use the `idlj` compiler from the JDK. Note that we will use a new folder for this example, as shown in the next screenshot, otherwise the `idlj` will overwrite files:

3. Implement the `CostTariffImpl` implementation class (see below).

4. Write the server process that creates an instance, and register it with the Naming Service.

5. Compile the source code.

6. Start the Naming Service and the server-side CORBA virtual component.

The implementation class `CostTariffImpl` for the CORBA virtual component written in Java looks like the following:

```
public class CostTariffImpl extends CostTariffPOA {

  public void calcCost (long durationInSeconds, short tariffUsed, Client c)
  {
    double cost = 0;

    // connect to the existing application and calculate
    System.out.println("Calculating...");
    Try {
      Thread.sleep(10000);
    } catch (Exception e) {};

    cost = durationInSeconds * 2;

    System.out.println("Notifying the client...");
    // notify the client
    try {
      c.operationFinished(cost);
    } catch (Exception e) {
      System.out.println(e);
    }
    System.out.println("Client notified...");
  }
}
```

The server process, `Server.java`, in its simplest form is presented as the next piece of code. As we know from previous examples, it initializes the ORB, creates a new instance of the virtual component, gets a reference to the root POA, activates the component instance with the POA, and binds it in the Naming Service:

```
import org.omg.CosNaming.*;
import org.omg.CosNaming.NamingContextPackage.*;
import org.omg.CORBA.*;
import org.omg.PortableServer.*;

public class Server {

  public static void main(String[] args) {

    try {
      ORB orb = ORB.init(args,null);

      CostTariffImpl c = new CostTariffImpl();

      POA rPOA = (POA)orb.resolve_initial_references("RootPOA");

      rPOA.the_POAManager().activate();

      rPOA.activate_object(c);

      org.omg.CORBA.Object objRef =
                        orb.resolve_initial_references("NameService");
      NamingContext ncRef = NamingContextHelper.narrow(objRef);

      NameComponent nc;
      NameComponent path[]={null};

      nc = new NameComponent("CostTariff", "");
      path[0] = nc;
      ncRef.rebind(path, rPOA.servant_to_reference(c));

      System.out.println("Server is ready...");

      orb.run();

    } catch (Exception e) {
      System.out.println(e);
    }
  }
}
```

The Client in RMI-IIOP

To run the example we will use the same client that we developed in the previous callback example
where we had RMI-IIOP on both sides, so there are no changes to this client required. This clearly
demonstrates the interoperability.

After compiling the source code, we should start the Naming Service and the CORBA virtual
component, as shown in the next screenshots. To start the client we use the identical command as in
previous example. In fact, we are actually using the same client from the previous example (notice
the directory change):

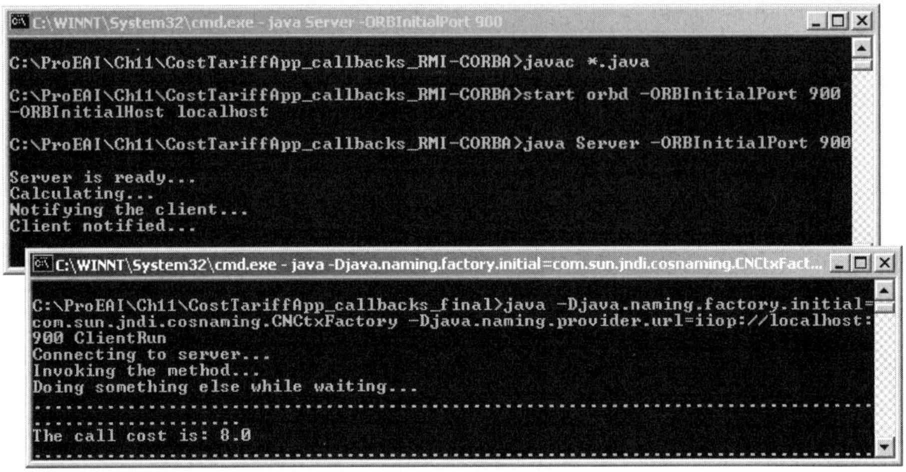

We have seen that implementing a callback between an RMI-IIOP client and a CORBA virtual component is not particularly difficult. Next we'll continue with the callback scenarios a little more when we take a look at the one way operations that CORBA provides particularly for this purpose.

Using One Way Operations with CORBA Clients

Instead of using a separate thread to invoke callback operations in CORBA we can use one way operations, which we can define in IDL. Accordingly, we will take a look at how to use one way operations to implement a callback. Obviously, an operation that is defined as one way must not return any result (it has to be `void`), and it should also immediately return control to the client. Therefore we do not need to invoke them in a separate thread.

To define an operation as one way we simply modify the `CostTariff.idl` file. We declare the `calcCost()` operation as `oneway`. This is a CORBA `IDL` keyword, as shown below:

```
/**
 * CostTariff.idl
 * Generated by rmic -idl. Do not edit
 */

#ifndef __Client__

    interface Client;

#endif

#include "orb.idl"

#ifndef __CostTariff__
#define __CostTariff__

    interface CostTariff {
```

```
            oneway void calcCost(
                in long long durationInSeconds,
                in short tariffUsed,
                in Client c);

    };

    #pragma ID CostTariff "RMI:CostTariff:0000000000000000"

    #include "Client.idl"
    #endif
```

Note that we do not have to make any modifications to the server-side code – the IDL compiler will generate the appropriate stubs that will return control to the client immediately.

Declaring operations as oneway will, however, not influence RMI-IIOP client. The RMI-IIOP client will not use the stub generated by the IDL compiler, but a stub generated by the rmic compiler. Therefore for the RMI-IIOP client we still have to use a separate thread. Consequently, in order to take full advantage of oneway operations we have to develop a CORBA client.

The next listing shows the CORBA client developed in Java:

```java
import org.omg.CosNaming.*;
import org.omg.CORBA.*;
import org.omg.PortableServer.*;

public class ClientImpl extends ClientPOA {

  private CostTariff ct = null;
  private static ORB orb = null;

  private void performOperation() {

    // Connect to the server virtual component
    System.out.println("Connecting to server...");

    try{
      org.omg.CORBA.Object objRef =
                      orb.resolve_initial_references("NameService");
      NamingContext ncRef = NamingContextHelper.narrow(objRef);

      NameComponent nc = new NameComponent("CostTariff", "");
      NameComponent path[] = {nc};
      ct = CostTariffHelper.narrow(ncRef.resolve(path));

      // Invoke the method
      System.out.println("Invoking the method...");

      POA poa = (POA)orb.resolve_initial_references("RootPOA");

      poa.the_POAManager().activate();
```

```
      poa.servant_to_reference(this);

      ct.calcCost((long)4, (short)2, this._this());

    } catch (Exception e) {
      System.out.println(e);
    }

    // Do something else while waiting for response
    System.out.println("Doing something else while waiting...");
    int i=0;
    while (i<500) {
      try{
        Thread.sleep(100);
      } catch (Exception e) {};
      System.out.print(".");
      i++;
    };
  }

  public void operationFinished(double r)
  {
    // Report the result
    System.out.println("");
    System.out.println("The call cost is: "+r);

  }

  public static void main(String[] args) {
    try{
      orb = ORB.init(args, null);

      ClientImpl c = new ClientImpl();
      c.performOperation();

    } catch (Exception e) {
      System.out.println(e);
    }


  }
}
```

Notice that the callback CORBA client implements the same interface as the RMI-IIOP client and that we used the Client.idl file, generated from Java interface declarations (we did that in the previous example). Therefore, the ClientImpl class has to extend the ClientPOA. Also, note that we initialize the ORB in the main() method and store the reference as an attribute.

We should not forget to create a POA for the client, to activate the POA manager, and to activate the servant. We should also notice how to send the client reference to the server side. We cannot simply use this, because it would forward the reference to the implementation class – the servant. The servant, however, provides the _this() method that returns the reference to the CORBA client object instance – exactly what we need. Furthermore, note that we used a normal method invocation that will return the control to the client immediately.

Using one way operations has the disadvantage that the client cannot be sure if the virtual component received the invocation request successfully. The stub returns the control directly to the client and does not wait for acknowledgement from the virtual component, so there is no way to figure out if something goes wrong. For instance, the virtual component could crash or communication might be interrupted for some other reason. According to the CORBA specification, best-effort semantics are expected of requests for this operation – our application should be aware of this.

To start this example we should first start the naming service (orbd) and the CORBA virtual component developed in the previous example. The necessary commands are shown in the next screenshot (together with the output after the client has been started). We should compile the CostTariff.idl and Client.idl IDL files using the idlj, and then compile the source files using javac. Finally, we need to start the client (ClientImpl.class):

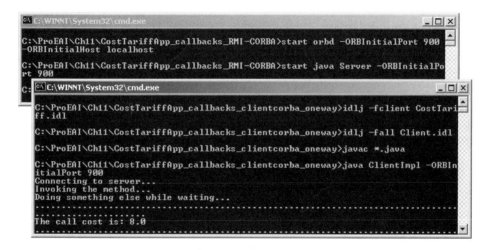

We have seen that the CORBA one way operations simplify the development of callback scenarios. In the next section we will look at another problem that might arise with integration. We will discuss how to achieve interoperability with RMI (which uses JRMP instead of IIOP).

Interoperability with RMI

Sometimes we will be faced with existing Java applications that use the original RMI, perhaps one that uses JRMP instead of IIOP. Porting these applications to RMI-IIOP is not very difficult because there is not much difference between them. However, if we do this then we also have to port all clients. Or we will want to provide access to virtual components from the original RMI in addition to RMI-IIOP. In other words, sometimes we need the RMI-IIOP virtual component (server object) to be accessed from an RMI-IIOP (including CORBA) client and from regular RMI clients (using the native JRMP protocol). Luckily, this is possible.

We can create so-called "dual export" RMI objects that expose their functionality through both IIOP and JRMP at the same time. To understand how it works, let us look at the class hierarchy of RMI-IIOP classes.

For this, let's briefly return to the first RMI-IIOP example presented in this chapter, in which we defined the `CostTariff` interface and the `CostTariffImpl` implementation class. The `CostTariff` interface had to extend the `Remote` interface. The `CostTariffImpl` class implemented the `CostTariff` interface and extended the `PortableRemoteObject` class. This class hierarchy is seen more clearly in a UML class diagram:

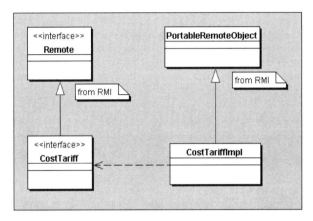

So, the essential difference between RMI-IIOP and RMI relates to the class from which the implementation class inherits. In RMI-IIOP this is `PortableRemoteObject`, while in RMI this should be the `UnicastRemoteObject`, which extends the `RemoteServer`, which in turn extends the `RemoteObject` class. To make sure this is clear, let's have a look at the RMI hierarchy for a direct comparison:

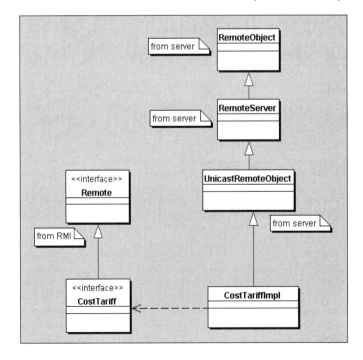

Obviously we cannot extend from these classes, `PortableRemoteObject` and
`UnicastRemoteObject`, simultaneously. However, we can use another fact: namely, that it is not
necessary to inherit from those classes to implement RMI or RMI-IIOP objects. We can also write
classes without inheritance, but then we have to export the objects manually. This fact will help us in
producing dual export server objects. We will carry out the following:

- ❏ The `CostTariffImpl` class will not inherit from any class but will simply implement the
  `CostTariff` interface
- ❏ We will manually export the object to both IIOP and JRMP
- ❏ We will register the name of the server object in the Naming Service and RMI Registry
- ❏ To configure the initial naming factory we will have to use Java `Properties`

The `CostTariffImpl` class will look very similar to before:

```
import java.rmi.RemoteException;

public class CostTariffImpl implements CostTariff  {

   public CostTariffImpl() throws RemoteException {
   }

   public double calcCost (long durationInSeconds,
                           short tariffUsed) throws RemoteException {

     double cost = 0;
     // connect to the existing application and calculate the cost

     return cost;
   }
}
```

The major changes will take place in the server process where we will have to export the object to
both naming services – the CORBA Naming Service and the RMI Registry:

```
import java.rmi.RemoteException;
import javax.rmi.PortableRemoteObject;
import javax.naming.*;
import java.util.Properties;

public class Server {

  public static void main(String[] args) {

    try {

      CostTariff ct = new CostTariffImpl();

      // Export the RMI-IIOP object
      javax.rmi.PortableRemoteObject.exportObject(ct);

      // Export the RMI object
```

```
       java.rmi.server.UnicastRemoteObject.exportObject(ct);

       // Register the RMI-IIOP object in CORBA Naming Service
       Properties cosProp = new Properties();
       cosProp.put("java.naming.factory.initial",
                   "com.sun.jndi.cosnaming.CNCtxFactory");
       Context iiopNamingContext = new InitialContext(cosProp);
       iiopNamingContext.rebind("CostTariff", ct);

       // Register the RMI object in RMI Registry
       Properties rmiProp = new Properties();
       rmiProp.put("java.naming.factory.initial",
                   "com.sun.jndi.rmi.registry.RegistryContextFactory");
       Context jrmpNamingContext = new InitialContext (rmiProp);
       jrmpNamingContext.rebind("CostTariff", ct);

       System.out.println("Server ready...");

    } catch (Exception e) {
       System.out.println(e);
       e.printStackTrace(System.out);
    }
  }
}
```

To test the example we also have to develop both clients. The RMI-IIOP client we have already developed in the first example in this chapter and we'll use it for this example too. The RMI (JRMP) client differs from the RMI-IIOP client in that it uses the `java.rmi.Naming` instead of `javax.naming`. The lookup for resolving the name and getting a reference to the server-side virtual component also differs, as we can see from the code below:

```
import java.rmi.Naming;

public class ClientJRMP {

  public static void main(String[] args) {

    CostTariff ct = null;

    // Resolve the name in the RMI Registry
    try {
       ct = (CostTariff)Naming.lookup("CostTariff");
    } catch (Exception e) {
       System.out.println(e);
    }

    // Invoke the method
    try {
       double r = ct.calcCost((long)4, (short)2);
       System.out.println(r);

    } catch (Exception e) {
       System.out.println(e);
    }
  }
}
```

To build the example we have to compile the source code, and generate the stubs and skeletons for both IIOP and JRMP. We'll use the `rmic` compiler for both, once with `-iiop` and once without. To run the example we have to start both the CORBA Naming Service (`orbd` or `tnameserv`) and the RMI Registry (`rmiregistry`). Then we have to start the server-side virtual component. The required commands are shown in the screenshot below:

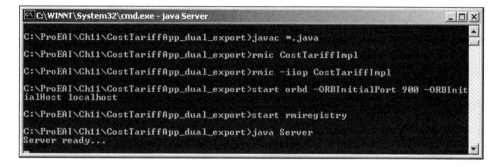

Notice that if you already have generated stubs and skeletons, you will see a warning when running `rmic` *again, which will warn you that you should remove previously generated stubs and skeletons, otherwise the object will be exported to IIOP instead to JRMP. For our purposes, we can ignore this warning because we export the object manually to both.*

Next we can run the clients. First let's run the RMI-JRMP client, using the following command:

Finally we can run the RMI-IIOP from the first example in this chapter (again, note the change in working directory):

We have seen that dual-exporting RMI virtual components is not particularly difficult. That way we can make them accessible by both RMI-IIOP and RMI-JRMP clients. In the next section we will address another important topic: how to persuade the IIOP protocol to cross firewalls.

IIOP and Firewalls

As with HTTP, the IIOP protocol is based on TCP/IP for communication and is used to invoke operations on distributed objects (virtual components in our case). In other words, clients from anywhere on the network can execute operations on virtual components. Clearly, this represents a potential security risk. We would not be happy if *anyone* from the local company network is able to invoke methods on virtual components and access the existing applications that way. Today, most local networks are connected to the Internet, so we will be even less happy if anyone with Internet access could access our virtual components.

Luckily, in most cases this will not be the case – the majority of firewalls today do not allow IIOP communication and actually block IIOP requests (indeed, most firewalls block JRMP requests too). This reduces security risks, but at the same time means that we will not be able to use IIOP by default for clients behind the firewall to communicate with virtual components.

There are two obvious solutions to this problem:

❑ We can open the firewall to allow IIOP protocol communication. Indeed, with the recent OMG specification this can be done safely.

❑ We can use HTTP tunneling to bypass the firewall restrictions.

Opening the firewall is the best approach to achieve communication with the IIOP protocol. However, in many cases it is not applicable – either we are not in a position to ask the network administrator to open the firewall, or we cannot convince them to. Probably the main reason is that IIOP clients from outside will be able to invoke methods (that is, to execute code) in the company's intranet. This is potentially dangerous, because a malicious client could do harm. Therefore (unfortunately) corporate policies will usually not allow us to do this.

If we cannot open the firewall we can use HTTP tunneling. With this technique client IIOP requests are simply wrapped with HTTP POST requests, before entering the firewall. Therefore, the firewall thinks they are simple HTTP messages. After entering the firewall they are unwrapped and forwarded to the recipient (virtual component). Using HTTP tunneling requires a special process on the company's web server, which does the wrapping and unwrapping (tunneling).

HTTP tunneling does, however, have several distinct disadvantages:

❑ It opens security holes to the system, because IIOP requests can now enter the intranet through the "back door". This is sometimes not recognized by systems/network administrators because they may not be aware of the HTTP tunneling process on the web server. If they were aware, it would probably be possible to convince them to open the firewall anyway.

❑ It makes it impossible to use callback scenarios, which can be a serious limitation. Callback scenarios require a connection in the other direction too – from the virtual component to the client, because the virtual component has to invoke a method on the client to report results (using IIOP, obviously). Firewalls usually block outgoing IIOP requests too. To do HTTP tunneling in this direction we would need a tunneling component on the client too. This is not practical in most cases.

❑ It has large implications on performance, at least an order of magnitude in terms of speed. The tunneling process has to intercept each IIOP request twice – before it enters the firewall, and once it's inside.

In fact, to achieve interoperability with external components a more valuable alternative than IIOP exists today. The Simple Object Access Protocol (SOAP) is an XML-formatted protocol that can be transferred over HTTP or other protocols (SMTP for example). It is also independent of the architecture, so it can also be used with technologies other than J2EE. We will cover SOAP in Chapter 18.

Summary

In this chapter we discussed RMI-IIOP and its role in EAI. We identified RMI-IIOP as a key communication technology between components and tiers in the J2EE integration architecture. RMI-IIOP is used by clients to access server-side components, including RMI-IIOP distributed objects, EJBs, and CORBA objects. The IIOP protocol is also used for communication between components.

In terms of integration, the role of RMI-IIOP is therefore twofold. It is important for building virtual components and it is important for achieving interoperability with CORBA component wrappers. We've covered both aspects and presented several examples with code.

First, we looked at how to implement virtual components with RMI-IIOP solely. Then we identified the need to achieve RMI-IIOP to CORBA communication. We have effectively investigated both scenarios:

❑ RMI-IIOP client communicating with a CORBA (C++) virtual component

❑ CORBA client communicating with an RMI-IIOP virtual component

We discussed the problems of multiple clients accessing an existing application through a virtual component simultaneously. To address this problem we discussed multi-threading, identified how to manage threads and how to write thread-safe code in Java. Then we showed how to control and limit the number of simultaneous clients with the Factory pattern and demonstrated how to implement the factory pattern with RMI-IIOP.

In some scenarios we may want to invoke methods on virtual components that are deferred synchronous. This means that the client will not wait for the completion. Rather, it will invoke a method and then continue with its work. The virtual component will delegate the work to the existing application and, once the existing applications finishes, the virtual component will call back the client and report the results.

Thus, we demonstrated how to build a callback scenario using RMI-IIOP. Then we introduced the CORBA virtual component instead of an RMI-IIOP virtual component and we saw that we can use exactly the same RMI-IIOP client to achieve callback interoperability with CORBA.

Finally, we discussed interoperability with RMI (using the JRMP protocol) and demonstrated how the same virtual component can be exported to both IIOP and JRMP. This means that RMI-JRMP, RMI-IIOP, and CORBA clients can use the same component simultaneously. Additionally, we discussed the IIOP and firewall issues related to accessing components that are located behind the firewall.

In the next chapter we will continue with our study of the J2EE technologies that are relevant to business level integration, turning our attention to the important topic of using EJBs to achieve EAI.

12
EJBs for Integration

The foremost technology for developing business logic or middle-tier components with the J2EE platform is **Enterprise JavaBeans (EJBs)**. EJBs offer a modern component architecture that simplifies the development of complex components. This architecture provides support for major enterprise technologies like transactions, security, and persistence. Moreover, it provides support for these services in a declarative and programmatic way, making the development of business components a relatively easy task.

Although EJB development is limited to the Java programming language, this does not necessarily represent a problem by itself, because Java is a modern, powerful language. However, problems may arise when we start to consider what to do with existing applications. Older applications were not necessarily developed with Java, so there is little likelihood of being able to port existing source code to EJB components easily. However, EJBs can still be used to reuse existing applications.

In this chapter will look at the possibility of using the EJB technology to achieve integration with existing applications. We will discuss the options available with EJB technology according to the J2EE integration architecture that we defined in earlier chapters. In view of this, we will consider EJBs as higher-level virtual components that, on one side, expose high-level business-oriented interfaces to the J2EE clients. On the other side they delegate the requests to lower-level virtual components and wrappers developed in CORBA, RMI-IIOP, JMS, and other technologies, and reuse the functionality of existing applications that way.

Using EJBs in this way for integration enables us to build a clean architecture through which we reuse the functionality of existing applications. It also enables us to re-engineer existing applications step-by-step, adhering to the EJB architecture. This way we can make a relatively easy and seamless transition from existing applications to newly developed solutions.

In this chapter we will examine the following:

- ❏   The role of EJBs in integration:
- ❏   Using entity beans to access existing databases directly and through existing applications
- ❏   Usage scenarios for bean-managed persistence and container-managed persistence
- ❏   Accessing CORBA component wrappers from entity beans
- ❏   How and when to use session beans to access the functions of existing applications
- ❏   Accessing RMI-IIOP virtual components from session beans
- ❏   How and when to use message-driven beans to integrate with Message-Oriented Middleware
- ❏   Performance-related issues

The Role of EJBs for EAI

EJBs have an important role in the application interface and business method integration phases. These phases, sometimes referred to with the common name "business level integration", focus on sharing and reusing the functionality of existing applications. EJBs also play an important role in data level integration phase, because they provide support for representing existing data as components.

The EJB 2.0 specification defines three types of Enterprise JavaBeans:

- ❏   **Entity beans**
   Entity beans represent business data and provide access to data through methods. We also say that they provide an OO view to the underlying persistent data. They represent a shared, transactional state. Typically, they are named with nouns, examples of which might include `Customer`, `Product`, `Order`, and so on. Clients access entity beans synchronously, using RMI-IIOP.

- ❏   **Session beans**
   Session beans model business processes – they are conversational and perform specific actions. They are typically named with verbs, like `checking account balance`, `authorizing credit card`, `disabling accounts with zero balance`, and so on. Clients access session beans synchronously, using RMI-IIOP.

- ❏   **Message-driven beans**
   Message-driven beans represent business processes, similar to session beans (they are named with verbs too). The fundamental difference is that clients access message-driven beans asynchronously, using JMS. Message-driven beans are therefore suitable for business processes that require a longer time to process and that do not return results immediately.

Enterprise beans execute in the **EJB container**, which provides an environment in which the EJBs run. It is also responsible for managing the beans and for providing services, such as transactions, security, and persistence. The container manages the beans so that it invokes the beans callback methods. We'll discuss callback methods shortly.

> *For more information on how the EJB container works and about the EJB architecture, refer to related literature, such as the book Professional EJB from Wrox Press, ISBN 1-861005-08-3.*

EJBs can thus be used in three integration phases: data level, application interface level, and business method level integration. To discuss the role of EJBs more comprehensively we will examine the following scenarios:

❑   Using EJBs to enable access to the functionality of existing applications

❑   Using EJBs to access and represent existing data

❑   Using EJBs to represent the functionality of existing applications in the J2EE architecture in a common way

Let us now make a quick synopsis of what we learned in Chapter 9, and discuss the role of EJBs for all three of these situations.

Using EJBs to Access the Functionality of Existing Applications

The first step in reusing functionality of existing applications is finding out how to access their functionality. Usually, applications provide access to their functions through the user interface, but in this case we need to access functions in a programmatic way, hopefully through existing APIs. Often, existing applications will not provide APIs, so we will have to wrap the existing application with a wrapper: by modification of source code or through screen scraping or terminal emulation.

> **EJBs are not appropriate for wrapping existing applications, neither with source code modification nor with screen scraping or terminal emulation.**

EJBs have to be implemented in Java, whereas existing applications will, in most cases, be written in some other language. Due to the programming limitations that the EJB specification sets, EJBs are not appropriate for wrapping. The most important restrictions in terms of wrapping include:

❑   The enterprise bean must not attempt to load a native library – this makes EJBs inappropriate for wrapping with source code modification or screen scraping

❑   An enterprise bean must not attempt to listen to a socket, accept connections on a socket, or use a socket for multicast – this also makes them inappropriate for wrapping with terminal emulation

Let's now discuss how to use EJBs to access and represent existing data.

Using EJBs to Access and Represent Existing Data

To represent existing data on the business logic tier in the form of components, and to provide access to this data through interfaces and methods, we will use entity beans. On one side, entity beans present a component interface through which J2EE clients can access the data through methods. In addition to simple methods to access data, such as getter and setter methods, entity beans can also provide methods that perform operations on that data.

On the other side entity beans access existing data. There are two possibilities of how they can access existing data:

- ❑ Entity beans can access existing databases directly

- ❑ Entity beans can access existing data through APIs, exposed by existing applications, or wrappers, added to existing applications.

> **Entity beans are suitable for representing existing data, either through direct access to databases, or through existing APIs and wrappers.**

Accessing Existing Data Directly

Entity beans can access the databases of existing applications directly. Before we can access the existing databases we first have to identify what data we are dealing with; we have to understand exactly what data is stored in the existing application database and how. We should be familiar with such an analysis after our study of the existing applications in Chapter 4.

Generally, existing data can be stored in a variety of formats, including relational, object, hierarchical, network, flat files, or proprietary formats, and the support for these formats differs between EJBs. A standard way to access data in J2EE architecture is through JDBC, which provides a transparent database access, independent of the underlying data store. However, JDBC is limited to accessing relational databases only.

Thus, if existing data is stored in relational format, entity beans will be able to access it directly using JDBC, as shown in the figure below:

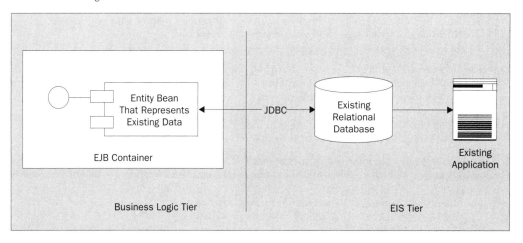

If the existing data is *not* stored in a relational format, then entity beans will not be able to use JDBC. They will have to find another way. For commercial databases, particularly object-oriented, but also hierarchical and network, the vendors might provide libraries that enable access to them from Java. In such cases entity beans will be able to access these databases directly too.

Accessing other existing data, particularly those stored in proprietary formats or in flat files, might not be possible directly. More specifically, the EJB architecture defines several programming restrictions for EJB (for more information have a look at section 24.1.2 in the *Enterprise JavaBeans Specification Version 2.0*, from Sun Microsystems – http://java.sun.com/products/ejb/docs.html). The programming restrictions relevant to integration of existing data are:

❑ An enterprise bean must not use the `java.io` package directly to access files and directories in the file system

❑ An enterprise bean must not attempt to directly read or write a file descriptor

In such cases the access to existing database is wrapped by a wrapper, which exposes an API through which entity beans can access existing data. These wrappers can be, for example, CORBA component wrappers (discussed in Chapter 10). This way entity beans do not access existing data directly, but through a wrapper.

Before we discuss access to the existing data through APIs or wrappers, let us remind ourselves that accessing the data with direct database access ignores database rules, which are usually coded in the existing applications. This can compromise database integrity. However, because entity beans provide access to the existing data through interfaces, they can in fact incorporate these database rules. A better approach is to access existing data through the existing applications.

Accessing Existing Data through APIs or Wrappers

The other possibility to consider is that the entity beans do not access existing databases directly, but use:

❑ Wrappers that wrap access to the database

❑ APIs exposed by existing applications that provide access to data through existing applications

❑ Wrappers that wrap access to existing applications

In the first case the existing databases are still accessed directly, thus database rules are avoided. Such access uses wrappers to access existing data through interfaces. Entity beans use these wrappers to access existing databases, usually because EJB programming restrictions do not allow them to access existing databases directly. This scenario is shown in the following figure:

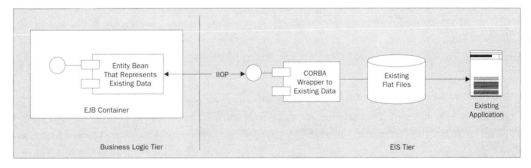

Entity beans can access data through existing applications too. In this case they do not ignore the database integrity rules, which is advantageous. As we have mentioned before, entity beans can use the APIs provided by existing applications, or they can use wrappers that add APIs to existing applications later (refer to Chapter 9 for a discussion of wrapping).

If existing applications already provide APIs with operations to access the existing data, entity beans will use those. Such APIs will use a variety of technologies to access them. If these technologies are compliant with the J2EE platform (like CORBA or JMS), entity beans can access them directly. Otherwise we should abstract such APIs with lower-level virtual components, which mask any technology differences. Such lower-level virtual component can be developed in RMI-IIOP or CORBA, for example.

The next figure shows the scenario where an entity bean represents existing data. For access, it uses an API exposed by an existing application, directly through JMS (other J2EE-compliant technologies would also be appropriate, such as CORBA, RMI-IIOP, JCA, and so on):

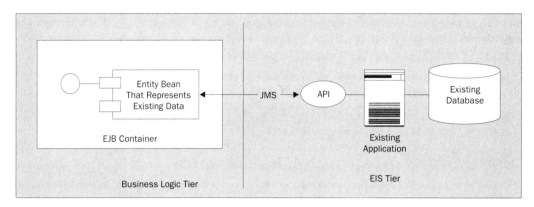

The other possibility is that the API exposed by the existing application uses some proprietary technology; therefore it requires a lower-level virtual component on the business logic tier, which masks the technology differences. The next figure shows a scenario in which the lower-level virtual component is developed in RMI-IIOP (although other technologies could be used, including CORBA and JMS):

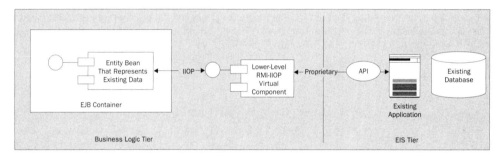

If, on the other hand, existing applications do not provide an API, or the API does not contain the necessary operations, then we can add an API and wrap the existing applications.

Entity beans can use wrappers to access data through the existing application, as shown in the next figure, where we show a wrapper developed in CORBA:

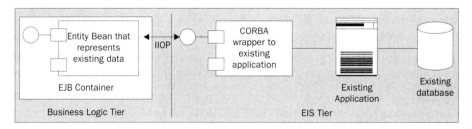

We will address the topic of using entity beans to represent existing data later in this chapter. In the next section we will consider the third issue: using EJBs to represent the functionality of existing applications in the J2EE architecture in a common way.

Using EJBs to Represent the Functionality of Existing Applications in the J2EE Architecture

So, we've now realized that EJBs are not appropriate for wrapping existing applications. Next we will discuss how appropriate EJBs are to represent the functionality of existing applications through interfaces on the business logic tier of the J2EE integration architecture. As we have identified in Chapter 9 we will use:

❏   **Lower-level virtual components** to expose lower-level APIs provided by existing applications

❏   **Higher-level virtual components** to expose high-level business-oriented interfaces

Existing applications, that already provide APIs, use a variety of different technologies to access these APIs. Lower-level virtual components are meant to mask these technology differences and present them on the business logic tier, so that J2EE clients can access them without knowing anything of these differences.

> **EJBs are not appropriate for developing lower-level virtual components.**

As a result of the programming restrictions (that we've mentioned earlier in this chapter), EJBs cannot use proprietary libraries, they cannot access native code, or communicate with proprietary protocols. They are therefore not appropriate for masking the technology differences.

Higher-level virtual components raise the abstraction of the methods to the level of business operations. Therefore we say that higher-level virtual components expose business-oriented interfaces. Higher-level virtual components will aggregate the behavior of lower-level virtual components and provide a higher abstraction level of functionality of existing applications. Higher-level virtual components will, on one side, expose high-level business methods to the clients. On the other side they will translate high-level methods into a series of calls to lower-level virtual components.

> **Session beans and message-driven beans are appropriate for developing higher-level virtual components.**

The difference between session and message-driven beans relates to the way in which J2EE clients access them. J2EE clients access session beans in a synchronous way, through remote method invocation, using RMI-IIOP or CORBA. Clients that access session beans have to wait for the session bean to complete the invoked method. Clients cannot do other tasks during remote method invocation (unless they use a different thread). Session beans are therefore appropriate for request/response operations (also sometimes called read operations) that require an immediate answer. Usually session beans will use RMI-IIOP or CORBA to access existing applications too, but this is not necessarily the case (they might also use JMS, JCA, or other J2EE technologies).

For communication with message-driven beans, J2EE clients use message-oriented middleware (MOM) through JMS. Message-driven beans are JMS message consumers; clients access them asynchronously, sending them a message. After they send a message, clients can continue with other work and do not have to wait for the message-driven bean to completes the process. Message-driven beans are appropriate for operations that might take longer to process and do not require an immediate response (update operations). Message-driven beans can use JMS, RMI-IIOP, CORBA, JCA, or other J2EE technologies, to access existing applications.

In the next figure we demonstrate a possible scenario in which two higher-level virtual components – a session and a message-driven bean, access lower-level virtual components, component wrappers, and APIs of existing applications. The session bean uses RMI-IIOP to access lower-level RMI-IIOP virtual component and CORBA to access a CORBA wrapper. Likewise, the message-driven bean uses CORBA to access a lower-level CORBA virtual component, and JMS to access an API of an existing application over MOM (note that not all possibilities are shown on this figure):

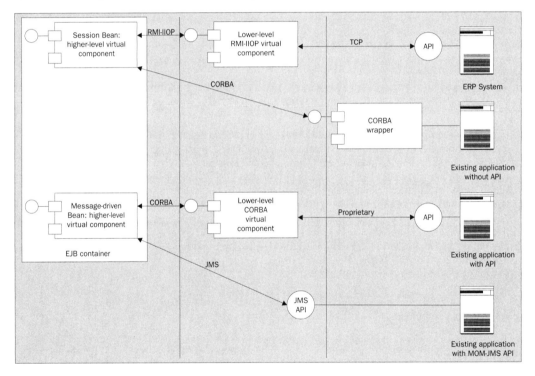

However, the challenge here is not only implementing the session and message-driven beans, but also how to define their interfaces. Remember that EJBs should expose business interfaces, and not the simple, low-level APIs of existing applications directly. Exposing APIs of existing applications through EJB interfaces directly may work at the beginning of the integration project, but will lead to considerable difficulties later. The APIs exposed by existing applications will barely meet the requirements of an integrated system and will usually not fit into the integrated information system as they are; they will usually be too low-level and too complex (but this will obviously depend on the quality and style of existing APIs). We have discussed this in Chapters 4 and 9.

It is therefore much better if we follow the integration process and define the global architecture together with the necessary interfaces. These interfaces will expose high-level, business-oriented methods. The EJB virtual components should therefore expose these methods rather than low-level functions, specific to existing applications. In this way we will achieve the business method level integration. Refer back to Chapter 9 for more information about how to define the interfaces and achieve business method level integration.

> **Reusing the functionality of existing applications with high-level EJBs that expose business methods through their interfaces adds great flexibility to our integration architecture.**

Specifically, clients will not see the complexity behind these business interfaces and will actually not be aware that there are existing applications in the background that do the actual work. Since most of the complexity remains hidden, the hidden components can be altered and/or replaced without the clients being bothered with the changes. This will give us a greater deal of flexibility when replacing and re-engineering existing applications. We will even be able to afford replacing existing applications part by part, as business needs dictate and as resources are available.

In this chapter we will address implementation activities and show how to develop different enterprise beans for the purpose of EAI. First, we should summarize some of the main points relevant to developing EJBs for integration to give context to what we will be demonstrating through examples.

Developing EJBs for Integration

EJBs fulfill two major roles in integration:

❏   Entity beans can be used to represent existing data

❏   Session and message-driven beans can be used for developing higher-level virtual components, which expose business methods to J2EE clients on the one side and reuse existing applications through lower-level virtual components, wrappers, or APIs on the other side:

    ❏   Session beans expose business methods to J2EE clients synchronously, through RMI-IIOP

    ❏   Message-driven beans expose business methods to J2EE clients asynchronously, using JMS

Accordingly, in the following sections of this chapter we will look at the scenarios that we discussed above:

❏   Using entity beans to represent existing data

❏   Using session beans to reuse functionality of existing applications

❏   Using message-driven beans to reuse functionality of existing applications

We will present examples of how to develop entity beans using bean-managed and container-managed persistence, and we will discuss when to use either type. We will show how to develop session and message-driven beans.

As we have seen in the previous discussion, all these beans will have to access existing applications (or databases). For this they will use a variety of technologies, most of which are covered in this book. This includes JDBC (Chapter 5) for accessing databases, and JMS (Chapter 8), CORBA (Chapter 10), RMI-IIOP (Chapter 11), and JCA (Chapter 13), for accessing APIs, wrappers, and lower-level virtual components. A demonstration of all of these possibilities is beyond the scope of this chapter, and the readers should refer to related chapters.

In addition to the development of entity, session, and message-driven beans, we will address the interoperability of EJBs with CORBA in this chapter in more detail. In this chapter, we will demonstrate how to access CORBA wrappers from within an entity, session, and message-driven bean.

Additionally, we'll discuss the performance considerations that are relevant to the use of EJBs for integration. When using EJBs for integration we have to deal with the problems of transaction and security integration too. More precisely, we have to find ways how to propagate transactional and security contexts from the J2EE platform to existing systems, and back. We will discuss these issues in Chapters 15 and 16.

First we will look at using EJBs for integration with existing data.

Using Entity Beans to Represent Existing Data

To represent the data from existing databases the most logical decision is to use entity beans, which are specifically intended to represent persistent data. We will first look at entity beans that access the existing databases directly. Although implementing entity beans is quite straightforward, connecting them to the existing database might prove to be difficult and, in practice, depends on the existing application and their databases.

Thus, how we use our entity beans depends on the type of data that we are accessing. Existing data can be stored in a variety of formats, including relational, object, hierarchical, network, flat files, or proprietary.

> **The format of existing data will dictate which of the two persistence models we will use.**

EJB provides two persistence models:

❑   **Bean-managed persistence (BMP)**

❑   **Container-managed persistence (CMP)**

The major difference between BMP and CMP is that with CMP the container takes care of persistence – it generates the necessary code for accessing the database, as its name suggests. Therefore we do not have to implement callback methods, such as `ejbLoad()`, `ejbStore()`, `ejbCreate()`, `ejbRemove()`, and `ejbFindXXX()`. This saves us some development effort and makes our EJBs more independent from the underlying data store. With CMP however we cannot access all databases, only relational databases. Using the CMP makes us rely on the object relational mapping provided by the container. This mapping can be implemented efficiently or not so efficiently, depending on the particular application server and EJB version we are using.

Even when using relational databases we can hit the limits of CMP. If we would like to present data that is partitioned through many different relational database tables in a single entity bean, requiring special tasks to be matched together, we might hit the limitations of CMP mappings. But it is worth noting that the CMP 2.0 model, part of the EJB 2.0 specification, provides a much more powerful relational mapping than CMP 1.1 did.

On the other hand, when using BMP we have to manually develop the code necessary for accessing existing databases, so we are not limited to relational databases and we can access data in other formats. We can even access the data through APIs, either those already provided by existing applications, or through wrappers added later.

If we have the choice between CMP and BMP we should choose CMP, mainly because it requires less development effort, and it also opens the door to container-managed optimizations. If we use a good application server the CMP should work faster and more efficiently than the average implemented BMP. Containers can implement several optimizations that would require a lot of effort to implement manually, the most important of which include:

❑   Generating optimized SQL for database access

❑   Reducing the number of database accesses

❑   Monitoring the bean's state to do only partial load/stores (and therefore not storing the data if it hasn't been changed)

❑   Implementing lazy bean loading

> **EJB 2.0 specification introduced the CMP 2.0 model that established significant changes.**

In fact, the changes in the latest version of CMP were so dramatic that all EJB 2.0-compliant application servers are now required to support both CMP 1.1 and CMP 2.0 models. The CMP 2.0 model is based on getter and setter methods, which handle persistent fields, rather than on the fields directly (therefore it is sometimes called method-based CMP). This makes it much more flexible, because in the methods the container can do additional tasks, such as looking into different relational tables. The CMP 2.0 model is also much more suitable for optimizations, and can easily inspect the state changes and supervise the relationships, as we will see a little later.

In this chapter we will present both CMP 2.0 and CMP 1.1 entity beans.

How to Define Entity Beans

When we develop new EJB applications, we will typically first create the design, and then define the entity beans based on this design. However, when we develop EJBs for integration purposes we are faced with an existing database schema.

It is very rare that the existing database schema will correspond to the requirements of the newly integrated system. In particular, when we are faced with an existing relational schema it is often a bad idea to map the tables directly to entity beans.

> **Modeling EJBs directly on the existing database schema is not recommended.**

Most importantly, existing database schemas will in many cases not represent the data in a format that is suitable for the newly integrated information system. Moreover, this approach would result in a large number of entity beans having fine-grained interfaces. Such beans would have many references to each other resulting in a complicated graph of connected objects thereby making the system less flexible and not adaptable in nature. Clearly this is contradictory to the requirements of EAI.

Mapping other database schemas, like object, network, or hierarchical databases would result in similar problems. For instance, objects stored in object databases should not be mapped directly to entity beans because objects are more finely grained than EJBs and have too many relationships.

Consequently, to define the entity beans we should go the opposite way. We should first analyze the integrated information system as we would like to have it, then we should build the design model and use it as a basis for defining the entity beans. Only then we should consider how these entity beans map to the existing databases.

> **The design of the entity beans should be oriented towards the requirements of the new system rather than the databases of existing applications.**

This approach will result in beans that offer cleaner interfaces and that fit into the enterprise architecture. Re-engineering such beans will also be quite straightforward. That way we will also easily identify which methods should be placed in the entity beans and which should be delegated to session or message-driven beans.

To decide which methods we should include in entity beans we can follow some simple guidelines:

❑ The entity bean should include methods that are self-contained – business-level components that are perfectly suitable to implement business logic that operate on the data contained on the entity bean.

❑ The methods should not introduce too many relationships to other entity beans – methods that introduce relationships to other entity beans are not self-contained and should be moved to session or message-driven beans. Dependencies between entity beans also introduce performance overhead. Therefore this is valid particularly for entity beans with remote interfaces.

❑ The entity bean should not manage workflows – entity beans are meant to represent a shared, transactional persistent state. For modeling workflows, session and message-driven beans should be used.

Remember that EJBs are middle tier components. The pre-EJB 2.0 entity beans had remote interfaces only – they did not have any notion of *local interfaces*. They also did not provide support for relationships between enterprise beans. So it is clear that the way in which we model entity beans depends of the EJB version we will use. Therefore, in the next two subsections we will discuss entity beans with remote and with local interfaces and offer guidelines with which the EAI developer will be able to choose the most appropriate interfaces and will design the operations in the interfaces appropriately.

Entity Beans with Remote Interfaces

EJB 1.1 entity beans and EJB 2.0 entity beans with remote interfaces expose their functionality through remote interfaces and should have coarse-grained interfaces. They should be self-contained with reduced relationships to the other EJBs. The coarse-grained remote interfaces effectively minimize the remote method overhead because the clients need to invoke a lower number of method invocations with coarse-grained interfaces (compared to fine-grained interfaces).

We should also minimize the relationships between the entity beans. When a client accesses a certain bean, the container will have to instantiate it. For this it will have to identify a free instance and load the state from the database. However, the container will also have to load all the related beans in case they are needed. If there are many relationships between beans, this can result in heavy loading efforts, thus reducing performance.

It is true that application servers can optimize loading of related beans by implementing strategies like lazy loading. With lazy loading, the container loads only the required bean and holds activation of related beans until they are really needed.

Entity Beans with Local Interfaces

The EJB 2.0 specification introduced local interfaces for enterprise beans. Local interfaces do not have the overhead of remote interfaces, because the communication does not go through the stubs and skeletons and there is no marshaling overhead. However, local interfaces are limited to the communication with other beans that have to be deployed in the same container (in the same JVM).

Local interfaces are an ideal concept for entity beans – they can have a fine-grained interface without any performance drawbacks. This does not mean that we should model the entity beans after the existing database schemas; it simply means that we can afford more fine-grained components.

Fine-grained components almost always introduce relationships with other components. In EJB 2.0, when using the CMP 2.0, the container manages the relationships through abstract methods that we define in the entity bean implementation class. We further define these relationships in the deployment descriptor. This gives the container enough information to perform several optimizations, including lazy loading. The design of CMP 2.0 entity beans with local interfaces is thus quite different to other entity beans.

However, as already mentioned, local interfaces limit the communication to clients that exist in the same JVM. In other words, clients from other tiers will not be able to access entity beans with local interfaces directly. As we will see, accessing entity beans directly from other tiers is not advisable anyway.

Distributed Façade

As we have seen, entity beans can expose remote interfaces through which clients from other tiers or from other containers can access them. Although this adds a lot of flexibility, it also introduces a considerable overhead and makes entity beans poorly scalable. In addition to the overhead of remote method invocations the direct access to entity beans requires database lookups. The database is shared with existing applications, thus the entity bean has to do a database lookup for each remote method invocation (unless done within a transaction). For a complete discussion of performance and scalability of EJB please refer to Chapter 15 of the book *Professional EJB* from Wrox Press.

The first problem with clients from other tiers (particularly the client and web component tiers) that access entity beans directly arises from the nature of entity beans. Entity beans store shared transactional data, so clients will access them to perform a certain business task or process. If the clients from user interface tiers access entity beans directly, it implicitly means that they include some business logic. This will become clearer with an example.

Consider a scenario in which we need to model orders as entity beans. Each order needs several order items, which will represent the number of products that have been ordered. Each order item will therefore have to be related to the product as well. This results in the following entity beans: `Order`, `OrderItem`, and `Product`. The relations and possible methods are presented in the following class diagram:

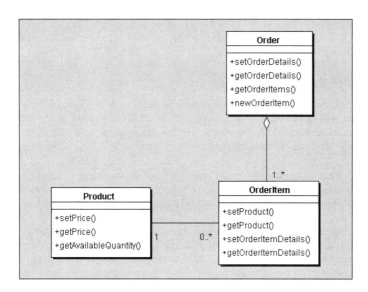

Suppose that the task is to calculate the sum of all orders. If this task is performed by the client from the user interface or web component tier, some code would have to be placed in the client on that tier to perform the following: we would iterate through all `Orders`, for each `Order` we would have to access all `OrderItems`, then for each `OrderItem` access the `Product` to get the price, and then multiply and sum. The code in the client would look similar to this:

```
...
Collection myOrders;
Collection myOrderItems;
Iterator myOrderIter;
Iterator myOrderItemIter;
Order myOrder;
OrderItem myOrderItem;
OrderItemDetails myOrderItemDetails;
Product myProduct;
double myPrice, myQuantity;
...
myOrderIter = myOrders.iterator ();
for (int i=0; i<myOrders.size(); i++ ) {
   myOrder = (Order) PortableRemoteObject.narrow
                        (myOrderIter.next (), Order.class);
   myOrderItems = myOrder.getOrderItems();
   myOrderItemIter = myOrderItems.iterator ();
   for (int j=0; j<myOrderItems.size(); j++ ) {
      myOrderItem = (OrderItem) PortableRemoteObject.narrow
                    (myOrderItemIter.next (), OrderItem.class);
      myOrderItemDetails = myOrderItem.getOrderItemDetails();
      myProduct = myOrderItemDetails.prod;
      myPrice = myProduct.getPrice();
      myQuantity = myOrderItemDetails.quantity;

      // multiply and add
   }
}
...
```

First of all, all the method invocations would have to be remote – the client from another tier cannot use local interfaces. Therefore in the above code excerpt we have marked the remote invocations bold. The above example already uses a coarse-grained interface. This is why it does not use several getter methods to acquire the necessary, but rather invokes the `getOrderItemDetails()` method, where a Value Object `OrderDetails`, that includes all the relevant information, is returned to the client. Remember, Value Objects are serializable Java objects that are sent to the client by value and instantiated there. Usually they include attributes that represent state and methods that work on these attributes, such as getter and setter methods, but also methods that perform input validation.

The Value Object `OrderDetails` might look like this:

```
import java.util.Date;

public class OrderDetails implements java.io.Serializable {
    public String customer;
    public Date orderDate;
    public Date deliveryDate;
    public String deliveryAddress;

    public boolean setDeliveryDate(Date deliveryDate) {
        if (deliveryDate.compareTo(orderDate)>=0) {
            this.deliveryDate = deliveryDate;
            return true;
        } else
            return false;
    }

    public Date getDeliveryDate() {
        return this.deliveryDate;
    }

    // Similar for other getter / setter methods
    ...
}
```

Although the client uses Value Objects to minimize the number of remote method invocations, there are still a large number of invocations needed to sum up the orders. For one hundred orders with ten items per order the client needs 2100 remote methods invocations. So we can see that the number of remote method invocations will increase dramatically in a real-world system where one hundred orders is not actually very much. We will more likely have some few hundred thousand orders in a typical large enterprise-scale system.

The large number of remote method invocations is not the only problem. Maybe an even bigger problem is transactional integrity. Designed like we have described, the only way to start a transaction, inside which the whole procedure should be performed, is from the client. Demarcating transactions from the client or web component tier is highly discouraged and brings several problems to the design. Starting a transaction from the client tier is also only possible explicitly – that is, programmatically. This way we cannot use declarative transaction management, one of the benefits of EJBs.

Even if we don't use transactions programmatically from the client, we are faced with problems. The first question is how to set the transaction attribute for the entity beans. Basically we can decide to use or not to use declarative transaction management. If we decide to use it, then each method invocation to the entity bean will start a new transaction. After starting the transaction the container will have to reload the state of the entity bean from the database, invoking the `ejbLoad()` method. This is necessary to ensure that the data has not changed directly in the database by some legacy or existing application.

Popular application servers have a toggle with which we can specify whether or not the database is shared with existing applications. If we say it is not, then the database lookup would be saved. However, keep in mind that we are talking about integration with existing databases here, so this solution may not be applicable for us.

After the transaction is finished the container will have to store the changes, invoking the `ejbStore()` method. Again, some containers provide optimizations here – for example, declaring a bean as read-only, or monitoring the changes of the state (particularly in EJB 2.0). Again, this will not solve our problem completely though.

The question we need to ask in order to solve our problem is whether or not the logic for summing up all orders should be placed in the client. This delegates some business responsibilities to the client, making it complicated. This also means that this logic would have to be placed in all different clients, making it closely coupled and very difficult to maintain the system. We should also keep in mind that placing the logic within the client increases network traffic considerably.

So, the best decision would be to place the business logic in the middle tier – the EJB tier. For this we can use a session or a message-driven bean. In EJB 2.0 we could also define home methods in entity bean remote home interfaces. The client would then invoke a simple method to sum up all the orders and receive the result. We could even use declarative transaction management, which would greatly reduce the number of database hits, ultimately making our system more flexible.

> **Such beans are called façade beans, because they provide a façade to distributed clients. The façade beans are modeled on the façade pattern, and this is one of the most important approaches that each EJB developer should be familiar with.**

For more information on façade patterns, please refer to the book *Design Patterns* by Erich Gamma, *et al.*, from Addison-Wesley, ISBN 0-201-63361-2. For more information about façade beans look into the book *Professional EJB* from Wrox Press, or follow this URL: http://java.sun.com/j2ee/blueprints/design_patterns/.

In our example we would simply define an `OrderFacade` bean (session, for example) that would perform the role of the Façade pattern, as shown in the figure below:

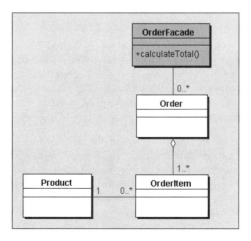

The distributed façade has several advantages:

- ❏ It exposes fewer (and coarser) grained interfaces to the clients

- ❏ It decouples the clients and the entity beans, which increases flexibility and maintainability

- ❏ It represents a transactional boundary, therefore enables declarative transaction management – the transaction can now be started declaratively on the façade, and the transaction does not spawn the client (or web component) tier anymore

- ❏ It improves the performance

The performance improvements are particularly important. A distributed façade enables calculating the sum of all orders inside a single transaction. This means that at the beginning of the transaction, locks are placed on all involved data in the database. The container places the locks, so it can be sure that no legacy application will change the data directly in that time. This reduces the number of times the `ejbLoad()` method has to be invoked on each bean, and also reduces the number of database updates.

The Façade pattern also greatly reduces the number of remote method invocations from the client tier to the EJB tier – from several thousand to only one. But we have to be aware that all those method invocations still have to be performed. The façade bean will have to call all the related entity beans.

With EJB 1.1 the façade bean must use the same remote interfaces to access entity beans. This would still have the overhead of remote invocation but speeds up the process because of transaction and database optimizations, mentioned previously. Several containers also optimize remote invocations inside the same container and bypass the stubs and skeletons. Examples of such containers include:

- ❏ WebLogic – http://www.bea.com/products/weblogic/server/index.shtml

- ❏ WebSphere – http://www-4.ibm.com/software/webservers/appserv/

- ❏ JBoss – http://www.jboss.org/jboss-overview.jsp

The other possibility we have with EJB 1.1 is not to model all fine-grained data objects as entity beans, but as simple Java objects instead, which brings us to the concept of **dependent objects**. Dependant objects do not expose remote interfaces; thus, they can only be accessed from the entity beans that created them. However, this also means that the entity bean can use local method invocations to access dependent objects, thereby speeding the performance. In our example we could model the `OrderItem` as a dependent object. It is highly unlikely that somebody would have to remotely access `OrderItem` without going through the `Order`. `Order` would, however, be able to access `OrderItem`s with local method invocations.

With EJB 2.0 we can use local interfaces for communication between the façade bean and entity beans deployed in the same container, and thus minimize the overhead. Remember, entity beans can have both local and remote interfaces, so this also does not compromise them.

However, many developers consider remote interfaces for entity beans as superfluous – exactly because of the fact that it is not wise to communicate with entity beans remotely. In many cases the decision could be to use only local interfaces for entity beans. The reason for remote interfaces concerns the need for communication between different containers in which entity beans can be deployed, and for clustering.

After familiarizing ourselves with how to define the interfaces of entity beans, let's have a look at the primary keys.

Primary Keys

Entity beans represent shared, transactional data. To access the data through entity beans, clients will first have to locate them and, as such, the entity beans need a unique identity. This identity is called the primary key and has a similar function as primary keys in relational databases.

Primary keys for entity beans are defined as Java classes that include the necessary information to uniquely identify them. For this purpose we can use existing Java classes like `java.lang.Integer`. We can also write our own classes for more complex primary keys. Note that the primary key attributes must be serializable.

For primary key classes we should implement the `equals()` and `hashCode()` operations and override the default implementations to guarantee correct comparison of keys. When using CMP we should also provide a constructor without any arguments because the container will need to create primary keys when necessary.

The major question we need to answer is how to define the primary key. In most cases the data will already have the primary key (particularly when dealing with relational data). If they don't we will almost always be able to find unique attributes, or a combination of them, that we can use for the primary key.

If we cannot identify a primary key from the existing data we will have to implement a synthetic key ourselves. One of the possibilities is to use a bean that creates primary keys from the data.

Implementing an Entity Bean to Access Existing Data

Now that we are familiar with the theory of entity beans, let's try to implement an entity bean that will access the database directly. To implement an entity bean we have to follow several steps:

❑   Define the component interface

❑   Define the home interface

❑   Define the primary key class

❑   Develop the implementation class

❑   Write the deployment descriptor

We will implement an entity bean to represent the customer data from our cell phone operator integration example, using the (fictional) relational database of the existing customer information application.

In the database the following data exists for each customer:

❑   Customer ID

❑   Name

❑   Address

❑   Number of phone accounts

First we will have a look at how to build a CMP 2.0 entity bean. We will use CMP to access the existing database directly and will presume that the existing data is in relational tables and that the mapping is straightforward. Let's start with the component interface.

Defining the Component Interface

In the component interface we will define the methods that will be accessed by clients. These methods will include getter and setter methods for attributes, but may also include other business logic methods, as we have identified earlier. For the needs of our example, we will show just the getter and setter methods.

As we have seen, an entity bean can have a remote or local interface – or both. Which interface to choose is actually a relatively simple decision. If remote clients will need to access the entity bean directly then we will have to implement the remote interface. We also need to be aware that remote clients can be other beans, like session and message-driven beans that are deployed in a remote container.

Note that the source code for all the examples in this book is available for download from http://www.wrox.com/. The first attempt to define the remote component interface of our example looks like the following:

```
package cmp1;

import javax.ejb.EJBObject;
import java.rmi.RemoteException;

public interface Customer extends EJBObject {

  public String getCustomerPrimaryKey() throws RemoteException;
  public String getCustomerName() throws RemoteException;
  public void setCustomerName(String name) throws RemoteException;
  public String getCustomerAddress() throws RemoteException;
  public void setCustomerAddress(String address) throws RemoteException;
  public int getCustomerNoOfPhoneAccounts() throws RemoteException;
  public void setCustomerNoOfPhoneAccounts(int noOfPhAcc) throws
                                             RemoteException;

}
```

This interface however has several disadvantages: in particular, the fine-grained approach is not suitable for remote interfaces. This approach requires many remote invocations, which adds too much overhead, and is therefore not effective.

So, it might be a good idea to add the coarse-grained method that would enable us to access and set all the attributes in one method invocation. Notice that in production systems we would usually have a much larger number of attributes than the four presented here. Instead of listing all attributes one by one we will introduce a Value Object, which is a regular Java object that should be serializable so that it can be transferred by value. It holds all the attributes and can also hold some methods, like getter and setter methods. These methods can also perform validation.

Therefore we will add the following two methods to the component interface:

```
...
  public CustomerData getCustomerData() throws RemoteException;
  public void setCustomerData(CustomerData custData) throws RemoteException;
...
```

We will also need to declare the Value Object `CustomerData`. The declaration will look like this:

```
package cmp1;

public class CustomerData implements java.io.Serializable {

  public String customerId = null;
  public String name = null;
  public String address = null;
  public int noOfPhoneAccounts = 0;

  public CustomerData () {
  }

  public CustomerData (String id, String nm, String ad, int na) {
    customerId = id;
    name = nm;
    address = ad;
    noOfPhoneAccounts = na;
  }

  public String getCustomerId() {
    return customerId;
  }
  public void setCustomerId(String id) {
    if (customerId==null)
      customerId = id;
  }

  public String getName() {
    return name;
  }
  public void setName(String nm) {
    name = nm;
  }

  public String getAddress() {
    return address;
  }
  public void setAddress(String ad) {
    address = ad;
  }

  public int getNoOfPhoneAccounts() {
    return noOfPhoneAccounts;
  }
  public void setNoOfPhoneAccounts(int pa) {
    noOfPhoneAccounts = pa;
  }

}
```

From the performance perspective it is not wise to access entity beans from clients in other tiers. Rather, the entity beans should be accessed through façade beans, which implement the Façade pattern – these can be session or message-driven beans (refer to the *Distributed Façade* subsection earlier in this chapter). Sometimes we know that these beans will be deployed in the same container as the entity beans, in which case it makes no sense to use the remote interface to access entity beans. Rather, we utilize the local interface.

We have also learned the ways in which local and remote interfaces differ, so there is no need for them to provide the same set of methods. The methods in the local interface must not throw remote exceptions, the parameters are transferred by reference rather than by value and we do not need to use the `PortableRemoteObject.narrow()` to cast object references, but just native Java casting. It is actually the deployment descriptor in which we tie together the interfaces and the implementation code.

Returning to our example, we will keep the local interface the same as the remote (which will make the explanation later a little shorter). The local interface for our example looks like this:

```
package cmp1;

import javax.ejb.EJBLocalObject;

public interface Customer extends EJBLocalObject {

  public String getCustomerPrimaryKey();
  public String getCustomerName();
  public void setCustomerName(String name);
  public String getCustomerAddress();
  public void setCustomerAddress(String address);
  public int getCustomerNoOfPhoneAccounts();
  public void setCustomerNoOfPhoneAccounts(int noOfPhAcc);

  public CustomerData getCustomerData();
  public void setCustomerData(CustomerData custData);

}
```

Having defined the component interface, next we will define the home interface.

Defining the Home Interface

The home interface provides methods to create and find entity beans. With EJB 2.0 the home interface can provide some business methods that are not related to a particular bean instance. We can use this for implementing the Distributed Façade pattern instead of using session or message-driven beans.

Let's first concentrate on the create and finder methods. The `create()` method will usually take the parameters that will set the initial state. We have to be aware that this method also creates the records in the underlying database, and we can overload it.

> *Sometimes it's not actually necessary to define the `create()` method. For example, if we were to access the existing data through EJBs, but do not add new data (therefore the only way to add new data would be by using the existing application), then we wouldn't need a `create()` method. However, in most cases it is useful to provide this method, even if it is not immediately required. In fact, such precaution makes future integration and development easier since most of the basics will already be in place.*

557

Then we have to define the finder methods. Each entity bean has to have at least one finder method that enables locating of the bean by the primary key. We can add several other finder methods that will return more than one entity bean as a result.

For our example we will define two create methods, one that takes the parameters one by one as arguments, and one that takes the four constituents of the Value Object (CustomerData) as arguments. We will also define two finder methods: one will locate entity beans by the primary key, and the other will locate them by name. The latter will return a Collection because it can happen that several customers have the same name.

We have already shown remote and local component interfaces for the Customer component. Now, we will show remote and local home interfaces for the Customer component. First, the remote home interface is presented below:

```
package cmp1;

import javax.ejb.CreateException;
import javax.ejb.EJBHome;
import javax.ejb.FinderException;
import java.util.Collection;
import java.rmi.RemoteException;

public interface CustomerHome extends EJBHome {

  public Customer create(String customerId, String name, String address,
                      int noOfPhAcc) throws RemoteException, CreateException;
  public Customer create(CustomerData custData)
                                throws RemoteException, CreateException;

  public Customer findByPrimaryKey(String primaryKey)
                                throws RemoteException, FinderException;
  public Collection findByName(String name)
                                throws RemoteException, FinderException;

}
```

The local home interface again differs in details. There should be no remote exceptions declared and it should extend the EJBLocalHome instead of EJBHome:

```
package cmp1;

import javax.ejb.CreateException;
import javax.ejb.EJBLocalHome;
import javax.ejb.FinderException;
import java.util.Collection;

public interface CustomerHome extends EJBLocalHome {

  public Customer create(String customerId, String name, String address,
                                int noOfPhAcc) throws CreateException;
  public Customer create(CustomerData custData) throws CreateException;
```

```
    public Customer findByPrimaryKey(String primaryKey)
                                     throws FinderException;
    public Collection findByName(String name) throws FinderException;

}
```

It's important to be aware that using remote finder methods that return a large number of entity beans (as a `Collection`), is not actually effective, particularly if all we want is just to access a single or a few attributes (such as name, for example). This would result in a large overhead. A much better idea is to use Value Objects and construct a Value Object with all the necessary data on the EJB tier and return that object only. The corresponding pattern is referred to as Value Object Assembler by Sun. Take a look at the book *Core J2EE Patterns: Best Practices and Design Strategies*, from Prentice Hall, ISBN 0-13-064884-1, or the URL http://java.sun.com/j2ee/blueprints/design_patterns/.

Defining the Primary Key Class

We already know why each entity bean requires a primary key – this is the identification of the entity bean to the clients primary key can be simple, as in our example, where we have used `String`. They can also be more complicated, constituted from several attributes (which are sometimes called composite keys). After identifying the primary key, we have to define a primary key class, which must follow certain rules:

❑　The attributes have to be unique for each bean

❑　The attributes have to be legal RMI/IDL types, which means that they must be serializable over RMI-IIOP

❑　The primary key has to implement the `hashCode()` and `equals()` methods so that they return suitable results

When using CMP, the primary key class must comply with some additional rules:

❑　It has to provide a public constructor without arguments

❑　A naming convention should be followed: the public attribute in the primary key should correspond to the equivalent attributes (used in get/set methods) of the entity bean implementation class

> **For our example we will use the Social Security Number (SSN) as the primary key for the customer (`CustomerId`).**

After we have defined the primary key we can continue with the development of the implementation class.

Developing the Implementation Class for CMP

The implementation class is the place where we provide implementations for all the methods from the component (local and/or remote) interface. In the implementation class we also implement the methods from the home interface and the required container callback methods. These include: `ejbLoad()`, `ejbStore()`, `ejbActivate()`, `ejbPassivate()`, `setEntityContext()`, `unsetEntityContext()`, `ejbCreate()`, `ejbRemove()`, and `ejbFindXXX()` methods. In addition to that, we also define the attributes. If we use CMP in EJB 2.0 we have to define abstract getter and setter methods for all persistent attributes, as we will see soon.

If we use CMP we will not have to implement all the mentioned methods; the container will provide implementations for `ejbLoad()` and `ejbStore()`. The same is true for `ejbFindXXX()` methods. However, we will have to specify additional information in the deployment descriptor. There we will have to define the persistent attributes and express the finder semantics using the EJB QL, which we will see a little later. At deployment we will also have to provide the exact mapping from persistent attributes to the database schema.

To implement the class for our Customer bean we will define the `CustomerBean` abstract class that implements the `EntityBean` interface. The class has to be abstract because the container will implement several methods, as we will see a little later. We will declare a private attribute to store the context and an empty constructor:

```
package cmp1;

import javax.ejb.*;

abstract public class CustomerBean implements EntityBean {

  private EntityContext ctx;

  public CustomerBean() {
  }
```

Notice that the implementation class is not explicitly tied to the remote or local component or home interfaces – there is no explicit connection between them. The fact is that the clients do not interact with bean implementation objects directly. Rather, the interaction with the component interface goes through `EJBObject` and `EJBLocalObject` objects. The first is a remote RMI-IIOP object, the second is a local object. These objects serve as interception points, where several container services are performed prior to *delegating* the request to the implementation object. The communication goes through `EJBHome` and `EJBLocalHome` objects in a very similar way.

This is also why the methods defined inside the bean implementation class do not explicitly throw remote exceptions. We also tie the implementation class to the local and/or remote interface in the deployment descriptor.

To continue with the implementation of our entity bean implementation class we have to define the container-managed attributes. In EJB 2.0, using CMP we have to define pairs of getter and setter methods for each attribute. At bean deployment the container will provide implementations for these methods. This is why we have to declare these methods abstract. This is also the reason why the whole class is declared abstract:

```
  // Container-managed fields
  abstract public String getCustomerId();
  abstract public void setCustomerId(String customerID);
  abstract public String getName();
  abstract public void setName(String name);
  abstract public String getAddress();
  abstract public void setAddress(String address);
  abstract public int getNoOfPhoneAccounts();
  abstract public void setNoOfPhoneAccounts(int noOfPhAcc);
```

In the next step we have to provide the implementations of the methods from the component interface. Note that our entity bean is relatively simple, so the implementation of these methods will also be simple. The fine-grained methods for get/set attributes will be implemented with simple method calls to the abstract getter/setter methods, defined earlier:

```
// Component interface
public String getCustomerPrimaryKey() {
  return getCustomerId();
}
public String getCustomerName() {
  return getName();
}
public void setCustomerName(String name) {
  setName(name);
}
public String getCustomerAddress() {
  return getAddress();
}
public void setCustomerAddress(String address) {
  setAddress(address);
}
public int getCustomerNoOfPhoneAccounts() {
  return getNoOfPhoneAccounts();
}
public void setCustomerNoOfPhoneAccounts(int noOfPhAcc) {
  setNoOfPhoneAccounts(noOfPhAcc);
}
```

We cannot simply expose the abstract get/set methods that will be implemented by the container, in the interface. This is why we had to add methods with a similar name in the component interface. In addition, we have also defined two coarse-grained methods, which use the Value Object CustomerData. Their implementation is as follows:

```
public CustomerData getCustomerData() {
  CustomerData cd = new CustomerData();
  cd.setCustomerId(getCustomerId());
  cd.setName(getName());
  cd.setAddress(getAddress());
  cd.setNoOfPhoneAccounts(getNoOfPhoneAccounts());
  return cd;
}

public void setCustomerData(CustomerData cd) {
  setCustomerId(cd.getCustomerId());
  setName(cd.getName());
  setAddress(cd.getAddress());
  setNoOfPhoneAccounts(cd.getNoOfPhoneAccounts());
}
```

Then we have to implement the methods for the home interface. We do not need to implement the ejbFindXXX() methods, but we do need to implement the ejbCreate() methods. As mentioned above, in our example we have two different methods, one that takes arguments one by one, and the four constituents of the Value Object (CustomerData) as arguments. The implementation is like this:

```
    // home methods
    public String ejbCreate(String customerId, String name, String address,
                                    int noOfPhAcc) throws CreateException {
      setCustomerId(customerId);
      setName(name);
      setAddress(address);
      setNoOfPhoneAccounts(noOfPhAcc);
      return null;
    }

    public void ejbPostCreate(String customerId, String name,
                              String address, int noOfPhAcc) {
    }

    public String ejbCreate(CustomerData cd) throws CreateException {
      setCustomerId(cd.getCustomerId());
      setName(cd.getName());
      setAddress(cd.getAddress());
      setNoOfPhoneAccounts(cd.getNoOfPhoneAccounts());
      return null;
    }

    public void ejbPostCreate(CustomerData cd) {
    }
```

We also have to declare other EJB-related methods that we have mentioned before. Luckily we can leave them blank, because we will use CMP and the container will do this for us:

```
    public void setEntityContext(EntityContext ctx) {
      this.ctx = ctx;
    }

    public void unsetEntityContext() {
      this.ctx = null;
    }

    public void ejbActivate() {
    }

    public void ejbPassivate() {
    }

    public void ejbLoad() {
    }

    public void ejbStore() {
    }

    public void ejbRemove() throws RemoveException {
    }
  }
```

This makes the bean implementation complete. In the next step we have to define a suitable deployment descriptor.

Writing the Deployment Descriptor

In the deployment descriptor we have to provide all the necessary additional information required to deploy the enterprise bean in the container. We will not discuss the finer details of the deployment descriptor here, and readers who are not familiar with this area are advised to refer to some EJB-specific literature for more explanations, for example the *Professional EJB* book from Wrox Press.

To define the deployment descriptor we will create the `ejb-jar.xml` file in which we will specify all the general information regarding our bean:

```xml
<?xml version="1.0"?>

<!DOCTYPE ejb-jar PUBLIC "-//Sun Microsystems, Inc.//DTD Enterprise JavaBeans
2.0//EN" "http://java.sun.com/dtd/ejb-jar_2_0.dtd">

<ejb-jar>
  <enterprise-beans>
    <entity>
      <ejb-name>eai1_Customer</ejb-name>
      <home>cmp1.CustomerHome</home>
      <remote>cmp1.Customer</remote>
      <ejb-class>cmp1.CustomerBean</ejb-class>
```

Then we will specify the persistence type the bean uses – in our example this is CMP. We will also specify the primary key class, and whether or not the bean is re-entrant:

```xml
      <persistence-type>Container</persistence-type>
      <prim-key-class>java.lang.String</prim-key-class>
      <reentrant>False</reentrant>
```

Then we will define the CMP version we use and declare which attributes should be container-managed. Notice the naming convention for the attributes – the names have to be the same as those used in getter and setter methods in the implementation class:

```xml
      <cmp-version>2.x</cmp-version>
      <abstract-schema-name>CustomerBean</abstract-schema-name>
      <cmp-field>
        <field-name>customerId</field-name>
      </cmp-field>
      <cmp-field>
        <field-name>name</field-name>
      </cmp-field>
      <cmp-field>
        <field-name>address</field-name>
      </cmp-field>
      <cmp-field>
        <field-name>noOfPhoneAccounts</field-name>
      </cmp-field>
      <primkey-field>customerId</primkey-field>
```

Next we have to define the finder methods, namely the `findByName()` from the home interface. For this we will use the **EJB Query Language (EJB QL)** (again, refer to the Wrox book *Professional EJB* for more information about EJB QL). Here's what the query segment of the deployment descriptor looks like:

```
        <query>
          <query-method>
            <method-name>findByName</method-name>
            <method-params>
              <method-param>java.lang.String</method-param>
            </method-params>
          </query-method>
          <ejb-ql>
            <![CDATA[SELECT OBJECT(a) FROM CustomerBean AS a
                                WHERE a.name LIKE ?1]]>
          </ejb-ql>
        </query>
      </entity>
    </enterprise-beans>
```

Finally we have to declare the transaction attributes:

```
    <assembly-descriptor>
      <container-transaction>
        <method>
          <ejb-name>eai1_Customer</ejb-name>
          <method-intf>Remote</method-intf>
          <method-name>*</method-name>
        </method>
        <trans-attribute>Required</trans-attribute>
      </container-transaction>
    </assembly-descriptor>
  </ejb-jar>
```

This completes the deployment descriptor. It is, however, important to realize that there are several other possibilities that could be included, for example security – the authorization required to invoke methods.

The standard deployment descriptor does not specify everything needed to deploy the bean. Therefore at the deployment we will have to specify at least the following:

❏   The JNDI name of the entity bean

❏   The data source and the mapping of bean attributes to the database schema

❏   Several other deployment parameters, like the number of the beans in the pool, and so on

We will have to do this in a proprietary way, within deployment descriptors specific to the particular the application server that we use, or directly through the user interface upon deployment.

WebLogic-Specific Deployment Descriptors

For our demonstration, we will use BEA WebLogic for these examples. WebLogic requires that we specify these parameters in the `weblogic-ejb-jar.xml` file, where we also specify the name of the file where the mappings between bean attributes and database schema will be defined. In our case this will be another deployment descriptor – the `weblogic-cmp-rdbms-jar.xml` file.

In its most simple form, the `weblogic-ejb-jar.xml` file is shown opposite. It specifies the persistence type and use, specific to WebLogic, the file with relational mappings and the JNDI name of the bean:

```
<?xml version="1.0"?>

<!DOCTYPE weblogic-ejb-jar PUBLIC
"-//BEA Systems, Inc.//DTD WebLogic 6.0.0 EJB//EN"
"http://www.bea.com/servers/wls600/dtd/weblogic-ejb-jar.dtd" >

<weblogic-ejb-jar>
  <weblogic-enterprise-bean>

    <ejb-name>eai1_Customer</ejb-name>

    <entity-descriptor>
      <persistence>
        <persistence-type>
          <type-identifier>WebLogic_CMP_RDBMS</type-identifier>
          <type-version>6.0</type-version>
          <type-storage>META-INF/weblogic-cmp-rdbms-jar.xml</type-storage>
        </persistence-type>
        <persistence-use>
          <type-identifier>WebLogic_CMP_RDBMS</type-identifier>
          <type-version>6.0</type-version>
        </persistence-use>
      </persistence>
    </entity-descriptor>

    <jndi-name>eai1-CustomerHome</jndi-name>

  </weblogic-enterprise-bean>

</weblogic-ejb-jar>
```

The `weblogic-cmp-rdbms-jar.xml` file that specifies the mapping from entity bean attributes to the database schema is also shown below:

```
<?xml version="1.0"?>

<!DOCTYPE weblogic-rdbms-jar PUBLIC
 '-//BEA Systems, Inc.//DTD WebLogic 6.0.0 EJB RDBMS Persistence//EN'
 'http://www.bea.com/servers/wls600/dtd/weblogic-rdbms20-persistence-600.dtd'>

<weblogic-rdbms-jar>
  <weblogic-rdbms-bean>

    <ejb-name>eai1_Customer</ejb-name>
    <data-source-name>cellphone-pool</data-source-name>
    <table-name>customers</table-name>
    <field-map>
       <cmp-field>customerId</cmp-field>
       <dbms-column>cId</dbms-column>
    </field-map>
    <field-map>
       <cmp-field>name</cmp-field>
       <dbms-column>cName</dbms-column>
    </field-map>
    <field-map>
       <cmp-field>address</cmp-field>
       <dbms-column>cAddress</dbms-column>
    </field-map>
```

```
      <field-map>
        <cmp-field>noOfPhoneAccounts</cmp-field>
        <dbms-column>cNoAcc</dbms-column>
      </field-map>

  </weblogic-rdbms-bean>
</weblogic-rdbms-jar>
```

Notice that this entity bean uses the `cellphone-pool` data source and the table with the name `customers`. You should create such a database in order to run this example – you can see from above how each attribute is mapped to the database column. Furthermore, before deploying the bean, you should register the appropriate data source and connection pool (and associated JNDI names) with your application server. With WebLogic, this can be achieved very simply via the server console. Alternatively, you can amend the file `%WL_HOME%\config\mydomain\config.xml` accordingly. For example, adding the following entry will register the `cellphone-pool` data source with the corresponding Cloudscape database (which should be created too):

```
<JDBCDataSource JNDIName="cellphone-pool" Name="cellphone-pool"
                PoolName="Cloudscape" Targets="myserver"/>
```

For more information about WebLogic deployment descriptors, and how to create database tables, please refer to the following URLs: http://edocs.bea.com/wls/docs61/ejb/index.html and http://edocs.bea.com/wls/docs61/index.html.

Building and Deploying the Bean

Before we can deploy the bean we have to compile the classes that we have created. For this purpose, we have to set the PATH, CLASSPATH , and other environment variables according to the application server that we are using. We will compile the source code into the directory `build` using the following command:

Then we have to pack the EJB to the JAR file. The JAR file must include all necessary classes and deployment descriptors. For our example we will need two directories: `cmp1` and `META-INF`. We will create the `eai1_Customer.jar`, using the following command:

Note that because we use WebLogic here, we need to include the two additional deployment descriptors, discussed above, which can be found within the source code package for this book, downloadable from http://www.wrox.com/:

❑   .\META-INF\weblogic-cmp-rdbms-jar.xml

❑   .\META-INF\weblogic-ejb-jar.xml

As we have mentioned, the further steps in the deployment are application-server-specific. EJB developers should always refer to the appropriate application server documentation for instructions on how to deploy a bean. Typically this procedure will include invoking an EJB compiler or going through GUI interfaces.

Deployment to WebLogic

To deploy our entity bean to WebLogic we may first need to compile the JAR file created earlier, using the ejbc compiler (supplied with WebLogic). Note, however, that since WebLogic versions 6.0 and above, WebLogic will automatically run the ejbc compiler on deployment – so this step may well be overkill in some cases (see http://edocs.bea.com/wls/docs61/ejb/deploy.html for more details). For completeness, we can use the following command, in which we will compile the eai1_Customer.jar to get eai1_CustomerDep.jar:

The eai1_CustomerDep.jar file is now ready for deployment. Start the WebLogic Server, start the Default Console, enter the corresponding username and password, right-click on the EJB on the left hand side and select Install a new EJB....

Next, we browse to and enter the full path and filename to the eai1_CustomerDep.jar file, which in our case is: C:\ProEAI\Ch12\cmp1\eai1_CustomerDep.jar, and then Upload this file.

Important Deployment Parameters

There are also at least two important, application server specific, deployment parameters that we will have to specify:

❑   Whether the database is shared with existing applications

❑   Whether our entity beans are read-only

The first parameter defines whether or not the database we use is shared with existing applications. This parameter is important for the container to decide how many times it has to invoke the ejbLoad() and ejbStore() methods to load or update the state of the entity bean to the database. If the database is not shared, the container can save several loading/storing operations. To make the database not shared in BEA WebLogic, for example, we just have to set the db-is-shared deployment parameter to false.

In fact, when concerned with integration, the databases will usually be shared, so it is important not to choose the wrong setting – which would result in data inconsistency. For example, consider a bean that loads a state by activation only. In the meantime, the existing applications might change the data. The entity bean would not be aware of the change, and would overwrite the state by passivation.

The second parameter, whether our entity beans are read-only, specifies how the container will use the `ejbStore()` method. Sometimes we will use entity beans to represent the existing data only, and we will not make any modifications to the data. In this case, and if our application server supports it, we can define entity beans as read-only, which are never modified by an EJB client. They can, however, be modified directly through database access, most often by an existing application. The application server does not call the `ejbStore()` method on a read-only bean, thus improving the performance. In BEA WebLogic, for example, we can denote beans as read-only through the `concurrency-strategy` deployment parameter, which we have to set to `ReadOnly`. If our application server does not provide this option, we could do it ourselves by using BMP and not implementing the body of the `ejbStore()` method. Read-only entity beans cannot take part in transactions.

There is another interesting deployment parameter that we can specify. Sometimes the existing applications update the data only occasionally. If we know the interval when this happens, we might consider using this interval for performance improvement; again, this depends on whether our application server supports this. Therefore we have to define the interval in which the data is reread from the persistent storage. This saves database lookups, because the container can omit calling the `ejbLoad()` method too often. We could implement this approach ourselves, if the application server does not provide this option – but we should consider whether it's actually worth the additional coding.

Client Application for the Entity Bean

After a successful deployment we will want to test the entity bean. For this we will have to write a simple client. Here we present a client application that invokes some of the methods on the remote component interface of the entity bean (to test the local interface we would have to develop another enterprise bean and deploy them in the same container). Note that the JNDI name used in this example is `eai1-CustomerHome` as specified in the `weblogic-ejb-jar.xml`:

```
package cmp1;

import java.rmi.*;
import javax.rmi.*;
import java.util.*;

import javax.ejb.*;
import javax.naming.*;

public class Client {

  public Client() {
  }

  public static void main(String[] args) {
    System.out.println("EAI CMP1 client");
    System.out.println();

    try {
      // Creates a new instance
```

```
      Client client = new Client();

      // Invokes the example() method
      client.example();

    } catch (Exception e) {
      System.out.println(e);
    }
  }

  public void example() {
    try {
      // Creates initial naming context
      Context ctx = new InitialContext();

      // Resolves to the home object and narrows
      CustomerHome home = (CustomerHome)PortableRemoteObject.narrow(
        (CustomerHome)ctx.lookup("eai1-CustomerHome"), CustomerHome.class);

      // Creates a new bean
      Customer c = home.create("1","Matjaz","Wrox",5);

      // Invokes a method and writes the result to console
      System.out.println("Customer name is: "+c.getCustomerName());

      // Removes the bean
      c.remove();

    } catch(Exception e) {
      System.out.println(e);
    }
  }
}
```

First we have to compile the Client class, together with the required interfaces Customer and CustomerHome and the Value Object CustomerData. We can use the following command:

```
C:\WINNT\System32\cmd.exe                                              _ □ ×

C:\ProEAI\Ch12\cmp1>javac Customer.java CustomerHome.java CustomerData.java Clie
nt.java

C:\ProEAI\Ch12\cmp1>_
```

Next we can run our simple client program. We have to specify the initial naming factory and the naming provider URL properties. Here, we are using WebLogic on the local computer and, as such, the initial naming factory should be weblogic.jndi.WLInitialContextFactory and the naming provider URL t3://localhost:7001. Upon running the client we should get the following result:

```
C:\WINNT\System32\cmd.exe                                              _ □ ×

C:\ProEAI\Ch12\cmp1>java -classpath %WL_HOME%\lib\weblogic.jar;. -Djava.naming.f
actory.initial=weblogic.jndi.WLInitialContextFactory -Djava.naming.provider.url=
t3://localhost:7001 cmp1.Client
EAI CMP1 client

Customer name is: Matjaz

C:\ProEAI\Ch12\cmp1>_
```

Using EJB 1.1 CMP

It may happen that we will already have an application server that does not support the EJB 2.0 specification. In this case we will have to use EJB 1.1. This model differs considerably from CMP 2.0, so we'll take a brief look at it.

As we have stated, EJB 1.1 does not support local interfaces, therefore we can only define remote home and remote component interfaces. Although the interface definitions and the primary key are in fact the same as in EJB 2.0, the major differences are in the implementation class, where we have to define public attributes instead of the getter/setter methods. A simple EJB 1.1 entity bean implementation class looks like this:

```
package cmp1;

import javax.ejb.*;

public class CustomerBean implements EntityBean {

  private EntityContext ctx;

  public CustomerBean() {
  }

  // Container-managed fields
  public String customerId;
  public String name;
  public String address;
  public int noOfPhoneAccounts;

  // Component interface
  public String getCustomerPrimaryKey() {
    return customerId;
  }
  public String getCustomerName() {
    return name;
  }
  public void setCustomerName(String n) {
    name = n;
  }
  public String getCustomerAddress() {
    return address;
  }
  public void setCustomerAddress(String a) {
    address = a;
  }
  public int getCustomerNoOfPhoneAccounts() {
    return noOfPhoneAccounts;
  }
  public void setCustomerNoOfPhoneAccounts(int noOfPhAcc) {
    noOfPhoneAccounts = noOfPhAcc;
  }

  public CustomerData getCustomerData() {
```

```
  CustomerData cd = new CustomerData();
  cd.setCustomerId(customerId);
  cd.setName(name);
  cd.setAddress(address);
  cd.setNoOfPhoneAccounts(noOfPhoneAccounts);
  return cd;
}
public void setCustomerData(CustomerData cd) {
  customerId = cd.getCustomerId();
  name = cd.getName();
  address = cd.getAddress();
  noOfPhoneAccounts = cd.getNoOfPhoneAccounts();
}

public void setEntityContext(EntityContext ctx) {
  this.ctx = ctx;
}

public void unsetEntityContext() {
  this.ctx = null;
}

public void ejbActivate() {
}

public void ejbPassivate() {
}

public void ejbLoad() {
}

public void ejbStore() {
}

public void ejbRemove() throws RemoveException {
}

// home methods
public String ejbCreate(String cId, String n, String a, int noOfPhAcc)
                                        throws CreateException {
  customerId = cId;
  name = n;
  address = a;
  noOfPhoneAccounts = noOfPhAcc;
  return null;
}

public void ejbPostCreate(String cId, String n, String a, int noOfPhAcc) {
}

public String ejbCreate(CustomerData cd) throws CreateException {
  customerId = cd.getCustomerId();
  name = cd.getName();
  address = cd.getAddress();
```

```
      noOfPhoneAccounts = cd.getNoOfPhoneAccounts();
      return null;
   }

   public void ejbPostCreate(CustomerData cd) {
   }
}
```

Note that we use the Value Object in this entity bean, so there is no need to declare the same attributes and getter/setter methods in the entity bean once again. We can use inheritance to simplify the entity bean a little. We can extend the Value Object, the `CustomerData` in our case, and inherit the attributes and the getter/setter methods. If we expose the same methods through the component interface we have to be careful that we name the methods exactly the same (which is not the case in our example). Here's the relevant code excerpt:

```
package cmp1;

import javax.ejb.*;

public class CustomerBean extends CustomerData implements EntityBean {

   // Attributes and getter/setter methods inherited from the Value Object
   ...
   // Other methods
   ...
}
```

Modifying the Bean to Use BMP

Container-managed persistence cannot satisfy all the requirements of integration, particularly with more complex relational schemes and data stored in non-relational formats we quickly hit the limits of CMP. Then we are forced to use bean-managed persistence. With BMP we do not use the container persistence service, but implement the necessary methods ourselves. This goes particularly for `ejbLoad()` and `ejbStore()` methods, and we also have to implement the finder methods by hand.

However, there is no difference in the component or home interface definitions, so the majority of changes will focus on the implementation class and on the deployment descriptor, as we will see later.

So, let's see how to write the BMP implementation class `CustomerBean` for our example. As with the previous example, we will use the Value Object `CustomerData`. In general we have to declare attributes in the bean implementation class that will hold the persistent data. But because we use the Value Object, we can simply define a relation to the data object and use their attributes and getter/setter methods. This saves a little coding.

Our BMP implementation class thus looks like this:

```
package bmp;

import javax.ejb.*;
import java.util.*;
```

```
public class CustomerBean implements EntityBean {

  private EntityContext ctx;

  public CustomerBean() {
  }

  private CustomerData cd;
```

Then we have to define the component interface methods:

```
// Component interface
public String getCustomerPrimaryKey() {
  return cd.getCustomerId();
}
public String getCustomerName() {
  return cd.getName();
}
public void setCustomerName(String name) {
  cd.setName(name);
}
public String getCustomerAddress() {
  return cd.getAddress();
}
public void setCustomerAddress(String address) {
  cd.setAddress(address);
}
public int getCustomerNoOfPhoneAccounts() {
  return cd.getNoOfPhoneAccounts();
}
public void setCustomerNoOfPhoneAccounts(int noOfPhAcc) {
  cd.setNoOfPhoneAccounts(noOfPhAcc);
}

public CustomerData getCustomerData() {
  return cd;
}
public void setCustomerData(CustomerData cd) {
  this.cd = cd;
}
```

Next we will define the home methods. The `ejbCreate()` methods are very similar to the CMP example:

```
// home methods
public String ejbCreate(String customerId, String name,
              String address, int noOfPhAcc) throws CreateException {
  // Connect to the existing database
  // and create a new record
  // Store this record in the value object
  cd = new CustomerData();
  cd.setCustomerId(customerId);
  cd.setName(name);
```

```
      cd.setAddress(address);
      cd.setNoOfPhoneAccounts(noOfPhAcc);
      return customerId;
   }

   public void ejbPostCreate(String customerId, String name, String address,
                                                   int noOfPhAcc) {

   }

   public String ejbCreate(CustomerData cd) throws CreateException {
      // Connect to the existing database
      // and create a new record
      // Store this record in the value object
      this.cd = new CustomerData();
      this.cd = cd;
      return cd.getCustomerId();
   }

   public void ejbPostCreate(CustomerData cd) {
   }
```

We also have to implement the `ejbFindXXX()` methods, so we have to declare and implement both methods – the `ejbFindByPrimaryKey()` and `ejbFindByName()`. Here we will have to access the database using any appropriate mechanism, the most common of which is the use of JDBC. On the other hand, to access existing data we will sometimes have to use other approaches, including access to other types of databases or calling component wrappers for data access, which we will discuss later. We will not show the code to access a database using JDBC here, because it is rather trivial (refer to Chapter 5 for an example). It is worth noting, however, that from the performance perspective it is always good to use prepared statements with JDBC. The skeletons of the necessary methods look like this (the full working code is included with the download package):

```
   public String ejbFindByPrimaryKey(String pk)
                                 throws ObjectNotFoundException{

     // Access the existing database
     // Locate the record by primary key
     // Return the primary key
     return "1";
   }

   public Collection ejbFindByName(String name) {
     Vector v = new Vector();

     // Access the existing database
     // Locate the records
     // Add primary keys to the vector
     v.addElement("1");
     // Return the vector
     return v;
   }
```

Then we have to implement the `ejbLoad()` and `ejbStore()` methods where we will load and update the state to the database, respectively, using the same mechanism as the finder methods:

```
public void ejbLoad() {
  cd = new CustomerData();

  // Access the existing database and load the data

  // Store the data to the value object
  cd.setCustomerId("1");
  cd.setName("Matjaz");
  cd.setAddress("Wrox");
  cd.setNoOfPhoneAccounts(5);
}

public void ejbStore() {
  // Access the existing database
  // Update the data from the bean to the database
}
```

Finally we have to provide other EJB-related methods:

```
public void setEntityContext(EntityContext ctx) {
  this.ctx = ctx;
}

public void unsetEntityContext() {
  this.ctx = null;
}

public void ejbActivate() {
}

public void ejbPassivate() {
}

public void ejbRemove() throws RemoveException {
}
}
```

For a BMP entity bean we also have to define a deployment descriptor that differs a little from the CMP bean deployment descriptor. We do not have to specify all the details of container-managed attributes and the finder methods as we had to do with the CMP bean, so the deployment descriptor is actually rather simpler. The changes when compared to the CMP descriptor are highlighted. Note that the <resource-ref> element was not present in the case of the CMP descriptor:

```
<?xml version="1.0"?>

<!DOCTYPE ejb-jar PUBLIC
'-//Sun Microsystems, Inc.//DTD Enterprise JavaBeans 2.0//EN'
'http://java.sun.com/dtd/ejb-jar_2_0.dtd'>

<ejb-jar>
  <enterprise-beans>
    <entity>
```

575

```
                <ejb-name>eai2_Customer</ejb-name>
                <home>bmp.CustomerHome</home>
                <remote>bmp.Customer</remote>
                <ejb-class>bmp.CustomerBean</ejb-class>
                <persistence-type>Bean</persistence-type>
                <prim-key-class>java.lang.String</prim-key-class>
                <reentrant>False</reentrant>
                <resource-ref>
                   <res-ref-name>jdbc/demoPool</res-ref-name>
                   <res-type>javax.sql.DataSource</res-type>
                   <res-auth>Container</res-auth>
                </resource-ref>

         </entity>
      </enterprise-beans>
      <assembly-descriptor>
         <container-transaction>
            <method>
               <ejb-name>eai2_Customer</ejb-name>
               <method-name>*</method-name>
            </method>
            <trans-attribute>Required</trans-attribute>
         </container-transaction>
      </assembly-descriptor>
   </ejb-jar>
```

Since this time the bean manages the persistence itself, we will have to specify fewer parameters for deployment as we did in the previous example. We will not need to specify the mappings to the relational schema for example. If we use WebLogic, we will only need the `weblogic-ejb-jar.xml` additional deployment descriptor (included with the source code for this chapter, downloadable from http://www.wrox.com/).

To build and run this example we should follow the same steps as in the previous example. First we should compile the code, and then build the EJB JAR file, as we have done previously, using the following command:

```
jar cv0f eai2_Customer.jar META-INF bmp
```

Next we have to deploy the JAR file to the application server. With WebLogic we can deploy through the server console, or by simply dropping the relevant EJB JAR file into the `%WL_HOME%\config\mydomain\applications` directory.

To test the example, we can use a similar client as in the first example. We just have to change the JNDI name for the `CustomerHome` interface. After compiling the client, upon running we should get the following result:

How to Support Both CMP and BMP

Sometimes when developing entity beans to integrate with existing databases we might not (or cannot) make the choice which persistence type to use until later stages of the integration project. For example, if we have not yet selected the application server, or if we would like to compare the performance of BMP and CMP. Or there might be other reasons why we would like to provide both the CMP and BMP varieties of our beans.

We can use inheritance to implement BMP entity beans out of CMP beans. In our example we would define the `CustomerBMPBean` class that would inherit from the `CustomerBean` class that we have implemented using EJB 2.0 CMP.

However, in the `CustomerBMPBean` class we would then have to implement all the abstract getter/setter methods for attributes, override the `ejbLoad()`, `ejbStore()`, `ejbCreate()`, and sometimes `ejbRemote()` methods. In addition, we would have to implement the `ejbFindXXX()` methods and declare the necessary attributes. All other methods, including business methods from the component interface, are inherited – we don't need to implement them once again.

Such a BMP entity bean implementation class is included in the source code package for book. You'll find `CustomerBMPBean.java` (including associated comments) in the `%BOOK_HOME%\Ch12\bmp\` directory.

Using Entity Beans to Access Existing Data Through APIs or Wrappers

It is not necessary for entity beans to access existing databases directly – they can use APIs exposed by existing applications, or wrappers added to existing applications later, to access data. Accessing data through APIs or wrappers does not go directly into the existing database, but uses the existing application logic. This way we use the database integrity rules, coded in existing applications. This minimizes the danger of compromising the database integrity.

Entity beans can use the following ways to access existing applications:

❑   Entity beans can use APIs exposed by existing applications directly if these APIs conform to a J2EE standard technology, such as CORBA, RMI-IIOP, JMS, or JCA

❑   Entity beans can access APIs of existing applications through lower-level virtual components if APIs use proprietary technology

❑   Entity beans can use wrappers that add interfaces to existing applications later, for example CORBA component wrappers

We will access the existing data through wrappers as if we use existing databases that we cannot access directly from entity beans. For example, we use a database that does not provide drivers for Java, but only for C++. Or our data is stored in flat files, which we cannot access directly from entity beans. Then we will build a database wrapper, so that we provide access to the data through the interface. For more discussion of these possibilities please refer to the first section in this chapter.

Often we may wonder which type of bean we should employ to access data through APIs or wrappers. The obvious answer is that we should use an enterprise bean that best suits the particular situation. This means that we should choose the same bean type that we would desire if we were building a new application from scratch. To represent shared, transactional persistent data we should therefore opt for entity beans, regardless of how we access the data. To represent business tasks and processes we will select session or message-driven beans instead, which we will explain shortly.

In this section we will demonstrate how to develop a `Customer` entity bean (similar to the previous example) that will represent the customers from the existing customer information application of the cell phone operation example. However, the `Customer` entity bean will not access the database directly. Rather, it will use the CORBA components wrapper for the customer information existing application, developed in Chapter 10.

Acquiring Resources

If we access the data of an existing application through component wrappers, APIs, or lower-level virtual components, we should pay attention to how to communicate with them in the most efficient way. Here we will discuss the scenario of communicating with the component wrapper, but the same is true for APIs and lower-level virtual components.

Developing an enterprise bean that communicates with the component wrapper requires obtaining a communication with the component wrapper and invoking methods. If this is a CORBA component wrapper we first have to acquire a connection to the ORB and then to the component wrapper, using the Naming Service, for example, to get the reference to the CORBA wrapper.

Acquiring the initial references and resolving the name are costly operations from a time perspective. For that reason, if we were to make them each time before invoking a method, it would be too time-consuming for real-world production systems. We have to find a way to acquire the connection only once, or as few times as is necessary or possible.

> **To solve this problem we first have to partition the resources to those that are independent of the bean instance state and those that are dependent on the state of the bean instance.**

We can acquire the bean-independent resources as soon as the bean instance is created in the container. Here, we're not so concerned with the `EJBObject`, but about the actual bean implementation class instance in the EJB container. When the container creates such an instance it calls the `setEntityContext()` method, where it associates the instance with the context.

For our example, a connection to the CORBA ORB is definitely a bean-independent resource, because all clients will use the same ORB. So we should make the connection here. All resources that we acquire with `setEntiyContext()` we should release with `unsetEntityContext()`.

The connection to the component wrapper can be a bean-dependent or -independent resource. If the component wrapper holds a state, then each entity bean will need a connection to a different wrapper. If the wrapper is, on the other hand, stateless, then all entity beans can use the same wrapper, and can therefore use the same connection. Therefore for stateless component wrappers we should also acquire a connection in the `setEntityContext()` method.

For bean-dependent resources, the right point to acquire them is the `ejbActivate()` method. Doing it in the `ejbLoad()` method would be wrong, because the container will usually call the `ejbLoad()` (as well as the `ejbStore()`) method several times during the life time of an entity bean to ensure that the entity bean represents the correct data. However we do not need a new connection each time. We should release the resources acquired in `ejbActivate()` in the `ejbPassivate()` method.

Accessing CORBA Wrappers from Entity Beans

For this example we will use the same component and home interfaces as shown in the previous examples in this book. The major differences will be in the entity bean implementation class, which will have to access the CORBA wrapper.

We will use the `Customer` CORBA wrapper, developed as the first example in the section *Building a CORBA Component Wrapper* in Chapter 10, which was designed to access the existing Customer Information application. Refer to Chapter 10 for more information on the `Customer` CORBA wrapper. We will now show how to access it from a BMP entity bean.

To build a CORBA client into the entity bean, we first have to identify which classes we need to use for the CORBA client. For this we will need the IDL file where the CORBA wrapper interfaces are specified. We will use the `CustomerInt.idl` file. To generate the necessary files (stubs) for the entity bean we will compile the IDL file using an IDL-to-Java compiler. A possibility is to use the `idlj` compiler that is included with the Java SDK (version 1.3 or 1.4). We will generate classes for the client side only, so we will use the `-fclient` switch, as shown on the next screenshot:

Compilation of the `CustomerInt.idl` file generates the `CustomerManagement` directory, which contains many Java classes out of which the following are used to build the entity bean:

- ❑ The `Customer` and `CustomerOperations` interfaces

- ❑ The `_CustomerStub` client-side stub class

- ❑ The `CustomerHelper` and `CustomerHolder` classes (although we will not use `CustomerHolder` in our example, we might need it at some later time)

- ❑ A `CustomerPackage` directory containing user-defined data types and exceptions

Now we will build a Customer client in the Customer entity bean (the `CustomerBean` class). For this, we have imported the `org.omg.CosNaming` and `org.omg.CORBA` packages, and declared a private attribute `cust` of type `CustomerManagement.Customer`. The `cust` attribute stores the reference to the CORBA component wrapper `Customer`. Here's how the code starts:

```
package bmp2;

import javax.ejb.*;
import java.util.*;
```

```
import org.omg.CosNaming.*;
import org.omg.CORBA.*;

public class CustomerBean implements EntityBean {

  private EntityContext ctx;
  private CustomerData cd;
  private CustomerManagement.Customer cust;
```

Next we will implement the component interface. We will do this the same way as we have done in the previous examples:

```
  // Component interface
  public String getCustomerPrimaryKey() {
    return cd.getCustomerId();
  }
  public String getCustomerName() {
    return cd.getName();
  }
  public void setCustomerName(String name) {
    cd.setName(name);
  }
  public String getCustomerAddress() {
    return cd.getAddress();
  }
  public void setCustomerAddress(String address) {
    cd.setAddress(address);
  }
  public int getCustomerNoOfPhoneAccounts() {
    return cd.getNoOfPhoneAccounts();
  }
  public void setCustomerNoOfPhoneAccounts(int noOfPhAcc) {
    cd.setNoOfPhoneAccounts(noOfPhAcc);
  }

  public CustomerData getCustomerData() {
    return cd;
  }
  public void setCustomerData(CustomerData cd) {
    this.cd = cd;
  }
```

Next we will provide the EJB-related methods. In the `setEntityContext()` we will acquire the connection to the ORB and will connect to the component wrapper, which in our case is a stateless wrapper. If it would be a stateful wrapper then we would use the `ejbActivate()` method. In our case `ejbActivate()` is empty. We will also release the resources in `unsetEntityContext()` and `ejbPassivate()`, respectively (in our case `ejbPassivate()` is empty):

```
  public void setEntityContext(EntityContext ctx) {
    this.ctx = ctx;
    try {
      // Connect with the ORB
```

```
      String args[] = new String[1];
      args[0] = "";
      ORB orb = ORB.init(args, null);

      // Connect with the component wrapper if stateless
      org.omg.CORBA.Object objRef =
                        orb.resolve_initial_references("NameService");
      NamingContext ncRef = NamingContextHelper.narrow(objRef);

      NameComponent nc = new NameComponent("CustomerWrapper", "");
      NameComponent path[] = {nc};
      cust = CustomerManagement.CustomerHelper.narrow(ncRef.resolve(path));
    } catch (Exception e) {
      System.out.println(e);
    }
  }

  public void unsetEntityContext() {
    // Disconnect with the component wrapper if stateless
    cust = null;

    this.ctx = null;
  }

  public void ejbActivate() {
    // Connect with the component wrapper if stateful
  }

  public void ejbPassivate() {
    // Disconnect with the component wrapper if stateful
  }
```

In all cases where we communicate with the wrapper we should handle the CORBA-related exceptions and react to them appropriately. We can forward them to the client, but we should actually only forward the relevant exceptions. The client should not be aware that we communicate with the CORBA wrapper, therefore we should not forward any CORBA-related exceptions to the client. Rather, we should translate them to EJB related exceptions and throw an appropriate exception, like we will see with the `ejbCreate()` method.

The other possibility is to first try to react to the exceptions, before forwarding them to the client. If, for example, we cannot invoke methods on the CORBA wrapper we might consider reconnecting to it first, before notifying the client of an error.

Let's continue with the implementation of the entity bean by implementing the `ejbLoad()` and `ejbStore()` methods. We will load and store the persistent state using the wrapper:

```
  public void ejbLoad() {
    cd = new CustomerData();

    try {
      // Acquire the data from the component wrapper
      StringHolder firstName = new StringHolder();
```

```
        StringHolder lastName = new StringHolder();
        StringHolder address = new StringHolder();
        ShortHolder numberOfPhoneAccounts = new ShortHolder();
        CustomerManagement.CustomerPackage.statusTypeHolder status =
                   new CustomerManagement.CustomerPackage.statusTypeHolder();

        String cId = (String) ctx.getPrimaryKey();
        int ciId = (new Integer(cId)).intValue();

        cust.getCustomer (ciId, firstName, lastName,
                                      address, numberOfPhoneAccounts, status);

        cd.setCustomerId(cId);
        cd.setName(lastName.value);
        cd.setAddress(address.value);
        cd.setNoOfPhoneAccounts(numberOfPhoneAccounts.value);
      } catch (Exception e) {
        System.out.println(e);
      }
    }

    public void ejbStore() {
      // Store the data in the component wrapper
      try {
        int r = cust.setCustomer(cd.getName(), "",
                     cd.getAddress(),
                     (short)cd.getNoOfPhoneAccounts(),
                     CustomerManagement.CustomerPackage.statusType.gold);
      } catch (Exception e) {
        System.out.println(e);
      }
    }
```

Then we will implement the home methods. First, the `ejbCreate()` methods:

```
    // home methods
    public String ejbCreate(String customerId, String name, String address,
                         int noOfPhAcc) throws CreateException {
      cd = new CustomerData();

      try {
        // Store to the bean
        cd.setCustomerId(customerId);
        cd.setName(name);
        cd.setAddress(address);
        cd.setNoOfPhoneAccounts(noOfPhAcc);

        // Create the corresponding record
        // in the existing system though wrapper
        int r = cust.setCustomer(cd.getName(), "",
              cd.getAddress(), (short)cd.getNoOfPhoneAccounts(),
              CustomerManagement.CustomerPackage.statusType.gold);
```

```
        // Return the primary key
        return customerId;
    } catch (Exception e) {
        System.out.println(e);
        throw new CreateException();
    }
}

public void ejbPostCreate(String customerId, String name,
                                    String address, int noOfPhAcc) {

}

public String ejbCreate(CustomerData cd) throws CreateException {
    try {
        this.cd = new CustomerData();
        this.cd = cd;

        // Create the corresponding record
        // in the existing system through the wrapper
        int r = cust.setCustomer(cd.getName(), "",
                cd.getAddress(), (short)cd.getNoOfPhoneAccounts(),
                CustomerManagement.CustomerPackage.statusType.gold);

        return cd.getCustomerId();
    } catch (Exception e) {
        System.out.println(e);
        throw new CreateException();
    }
}

public void ejbPostCreate(CustomerData cd) {
}

public void ejbRemove() throws RemoveException {
}
```

Finally we have to implement the finder methods. The implementation of the `ejbFindByPrimaryKey()` is straightforward:

```
public String ejbFindByPrimaryKey(String pk)
                            throws ObjectNotFoundException {
    cd = new CustomerData();

    try {
        StringHolder firstName = new StringHolder();
        StringHolder lastName = new StringHolder();
        StringHolder address = new StringHolder();
        ShortHolder numberOfPhoneAccounts = new ShortHolder();
        CustomerManagement.CustomerPackage.statusTypeHolder status =
                new CustomerManagement.CustomerPackage.statusTypeHolder();

        int ciId = (new Integer(pk)).intValue();
```

```
        cust.getCustomer (ciId, firstName, lastName,
                            address, numberOfPhoneAccounts, status);

        cd.setCustomerId(pk);
        cd.setName(lastName.value);
        cd.setAddress(address.value);
        cd.setNoOfPhoneAccounts(numberOfPhoneAccounts.value);

        return pk;
    } catch (Exception e) {
      System.out.println(e);
      throw new ObjectNotFoundException();
    }
  }
```

The implementation of the `ejbFindByName()` requires some further thought because the current component does not provide a suitable method. The solution might be to iterate through all customers comparing each name, but this would require several remote method invocations, which would negatively influence the network traffic and would place additional load on the EJB server and component wrapper.

So, a much better solution is to modify the component wrapper (assuming that we have access to the code, and the authority to modify it) and add the necessary method to locate customers by name. Such a method would then return a list of primary keys, exactly what we need for the entity bean. We won't go into the fine details here, because it is a relatively easy task:

```
    public Collection ejbFindByName(String name) {
      Vector v = new Vector();

      // Delegate the search to the wrapper
      return v;
    }
  }
```

Building and Deploying the Entity Bean

The deployment descriptor of this entity bean is almost exactly the same as the deployment descriptor of the BMP entity bean that we developed in the previous example:

```
    <?xml version="1.0"?>

    <!DOCTYPE ejb-jar PUBLIC
    '-//Sun Microsystems, Inc.//DTD Enterprise JavaBeans 2.0//EN'
    'http://java.sun.com/dtd/ejb-jar_2_0.dtd'>

    <ejb-jar>
      <enterprise-beans>
        <entity>
          <ejb-name>eai3_Customer</ejb-name>
          <home>bmp2.CustomerHome</home>
```

```
      <remote>bmp2.Customer</remote>
      <ejb-class>bmp2.CustomerBean</ejb-class>
      <persistence-type>Bean</persistence-type>
      <prim-key-class>java.lang.String</prim-key-class>
      <reentrant>False</reentrant>
      <resource-ref>
        <res-ref-name>jdbc/demoPool</res-ref-name>
        <res-type>javax.sql.DataSource</res-type>
        <res-auth>Container</res-auth>
      </resource-ref>

    </entity>
  </enterprise-beans>
  <assembly-descriptor>
    <container-transaction>
      <method>
        <ejb-name>eai3_Customer</ejb-name>
        <method-name>*</method-name>
      </method>
      <trans-attribute>Required</trans-attribute>
    </container-transaction>
  </assembly-descriptor>
</ejb-jar>
```

We also need an application-server-specific deployment descriptor, such as the `weblogic-ejb-jar.xml` for BEA WebLogic, which is almost exact as in previous example (except for the bean name and the JNDI name) and is included in the code that can be downloaded from http://www.wrox.com/.

To build the entity bean in the correct order, we should first generate the client-side mapping from the `CustomerInt.idl`, using an IDL compiler, for example Sun's `idlj`, as we've shown earlier in this example. Then we should compile the source code files, including the generated interfaces and classes to access the CORBA wrapper:

Finally, we should pack all the files in our `build` folder (from the `META-INF`, `bmp2`, and `CustomerManagement` directories) into the `eai3_Customer.jar` file, using the JAR command shown earlier. We will then deploy this to the container. Remember, for deploying the JAR in BEA WebLogic we should first use the `ejbc` compiler, and then use the server console for deployment.

We should also start the CORBA wrapper from Chapter 10. First we should run the CORBA Naming Service (`tnameserv`) and then the CORBA wrapper server-side object. The necessary commands are shown in the next screenshot:

```
C:\WINNT\System32\cmd.exe - java CustomerManagement.Server                    _ □ ×

C:\ProEAI\Ch10\CustomerInformation1>start tnameserv

C:\ProEAI\Ch10\CustomerInformation1>java CustomerManagement.Server
Server is ready...
```

To test the entity bean we will use a simple client, almost exactly the same as in the previous example. Again, the major difference will be the correct JNDI name of our new entity bean (`eai3-CustomerHome`), and that we use the `bmp2` package here.

After compiling the client source code, we should run it with the command shown below. Here's what the output looks like this time:

```
Select C:\WINNT\System32\cmd.exe

C:\ProEAI\Ch12>java -classpath %WL_HOME%\lib\weblogic.jar;. -Djava.naming.factor
y.initial=weblogic.jndi.WLInitialContextFactory -Djava.naming.provider.url=t3://
localhost:7001 bmp2.Client
EAI BMP2 client

Customer name is: B. Good

C:\ProEAI\Ch12>_
```

Using Session Beans to Reuse Functionality of Existing Applications

While entity beans are appropriate for accessing existing data, either through direct access to existing databases or over existing applications, session beans are more suitable to represent business logic and tasks. Session beans are not persistent components and they should model the conversation between the client and the business logic tier. They are appropriate when we access functions of existing applications that are not data related but rather represent a certain business operation or a workflow.

> **Session beans will often be used in integration to model the access to several existing applications.**

In other words, a business method that a session bean provides through its component interface will often require several operations on one or more existing applications. Session beans will therefore represent higher-level virtual components that will form a façade through which the clients from other tiers will access business logic of the integrated information system. On the other side the session beans will communicate with existing applications through lower-level virtual components, component wrappers, or with APIs. Please refer to the first section of this chapter for more discussion about the role of session beans in integration.

Using session beans as higher-level virtual components to provide common façades through which business logic is accessed has several advantages:

- They introduce a control layer between clients and the business logic tier.
- They model the integrated system in several abstraction layers. Session beans, as higher-level virtual components, will expose service-oriented interfaces focused on business functions. To implement them, session beans will communicate with lower-level virtual components, component wrappers, and APIs of existing applications.

❑ Uniform high-level, coarse-grained interfaces will be presented to the clients. This improves performance, lowers the number of remote method invocations, and reduces network traffic.

❑ They provide single entry points for services. This centralizes transaction and security management and fits with declarative transactions and security, as provided by the EJB container.

❑ They effectively decouple clients from details of how business logic is implemented. Clients will not be aware that existing applications are performing the actual work in the background.

> **Session beans as higher-level virtual components (or façades) will be the entry points for clients to access services.**

Therefore session beans will be a perfect place for transaction demarcation – for starting and ending transactions. When starting a transaction in the session bean, such transaction will include all interactions with lower-level virtual components, with component wrappers and APIs of existing applications. Starting and ending the transactions in the session beans on the business logic tier is the preferred way and also much better than starting them on the client or web component tier (which should not be done at all).

Session beans can demarcate (start and end) the transactions or they can only take part in already started transactions. Session beans can decide to use the container to manage the transactions – these are called **container-managed transactions** or declarative transaction demarcation. They are called declarative because the bean only has to declare how transactions should behave in the deployment descriptor (shown a little later).

Session beans can also demarcate transactions themselves and provide code that will start and end transactions. This is called a **bean-managed transaction** or programmatic transaction demarcation. Usually the preferred way will be to use container-managed transactions. For further discussion of transactions please refer to Chapter 15 of this book or to Chapter 9 of the *Professional EJB* book.

How to Identify Session Beans

Session beans should be identified at the problem domain analysis and design activities of the business method level integration phase. In Chapter 9 we described the steps of problem domain analysis and design in detail. For the purposes of integration, session beans will be used as higher-level service-oriented façades that will expose business logic to the clients.

As we have seen in Chapter 9, session beans that will expose high-level business-oriented service interfaces are identified by the analysis of use cases. However, it is not a good idea to map every use case to a separate session bean for the following reasons:

❑ It will result in a large number of session beans

❑ Such session beans will not provide coarse-grained interfaces

❑ This defeats the point of having high-level operations exposed to the clients to lower the number of remote method invocations in order to reduce network traffic

Undoubtedly, we should gather and consolidate use cases to a lower number of session beans. We should join them based on their functionality.

> Joining related use cases and aggregating related interactions to single session beans results in coarse-grained controllers with high-level business methods.

Stateless and Stateful Session Beans

Session beans model business processes and therefore simple business processes session beans do not have to preserve any client-related persistent state. The client will create a session bean, invoke a method and get a result. Such beans are called **stateless session beans** and are the most simple session beans. They do not have to store any client-related state, so they place the lowest overhead on the container, which can manage the instances in a highly efficient way, because it can pool the instances without considering the state.

However, not all business operations will be so simple that they can be performed with a single method invocation. Often the client will have to invoke more than one method within any given session or it would be very desirable if the session bean could hold some state between the client method invocations. Such state is called 'conversational' state, which is client-dependent. It exists only for the duration of a conversation between the client and the session bean – from the time the client creates a new session bean instance to the time when the clients removes the instance.

Stateful session beans enable us to store conversational state. They are appropriate for modeling business interactions that require several method invocations, but a client-dependent state has to be preserved between method invocations. Note also that conversational state is not stored to a database.

Since they hold state, the container cannot pool stateful session beans in the same way as stateless session beans. However, to achieve efficiency, a session bean container may need to temporarily transfer the state of an idle stateful session bean instance to some form of secondary storage. The transfer of a stateful session bean to secondary storage is called passivation. The container restores a session bean when the client invokes the bean – this return process is called activation, and the container does this using serialization. Hence, the state of a stateful session bean has to be serializable. Managing the state places additional overhead on stateful session beans, which obviously require more resources than stateless session beans.

This additional use of resources should not, however, influence the decision regarding which type of beans to use. If we need the conversational state we should choose stateful session beans and not stateless session beans (and implement the state management ourselves).

> We should select the appropriate session bean type based on business processes that we implement. If the business process can be implemented with a single method invocation, then we should select stateless session beans. If on the other hand a business process requires several method invocations, we should select stateful session beans that will preserve the conversational state.

Where to Store the Conversational State

Stateful session beans store the conversational state on the business logic tier, though this is not the only place to store conversational state. The other possibility is to store the state on the presentation tier, meaning the client or web component tier. A particularly popular choice among the developers is to store the state in the `HttpSession`. Other possibilities include storing the state in Java applications and other types of clients.

Not storing the state on the business logic tier enables us to use stateless session beans instead of stateful, which might improve the scalability of the EJBs. However, this approach has several drawbacks:

❏   If we do not store the conversational state on the business logic tier then we have to implement state for all different types of clients separately. Web clients will store the state in a different way to applications, leading to redundancy and maintainability problems.

❏   Storing the state on the presentation tier requires transmitting state by each method invocation, which increases network traffic and prolongs remote method invocation overhead.

❏   The decision where to store the state influences clustering and replication selection.

Developing a Stateless Session Bean

Session beans are even simpler than entity beans, which we already know how to develop. Session beans have two interfaces: a component interface and a home interface, through which the session beans expose business methods and provide life-cycle methods, respectively. Component and home interfaces can be remote, which allows remote clients to access the methods over RMI-IIOP. Furthermore, in EJB 2.0 session bean interfaces can also be local, which reduces the remote overhead for clients deployed in the same JVM (this will typically be other enterprise beans).

Remember – session beans do not represent persistent, shared state, so a single client uses each session bean at a time. In other words, session beans do not expose their identity to clients, so clients cannot locate them. They can just create a new session bean instance and use it for a certain period of time, and then they can remove the instance. Session beans do not have a client-recognizable identity, therefore they do not have primary keys either.

Accordingly, the home interface of session beans only provides the create methods that can be overloaded by entity beans, and a remove method. There are no finder methods applicable to session beans.

Although the client uses explicit create and remove methods, these methods do not create and remove session bean instances in the container. These methods result in creating or removing the `EJBObject` (if we use remote interface) or `EJBLocalObject` (if we use local interface). The actual session bean instances are under the control of the container or, more explicitly, the instance management algorithm *inside* the container, which may implement complex techniques like pooling in order to manage the instances.

To implement a session bean, regardless of whether it is stateless or stateful, we have to perform the following steps:

❏   Define the component interface

❏   Define the home interface

❏   Develop the implementation class

❏   Write the deployment descriptor

As a demonstration, we will develop a stateless session bean representing a higher-level virtual component that will expose a high-level business method for the integration example of our ongoing cell phone operator application that would calculate the current balance of cell phone accounts. We have identified this functionality in Chapter 9 as a part of our problem domain analysis and design activities.

In Chapter 9 we have figured out that the existing applications support calculating the current cell phone account balance. However, the functionality is not gathered inside a single existing application, so the high-level virtual component will have to depend on more than one existing application. To be precise, we will not use the existing applications directly. Rather, we will use the lower-level virtual components that present the functions of existing applications in a J2EE compliant way on the business logic tier.

To calculate the current balance of a cell account the higher-level virtual component will have to interact with the following existing applications, that is, with the lower-level virtual components that represent these existing applications:

- ❏ *Account balance management*
- ❏ *Domestic cell phone evaluation*
- ❏ *International cell phone evaluation*
- ❏ *Cost and tariff management*

In Chapter 9 we have also shown how we should identify the necessary interaction with existing applications and the sequence of operations that should be performed.

Building such session bean (higher-level virtual component) would require accessing lower-level virtual components for all these four existing applications.

In the previous chapter we did not develop lower-level virtual components for all four existing applications from our example. Therefore, to be able to actually run the example, we will simplify it a little. Our session bean will call only one of the existing applications – the Cost and Tariff Management existing application, through the lower-level virtual component developed in RMI-IIOP in Chapter 11. We will, however, show where we would have to make connections to other existing applications. We will develop the session bean, called `CheckBalance`, which will provide a method `calculateBalance()`. For the implementation of this method, the session bean will contact the lower-level RMI-IIOP virtual component `CostTariff` (from Chapter 11). This `CostTariff` lower-level virtual component will access the existing application to do the actual work.

We will reveal how to build a session bean and access a virtual component in RMI-IIOP. In the previous example with the entity bean we have shown how to call a CORBA wrapper. Therefore here we will show how to call the RMI-IIOP virtual component, developed in Chapter 11.

Defining the Component Interface

First we have to define the component interface for our session bean (`CheckBalance`), which can be remote or local. We will define a single method `calculateBalance()`, but note that it is not necessary that remote and local interfaces provide the same methods. If we pay attention to the way enterprise beans are developed we will see that the implementation is not directly related to the interfaces and that this relation is set in the deployment descriptor.

The remote component interface for our session bean is as follows:

```
package session1;

import java.rmi.RemoteException;
import javax.ejb.EJBObject;
```

590

```
public interface CheckBalance extends EJBObject {

  public double calculateBalance(int accountNo) throws RemoteException;

}
```

The local interface does not differ significantly in the way it should be declared. The major differences are that the local interface extends the `EJBLocalObject` instead of `EJBObject` and that the methods must not throw remote exceptions. The local interface is presented below, where we can see that it exposes the same method as the remote interface:

```
package session1;

import javax.ejb.EJBLocalObject;

public interface CheckBalance extends EJBLocalObject {

  public double calculateBalance(int accountNo);

}
```

After we have defined the remote interface we have to define the home interface.

Defining the Home Interface

The home interface provides the methods for the session bean life cycle. We have already identified that the session beans do not expose their identity to clients, so the home interface will have only create methods – in our case only a single create method. As with component interfaces, home interfaces can also be remote or local. A remote home interface declaration is shown in the next listing:

```
package session1;

import java.rmi.RemoteException;
import javax.ejb.CreateException;
import javax.ejb.EJBHome;

public interface CheckBalanceHome extends EJBHome {

  public CheckBalance create() throws CreateException, RemoteException;

}
```

The local home interface extends `EJBLocalHome` instead of `EJBHome` and the methods must not throw remote exceptions:

```
package session1;

import javax.ejb.CreateException;
import javax.ejb.EJBLocalHome;
```

```
public interface CheckBalanceHome extends EJBLocalHome {

  public CheckBalance create() throws CreateException;

}
```

After we have defined both interfaces we can continue with the development of the implementation class.

Developing the Implementation Class

In the implementation class we will have to provide implementations for all methods declared in the component and home interfaces. We will also have to implement certain container callback methods: `ejbActivate()`, `ejbPassivate()`, `setSessionContext()`, `ejbCreate()`, and `ejbRemove()` methods.

Session beans are simpler than entity beans and therefore require less EJB-related methods. We will declare the `CheckBalanceBean` class, which will have to implement the `SessionBean` interface. The implementation class is very simple, including all the necessary methods. We will start with the declaration:

```
package session1;

import javax.ejb.*;
import javax.naming.*;
import javax.rmi.PortableRemoteObject;
import java.util.*;

public class CheckBalanceBean implements SessionBean {
```

The session bean that we present here will call the `CostTariff` RMI-IIOP virtual component that we have developed in Chapter 11 in the section *Developing a Virtual Component in RMI-IIOP*. Although a real-world session bean would have to call more than one virtual component, here we show a simplified solution because our objective is to demonstrate the technical aspects.

If we will call the RMI-IIOP virtual component it would be wise to connect to the virtual component when the session bean instance is created, and store the connection. Making the connection requires a lookup in the naming service and narrowing the reference. These are costly operations and from the performance perspective it would not be efficient to make the connection each time before a method invocation.

When we have developed the entity bean to access the existing application (through CORBA wrapper), it is reasonable to partition the resources to those that are client dependent and those that are not. With stateless session beans we will not have this problem, because the beans themselves are stateless and therefore cannot store any client-related state. If we need to store client-related state we should use stateful session beans, which we will discuss later.

We will continue our session bean implementation class by declaring private attributes. One will store the session context, the other the connection to the `CostTariff` virtual component. Notice that stateless session bean can store client-independent state. Therefore we can store the connection to the virtual component in the bean. We will also declare several EJB-related methods that we do not need to implement in this simple example:

```
private SessionContext ctx;
private CostTariff ct;

public void ejbActivate() {
}

public void ejbRemove() {
}

public void ejbPassivate() {
}

public void setSessionContext(SessionContext ctx) {
  this.ctx = ctx;
}
```

Next we will implement the create method from the home interface. The `ejbCreate()` method is called by the container after calling the `setSessionContext()`, this is after the bean instance has been created in the container. Therefore the `ejbCreate()` method is an appropriate place where we can establish a connection to the `CostTariff` RMI-IIOP virtual component.

We will use the example from Chapter 11, where in the section *Developing a Virtual Component in RMI-IIOP* we have developed the `CostTariff` RMI-IIOP example. We'll simply build the RMI-IIOP client into the session bean. In the `ejbCreate()` method therefore we have to acquire the initial context, make a lookup after the `CostTariff` RMI-IIOP virtual component, and narrow the object reference. This is basically the same as we have done in the RMI-IIOP client.

However, in the RMI-IIOP client we have specified two important parameters with command-line switches when we started the client:

❑   The initial context factory

❑   The naming provider URL

With these parameters we specify which naming service we will use. For example, if we decided to use the naming service provided by Sun, more specifically `tnameserv` or `orbd`, then we would use the same settings as in Chapter 11. However, in a session bean we cannot specify it from the command line, so we have to use Java properties, and stipulate it that way:

```
// home
public void ejbCreate() throws CreateException {
  System.out.println("create: Connecting to the virtual component");
  try {
      // Define initial naming factory and URL as properties
      Properties h = new Properties();
      h.put(Context.INITIAL_CONTEXT_FACTORY,
          "com.sun.jndi.cosnaming.CNCtxFactory");
      h.put(Context.PROVIDER_URL, "iiop://localhost:900");

      // Obtain a reference to initial naming context
      Context inc = new InitialContext(h);
```

```
            // Resolve the CostTariff virtual component and narrow
            ct = (CostTariff)PortableRemoteObject.narrow(
                              inc.lookup("CostTariff"),CostTariff.class);
      } catch (Exception e) {
            System.out.println(e);
            throw new CreateException();
      }
   }
```

With this setting we do not have to modify the RMI-IIOP server, developed in Chapter 11. However, if we would rather use the naming service provided by the application server, we would have to modify the settings. With WebLogic, for example, we would have to:

❑   Set the initial context factory to: `weblogic.jndi.WLInitialContextFactory`

❑   Set the naming provider URL to: `t3://localhost:7001` (WebLogic uses port 7001 by default and uses `t3` protocol for communication with the JNDI)

Note that we would also have to modify the RMI-IIOP server to use the same naming service to register it.

We should also manage the exceptions. In the above example we have decided to forward any exceptions that may occur during the connection to the RMI-IIOP server as create exceptions. In production systems we would build in a more sophisticated exception management mechanism.

Finally we have to implement our business method, that is, the `calculateBalance()` method. As already mentioned, this method would normally call several existing systems. Here, to keep things simple so we can focus on the technical issues, we will call only a single RMI-IIOP virtual component:

```
   // business method
   public double calculateBalance(int accountNo) {
      double result = 0;
      System.out.println("calculateBalance:
                          invoking remote method on the virtual component");
      try {
         // invoke the method on the virtual component
         result = ct.calcCost((long)accountNo, (short)2);

      } catch (Exception e) {
         System.out.println(e);
      }
      return result;
   }
}
```

With this we have finished the implementation class for our stateless session bean. Next we have to define the deployment descriptor and build the example into a JAR file, and then we can deploy and test it.

Writing the Deployment Descriptor

After we have written the necessary code, we have to write the deployment descriptor (`ejb-jar.xml`), which is relatively straightforward for stateless session beans, so we will simply show it opposite without comments:

```
<?xml version="1.0"?>

<!DOCTYPE ejb-jar PUBLIC
'-//Sun Microsystems, Inc.//DTD Enterprise JavaBeans 1.1//EN'
'http://java.sun.com/j2ee/dtds/ejb-jar_1_1.dtd'>

<ejb-jar>
  <enterprise-beans>
    <session>
      <ejb-name>eaiSS_CheckBalance</ejb-name>
      <home>session1.CheckBalanceHome</home>
      <remote>session1.CheckBalance</remote>
      <ejb-class>session1.CheckBalanceBean</ejb-class>
      <session-type>Stateless</session-type>
      <transaction-type>Container</transaction-type>
    </session>
  </enterprise-beans>
  <assembly-descriptor>
    <container-transaction>
      <method>
        <ejb-name>eaiSS_CheckBalance</ejb-name>
        <method-name>*</method-name>
      </method>
      <trans-attribute>Required</trans-attribute>
    </container-transaction>
  </assembly-descriptor>
</ejb-jar>
```

Note that we might need an application-server-specific deployment descriptor. For WebLogic we will need the `weblogic-ejb-jar.xml` descriptor, which is very simple for our session bean and only specifies the JNDI name:

```
<?xml version="1.0"?>

<!DOCTYPE weblogic-ejb-jar PUBLIC
'-//BEA Systems, Inc.//DTD WebLogic 6.0.0 EJB//EN'
'http://www.bea.com/servers/wls600/dtd/weblogic-ejb-jar.dtd'>

<weblogic-ejb-jar>
  <weblogic-enterprise-bean>
    <ejb-name>eaiSS_CheckBalance</ejb-name>

    <jndi-name>eaiSS-CheckBalanceHome</jndi-name>

  </weblogic-enterprise-bean>
</weblogic-ejb-jar>
```

Building and Deploying

Finally we can compile the source files and gather all the necessary files into the JAR file. The usual files that are required are:

❑   Component and home interfaces (`CheckBalance.class` and `CheckBalanceHome.class`)

❑   Bean implementation class (`CheckBalanceBean.class`)

❑   Deployment descriptor (`ejb-jar.xml` and any necessary application-server-specific descriptors)

Additionally, we must not forget to include the RMI-IIOP interface `CostTariff` (`CostTariff.class`) and the necessary stub (`_CostTariff_Stub.class`). We can use the same stub that we have built in Chapter 11, or can build the stub again using the following command:

```
rmic -iiop CostTariffImpl
```

The command to build the JAR file is as follows (run from the `build` directory):

```
jar cv0f eaiSS_CheckBal.jar META-INF session1
```

Now we're ready to deploy the session bean to the application server. We should follow the specific steps relating to the particular application server we choose to deploy on. With WebLogic we can simply drop the `eaiSS_CheckBal.jar` file into the `%WL_HOME%\config\mydomain\applications` directory of our WebLogic installation.

More information on EJB deployment can be found in your application server's documentation, or in the Wrox book Professional EJB (in particular, the Appendices of Professional EJB demonstrate the deployment procedure for some of the more popular application servers).

Client

To be able to test the session bean we will write a simple client that will test the functionality through the remote interface. The client code that is shown below assumes that we have registered the session bean with the JNDI under the name `eaiSS-CheckBalanceHome`:

```
package session1;

import java.rmi.*;
import javax.rmi.*;
import java.util.*;

import javax.ejb.*;
import javax.naming.*;

public class Client {

  public Client() {
  }

  public static void main(String[] args) {
    System.out.println("EAI stateless session client");
    System.out.println();

    // Create a new instance and invoke the example() method
    try {
      Client client = new Client();
      client.example();
    } catch (Exception e) {
      System.out.println(e);
    }
  }

  public void example() {
```

```
      try {
        // Obtain a reference to the initial naming context
        Context ctx = new InitialContext();

        // Resolve the JNDI home name and narrow
        CheckBalanceHome home = (CheckBalanceHome)PortableRemoteObject.narrow
                    ((CheckBalanceHome)ctx.lookup("eaiSS-CheckBalanceHome"),
                                                       CheckBalanceHome.class);

        // Create a new session bean instance
        CheckBalance cb = home.create();

        // Invoke the method
        System.out.println("The balance of account no. 1 is: "
                                     +cb.calculateBalance(1));

        // Remove the session bean instance
        cb.remove();

      } catch(Exception e) {
        System.out.println(e);
      }
    }
  }
```

Running the Example

To run the session bean we should perform the following steps:

1. Deploy the bean to the application server
2. Run the naming service (`tnameserv`)
3. Run the RMI-IIOP server-side object – the `CostTariff` virtual component that we have developed in Chapter 11. We should use the command shown in the following screenshot (Note that this command works only when we use the `tnameserv` as the naming provider. Obviously, if we use any other naming service we have to specify it accordingly.):

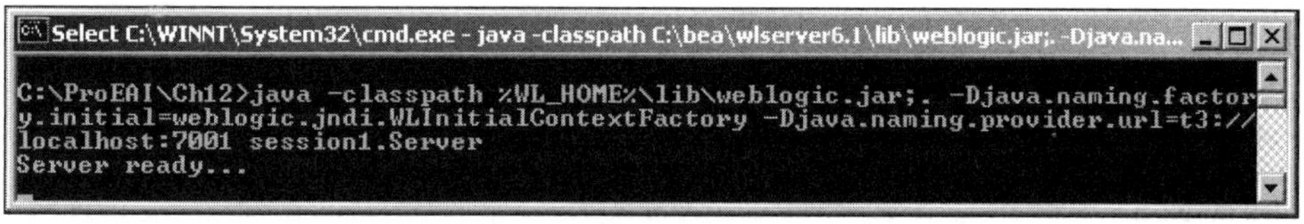

Select C:\WINNT\System32\cmd.exe - java -classpath C:\bea\wlserver6.1\lib\weblogic.jar;. -Djava.na...
C:\ProEAI\Ch12>java -classpath %WL_HOME%\lib\weblogic.jar;. -Djava.naming.factor
y.initial=weblogic.jndi.WLInitialContextFactory -Djava.naming.provider.url=t3://
localhost:7001 session1.Server
Server ready...

4. Finally we can run the EJB client using the following command:

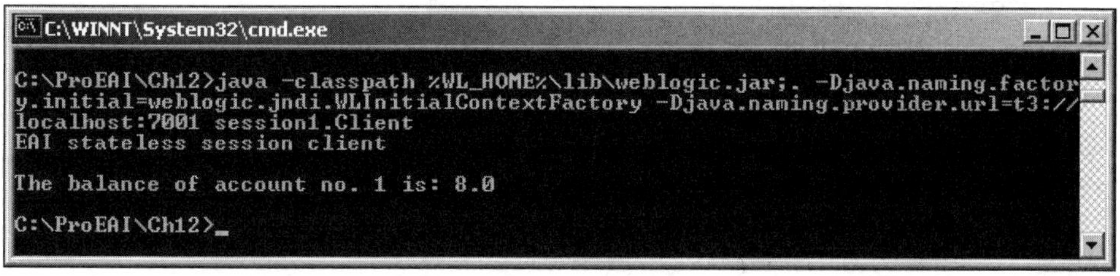

C:\WINNT\System32\cmd.exe
C:\ProEAI\Ch12>java -classpath %WL_HOME%\lib\weblogic.jar;. -Djava.naming.factor
y.initial=weblogic.jndi.WLInitialContextFactory -Djava.naming.provider.url=t3://
localhost:7001 session1.Client
EAI stateless session client
The balance of account no. 1 is: 8.0
C:\ProEAI\Ch12>_

We should also see from the `Server` window that the RMI-IIOP virtual component has actually processed the request:

```
C:\WINNT\System32\cmd.exe - java -Djava.naming.factory.initial=com.sun.jndi.cosnaming.CNCtxFact...
C:\ProEAI\Ch12>java -Djava.naming.factory.initial=com.sun.jndi.cosnaming.CNCtxFa
ctory -Djava.naming.provider.url=iiop://localhost:900 session1.Server
Server ready...
Processing the request...
```

Stateful Session Beans

We have already identified that we will use stateful session beans if we need to preserve the conversational state between different method invocations from the client. Developing a stateful session bean is very similar to the process for a stateless one. The major difference is that in the implementation class we declare public attributes in which the stateful session bean will preserve the conversational state.

The container will preserve the state of these public attributes and will temporarily store them if it needs to reuse the same bean instance. The container will use serialization to store the state, so, as we emphasized earlier, all attributes that maintain conversational state should be serializable. Furthermore, a stateful session bean can be passivated and activated, which means that we should partition the resources that we use in the bean in a similar way as we did with entity beans. The resources that are client-dependent should be acquired in the `ejbActivate()` method and released in `ejbPassivate()`. Client-independent resources show be acquired in `ejbCreate()` and released in `ejbRemove()`.

The next difference is quite obvious: we should specify in the deployment descriptor that we have developed a stateful session bean:

```
    ...
        <session-type>Stateful<session-type>
    ...
```

Session beans can participate in transactions, as we learned in the beginning of this section. They can use bean-managed or container-managed transactions. When they use bean-managed transaction the bean is responsible for starting and committing or rolling back the transaction.

If, however, we use a container-managed transaction, then stateful session beans can participate in the transaction through `SessionSynchronization`. Stateful session beans have to implement this interface, which adds three callback methods that the container invokes and the bean can do the necessary bookkeeping activities:

❑ `afterBegin()`

❑ `beforeCompletion()`

❑ `afterCompletion(Boolean)`

The `afterBegin()` method is called after the container starts the transaction, while before completion the container calls the `beforeCompletion()` method, as its name suggests. Finally, the container notifies the bean about the transaction success by calling the `afterCompletion()`. If the `Boolean` parameter is `true`, then the transaction has been committed; otherwise it has been rolled back.

Using Message-Driven Beans to Reuse Functionality of Existing Applications

Session beans are appropriate for exposing business methods, as we have seen in the previous section. However, session beans require synchronous RMI-IIOP communication with remote clients, which means that the client that invokes a method on a session bean waits for response.

This synchronous nature has several consequences. The client is blocked, so it would be advantageous if the operation were performed relatively quickly. Of course, with certain operations this is not possible, or it would require too much resource from the EJB tier. In many information systems we are faced with peak usage times, where we have a large number of simultaneous clients.

The solution is to use message-driven beans that communicate asynchronously, using the JMS. With asynchronous communication we can store the requests and process them in off-peak hours. The fact is that we cannot return results to clients, therefore message-driven beans will be appropriate for update operations that do not need to return the results to clients, or can use some other mechanism to report them.

We also know that JMS is an interface to MOM products, which have been very popular for simple, partial point-to-point integrations between applications in the past. This also means that with message-driven beans we can build EJBs that will react to messages sent from existing applications – and therefore enable integration between them. We have already looked at JMS in Chapter 8. Here we will show how to develop message-driven beans.

A message-driven bean is nothing but a JMS message consumer. It can register itself to a `Queue` or `Topic`. Queues are used for point-to-point communication, where there is one, and only one, message consumer for each message. Topics are used for publish/subscribe model, where each message is delivered to more than one consumer.

A message-driven bean has to implement the `MessageListener` interface, with which it waits for incoming messages and then processes them. As a consequence of their nature, message-driven beans are always stateless, and because they react on messages they do not need a home or component interface. The only way to communicate with them is over JMS, therefore we cannot talk about local interfaces either.

> **Message-driven beans are appropriate for implementing higher-level virtual components, particularly for update operations, that is, for operations that require a longer time to process and that do not return results to the clients.**

If we build message-driven virtual components after use cases we should follow the same guidelines as with session beans: we should not map each use case to a separate message-driven bean, but should rather aggregate related interactions and develop a lower number of message facades.

We will build a simple message-driven bean for the cell phone operator integration scenario (introduced in Chapter 4). We will develop `DisableAccountsBean`, a message-driven bean that will search and disable accounts that have had zero balance for three months or longer. Searching and disabling accounts will be done using the account balance management existing application. This is usually a task that requires a lot of time, and does not require that a result be immediately sent to the client who initiated to operation. A message-driven bean is therefore a perfect choice.

Our message-driven bean will register to a `Topic`. A client will initiate a corresponding message to the `Topic`. The `DisableAccountsBean` will accept the message and start processing, as shown in the figure below:

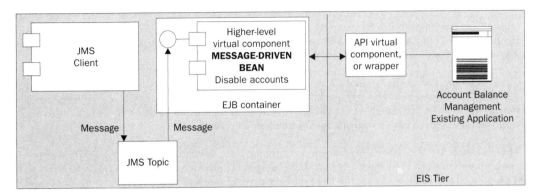

Developing a Message-Driven Bean

A message-driven bean has to implement two interfaces: `MessageDrivenBean` and `MessageListener`. The first interface requires the implementation of EJB container callback methods, like `setMessageDrivenContext()` and `ejbRemove()`, that enable the container instance pooling. The second interface requires the implementation of the `onMessage()` method. This method is also how the message-driven bean gets requests. More specifically, the message-driven bean will get a message through the `onMessage()` method and will then have to parse and react to the message accordingly.

We can see that message-driven beans are more loosely coupled and that they can react to different messages with the `onMessage()` method. There is no compile type checking and the parsing of the messaging must be done by hand.

Implementation of the message-driven bean will therefore have only the implementation class. As such, in our example we'll define the `DisableAccountsBean` implementation class that will implement the above mentioned interfaces. In the bean we will implement the `onMessage()` method which will perform the search for old accounts and disable them:

```
package msg;

import javax.ejb.*;
import javax.jms.*;

public class DisableAccountsBean implements MessageDrivenBean, MessageListener {

  private MessageDrivenContext mctx;

  public void ejbRemove() {
  }

  public void setMessageDrivenContext(MessageDrivenContext ctx) {
    mctx = ctx;
  }
```

```
public void ejbCreate () throws CreateException {
}

// Implementation of MessageListener

public void onMessage(Message msg) {
  try {
    // Extract the message
    TextMessage tm = (TextMessage) msg;
    String text = tm.getText();
    System.out.println("Received request: " + text);

    // Process the request
    System.out.println("Processing the request: disabling accounts...");

    // Contact the existing application
    // Search for accounts and disable them
  }
  catch(JMSException ex) {
    ex.printStackTrace();
  }
}
}
```

Deployment

After we have defined the implementation class we need to write the deployment descriptor. The particularly interesting tags are the `<message-driven-destination>` and the `<destination-type>`. They define whether the bean is subscribed to a topic or a queue:

```
<?xml version="1.0"?>

<!DOCTYPE ejb-jar PUBLIC "-//Sun Microsystems, Inc.//DTD Enterprise JavaBeans
2.0//EN" "http://java.sun.com/dtd/ejb-jar_2_0.dtd">

<ejb-jar>
  <enterprise-beans>
    <message-driven>
      <ejb-name>eaimsg_DisableAccounts</ejb-name>
      <ejb-class>msg.DisableAccountsBean</ejb-class>
      <transaction-type>Container</transaction-type>
      <message-driven-destination>
        <destination-type>javax.jms.Topic</destination-type>
      </message-driven-destination>
    </message-driven>
  </enterprise-beans>
</ejb-jar>
```

We will also need to specify the name of the topic. This will be done using an application-server-specific way. WebLogic requires the `weblogic-ejb-jar.xml` deployment descriptor, which is shown on the next listing. For this example, the topic name is defined as `disableAccounts`:

```
<?xml version="1.0"?>

<!DOCTYPE weblogic-ejb-jar PUBLIC "-//BEA Systems, Inc.//DTD WebLogic 6.0.0
EJB//EN" "http://www.bea.com/servers/wls600/dtd/weblogic-ejb-jar.dtd">

<weblogic-ejb-jar>
  <weblogic-enterprise-bean>
    <ejb-name>eaimsg_DisableAccounts</ejb-name>
    <message-driven-descriptor>
      <destination-jndi-name>disableAccounts</destination-jndi-name>
    </message-driven-descriptor>
    <jndi-name>eaimsg-DisableAccounts</jndi-name>
  </weblogic-enterprise-bean>
</weblogic-ejb-jar>
```

Next we have to compile the source files, prepare the JAR file that will include the
`DisableAccountsBean.class` and the deployment descriptors, and deploy the JAR file to the
application server.

We also have to create a JMS `Topic` with the name `disableAccounts`. In the WebLogic Console, we go
to **Services | JMS | Servers** in the left-hand side tree view, create a new JMS server (`MyJMSServer`, for
example), and then select **Create a new JMSTopic....** Then we enter the `dissableAccounts` name, as
shown in the screenshot below:

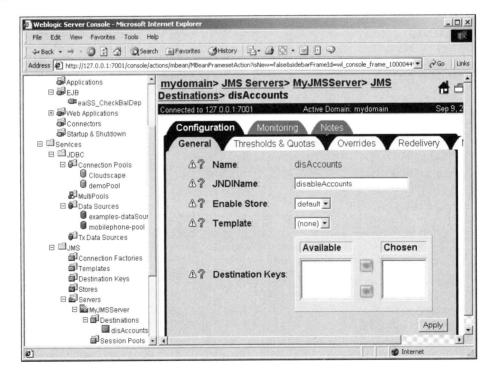

Client

The client for the message-driven bean can be any client that delivers messages to a certain topic (or queue if we had used `Queue` instead of `Topic`). This can be a Java client using JMS, or an existing application that uses a compliant MOM. Hence, message-driven beans are suitable to process requests from existing applications.

Here we will show a simple JMS client in Java, which will create a topic connection and start it, create a new topic session, create a topic publisher, create a text message, and publish it:

```
package msg;

import java.rmi.RemoteException;
import java.util.Properties;
import javax.jms.*;
import javax.naming.*;
import javax.ejb.CreateException;
import javax.ejb.RemoveException;
import javax.rmi.PortableRemoteObject;

public class Client {
    // The name of the topic the client and the message bean use
    static private String TOPIC_NAME = "disableAccounts";

    public Client() {
    }

    public static void main(String[] args) {
        System.out.println("EAI message client");
        System.out.println();

        try {
            Client client = new Client();
            client.example();
        } catch (Exception e) {
            System.out.println(e);
        }
    }

    public void example() {
        try {
            // Create a message context
            Context mctx = new InitialContext();

            // Create the topic connection and start it
            TopicConnectionFactory cf = (TopicConnectionFactory)
                            mctx.lookup("weblogic.jms.ConnectionFactory");
            TopicConnection mTopicConn = cf.createTopicConnection();
            mTopicConn.start();

            Topic newTopic = null;
            TopicSession session = null;

            try {
                // Create a new topic session
                session = mTopicConn.createTopicSession(
                                false,   // non transacted
                                Session.AUTO_ACKNOWLEDGE);
```

```
            // Look up the topic name (if exist, otherwise exception)
            newTopic = (Topic) mctx.lookup(TOPIC_NAME);

        } catch(NamingException ex) {

            // If the topic doesn't exist create it
            newTopic = session.createTopic(TOPIC_NAME);
            mctx.bind(TOPIC_NAME, newTopic);
        }

        // Create a topic publisher
        TopicPublisher sender = session.createPublisher(newTopic);

        // Create a text message
        TextMessage tm = session.createTextMessage();
        tm.setText("EAI-dissableAccounts");

        // Publish the message
        sender.publish(tm);

    } catch(Exception ex) {
        ex.printStackTrace();
    }
  }
}
```

For more information about JMS and a discussion of MOM refer to Chapter 8.

To run the client we have to compile it first. We have to run it specifying the initial naming factory and the naming provider URL (similar to previous examples). The screenshot below shows the necessary commands:

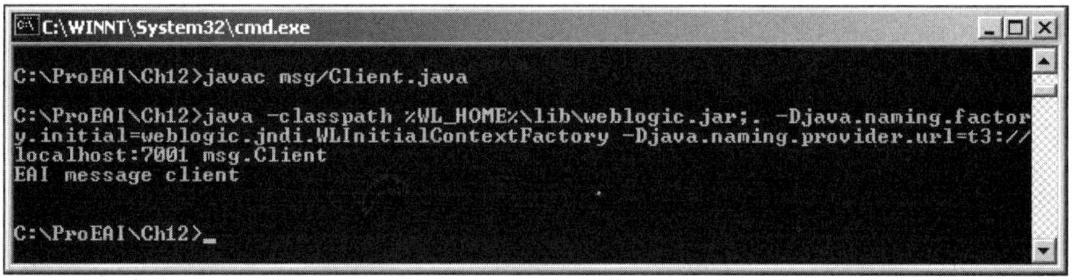

Notice that the client did not output any result, because the operation that it requested is not finished yet. The client has, however, returned the control to the operating system (the client is not blocked for the duration of performing the operation). We have to look into the application server window to see that our message-driven bean is actually peforming the work:

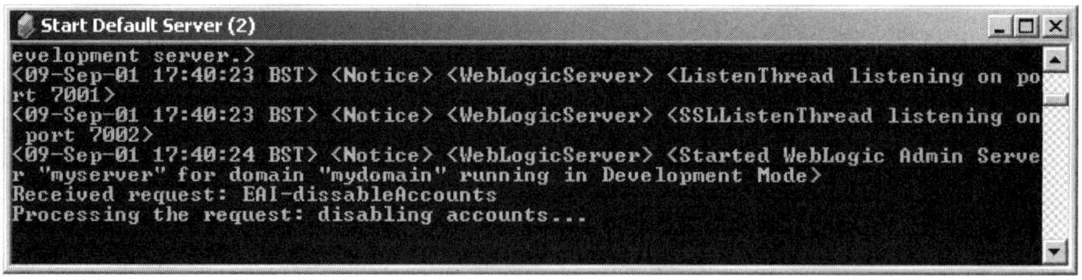

Performance Considerations

EJBs, like all distributed architectures, hide much of their complexity from the developer. However, to develop efficient applications we have to be aware of any potential performance bottlenecks.

As we have noted earlier in the chapter, prior to EJB 2.0, enterprise beans provided only remote interfaces, meaning that clients had to use remote method invocations. Such remote methods introduce performance issues due to stubs, skeletons, marshaling, and network overhead, so we should keep the number of remote method invocations as low as possible. This can be done with various approaches, including:

- ❑ Using coarse-grained interfaces
- ❑ Using Value Objects
- ❑ Using the Distributed Façade pattern

EJB 2.0 introduced local interfaces for session and entity beans. When developing virtual components to access existing applications, we have seen that we will often chain the virtual components, where a high-level virtual component will communicate with lower-level virtual components. To optimize communication between virtual components we should consider using local interfaces, which speed up the communication considerably.

To further optimize virtual components we should reuse resources as much as possible. We should partition our resources into client dependent and client independent and acquire and release them at appropriate times. We have demonstrated this with the development of the entity bean that accessed the CORBA wrapper, earlier in this chapter.

Using entity beans to access existing data also hides a lot of performance traps. We should notify the application server that we used a database that is shared with existing applications. This will increase the number of database loads and stores, because the container will have to preserve data integrity. With this in mind, it is even more important to access entity beans effectively. This includes:

- ❑ Accessing entity beans through session or message façade
- ❑ Accessing entity beans inside a transaction, which locks the underlying data and minimizes the number of database lookups

We can also influence the performance greatly at the bean deployment stage. For instance, regarding the pool size we will typically have to specify the minimum (or initial) and maximum numbers of bean instances in the pool, and determining the right number is indeed very tricky. A small number of instances will result in heavy passivation and activation by the container, thus lowering the performance. Too large a number, on the other hand, will waste resources. Selecting the ideal number of instances would prevent excessive context switching and would not leave any instances unused.

We can use profilers to identify the ideal number. As a rule of thumb, it is appropriate to select as many session or message-driven bean instances as we have simultaneous clients (or a few more). This limits the time that a client has to wait due to unavailable free instances. For entity beans, we should identify how many different instances of the same entity bean we use simultaneously.

Some application servers allow us to define the timeout value for stateful session and entity beans. This value defines how long a bean instance will remain activated, so after this time the container will remove the instance. To reach the optimal value it is useful to know the delay between the client method invocations. The worst possible value is to have it a little lower than the delay between method invocations and the same stateful session or entity bean. This would require unnecessary passivation and activation.

Another important deployment property is transaction isolation, if offered by the container vendor. Selecting the highest isolation level will result in poor performance. Selecting too low an isolation level can on the other hand result in data inconsistency. For the best performance, we should select the lowest isolation level that guarantees error-free operation.

Sometimes we can select whether the persistent storage is updated at the end of a transaction only, or also during a transaction. The first option usually offers better performance, because it avoids unnecessary database updates.

Particularly for integration, it is important if our EJB container supports read-only entity beans. Read-only entity beans are never modified by an EJB client, but they can, however, be modified directly through database access, most often by a legacy application. With read-only beans the application server does not need to call the `ejbStore()` method, thus improving the performance. In BEA WebLogic, for example, we can denote beans as read-only through `concurrency-strategy` deployment parameter, which we have to set to `ReadOnly`. If our application server does not provide this option, we could do it ourselves using BMP and not implementing the body of the `ejbStore()` method. Read-only entity beans cannot take part in transactions.

Some application servers support a setting for entity beans that are updated only occasionally, so we have to define the interval in which the data is reread from the persistent storage. This saves database lookups, because the container can omit calling the `ejbLoad()` method too frequently. Again, if the application server does not provide this option, we could implement this approach ourselves.

There are several other factors that influence the performance of EJBs. For further discussion on EJB performance and scalability take a look into the *Profession EJB* book from Wrox Press, which has a whole chapter dedicated to performance issues.

Summary

In this chapter we discussed the role of EJBs for integration. EJBs are one of the most important J2EE technologies; they are focused on the development of the business logic components. In integration, EJBs should present the business logic through their interfaces making the clients think that they are dealing with a newly developed information system – EJBs should realize higher-level virtual components. However, instead of implementing the functionality themselves, the EJBs should delegate it to the existing applications. They can do this with lower-level virtual components, wrappers, like those developed in CORBA and RMI-IIOP, through JMS, Connectors, or other proprietary APIs, exposed by existing applications.

On account of the relative importance of EJBs to integration, we covered all of their possible roles. First we discussed how to use entity beans to represent existing data, either through direct database access or through existing applications. We noted that we should not model entity beans after existing schemas, but rather design a new architecture model. We also discussed the situations in which we use CMP and BMP and have found that with relational data we can only use CMP. We also saw how to develop both CMP and BMP entity beans using the EJB 2.0 and EJB 1.1 persistence model.

Then we showed how to use entity beans to access data through existing applications over APIs, wrappers, or lower-level virtual components. We discussed when to use entity beans and when to use session beans, and showed how to partition resources so that we use them in the most effective way. Then we showed how to access a CORBA component wrapper from an entity bean.

Next we investigated session and message-driven beans. We identified that session and message-driven beans are particularly suitable for developing higher-level virtual components that expose business methods to the clients on one side, and reuse existing application through lower-level virtual components, wrappers, or APIs, on the other side.

We showed how to select between stateless and stateful session beans, how to design them, and finally how to implement them. We demonstrated how to access an RMI-IIOP virtual component from a session bean.

Then we discussed message-driven beans, presenting arguments for using message-driven beans instead of session beans. We also saw how to develop a message-driven bean and how to use them to integrate existing applications that use MOM.

Finally, we discussed performance-related questions and summarized the most important EJB performance issues.

In the next chapter, we'll change our focus slightly and take a look at the J2EE Connector Architecture (JCA). The JCA is a recent addition to the J2EE platform that provides a standardized API, thereby allowing J2EE components to interact with heterogeneous Enterprise Information Systems. We'll examine the finer details of the JCA and learn how to develop EAI applications using Connector components.

The J2EE Connector Architecture

This chapter presents the **J2EE Connector Architecture (JCA),** which was introduced in version 1.3 of Java 2 Platform, Enterprise Edition (J2EE). It is an EAI initiative to provide a standardized API architecture that enables J2EE components to interact with heterogeneous **Enterprise Information Systems (EIS)**, including Enterprise Resource Planning (ERP), transaction processing, and legacy database systems.

We will study the JCA and developing EAI applications using J2EE Connector components to integrate and interact with back-end EIS resources. In particular, we will be focusing on:

- ❑ The role of JCA in an EAI environment
- ❑ The architecture, services, and API of JCA
- ❑ How JCA works in a J2EE framework
- ❑ Programming with the Common Client Interface (CCI)
- ❑ The rules that a JCA developer must follow
- ❑ How to deploy and test JCA components
- ❑ The potential benefits of using JCA
- ❑ The current limitations and issues of JCA

The JCA specification is available from http://java.sun.com/j2ee/connector/. At the time of writing, only the J2EE 1.3 Reference Implementation had a complete JCA implementation, although some vendors have implemented beta versions of JCA for their J2EE application servers. A list of EIS vendors that provide EIS-specific resource adapters is available from http://java.sun.com/j2ee/connector/products.html, although at the time of writing no EIS vendors had made their resources adapters available for production use.

The Role of J2EE Connector Architecture in EAI

The integration of business applications has always been crucial to their successful use. Today, we might design our applications to integrate across the Internet. However, in earlier times many companies invested heavily in business and management information application systems such as:

❑   ERP applications – for example SAP R/3 and BAAN

❑   Customer Relationship Management (CRM) applications – for example Siebel and Clarify

❑   Mainframe transaction processing applications – for example CICS

❑   Legacy database systems – for example IMS

All these types of systems are known as **Enterprise Information Systems (EIS)**.

> **An EIS provides the information infrastructure and services for an enterprise. This information could be a set of records in a database, a business object in an ERP, a workflow object in a CRM, or a transaction program in a TP Monitor based application.**

Leveraging these complex business applications (within an EAI environment) so that they interact with each other is often a challenging task, and implementing this interaction for a high-availability web application can be time-consuming and difficult.

Prior to JCA, application server vendors would provide custom adapters for integrating EIS systems. These adapters would provide developers with custom native interfaces, which were complex to understand and limited in their effort to support a standard architecture. The limitations of this approach included:

❑   Application programming for EIS is proprietary by its very nature. The variety of application systems means there can be no generic interface mechanism for integration with open architectures.

❑   Most large-scale EAI-based applications require high-availability and scalability with regard to the number of clients and connection management. Unfortunately adding clients to an application could involve expensive additional license fees. Custom adapters lacked support for the connection management features provided by J2EE application servers.

❑   The lack of a standard infrastructure that provides a security mechanism and generic transaction management support means that managing security and distributed transactions over multiple back-end applications can be extremely complex.

> **JCA provides EAI-based application developers with a standardized method for integrating EIS with J2EE components. It does this by defining a common API and a common set of services that the developer can use from within the J2EE environment.**

The following diagram shows how a J2EE environment that uses JCA might be arranged:

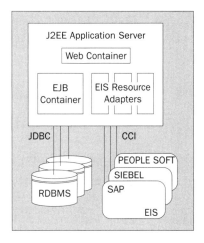

In an EAI environment that requires the integration of a J2EE-based application with an existing EIS, we simply need to install the appropriate EIS-specific J2EE connector (a JCA-compliant **resource adapter**) into our application server.

Once the resource adapter is installed, we can develop J2EE components to interface with the EIS using the **Common Client Interface (CCI)** API. We can use the CCI API in the same way that we make use of JDBC to interface with relational databases. This means that development is simplified by not having any EIS-specific programming outside the adapter, and having configuration completely independent of the back-end EIS.

It is intended that eventually all J2EE application server vendors will implement JCA services and that the EIS vendors will implement JCA-compliant EIS resource adaptors. This would boost the productivity of both the EAI and J2EE application developer, reduce developments costs, and protect existing investment in EIS systems by providing a scalable EAI solution through J2EE.

The Elements of JCA

JCA is implemented in a J2EE 1.3 application server, and the resource adapters are implemented and provided by an EIS vendor. Resource adapters are EIS-specific, pluggable J2EE components for the application server, and provide a standard interface for communicating with the underlying EIS system.

JCA defines the following list of elements and services:

❑   **System-level contracts and services**
    These define the standard interface between the J2EE components, the application server provider, and the EIS system. The contracts and services are implemented in the application server by the J2EE server provider and in the resource adapter by the EIS vendor. The implementation of contracts and services defines a logical (not physical) separation between the application server and the resource adapter. This separation is defined in terms of system-level roles and responsibilities, which allows the J2EE server and the resource adapter to collaborate with each other's underlying mechanisms (for example, connection pooling, security, and transactions). The separation also enables a JCA-compliant resource adapter to plug in to any J2EE server.

❑ **The JCA Common Client Interface (CCI)**
This defines a client API that J2EE components (such as JSP pages and EJBs) can use to connect and interact with EIS systems. In addition to J2EE client components, the CCI also allows non-managed applications (such as Java applets and application clients) to integrate with an EIS using a JCA-compliant resource adapter.

❑ **Packaging and deployment interfaces**
These allow various EIS resource adapters to plug into J2EE applications. We'll understand how this is done in *Packaging and Deploying a Resource Adapter*.

The following diagram illustrates how the JCA and components access EIS resources:

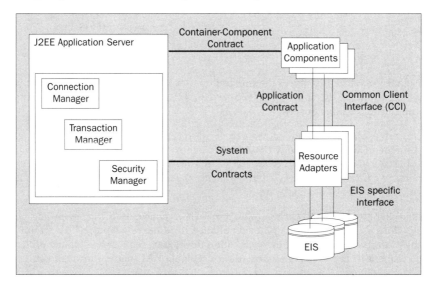

The resource adapter is the fundamental component of the JCA; it serves as the central connector among the J2EE components, the application server, and the EIS system.

In a J2EE application framework that uses JCA, an EIS vendor will provide JCA-compliant resource adapters with CCI as a part of its implementation. J2EE server vendors provide application servers that support JCA system-level contracts. These contracts enable resource adapters to plug into the application server to provide connectivity to the underlying EIS resources. This allows J2EE application developers to develop integration components using CCI and allows them to avoid the connection, security, and transaction mechanisms that are meant for connectivity with one or more EIS resources.

The JCA specification supports two types of environments for the client application that uses the resource adapter:

❑ **Managed Environment**
A managed environment defines a multi-tier, web-enabled, J2EE-based application that accesses one or more EIS. The application may contain one or more application components (for example, EJBs, JSP pages, and servlets), which are deployed in their respective containers. In the JCA context, these applications are referred to as **managed applications**.

❑ **Non-managed Environment**
JCA also supports access to one or more EIS systems from non-managed application clients, such as applets or Java client applications. Typically, this is in a two-tier architecture in which an application client directly uses a resource adapter library. In this case, the resource adapter provides its low-level transactions and security to its clients. In the JCA context, these applications are referred as **non-managed applications**.

Comparing JCA with JDBC

JCA and JDBC have identical mechanisms to deal with connection and transaction management.

> **Resource adapters for EIS systems are analogous to JDBC drivers for relational databases.**

The following table compares the features of JDBC and JCA:

JDBC 3.0	JCA 1.0
Provides a generic interface to interact with relational databases	Provides a standard architecture for J2EE and Java applications to integrate and interact with EIS resources
The JDBC API defines a standard Java API to access relational databases	The JCA Common Client Interface (CCI) provides an EIS-independent API
Uses JDBC drivers specific to a RDBMS	Uses an EIS-specific resource adapter to interact with an EIS
J2EE servers implement JDBC connection pool mechanisms to create connections to a database	J2EE servers implement JCA service contracts to establish a connection factory and manage connections with an EIS
Supports non-managed applications (two-tier applications), which use JDBC	Supports non-managed applications (two-tier applications), which use CCI
JDBC 3.0 provides support and relationship with JCA Service Provider Interface	Defines Service Provider Architecture for integrating application server services (such as transaction, connection, and security)
Supports both XA and non-XA transactions with underlying XA data sources	Supports both XA and non-XA transactions with underlying EIS resources
Provides an interface to support the Java Transaction API (JTA) and Java Transaction Service (JTS)	Supports JTA with a contract between the J2EE transaction manager and the EIS resource manager

The JCA Resource Adapter

The JCA resource adapter contains an EIS-specific library (which can be written in Java or with native interface components). This library provides connectivity to the EIS it represents. The resource adapter runs in the J2EE application server's address space and manages the connectivity to the underlying EIS.

JCA requires that all JCA-compliant EIS resource adapters and J2EE application servers support the system-level contracts.

> A contract sets out the responsibilities between layers of the application and implements a standard interface between those layers.

JCA also recommends (but does not mandate) that all resource adapters support CCI as their client API. This provides a J2EE-based solution for application development that integrates multiple EIS. It also enables EIS resource adapters to plug into an application server and collaborate with all system-level mechanisms.

Resource Adapter Contracts

As per the JCA specification, resource adapters implement two types of contracts:

- **Application contracts**
  Application contracts define the CCI API through which a J2EE client component (such as an EJB or servlet) or a non-managed client (such as an applet) communicates with the underlying EIS resources. For more information on CCI, you should refer to the later section on *The Common Client Interface.*

- **System-level contracts**
  System-level contracts enable the resource adapter to link with the application server services, in order to manage connections, transactions, and security.

The JCA 1.0 specification defines the following system-level contracts for the resource adapter to access, and the J2EE application server to implement.

Connection Management

Connection management is a service contract that enables an application server to offer its own services to create and manage connection pools with the underlying EIS resource. It provides a scalable connection management facility to support a large number of clients. The connection management contract is intended to:

- Establish a consistent application programming practice for providing connection acquisition for both managed (J2EE applications) and non-managed (two-tier) applications

- Enable an EIS resource adapter to provide a connection factory and connection interfaces based on the CCI, specific to the type of resource adapter and EIS

- Provide a generic mechanism for the J2EE-managed components by which a J2EE application server can provide services such as transactions, security, advanced pooling, and error tracing/logging

- Provide support for connection pooling services as part of a J2EE application server

Transaction Management

The transaction management contract extends the applications server's transactional capability to the underlying EIS resource managers. An EIS resource manager manages a set of shared EIS resources that participate in a transaction. A resource manager can manage two types of transaction:

- ❑ Transactions controlled and coordinated by external transaction managers
- ❑ Transactions managed internally that involve no external transaction managers

The transaction manager provided within the application server can manage transactions across multiple EIS resource managers. Resource adapters utilizing the J2EE transaction manager services provide three different levels of transaction support:

- ❑ XA transactions
- ❑ Location transactions
- ❑ No transactions

XA transactions support a JTA XA resource-based transaction management contract with a JCA-compliant resource adapter and its underlying EIS resource manager. This means that participating EIS resources also support JTA based XA transactions by implementing a XAResource interface through its resource adapter.

> **The JTA XAResource interface enables two or more resource managers to participate in transactions coordinated by an external transaction manager.**

XA transactions allow a transaction to be managed by a transaction manager that is external to the resource adapter. When a J2EE application component demarcates an EIS connection request as part of a transaction, the application server is responsible for enlisting the XA resource with the transaction manager. When the client closes that connection, the application server de-lists the XA resource from the transaction manager. Once the transaction is completed, it cleans up the EIS connection. This allows the business component to participate in two-phase commits.

Local transactions are demarcated by the J2EE server container (container-managed) or by the J2EE component (component-managed). This allows the application server to manage resources local to the application and its resource adapter. In component-managed transactions, the J2EE component uses the JTA UserTransaction interface or the transaction API specific to the EIS.

When an application component requests an EIS connection, the application server starts a local transaction using the currently available transaction context. When the application component closes that connection, the application server commits, or rolls back on the local transaction and cleans up the EIS connection.

No transactions occur when a resource adapter does not require or support an XA or local transaction.

We'll look at transactions again in more detail in Chapter 15.

Security Management

The security management service defines the security mechanism between the application server and the EIS resource. There are a variety of mechanisms used to protect an EIS against unauthorized access (and other security threats), including:

❑   User identification, authentication, and authorization of principals

❑   Secure communication between the application server and the EIS resource, using open network communication security protocols such as Kerberos, which provides end-to-end security with authentication and confidentiality services (for more information on Kerberos security mechanisms refer to Chapter 16)

❑   An EIS-specific security mechanism, such as exists in Lotus Domino, SAP, or BAAN

The security contract between the J2EE server and the EIS resource adapter extends the connection management contract. It provides the following EIS sign-on mechanism:

❑   It passes the connection request from the resource adapter to the J2EE application server and enables the server with its authentication and authorization services

❑   It propagates the security context with security credentials from the application server to the resource adapter

We'll explore security in more detail in Chapter 16.

EIS Sign-on

The creation of an EIS connection usually involves the creation of a sign-on process. This is based on the security context, which creates an authentication and authorization process. If the security context changes the connection must be re-authenticated. An EIS sign-on requires one or more of the following steps:

❑   Determine the resource principal (the identity of the initiating caller) under whose security context a new connection to an EIS will be established

❑   Authenticate the resource principal if the connection is not already authenticated

❑   Establish a secure association between the application server and the EIS (additional mechanisms such as SSL or Kerberos can also be deployed)

❑   Control access to EIS resources

Once a secure association is established, the connection is associated with the security context of the initiating user. Subsequently, all application-level invocations of an EIS instance using the connection occur under the security context of that user.

JCA recommends that J2EE application server vendors provide and support container-managed sign-on for J2EE-managed applications and application-managed sign-on for non-managed applications:

❑   **Application-managed sign-on**
    The client component provides security credentials (typically a username and password) when it requests a connection to an EIS.

❑ **Container-managed sign-on**

The J2EE client component does not present any security credentials. It is the J2EE container's responsibility to find the necessary sign-on credentials and provide them to the resource adapter when it requests a connection to an EIS. In this scenario, the container must find the resource principal and provide this information to the resource adapter in the form of a Java Authentication and Authorization Service (JAAS) subject.

Packaging and Deploying a Resource Adapter

JCA defines packaging and deployment interfaces, which enable various resource adapters to plug easily into a J2EE application server in a modular and portable manner. The resource adapter module (which has a file extension of `.rar`) is similar to J2EE application module (which has a file extension of `.ear`). The following figure illustrates the steps involved in the packaging and deployment of a resource adapter module intended to connect a J2EE application with an EIS resource. This process is very similar to how we deploy EJBs and web components in a J2EE container:

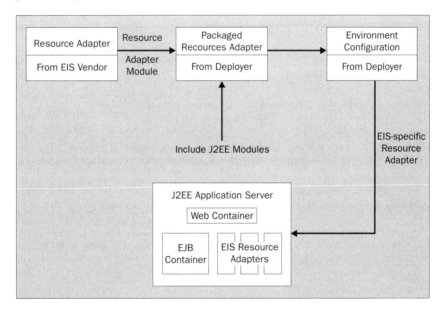

The packaging and deployment process of a resource module follows these steps:

1. The EIS resource adapter provider (usually the EIS vendor) develops a set of Java interfaces and utility classes as part of the resource adapter implementation. These Java classes implement the JCA contracts and EIS-specific functionality provided by the resource adapter.

2. The Java classes, the native libraries provided by the resource adapter provider, and a deployment descriptor (which details the environment configuration) are packaged into a **resource adapter module (RAR)**. As with other J2EE component deployment descriptors, the resource adapter module deployment descriptor defines the service contract attributes for the deployment of a resource adapter.

3. During deployment, the application deployer installs a resource adapter module on an application server and then configures it with the J2EE applications server and the underlying target EIS environment.

We mentioned earlier that the packaging and deployment process of a resource adapter module for an application is similar to other J2EE packaging and deployment processes, especially for web and EJB components. However, the roles and responsibilities involved in packaging and deploying the resource adapter are slightly different when compared to other J2EE components.

Packaging a Resource Adapter

An EIS resource adapter is a J2EE server component contained in a `.rar` archive. We can place one or more resource adapters in a directory and package them as `.rar` file(s). The following steps detail the typical packaging of a resource adapter:

1. Create a temporary staging directory.

2. Compile and/or copy the resource adapter Java classes into the staging directory.

3. Create a JAR in which to store the resource adapter Java classes, then add it to the top level of the staging directory.

4. Create a subdirectory named `META-INF` in the staging directory.

5. Create a deployment descriptor file (named `ra.xml`) in the `META-INF` subdirectory and add entries for the resource adapter (we will see examples of these entries shortly). The DTD for `ra.xml` is available at http://java.sun.com/dtd/connector_1_0.dtd.

6. Create a J2EE vendor-specific deployment descriptor in the `META-INF` subdirectory and add entries for the resource adapter (again, we will see examples shortly).

7. When all of the resource adapter classes and deployment descriptors are made available in the staging directory, you can create the resource adapter module RAR file by running the following command from within the directory:

```
jar cvf wroxResourceAdapter.rar -C staging-dir .
```

This command creates a RAR that we can deploy on any JCA-compliant J2EE server. Alternatively we could package it in an application JAR file. (The `-C staging-dir` option defines the `jar` command to change to the `staging-dir` directory so that the directory path defined in the RAR is relative to the directory where you staged the resource adapters.)

A packaged resource adapter module defines the contract between an EIS resource adapter provider and deployer and includes the following elements:

❏ Java classes and interfaces that are required for the implementation of both the JCA contracts and the functionality of the resource adapter

❏ Utility Java classes for the resource adapter

❑ Platform-dependent native libraries required by the resource adapter

❑ Help files and documentation specific to the resource adapter

❑ Descriptive meta information that ties these elements together

The deployment process begins with the RAR or a deployment directory, both of which contain the compiled resource adapter interfaces and implementation classes provided by the EIS resource adapter provider. Resource adapters in a J2EE environment use a common directory format, for example:

```
\J2EEServerHome
\config
\wroxdomain
\applications\
           wroxResourceAdapter\
                             readme.html
                             eis.jar
                             utilities.jar
                             windos.dll
                             solaris.so
                             images\
                                   ra.jpg
                             META-INF\
                                     ra.xml
                                     J2EEServerProvider-ra.xml
```

In this structure, `ra.xml` is the deployment descriptor for the resource adapter and `J2EEServerProvider-ra.xml` is the J2EE vendor deployment descriptor, which defines the operational parameters unique to the server provider. The `eis.jar` and `utilities.jar` archives contain Java interfaces along with implementation classes of the EIS resource adapter. `windos.dll` and `solaris.so` are examples of native libraries.

This same format can be used when a resource adapter provided by the EIS vendor is packaged as RAR. It is similar to the process of deploying an enterprise application (.ear) in a J2EE environment. After copying a RAR, our J2EE server installation looks like this:

```
\J2EEServerHome
\config
\wroxdomain
\applications\
           wroxResourceAdapter.rar
```

The Deployment Descriptor (ra.xml)

EIS resource adapters use descriptors to define the contract between an EIS resource adapter provider and a deployer of that environment. It provides the attributes that allow the deployer to deploy an EIS resource adapter in its environment. The J2EE vendor requires an additional deployment descriptor, which defines those operational attributes unique to the server provider.

A resource adapter module also includes those deployment requirements specified by the resource adapter provider in the deployment descriptor. The `ra.xml` file contains the deployment attributes of a resource adapter. Therefore, to set the necessary deployment properties for the resource adapter we would need to edit the `ra.xml` file packaged with it.

The resource adapter provider is responsible for providing the deployment descriptor for an EIS-specific resource adapter. For JCA 1.0, certain information is required from a resource adapter deployment descriptor provided by an EIS resource adapter provider. General information about a resource adapter can include:

- The name of the resource adapter
- The name of the vendor who provides the resource adapter
- The type of the supported EIS system supported (for example, ERP)
- The version of the JCA supported

For example:

```
<display-name>BlackBoxNoTx</display-name>
<vendor-name>Java Software</vendor-name>
<spec-version>1.0</spec-version>
<eis-type>JDBC Database</eis-type>
<version>1.0</version>
```

The provider specifies the fully qualified name of the Java class that implements the `javax.resource.spi.ManagedConnectionFactory` interface:

```
<managedconnectionfactory-class>
  com.sun.connector.blackbox.NoTxManagedConnectionFactory
</managedconnectionfactory-class>
```

The provider specifies the fully qualified name of the Java interface and implementation class for the connection factory:

```
<connectionfactory-interface>javax.sql.DataSource</connectionfactory-interface>
<connectionfactory-impl-class>
  com.sun.connector.blackbox.JdbcDataSource
</connectionfactory-impl-class>
```

The provider specifies the fully qualified name of the Java interface and implementation class for the connection interface:

```
<connection-interface>java.sql.Connection</connection-interface>
<connection-impl-class>
  com.sun.connector.blackbox.JdbcConnection
</connection-impl-class>
```

The provider specifies the level of transaction support provided by the resource adapter implementation. The level of transaction support is usually one of `NoTransaction`, `LocalTransaction`, or `XATransaction`:

```
<transaction-support>NoTransaction</transaction-support>
```

The provider defines name, type, description, and optional default values for the properties that have to be configured on each `ManagedConnectionFactory` instance. The following example uses a Cloudscape database:

```
<config-property>
  <config-property-name>ConnectionURL</config-property-name>
  <config-property-type>java.lang.String</config-property-type>
  <config-property-value>
    jdbc:cloudscape:rmi:CloudscapeDB;create=true
  </config-property-value>
</config-property>
```

The provider specifies all the authentication mechanisms supported by the resource adapter. This includes the support provided by the resource adapter implementation but not by the underlying EIS instance. The standard values are: `BasicPassword` and `Kerbv5`:

```
<authentication-mechanism>
  <authentication-mechanism-type>BasicPassword</authentication-mechanism-type>
  <credential-interface>
    javax.resource.security.PasswordCredential
  </credential-interface>
</authentication-mechanism>
```

The provider specifies whether its resource adapter supports re-authentication of an existing connection. The default value is specific to the EIS resource adapter:

```
<reauthentication-support>false</reauthentication-support>
```

Roles and Responsibilities in Deployment

There are four roles during deployment and they each have different responsibilities. They are:

- ❑ The resource adapter provider
- ❑ The application server vendor
- ❑ The application component provider
- ❑ The deployer

The Resource Adapter Provider

The resource adapter provider is responsible for providing a resource adapter for an EIS. An EIS vendor or a third-party vendor typically provides the resource adapter and its application deployment tools system. The resource adapter provider is also responsible for specifying the deployment descriptor (we just looked at what needs to go into this deployment descriptor).

The Application Server Vendor

The application server vendor provides the JCA implementation for the J2EE application server, along with support for JCA component-based applications. This isolates the J2EE application components from the details of the underlying system-level services.

621

The Application Component Provider

The application component provider develops the J2EE application component that interacts with EIS systems to provide its application functionality (the application component provider develops programs using CCI). The application component provider does not create code that includes transactions, security, concurrency, and distribution; the J2EE server is responsible for providing these services.

The Deployer

The deployer is responsible for configuring a resource adapter for the target J2EE environment. The configuration of a resource adapter is based on attributes defined in the deployment descriptor, which is part of the resource adapter module. The deployer must typically configure:

❑   The property for creating connections to underlying EIS instances (set per `ManagedConnectionFactory`)

❑   The application server for the transaction management, based on the level of transaction support specified by the resource adapter

❑   Security in the operational environment, based on the security requirements specified by the resource adapter in its deployment descriptor

Deployment Options

It is possible to deploy a resource adapter in two different ways in Sun's J2EE Reference Implementation (J2EE RI). It can be deployed using the deploy tool (either at the command line or using the GUI version). On the command line, we would run something like:

```
deploytool -deployConnector %J2EE_HOME%/lib/connector/blackbox-tx.rar localhost
```

A resource adapter could also be deployed as part of a J2EE application deployed as an EAR.

Deploying a Resource Adapter as a J2EE Application

JCA allows us to include a RAR inside an EAR (just as we can include a WAR or JAR), and then deploy the application in a J2EE server. To deploy a J2EE application that contains a RAR we must first create a valid `application.xml` file and place it in the `META-INF` directory of the EAR. When we create `application.xml` we must ensure that it contains the new `<connector>` element that identifies the resource adapter within the EAR. For example:

```
<connector>wroxBlackBoxNoTx.rar</connector>
```

Let's take a quick check of what we've covered so far. We've looked at resource adaptors, resource adapter contract, and how to package and deploy a resource adaptor. Our next task is to demonstrate the configuration and deployment of resource adapters using the black box resource adapters provided by the J2EE RI.

At the time of writing, even beta versions of EIS resource adapters were hard to find. Therefore, the examples are discussed using the black box resource adapters provided with the J2EE 1.3 RI. The adapters are meant for testing the packaging and deployment process as well as to test CCI.

Black Box Resource Adapters

> Black box adapters are included as part of the J2EE 1.3 RI to support and demonstrate JCA compliance. They are the same as EIS resource adapters but use a relational database as an underlying EIS and are intended for testing purposes only.

Black box resource adapters are primarily used for testing end-to-end connectivity with a JCA-compliant J2EE application server and its J2EE compatibility as per the JCA 1.0 specification. The black box resource adapters provided with the J2EE RI use JDBC calls to interact with a DBMS, which provides a simple mock environment for testing purposes.

Using a Black Box Adapter

We'll examine the `DemoConnector` example, which demonstrates a black box resource adapter accessing a Cloudscape database using JDBC. The example uses an entity EJB that performs transactions using the black box adapter configured with a database, and then displays the output. As we work through this example, we'll look at how to:

- ❑ Select a black box adapter and transaction level from the J2EE RI
- ❑ Configure and deploy the black box adapter
- ❑ Test the black box adapter within a transaction using an entity bean as a managed client

Selecting a Black Box Adapter

Let's look at the black box adapters available in the J2EE 1.3 RI. First, check that your installation includes the black box resource adapters. Usually they are located in `%J2EE_HOME%\lib\connector\`. There should be five black box resource adapters (identified by their `.rar` extensions) which support the different transaction levels we discussed earlier:

- ❑ `blackbox-notx.rar` – To support `NO_TRANSACTION`
- ❑ `blackbox-tx.rar` – To support `LOCAL_TRANSACTION`
- ❑ `blackbox-xa.rar` – To support `XA_TRANSACTION`
- ❑ `cciblackbox-tx.rar` – To support `LOCAL_TRANSACTION`
- ❑ `cciblackbox-xa.rar` – To support `XA_TRANSACTION`

In our example, we'll be using the `blackbox-tx.rar` resource adapter in order to demonstrate how to use local transactions.

XA and Non-XA Transactions Using a Black Box Adapter

The black box resource adapters require an URL in order to create connection factories with underlying EIS. The black box resource adapters generally use JDBC drivers to connect with the database. For non-XA transactional resources, this requires the configuration of the `ConnectionURL` property. For XA-supported resources, we need to configure the `XADataSource` property.

623

Our example uses the Cloudscape database server provided in the J2EE RI. There are default values provided in the deployment descriptor of a black box adapter. For non-XA black box adapters (using non-XA transaction levels) the default value of ConnectionURL is jdbc:cloudscape:rmi:CloudscapeDB;create=true. For XA black box adapters (using XA transaction levels) the default value of XADataSourceName is jdbc/XACloudscape_xa.

Deploying the Black Box Resource Adapter

To configure and deploy a black box resource adapter, we need to:

❑   Configure our database, JDBC drivers, and create our application specific tables

❑   Deploy our packaged black box resource adapter module into a running J2EE server

Configuring the Database

Deploying and testing this black box resource adapter example (blackbox-tx.rar) requires a database table. We'll be using the Cloudscape database provided with the J2EE RI. To create the table, start the Cloudscape engine:

```
%J2EE_HOME%\bin\cloudscape -start
```

Then run the following SQL script:

```
CREATE TABLE demoaccount (
            accountid VARCHAR(3) CONSTRAINT Demoaccount_pk PRIMARY KEY,
            firstname VARCHAR(25),
            lastname  VARCHAR(25),
            balance   DECIMAL(12,2)
          );
```

We've configured our database, but don't close down the database process just yet.

Deploying the Resource Adapter

Now we need to start the J2EE server:

```
%J2EE_HOME%\bin\j2ee -start
```

Once the server is up and running, we can deploy the black box adapter with the application deploy tool (run using deploytool from the command line). First, we'll create a new application for our example, called Blackbox. Select New I Application and enter the following data in the dialog box:

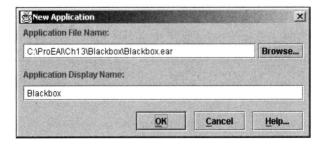

Then select **Add to Application | Resource Adapter RAR** from the **File** menu. From the resulting open dialog: browse to where the RAR files are located (`%J2EE_HOME%\lib\connector`), select the `blackbox-tx.rar` file, and add it to the application:

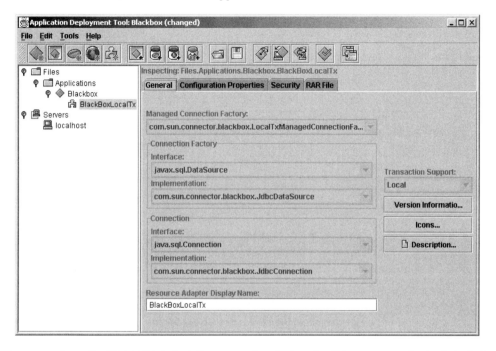

We can see from the **General** tab that the connection factory for this resource adapter is in fact simply a `javax.sql.DataSource` class.

To use this adapter we need to deploy the adapter. Select the `Blackbox` application and use **Deploy** from the **Tools** menu, clicking straight through to finish without altering the default settings:

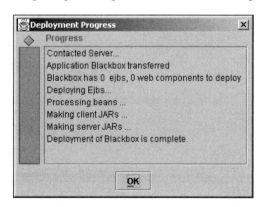

Next, expand the **Servers** node so that you can see localhost, and then select it. In the right-hand pane switch to the **Resource Adapters** tab. Press the **New...** button to add a new connection factory. You'll see that the `blackbox-tx.rar` adapter is already selected, so all we need to do is to add the **Connection Factory JNDI Name**. In this case, we will use `eis/WroxEIS` (note that the ConnectionURL property is pointing to a Cloudscape database):

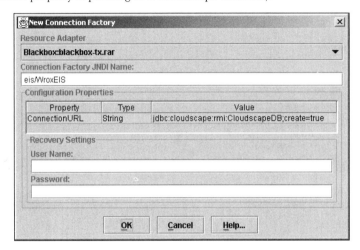

Press the OK button and if everything worked out, you'll get a confirmation prompt:

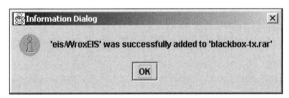

Select the **Resource Adapters** tab and expand the `Blackbox` adapter; it should look like this:

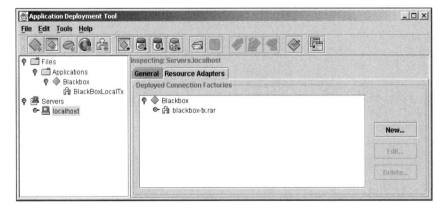

Now we're ready to create the entity bean that we can use to test this adapter.

Testing the Black Box Resource Adapter

The `DemoConnector` example is an entity bean that will serve as a simple (non-managed) client. It will use the black box resource adapter to perform transactions with a Cloudscape database.

The Home Interface

The home interface defines methods to create an account, find an account using the account ID, find accounts by last name, and find accounts between a range of values:

```
import java.util.Collection;
import java.rmi.RemoteException;
import javax.ejb.*;

public interface DemoAccountHome extends EJBHome {

  public DemoAccount create(String accountid, String firstName,
                            String lastName, double balance)
    throws RemoteException, CreateException;

  public DemoAccount findByPrimaryKey(String accountid)
    throws FinderException, RemoteException;

  public Collection findByLastName(String lastName)
    throws FinderException, RemoteException;

  public Collection findInRange(double low, double high)
    throws FinderException, RemoteException;
}
```

The Remote Interface

The remote interface defines methods to debit funds from the account, credit funds to the account, get the first name, get the last name, and get the balance of the account:

```
import javax.ejb.EJBObject;
import java.rmi.RemoteException;

public interface DemoAccount extends EJBObject {
  public void debit(double amount) throws ProcessingException, RemoteException;
  public void credit(double amount) throws RemoteException;
  public String getFirstName() throws RemoteException;
  public String getLastName() throws RemoteException;
  public double getBalance() throws RemoteException;
}
```

The Bean Implementation Class

Next, we create the implementation of our bean:

```
import java.sql.*;
import javax.sql.*;
import java.util.*;
```

```
import javax.ejb.*;
import javax.naming.*;

public class DemoAccountBean implements EntityBean {

  private String accountid;
  private String firstName;
  private String lastName;
  private double balance;
  private EntityContext context;
  private Connection con;
```

Here we define the JNDI name of the EIS resource:

```
private String eisName = "java:comp/env/eis/WroxEIS";
```

Then we provide the implementations of the methods we defined in the home and remote interfaces:

```
public void debit(double amount)  throws ProcessingException {
  if (balance - amount < 0) {
    throw new ProcessingException();
  }
  balance -= amount;
}

public void credit(double amount) {
  balance += amount;
}

public String getFirstName() {
  return firstName;
}

public String getLastName() {
  return lastName;
}

public double getBalance() {
  return balance;
}
```

Now we define those methods required for all EJBs:

```
public String ejbCreate(String accountid, String firstName,
                        String lastName, double balance)
    throws CreateException {
  if (balance < 0.00) {
    throw new CreateException("Negative balance value not permitted.");
  }
  try {
    insertRow(accountid, firstName, lastName, balance);
```

```
    } catch (Exception ex) {
      throw new EJBException("ejbCreate: " + ex.getMessage());
    }
    this.accountid = accountid;
    this.firstName = firstName;
    this.lastName = lastName;
    this.balance = balance;

    return accountid;
  }

  public String ejbFindByPrimaryKey(String primaryKey) throws FinderException {
    boolean result;
    try {
      result = selectByPrimaryKey(primaryKey);
    } catch (Exception ex) {
      throw new EJBException("ejbFindByPrimaryKey: " + ex.getMessage());
    }
    if (result) {
      return primaryKey;
    } else {
      throw new ObjectNotFoundException("Account Id " + primaryKey +
                                " not found.");
    }
  }

  public Collection ejbFindByLastName(String lastName)
      throws FinderException {
    Collection result;
    try {
      result = selectByLastName(lastName);
    } catch (Exception ex) {
      throw new EJBException("ejbFindByLastName " + ex.getMessage());
    }
    return result;
  }

  public Collection ejbFindInRange(double low, double high)
      throws FinderException {
    Collection result;
    try {
      result = selectInRange(low, high);
    } catch (Exception ex) {
      throw new EJBException("ejbFindInRange: " + ex.getMessage());
    }
    return result;
  }

  public void ejbRemove() {
    try {
       deleteRow(accountid);
    } catch (Exception ex) {
      throw new EJBException("ejbRemove: " +  ex.getMessage());
    }
  }
}
```

Create a method to set the entity context and initialize connections:

```
public void setEntityContext(EntityContext context) {
  this.context = context;
  try {
    makeConnection();
  } catch (Exception ex) {
    throw new EJBException("database failure " + ex.getMessage());
  }
}
```

Define a method to unset entity context for closing connections:

```
public void unsetEntityContext() {
  try {
    con.close();
  } catch (SQLException ex) {
    throw new EJBException("unsetEntityContext: " + ex.getMessage());
  }
}
```

We define some more methods that are required for our EJB:

```
public void ejbActivate() {
  accountid = (String)context.getPrimaryKey();
}

public void ejbPassivate() {
  accountid = null;
}

public void ejbLoad() {
  try {
    loadRow();
  } catch (Exception ex) {
    throw new EJBException("ejbLoad: " + ex.getMessage());
  }
}

public void ejbStore() {
  try {
    storeRow();
  } catch (Exception ex) {
    throw new EJBException("ejbStore: " + ex.getMessage());
  }
}

public void ejbPostCreate(String accountid, String firstName,
                          String lastName, double balance) { }
```

This is a method to make connections to an EIS resource:

```
private void makeConnection() throws NamingException, SQLException {
  InitialContext ic = new InitialContext();
  DataSource ds = (DataSource) ic.lookup(eisName);
  con = ds.getConnection();
}
```

This method inserts account data:

```
private void insertRow (String accountid, String firstName,
                         String lastName, double balance)
    throws SQLException {

  String insertStatement = "INSERT INTO demoaccount VALUES ( ? , ? , ? , ? )";
  PreparedStatement prepStmt = con.prepareStatement(insertStatement);
  prepStmt.setString(1, accountid);
  prepStmt.setString(2, firstName);
  prepStmt.setString(3, lastName);
  prepStmt.setDouble(4, balance);
  prepStmt.executeUpdate();
  prepStmt.close();
}
```

This method deletes an account using the account ID:

```
private void deleteRow(String accountid) throws SQLException {
  String deleteStatement = "DELETE FROM demoaccount WHERE accountid = ? ";
  PreparedStatement prepStmt = con.prepareStatement(deleteStatement);
  prepStmt.setString(1, accountid);
  prepStmt.executeUpdate();
  prepStmt.close();
}
```

This method selects accounts using the primary key:

```
private boolean selectByPrimaryKey(String primaryKey)
    throws SQLException {

  String selectStatement = "SELECT accountid " +
                   "FROM demoaccount WHERE accountid = ? ";
  PreparedStatement prepStmt = con.prepareStatement(selectStatement);
  prepStmt.setString(1, primaryKey);
  ResultSet rs = prepStmt.executeQuery();
  boolean result = rs.next();
  prepStmt.close();
  return result;
}
```

This method selects accounts using the last name:

```
private Collection selectByLastName(String lastName)
    throws SQLException {

  String selectStatement = "SELECT accountid " +
                      "FROM demoaccount WHERE lastname = ? ";
  PreparedStatement prepStmt = con.prepareStatement(selectStatement);
  prepStmt.setString(1, lastName);
  ResultSet rs = prepStmt.executeQuery();
  ArrayList al = new ArrayList();
  while (rs.next()) {
    String accountid = rs.getString(1);
    al.add(accountid);
  }
  prepStmt.close();
  return al;
}
```

This method selects accounts for a given range of balance:

```
private Collection selectInRange(double low, double high)
    throws SQLException {

  String selectStatement = "SELECT accountid from demoaccount " +
                      "WHERE balance BETWEEN  ? AND ?";
  PreparedStatement prepStmt = con.prepareStatement(selectStatement);
  prepStmt.setDouble(1, low);
  prepStmt.setDouble(2, high);
  ResultSet rs = prepStmt.executeQuery();
  ArrayList al = new ArrayList();
  while (rs.next()) {
    String accountid = rs.getString(1);
    al.add(accountid);
  }
  prepStmt.close();
  return al;
}
```

This method is used to select an account:

```
private void loadRow() throws SQLException {
  String selectStatement = "SELECT firstname, lastname, balance " +
                      "FROM demoaccount WHERE accountid = ? ";
  PreparedStatement prepStmt = con.prepareStatement(selectStatement);
  prepStmt.setString(1, this.accountid);
  ResultSet rs = prepStmt.executeQuery();
  if (rs.next()) {
    this.firstName = rs.getString(1);
    this.lastName = rs.getString(2);
    this.balance = rs.getDouble(3);
    prepStmt.close();
```

```
    } else {
      prepStmt.close();
      throw new NoSuchEntityException("Account " + accountid + " not found");
    }
  }
}
```

Our final method is used to update account information and balances:

```
private void storeRow() throws SQLException {
  String updateStatement = "UPDATE demoaccount SET firstname = ? ," +
                           "lastname = ? , balance = ? " +
                           "WHERE accountid = ?";
  PreparedStatement prepStmt = con.prepareStatement(updateStatement);
  prepStmt.setString(1, firstName);
  prepStmt.setString(2, lastName);
  prepStmt.setDouble(3, balance);
  prepStmt.setString(4, accountid);
  int rowCount = prepStmt.executeUpdate();
  prepStmt.close();
  if (rowCount == 0) {
    throw new EJBException("Account update" + accountid + " failed.");
  }
}
}
```

The ProcessingException Class

```
public class ProcessingException extends Exception {

  public ProcessingException() {}

  public ProcessingException(String msg) {
    super(msg);
  }
}
```

The EJB Deployment Descriptor

```
<?xml version="1.0" encoding="UTF-8"?>

<!DOCTYPE ejb-jar PUBLIC '-//Sun Microsystems, Inc.//DTD Enterprise JavaBeans
2.0//EN' 'http://java.sun.com/dtd/ejb-jar_2_0.dtd'>

<ejb-jar>
  <display-name>DemoAccount</display-name>
  <enterprise-beans>
    <entity>
      <display-name>DemoAccount</display-name>
      <ejb-name>DemoAccount</ejb-name>
      <home>DemoAccountHome</home>
      <remote>DemoAccount</remote>
      <ejb-class>DemoAccountBean</ejb-class>
      <persistence-type>Bean</persistence-type>
```

```
        <prim-key-class>java.lang.String</prim-key-class>
        <reentrant>False</reentrant>
        <security-identity>
          <description></description>
          <use-caller-identity></use-caller-identity>
        </security-identity>
        <resource-ref>
          <res-ref-name>eis/WroxEIS</res-ref-name>
          <res-type>javax.sql.DataSource</res-type>
          <res-auth>Container</res-auth>
          <res-sharing-scope>Shareable</res-sharing-scope>
        </resource-ref>
      </entity>
    </enterprise-beans>
  </ejb-jar>
```

Deploying the Bean

Compile the various Java files and create the EJB JAR file called `DemoAccount.jar`, which should have the following structure:

```
Blackbox/
        DemoAccount.class
        DemoAccountBean.class
        DemoAccountHome.class
        ProcessingException.class
        META-INF/
                ejb-jar.xml
```

Now select the `Blackbox` application and add the newly created JAR file to the application, using Add to Application | EJB JAR...:

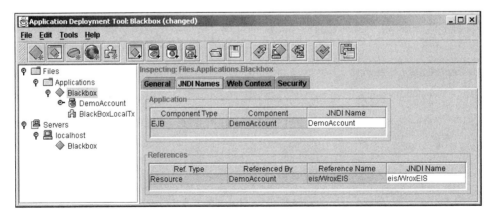

Provide the application with the JNDI names shown. Finally, deploy the `Blackbox` application into the running server, remembering to click the Return Client Jar box to create the client JAR file.

The Client

```
import java.util.*;
import javax.naming.*;
import javax.rmi.PortableRemoteObject;

public class DemoAccountClient {

  public static void main(String[] args) {
    try {
      Context initial = new InitialContext();
```

Get the JNDI lookup for our EJB:

```
      Object objref = initial.lookup("DemoAccount");
```

Then get the EJB home object:

```
      DemoAccountHome home = (DemoAccountHome)PortableRemoteObject.narrow(objref,
                                                     DemoAccountHome.class);
```

We demonstrate the use of the `create()`, `credit()`, and `debit()` methods of our EJB for a variety of accounts:

```
      DemoAccount ramesh = home.create("100", "Ramesh", "Roger", 0.00);
      ramesh.credit(50.00);
      ramesh.debit(10.15);
      double balance = ramesh.getBalance();
      System.out.println("Account Balance = " + String.valueOf(balance));
      ramesh.remove();

      DemoAccount craig = home.create("200", "Craig", "Berry", 0.00);
      craig.credit(100.59);

      DemoAccount nikki = home.findByPrimaryKey("200");
      nikki.debit(2.00);
      balance = nikki.getBalance();

      System.out.println("Account Balance = " + String.valueOf(balance));
      DemoAccount bill = home.create("300", "Bill", "Clinton", 0.00);
      bill.credit(2000.00);

      DemoAccount bob = home.create("400", "Bob", "Clinton", 0.00);
      bob.credit(1000.00);

      DemoAccount jim = home.create("500", "Jimmy", "Clinton", 0.00);
      jim.credit(1000.00);
```

We find accounts by account by last name `Clinton`:

```
Collection c = home.findByLastName("Clinton");
Iterator i = c.iterator();

while (i.hasNext()) {
  DemoAccount account = (DemoAccount)i.next();
  String accountid = (String)account.getPrimaryKey();
  double amount = account.getBalance();
  System.out.println(accountid + ": " + String.valueOf(amount));
}
```

Then, we find accounts by a range of values:

```
c = home.findInRange(20.00, 99.00);
i = c.iterator();

while (i.hasNext()) {
  DemoAccount account = (DemoAccount)i.next();
  String accountid = (String)account.getPrimaryKey();
  double amount = account.getBalance();
  System.out.println(accountid + ": " + String.valueOf(amount));
}

System.exit(0);

} catch (ProcessingException ex) {
  System.err.println("Caught a ProcessingException: " + ex.getMessage());
} catch (Exception ex) {
  System.err.println("Caught an exception." );
  ex.printStackTrace();
}
}
}
```

Once it's compiled, we can run the client using this command:

```
java -classpath %J2EE_HOME%\lib\j2ee.jar;BlackboxClient.jar;. DemoAccountClient
```

The client should display the following results in your command window:

The Common Client Interface (CCI)

The **Common Client Interface (CCI)** provides us with a simple approach to the problem of writing a more complex Java interface to an underlying EIS resource. Until the emergence of CCI, this problem had been an issue between the Java developers and EIS vendors commonly known as 'integration chaos'. By implementing CCI in resource adapters, EIS vendors can provide a Java interface to their EIS products that will run on any J2EE 1.3 application server.

The CCI defines an EIS-independent client API that enables J2EE components to integrate and interact across heterogeneous EIS resources. It defines the remote-function call interfaces for executing queries and transactions with an EIS as well as interfaces to obtain the results.

> **CCI provides function call APIs for J2EE application servers and its components (via a JCA resource adapter) to create and manage connections with an EIS resource; to execute an operation with an EIS resource; to manage data objects/records as input, output, or return values.**

The JCA specification recommends that the CCI be the basis for richer functionality as an extensible programming model provided by the EIS resource adapter vendors, rather than being the API to be used by most application developers. Although the CCI is independent of a specific EIS (for example, data types specific to an EIS), the CCI is capable of being driven by EIS-specific meta data from a repository. The CCI is also designed to use the JavaBeans architecture and Java Collections framework.

> For example, a resource adapter can implement the `ManagedConnectionFactory` interface as a JavaBean. This improves the ability of tools to manage the configuration of `ManagedConnectionFactory` instances.

The JCA 1.0 specification recommends (but does not mandate) that all EIS resource adapters implement CCI as their client API. It also requires that these resource adapters provide the system contracts with a J2EE application server. It is important to note that a resource adapter may also choose to have another client API in addition to the CCI (similar to the vendor-provided client API available in JDBC implementations).

The benefits of using CCI are faster developer productivity, reduced cost of integration, portable code, scalable application frameworks, and easier maintainability.

CCI Interfaces and Classes

JCA defines CCI interfaces and classes that fit within five types.

Connection Interfaces

These represent the connection factory that enables connections to an EIS instance via the resource adapter:

```
javax.resource.cci.ConnectionFactory
javax.resource.cci.Connection
javax.resource.cci.ConnectionSpec
javax.resource.cci.LocalTransaction
```

`javax.resource.cci.ConnectionFactory` is a public interface that enables connections to an EIS instance via the resource adapter. The EIS resource adapter usually provides this interface. An application looks up a `ConnectionFactory` instance from the JNDI namespace and uses it to obtain EIS connections. `ConnectionFactory` has the following methods:

```
public RecordFactory getRecordFactory() throws ResourceException;
public Connection getConnection() throws ResourceException;
public Connection getConnection(javax.resource.cci.ConnectionSpec properties)
  throws ResourceException;
public ResourceAdapterMetaData getMetaData() throws ResourceException;
```

The `getConnection()` method creates a `Connection` instance. Using the `getConnection()` method with the `javax.resource.cci.ConnectionSpec` parameter requires security information and connection parameters. The `getRecordFactory()` method creates a `RecordFactory` instance, which creates `Record` objects.

`ConnectionSpec` provides the connection request-specific information and properties like username, password, and other parameters to the `ConnectionFactory` while making a connection to an EIS. The `Connection` class represents a connection to an EIS resource. It is used for subsequent operations with an underlying EIS.

Interaction Interfaces

These provide a component to drive an interaction executing specific operation with an EIS instance (specified using an `InteractionSpec` which provides the EIS-specific object properties):

```
javax.resource.cci.Interaction
javax.resource.cci.InteractionSpec
```

`Interaction` creates an interaction with a connected EIS with specific operations and has the following methods:

```
public Connection getConnection();
public void close() throws ResourceException;
public boolean execute(InteractionSpec ispec, Record input, Record output)
  throws ResourceException;
public Record execute(InteractionSpec ispec, Record input)
  throws ResourceException;
```

`InteractionSpec` defines the *interaction* providing the EIS-specific object properties (for example, data types, or schema) associated with an EIS.

Data Representation Interfaces

These are used to represent data structures involved in an interaction with an EIS instance:

```
javax.resource.cci.Record
javax.resource.cci.MappedRecord
javax.resource.cci.IndexedRecord
javax.resource.cci.RecordFactory
javax.resource.cci.Streamable
javax.resource.cci.ResultSet
java.sql.ResultSetMetaData
```

A `Record` is the Java representation of a data structure used as input or output to an EIS function. `RecordFactory` creates `Record` objects (such as `IndexedRecord`, `ResultSet`, or `MappedRecord`). `LocalTransaction` creates a transaction context to perform a local transaction using the Java Transaction API (for example, `javax.transaction.UserTransaction`) and manages its own transaction and persistence. The `javax.resource.cci.LocalTransaction` class defines a transaction demarcation interface for resource manager local transactions and has the following methods:

```
public void begin() throws ResourceException;
public void commit() throws ResourceException;
public void rollback() throws ResourceException;
```

Meta Data Interfaces

These provide basic meta data information about a resource adapter implementation and an EIS-specific connection:

```
javax.resource.cci.ConnectionMetaData
javax.resource.cci.ResourceAdapterMetaData
javax.resource.cci.ResultSetInfo
```

Exception and Warning Classes

These provide exception handling and resource warning during interaction with an EIS resource:

```
javax.resource.ResourceException
javax.resource.cci.ResourceWarning
```

To establish a connection to an EIS resource and to perform interactions such as querying and transactions the developer needs to adhere to a standard approach defined by the JCA 1.0 specification. The specification explains two scenarios for obtaining a connection to an EIS. These are discussions about:

❑   Connection to a managed application (J2EE Application)

❑   Connection to a non-managed application (Applets or two-tier Java applications)

Let's discuss these two scenarios and the steps involved for connecting and interacting with each.

Connection with a Managed Application

In this scenario, the application obtains a connection provided by the connection factory, which is configured during the deployment of a resource adapter module in the J2EE server. This connection factory is usually defined in the deployment descriptor of the resource adapter.

The following UML diagram shows the steps that are involved when a managed application obtains a connection to an EIS instance from a connection factory and then interact with an EIS:

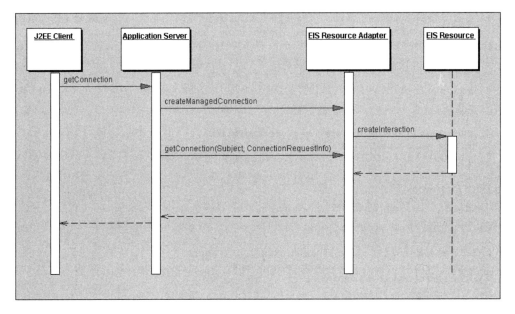

Let's take a closer look at the steps involved:

1. The application assembler specifies the connection factory requirements for a J2EE application component using its deployment descriptor (for example, web.xml or ejb-jar.xml). An EJB assembler specifies the following elements in the deployment descriptor for a connection factory reference. This connection factory reference is part of the deployment descriptor for EJB or the web component and not the resource adapter:

```
<res-ref-name>eis/wroxEIS</res-ref-name>
<res-type>javax.resource.cci.ConnectionFactory</res-type>
<res-auth>Application or Container</res-auth>
```

2. The J2EE application server uses the configured resource adapter to create connections to the underlying EIS resource.

3. The J2EE component looks up a connection factory instance in the environment using JNDI services.

```
Context initctx = new InitialContext();

javax.resource.cci.ConnectionFactory cf =
                (javax.resource.cci.ConnectionFactory)
                initctx.lookup("java:comp/env/eis/wroxEIS");
```

The JNDI lookup results in a connection factory instance of type java.resource.cci.ConnectionFactory, as specified in the application's deployment descriptor.

4. The application invokes the `getConnection()` method on the connection factory to obtain an EIS connection. It returns a `Connection` instance, which represents a physical handle to an EIS. The application component can obtain multiple connections by calling the `getConnection()` on the connection factory as required:

```
javax.resource.cci.Connection cx =
                    (javax.resource.cci.Connection)cf.getConnection();
```

5. Then the application uses the `Connection` object's `createInteraction()` method to create an `Interaction` instance. The `javax.resource.cci.Interaction` enables a component to execute EIS functions.

6. Create `Record` instances using the `RecordFactory` create method (methods also include `createIndexedRecord()` and `createMappedRecord()`).

7. Use `LocalTransaction` by defining a transaction context to perform operations with an EIS. `javax.resource.cci.LocalTransaction` defines a transaction demarcation interface for resource manager local transactions. The J2EE application component uses the `LocalTransaction` interface to demarcate local transactions.

8. Once the J2EE application finishes with the connection, it closes the connection using the `close()` method on the `Connection` interface. If the application attempt to close an allocated connection method fails after its use, the connection is considered as unused and the application server takes care of the cleanup of unused connections.

Connection with a Non-Managed Application

In a non-managed application connection scenario (which might involve an applet or two-tier Java application) it is the application developer's responsibility to create a connectivity model by using low-level APIs. These are exposed by the resource adapter, equivalent to that of a configured managed-application in a J2EE environment. Typically, a non-managed application involves the lookup of a connection factory instance, obtaining an EIS connection, using the connection for EIS operations, and closing the connection. This model is similar to the way a two-tier JDBC application client accesses a database system in a non-managed environment.

The following UML diagram details the steps involved when a non-managed application obtains a connection to an EIS instance from a connection factory. It then interacts with an EIS:

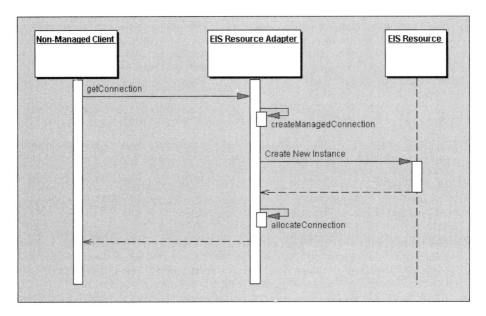

Again, let's take a closer look at the steps involved:

1. The non-managed application component calls a method on the
    `javax.resource.cci.ConnectionFactory` instance (returned from the JNDI lookup)
    to get a connection to the underlying EIS resource.

2. The `ConnectionFactory` instance delegates the connection request from the non-
    managed application to the default `ConnectionManager` instance provided by the
    resource adapter. As per the JCA 1.0 specification, in a non-managed environment the
    EIS resource adapter provides the `ConnectionManager` implementation as equivalent to
    the J2EE server environment.

3. The `ConnectionManager` instance then creates a new connection to the EIS resource by
    calling the `createManagedConnection()` method of `ManagedConnectionFactory`.

4. The `ManagedConnectionFactory` instance handles the `createManagedConnection()`
    method by creating a new connection to the underlying EIS resource represented by a
    `ManagedConnection` instance. The `ManagedConnectionFactory` uses the
    `ConnectionRequestInfo`, and its configured set of properties (like port number, server
    name) to create a new `ManagedConnection` instance.

5. The `ConnectionManager` instance calls the `getConnection()` method of
    `ManagedConnection` to get an application-level connection handle. This actually
    provides a temporary handle that the non-managed application client can use to access
    the underlying `ManagedConnection` instance.

6. The `ConnectionManager` instance returns the connection handle to the
    `ConnectionFactory` instance, which then returns the `Connection` to the non-managed
    application client that initiated a connection request.

7. Then the application uses the `Connection` object's `createInteraction()` method to create an `Interaction` instance, which enables a component to execute EIS functions.

8. Create `Record` instances using `RecordFactory` create methods (including `createIndexedRecord()` and `createMappedRecord()`).

9. Use `LocalTransaction` by defining a transaction context to perform operations with an EIS.

10. Once the non-managed application finishes with the connection, it must close the connection using the `close()` method on the `Connection` interface.

Next, we'll use CCI black box resource adapters and learn how to write J2EE application clients to invoke CCI API methods available from the resource adapter. We'll also discuss how to use the different interfaces and classes defined by the CCI to access a resource adapter for a database or EIS.

Using a CCI Black Box Adapter

This example is a fictitious bookstore application that allows us to add new books and to get the total quantity of books available from a database. We'll implement a stateful session bean, which uses a CCI black box adapter to run SQL stored procedures for querying and executing transactions with a RDBMS. It is quite similar to a JDBC application but instead of using JDBC calls, the CCI API is used to pass parameters and execute the SQL stored procedures on an underlying database.

The steps involved in implementing the `BookStore` example using a CCI black box adapter are as follows:

❑   Implement the session bean using CCI

❑   Deploy the CCI black box adapter

❑   Deploy the session bean

❑   Test the CCI black box adapter

Developing a Session Bean with CCI

In this example, a stateful session bean is used to invoke CCI calls on a CCI black box adapter to execute stored procedures in a database. Like any other EJB, it contains a home interface (`BookStoreHome`), a remote interface (`BookStore`) and a bean implementation class (`BookStoreBean`).

The Home Interface

BookHome simply defines a `create()` method to return a reference to the `Book` remote interface:

```
import javax.ejb.*;
import java.rmi.RemoteException;

public interface BookStoreHome extends EJBHome {
  BookStore create() throws RemoteException, CreateException;
}
```

The Remote Interface

Book contains the definition for two business methods:

```
import javax.ejb.EJBObject;
import java.rmi.RemoteException;

public interface BookStore extends EJBObject {
  public void insertBooks(String name, int quantity) throws RemoteException;
  public int getBooksCount() throws RemoteException;
}
```

The Bean Implementation Class

BookBean is the bean implementation class, which uses CCI. BookBean imports the CCI interfaces (that is, `javax.resource.cci.*`) and the interface classes (`com.sun.connector.cciblackbox.*`) specific to the black box adapter, along with `javax.resource.ResourceException`:

```
import java.math.*;
import java.util.*;
import javax.ejb.*;
import javax.resource.cci.*;
import javax.resource.ResourceException;
import javax.naming.*;
import com.sun.connector.cciblackbox.*;

public class BookStoreBean implements SessionBean {
```

In the `setSessionContext()` method, the bean uses environmental variables for the username and password to instantiate a `ConnectionFactory` for the CCI black box adapter:

```
private SessionContext sc;
private String user;
private String password;
private ConnectionFactory cf;

public void ejbRemove() {}
public void ejbActivate() {}
public void ejbPassivate() {}
public void ejbCreate() throws CreateException {}

public void setSessionContext(SessionContext sc) {
  try {
    this.sc = sc;
    Context ic = new InitialContext();
    user = (String) ic.lookup("java:comp/env/user");
    password = (String) ic.lookup("java:comp/env/password");
    cf = (ConnectionFactory) ic.lookup("java:comp/env/eis/WroxCCIEIS");
  } catch (NamingException ex) {
    ex.printStackTrace();
  }
}
```

The bean uses its private method getCCIConnection() to establish a connection with the database using the black box adapter. In the getCCIConnection() method, it instantiates a new CciConnectionSpec object which represents the implementation of the ConnectionSpec interface, with the user and password values obtained from the bean's context, and then calls the getConnection() method to obtain the connection. This creates a connection handle to the underlying EIS resource:

```
private Connection getCCIConnection() {
  Connection con = null;
  try {
    ConnectionSpec spec = new CciConnectionSpec(user, password);
    con = cf.getConnection(spec);
  } catch (ResourceException ex) {
    ex.printStackTrace();
  }
  return con;
}
```

The bean also contains a private method closeCCIConnection() to close a connection with the resource manager. The session bean uses this method internally to invoke a Connection object's close() method:

```
private void closeCCIConnection(Connection con) {
  try {
    con.close();
  } catch (ResourceException ex) {
    ex.printStackTrace();
  }
}
```

Now that we have defined the methods that allow our bean to interact with the underlying resource using CCI, let's create the methods to perform operations with the resource, in this case a database.

The BookStore session bean implements an insertBooks() method, which executes a local transaction to insert new records into the Book database table. This method invokes the database-stored procedure INSERTBOOKS that adds a new record with two values as arguments. Typical to a JDBC method call, the insertBooks() method first establishes a connection to the database via the black box adapter using getCCIConnection(), and then creates a new Interaction instance. Then the bean instantiates a new CciInteractionSpec object to define the database interaction properties required to communicate with a database (such as setting the stored procedure name and its parameters):

```
public void insertBooks(String name, int qty) {

  Connection con = null;
  try {
    con = getCCIConnection();
    Interaction ix = con.createInteraction();
    CciInteractionSpec iSpec = new CciInteractionSpec();
    iSpec.setFunctionName("INSERTBOOKS");
    iSpec.setSchema(user);
    iSpec.setCatalog(null);
```

```
        RecordFactory rf = cf.getRecordFactory();
        IndexedRecord iRec = rf.createIndexedRecord("InputRecord");
        boolean flag = iRec.add(name);
        flag = iRec.add(new Integer(qty));
        ix.execute(iSpec, iRec);
        } catch(ResourceException ex) {
          ex.printStackTrace();
        } finally {
          closeCCIConnection(con);
          System.out.println("Closed connection");
        }
      }
    }
```

The getBooksCount() method, using CCI, reads records from an underlying database table by
running the stored procedure COUNTBOOKS. The method uses an IndexedRecord (this is the only
Record currently supported by the CCI black box adapter), which holds its elements in an indexed
collection based on java.util.List:

```
    public int getBooksCount() throws ResourceException{
      int count = -1;
      Connection con = null;
      try {
        con = getCCIConnection();
        Interaction ix = con.createInteraction();
        CciInteractionSpec iSpec = new CciInteractionSpec();
        iSpec.setSchema(user);
        iSpec.setCatalog(null);
        iSpec.setFunctionName("COUNTBOOKS");
        RecordFactory rf = cf.getRecordFactory();
        IndexedRecord iRec = rf.createIndexedRecord("InputRecord");
        Record oRec = ix.execute(iSpec, iRec);
        Iterator iterator = ((IndexedRecord)oRec).iterator();
        while(iterator.hasNext()) {
        Object obj = iterator.next();
        if(obj instanceof Integer) {
          count = ((Integer)obj).intValue();
        } else if(obj instanceof BigDecimal) {
          count = ((BigDecimal)obj).intValue();
        }
      }
    } finally {
      closeCCIConnection(con);
      System.out.println("Closed Connection");
    }
    return count;
  }
```

The EJB Deployment Descriptor

```
    <?xml version="1.0" encoding="UTF-8"?>
    <!DOCTYPE ejb-jar PUBLIC
                '-//Sun Microsystems, Inc.//DTD Enterprise JavaBeans 2.0//EN'
                'http://java.sun.com/dtd/ejb-jar_2_0.dtd'>
    <ejb-jar>
```

```
<display-name>BookStore</display-name>
<enterprise-beans>
  <session>
    <display-name>BookStore</display-name>
    <ejb-name>BookStore</ejb-name>
    <home>BookStoreHome</home>
    <remote>BookStore</remote>
    <ejb-class>BookStoreBean</ejb-class>
    <session-type>Stateful</session-type>
    <transaction-type>Bean</transaction-type>
    <env-entry>
      <env-entry-name>user</env-entry-name>
      <env-entry-type>java.lang.String</env-entry-type>
    </env-entry>
    <env-entry>
      <env-entry-name>password</env-entry-name>
      <env-entry-type>java.lang.String</env-entry-type>
    </env-entry>
    <security-identity>
      <description></description>
      <use-caller-identity></use-caller-identity>
    </security-identity>
```

Note that the `<resource-ref>` element is of type `javax.resource.cci.ConnectionFactory`:

```
    <resource-ref>
      <res-ref-name>eis/WroxCCIEIS</res-ref-name>
      <res-type>javax.resource.cci.ConnectionFactory</res-type>
      <res-auth>Container</res-auth>
      <res-sharing-scope>Shareable</res-sharing-scope>
    </resource-ref>
  </session>
</enterprise-beans>
</ejb-jar>
```

The Client

The client invokes the `getBooksCount()` and `insertBooks()` methods on the session bean to test the CCI black box adapter:

```
import java.util.*;
import javax.naming.Context;
import javax.naming.InitialContext;
import javax.rmi.PortableRemoteObject;

public class BookStoreClient {

  public static void main(String[] args) {
    try {
      Context initial = new InitialContext();
      Object objref = initial.lookup("BookStore");

      BookStoreHome home =
        (BookStoreHome)PortableRemoteObject.narrow(objref, BookStoreHome.class);

      BookStore book = home.create();

      int count = book.getBooksCount();
```

```
        System.err.println("Current Book count = " + count);

        System.err.println("Inserting 2 new books...");
        book.insertBooks("USA Tour guide", 100);
        book.insertBooks("Europe Tour guide", 20);

        count = book.getBooksCount();
        System.err.println("Current Book count = " + count);
    } catch (Exception ex) {
        System.err.println("Caught an unexpected exception!");
        ex.printStackTrace();
    }
  }
}
```

Deploying the CCI Black Box Resource Adapter

As with the DemoAccount example we saw earlier, deploying the resource adaptor is a two-stage process. First, we need to configure the database to create the table and add the stored procedures, and then we need to deploy the adapter itself.

Configuring the Database

Configuring the database is a slightly more complex process than before, as besides creating the books table we also need to create the two stored procedures. We'll be using Cloudscape again however, the Cloudscape database has a rather unusual method of handling stored procedures. We'll explain what that method is in just a moment, but first let's create the books table. Use the following SQL to create the very simple books table:

```
CREATE TABLE books (name VARCHAR(32), qty INTEGER);
```

Now let's get back to the stored procedures. In order to use them with Cloudscape we need to write a Java class that provides the implementation of the procedure using basic JDBC. Then within the database, we create aliases for the stored procedures that point to this class. So for our COUNTBOOKS stored procedure, we'll add a method to our class that looks like this:

```
import java.lang.Integer;
import java.sql.*;
import java.io.*;

public class BookProcs implements Serializable {

  public static int countBooks() {
    int count = 0;
    try {
      Connection con =
      DriverManager.getConnection("jdbc:cloudscape:;current=true");
      PreparedStatement ptstmt =
      con.prepareStatement("SELECT COUNT(*) FROM books");
      ResultSet rs = ptstmt.executeQuery();
      while (rs.next()) {
        count = rs.getInt(1);
      }
      ptstmt.close();
    } catch (Exception ex) {
      ex.printStackTrace();
```

```
      }
    return count;
  }
}
```

Then we can add the following ALIAS to the Cloudscape database:

```
CREATE METHOD ALIAS COUNTBOOKS FOR BookProcs.countBooks;
```

In order for this to work, we need to make sure that the BookProcs class is in the classpath of the database. The easiest way to do this is to modify the %J2EE_CLASSPATH% variable (set in the userconfig.bat file).

For the INSERTBOOKS stored procedure, we need to add another method to BookProcs:

```
public static void insertBooks(String name, int qty) {
  try {
    Connection con =
    DriverManager.getConnection("jdbc:cloudscape:;current=true");
    PreparedStatement ptstmt =
    con.prepareStatement("INSERT INTO books VALUES (?,?)");
    ptstmt.setString(1, name);
    ptstmt.setInt(2, qty);
    ptstmt.executeUpdate();
    ptstmt.close();
  } catch(Exception ex){
    ex.printStackTrace();
  }
}
```

Then we can add the following ALIAS:

```
CREATE METHOD ALIAS INSERTBOOKS FOR BookProcs.insertBooks;
```

Deploying the Adapter

To deploy the adapter we'll use a similar method as before, except this time of course we'll be deploying the cciblackbox-tx.rar file. With the J2EE 1.3 Reference Implementation server running, open the deployment tool and create a new application called CCIAdapter. If you changed the userconfig.bat file, you will need to restart the server:

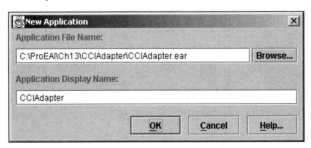

Then add an existing RAR file as before but this time select the %J2EE_HOME%\lib\connector\cciblackbox-tx.rar file. Then deploy the application.

Expand the Servers node until you can see your running server (most likely localhost) and select the server in the left-hand pane. On the right-hand pane, switch to the Resource Adapters tab, and hit the New button. On the New Connection Factory dialog, select the CCIAdapter:cciblackbox-tx.rar as the Resource Adapter and give it a JNDI Name of eis/WroxCCIEIS:

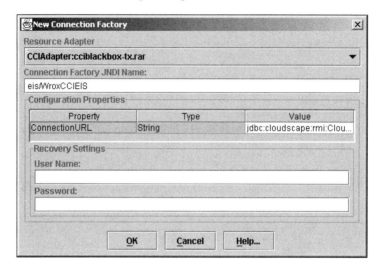

Make sure that the ConnectionURL property is pointed to the correct database and press OK to add the adapter:

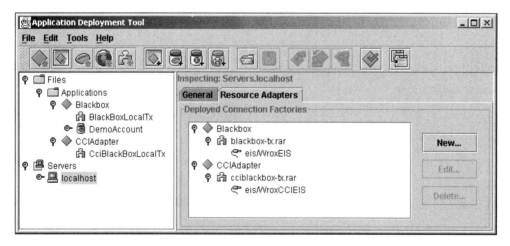

Now that we've deployed the CCI black box resource adapter module with a connection factory into the J2EE RI server, created the database tables, and stored procedures, let's deploy the session bean and run the client.

Deploying and Testing the CCI Application

Compile the EJB `java` files (you will need to add the `cciblackbox.tx.jar` file, found within the `cciblackbox-tx.rar` archive, to your class path), and then add them to the application:

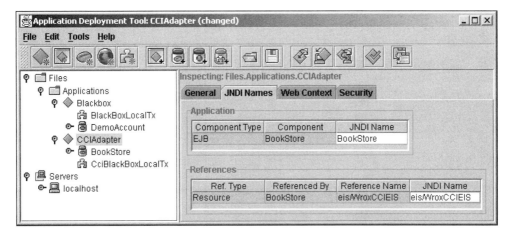

Add the relevant JNDI names (as shown) and deploy the application again, remembering to create the client JAR. To run the client, use the following command:

```
java -classpath %J2EE_HOME%\lib\j2ee.jar;CCIAdapterClient.jar;. BookStoreClient
```

If everything works successfully, you will get the following output:

```
C:\ProEAI\Ch13\CCIAdapter>java -classpath %J2EE_HOME%\lib\j2ee.jar;CCIAdapterCli
ent.jar;. BookStoreClient
Current Book count = 2
Inserting 2 new books...
Current Book count = 4

C:\ProEAI\Ch13\CCIAdapter>_
```

The SAP Resource Adapter

In this section, we'll discuss using a beta version of SAP Resource Adapter (SAP-RA) provided by In-Q-My Technologies Inc. A free demo download is available from http://www.inqmy.com/download/download.htm. To try out this snippet you would require a SAP R/3 system and an In-Q-My application server implementation that provides the system contracts for the SAP-RA (beta).

> *Although it is unlikely that you will have access to a SAP system, this section should still prove instructive, as it will demonstrate further the techniques we have looked at so far.*

In-Q-My SAP-RA is a pluggable JCA resource adapter component that allows J2EE 1.3 application servers to integrate with a SAP system. SAP-RA complies and supports the JCA 1.0 and can be used with any J2EE server that supports the JCA 1.0 specification.

SAP-RA implements the CCI interface of the JCA 1.0 and maps it to the native methods of another Java-library referred to as JCO (SAP Java Connector). JCO uses a SAP native interface to establish and manage connections with an underlying SAP system. It also invokes calls to the functions of a SAP system using native remote functions calls (RFCs).

The following diagram illustrates how the J2EE server and components use SAP-RA to access a SAP system:

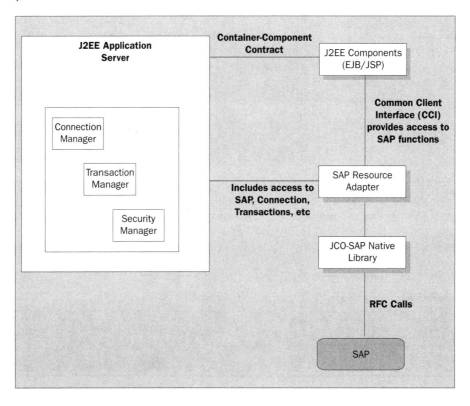

Using CCI with SAP-RA

The following is a 'Hello World' example snippet that uses SAP-RA to connect to a SAP R/3 system. Using JCA-CCI, it calls the remote-function STFC_CONNECTION. This function uses the "Hello World to In-Q-My SAP-RA"string as an input-parameter. The string is returned to the system by the echo function (this functionality is provided by SAP) followed by another string, which provides brief information about the SAP system.

We perform a JNDI lookup for the connection factory:

```
InitialContext initialcontext = new InitialContext();
ConnectionFactory sapConnectionFactory = (ConnectionFactory)
initialcontext.lookup("java:comp/env/EIS/MySAPConnectorFactory");
```

Then we define the connection credentials: client, language, username, and password:

```
ConnectionSpec sapConnectionSpec =
                    new SAPConnectionSpec("000", "EN", "username","password");
```

Then we establish the SAP connection:

```
Connection sapConnection = sapConnectionFactory.getConnection(sapConnectionSpec);
```

We create a mapped record:

```
MappedRecord input = sapConnectionFactory.getRecordFactory()
                    .createMappedRecord("STFC_CONNECTION");
```

We declare and populate some result sets:

```
ResultSet importResultSet = (ResultSet) input.get("import");
ResultSet exportResultSet = (ResultSet) input.get("export");
```

Now we can set the input string:

```
importResultSet.updateString("REQUTEXT", "Hello World using In-Q-My SAP-RA.");
```

We create an `Interaction` object and make use of its `execute()` method:

```
Interaction interaction = sapConnection.createInteraction();
interaction.execute(null, input);
```

Finally, we extract the results:

```
System.out.println("The SAP-RA returned the following:");
System.out.println("ECHOTEXT : " + exportResultSet.getString("ECHOTEXT"));
System.out.println("RESPTEXT : " + exportResultSet.getString("RESPTEXT"));
```

Missing Elements in JCA 1.0

We'll finish this chapter by briefly discussing what's missing from version 1.0 of the JCA specification. The two key missing elements are:

❑   The current specification does not support asynchronous communication, and it supports only synchronous request/reply communication models. This could be a limiting problem to connect with message queues.

❑   There is no built-in XML support mechanism available to retrieve XML data. But CCI can be used to support XML.

These limitations are due to be resolved in the next version of the specification – JCA 1.1. For further details, you should refer to http://java.sun.com/j2ee/connector/.

Summary

JCA provides a standard architecture, which fixes some shortfalls of common EAI solutions. With a long list of EIS vendors providing EIS-specific resource adapters and the success of J2EE in web-based enterprise applications, it is anticipated that JCA will emerge as the primary integration mechanism for back-end EIS resources. The major benefits of JCA are that it:

❑   Enables organizations to leverage both the advantages of their existing EIS systems and J2EE

❑   Allows developers to write (or rewrite) new applications using J2EE and also encapsulating functional parts of existing applications in EJB or Web components

In this chapter, we studied how we can use the J2EE Connector Architecture 1.0. We looked at some examples of its use as well as its relevance for EAI implementation. We discussed how JCA solves EAI integration issues faced by the industry today. We also explained and demonstrated the steps involved in integrating and interacting with an EIS by using the black box adapters provided with the J2EE RI.

In the next chapter, we will look at how we can use COM bridges, which will allow us to integrate our applications with COM-based applications on Microsoft Windows.

14

COM Bridges for Windows Integration

This chapter presents some techniques and implementation strategies to enable integration between Java/J2EE-based applications and Microsoft Win32/COM-based application components. In other words, we'll discuss how to implement a component wrapper that accesses an existing application written and deployed in Windows' COM architecture.

To enable us to integrate COM-based applications with those that are not, we need to use some form of bridge or adapter to cross the differences in connectivity mechanisms, operating systems, communication protocols, standards, data formats, and so on. Unfortunately, due to a lack of a common platform or a standards-based approach, there is no real standard way for integrating COM-based applications with non-Windows-based applications. As a result we will explore a number of the different options that are available.

This chapter explores traditional development approaches, commercially available integration technologies, and implementation strategies for COM integration with J2EE-based EAI applications, focusing on the following:

- ❑ Overview of the COM Architecture
- ❑ Java-COM integration
- ❑ Commercial bridges for Java-COM integration
- ❑ Developing a custom Java bridge to COM applications
- ❑ Common issues and limitations

An Overview of the Microsoft COM Architecture

The Microsoft **Component Object Model (COM)** defines the way that Windows-based software components communicate with each other by defining a binary and network standard regardless of location, network, operating system (providing COM is supported – but in reality Windows is the only real executable platform) and Windows programming language. Windows 2000 also introduced COM+ as an extension to COM to provide runtime services. This allows for managed components, akin to the container architecture of J2EE, and supports services such as life-cycle management, type information, naming, database access, data transfer, registry, and asynchronous communication.

COM Architectural Elements and Characteristics

In a COM implementation, a COM client object gets a **pointer** to a COM server and uses its services by calling methods on the server's interfaces. A COM server is an object that provides services to its clients; these services are in the form of COM interface implementations that can be called by any client that is able to get a pointer to the interfaces on the server object:

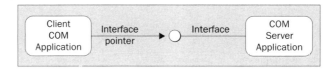

A COM object is defined by a COM class (written in any language that can produce binary-compatible code, such as C, Visual C++, Visual J++, and Visual Basic), which acts as a template for the creation of a COM object. The actual creation of a COM object is controlled by the **COM runtime**.

COM defines a binary standard to describe the interface contract between COM objects. The interface contract (the order of the methods, parameters, and so on) is fixed at compilation time into a binary file. This COM interface is really a virtual method array, which contains pointers to the method implementations:

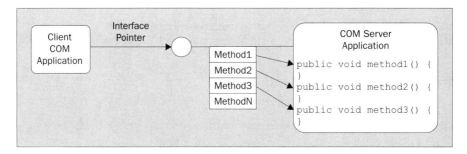

COM uses a standard interface, called IUnknown, to identify and discover what interfaces a component makes available for client invocation. The IUnknown interface provides a QueryInterface() method, which enables a client to query a COM object for the interfaces that it exposes. If the object supports the requested interface, the method must return a pointer to that interface. This permits an object to navigate freely through the interfaces provided by a COM object.

COM uses **globally unique identifiers (GUIDs)** to identify every interface and every component object class. These GUIDs are 128-bit (16 byte) numbers described as a string. Fortunately, we don't have to generate these numbers ourselves, as the COM runtime will do it for us. The COM runtime will generate Class IDs (CLSIDs) to identify COM classes, and Interface IDs (IIDs) to identify interfaces. These GUIDs are stored in the Windows registry the `HKEY_CLASSES_ROOT\CLSID` key. The COM runtime will use the registry to locate and then create any requested COM objects.

The following diagram represents the creation of a COM object:

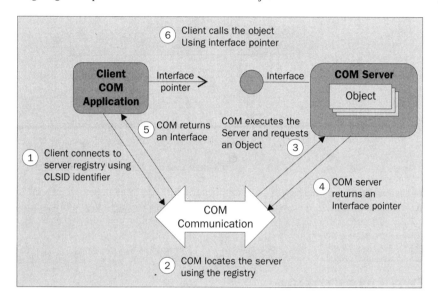

In a typical scenario, a client application will invoke a COM server object as follows:

1. The client initiates a request to create the server object

2. The COM runtime uses the registry to locate the server object

3. The COM runtime then creates an instance of the server object

4. The COM runtime returns a reference for the server object's `IUnknown` interface to the client

5. The client can then use the `IUnknown` interface to locate functional interfaces on the server, from which it can call methods

The COM runtime creates the server object in a process space as defined by the binary executable of the object. This can either be in-process (where the server object is created within the same process space of the client – DLLs) or out-of-process (where the server object is created in a separate process space to the client – EXEs). Obviously DLLs can only be used on the same local machine.

DCOM

The **Distributed Component Object Model (DCOM)** extends COM support to objects across a network, allowing COM applications to be distributed in multiple locations. DCOM defines the inter process communication through a network protocol. At run time, COM components provide services to clients and components using RPC, also conforming to the DCOM protocol standard.

The following diagram represents the COM architecture using DCOM:

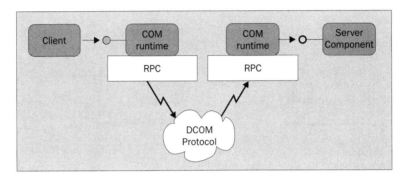

Clients are essentially unaware that they are communicating with a remote object, as DCOM employs a stub and skeleton mechanism, akin to the way CORBA provides language and platform independence. When the server object is registered in the client's registry, the location of the object is indicated as being on another machine somewhere on the network.

Java-COM Integration

Application Development Trends (Magazine), August 1996 declared: "Java provides the nirvana of cross-platform development and will continue to do so for sometime". This is *true* even today; Java is the de facto standard programming language and tool for cross platform development. The major strength of Java technology is its portability of applications over a variety of operating environments, applications, and databases.

At the same time, the Win32/COM environment has become the de facto standard for client development on the desktop, through applications such as MS Office and the RAD development environment of VB. Therefore, with the popularity of Java on the server-side and COM on the client-side it is becoming increasingly necessary to integrate the two platforms. In addition, MS has recently been trying to push itself as a viable server-side deployment platform, so there is increasingly a need to integrate server-side COM components as well.

In an EAI environment, Java-COM application integration helps EAI developers to seamlessly integrate components written in any COM-compliant language with Java applications. This allows COM objects to share data and interact with applications from many different types of multiple operating systems, applications, and services.

Java-COM Integration Technologies

Currently, there are numerous options and ways to enable Java-COM application integration, dependent upon the complexity and nature of the target environment. The most common Java-COM integration strategies using products and custom techniques are as follows:

❑ **J2EE Client Access Services COM Bridge**
As part of Sun Java Developer Connection, Sun released the J2EE Client Access Services COM Bridge that provides a bundle of COM objects. These objects allow COM components to establish a connection to an application server and obtain references to EJB components. This bridge only provides uni-directional access from COM objects to J2EE components.

❑ **The Microsoft JVM**
Microsoft's JVM provides an environment for developing Java wrappers for COM components by specifying Java object mapping to their COM equivalent and vice versa. When the Microsoft VM compiler compiles these source files, they are converted into Java classes.

❑ **Off-the-Shelf and Open-Source Solutions**
Commercial off-the-shelf applications such as J-Integra (Linar), WebLogic jCOM (BEA) and open-source applications such as Bridge2Java (IBM Alphaworks), the JACOB project, and JAWIN (DevelopMentor) provide Java-COM integration solutions to solve a wide range of application integration issues.

❑ **Custom Bridges**
Traditionally, experienced developers built their own custom bridges to provide the same or more precise functionality than commercially available bridges.

❑ **XML and SOAP**
XML and SOAP provide a common format for message-based integration solutions to share data between applications. This emerging technique would provide interoperability solutions using SOAP Messaging.

Although these products and technologies are promising for Java-COM integration, the following factors influence the choice of the correct integration tool depending upon the target deployment environment:

❑ **OS environment**
The target operating environment – is it a Microsoft, Unix environment, and so on?

❑ **Application deployment**
Is the application Internet, or intranet-based, or standalone? How many maximum users? Does it require participation in transactions? What user interfaces are there?

❑ **Data format**
Any specific data exchange format to be supported with the underlying COM application (binary data/XML, and so on).

❑ **Application nature**
Is it multi-threaded? Any specific protocols for communication?

❑ **Other requirements**
N-Tier architecture-based, reusability, portability, scalability, and performance-related requirements.

In earlier chapters we defined our integration architecture, so we know that we want to build our integrated system using lower-level virtual components to wrap existing applications. Therefore, although there are numerous methods to integrate Java and COM, in this chapter we will focus only on those that would be appropriate from an application-wrapping perspective. Consequently, we will focus on the following techniques:

- ❏ J-Integra
- ❏ Combining RMI and the MS JVM

Let's take a closer look at some of these different technologies, and how we can use them to solve Java-COM integration for EAI applications.

Using Commercial Java-COM Bridges

In this section we'll discuss using Linar's **J-Integra** Java-COM bridge that enables seamless Java integration with COM components.

J-Integra is a popular bi-directional Java-COM bridge developed by Linar Ltd (now owned by Intrinsyc Software) – http://www.intrinsyc.com/products/bridging/jintegra.asp. It provides integration of Java and Microsoft COM components and works well with all Java VMs and their supporting operating systems.

J-Integra for Java-COM Integration

J-Integra provides a variety of Java-COM bridging tools allowing Java-COM integration running on all operating systems and also J2EE application servers. As part of a J-Integra suite the following Java-COM bridges are available to solve different types of application integration scenarios involving Java and COM:

- ❏ Active Server Page-to-Java Bridge
- ❏ Servlet-to-COM Bridge
- ❏ Visual Basic-to-EJB Bridge
- ❏ Java-to-Excel Bridge
- ❏ Java-to-Exchange Bridge

J-Integra itself is a Java-based run time that translates Java calls to COM calls and vice versa, by using DCOM calls through the use of standard Java networking classes:

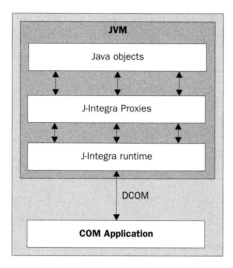

In this chapter, we'll look at creating an EJB component wrapper to access the data in a MS Excel application, using the Java-to-Excel bridge. To relate it to our cell phone operator example, we might find out that some employees for the operator run their own spreadsheet apps to help the track user data. By treating these spreadsheet apps as existing applications and wrapping them as we have other existing applications, we can incorporate these subsidiary applications into our integrated system architecture.

Accessing an MS Excel Application from Java

Upon downloading and installing the Java-to-Excel bridge from the Intrinsyc web site, we get two components. One is the J-Integra runtime as described above, while the other is the **Excel JAPI** – a set of proxy classes that we can use to manipulate the Excel object model:

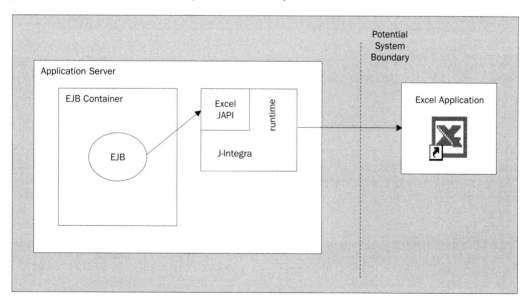

In our example, we'll write a simple EJB component that will use the Java-to-Excel bridge to read data from an Excel spreadsheet. We'll use a sample spreadsheet that comes with the installation of MS Office, and can be found in `\Program Files\Microsoft Office\Office\Samples\SOLVSAMP.XLS`:

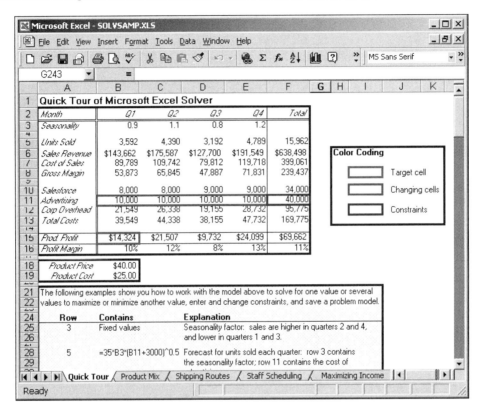

We'll write a BMP entity bean that reads a few lines of data off the first worksheet of this spreadsheet. In order to do this, we really need to understand the Excel VBA (Visual Basic for Applications) object model. However, explaining VBA and the Excel object model is really beyond the scope of this book, so we'll just present the necessary code.

A good reference to the Excel object model can be found in the book, Excel 2000 VBA Programmer's Reference, by John Green, Wrox Press; ISBN 1-861002-54-8.

If you are familiar with VBA, you may find that the J-Integra mapping of the Excel object model means that the programming style can be a bit awkward, as VBA is designed for rapid development. Thus tricks that the VBA language can employ to shorten coding, need to be done the long way round when we come to Java, as we'll soon see.

Setting Up the Environment

Before we can successfully use J-Integra we need to make sure that a few environmental settings are configured correctly:

❑   Add a reference to the `<J-INTEGRA_HOME>\bin` directory into your path. As we will be deploying our bean into the WebLogic Server, we need to modify the startup scripts to include this directory. If we fail to do this, we will get unpleasant `General Access Denied` errors when we try to launch the Excel executable.

❑   We also need to add the J-Integra runtime files, in the form of the `jintegra.jar` file into our classpath. This JAR file is located in the `\lib` directory of the J-Integra installation.

❑   Finally, we also need to add the Excel JAPI files that represent the Excel VBA object model to our classpath. The J-Integra Java-to-Excel bridge comes with precompiled versions of these classes in the `\lib` directory for Excel 97, Excel 2000, and Excel XP. However, J-Integra also provides a tool called `exl2java.exe` that allows you to generate the source Java files for the VBA object model yourself. Refer to the documentation on how to do this – we will use the precompiled libraries for simplicity.

Reading Data from an Excel Spreadsheet in Java

We'll start by examining the Excel-specific code that we will use to open the spreadsheet and read the data, without looking at the EJB code.

With the Javafied-version of the Excel VBA object model located in the `excel.*` package, we can access the functions of Excel as if we were using VBA directly. In fact it is a good idea to prototype your code in VBA itself before translating it to Java.

The first step in working with Excel is to access the `Application` object. This is the root object for all the others and represents an instance of Excel itself. By creating a new instance of the `Application` object we start up a new instance of Excel:

```
import excel.*;

Application app = new Application();
app.setVisible(true);
```

In this case, we have also made the instance visible so we can track what's going on ourselves.

Having started an instance of Excel we now need to open the spreadsheet we are interested in. In Excel parlance, this means opening a workbook, passing in the path to the file we want to open:

```
app.getWorkbooks().open("C:\\Program Files\\Microsoft Office\\Office\\" +
                        "Samples\\SOLVSAMP.XLS", null, null, null, null, null,
                        null, null, null, null, null, null, null);
```

You'll note that we also pass in a lot of null values as well. VBA allows methods to have optional parameters, but unfortunately as Java does not we need to provide a value for every parameter. This is why it is handy to keep a reference to the object model handy when you do this kind of development.

Having opened the spread, we now need to get a reference to the particular sheet of the workbook we are interested in:

```
Integer i = new Integer(1);
workSheet = new Worksheet (app.getWorksheets().getItem(i));
```

As you can see, we've pretty much hard-coded this reference to simplify this example. We also need to use a more long-winded syntactical style than VBA in order to navigate through the collections.

Having obtained our reference to the desired sheet, we can now go about reading the data from it. Again we will hard code in the exact cell references but it would probably be more realistic to use a more dynamic mechanism to look for the data we need. In this case, we'll simply read a few lines off the table on the sheet. Here's the routine that will do this and return the data as a string:

```
public String getData(String dataRequired) {

  String data = "";

  try {

    if(dataRequired.equals("Prod. Profit")) {

        Double d = new Double(0);
        d = (Double) workSheet.getRange("B15", null).getValue();
        data = "Q1:$" + Math.round(d.doubleValue()) + "|";
        d = (Double) workSheet.getRange("C15", null).getValue();
        data += "Q2:$" + Math.round(d.doubleValue()) + "|";
        d = (Double) workSheet.getRange("D15", null).getValue();
        data += "Q3:$" + Math.round(d.doubleValue()) + "|";
        d = (Double) workSheet.getRange("E15", null).getValue();
        data += "Q4:$" + Math.round(d.doubleValue()) + "|";
        d = (Double) workSheet.getRange("F15", null).getValue();
        data += "Total:$" + Math.round(d.doubleValue()) + "|";

    } else if (dataRequired.equals("Profit Margin")) {

        Double d = new Double(0);;
        d = (Double) workSheet.getRange("B16", null).getValue();
        data = "Q1:" + Math.round(d.doubleValue() * 100) + "%|";
        d = (Double) workSheet.getRange("C16", null).getValue();
        data += "Q2:" + Math.round(d.doubleValue() * 100) + "%|";
        d = (Double) workSheet.getRange("D16", null).getValue();
        data += "Q3:" + Math.round(d.doubleValue() * 100) + "%|";
        d = (Double) workSheet.getRange("E16", null).getValue();
        data += "Q4:" + Math.round(d.doubleValue() * 100) + "%|";
        d = (Double) workSheet.getRange("F16", null).getValue();
        data += "Total:" + Math.round(d.doubleValue() * 100) + "%|";
    }

  } catch(Exception e) {
  }

  return data;
}
```

Finally, we'll also make sure there is a call to the J-Integra runtime to clean up after us:

```
// Release all remote objects that haven't already been garbage collected.
com.linar.jintegra.Cleaner.releaseAll();
```

Accessing an MS Excel Application from an EJB

Now let's take the business logic we discussed above and place it into an EJB for deployment. As we've already discussed EJBs in detail in Chapter 12, we don't go into the EJB framework code here.

The Home Interface

```
import javax.ejb.*;
import java.rmi.RemoteException;

public interface ExcelSolverHome extends EJBHome {

  ExcelSolver create() throws RemoteException, CreateException;
  ExcelSolver findByPrimaryKey(String key) throws RemoteException,
    FinderException;

}
```

The Remote Interface

```
import javax.ejb.*;
import java.rmi.RemoteException;

public interface ExcelSolver extends EJBObject {

  String getData(String dataRequired) throws RemoteException;
}
```

The Bean Implementation Class

It is here that our Excel code is included:

```
import javax.ejb.*;
import java.rmi.RemoteException;
import excel.*;

public class ExcelSolverEJB implements EntityBean {

  private Worksheet workSheet;

  public void setEntityContext(EntityContext entityContext) {

    try {
        // Create an instance of Excel.Application.
        Application app = new Application();
        app.setVisible(true);

        app.getWorkbooks().open("C:\\Program Files\\Microsoft Office\\" +
                        "Office\\Samples\\SOLVSAMP.XLS", null,
                        null, null, null, null, null, null,
                        null, null, null, null);
        Integer i = new Integer(1);
        workSheet = new Worksheet (app.getWorksheets().getItem(i));
```

667

```
        } catch (Exception e) {
            e.printStackTrace();
        }
    }

    public void unsetEntityContext() {
        // Release all remote objects that haven't already been garbage collected.
            com.linar.jintegra.Cleaner.releaseAll();
    }

    public String ejbFindByPrimaryKey(String key) {
        return "C:\\Program Files\\Microsoft Office\\Office\\Samples\\SOLVSAMP.XLS";
    }

    public void ejbLoad() {};
    public void ejbStore() {} ;
    public void ejbRemove() {};

    public String ejbCreate() {
        return "C:\\Program Files\\Microsoft Office\\Office\\Samples\\SOLVSAMP.XLS";
    }

    public void ejbPostCreate() {};
    public void ejbActivate() {};
    public void ejbPassivate() {};

    public String getData(String dataRequired) {

        String data = "";

        try {

            if(dataRequired.equals("Prod. Profit")) {

                Double d = new Double(0);
                d = (Double) workSheet.getRange("B15", null).getValue();
                data = "Q1:$" + Math.round(d.doubleValue()) + "|";
                d = (Double) workSheet.getRange("C15", null).getValue();
                data += "Q2:$" + Math.round(d.doubleValue()) + "|";
                d = (Double) workSheet.getRange("D15", null).getValue();
                data += "Q3:$" + Math.round(d.doubleValue()) + "|";
                d = (Double) workSheet.getRange("E15", null).getValue();
                data += "Q4:$" + Math.round(d.doubleValue()) + "|";
                d = (Double) workSheet.getRange("F15", null).getValue();
                data += "Total:$" + Math.round(d.doubleValue()) + "|";

            } else if (dataRequired.equals("Profit Margin"))  {

                Double d = new Double(0);;
                d = (Double) workSheet.getRange("B16", null).getValue();
                data = "Q1:" + Math.round(d.doubleValue() * 100) + "%|";
                d = (Double) workSheet.getRange("C16", null).getValue();
                data += "Q2:" + Math.round(d.doubleValue() * 100) + "%|";
                d = (Double) workSheet.getRange("D16", null).getValue();
```

```
            data += "Q3:" + Math.round(d.doubleValue() * 100) + "%|";
            d = (Double) workSheet.getRange("E16", null).getValue();
            data += "Q4:" + Math.round(d.doubleValue() * 100) + "%|";
            d = (Double) workSheet.getRange("F16", null).getValue();
            data += "Total:" + Math.round(d.doubleValue() * 100) + "%|";
        }

    } catch(Exception e) {
      throw new EJBException(e);
    }

    return data;
  }

}
```

The Deployment Descriptors

Firstly, the standard `ejb-jar.xml` file:

```
<?xml version="1.0" encoding="UTF-8"?>

<!DOCTYPE ejb-jar PUBLIC '-//Sun Microsystems, Inc.//DTD Enterprise JavaBeans
2.0//EN' 'http://java.sun.com/dtd/ejb-jar_2_0.dtd'>

<ejb-jar>
  <display-name>ExcelSolver</display-name>
  <enterprise-beans>
    <entity>
      <display-name>ExcelSolverEJB</display-name>
      <ejb-name>ExcelSolverEJB</ejb-name>
      <home>ExcelSolverHome</home>
      <remote>ExcelSolver</remote>
      <ejb-class>ExcelSolverEJB</ejb-class>
      <persistence-type>Bean</persistence-type>
      <prim-key-class>java.lang.String</prim-key-class>
      <reentrant>False</reentrant>
    </entity>
  </enterprise-beans>

</ejb-jar>
```

And the WebLogic-specific version:

```
<?xml version="1.0"?>

<!DOCTYPE weblogic-ejb-jar PUBLIC
'-//BEA Systems, Inc.//DTD WebLogic 6.0.0 EJB//EN'
'http://www.bea.com/servers/wls600/dtd/weblogic-ejb-jar.dtd'>

<weblogic-ejb-jar>

  <weblogic-enterprise-bean>
```

```
            <ejb-name>ExcelSolverEJB</ejb-name>
            <jndi-name>ExcelSolver</jndi-name>
        </weblogic-enterprise-bean>

    </weblogic-ejb-jar>
```

The Client

Finally, here is a simple client that we can use to test if our EJB wrapper is working correctly:

```java
import javax.ejb.*;
import javax.naming.*;
import ExcelSolverHome;
import ExcelSolver;
import java.util.Properties;
import javax.rmi.PortableRemoteObject;

class ExcelClient
{
  public static void main(String[] args)    {

    try {
      Properties prop = new Properties();
      prop.put(Context.INITIAL_CONTEXT_FACTORY,
              "weblogic.jndi.WLInitialContextFactory");
      prop.put(Context.PROVIDER_URL, "t3://localhost:7001");

      Context ic = new InitialContext(prop);
      Object objRef = ic.lookup("ExcelSolver");

      ExcelSolverHome home = (ExcelSolverHome)
           PortableRemoteObject.narrow(objRef, ExcelSolverHome.class);

      ExcelSolver solver = home.create();
      System.out.println(solver.getData("Prod. Profit"));
      System.out.println(solver.getData("Profit Margin"));

    } catch (NamingException ne) {
      System.out.println(ne);
    } catch (Exception e) {
      System.out.println(e);
      e.printStackTrace();
    }

  }
}
```

Running the Example

Assuming you have set up your environment correctly, and configured your WebLogic startup scripts to have the relevant path and classpath information, you should be able to deploy the bean and run the client to get the following result:

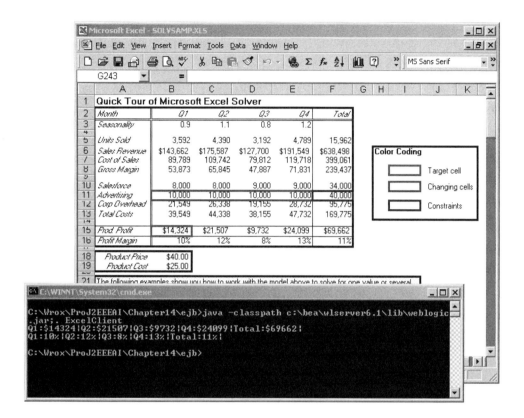

WebLogic jCOM

BEA has recently released a beta of their own Java-COM bridge called jCOM. However, jCOM is really J-Integra under the covers and runs in the same manner. The packaging, examples, and documentation are different but currently the binary is the same as the J-Integra suite 1.4.1.

Building Custom Java-COM Bridges

In this section we will combine a number of techniques to build our own Java-COM bridge. The underlying mechanism of this custom solution uses Java RMI. RMI requires Java objects to be serializable in order for them to be sent over the network. Fortunately, almost all classes in Java can be serializable, as long as they are declared to be so. The exceptions are classes containing only static or transient fields, and classes that represent the characteristics of a virtual machine.

The implementation of this custom bridge uses the Sun JVM to run the Java RMI client and the Microsoft JVM for running the RMI server invoking Java COM wrappers that we'll build using Visual J++:

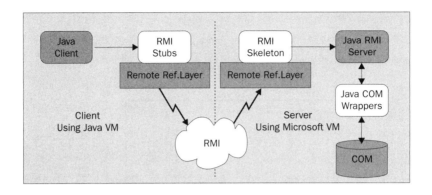

The Microsoft JVM for Java-COM Integration

The **Microsoft Java Virtual Machine (MS JVM)** provides automatic mapping for COM objects, which enables a Java object to be accessible as a COM object, and a COM object to be accessible as a Java object.

To accomplish the usage of a COM object in a Java environment, the MS JVM requires the COM object to expose its functionality through a **Java Callable Wrapper (JCW)**. The JCW for a COM component can be generated automatically using the JActiveX tool (provided in the Microsoft SDK for Java) or using Visual J++. The generated JCW class contains MS JVM-specific attributes (@com directives), and enables the Microsoft VM to map the JCW class back to the COM object.

> There are some caveats to using the MS JVM, however. It is designed to run only on Microsoft Windows platforms, and because of well-documented legislation between Sun and Microsoft, it is rather out of date (JDK 1.1) and no longer supported.

However, as we'll see later we can overcome some of the limitations of the MS JVM so that we can still use this method to construct a wrapper for Java 2-based components.

Accessing COM Components Via the Microsoft JVM

In our example, we'll build a simple COM component that represents a Customer Relations Management application, accessing a database (crm.mdb). We'll use Microsoft Visual J++ 6.0 to generate the Java COM Wrappers for the COM component, which can be called from a Java class executing in the MS JVM.

The steps involved for implementing this example are as follows:

❑ Creating a COM component

❑ Creating the Java-COM Wrapper

❑ Creating the Java-application

❑ Testing the Java-COM integration

Let's take a closer look at the implementation-level details of these steps.

Creating the CRM COM Component

You can find the compiled component and database in the source code for this chapter (available from http://www/wrox.com). However, we'll briefly go over the steps required to build the component with Visual Basic.

Create a new ActiveX DLL Project in Microsoft Visual Basic, and add a reference to the **Microsoft ActiveX Data Objects** library (the version will depend on your Windows version) using the **References** option from the **Project** menu.

Rename the project to CRM and the class module to CustomerData. Then add the following code to the class module:

```
Option Explicit

'Database connection variable
Private con As ADODB.Connection

' Property variables for Customer data
Private mstrCustName As String
Private mstrCompanyName As String
Private mstrAddress As String
Private mstrCity As String
Private mstrState As String
Private mstrCountry As String
Private mstrZipcode As String
Private mstrEmailAddress As String
Private mstrPhoneNum As String

'Get/Set methods for the Customer data properties
Public Property Let PhoneNum(ByVal vData As String)
  mstrPhoneNum = vData
End Property

Public Property Get PhoneNum() As String
  PhoneNum = mstrPhoneNum
End Property

Public Property Let EmailAddress(ByVal vData As String)
  mstrEmailAddress = vData
End Property

Public Property Get EmailAddress() As String
  EmailAddress = mstrEmailAddress
End Property

Public Property Let Zipcode(ByVal vData As String)
  mstrZipcode = vData
End Property

Public Property Get Zipcode() As String
  Zipcode = mstrZipcode
End Property

Public Property Let Country(ByVal vData As String)
  mstrCountry = vData
End Property
```

```
Public Property Get Country() As String
  Country = mstrCountry
End Property

Public Property Let State(ByVal vData As String)
  mstrState = vData
End Property

Public Property Get State() As String
  State = mstrState
End Property

Public Property Let City(ByVal vData As String)
  mstrCity = vData
End Property

Public Property Get City() As String
  City = mstrCity
End Property

Public Property Let Address(ByVal vData As String)
  mstrAddress = vData
End Property

Public Property Get Address() As String
  Address = mstrAddress
End Property

Public Property Let CompanyName(ByVal vData As String)
  mstrCompanyName = vData
End Property

Public Property Get CompanyName() As String
  CompanyName = mstrCompanyName
End Property

Public Property Let CustName(ByVal vData As String)
  mstrCustName = vData
End Property

Public Property Get CustName() As String
  CustName = mstrCustName
End Property

'This method inserts a record in to the Customers table
Public Function AddCustomer() As Boolean

  Dim strSQL As String
  Dim cmd As ADODB.Command

  On Error GoTo errh:

  If con Is Nothing Or con.State = adStateClosed Then
    AddCustomer = False
  Else
    strSQL = "INSERT INTO Customers ("
    strSQL = strSQL + "CONTACT_NAME, COMPANY_NAME, ADDRESS, CITY, " & _
                      "STATE, ZIPCODE, COUNTRY, EMAILADDRESS, PHONENUMBER )"
    strSQL = strSQL + " VALUES ( '" & mstrCustName & "', '" & _
```

```
                              mstrCompanyName & "', '" & mstrAddress & "', '" & _
                              mstrCity & "', '" & mstrState & "', '" & _
                              mstrZipcode & "', '" & mstrCountry & "', '" & _
                              mstrEmailAddress & "', '" & mstrPhoneNum & "')"

        Set cmd = New ADODB.Command
        Set cmd.ActiveConnection = con
        cmd.CommandText = strSQL
        cmd.Execute
        AddCustomer = True
    End If

    Exit Function
errh:
        AddCustomer = False

End Function

'This method establishes a connection to the database
Public Function connectToDatabase(ByVal DSN As String) As Boolean

    On Local Error GoTo ERR_Conn

    Set con = New ADODB.Connection
    con.ConnectionString = "DSN=" & DSN
    con.Open
    connectToDatabase = True
    Exit Function

ERR_Conn:
    connectToDatabase = False

End Function

Public Sub disconnect()

    If con.State <> adStateClosed Then
        con.Close
    End If
    Set con = Nothing

End Sub
```

All this class basically does is allow a new customer to be added to the database through the use of a lot of property routines.

Compile the DLL using the menu option File | Make CRM.dll. Building the DLL registers the COM component into the local registry. To use the DLL on a different machine, we need to register the DLL manually into that machines registry. This can be done using the `regsvr32` utility:

```
regsvr32 <PATH_TO_DLL>\CRM.dll
```

In order to use this component properly, we also need to set up a data source name (DSN) that points to the `crm.mdb` database. This can be configured through the Data Sources (ODBC) dialog:

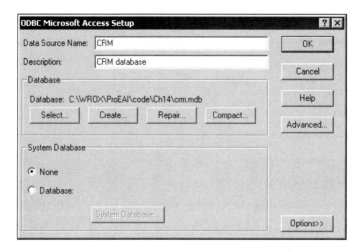

Creating the Java COM Wrapper

Java COM wrappers can be generated using either Microsoft Visual J++ or the JActiveX (provided by Microsoft SDK for Java) command-line utility. In this example we'll use Microsoft Visual J++ 6.0.

Create a new Console Application project using Microsoft Visual J++, and call it CRMJavaWrapper. Then choose Add COM Wrapper from the Project menu, as shown below:

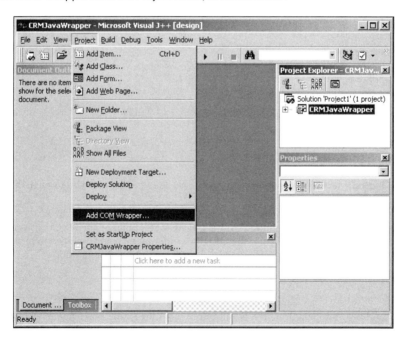

A dialog box displays a list of COM components that are registered in the registry:

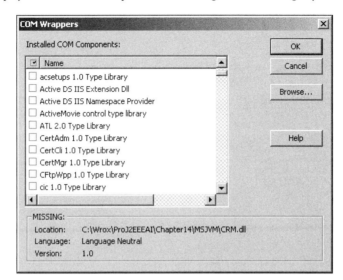

Choose the CRM component from the list and click OK. If you don't see our CRM component in the list then use the Browse button to navigate to it manually. Java classes are created for the COM component and they are grouped in a package using the name of component:

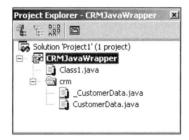

Build the project using the Build option on the Build menu. This creates a package of Java-COM wrapper classes in the project's directory. Make sure to include this package in the classpath.

Creating the Java Application

The Java application (`ImportCustomer`) uses the Java-COM wrapper to add customer details to the database.

The following is the code for `ImportCustomer.java`:

```
package wrapper;

// Import Java Com Wrapper package and the
// com exceptions classes provided by Microsoft SDK
import com.ms.com.*;
import crm.*;
```

677

```
/** The ImportCustomer class is used to access the Java-COM Wrapper,
CustomerData's methods to add customer details in a Microsoft Access database */

public class ImportCustomer {

  // Java COM Wrapper, CustomerData
  private CustomerData custData;

  // The following member variables are to store Customer details
  private String mCompName;
  private String mCustName;
  private String mAddress;
  private String mCity;
  private String mState;
  private String mCountry;
  private String mZip;
  private String mEmailAddr;
  private String mPhoneNum;

  public ImportCustomer() throws Exception {
    try {
      //Instantiate the Java-COM Wrapper
      custData = new crm.CustomerData();

    } catch (ComFailException ce) {
      throw new Exception(ce.getHResult() + " " +
                        ce.getSource() + " " + ce.getMessage());
    }
  }

  // connectToDatabase and disconnect methods

  public synchronized boolean connect(String DSN) throws Exception {
    boolean ret = false;
    try {
      ret = custData.connectToDatabase(DSN);
    } catch (ComFailException ce) {
      throw new Exception("COMFailException in connect: "+
                        ce.getSource() + " " + ce.getMessage());
    }
    return ret;
  }

  // Disconnect
  public synchronized void disconnect() throws Exception {
    try {
      custData.disconnect();
    } catch (ComFailException ce) {
      throw new Exception("COMFailException in disconnect: "+
                        ce.getSource() + " " + ce.getMessage());
    }
  }

  // Use the member variable to set the CustomerData object and invoke to
  // the AddCustomer method
  public synchronized boolean addCustomer() throws Exception {
    boolean ret = false;
    try {
      custData.setCustName(mCustName);
```

```
        custData.setCompanyName(mCompName);
        custData.setAddress(mAddress);
        custData.setCity(mCity);
        custData.setState(mState);
        custData.setZipcode(mZip);
        custData.setCountry(mCountry);
        custData.setEmailAddress(mEmailAddr);
        custData.setPhoneNum(mPhoneNum);
        ret  = custData.AddCustomer();

    } catch (ComFailException ce) {
      throw new Exception("COMFailException in addCustomer: " +
                          ce.getSource() + " " + ce.getMessage());
    }
    return ret;
  }

  public String getPhoneNumber() { return mPhoneNum; }
  public void setPhoneNumber(String s) { mPhoneNum = s; }

  public String getEmailAddress() { return mEmailAddr; }
  public void setEmailAddress(String s) { mEmailAddr = s; }

  public String getZipcode() { return mZip; }
  public void setZipcode(String s) { mZip = s; }

  public String getCountry() { return mCountry; }
  public void setCountry(String s) { mCountry = s; }

  public String getState() { return mState; }
  public void setState(String s) { mState = s; }

  public String getCity() { return mCity; }
  public void setCity(String s) { mCity = s; }

  public String getAddress() { return mAddress; }
  public void setAddress(String s) { mAddress = s; }

  public String getCustomerName() { return mCustName; }
  public void setCustomerName(String s) { mCustName = s; }

  public String getCompanyName() { return mCompName; }
  public void setCompanyName(String s) { mCompName = s; }

// Test program
public static void main(String[] argv) {
  try {
    ImportCustomer ic = new ImportCustomer();
    ic.setCustomerName("Mark Lee");
    ic.setCompanyName("NICE FOOD COMPANY");
    ic.setAddress("77 Third Ave");
    ic.setCity("Wayland");
    ic.setState("MA");
    ic.setZipcode("09711");
    ic.setCountry("USA");
    ic.setEmailAddress("mlee@nicefood.com");
    ic.setPhoneNumber("781-666-4398");
    if (ic.connect("CRM")) {
      boolean ret  = ic.addCustomer();
      if (ret) {
```

```
          System.out.println("Add Successful");
        } else {
          System.out.println("Fail to add");
        }
        ic.disconnect();
      } else {
        System.out.println("Unable to connect to database");
      }
    } catch (Exception e) {
      e.printStackTrace();
    }
  }
}
```

To compile the class we need to use the `jvc` command utility provided by Visual J++/Microsoft SDK for Java as follows (remembering to make sure that the `crm` package is in the classpath):

```
jvc wrapper\ImportCustomer.java
```

Execute the program using the `jview` command utility provided by Visual J++/Microsoft SDK for Java as follows:

```
jview wrapper.ImportCustomer
```

The successful execution of the program inserts a customer record into the database and then displays an **Add Successful** message:

Implementing the Custom Java-COM Bridge

In this section, we'll expand the previous Microsoft JVM-based example by enabling it to be accessed over RMI. We get round the differing JVM implementations by passing a serializable value object between the RMI client and server.

The RMI Client sends a `CustomerObj` class (a value object) to the RMI server. The server unmarshals the object, reads the data in the value object, and then writes the data to the database using the Java COM wrapper.

The following steps are involved in the `CRMAdapter` implementation:

❑   Create the RMI server classes – a remote Interface and the server implementation.

❑   Generate the stubs and skeleton classes.

❑   Create the client RMI application

❑   Test the Java COM Integration

Create the RMI Server Classes

Create a remote interface, which declares a method `addCustomerData()`. The following is the code for the remote interface of the `CRMAdapter` – `ICRMAdapter.java`:

```
package adapter;

import java.rmi.Remote;
import java.rmi.RemoteException;

/** This interface declares methods for CRMAdapter, which can be called from other
 ** JVMs
 */

public interface ICRMAdapter extends Remote {

    // This method adds Customer data to the database
    public boolean addCustomerData(CustomerObj cObj, String DSN)
        throws RemoteException, Exception;
}
```

Create a RMI server that implements the remote interface `ICRMAdapter`:

```
package adapter;

import java.rmi.Naming;
import java.rmi.RemoteException;
import java.rmi.RMISecurityManager;
import java.rmi.server.UnicastRemoteObject;

import wrapper.*;
```

This is the `CRMAdapter` class using the RMI server program for accessing our COM component. It implements all the methods defined in the interface:

```
// The RMI Server is registered in the main method
public class CRMAdapter extends UnicastRemoteObject implements ICRMAdapter {
  public CRMAdapter() throws RemoteException {
    super();
  }
}
```

The `addCustomerData()` method implements the business logic to adding customer data to the database:

```
    public synchronized boolean addCustomerData(CustomerObj cObj, String DSN)
        throws Exception {

      try {
        boolean ret = false;
```

```
          ImportCustomer ic = new ImportCustomer();
          ic.setAddress(cObj.getAddress());
          ic.setCity(cObj.getCity());
          ic.setCompanyName(cObj.getCompanyName());
          ic.setCountry(cObj.getCountry());
          ic.setCustomerName(cObj.getCustomerName());
          ic.setEmailAddress(cObj.getEmailAddress());
          ic.setPhoneNumber(cObj.getPhoneNumber());
          ic.setState(cObj.getState());
          ic.setZipcode(cObj.getZipcode());
          boolean con = ic.connect(DSN);
          if (con) {
            ret = ic.addCustomer();
          }
          ic.disconnect();
          return ret;
        } catch (Exception e) {
          e.printStackTrace();
          throw e;
        }
      }

      public static void main(String args[]) {
        // Instantiation of the RMI Server
        if (System.getSecurityManager() == null) {
          System.setSecurityManager(new RMISecurityManager());
        }
        try {
          CRMAdapter cAdapter = new CRMAdapter();
          // Binds the object instance to the RMI registry
          Naming.rebind("//" + args[0] + "/CRMAdapter", cAdapter );
          System.out.println( "CRMAdapter bound to registry" );
        } catch (ArrayIndexOutOfBoundsException ae) {
          System.out.println("Usage: jview CRMAdapter <HostName>");
        } catch ( Exception e ) {
          System.out.println( "CRMAdapter EXCEPTION: " + e.getMessage( ) );
          e.printStackTrace( );
        }
      }
    }
```

The following is the code for the CustomerObj class – this class is used pass data from the client JVM to the server JVM:

```
package adapter;

import java.io.Serializable;

public class CustomerObj implements Serializable {
  private String mCompName;
  private String mCustName;
  private String mAddress;
  private String mCity;
```

```
    private String mState;
    private String mCountry;
    private String mZip;
    private String mEmailAddr;
    private String mPhoneNum;

    // Get/Set methods are provided to access data variables

    public String getPhoneNumber() { return mPhoneNum; }
    public void setPhoneNumber(String s) { mPhoneNum = s; }

    public String getEmailAddress() { return mEmailAddr; }
    public void setEmailAddress(String s) { mEmailAddr = s; }

    public String getZipcode() { return mZip; }
    public void setZipcode(String s) { mZip = s; }

    public String getCountry() { return mCountry; }
    public void setCountry(String s) { mCountry = s; }

    public String getState() { return mState; }
    public void setState(String s) { mState = s; }

    public String getCity() { return mCity; }
    public void setCity(String s) { mCity = s; }

    public String getAddress() { return mAddress; }
    public void setAddress(String s) { mAddress = s; }

    public String getCustomerName() { return mCustName; }
    public void setCustomerName(String s) { mCustName = s; }

    public String getCompanyName() { return mCompName; }
    public void setCompanyName(String s) { mCompName = s; }
}
```

Create the RMI Stub and Skeleton Classes

Once we've compiled our server classes we need to generate the RMI proxy classes so that they can be used across RMI. Run the `rmic` compiler from the command prompt:

```
rmic adapter.CRMAdapter
```

Create the RMI Client Application

The following is the code for the RMI client application:

```
package client;

import java.io.IOException;
import java.rmi.Naming;
import java.rmi.RemoteException;
import java.rmi.server.*;

import adapter.*;

public class CRMClient {
```

683

```
  public boolean createCustomer(ICRMAdapter ic) {

    boolean ret = false;
    try {
      CustomerObj cObj = new CustomerObj();
      cObj.setCustomerName("Mark Lee");
      cObj.setCompanyName("NICE FOOD COMPANY");
      cObj.setAddress("77 Third Ave");
      cObj.setCity("Wayland");
      cObj.setState("MA");
      cObj.setZipcode("09711");
      cObj.setCountry("USA");
      cObj.setEmailAddress("mlee@nicefood.com");
      cObj.setPhoneNumber("781-666-4398");

      ret = ic.addCustomerData(cObj, "CRM");

    } catch (Exception e) {
      System.err.println("Exception: " + e.getMessage());
      e.printStackTrace();
    }
    return ret;
  }

  // Test the application
  public static void main(String args[]) {
    try {
      // Lookup the CRMAdapter in RMI Registry
      String name = "//" + args[0] + "/CRMAdapter";
      ICRMAdapter ca = (ICRMAdapter) Naming.lookup(name);

      CRMClient cc = new CRMClient();

      boolean ret = cc.createCustomer(ca);
      if (ret) {
        System.out.println("Add Successfull");
      } else {
        System.out.println("Fail to add");
      }
    } catch (IOException ie) {
      System.err.println("IOException: " + ie.getMessage());
      ie.printStackTrace();
    } catch (ArrayIndexOutOfBoundsException ae) {
      System.out.println("java client.CRMClient <hostname>");
    } catch (Exception e) {
      System.err.println("Exception: " + e.getMessage());
      e.printStackTrace();
    }
  }
}
```

Testing the Java-COM Integration Bridge

To enable the Microsoft JVM for handling RMI classes, create a library file (`rmi.zip`) containing the Java RMI-specific classes and packages from the Sun JDK:

❑ `java.rmi.*`

❑ `sun.rmi.*`

❑ `sun.applet.*`

Make sure this `rmi.zip` file is available in the classpath for the Microsoft JVM.

The following steps are involved in testing this application:

❑ Start the RMI registry:

```
start rmiregistry
```

❑ Start the RMI server (you need `rmi.zip` and the `crm` package in the classpath):

```
jview /d:java.rmi.server.codebase=file:/<path to parent directory of adapter>
    adapter.CRMAdapter <Host Machine Name>
```

❑ Start the RMI client:

```
java client.CRMClient <Host Machine Name>
```

When started, the client looks up the RMI server in the RMI registry. When successful, it invokes the `addCustomer()` method and sends the `CustomerObj` object as its parameter. This in turn invokes the Java-COM Wrapper method to call the COM method to add the customer record to the database. The screenshot below shows the command window displaying the status of the execution:

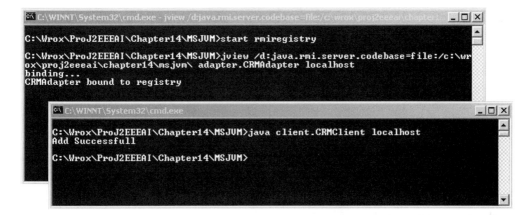

Common Issues and Limitations of COM Bridges

In general COM bridges offer promising solutions for enabling EAI with Microsoft-based applications. Typical to other tightly-coupled integration solutions, the following issues and limitations are to be noticed when using COM bridges:

- ❏ There are no industry standards to define standard COM bridges and to support true integration, defining the basic features to address EAI-specific requirements.

- ❏ Performance issues are observed during runaway processes at the COM server end and also during the reporting of service time out errors.

- ❏ Integrating multi-threaded applications is usually quite complex as there is no control to programmatically manage the threading model at the COM server end.

- ❏ Implementing high availability to enable load balancing and fail-over recovery is another problem especially at the back-end COM connectivity.

- ❏ Due to the tightly-coupled integration, COM bridges affect application extensibility – it requires complete rebuilding of the Java COM wrappers every time.

- ❏ Security credentials are required to be hard coded every time when connecting to COM components.

- ❏ Distributed transactions using custom COM bridges lack supporting standards and reliability mechanisms.

- ❏ High maintenance effort required during application upgrades and enhancements.

Although these issues are not pertinent to all scenarios it depends upon the specific problem domain and its complexity of implementation. The good news is that due to the fast growing EAI frameworks, which demand integration with Microsoft-based applications, Java-COM bridges are the only promising technology with proven design and implementation to reduce the cost to build and make it possible in a shorter development time to build portable and fully-featured EAI solutions.

Summary

In this chapter, we studied the different strategies and techniques of implementing COM bridges for integrating Microsoft-based applications. We discussed using traditional approaches and commercial COM bridge solutions with examples and its relevance for EAI implementation. This chapter also explained and demonstrated the steps involved in integrating and interacting with a COM component exposed by a Microsoft environment.

In general, we have looked at:

- ❏ The role of COM Bridges in EAI

- ❏ Microsoft COM Architecture and Java integration

- ❏ Commercially available Java-COM bridges

- ❏ Developing a Custom Java bridge for COM integration

- ❏ Potential issues and limitations.

In the following chapter we will cover transaction management in EAI implementations.

15

Transaction Management in EAI

This chapter focuses on the different strategies and solutions used for implementing transactions within an EAI framework. Creating a flexible EAI infrastructure poses several challenges and one of the most important is the integration of business functionality with unique transactional behavior bridging heterogeneous distributed resources.

Access to distributed transactions is important for EAI because it enables concurrent access to data shared between disparate applications, while maintaining integrity, consistency, performance, and recoverability of deliverable data across disparate applications. It is often quite complex to implement a transactional EAI framework that maintains the integrity of the data participating in transactions with heterogeneous, and potentially, legacy resources.

This chapter explores a variety of distributed transaction techniques for J2EE-based EAI frameworks, addressing the challenges associated with their implementation. We will be discussing:

- ❑ Basics of the transactional behavior and different models
- ❑ Transaction processing standards
- ❑ The two-phase commit protocol
- ❑ X/Open DTP (Distributed Transaction Processing)
- ❑ CORBA – OTS (Object Transaction Service)
- ❑ JTS/JTA – Java Transaction Services
- ❑ Transaction Management in J2EE infrastructure
- ❑ Transactions using J2EE components
- ❑ Transaction integration with TP Monitors

As the implementation of CORBA-based technologies is also proven to be effective and successful in EAI transactions, this chapter illustrates these topics with Java code snippets of CORBA transaction scenarios.

Basics of Transactional Behavior

Although the concept of a transaction should be reasonably familiar to you, in this section we will briefly review the basic transactional concepts, so that they are fresh in your mind when we consider more advanced concepts later in the chapter.

There are many situations in which we might want to ensure that actions performed during a process are completed successfully. The classic example is the transfer of funds between bank accounts. If something goes wrong during the transfer, we don't want funds to be partially transferred, or even lost. We need to make sure that either all of the funds are transferred successfully, or if something does go wrong, that any partial transfer of funds is reversed: in other words the system is **rolled back** to its original state.

This implies that we need to be able to group together a set of associated actions as one unit of work, and only accept the results of the actions if all of them execute successfully. When we treat a group of actions as one unit of work, the unit of work is known as a **transaction**.

For example, in our fund transfer example, we would group together all of the actions needed to perform the transfer into a transaction. If all of the actions were executed successfully, then the transaction would be **committed**: in other words all of the actions bundled together in the transaction would be accepted. However, if any of the actions failed, the transaction would fail too, and the system would be rolled back to the state it was in before any of the actions associated with the transaction were performed.

Another way of looking at transactions is that they allow us to make sure that a system moves from one **consistent state** to another. In the case of the bank funds transfer, we are only interested in two states: either the funds are transferred, or they are not. Although the transfer is performed via a number of actions, implying that there are a number of intermediate states between the two we are interested in, these intermediate states should only be temporary. By combining the actions into a transaction, we can make sure that the system cannot end up in one of the intermediate states.

ACID Properties

To take a system from one consistent state to another, a transaction must have four properties:

❑ **Atomicity**
However many actions the transaction involves, the transaction is treated as one unit of work. If the transaction fails for any reason, everything changed during the transaction can be restored to the state it was in prior to the start of the transaction, via a rollback operation.

❑ **Consistency**
On completion, the transaction must leave the system in a valid and consistent state.

❑ **Isolation**
The changes made by a transaction in process (not yet committed) are not made visible to other transactions until it is committed. In other words, interactions between transactions are well defined.

❑ **Durability**
The changes made to the state of the system following the completed transaction are persistent, and are saved by the system such that, even in the event of a system failure and subsequent system restart, the data will be available in its correct state.

Since the first letters of these properties form the acronym "ACID", these properties are often known as the ACID properties. The concept of ACID transactions is especially important when the transactions are occurring simultaneously.

Transaction Types

Transactions are generally categorized into three types and as implemented by the participating application:

❑ **Flat Transactions**
Also referred to as the simple transactional model. The transaction demarcation for a flat transaction is identified by a definite beginning, which initiates the transaction, and a definite endpoint, which saves the changes or aborts the changes

❑ **Chained Transactions**
Chained transactions are similar to hard save points (which preserve the atomicity of an update) in a database system. The transaction is broken into several actions where each action is typically controlled as a flat transaction. Once an action is complete, it is committed or rolled back independent of the state of the other actions.

❑ **Nested Transactions**
In a nested transaction, the transaction itself contains other transactions: in other words, it is a tree of transactions. Each node of the tree is defined as a flat transaction. This is quite similar to chained transactions, except that all sub transactions must execute successfully for the original transaction to commit.

Today, it is widely accepted that transactions are the key to constructing reliable distributed applications. Lately, the transaction concept has been extended to the broader context of distributed computing involving transactions across disparate applications.

Distributed Transaction Processing

An environment where transactions span multiple application resources is usually referred to as a **distributed transaction processing environment**. To enable distributed transaction processing, we require a transaction processing framework that enables shared access and coordinates actions across application resources to reliably deliver business-critical functions, whilst ensuring transactional integrity and consistency.

A distributed transaction is a transaction whose context spans more than one resource and/or whose context is propagated or shared by more than one component. Distributed transactions support scenarios such as:

❑ A component needs to communicate with multiple resources within the same atomic operation. A bank account session bean might debit funds from an account in one database and credit the funds in another database.

❑ Multiple components need to operate within the same atomic operation. Our banking system could debit the balance in one account entity bean, credit the funds to another entity bean, and create an audit log entry by calling a third session bean.

A distributed transaction requires the cooperation of several different **transaction managers**. A master transaction manager known as a **distributed transaction manager** coordinates the other transaction managers. It is the responsibility of the distributed transaction manager to control the propagation, demarcation, and resolution of a single transaction across several participating *local* transaction managers. A local transaction manager is a transaction manager that participates, or is "enlisted", in a distributed transaction.

The following diagram illustrates one possible configuration:

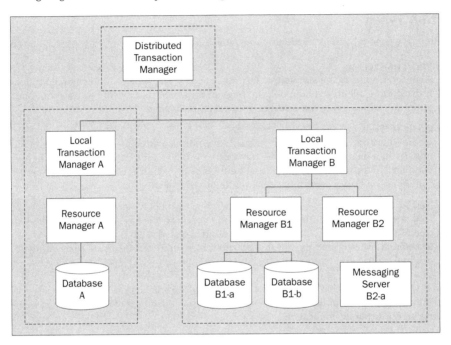

Four resources exist on two different systems. The resources are three databases (named Database A, Database B1-a, and Database B1-b) and a messaging server (Messaging Server B2-a). Database A is managed by Resource Manager A. Typically, the two together comprise a database management system (DBMS). Here, they are shown separately to distinguish between the physical data and the component responsible for managing that data. Resource Manager A's transactional context is managed by Local Transaction Manager A. For almost all databases, the transaction manager is coupled with the resource manager.

This topology also applies to Database B1-a and Database B1-b. The messaging server also has an associated resource manager, B2. For the purpose of our example, the database and the messaging server are managed by the same transaction monitor (perhaps they are part of a vendor's integrated solution). However, more often than not, these resource managers will have separate transaction managers.

The distributed transaction manager at the top is responsible for coordinating the efforts of the underlying local transaction managers when the resources associated with the local managers are involved within a distributed transaction.

Today a variety of transaction-processing applications are commercially available to provide distributed transaction frameworks and also to solve a variety of business-specific transaction problems. In addition, there are some industry standardization efforts so that applications can support and provide a standardized distributed transaction processing system.

The following industry standards committees release the most common transaction models:

❑ The Open Group (OSF or X/Open) – http://www.opengroup.org/

❑ Open System Interconnection (OSI) – http://www.acm.org/sigcomm/standards/iso_stds/OSI_MODEL/

❑ Object Management Group (OMG) – http://www.omg.org/

These have provided specifications for standardized distributed transaction architectures that enable interoperable transaction application solutions. We will discuss some of these in much more depth later in the chapter.

The Two-Phase Commit Protocol

The **two-phase commit protocol** (2PC) is a method of communication for the coordination of transactions across multiple servers and/or resources. The Open Group manages a standardized version of the two-phase commit protocol. However, not all vendors support the standardized protocol, preferring to implement their own. EJB supports the X/Open standard via the Java Transaction API. For consistency and compatibility across different platforms, you should make sure that your application server supports the X/Open specification.

When a transaction requires the services of multiple resources, the transaction processing of these resources will be managed using the two-phase commit protocol. Although we have primarily discussed databases, know that any resource manager that supports the two-phase commit protocol can participate in a distributed transaction.

As its name suggests, the two-phase commit protocol consists of two phases: the "prepare" phase and the "commit" phase.

In the prepare phase, the following happens:

❑ The distributed transaction manager tells the various local transaction managers to prepare for the requested data operations.

❑ The local transaction manager writes the details of the data operation to a transaction log. In the event that a failure occurs and the data operation was not submitted successfully to the resource manager, the transaction manager has a 'local' copy from which it can try and recreate this transaction.

❑ The local transaction managers will create a local transaction and notify their respective resource managers of the operations.

❑ Once the data operation has been executed, the resource manager will notify its transaction manager that it is ready to commit or that it needs to roll back.

❑ The resource manager will then wait for further instructions from the transaction manager.

❑ The local transaction manager will then notify the distributed transaction manager of the success or failure of their transaction.

In the commit phase:

- ❏ The distributed transaction manager notifies the enlisted transaction managers to commit or roll back. This decision is based on the results from the various local transaction managers in the prepare phase.

- ❏ The local transaction managers notify their resource managers to commit or roll back their changes.

- ❏ The resource managers comply and report the outcome back to their local transaction manager.

- ❏ Finally, the local transaction manager reports the results to the distributed transaction manager, which likewise returns the result to the calling application.

The following diagram summarizes this process:

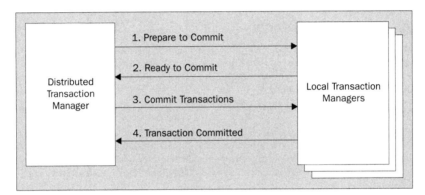

Should a local transaction manager determine that it cannot commit its transaction, the distributed transaction manager will notify the other local transaction managers to abort – as illustrated below:

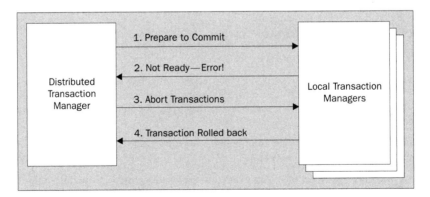

While it appears to the programmer that utilizing a distributed transaction is rather straightforward (and indeed it is), the actual implementation is extremely complex and difficult. So much so that some J2EE vendors simply do not support distributed transactions. When we look at some of the problems inherent in implementing a distributed transactional system, it's easy enough to understand why:

❏ Failure recovery cannot be relied on, if it exists at all. A transaction can fail due to connection problems, server crashes, transaction timeouts and deadlocks or other situations that might cause a transaction to get "stuck".

❏ What if our distributed transaction has three enlisted resource managers and the third resource manager fails during the commit phase? The other two resource managers have already committed their local transactions. Once data is committed, it usually cannot be rolled back. As a result, our data is now in an inconsistent, or corrupt, state. Worse still, other transactions may have executed against the now-committed data, compounding the problem and making recovery horrifically difficult if not outright impossible.

❏ If a distributed transaction does fail, how does our application determine where the failure occurred? How can we implement compensating transactions if we don't know where to apply them?

❏ While many transaction managers have logs that can be consulted to assist in recovery, this is often a manual process. In fact, you'd be surprised by how many organizations do not have a process in place to support transactional failures. The most common resolution is to restore from an earlier backup. This works provided, of course, that the organization is diligent with maintaining backups. The organization also has to be willing to accept the loss of work completed prior to the failure – most are not.

❏ The performance of distributed transactions is very slow compared to traditional, local transactions. Distributed transactions require a large amount of resources potentially spanning several servers. The two-phase commit protocol requires more communication than local transactions and this communication is conducted over a network, which can present all sorts of connectivity problems.

❏ Distributed transactions are typically longer-lived than local transactions, affecting overall system response time. This is due to the increased number of enlisted transaction managers and resource managers involved.

❏ Distributed transactions typically use the strictest form of isolation due to their higher-risk nature. This increases data contention and presents additional bottlenecks. Add to these performance issues the various schemes for ensuring stability, caching, logging and recovery support, and the performance implications become substantial.

❏ By their very nature, the design of distributed transactional systems is much more complex. Special care must be taken to ensure that one transaction does not rely on the data affected, and thus locked, by another transaction.

The use of distributed transactional processing is more complex than the code to implement it would imply. The increased scalability and capability comes at the expense of performance and the added cost of pre-planning. There is greater risk for failure and more effort required for recovery tactics. Some systems do provide support for recovery methods. However, effective recovery relies on not just the automated capabilities of the application server, but on corporate policy, as well. Without a proper contingency plan and standardized, agreed-upon, rules for data reconciliation, data recovery success will be minimal at best.

X/Open Distributed Transaction Processing

X/Open is a consortium of users, software vendors, and hardware vendors that defines standard programming interfaces for application portability. X/Open specified the DTP model that is widely adopted and implemented by database vendors and transaction application providers. The transaction processing standards proposed by OMG and Sun also use **X/Open DTP** as their basis for building distributed transaction application frameworks.

The X/Open DTP standard defines a standard communication architecture through which multiple application programs may share resources, while coordinating their work into transactions that can execute concurrently. It describes several components and their interfaces, a few instances of system architecture, as well as several protocols including the two-phase commit protocol. It also includes an application programming interface that allows applications to be portable. In general, X/Open DTP defines an open distributed transaction model that describes how components of a distributed transaction system can interoperate.

The X/Open DTP model defines three basic modules for a transaction processing application which include:

❑ **Application Programs (AP)**
   A client program that uses the interfaces provided by the DTP application system

❑ **Transaction Managers (TM)**
   An application that coordinates the transactions and controls their execution over the underlying shared resources

❑ **Resource Managers (RM)**
   Manages access to the underlying shared resources – usually X/Open-compliant database applications, message brokers, and legacy applications

The following figure represents the X/Open DTP model:

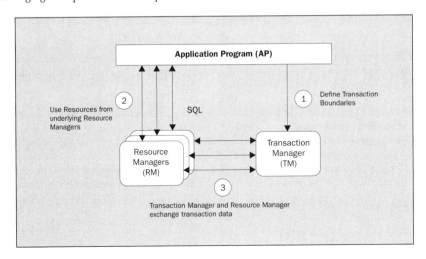

The application program interfaces with the transaction manager using the TX interface, and the transaction manager interfaces with the resource manager using the XA interface. The application program also communicates using native interfaces with the resource managers using languages such as ISAM, SQL and so on. Let's now take a closer look at these interfaces.

The TX Interface

We noted above that the TX interface defines the interaction between the application program and the transaction manager. The interface defines the transaction boundaries, the status of the transaction, and control operations.

The commonly used TX interface calls are:

Method Call	Description
tx_info()	Returns the status of the transaction
tx_begin()	Starts the transaction
tx_commit()	Commits the transaction
tx_rollback()	Rolls the transaction back

The XA Interface

The XA interface describes the protocol for transaction coordination, commitment, and recovery. It defines a bi-directional interface enabling interaction between the transaction manager and resource managers. The XA interface enables a transaction manager to coordinate the work of resource managers of participating databases. Resource managers supporting the XA protocol are capable of two-phase commits and use a transaction log for the second phase.

The commonly used XA interface calls are:

Method Call	Description
xa_prepare()	Prepares a transaction in 2PC
xa_start()	Starts the transaction
xa_commit()	Commits the transaction
xa_end()	Ends the transaction
ax_reg()	Registers a resource manager with a transaction manager

The X/Open DTP model was defined initially to support a single network domain and does not address how the application components communicate each other across network domains. The latest X/Open DTP model adds another component referred to as the **Communication Resource Manager (CRM)**. The CRM enables communications between applications across a network using standard network protocols. To handle the above issues, the X/Open CRM model provides the following interfaces:

❑ **XA+ interface**
This interface enables interaction between a transaction manager and CRM components.

697

❑ **TxRPC interface**
This defines the transactional RPC mechanism to communicate with the CRM.

❑ **XATMI Interface**
This allows a conversational mode of sending a synchronous request for an application that is executed remotely. This interface is based on BEA's Tuxedo application transaction management interface and it is accepted as an X/Open standard.

❑ **CPI-C Interface**
Otherwise known as the Common Programming Interface for Communications. It is based on the IBM CICS API and LU6.2 and allows applications that run on various systems to maintain conversational communication.

The Object Transaction Service (OTS)

The Object Management Group's **Object Transaction Service (OTS)** defines interfaces that integrate transactions into a CORBA-based distributed object framework. The OMG OTS interfaces allow developers to manage transactions involving distributed objects. OTS defines the transaction-processing framework in distributed environments, which use a CORBA ORB to locate the objects on the network.

OTS is envisioned as a standard for distributed transaction processing, supporting integration with existing transaction processing standards provided by legacy applications. The important features of an OTS implementation (provided by an ORB vendor that complies with the OTS specification) are as follows:

❑ **Application portability**
OTS defines an interface between the application and the underlying transaction service, which allows portability across ORB implementations.

❑ **Multiple transaction model support**
Supports all flat, chained and nested transaction models.

❑ **Existing applications integration**
Allows us to wrap existing applications in CORBA transactional objects so that they can be deployed into the CORBA application framework (refer to Chapter 10 for more information about wrapping existing applications with CORBA). This allows us to use OTS transaction services with existing applications.

❑ **Model and Network Interoperability**
OTS allows us to interoperate transactional objects with existing transaction managers based on the X/Open DTP model. It also allows transactional objects to interoperate in single ORB or multiple ORB environments.

❑ **Transaction propagation control**
The OMG OTS interface allows developers to manage and control transactions under two different models of transaction demarcation – implicit and explicit:

    ❑ In the implicit model, the transaction context, which defines the transaction meta-information, is managed automatically by OTS. Transaction context is associated with the client thread; when client requests are made on transactional objects, the transaction context associated with the thread is propagated to the transactional objects implicitly.

❑ In the explicit model, the transaction context must be passed explicitly (manually) when the client requests are made on transactional objects in order to propagate the transaction context to the object.

OTS Implementation and Characteristics

A typical OTS implementation consists of the following components:

❑ **Transaction Client**
A transaction client is an application program that initiates the request to invoke operations of many transactional objects in a single unit of a transaction. The transaction client that starts the transactions is called transaction originator.

❑ **Transactional Object**
A transactional object is an object invoked within the scope of a transaction. A transactional object contains or references persistent data that can be modified by requests. The transaction service does not require that all requests have transactional behavior, even when issued within the scope of a transaction. A transactional object can choose to support, or not to support, transactional behavior at its own discretion. In the case of a non-transactional object that does not support transactional behavior whose operations are affected by being invoked, the changes produced by the request may not survive a failure and the changes cannot be rolled back. In an OTS implementation transactional objects are used to implement two types of server:

  ❑ **Transactional Server**
  A transactional server is a collection of one or more objects affected by the transaction, associated with no recoverable states of their own. Instead, it implements transactional changes using other recoverable objects. A transactional server does not participate in the completion of the transaction, but it forces the transaction to roll back.

  ❑ **Recoverable Server**
  A recoverable server is a collection of objects of which at least one of them is recoverable. It registers all the resource objects with the transaction service and participates in the transaction coordination. The transaction service issues the commit requests to the resources registered for a transaction.

❑ **Recoverable Objects and Resource Objects**
Recoverable objects and resource objects inherit from transactional objects. An object whose data is affected by committing or rolling back a transaction is called a recoverable object. A recoverable object must support and participate in the transaction service protocols. The transaction service drives the commit protocol by issuing requests to the resources registered for a transaction.

The following figure represents an OTS implementation and its components:

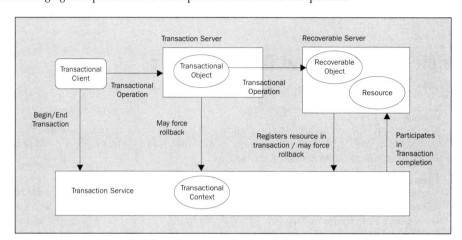

And it should be noted that the transaction service relies completely on the application to provide transaction integrity. Throughout the transaction life cycle, the ORB maintains the transactional context.

OTS Service Architecture

The transaction originator is the application that initiates the transaction. The recoverable server implements an object with recoverable state. The transaction server and recoverable server are invoked directly or indirectly by the transaction client through one or more transactional objects within the scope of the transaction. The way the transaction originator and transaction clients start and interact with the transaction depends on how the transaction context is propagated. Transaction context can be propagated implicitly or explicitly:

❏   The implicit approach is based on the OTS `Current` interface that provides operations to create and terminate a transaction. When the transaction is begun it is implicitly tied up with its originating thread. When the request is made to the transactional object, the transaction context is propagated by the ORB to the thread executing the method on the transactional object automatically.

❏   With explicit transaction context propagation the transaction client has to provide the necessary code to propagate the transaction context. Therefore, the explicit approach adopts more than one OTS interface to start, manage, and control the transaction. The transaction originator creates a transaction using an OTS interface `TransactionFactory`; a `Control` interface is returned and it provides access to a `Terminator` and a `Coordinator` interface. The transaction originator uses the `Terminator` interface to commit or roll back the transaction. The `Coordinator` interface is made available to recoverable servers and provides means for them to take part in the transaction.

As per the OTS 1.2 specification, the following diagram represents the OTS service architecture:

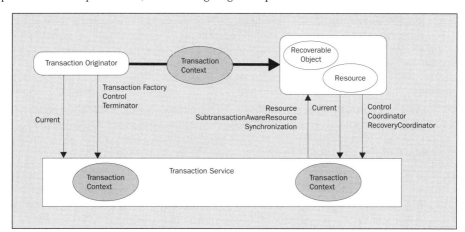

- ❏ A recoverable server registers a `Resource` with the `Coordinator`.

- ❏ The `Resource` implements the two-phase commit protocol, which is driven by the transaction service. A recoverable server may also register a `Synchronization` with the `Coordinator`.

- ❏ The `Synchronization` implements a dependent object protocol driven by the transaction service.

- ❏ A recoverable server can also register a specialized resource called a `SubtransactionAwareResource` to track the completion of sub transactions in the nested transactional model.

- ❏ A `Resource` uses a `RecoveryCoordinator` in failure cases to determine the outcome of the transaction and to coordinate the recovery process with the transaction service.

OTS Services

We have already mentioned that with implicit transaction context propagation, the transaction originator uses the OTS `Current` interface to begin a transaction, which becomes associated with the transaction originator's thread. The transaction originator then issues requests. When a request is issued to a transactional object, the transaction context associated with the invoking thread is automatically propagated to the thread executing the method of the target object. The propagation of the transaction context can extend to multiple levels if a transactional object issues a request to another transactional object.

Using the `Current` interface, the transactional object can request a rollback of the transaction and can inquire about the current state of the transaction. Using the `Current` interface, the transactional object also can obtain an OTS `Coordinator` interface for the current transaction. Using `Coordinator`, a transactional object can determine the relationship between two transactions, to implement isolation among multiple transactions.

Some transactional objects are also recoverable objects. A recoverable object has persistent data that must be managed as part of the transaction. A recoverable object uses the `Coordinator` interface to register a `Resource` object as a participant in the transaction. The `Coordinator` uses the resource to perform the two-phase commit protocol on the recoverable object's data. After the computations involved in the transaction have been completed, the transaction originator uses the `Current` interface to request that the changes be committed using a two-phase commit protocol.

OTS Interfaces

The OTS is specified using CORBA IDL. The OTS specification defines two major modules called `CosTransactions` and `CosTsPortability`. We will cover the `CosTransaction` module only. For information of `CosTsPortability` please refer to the CORBA Object Transaction Service Specification: ftp://ftp.omg.org/pub/docs/formal/01-05-02.pdf

CosTransactions

The `CosTransactions` module defines interfaces and supporting data types that allow transactional objects, resources, resource managers and transaction managers to interoperate with each other.

The interfaces in the `CosTransactions` module defined by the transaction service are as follows:

❑   **The Current interface**
It defines the simple transaction operations required by the CORBA transactional applications. These operations can be used to begin and end transactions, allow implicit propagation of transaction context to transactional objects and to obtain information about the current transaction.

```
interface Current : CORBA::Current {

  // Starts a new transaction
  void begin();
  // Commits a transaction
  void commit(in boolean report_heuristics);

  // Rolls back transactions
  void rollback();
  // Marks transaction for rollback only
  void rollback_only();
  // Returns the Status interface
  Status get_status();
  // Returns the transaction name
  string get_transaction_name();
  // Sets the timeout for transaction in seconds
  void set_timeout(in unsigned long seconds);
  // Returns Control interface for the current transaction
  Control get_control();
  // Suspends the current transaction and returns the Control
  // interface to resume it later
  Control suspend();
  // Resumes a suspended transaction
  void resume(in Control which);
};
```

❑   **The TransactionFactory interface**
The `TransactionFactory` interface is provided to allow the transaction originator to begin a transaction, if it chooses to use the explicit transaction context propagation. It provides `create()` and `recreate()` methods that a client can invoke to get a `Control` object for a transaction or to obtain a previously used control object.

```
interface TransactionFactory {
  Control create(in unsigned long time_out);
  Control recreate(in PropagationContext ctx);
};
```

❑ **The Control interface**
The `Control` interface provides methods to obtain the `Terminator` and `Coordinator` interfaces. For this it provides the `get_terminator()` and `get_coordinator()` methods.

```
interface Control {
  Terminator get_terminator() raises(Unavailable);
  Coordinator get_coordinator() raises(Unavailable);
};
```

❑ **The Terminator interface**
The `Terminator` interface supports operations to commit or roll back a transaction.

```
interface Terminator {
  void commit(in boolean report_heuristics);
  void rollback();
};
```

❑ **The Coordinator interface**
The `Coordinator` interface provides operations that are used by participants for creation and control of transactions to get status, transaction context and so on. These participants are typically either recoverable objects or agents of recoverable objects, such as subordinate coordinators. Each object supporting the `Coordinator` interface is implicitly associated with a single transaction.

```
interface Coordinator {
  Status get_status();
  Status get_parent_status();
  Status get_top_level_status();
  boolean is_same_transaction(in Coordinator tc);
  boolean is_related_transaction(in Coordinator tc);
  boolean is_ancestor_transaction(in Coordinator tc);
  boolean is_descendant_transaction(in Coordinator tc);
  boolean is_top_level_transaction();
  unsigned long hash_transaction();
  unsigned long hash_top_level_tran();
  RecoveryCoordinator register_resource(in Resource r);
  void register_synchronization (in Synchronization sync);
};
```

❑ **The RecoveryCoordinator interface.**
The recoverable object uses a `RecoveryCoordinator` interface to handle the recovery process in certain recovery situations.

```
interface RecoveryCoordinator {
  Status replay_completion(in Resource r);
};
```

❑ **The Resource interface**
The `Resource` interface defines the operations invoked by the transaction service on the defined resources while using the two-phase commit protocol. The recoverable objects implement this interface.

```
interface Resource {

  Vote prepare();
  void rollback();
  void commit();
  void commit_one_phase();
  void forget();
};
```

❑ **The Synchronization interface**
This interface defines the protocol for the transaction service with a transient state by ensuring that transacted data is notified to the resource manager before commencing the two-phase commitment protocol, and after its completion. This enables notifying the resource manager before and after the two-phase commit.

```
interface Synchronization : TransactionalObject {
  void before_completion();
  void after_completion(in Status status);
};
```

❑ **The SubtransactionAwareResource interface**
Recoverable objects using the nested transaction behavior support a specialization of the Resource interface called the SubtransactionAwareResource interface. A recoverable object requires a notification of the completion of a sub transaction by registering a specialized resource object that offers the SubtransactionAwareResource interface with the transaction service.

```
interface SubtransactionAwareResource : Resource {
  void commit_subtransaction(in Coordinator parent);
  void rollback_subtransaction();
};
```

❑ **The TransactionalObject interface**
It controls the transaction behavior of an object and is an abstract interface with no operations (a marker interface). To enable an object as a transactional object, it is required to inherit from TransactionalObject.

```
interface TransactionalObject {
};
```

Implementing an OTS Transactional CORBA Component Wrapper

In Chapter 10 we learned how to implement CORBA component wrappers that abstract access to existing applications and provide their functionality through CORBA interfaces. Here we will look at the programming steps to develop a simple transactional CORBA-based component wrapper. The transactional CORBA wrapper will use OTS to integrate with the transaction system of the existing application. For this to work the transaction system of existing application has to be X/Open DTP-compliant.

We will show how to develop an OTS transactional CORBA component wrapper that will provide access to accounts, managed by an existing application. To demonstrate the transactional functionality we will provide an additional interface that will provide functionality to transfer funds between accounts. The transfer is performed using two operations: a withdrawal (debit) from the source account and a deposit (credit) to the destination account. By performing these two operations within a transaction, we ensure that either both operations succeed or neither of them succeeds.

The steps involved in writing this are:

1. Obtain a reference to the OTS `Current` interface from the ORB

2. Create a new transaction

3. Transfer the money between the two accounts

4. Complete the transaction by either committing it or rolling it back

For our example we will define two interfaces:

❑ The `Account` interface will provide access to the functionality of the accounts (implemented by the existing application)

❑ The `BankATM` interface that will perform the transactional transfer between accounts

The IDL interface `Account` will provide operations to deposit and withdraw money (`debit()`, `credit()`). The `Account` component wrapper is a transactional object that stores state that is altered during the transaction. Therefore, `Account` will extend the `TransactionalObject` marker interface and the `Resource` interface of the OTS. There are namely two aspects to managing transactions on the server side:

❑ Ensure that the transaction is propagated to the application objects

❑ Ensure that any updates to the persistent state of the object are consistent with the outcome of the transaction

For the `Account` interface we will also define a user exception `InsufficientFundsException` through which we will signalize that funds are insufficient for withdrawal.

The second interface, the `BankATM` interface, will implement the method to transfer the money between two accounts. This transfer will be done within a transaction.

Please notice that this example demonstrates a transactional CORBA component wrapper that integrates with the transaction system used by existing application. For this it uses the CORBA OTS compatibility with the X/Open DTP model. Therefore, OTS will handle the propagation of transactional context between the wrapper and the existing application automatically – under the condition that the transaction system of the existing application is X/Open DTP-compliant.

Defining the Interfaces

The IDL definition of the `Account` and `BankATM` interfaces is shown below:

```
#include "CosTransactions.idl"

module bankatm {

  // Exception is used to signalize insufficient money
  exception InsufficientFundsException{};

  // Component wrapper for account
  interface Account :
    ::CosTransactions::Resource,
    ::CosTransactions::TransactionalObject {

    void credit( in float amount );

    void debit( in float amount )
      raises( InsufficientFundsException );
  };

  // Wrapper that provides transactional money transfer
  interface Bank_ATM {

    void transfer( in Account source, in Account destination,
                   in float amount )
      raises( InsufficientFundsException );
  };
};
```

Implementing the Component Wrapper in Java

After we have defined the interfaces in IDL we have to map them to the programming language used for implementing the component wrapper. For simplicity we will use Java for our example. Please refer to Chapter 10 for more information on how to compile the IDL interfaces to Java and about IDL-to-Java language mapping.

To develop the classes that will implement the functionality of the generated interfaces (and delegate it to the existing application) we will use the Basic Object Adapter with the inheritance approach (refer to Chapter 10 on tie approach for a discussion between inheritance and delegation). To implement the `Account` and `BankATM` interfaces we will define Java classes that will extend from the generated implementation base classes.

The implementation class (`AccountImpl.java`) of the `Account` interface is as follows:

```
package bankatmImpl;

import bankatm.*;

import org.omg.CORBA.*;
import org.omg.CORBA.ORBPackage.*;
import org.omg.CosTransactions.*;

//Account class Implementation
```

```
public class AccountImpl extends _AccountImplBase {

  private float balance;
  private float newBalance;
  private float amount;
  private boolean credit;
  private ORB orb;
  private String name;
  private Lock lock;

  public AccountImpl( ORB orb, String name, float deposit ) {

    super( name );
    this.name = name;
    this.orb = orb;

    // CONNECTION TO EXISTING APPLICATION
    // OBTAIN THE ACCOUNT BALANCE FROM EXISTING APPLICATION
    balance = deposit;

    // Create Lock instance to lock the access to the object
    // for the duration of the method invocation
    lock = new Lock();
  }

  public synchronized void credit( float amount ) {

    try {

      // Lock account
      lock.lock();

      this.amount = amount;
      credit = true;

      // Obtain transaction Current object
      org.omg.CORBA.Object obj =
        orb.resolve_initial_references("TransactionCurrent");

      org.omg.CosTransactions.Current current =
        org.omg.CosTransactions.CurrentHelper.narrow( obj );
      if( current == null ) {
        System.err.println("Improper type");
        System.exit( 1 );
      }

      // Get control and coordinator
      System.err.println("Status of the transaction: "
        + current.get_status());

      Control control = current.get_control();

      Coordinator coordinator = control.get_coordinator();

      // Register resource
      // please notice that Account stores state therefore it
      // has to implement the functionality of Resource
      RecoveryCoordinator recCoordinator =
        coordinator.register_resource( this );
```

```
      // CONNECTION TO EXISTING APPLICATION
      // INVOKE CREDIT ON ACCOUNT USING EXISTING APPLICATION
      // Obtain new balance FROM EXISTING APP
      newBalance = balance + amount;
      System.out.println(" credit $" + amount );
      System.out.println(" new balance is $" + newBalance );
    }
    catch( Exception ex ) {
      System.err.println("Account exception: " + ex );
    };
  }

  public synchronized void debit( float amount )
    throws bankatm.InsufficientFundsException {

    try {

      // Lock account
      lock.lock();

      this.amount = amount;
      credit = false;

      // Obtain current object
      System.err.println("Obtaining transaction current");

      org.omg.CORBA.Object obj =
        orb.resolve_initial_references("TransactionCurrent");

      org.omg.CosTransactions.Current current =
        org.omg.CosTransactions.CurrentHelper.narrow( obj );

      if( current == null ) {
        System.err.println("Improper expected type");
        System.exit( 1 );
      }

      // Get control and coordinator
      System.err.println("Getting status of the transaction: "
        + current.get_status());

      Control control = current.get_control();

      Coordinator coordinator = control.get_coordinator();

      // Register resource
      RecoveryCoordinator recCoordinator =
        coordinator.register_resource( this );
      System.out.println("Resource registered");

      if( amount > balance ) {
        System.out.println("Insufficient funds");
        lock.unlock();
        System.out.println("Resource: " + name + " account unlocked");
        throw new InsufficientFundsException();
      }

      // CONNECTION TO EXISTING APPLICATION
```

```
        // INVOKE CREDIT ON ACCOUNT USING EXISTING APPLICATION

        newBalance = balance - amount;
        System.out.println(" debit $" + amount );
        System.out.println(" new balance is $" + newBalance );

    }
    catch( InvalidName in ) {
      System.err.println("Account exception: " + in );
    }
    catch( Unavailable u ) {
      System.err.println("Account exception: " + u );
    }
    catch( Inactive i ) {
      System.err.println("Account exception: " + i );
    }
    catch( SystemException se ) {
      System.err.println("Account exception: " + se );
    }
  }

  // Implement methods of the Resource interface
  // Through these methods the Account, which is a resource
  // in transaction, will take part at transaction completion
  public Vote prepare() {
    if( balance == newBalance )
      return Vote.VoteReadOnly;
    return Vote.VoteCommit;
  }

  public void rollback() {
      lock.unlock();
    System.out.println("Resource: " + name + " account unlocked");
  }

  public void commit() {
    // Move data to final storage
    System.out.println("Resource " + name + " : commit()");
    balance = newBalance;
    lock.unlock();
    }

  public void commit_one_phase() {
    // store data immediately at final destination
    System.out.println("Resource " + name + " : commit_one_phase()");
    if(prepare() == Vote.VoteCommit) {
      commit();
    }
  }

  public void forget() {
      System.out.println("Resource " + name + " : forget()");
  }
}
```

After we have implemented the `Account` component wrapper, we have to implement the `BankATM` interface that will transfer the money between two accounts, using an OTS transaction (propagated to the existing application, as discussed before).

The implementation of the `BankATM` interface, `BankATMImpl.java` is as follows:

```
package bankatmImpl;

import bankatm.*;

import org.omg.CORBA.*;
import org.omg.CORBA.ORBPackage.*;
import org.omg.CosTransactions.*;

public class BankATMImpl extends _ATMImplBase {

  private ORB orb;

  public BankATMImpl( ORB orb ) {
    this.orb = orb;
  }

  public void transfer( Account source, Account destination, float amount )
    throws InsufficientFundsException {

    org.omg.CosTransactions.Current current = null;

    try {
      // Obtain current object
      System.err.println("resolve transaction current");
      org.omg.CORBA.Object obj =
          orb.resolve_initial_references("TransactionCurrent");
      current = CurrentHelper.narrow(obj);
      if( current == null ) {
            System.err.println("Unknown type - exit");
        System.exit( 1 );
      }

      // Start the transaction
      System.err.println("Starting transaction");
      current.begin();
      System.err.println("transaction status: " + current.get_status() );

      // Debit money on source account
      source.debit( amount );

      System.err.println("debited");

      // Credit money on destination account
      destination.credit( amount );

      System.err.println("credited");

      // Commit the transaction
      System.err.println("commit transaction");
      current.commit( true );
      System.err.println("transaction committed");
    }
    // Roll back transaction in case of exceptions
    catch( InsufficientFundsException isf ) {
      try {
        current.rollback();
      } catch( NoTransaction nt ) {
        System.err.println("No transaction : " + nt );
```

```
          System.exit( 1 );
      }
      throw( isf );
    } catch( InvalidName in ) {
      System.err.println("Initialization failure: " + in );
      System.exit( 1 );
    } catch( UserException ue ) {
      System.err.println("Transactional failure " + ue );
      System.exit( 1 );
    } catch( SystemException se ) {
      System.err.println("System exception - rollback transaction: " + se );
      try {
        //  Rollback
        current.rollback();
      } catch( NoTransaction nt ) {
        System.err.println("No transaction: " + nt );
        System.exit( 1 );
      }
      throw( se );
    }
  }
}
```

As we have learned in Chapter 10, we have to provide a server process where we will instantiate the component wrapper instances. We will do this in the ATMServer class. The implementation of the ATMServer class includes a main() method, where it initializes the ORB and the object adapter, and then instantiates several accounts and waits for invocation by the client. ATMServer.java is as follows:

```
package bankatmImpl;

import bankatm.*;
import java.util.*;
import org.omg.CORBA.*;
import org.omg.CosTransactions.*;
import org.omg.CORBA.ORBPackage.*;

public class ATMServer {

  public static void main(String[] args) {

    if( args.length < 2 ) {
      System.err.println(
        "Usage: bankatmImpl.ATMServer <account number>");
        System.exit( 1 );
    }

    try {
      Properties props = new Properties();

        // Initialize the ORB
        // Use your ORB Implementation here
        // For example, Visigenic ORB implementation
      props.put("ORBservices", "com.visigenic.services.CosTransactions");
      ORB orb = ORB.init( args, props );

        // Initialize the basic object adapter
      BOA boa = orb.BOA_init();
      Hashtable accounts = new Hashtable();
```

```
            Random random = new Random();

            for( int i = 0; i < args.length; i++ ) {

              //Randomly generate an account deposit
              float deposit = random.nextFloat() * 100;
              AccountImpl accountImpl = new AccountImpl(orb, args[i], deposit );

              // Server is ready to use
              boa.obj_is_ready( (Account)accountImpl );
              System.out.println( "account " + args[i] + " created" );
              System.out.println( "with initial deposit: $" + deposit );
            }
            boa.impl_is_ready();
          } catch(SystemException se) {
            System.err.println(se);
          }
        }
      }
```

Developing the Client

To test the functionality of the component wrapper we will implement a simple client. The client will invoke transactional transfer of funds between accounts using the BankATM interface.

The following code is for the client implementation (ATMClient) that acts as a transaction originator for the ATMServer. ATMClient.java is as follows.

```
package bankatmImpl;

import bankatm.*;
import java.util.*;
import org.omg.CORBA.*;
import org.omg.CORBA.ORBPackage.*;
import org.omg.CosTransactions.*;

public class ATMClient {

  public static void main(String[] args) {

    if( args.length != 3 ) {
      System.err.println("Usage: bankatmImpl.ATMClient " +
                         "<source ex.'checking'> " +
                         "<destination ex.'savings'> " +
                         "<amount ex. 0.00>");
      System.exit( 1 );
    }

    try {
      Properties props = new Properties();
      // Initialize the ORB and Object adapter
      props.put("ORBservices", "com.visigenic.services.CosTransactions");
      ORB orb = ORB.init( args, props );
      BOA boa = orb.BOA_init();

      // Create an instance of the ATM object
      BankATMImpl atmImpl = new BankATMImpl(orb);
```

```
        boa.obj_is_ready( (Bank_ATM)atmImpl );

        // Locate the account objects (For.ex - checking, Savings)
        Account source = AccountHelper.bind( orb, args[0] );
        Account destination = AccountHelper.bind( orb, args[1] );

        // Call the transfer method.
        atmImpl.transfer( source, destination, args[2] );
    } catch(InsufficientFundsException nsf) {
        System.err.println(nsf);
    } catch(SystemException se) {
        System.err.println(se);
    }
  }
}
```

To run the above example we need a CORBA implementation such as Inprise/Borland Visibroker for Java and a CORBA OTS implementation. Unfortunately, OTS implementations are not very portable so you will probably find you will need to modify the code from the above. Complete instructions for a particular ORB and OTS implementation can be found in the code download for this chapter.

Now the system will display the transaction debit and credit as committed transactions. Also try to execute a large transfer to induce an `InSufficientFundsException` and to roll back the transaction. Take a look at the ORB server logs to view the events of the transaction coordinator.

With this example we have become familiar with the functionality of CORBA OTS and have seen how to develop transactional component wrappers for integration with existing transactional applications, compliant with the X/Open DTP standard. Next we will look at Java Transaction Service (JTS) and identify the relation between OTS and JTS.

The Java Transaction Service

As a part of the J2EE initiative, Sun released the **Java Transaction Service (JTS)**. JTS specifies the implementation of a Java-based transaction manager supporting a high-level **Java Transaction API (JTA)**.

> **Java Transaction Service (JTS) is the mapping of the OMG CORBA Object Transaction Service (OTS) version 1.1 to Java.**

The Java mapping of OTS 1.1 interfaces uses CORBA standard IDL and Java programming language mapping. The OTS modules `CosTransactions` and `CosTSPortability` are mapped to corresponding Java packages:

❑ `org.omg.CosTransactions`

❑ `org.omg.CosTSPortability`

JTS uses the standard CORBA OTS and ORB interfaces (and the IIOP protocol) for generating and propagating transaction context between JTS-based transaction managers. The Java Transaction API (API) defines the API interface for applications wishing to use JTS. It provides a generic interface to use JTS-based transaction services and allows programmatic control of the transaction boundaries. This enables JTA/JTS-compliant applications to use transactions independent of the specific implementation and also allows interoperation with other OTS 1.1-compliant applications through standard IIOP. Due to the interoperability of OTS with existing transactional systems compliant with X/Open DTP, this means that JTS is also interoperable with X/Open DTP-compliant transaction systems – that is with existing transactional applications.

The JTS specification defines the JTS infrastructure with the following basic components:

❏   **Transaction Manager**
This provides the basic services for managing and controlling the creation of JTA-based transactions by providing transaction demarcation, propagation of transaction context, synchronization, initiation and coordination of two-phase commit, and recovery protocols with resource managers.

❏   **Application Server**
This provides the runtime environment and transaction services for JTA-based components. It manages the creation and control of transactions allowing the developers to focus on the business logic independent of transaction services. In the JTS context, the application server uses the `javax.transaction.TransactionManager` interface.

❏   **Resource Manager**
This allows an application to access the resources. It implements the transaction resource interface used by the transaction manager for participating in transactions, which include support to the two-phase commit protocol. In the JTS context, the resource manager uses the `javax.transaction.xa.XAResource` interface.

❏   **Transaction Application**
This initiates transactions and interacts with underlying resources using the services provided by the application server environment. In the case of unmanaged stand alone Java applications, the transaction boundaries are managed using interfaces provided by a transaction manager of the underlying resource. In the JTS context, the application uses the `javax.transaction.UserTransaction` interface.

❏   **Communication Resource Manager (CRM)**
This allows the transaction manager to participate in transactions by supporting the transaction context obtained from other transaction managers. The JTS specification does not define a protocol but it assumes an implementation of CRM as per the CORBA OTS and GIOP specifications.

The following diagram represents a JTS-compliant infrastructure and its components supporting JTA interfaces:

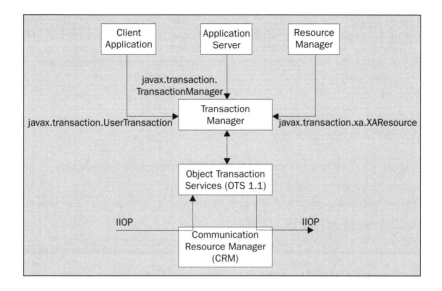

The Java Transaction API

As part of the Java Community Process, Sun Microsystems (in co operation with leading transaction processing and database system vendors in the industry, such as IBM, TIBCO, and BEA) released the JTA specification and it is available at http://java.sun.com/products/jta/index.html.

Let's now discuss the most important interface classes of the Java Transaction API:

The javax.transaction.UserTransaction Interface

The UserTransaction interface provides Java applications with the ability to programmatically control transaction boundaries. It is implemented by the transaction manager services exposed by the application server, and is called by the client application.

```
public interface javax.transaction.UserTransaction {

   public void begin();
   public void commit();
   public void rollback();
   public int getStatus();
   public void setRollbackOnly() ;
   public void setTransactionTimeout (int seconds);
}
```

The use of the UserTransaction interface is very straightforward, as detailed below:

❑   Begin the transaction by invoking begin()

❑   Execute any business logic to be contained within the transaction

❑   Complete the transaction by either invoking commit() or rollback()

715

The setRollbackOnly() method will mark a transaction for rollback without actually rolling the transaction back. This is desirable when other methods within the transaction need to run regardless of whether the transaction will commit or roll back. When the setRollbackOnly() method is used, the transaction's status should be checked before the end of the transaction and handled accordingly. This is done by invoking the getStatus() method which will return the status of the current transaction. getStatus() returns one of the following values (embodied in the javax.transaction.Status interface):

❑ STATUS_ACTIVE
   A transaction is associated with the component and is in the active state.

❑ STATUS_COMMITTED
   A transaction is associated with the component and has been committed.

❑ STATUS_COMMITTING
   A transaction is associated with the component and is in the process of committing.

❑ STATUS_MARKED_ROLLBACK
   A transaction is associated with the component and has been marked for rollback.

❑ STATUS_NO_TRANSACTION
   No transaction is associated with the component.

❑ STATUS_PREPARED
   A transaction is associated with the component and has been prepared for committing in a two-phase commit (discussed later). It is waiting for a commit instruction from the transaction manager.

❑ STATUS_PREPARING
   A transaction is associated with the component and is in the process of preparing for a two-phase commit, but has not yet completed the preparation.

❑ STATUS_ROLLEDBACK
   A transaction is associated with the component and has been rolled back.

❑ STATUS_ROLLING_BACK
   A transaction is associated with the component and is in the process of rolling back.

❑ STATUS_UNKNOWN
   A transaction is associated with the component but its status cannot be determined.

The following state diagram shows the relationship of the statuses to the transaction life cycle:

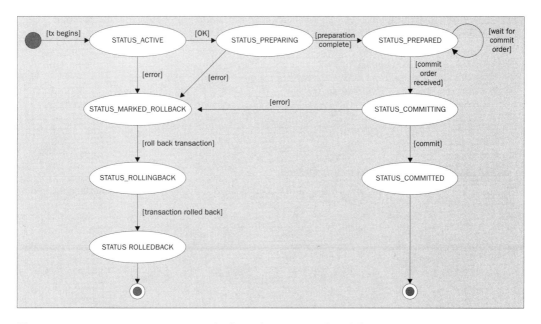

The setTransactionTimeout() method sets the timeout value of the transaction that is associated with the current thread. If a transaction does not complete within the specified length of time, a SystemException will be thrown. Generally, the timeout value for a transaction is defined through the application server's configuration. As such, it is better to set the timeout value at the server level, than at the method level.

We'll look at how to use the UserTransaction interface to manage transactions in EJBs shortly.

The javax.transaction.TransactionManager Interface

This interface allows the application server to demarcate the transactional boundaries on behalf of the client application. In container-managed transactions, it allows the bean to mark the transaction, especially for rollback. The transaction manager implements the TransactionManager interface and it is called by the application server.

```
interface javax.transaction.TransactionManager
{
  public abstract void begin() ;
  public abstract void commit();
  public abstract int getStatus();
  public abstract Transaction getTransaction();
  public void resume(Transaction tobj);
  public abstract void rollback();
  public abstract void setRollbackOnly();
  public abstract void setTransactionTimeout(int seconds);
  public abstract Transaction suspend() ;
}
```

For example, in an application server, the application server handles the transaction demarcation. The necessary commands are shown below:

```
// Start the transaction
Transaction tx = TransactionManager.begin();

// Executes operations ...

// Commit the transaction
TransactionManager.commit;
```

The javax.transaction.xa.XAResource Interface

The XAResource interface provides the Java mapping of the XA resource manager interface defined by the X/Open specification:

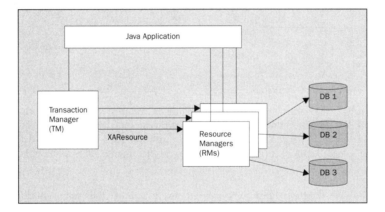

It enables the transaction manager to perform the following operations:

❏   Associate and disassociate transaction work with underlying resources during transaction commit and rollback scenarios

❏   Use the two-phase commit protocol and coordinate completion of transaction

❏   Recover a transaction after a crash

The resource manager or a compliant driver implements the XAResource interface, and the resource adapter or a compliant driver to the transaction manager exposes it. The javax.transaction.xa.Xid interface is a Java mapping of the X/Open transaction identifier.

```
public interface javax.transaction.xa.XAResource {
  public abstract void commit(Xid xid, boolean onePhase);
  public abstract void end(Xid xid, int flags);
  public abstract void forget(Xid xid);
  public abstract int getTransactionTimeout();
  public abstract boolean isSameRM(XAResource xares);
  public abstract int prepare(Xid xid);
  public abstract Xid[] recover(int flag);
```

```
    public abstract void rollback(Xid xid);
    public abstract boolean setTransactionTimeout(int seconds);
    public abstract void start(Xid xid, int flags);
}
```

One possibility to use JTA for integration with existing data is to develop lower-level virtual components that abstract access to existing databases, which require transactional access. Then we can use JTA, which will propagate the transactional context automatically if the existing databases are X/Open DTP-compliant and provide the XA interface. Fortunately the majority of existing databases are X/Open DTP-compliant and provide the XA interface. Therefore transactional integration is seamless.

The following code snippet illustrates the necessary commands for developing a lower-level virtual component for data integration, using Oracle XA drivers to execute an XA transaction using JTA-based XAResource interfaces. Please notice that using drivers for other databases would make the same code work with any XA-compliant database.

```
// imports
import java.sql.*;
import javax.sql.*;
import oracle.jdbc.driver.*;
import oracle.jdbc.pool.*;
import oracle.jdbc.xa.OracleXid;
import oracle.jdbc.xa.OracleXAException;
import oracle.jdbc.xa.client.*;
import javax.transaction.xa.*;
import oracle.jdbc.xa.OracleXid;

public class TestOracleXA {

  public static void main(String[] args) {

    double savingsBalance=0;
    double checkingsBalance=0;
    double transferValue;

    XAConnection xacon1 =n ull, xacon2 = null;
    Connection c1 = null, c2 = null;

    try {

      DriverManager.registerDriver(new OracleDriver());

      // Create XADataSource instances and set properties.
      OracleXADataSource ds1 = new OracleXADataSource ();
      ds1.setURL("jdbc:oracle:thin:@dbserver:1521:ejb");
      ds1.setUser("scott");
      ds1.setPassword("tiger");

      OracleXADataSource ds2 = new OracleXADataSource ();
      ds2.setURL("jdbc:oracle:thin:@(description=(address=(host=" +
              "xadb.wrox.com)(protocol=tcp)(port=5521))" +
              "(connect_data=(sid=java)))");
      ds2.setUser("scott");
      ds2.setPassword("tiger");

      // Obtain the XA Connection to the underlying data sources
```

719

```
xacon1 = ds1.getXAConnection ();
c1 = xacon1.getConnection ();
xacon2 = ds2.getXAConnection ();
c2 = xacon2.getConnection ();

//Get current balances
Statement stmt1 = c1.createStatement ();
Statement stmt2 = c2.createStatement ();

ResultSet rset1 = stmt1.executeQuery (
        "SELECT balance FROM savings_account2 WHERE accountid='" +
        args[0] + "'");
ResultSet rset2 = stmt2.executeQuery (
        "SELECT BALANCE FROM checking_account WHERE accountid='" +
        args[0] + "'");

while (rset1.next())
  savingsBalance = rset1.getDouble(1);

while (rset2.next())
  checkingsBalance = rset2.getDouble(1);

transferValue = (Double.valueOf(args[1])).doubleValue();

System.out.println("Current savings balance is: " + savingsBalance);
System.out.println("Current checkings balance is: " +
                    checkingsBalance);

// Get the XA Resources
XAResource xares1 = xacon1.getXAResource ();
XAResource xares2 = xacon2.getXAResource ();

// Create an X/Open identifier choosing a value
Xid xid1 = createXid(1);
Xid xid2 = createXid(1);

// Start the Transaction
xares1.start (xid1, XAResource.TMNOFLAGS);
xares2.start (xid2, XAResource.TMNOFLAGS);

// Transfer money from savings to checkings
stmt1.execute ("UPDATE savings_account2 SET balance=" +
                (savingsBalance - transferValue) +
                " WHERE accountid='" + args[0] + "'");
stmt1.execute ("UPDATE checking_account SET balance=" +
                (checkingsBalance + transferValue) +
                " WHERE accountid='" + args[0] + "'");

// END both the branches
xares1.end (xid1, XAResource.TMSUCCESS);
xares2.end (xid2, XAResource.TMSUCCESS);

// Prepare the resource managers for 'prepare phase'
int prep1 = xares1.prepare (xid1);
int prep2 = xares2.prepare (xid2);

System.out.println("prepare 1 is " + prep1);
System.out.println("prepare 2 is " + prep2);
```

```
      if (prep1 == XAResource.XA_OK && prep2 == XAResource.XA_OK) {
        // Commit the Transaction
        xares1.commit (xid1, false);
        xares2.commit (xid2, false);
        System.out.println("committed");
      } else {
        // Roll back the transaction
        xares1.rollback (xid1);
        xares2.rollback (xid2);
        System.out.println("rolledback");
      }

    } catch (SQLException sqe) {
      sqe.printStackTrace();
    } catch (XAException xae) {
      if (xae instanceof OracleXAException) {
        System.out.println("XA Error is " +
                        ((OracleXAException)xae).getXAError());
        System.out.println("SQL Error is " +
                        ((OracleXAException)xae).getOracleError());
        System.out.println(xae);
      }
    } finally {
      try {
        c1.close();
        c2.close();
        xacon1.close();
        xacon2.close();
      } catch (SQLException sqle)  {
        System.out.println("Error closing connections: "+ sqle);
      }
    }

  }

  static Xid createXid(int bids) throws XAException  {
    byte[] gid = new byte[1]; gid[0]= (byte) 9;
    byte[] bid = new byte[1]; bid[0]= (byte) bids;
    byte[] gtrid = new byte[64];
    byte[] bqual = new byte[64];
    System.arraycopy (gid, 0, gtrid, 0, 1);
    System.arraycopy (bid, 0, bqual, 0, 1);
    Xid xid = new OracleXid(0x1234, gtrid, bqual);
    return xid;
  }

}
```

Advantages of Using JTS/JTA for Business Transactions

In general, JTA provides the following support for handling business transactions:

❑   Defines a unique transaction identifier when the transaction is originated by a client application.

❑   It runs within a J2EE application server infrastructure or a JTS supported transaction manger running the transactional objects, and coordinates the transaction to commit or roll back.

❑   Notifies the resource managers (databases) on behalf of a transaction. Resource managers then lock the accessed records until the end of the transaction.

721

❑ Manages the two-phase commit during the execution of the transaction, ensuring all the participants in the transaction commit their updates simultaneously. It also coordinates the commit with any databases supporting X/Open specifications.

❑ Executes the rollback procedure when the transaction needs to be terminated.

❑ Executes the recovery procedure after failure. It determines the active transactions at the time of the crash, and identifies which transactions need to be rolled back or committed.

❑ Manages transaction timeouts for transaction operations that exceed the timeout period. It issues a timeout for the transaction and frees the locked resource manager/database resources.

JTA Support in J2EE Infrastructure

J2EE allows J2EE components to participate in local and distributed transactions. It defines two basic approaches for handling transactions, as follows:

❑ **Declarative Transactions**
The separation of transaction handling from the business logic by declaring the transaction attributes through a deployment descriptor

❑ **Programmatic Transactions**
Programmatic control over transaction mechanisms using JTA

As per J2EE 1.3, the following J2EE API-based components deployed in a J2EE server can participate in transactions:

❑ EJBs (Enterprise JavaBeans) use JTA for distributed transaction support. EJBs provide a declarative transaction mechanism, using deployment descriptor attributes, to support transaction handling.

❑ JDBC provides standard interfaces for accessing relational database systems from Java code. JTA provides transaction support on connections retrieved using a JDBC driver and transaction data source.

❑ J2EE Connector Architecture, in the form of Client Connectivity Interfaces, provides standard interfaces for accessing EIS resource systems from Java. JTA provides transaction support for connections retrieved using a resource adapter from an EIS resource.

❑ JMS (Java Message Service) uses JTA to support transactions across multiple data resources. Most JMS implementations provide an XA-compliant resource manager to support JTS/JTA transactions.

Using Transactions in EJBs

In Chapter 12 we identified the role of EJBs in integration. There we figured out that EJBs are best suited for higher-level virtual components. Often transactional support is required in such higher-level virtual components. Here we will look at the support for transactions in EJBs. The EJB 2.0 specification defines EJBs' participation in transactions in two different ways:

❑ The EJB is invoked based on a declarative transactional context as a container-managed transaction.

❑ The EJB runs a bean-managed transaction using the `UserTransaction` interface in a bean method invoked by the client, and it does *not* suspend or terminate that transaction upon completion.

The key feature of using EJBs in transactions is the support for both declarative and programmatic transactions:

❑ In the declarative transaction model, the transaction attributes are associated with beans at deployment time and it is the EJB container's responsibility, based on the attribute value, to demarcate and transparently propagate transactional context. Declarative transactions are supported by entity beans using container-managed mechanisms, because the container uses the transaction manager directly to ensure that all participants in the transaction are consistent.

❑ For programmatic control and demarcation of transactions, the EJB developer controls all aspects of transaction management, using JDBC, JTA, and the `UserTransaction` interface. It is usually done using bean-managed transactions similar to JDBC, but it allows participation in global transactions.

Let's take a look at EJB container-managed and bean-managed transactions, focusing on global transactions.

Container-Managed Transactions

In an EJB with container-managed persistence, the EJB container sets the boundaries of the transactions using a declarative transaction context provided in the EJB deployment descriptor (**container-managed transactions**). This simplifies EJB development because the bean implementation does not need to include the transaction boundaries such as `begin()` and `commit()`. Instead the EJB container uses declarative transaction attributes to control the transactions. The transaction attributes define and specify the scope of transactions associated with the bean methods. In a container-managed transaction the application assembler can specify the following transaction attributes:

❑ **TX_REQUIRED**
Used as a default value in most transactions. In this case, the client is already part of a transaction and when it invokes the EJB's method the method executes within a transaction. If the client is not part of a transaction, then a new transaction is created before invoking the EJB's method.

❑ **TX_REQUIRES_NEW**
This requires that the container start a new transaction when a method is invoked. The container attempts to commit the transaction when the bean's method call completes. When a client calls into a bean with this attribute, the container suspends the client's transaction before starting the bean's new transaction. Upon completing the bean's transaction, the container resumes the client's suspended transaction.

❑ **TX_MANDATORY**
The container invokes the EJB's method using the transaction context associated with the client application. The EJB's method will not start unless the client is in a transaction, or it will throw a `TransactionRequiredException`.

❑ **TX_NOTSUPPORTED**
When this attribute is specified, if the client is running within a transaction and it invokes the EJB's method then the container suspends the transaction before the invocation of the method. You should use this attribute to ensure that the method will never run within a transaction managed by the container.

❏ **TX_SUPPORTS**
In this case, if the client is part of a transaction, then the EJB's method will also be part of the transaction. Otherwise the method is invoked with no transaction context.

Using Container-Managed Transactions in EJB

Container-managed transactions typically work in the following order:

❏ In the EJB deployment descriptor we define the transaction type for container-managed transactions by setting the `<transaction-type>` element to `<Container>`.

❏ In the EJB deployment descriptor we specify the default transaction attribute element for the EJB as one of the following: `Required`, `RequiresNew`, `NotSupported`, `Supports`, `Mandatory`, or `Never`, as described above.

❏ Additionally, in the EJB deployment descriptor we can also specify the method level `<trans-attribute>` for the bean methods. During a client application invocation of a method in the EJB, the EJB container checks the `<trans-attribute>` setting in the deployment descriptor for that method. If it is not provided for that particular method then it uses the EJB's default `<trans-attribute>`.

❏ When the client application invokes a bean method, the EJB container identifies the `<trans-attribute>` setting in the deployment descriptor for the bean method. If no attribute is specified, it chooses the default setting made for the EJB.

❏ The EJB container executes the operation based on the provided `<trans-attribute>`.

❏ In the invocation process of the business method, if the bean method determines a rollback is required, then the bean method invokes the `EJBContext.setRollbackOnly()` method. In turn, the container makes the transaction roll back at the end of the method invocation.

Rollback Mechanism in Container-Managed Transaction

In a container-managed transaction scenario, the container invokes the transaction rollback in the following two ways:

❏ During an exception (`EJBException`) thrown by the bean method

❏ By invoking the `setRollbackOnly()` method of the `EJBContext` interface

Container-Managed Transactions EJB Example

We'll put together an EJB version of our account transfer example, which uses two entity beans to represent the two accounts and a session bean to control the transfer. First, we'll demonstrate how to declaratively set the transaction attributes for container-managed transactions (entity beans can only use CMT anyway). The complete code can be found in the download for this chapter from http://www.wrox.com.

The most interesting class in this example, is the session bean's implementation class:

```
package atm;

import javax.ejb.*;
import checking.*;
import saving.*;
```

```java
import javax.naming.InitialContext;
import javax.naming.NamingException;
import javax.transaction.*;

public class ATMEJB implements SessionBean {

  private SessionContext sessionCtx = null;

  public void transferFromSavingsToCheckings(String accountId,
                                             double amount)
      throws InsufficientFundsException {

    try {

      InitialContext ctx = new InitialContext();
      CheckingAccountHome checkHome = (CheckingAccountHome)
          javax.rmi.PortableRemoteObject.narrow(
              ctx.lookup("CheckingAccount"), CheckingAccountHome.class);
      CheckingAccount checkAccount = checkHome.findByPrimaryKey(accountId);

      SavingAccountHome saveHome = (SavingAccountHome)
          javax.rmi.PortableRemoteObject.narrow(
              ctx.lookup("SavingAccount"), SavingAccountHome.class);
      SavingAccount saveAccount = saveHome.findByPrimaryKey(accountId);

      if (saveAccount.getBalance() < amount) {
        sessionCtx.setRollbackOnly();
        throw new InsufficientFundsException();
      } else {
        saveAccount.setBalance( (saveAccount.getBalance()) - amount);
        checkAccount.setBalance( (checkAccount.getBalance()) + amount);
      }

    } catch (NamingException ne) {
      throw new EJBException(ne);
    } catch (Exception e) {
      throw new EJBException(e);
    }
  }

  public void ejbCreate() {}
  public void ejbPostCreate() {}
  public void ejbRemove() {}

  public void unsetSessionContext() {
    this.sessionCtx = null;
  }
  public void setSessionContext(SessionContext ctx) {
    this.sessionCtx = ctx;
  }
  public void ejbActivate() {}
  public void ejbPassivate() {}

}
```

As you can see there is virtually no transactional code in this class. The only line is demonstrating the use of the `setRollbackOnly()` method. This is because all the transactional settings are configured in the deployment descriptor. Here are the relevant sections:

```xml
<?xml version="1.0" encoding="UTF-8"?>

<!DOCTYPE ejb-jar PUBLIC '-//Sun Microsystems, Inc.//DTD Enterprise JavaBeans
2.0//EN' 'http://java.sun.com/dtd/ejb-jar_2_0.dtd'>

<ejb-jar>
  <display-name>Beans</display-name>
  <enterprise-beans>
    <entity>
      <display-name>SavingAccount</display-name>
      <ejb-name>SavingAccount</ejb-name>
      <home>saving.SavingAccountHome</home>
      <remote>saving.SavingAccount</remote>
      <ejb-class>saving.SavingAccountEJB</ejb-class>
      <persistence-type>Container</persistence-type>
      <prim-key-class>java.lang.String</prim-key-class>
      <reentrant>False</reentrant>
      <cmp-version>1.x</cmp-version>
      <cmp-field>
        <description>no description</description>
        <field-name>balance</field-name>
      </cmp-field>
      <cmp-field>
        <description>no description</description>
        <field-name>accountId</field-name>
      </cmp-field>
      <primkey-field>accountId</primkey-field>
    </entity>
    <entity>
      <display-name>CheckingAccount</display-name>
      <ejb-name>CheckingAccount</ejb-name>
      <home>checking.CheckingAccountHome</home>
      <remote>checking.CheckingAccount</remote>
      <ejb-class>checking.CheckingAccountEJB</ejb-class>
      <persistence-type>Container</persistence-type>
      <prim-key-class>java.lang.String</prim-key-class>
      <reentrant>False</reentrant>
      <cmp-version>1.x</cmp-version>
      <cmp-field>
        <description>no description</description>
        <field-name>balance</field-name>
      </cmp-field>
      <cmp-field>
        <description>no description</description>
        <field-name>accountId</field-name>
      </cmp-field>
      <primkey-field>accountId</primkey-field>
      <security-identity>
        <description></description>
        <use-caller-identity></use-caller-identity>
      </security-identity>
    </entity>
    <session>
      <display-name>ATM</display-name>
      <ejb-name>ATM</ejb-name>
```

```
      <home>atm.ATMHome</home>
      <remote>atm.ATM</remote>
      <ejb-class>atm.ATMEJB</ejb-class>
      <session-type>Stateless</session-type>
      <transaction-type>Container</transaction-type>
      <ejb-ref>
        <ejb-ref-name>CheckingAccount</ejb-ref-name>
        <ejb-ref-type>Entity</ejb-ref-type>
        <home>checking.CheckingAccountHome</home>
        <remote>checking.CheckingAccount</remote>
      </ejb-ref>
      <ejb-ref>
        <ejb-ref-name>SavingAccount</ejb-ref-name>
        <ejb-ref-type>Entity</ejb-ref-type>
        <home>saving,SavingAccountHome</home>
        <remote>saving.SavingAccount</remote>
      </ejb-ref>
    </session>
  </enterprise-beans>
  <assembly-descriptor>
    <container-transaction>
      <method>
        <ejb-name>SavingAccount</ejb-name>
        <method-intf>Remote</method-intf>
        <method-name>setBalance</method-name>
        <method-params>
          <method-param>double</method-param>
        </method-params>
      </method>
      <trans-attribute>Required</trans-attribute>
    </container-transaction>
    <container-transaction>
      <method>
        <ejb-name>SavingAccount</ejb-name>
        <method-intf>Remote</method-intf>
        <method-name>getBalance</method-name>
        <method-params />
      </method>
      <trans-attribute>Required</trans-attribute>
    </container-transaction>
    <container-transaction>
      <method>
        <ejb-name>SavingAccount</ejb-name>
        <method-intf>Remote</method-intf>
        <method-name>remove</method-name>
        <method-params />
      </method>
      <trans-attribute>Required</trans-attribute>
    </container-transaction>
    <container-transaction>
      <method>
        <ejb-name>CheckingAccount</ejb-name>
        <method-intf>Remote</method-intf>
        <method-name>setBalance</method-name>
        <method-params>
          <method-param>double</method-param>
        </method-params>
      </method>
      <trans-attribute>Required</trans-attribute>
    </container-transaction>
```

```
<container-transaction>
  <method>
    <ejb-name>CheckingAccount</ejb-name>
    <method-intf>Remote</method-intf>
    <method-name>getBalance</method-name>
    <method-params />
  </method>
  <trans-attribute>Required</trans-attribute>
</container-transaction>
<container-transaction>
  <method>
    <ejb-name>CheckingAccount</ejb-name>
    <method-intf>Remote</method-intf>
    <method-name>remove</method-name>
    <method-params />
  </method>
  <trans-attribute>Required</trans-attribute>
</container-transaction>
<container-transaction>
  <method>
    <ejb-name>ATM</ejb-name>
    <method-intf>Remote</method-intf>
    <method-name>transferFromSavingsToCheckings</method-name>
    <method-params>
      <method-param>java.lang.String</method-param>
      <method-param>double</method-param>
    </method-params>
  </method>
  <trans-attribute>Required</trans-attribute>
</container-transaction>
</assembly-descriptor>
</ejb-jar>
```

Transaction Notification

In the case of a stateful session bean that uses container-managed transactions, the bean requires notification of failure as it has in-memory state that needs to be rolled back. To handle this issue, a stateful session bean using container-managed transactions can implement the `javax.ejb.SessionSynchronization` interface to provide transaction synchronization notifications:

```
public interface javax.ejb.SessionSynchronization {

  public void afterBegin() throws EJBException, RemoteException;

  public void afterCompletion(boolean committed) throws EJBException,
                                                        RemoteException;

  public void beforeCompletion() throws EJBException, RemoteException;
}
```

In addition, all methods on the stateful session bean must support one of the following transaction attributes: REQUIRES_NEW, MANDATORY or REQUIRED. This helps the bean in the following ways:

❑ Alerts the stateful session bean in case of transaction failure enabling it to act like a transactional resource, undoing state changes

❑ Alerts the transaction boundaries enabling the database to cache the data for performance

If a stateful session bean implements `SessionSynchronization`, the EJB container needs to make the following callbacks to the bean during its life cycle:

- ❏ `afterBegin()` – The container calls this method before the transaction notifying the bean that a new transaction is about to begin.

- ❏ `beforeCompletion()` – The container calls this method when it is ready to execute the transaction before a commit.

- ❏ `afterCompletion()` – The container calls this method when the transaction is committed or rolled back.

The EJB container can additionally call other EJBs or involve additional XA resources in the `beforeCompletion()` method with a condition that the number of calls is limited by the `beforeCompletionIterationLimit` attribute. This attribute specifies how many cycles of callbacks are processed before the transaction is rolled back. This attribute ensures that synchronization cycles do not run indefinitely.

Bean-Managed Transactions

In bean-managed transactions, the EJB developer manages the transaction demarcation within the bean implementation class. The EJB makes explicit method invocations on the `javax.transaction.UserTransaction` object to begin, commit or roll back transactions.

Bean-managed transactions can be done in session and message-driven beans by setting the `<trans-attribute>` element to `Bean` in the deployment descriptor. Entity beans cannot use bean-managed transactions. For stateful session beans, the entering and exiting transaction contexts may not have to match as the EJB container maintains associations between the bean and the non-terminated transaction. This is to avoid performance-related issues. In the case of stateless session beans, the entering and exiting transaction contexts must match at the end of session termination.

Session beans with bean-managed transactions cannot use the `setRollbackOnly()` and `getRollbackOnly()` methods of the `javax.ejb.EJBContext` interface as it is intended for container-managed transactions only.

Using Bean-Managed Transactions in EJB

An EJB-based bean-managed transaction typically works in the following order:

- ❏ The EJB deployment descriptor defines the transaction type for container-managed demarcation as `Bean`.

- ❏ The application uses JNDI to obtain an object reference to the `UserTransaction` object.

- ❏ The application begins the transaction using the `UserTransaction.begin()` method and all of the operations will be executed within the scope of the particular transaction.

- ❏ In the case of operation failure it raises an exception and the transaction will be rolled back using the `UserTransaction.rollback()` method.

- ❏ In the case of no exceptions, the `UserTransaction.commit()` method enables the EJB container to call the transaction manager to complete the transaction.

- ❏ The transaction manager is responsible for coordinating with all the underlying resource managers.

729

Let's update our session bean from the previous example to use bean-managed transactions instead:

```java
package atm;

import javax.ejb.*;
import checking.*;
import saving.*;
import javax.naming.InitialContext;
import javax.naming.NamingException;
import javax.transaction.*;

public class ATMEJB implements SessionBean {

    private SessionContext sessionCtx = null;

  public void transferFromSavingsToCheckings(String accountId,
                                             double amount)
      throws InsufficientFundsException {

    UserTransaction tx = null;
    try {
      tx = sessionCtx.getUserTransaction();
      tx.begin();

      InitialContext ctx = new InitialContext();
      CheckingAccountHome checkHome = (CheckingAccountHome)
          javax.rmi.PortableRemoteObject.narrow(
              ctx.lookup("CheckingAccount"), CheckingAccountHome.class);
      CheckingAccount checkAccount = checkHome.findByPrimaryKey(accountId);

      SavingAccountHome saveHome = (SavingAccountHome)
          javax.rmi.PortableRemoteObject.narrow(
              ctx.lookup("SavingAccount"), SavingAccountHome.class);
      SavingAccount saveAccount = saveHome.findByPrimaryKey(accountId);

      if (saveAccount.getBalance() < amount) {
        throw new InsufficientFundsException();
      } else {
        saveAccount.setBalance( (saveAccount.getBalance()) - amount);
        checkAccount.setBalance( (checkAccount.getBalance()) + amount);
      }

      tx.commit();

    } catch (NamingException ne) {
      throw new EJBException(ne);
    } catch (Exception e) {
      try {
        tx.rollback();
      } catch (Exception newe) {
        throw new EJBException("Rollback failed: " + newe);
      }
    }

  }

  public void ejbCreate() {}
  public void ejbPostCreate() {}
  public void ejbRemove() {}
```

```
      public void unsetSessionContext() {
        this.sessionCtx = null;
      }
      public void setSessionContext(SessionContext ctx) {
        this.sessionCtx = ctx;
      }
      public void ejbActivate() {}
      public void ejbPassivate() {}

}
```

We also need to modify the deployment descriptor to indicate that we are using BMT now:

```
    <session>
      <display-name>ATM</display-name>
      <ejb-name>ATM</ejb-name>
      <home>atm.ATMHome</home>
      <remote>atm.ATM</remote>
      <ejb-class>atm.ATMEJB</ejb-class>
      <session-type>Stateless</session-type>
      <transaction-type>Bean</transaction-type>
      <ejb-ref>
        <ejb-ref-name>CheckingAccount</ejb-ref-name>
        <ejb-ref-type>Entity</ejb-ref-type>
        <home>checking.CheckingAccountHome</home>
        <remote>checking.CheckingAccount</remote>
      </ejb-ref>
      <ejb-ref>
        <ejb-ref-name>SavingAccount</ejb-ref-name>
        <ejb-ref-type>Entity</ejb-ref-type>
        <home>saving,SavingAccountHome</home>
        <remote>saving.SavingAccount</remote>
      </ejb-ref>
    </session>
```

Transaction Isolation

The ACID property **isolation** requires that a transaction must be able to operate without regard for and without being affected by other active transactions in the system. In a concurrent system, several transactions may be executing at once – often on the same data. It may be necessary to protect one transaction from the efforts of another. Transaction isolation is achieved via locking and the serialization of data requests.

Locking controls access to a given set of data. The two primary types of locks are read locks and write locks. Read locks are **non-exclusive** locks – they will allow multiple transactions to read data simultaneously. Write locks are **exclusive** locks – they will only allow a single transaction to update a set of data.

Serialization guarantees that concurrently executing transactions will behave as if they were executing sequentially, not concurrently. Of course, the transactions will be executing concurrently, but they will appear to be executing in series. The result of serialization is the appearance that multiple transactions are working with data one at a time, in order.

Isolation levels specify concurrency control at a high level. The types of locks and serialization used, as well as the extent to which they are applied, determines the level of isolation that a transaction will execute under. The actual implementation is up to the resource manager and/or transaction manager. Isolation levels vary from very relaxed to very strict. As might be expected, the stricter the level of concurrency control, the greater the impact on performance. As with so many other issues in designing concurrent systems, special care must be taken when determining which isolation level to use.

J2EE provides support for four types of isolation levels, as defined in the `java.sql.Connection` interface (we will see how to set these later):

- ❏ `TRANSACTION_READ_UNCOMMITTED`

- ❏ `TRANSACTION_READ_COMMITTED`

- ❏ `TRANSACTION_REPEATABLE_READ`

- ❏ `TRANSACTION_SERIALIZABLE`

In transactional processing, there are three major types of concurrency issues that the isolation levels attempt to address:

- ❏ Dirty reads

- ❏ Unrepeatable reads

- ❏ Phantom reads

The following discusses the various problems as well as the appropriate isolation level to use to resolve these problems.

Dirty Reads

A dirty read occurs when a transaction reads data that has been written by another transaction but has not been yet been committed. This happens when there is a complete lack of synchronization on the data. We return to our banking system for an example of a dirty read:

- ❏ A client's bank account has $1000.

- ❏ Transaction 1 deposits $500 into the account, but does not yet commit the operation.

- ❏ Transaction 2 is posting a check for $1500, reads the account and sees the balance is $1500. It then processes the check against the account and commits.

- ❏ Transaction 1, which is still active, rolls back its operation. The balance is restored to the $1000 that it was at before transaction one started.

- ❏ The $1500 check has still been cleared and the bank just lost the money!

A dirty read can occur if we use the lowest level of transactional isolation, `TRANSACTION_READ_UNCOMMITTED`. The only time that this level of isolation should be used in a system is when the transaction will be the only one accessing the data. Similarly, we should also use it when the data is, and always will be, read-only.

An example of this would be a static lookup table. Even in this case, we might want to implement some sort of read/write control mechanism in the rare event that the data might need to be updated. `TRANSACTION_READ_UNCOMMITTED` is used by the reading transactions, but the reads are blocked when a writing transaction is active.

The use of `TRANSACTION_READ_COMMITTED` avoids the dirty read problem. It requires that a transaction can only read data that has been committed. It cannot read data that is in the scope of another active transaction. This is the most common level of isolation and, in fact, is the default isolation method for most databases servers. However, since we will be using Enterprise JavaBeans which are concurrent by nature, we try to avoid using `TRANSACTION_READ_UNCOMMITTED` whenever possible.

Unrepeatable Reads

An unrepeatable read occurs when a transaction reads data from a database, but gets a different result if it tries to read the same data again within the same transaction. This typically happens when another transaction writes over some of the data that was read in by the first transaction.

Consider an order entry system where a customer's invoice is being reviewed:

❏ Clerk 1 is reading an invoice

❏ Clerk 2 makes changes to the invoice's line items updating the unit price

❏ Clerk 1 fulfills the invoice at the original price

❏ The company has charged the client the wrong amount for the order!

The second clerk should not be allowed to modify the order while the first clerk is working with it.

If this behavior needs to be prevented, the `TRANSACTION_REPEATABLE_READ` isolation level should be used. `TRANSACTION_REPEATABLE_READ` provides more reliable transactions where data must be read and subsequently reread. This isolation level works by locking the data so that other transactions cannot make changes to it. Once the transaction is completed, the other transactions will then be permitted to continue.

Phantom Reads

A phantom read occurs when a transaction executes multiple reads against a set of data and, in between two of the read operations, another transaction slips in and inserts additional data. This differs from the unrepeatable read problem in that here data is being inserted into our data set, rather than that data merely being updated.

Returning again to our example of an order-entry system, let's say we were fulfilling an order:

❏ The shipping department reviews the order, packages the items and sends them on their way.

❏ Meanwhile, here comes Clerk 2 again who adds an additional item to the order.

❏ If the shipping department were to review the order again, they would see that another item has magically appeared. The client does not get their correct order and is very upset!

It is desirable that Clerk 2 should not be allowed to add items to this invoice while another person is working on it.

Using the transaction isolation level `TRANSACTION_SERIALIZABLE` prevents this from occurring. This level of isolation provides the strictest form of transaction management available.

Specifying Isolation Level

In container-managed transaction demarcation, the isolation level is determined by the container. Since EJB 1.1, there is no support for specifying the isolation level in the deployment descriptor. While some containers provide the ability to specify the isolation level at the resource manager-level, you should not rely on this. It is generally best to leave this decision to the container.

In bean-managed transaction demarcation, the isolation level is specified by directly interacting with the resource manager's API. In the case where a database is being used, this would be via the `java.sql.Connection.setTranactionIsolation()` method.

> Be forewarned that support for transaction isolation by a resource manager is not a requirement. Therefore, caution should be adhered to when specifying a transaction's isolation level. In fact, many resource managers will prevent you from doing this (database managers especially).

When determining the proper isolation level to use, it is important to remember that stricter levels of control will have a greater impact on performance. It is for this reason that each transaction will have to be considered on an individual basis. One isolation level will not be applicable across all transactions.

An isolation level is associated with a resource manager. As such, if a bean interacts with multiple resource managers (say, two database servers), a separate isolation level can be specified for each resource manager. However, most resource managers require that all access to that resource manager within a given transaction must be executed at the same isolation level.

It is very important that you do not attempt to switch isolation levels mid-way through a transaction, as this could cause the transaction to commit prematurely, among other erratic behavior. This is because you would be changing the rules governing locking and serialization in the middle of the transaction. This gets even more complex when you have multiple beans accessing the same resource manager within the same transaction. Certainly, a great deal of caution, coordination, and planning is required.

Alternatives to Isolation Control

Strict transaction isolation comes at a price – the greater the level of control, the greater the performance cost. When strict isolation is required, the negative performance impact could require us to see alternative control methods. Two such methods are **optimistic locking** and **pessimistic locking**.

Optimistic locking allows many clients to access the same data concurrently. Optimistic locking is called so because we are "optimistic" that the data will not change while we are using it. When one of the clients needs to update the data, it submits the changes to a controller (say, an entity bean) for consideration. The controller compares the data in the database (or similar) to the data that was originally provided to the client. If they match, that is if no changes have occurred between the time that the client read the data and when the client requested to change the data, then the update is allowed to proceed. If, on the other hand, the data has changed since it was initially provided to the client, the client is notified that it must refresh its copy of the data and resubmit the update request. As this can result in a duplication of effort, optimistic locking is best suited for situations where most of the clients will be reading, not updating.

Pessimistic locking takes the view that there is a high probability that someone will want to change data while we are working with it, thus the data must be protected. Pessimistic locking is usually achieved through the use of transactions. However, where transactions are not available or could be very long-lived, a semaphore can be used in its place. In this case, the master data record contains a flag that indicates whether the data is currently in use by a client for either viewing or editing.

Pessimistic locking is achieved by utilizing read locks every time data is read, and write locks every time the data is to be updated. These locks are held for the duration of the transaction in which the data is being used. Clients may obtain a read lock on the data provided that no other transactions have write locks. Write locks are used to update the data and other clients are still allowed to read the data provided that they do not require a read lock. However, a write lock will not allow another transaction to read its changing data until those changes have been committed.

Behavior of Exceptions in Container-Managed Transactions

The behavior of exceptions when using container-managed transactions depends on the type of transaction being used, who initiated the transaction, and the type of exception occurring. Let's briefly review how exceptions work in EJB.

Recall that there are two categories of exceptions in EJB:

❏ Application exceptions

❏ System exceptions

Application exceptions are basically any exceptions that are declared in the `throws` clause of the methods of a bean's home or remote interfaces. Put another way, application exceptions are those exceptions that will be propagated to a bean's client.

The purpose of an application exception is to indicate an abnormal application-level condition. For example, an invalid account balance, an invalid account number, or attempting to access prohibited data could all result in an application exception.

Typically, an application exception is defined by the bean developer and represents a business-logic exception more than a system exception. `InsufficientFundsException`, `AccountNotFoundException`, and `AccessDeniedException` are all examples of application exceptions. In addition, `javax.ejb.CreateException`, `RemoveException`, and `FinderException` are also considered application exceptions, despite the fact that they do not represent business logic exceptions. However, it is desirable that these exceptions be propagated back to the client.

System exceptions are any non-application exceptions. When a system exception occurs, it is due to a system-level error, not a business-level error. System exceptions are not returned to the client. Instead, they are caught at the server level and dealt with there. If an exception is to be returned to the client, either an `EJBException` will be thrown or an application exception will be created and thrown instead.

There are no hard and fast rules regarding the behavior of system exceptions, but the following guidelines usually apply:

❑ If a `RuntimeException` or `Error` occurs, it will be propagated to the container

❑ If the exception is not a `RuntimeException`, it will be wrapped in an `EJBException` and returned to the bean

❑ Any other type of unexpected error will result in an `EJBException`

Exception Scenarios

When an exception occurs within the bounds of a transaction, the results vary depending on the type of error and where the transaction originated. The following sections detail the different possible exception scenarios.

Scenario One

The transaction originated on the client and the transactional attribute for the bean's method is either `Required`, `Mandatory` or `Supports`.

When an application exception occurs within this context, the container will still attempt to commit the transaction. Since an application exception does not necessarily indicate an error with the data operation itself, the container cannot assume on its own that the transaction should be rolled back. Furthermore, as the container did not start the transaction itself, it cannot safely guess the use of the transaction.

If we raise an application exception and know that the transaction should be rolled back, we should invoke the `setRollbackOnly()` method on the `EJBContext` object. This should be done within our bean's method where the application exception would be raised.

It is at the discretion of the client whether or not to continue a transaction when an application exception occurs. A good example of this would be an `InsufficientFundsException` being thrown when posting a check within our banking system. The client may wish to try posting the check to another account, such as a savings account or overdraft account. When a client does receive an application exception, however, they should check the `getRollbackOnly()` or `getStatus()` methods.

When a system exception or error occurs within this context, the container will:

❑ Log the exception or error for later review by the system administrator

❑ Mark the transaction for rollback, via the `setRollbackOnly()` method

❑ Discard the instance of the bean

❑ Throw a `TransactionRolledBackException` or `TransactionRolledBackLocalException` back to the client

Scenario Two

The transaction is started by the container, with the transactional attributes `Required` or `RequiresNew`.

When an application exception is thrown, if the bean's method where the exception was thrown marked the transaction for rollback via the `setRollbackOnly()` method, the container will roll back the transaction. Otherwise the container will attempt to commit the transaction. The container will then rethrow the application exception back to the client.

When a system exception occurs, the container will:

❑ Log the exception or error for later review by the system administrator

❑ Mark the transaction for rollback, via the `setRollbackOnly()` method

❑ Discard the instance of the bean

❑ Throw a `RemoteException` or `EJBException` back to the client

This is similar to the behavior of a transaction started by the client, except that a `RemoteException` or `EJBException`, depending on client location, is thrown. Since the transactional context is limited to the bean's method, it would not make sense to return a `TransactionRolledBackException`, or `TransactionRolledBackLocalException`, as above.

Scenario Three

The bean method is invoked with an unspecified transaction context, such as when the transaction attributes `NotSupported` or `Never` are used, or when the bean's method is marked as `Supports` but is invoked by an unspecified transaction context:

The container will not roll back the transaction if an application error is thrown, simply rethrowing the application exception that occurred. Remember that a transaction cannot be marked for rollback within an unspecified transaction context. The `setRollbackOnly()` method is only supported for methods with the transaction attribute `Required`, `RequiresNew`, or `Manadatory`. Attempting to set a transaction for rollback within an unspecified transaction context will result in a `java.lang.IllegalStateException`.

When a system error occurs, the container will log the exception or error, discard the instance of the bean, and throw a `RemoteException` or `EJBException`.

Scenario Four

The method is part of a session bean or message-driven bean and the transaction is bean-managed:

When an application exception is thrown, the client will receive the application exception.

When a system error occurs, the container will:

❑ Log the exception or error for later review by the system administrator

❑ Mark the transaction for rollback, via the `setRollbackOnly()` method

❑ Discard the instance of the bean

❑ Throw a `RemoteException` back to the client

When dealing with container-managed transactions, if a transaction was rolled back due to the `setRollbackOnly` flag being set, the container will roll the transaction back, but will not throw a `RemoteException`. Instead, the container will either return the normal result of the method or, if one was thrown, an application exception.

In container-managed transactions, if an exception occurs, the container will release any connections to any managed resources. A managed resource is any resource (such as a database) that the bean's instance might have obtained via the container's resource factory. However, the container cannot release any *unmanaged* resources (such as a network socket) that the bean instance might have obtained through the standard JDK APIs. Unmanaged connections will be released during regular garbage collection. If you are using unmanaged connections, you should be careful to release them in the event of an exception.

When a system exception occurs, the transaction may not necessarily be marked for rollback. For example, a communication problem prevents the remote bean from even begin called. In this case, the server won't have the opportunity to mark the transaction for rollback because it never even got the transaction in the first place.

The Role of Transaction Processing Monitors

Today, OLTP (Online Transaction Processing) systems represent over 25 percent (as per Internet Week survey) of all transaction processing frameworks, especially in large-scale enterprise applications such as airline reservation, electronic banking, securities trading, inventory and production control, communications switching, military command and control, and government services. The reason is that these TP systems provide a scalable transaction processing framework architecture for implementing mission-critical distributed transaction applications that support a wide range of application resources. In general an OLTP system is an integrated suite of products that supports TP applications.

Transaction Processing (TP) monitors ease development and management of OLTP systems. The TP monitor coordinates and control the flow of transaction requests between client application terminals and the TP applications that process the requests, by accessing shared resources on behalf of the client application. TP monitors automatically manage the entire environment that a business system runs including transactions, resource management, fault tolerance and so on.

The business logic defined in TP monitors is based on procedural applications that are often accessed through network-based message-oriented middleware (MOM) or remote procedural calls (RPC). Although there is no standard defined for TP monitors, it should be noted that the most popular TP monitors implement and support the X/Open and OMG CORBA specifications that allow integration of heterogenous data sources and applications. TP monitors typically provide functionality such as resource management and administration, connection management, naming services, data-driven routing, high availability, load balancing, and support for distributed transaction management, for X/Open and OMG standards-compliant applications.

Popular TP Systems

The most popular TP systems are as follows:

❑   **IBM CICS family** (http://www.ibm.com/software/ts/cics/)
    IBM CICS is general-purpose online transaction processing (OLTP) software. It provides a powerful TP application server and a management system (TP monitor) that runs on a range of operating systems from the smallest desktop to the largest mainframe. It is also well integrated with IBM WebSphere Application Server Enterprise Edition suite 4.x so that it can take part in e-business and EAI-based applications.

❑ **IBM Encina family** (http://www.ibm.com/servers/aix/products/ibmsw/db_dm_tp/encina.html)
Encina provides a flexible, open, distributed online transaction processing (OLTP)
programming and runtime environment for heterogeneous, multi-vendor, network computing
environments. It runs on the IBM AIX-based Unix environment and it supports X/Open XA
and TxRPC specifications. It is also well integrated with IBM WebSphere Application Server
Enterprise Edition suite.

❑ **BEA Tuxedo** (http://www.beasys.com/products/tuxedo/index.shtml)
BEA Tuxedo is an integral component of the BEA WebLogic E-Business Platform suite 6.x of
applications for mission-critical e-business and transaction applications. Tuxedo provides a TP
environment that allows clients and servers to participate in a distributed transaction that
involves coordinated updating of multiple databases and heterogenous applications. It also
features compliance with the X/Open standards, and supports the CORBA specification for
distributed application development.

Limitations of TP Monitors

The known limitations of TP monitors are as follows:

❑ They do not provide an object-oriented development environment

❑ They are based on procedural code to perform mission-critical tasks without an identity

❑ Executes static methods using RPC and there is no support for distributed computing and
transactions over heterogenous applications

For the rest of the discussion in this section, we will use that BEA Tuxedo and BEA WebLogic Enterprise
suite to examine transaction management and transaction integration over heterogenous applications.

Transaction Integration with TP Monitors

In this section, to demonstrate the transaction integration scenerios with TP monitors using J2EE, we will use
the BEA WebLogic product family. In particular we will use the following BEA product solutions:

❑ BEA Tuxedo as the TP environment

❑ BEA Jolt as the Java interface to Tuxedo

❑ BEA WebLogic Server as the J2EE-based integration platform to leverage the applications in a
J2EE-based EAI application environment

Using BEA Tuxedo as a TP Monitor

BEA Tuxedo provides a middleware platform for communicating between applications across multiple
platforms, databases, and operating systems using message-based communications and also enabling
distributed transaction processing.

In a nutshell, the BEA Tuxedo system provides the following features:

❑ Defines a standard for creation and administration of distributed online transaction
applications in a heterogeneous client/server environment.

❑   It eases distributed application development by providing a middleware environment, by keeping the developers away from the issues like identifying server locations or routing mechanisms or OS platforms used.

The BEA Tuxedo system provides the ability to manage transactions for applications that support XA interfaces.

ATMI (Application-to-Transaction Monitor Interface) is a superset of X/Open's XATMI interface that allows writing distributed applications using Tuxedo. And the Tuxedo system also provides interfaces to X/Open TX and X/Open XA-compliant applications and transaction systems.

To implement XA transactions in Tuxedo, it is required to use the following ATMI functions:

❑   tpbegin() – Starts the transaction.

❑   tpcall() – Calls the application services

❑   tpcommit() – Starts the commit process.

❑   tpabort() – Aborts the transaction.

The following diagram illustrates how Tuxedo handling distributed transactions:

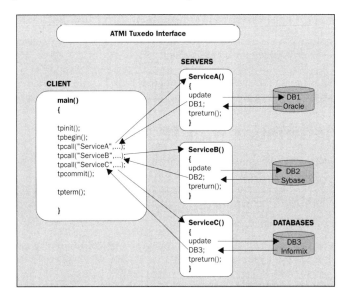

Using BEA Weblogic Server as J2EE Application Server

BEA WebLogic Server is an application server that complies with the J2EE specification, and provides a reliable server infrastructure to run mission-critical e-business and integration applications. It implements all of the components specified by the J2EE platform specification. J2EE services provide access to standard network protocols, database, and messaging systems.

It also supports and integrates seamlessly with the BEA family of products, popular relational databases, messages queues, and legacy systems.

Using BEA Jolt as the Java Interface to Tuxedo

BEA Jolt provides a Java-based interface to interact with BEA Tuxedo transaction processing and enabling access to Tuxedo capabilities to the J2EE-based application server (BEA WebLogic server). It manages requests to BEA Tuxedo services using a Jolt Service Listener (JSL) running on the Tuxedo server. The Jolt API is implemented within the WebLogic API library, and is accessible from a servlet or any BEA WebLogic application. The Jolt components translate Java client requests into Tuxedo application calls, and return the results to the client.

The basic features of BEA Jolt for BEA WebLogic Server are as follows:

❑   Allows Java servlets/EJBs to interact with Tuxedo applications

❑   Provides session pooling to use Tuxedo resources

❑   Supports transactions with Tuxedo

BEA Jolt for WebLogic does not support asynchronous Tuxedo event notifications.

Transaction Integration with Legacy Systems

As we saw in Chapter 13, J2EE 1.3 introduced the J2EE Connector Architecture (JCA) to provide a consistent access mechanism to EIS resources in the form of resource adapters. Incorporated as part of this architecture is the management of transactions between the J2EE components (running in the application server) and the EIS resources.

Under the JCA model there are two transaction scenarios:

❑   **Transactions across multiple resource managers**
In this scenario, an external transaction manager is used to manage the transaction across multiple resource managers and to support the propagation of transaction context across distributed systems.

The resource managers must implement the JTA `XAResource` interface to enable them to participate in transactions coordinated by the external transaction manager.

❑   **Local Transaction Management**
Conversely, in this scenario, no external transaction managers are required. As with the EJB transactions we discussed earlier, local transactions are either demarcated by the container or by an application component. For a component-managed demarcation transaction, the component can either use the JTA `UserTransaction` interface or an API specific to the EIS.

Should multiple resource managers be required in the transaction, then a transaction manager will be used for coordination via the `XAResource` interface.

For more information on the J2EE Connector Architecture see its specification available at http://java.sun.com/j2ee/download.html#connectorspec.

Summary

In this chapter, we discussed a variety of distributed transaction models and mechanisms available for implementing EAI applications. We discussed using transaction models provided by J2EE and CORBA with examples and its relevance for EAI implementation. We also looked at the concepts of handling transaction integration with TP monitors and legacy systems.

In general, we have looked at:

❑   Basics of the transaction behavior and different transaction models

❑   Industry standards for distributed transaction processing defined by X/Open, OSI and OMG

❑   Understanding the X/Open DTP (Distributed Transaction Processing) and its features

❑   Using CORBA – OTS (Object Transaction Service)

❑   Using JTS/JTA – Java Transaction Services and API

❑   Handling transaction scenarios in J2EE environment especially in EJB

In the next chapter we'll move on to look at security management in an integrated information architecture.

16

Security Management in EAI

Applications have to be secure. An unsecured application can have its service disrupted and can suffer intrusion, which can lead to the exploitation, manipulation, or destruction of sensitive and confidential information. Accordingly, applications are designed to be secure, which means that when we come to integrate them, we need to use their existing security mechanisms – both to ensure that the applications remain secure, and so that we don't recreate functionality that already exists.

Imagine that we have several integrated applications, and that each of these applications requires users to be authenticated and authorized. Using our integrated application is going to be a pretty tedious experience if we have to log on several times. It should appear to a user as a single application, one that they only have to log in once for.

What we need is a way to propagate one authentication throughout the integrated application. We need a standardized security model that can handle a wide range of distributed applications. It should be able to establish end-to-end security throughout the logical tiers of our application, and provide a single point at which a user is authenticated.

In this chapter we're going to explore the J2EE and CORBA security models, as these are the most commonly found security models in a J2EE-based EAI environment. We'll also look at how we can perform authentication in our applications – we'll pay particular attention to the Kerberos authentication service. Finally, we'll explore a commercially available security infrastructure that provides single sign-on support – Netegrity SiteMinder.

This chapter *doesn't* include a detailed discussion of security at the system and network level. Knowledge of concepts such as firewalls and gateway security solutions is assumed. For more information on these topics, as well as Java security in general, you should refer to *Professional Java Security (ISBN 1-861004-25-7) by Wrox Press.*

Application Security

Whether a security threat is internal or external it is equally important to deal with it, but implementing an integrated security model is a difficult problem, both in terms of scope, and solution. Let's consider what we require of a security model.

Our model must be able protect the integrity of applications and their transactions. The applications themselves must maintain a high level of availability and reliability. The integrity of the data moving within the system must be assured. Any processes that operate on the data must be reliable, compliant with regulatory requirements, comprehensive, and systematic. The model must prevent any unauthorized access, destruction, or alteration of the data. Information and data exchanged in an integrated application must be kept confidential, and made available only to those authorized to receive it. Our model must be able to verify the identity of both users and applications. Accordingly, when a user or application asserts their identity the model must authenticate this assertion.

Specifically, our model must be able to:

❑   Verify the accuracy and authenticity of data

❑   Verify claims of identity by users and applications

❑   Verify attributes related to resources, such as access levels and administrative rights

❑   Control access to resources by applying security policies

❑   Monitor and log user and system activities

❑   Stop users from denying a transaction took place (known as non-repudiation)

❑   Allow control over how security is applied to users and applications

In an EAI framework, the process of building a request, acquiring data from multiple sources, executing a transaction, and sending a response must all be augmented with the above security functionalities to ensure that the security of the particular domain is enforced. It is very difficult to address this in both an effective and standard way.

Standard security mechanisms are available for *specific* application environments. They provide end-to-end security, which allows us to protect access and data across the network. We're going to look at two such models – the Java and the CORBA security models – to help us better understand the requirements we've set out.

The Java Security Model

Java has a policy-driven, domain-based security model and is considered a secure platform on which to run distributed applications. The security features provided by Java include:

❑   Policy-driven restricted access to resources

❑   Rules-based class loading and verification of byte code

❑   A system for signing code and assigning levels of capability

The Java Virtual Machine (JVM) executes code within a **sandbox**, which provides a restricted access environment in which applications run. The Java 2 security model has many capabilities such as fine-grained access control, configurable security policies, and an extensible access control structure.

Java provides extension packages to support a variety of security infrastructures and services, including: cryptographic services; certificate interfaces and classes for managing digital certificates based on the X.509 version 3 implementation; **Public Key Infrastructure (PKI)** interfaces and classes to access, modify, and manage a repository of keys and certificates; and **Secure Socket Extension (SSE)**, which helps to protect the privacy and integrity of data transferred across a network.

The following packages were initially introduced as optional but have been integrated into J2SE 1.4:

❑ **Java Authentication and Authorization Service (JAAS)** – provides a framework of services for enabling authentication and user/group/role-based access control

❑ **Java Secure Socket Extension (JSSE)** – provides packages for enabling secure communications using SSL and Transport Layer Security (TLS) protocols and also includes functionality for data encryption, server authentication, message integrity, and client authentication

❑ **Java Cryptography Extension (JCE)** – provides a framework and implementation for encryption, key generation and key agreement, and Message Authentication Code (MAC) algorithms

Starting with JAAS, we'll look at how these enhancements help to provide the security infrastructure required by EAI.

Java Authentication and Authorization Service

The J2EE 1.3 specification requires that all J2EE application servers use JAAS API in EJB and web containers, particularly to support J2EE Connector components. The JAAS specification and packages are available at http://java.sun.com/products/jaas/.

The JAAS API is based on two concepts:

❑ **Authentication** – a reliable and secure mechanism to determine who is executing the code regardless of whether the running code is an application, an applet, a servlet, or a JSP page

❑ **Authorization** – ensures that the users have access control rights and privileges required to execute the required functions

JAAS Authentication

JAAS does not provide an authentication model itself. Instead, it allows different authentication models to be plugged in at run time, allowing applications to remain independent from the underlying authentication technologies. It also allows new authentication components to be plugged into a JAAS-based application without the application itself being modified.

Client applications enable the JAAS authentication process by instantiating a `LoginContext` object. This `LoginContext` then communicates with a `LoginModule`, which performs the actual authentication process. As the `LoginContext` uses a generic interface provided by all `LoginModule` classes, changing authentication algorithms at run time is easy.

A typical `LoginModule` will prompt for, and verify, a username and password. There are also more sophisticated biometric authentication schemes that can verify a voiceprint, a fingerprint, or a retina pattern.

Using JAAS Authentication

Let's walk through the process of creating a JAAS Authentication client. To create a new login context we require a configuration file that specifies the classes that implement the authentication technology, and a reference to the `CallbackHandler`:

```
LoginContext loginContext = null;
  try {
```

We will use a Kerberos authentication module and a `TextCallbackHandler`:

```
    loginContext = new LoginContext("WroxKerberosModule",
                              new TextCallbackHandler());
  } catch (LoginException le) {
    System.err.println("Cannot create LoginContext. " + le.getMessage());
    System.exit(-1);
  } catch (SecurityException se) {
    System.err.println("Cannot create LoginContext. " + se.getMessage());
    System.exit(-1);
  }
```

The configuration file `WroxKerberosModule.conf` specifies the authentication module `Krb5LoginModule` from the `com.sun.security.auth.module` package, which implements the Kerberos login authentication mechanism:

```
WroxKerberosModule {
  com.sun.security.auth.module.Krb5LoginModule required;
};
```

The `LoginModule` obtains a username and password. It invokes a `javax.security.auth.callback.CallbackHandler` to obtain them. The `LoginModule` passes an array of `javax.security.auth.callback` objects to the `handle()` method of `CallbackHandler`. The `CallbackHandler` performs the requested user interaction and sets appropriate values:

```
    public void handle(Callback[] callbacks)
      throws IOException, UnsupportedCallbackException {

      for (int i = 0; i < callbacks.length; i++) {
        if (callbacks[i] instanceof TextOutputCallback) {
```

Here we would display a message according to the specified type:

```
        } else if (callbacks[i] instanceof NameCallback) {
```

We prompt the user for a username:

```
            NameCallback nc = (NameCallback)callbacks[i];
            System.err.print(nc.getPrompt());
            System.err.flush();
            nc.setName((new BufferedReader
                        (new InputStreamReader(System.in))).readLine());
        } else if (callbacks[i] instanceof PasswordCallback) {
```

We prompt the user for a password:

```
            PasswordCallback pc = (PasswordCallback)callbacks[i];
            System.err.print(pc.getPrompt());
            System.err.flush();
```

We use the `readPassword()` method and set the password in our `PasswordCallback`:

```
            pc.setPassword(readPassword (System.in));
        } else {
            throw new UnsupportedCallbackException (callbacks[i],
                                        "Callback Unrecognized ");
        }
      }
    }
```

Once the login context has been created, we can perform the login process by calling the `login()` method:

```
    try {
      loginContext.login();
    } catch (LoginException le) {
      System.err.println("Authentication failed:");
      System.err.println("   " + le.getMessage());
    }
```

The `login()` method of `LoginContext` calls methods in the `WroxLoginModule` to perform the login and authentication. `WroxLoginModule` uses `TextCallbackHandler` to obtain the username/password, which it then verifies. If authentication is successful, `WroxLoginModule` populates the `Subject` with a `Principal` representing the user. The calling application can retrieve the authenticated `Subject` by calling the `getSubject()` method of `LoginContext`.

Let's put this all together as a JAAS authentication client that uses Kerberos authentication:

```
    package eaisecurity;

    import java.io.*;
    import java.util.*;
    import javax.security.auth.login.*;
    import javax.security.auth.*;
    import javax.security.auth.callback.*;
    import com.sun.security.auth.callback.*;

    public class JAASAuthenticationClient {
```

```
        public static void main(String[] args) {

     LoginContext loginContext = null;
        try {
          loginContext = new LoginContext("WroxKerberosModule",
                                        new TextCallbackHandler());
        } catch (LoginException le) {
          System.err.println("Cannot create LoginContext. " +
                              le.getMessage());
          System.exit(-1);
        } catch (SecurityException se) {
          System.err.println("Cannot create LoginContext. " +
                              se.getMessage());
          System.exit(-1);
        }
```

We'll attempt to authenticate three times:

```
        for (int i = 0; i < 3; i++) {
          try {
            loginContext.login();
```

We break if authentication succeeded:

```
            break;
          } catch (LoginException le) {
            System.err.println("Authentication failed:");
            System.err.println("  " + le.getMessage());
            try {
              Thread.currentThread().sleep(3000);
            } catch (Exception e) {}
          }
        }

     if (i == 3) {
       System.out.println("Authentication failed - 3 Times");
       System.exit(-1);
     }

     System.out.println("Authentication using Kerberos is successful");
   }
}
```

To run the example, you'll need to have a Kerberos installation with a Kerberos Key Distribution Center (KDC) installed. A KDC implementation is part of a Kerberos installation, not a part of the JDK.

Kerberos V5 is supported in Microsoft Windows 2000 Server, Solaris 8, and the latest Linux distributions. In Windows 2000 Server, the environment KDC is implemented as a domain service and uses the Active Directory as its account database.

750

To run our `JAASAuthenticationClient` application we need to compile `JAASAuthenticationClient` and place it in a JAR named `JAASAuthenticationClient.jar`. Then we need to create a policy file named `JAASAuthenticationClient.policy`:

```
grant codebase "file:./JAASAuthenticationClient.jar " {
  permission javax.security.auth.AuthPermission
  "createLoginContext.WroxKerberosModule";
};
```

Then we can run our client application with the following command:

```
java -classpath JAASAuthenticationClient.jar -Djava.security.manager
-Djava.security.krb5.realm="localhost"
-Djava.security.krb5.kdc="localhost"
-Djava.security.policy=JAASAuthenticationClient.policy
-Djava.security.auth.login.config=WroxKerberosModule.conf
eassecurity.JAASAuthenticationClient
```

We use `-Djava.security.manager` to install the basic Java Security Manager; `-Djava.security.krb5.realm=<kerberos5_realm>` to define the Kerberos realm; `-Djava.security.krb5.kdc=<kerberos_kdc>` to provide a Kerberos Key Distribution Center (KDC); `-Djava.security.policy=security.policy` to define the security policy; and `-Djava.security.auth.login.config=jaasloginModule.conf` to define the login module configuration.

The specified policy files contain an entry granting `JAASAuthenticationClient` permission to instantiate a `LoginContext` and continue execution. You will be prompted for your Kerberos username and password, and the underlying Kerberos authentication mechanism specified in the login configuration file will log you into Kerberos. If your login is successful, you will see the message `"Authentication successful!"`.

It's always good practice to log out as soon as the user-specific actions have been performed, or at least before exiting the application. We can use the login context to perform the logout by calling the `logout()` method in `loginContext`:

```
try {
  loginContext.logout();
}  catch (LoginException e) {
  System.out.println(e.getMessage());
}
```

Calling the `logout()` method on the login context results in the `logout()` method on the login module. When a client uses the login context to perform a login or logout, the calls are ultimately forwarded to the underlying authentication module.

JAAS Authorization

JAAS authorization enhances the Java security framework by adding user/group/role-based access controls and allows user/operational level access privileges based on who executes the code.

When a client runs JAAS authentication to authenticate the user, a `Subject` is created as a result of authentication. The `Subject` represents an authenticated entity. A `Subject` usually contains a set of principals, where each `Principal` represents a caller of the application. Permissions are granted using the policy for selective principals. Once the user login is authenticated, the application associates the `Subject` with the `Principal` based on the current access control context.

To implement a user authorization we must:

- ❑ Use JAAS authentication to authenticate the user
- ❑ Define a security policy file with `Principal`-based entries
- ❑ Associate the `Subject` with the authenticated user with an `AccessControlContext`

Creating a JAAS Principal-Based Policy File

The `Principal`-based policy file provides grant statements to include one or more `Principal` fields Adding `Principal` fields in the policy file defines the users or entities with designated permissions to execute the specific application code or other privileges associated with the application or resources.

The basic format of a `grant` statement is:

```
grant <signer(s) field>, <codeBase URL>
   <Principal Principal_class Principal_name > {
   permission class_name "target_name", "action";
   permission class_name "target_name", "action";
};
```

The `signer` field usually defines the application code base followed by the code base location. The `Principal` field defines the `Principal_class` (defined by the authentication module) and the associated username. The usernames (`Principal_Name`) for `KerberosPrincipals` are usually in the form `username@realm`. For example, if the username is `nramesh` and the Kerberos realm is `sun.com`, then the `principal_name` designation to use in the grant statement is `nramesh@sun.com`.

It is possible to include more than one `Principal` field in a grant statement. If multiple `Principal` fields are provided, then the permissions are granted from that grant statement only if the `Subject` associated with the current access control context contains all of those as authenticated `Principals`. To grant the same set of permissions to multiple `Principals`, we need to create multiple grant statements listing all the permissions, each containing a single `Principal` field designating one of the `Principals`.

Associating the Subject with Access Control

To associate a `Subject` with the access control context we need to authenticate the user using JAAS authentication. Then we call the `doAs()` method available in the `Subject` class, passing the authenticated subject and either a `java.security.PrivilegedAction` or `java.security.PrivilegedExceptionAction` object.

The `doAs()` method associates the `Subject` with the current access control context and invokes the `run()` method from the action, which contains all the necessary code to be executed. The `doAsPrivileged()` method from the `Subject` class can be called instead of the `doAs()` method with `AccessControlContext` as an additional parameter. This enables the `Subject` to associate with only the `AccessControlContext` provided.

The following example uses our previous example illustration of `JAASAuthentication.java` to implement a JAAS authorization:

```java
package eaisecurity;

import java.io.*;
import java.util.*;
import javax.security.auth.login.*;
import javax.security.auth.*;
import javax.security.auth.callback.*;
import com.sun.security.auth.callback.*;
import java.security.PrivilegedAction;

public class JAASClient {

  public static void main(String[] args) {
```

Create a `LoginContext`; then use the Kerberos authentication module specified in the JAAS login configuration file and the `TextCallbackHandler`:

```java
    LoginContext loginContext = null;
    try {
      loginContext = new LoginContext("WroxKerberosModule",
                              new TextCallbackHandler ());
    } catch (LoginException le) {
      System.err.println("Cannot create LoginContext. " + le.getMessage());
      System.exit(-1);
    } catch (SecurityException se) {
      System.err.println("Cannot create LoginContext. " + se.getMessage());
      System.exit(-1);
    }
```

We attempt to authenticate three times:

```java
    for (int i = 0; i < 3; i++) {
      try {
        loginContext.login();
        break;
      } catch (LoginException le) {
        System.err.println("Authentication failed:");
        System.err.println("  " + le.getMessage());
        try {
          Thread.currentThread().sleep(3000);
        } catch (Exception e) {}
      }
    }

    if (i == 3) {
      System.out.println("Authentication failed - 3 Times");
      System.exit(-1);
    }

    System.out.println("Authentication successful");
```

Authorize the execution of `WroxAction` as the authenticated `Subject`:

```
    Subject mySubject = loginContext.getSubject();
    PrivilegedAction action = new WroxAction();
    Subject.doAsPrivileged(mySubject, action, null);
  }
}
```

The code is to be executed after we have associated the `Subject` with the current access control context:

```
import java.io.*;
import java.security.PrivilegedAction;

public class WroxAction implements PrivilegedAction {
```

This method is called by `doPrivileged()` after enabling privileges:

```
    public Object run() {
```

We try to write a dummy file named `WroxAuthor.txt`:

```
    try {
      FileOutputStream outFile = new FileOutputStream("WroxAuthor.txt");
      outFile.write('Java Rules');
      outFile.close();
    } catch(IOException ie){
      System.out.println("File Not accessible to the user" +
                    ie.getMessage());
    }
  }
}
```

Again, you'll need to have a Kerberos installation along with a Kerberos Key Distribution Center to run this example.

Then, create a JAR file (named `JAASClient.jar`) containing all the class files and create a policy file to grant `JAASClient.jar` access to the privileged users (in the current directory) that have the required permissions:

```
grant codebase "file:./JAASClient.jar " {
  Principal javax.security.auth.kerberos.KerberosPrincipal
    "nikki@myjaas.wrox.com"  {
    permission java.io.FilePermission "WroxAuthor.txt", "write";
  }

  Principal javax.security.auth.kerberos.KerberosPrincipal
    "cberry@myjaas.wrox.com"  {
    permission java.io.FilePermission "WroxAuthor.txt", "write";
  }
};
```

Then run the application with the following command:

```
java -classpath JAASClient.jar WroxAction.jar -Djava.security.manager
    -Djava.security.krb5.realm="myjaas.wrox.com"
    -Djava.security.krb5.kdc="wroxkdc.wrox.com"
    -Djava.security.policy=JAASClient.policy
    -Djava.security.auth.login.config=WroxKerberosModule.conf
    eaisecurity.JAASClient
```

The specified policy files contain an entry granting the code the required permission; JAASClient will be allowed to instantiate a LoginContext and continue execution. Again, you'll be prompted for your Kerberos username and password, and the underlying Kerberos authentication mechanism specified in the login configuration file will log you into Kerberos. If your login is successful, you will see the message "Authentication successful!".

Upon successful authentication, the action defined in the WroxAction class will be executed based on the user access privileges defined in the policy file providing grant permissions. The JAASClient.policy policy file grants the required permissions, and provides write access to a file named WroxAuthor.txt in the current directory.

Using JAAS with EAI

JAAS helps us to build our own EAI security infrastructure. It allows us to wrap the underlying EAI applications in the same authentication and authorization process – using industry standard authentication modules such as Kerberos.

JSSE and JCE

JSSE enables secure Internet communications by using the SSL and TLS protocols, both of which are designed to protect the privacy and integrity of data as it is transferred across the network.

JCE provides a framework and implementation for encryption, key generation and agreement, and Message Authentication Code (MAC) algorithms. It supports encryption, which includes symmetric, asymmetric, block, and stream ciphers. As part of the software it also supports secure streams and sealed objects. The JCE API can implement the following key cryptographic mechanisms:

- ❑ Encryption and Decryption
- ❑ Password-Based Encryption
- ❑ Cipher
- ❑ Key Agreement protocol
- ❑ Message Authentication Code (MAC)

The J2EE Server Security Infrastructure

J2EE server applications are essentially components running in different tiers of a multi-tier enterprise application, each of which could be deployed in different application containers. The security features provided by a J2EE server also allow us to establish secure connections to the J2EE applications from browsers, Java clients, and other connected servers.

J2EE application servers commonly provide the following security features:

❑ Security realms, which represent a logical grouping of users, groups, and Access Control Lists (ACLs) that protect server resources

❑ Authentication of clients requesting access to J2EE server resources – authentication can be accomplished using a username-password combination or digital certificates, with which a client is authenticated using the identity inside of the X.509 digital certificate provided to the J2EE server as part of an SSL connection

❑ Authorization of users and groups through ACLs

❑ The JAAS implementation in the J2EE server enables `LoginContext` authentication and `Subject` authorization

❑ Data integrity and confidentiality through the SSL protocol. Clients can establish SSL sessions with J2EE Server using HTTPS, or RMI IIOP

❑ Auditing and logging of events – to identify failed login attempts, authentication requests, rejected digital certificates, and invalid ACLs

❑ Filtering of client connections for the purpose of accepting or rejecting the client request based on the origin (host name or network address) or protocol of the client

❑ Propagation of the security context from J2EE server security realms to other connected server domains using single sign-on authentication mechanisms such as Kerberos 5

In a J2EE-based EAI application framework the application-level security is addressed in all logical tiers in order to achieve an end-to-end security in all deployed components. This allows the propagation of the security context for an EAI user across all logical tiers (web, business, and resource), its associated components, and its method invocation.

Web Tier Security

To enable access to a protected web resource the J2EE web container activates the authentication mechanism that has been configured for that resource. The J2EE web container usually supports the following authentication mechanisms:

❑ **HTTP basic authentication** – the HTTP server will authenticate a user by using the username/password provided with the basic realm of the J2EE web client.

❑ **Form-based authentication** – a customized web client login screen (and associated error pages) are presented to the end user.

❑ **Client certificate authentication** – the HTTP server will authenticate the client using a X.509 certificate. Also, by using HTTP over SSL (HTTPS) the server and the client can authenticate each other with signed Public Key Certificates.

- ❑ **Declarative security** – usually defined in the deployment descriptor or using the server console that allows mapping the security mechanisms provided by the J2EE server.

- ❑ **Programmatic security** – when declarative security alone is not sufficient to express the security model of the application. Programmatic security consists of the following methods of the `HttpServletRequest` interface:

  - ❑ `getRemoteUser()` – determines the username with which the client authenticated

  - ❑ `IsUserInRole()` – determines if a user is in a specific security role

  - ❑ `getUserPrincipal()` – gets a `java.security.Principal` object as the initiating user

Using programmatic security in J2EE allows operations to be based on the logical role of the remote user.

Business Tier Security

The J2EE server allows us to protect any business logic tier (otherwise know as the EJB tier) resources adopting declarative or programmatic security in the following ways:

- ❑ **Declarative security** – allows the definition and declaration of method level security permissions of an EJB and it is mapped to J2EE users and groups. It is usually defined in an EJB deployment descriptor.

- ❑ **Programmatic security** – uses the `getCallerPrincipal()` and the `isCallerInRole()` methods in EJBs to determine the caller of the EJB and to determine the caller's role.

Resource Tier Security

In the back-end resource, an application component requests a connection to a database or an Enterprise Information System (EIS) resource. As part of this connection, the back end database or EIS may require a sign-on to the resource. For a typical database connection, based on a username and password, the JDBC driver obtains pooled connections.

J2EE 1.3 also supports the J2EE Connector Architecture 1.0 specification, which encompasses two sign-on techniques:

- ❑ **Container-managed sign-on approach** – the application component lets the container take the responsibility of configuring and managing the EIS sign on

- ❑ **Component-managed sign-on approach** – the application component code manages the EIS sign-on by including code that performs the sign-on process to an EIS

These tier-level security features help us to implement a secure J2EE-based EAI framework by propagating the security context from J2EE-based components to the underlying resources, including databases, EIS resources, mail, messaging applications, and URLs.

In an EAI framework that involves the integration of non-Java applications and resources, enabling J2EE-based security may not help achieve end-to-end security. Industry experts usually choose CORBA-based application servers with Java support to build security infrastructure for non-Java applications.

The CORBA Security Model

The CORBA security service provides a security architecture that can support a variety of security policies to meet different application security requirements – the framework it defines is neutral to the choice of security technology. The **Common Object Services (COS)** specification, available from the OMG (http://www.omg.org/), describes the security-related tasks and requirements for CORBA.

The CORBA security service functionality defined in the specification includes:

❑ Identification and authentication of principals

❑ Authorization- and infrastructure-based access control

❑ Security auditing to make users accountable for their security related actions

❑ Secure communication between objects

❑ Non-repudiation

We can implement CORBA security on a wide variety of legacy systems, reusing the security mechanisms and protocols native to each. The security service can control access to an application object without awareness of the underlying security. This allows it to be ported to environments that enforce different security policies and use different security mechanisms. However, if an object requires application-level security, the security attributes must be delegated and access control must be made available to the application.

The CORBA security service defines two levels of CORBA security conformance, **Security Level 1** and **Security Level 2**:

❑ At Security Level 1 all programs are security unaware; authentication, encryption, data integrity, object invocation authorization, audit trails, and security domain administration must be provided. We just need to catch unauthorized exceptions when we try to bind to a remote object or call a remote method. The ORB mechanism (implemented by the ORB provider) handles security checks for object access within the application software.

❑ At Security Level 2 programs can be security aware, and there is a rich set of security APIs that can be used to allow the application to check access to objects, write to audit trails, and verify digital signatures. We should bear in mind that doing this can require a lot of extra work, as Interface Definition Language scripts must be provided.

The CORBA security service specification defines the interfaces to be used by the application developers, ORB providers, security service providers and security administrators. The security model in an ORB system uses the concepts of application clients, target objects, and invocations. The process of building a request, transmitting it to the target object over a network, executing an operation, and sending a reply with augmented levels of security procedures, insures that all the security levels of the domain are enforced.

The CORBA Security Reference Model

The developers of the CORBA Security Service specification produced a general **Security Reference Model (SRM)**. With the SRM, it's possible to implement the specific security policies that enterprises require.

Authentication, Identity, and Privilege

The SRM conceptualizes entities that are the causes of security events. A **principal** is a user or system entity that is registered and authenticated to the system and **initiating principals** are those that initiate activities. An initiating principal can be authenticated in a number of ways, but there are two common methods:

- ❑ For users, a password is usually validated
- ❑ For system entities, a long-term key is commonly used as the authentication information needs to be associated with the object

The principal is associated with sets of attributes that represent all of the information that the CORBA security service requires to make decisions about what the principal is and isn't allowed to do. The SRM defines two types of attributes:

- ❑ **Identity attributes**, which may be used for principal accountability, signing messages, access control, and object implementation usage charging. Depending on the system policy, a principal can have a separate identity attribute for each use or a single identity attribute for all uses.
- ❑ **Privilege attributes**, which provide the basis for access decisions within the CORBA security service. The privilege attributes available to a principal are determined by the access policies enforced by the system (as well as any predefined access restrictions on the principal).

Within the SRM, the principal is not an actual object. Information that represents the system's knowledge about the principal is encapsulated within a `Credentials` object. A `PrincipalAuthenticator` object performs the authentication operation using the security name, the authentication information, and the requested privilege attributes supplied by the principal.

Security Associations and Message Protection

A CORBA system deals exclusively with operation requests, and the responses to those requests. The ORB maintains a persistent connection between the client and the object. The CORBA security service uses this persistent connection as the basis for secure associations, which provides:

- ❑ Identification and authentication of the client to the object and of the object to the client
- ❑ The protected transfer of credentials between the client and the object
- ❑ Negotiation about the minimum transport message protection that is acceptable to both the client and the object

The techniques used to establish a security association, and characteristics of the resulting connection, depend on:

- ❑ The individual administrative and technical security policies of the client and the object
- ❑ The common security mechanisms available between the client and the object

The CORBA security service specification defines a set of administrative interfaces and option names for setting secure association policies on both the client and object.

Object Invocation Access Control

The SRM incorporates two levels of access control. At the lower level are access controls that the ORB can enforce between object interfaces (and implementations of those interfaces), each time that an object makes an object invocation on another object. At the higher level are the access controls that the object implementations can implement themselves, each time an invocation is received.

The object invocation access control service is based on the concept of an object invocation access policy. This policy governs whether the client acting on behalf of the current user can invoke the requested operation on this target object. The ORB enforces this policy and the security services it uses for all applications, whether they are aware of security or not. A CORBA security service access policy is expressed in terms of the principal's privilege attributes, which are encapsulated by the CORBA security service `Credentials` object; and the target object's control attributes, which are encapsulated by the CORBA security service `AccessDecision` object. The control attributes, which are always associated with an object that accepts invocations, describe what a principal must possess in order to be allowed to invoke the requested operation on a specific object implementation.

Security Auditing

Recording security events as they occur assists in the detection and investigation of security violations in a system. As the definition of a security event varies from system to system, both the CORBA security service SRM and specification use the concept of a security audit policy to specify what events are to be audited, and under what circumstances.

The two categories of audit policies are:

❑ **System audit policies**, which control the auditing of ORB and CORBA security service events

❑ **Application audit policies**, which control the auditing of events that occur in or at the boundary of applications

Delegation

Access control in a CORBA application is complicated by the fact that a target object, upon receiving an invocation from an authorized client, may have to become the client of other objects in the system in order to form the response to the original request.

From the point of view of an access control, the question becomes: what set of privileges can and should be used for the second (and higher) order requests spawned by the first order request from the client to the target?

The issue is one of delegation, and the CORBA security service specification addresses it using the concept of privilege delegation, in both the SRM and the specified interfaces. The initiating principal's privilege attributes are delegated to intermediate objects until they reach a final target, which then uses the delegated privilege attributes to make an decision on access.

The CORBA security service specification identifies five types of delegation policies:

❑ **No delegation**, in which the intermediate object uses only its own privilege attributes.

❑ **Simple delegation or impersonation**, in which the intermediate object simply uses the initiating principal's privileges in place of its own.

❑ **Combined privileges delegation**, in which the initiating principal's privileges are combined with those of the intermediate object such that the target cannot distinguish the source of the privileges.

❑ **Composite delegation**, in which the privileges of both the initiating principal and the intermediate object are passed to the target, which then checks both sets of privileges against its access policy.

❑ **Traced delegation**, which is an extension of the composite delegation policy such that every intermediate object in the delegation chain passes the privileges of itself and all previous intermediates. The final target will then be able to trace the sequence of delegations and optionally check its access policy against the privileges of any or all of the intermediates.

Non-Repudiation

A non-repudiation (NR) security service generates irrefutable evidence about a claimed event or action. Although we might want to securely store this information, the CORBA security NR service does not include that capability. It is designed for use by security-aware applications and not for use within the standard CORBA Security Service or the ORB.

The CORBA security NR service allows for the creation of NR evidence relating to both the creation (origination) and receipt (delivery) of a message (as well as other sorts of evidence that may be relevant only within the context of the application using the NR service). The NR service does not provide evidence that a request on an object was successfully carried out, as this would require use of the NR service within the ORB.

The CORBA security NT service can:

❑ Generate evidence of an action

❑ Verify evidence of an action

❑ Generate a request for evidence related to a message sent to a recipient

❑ Receive a request for evidence related to a message received

❑ Analyze the evidence of an action

❑ Collect evidence required for long-term storage

Security Management and Administration

The unique communications and control flow nature of the CORBA environment leads to a different approach from that found in traditional storage-oriented systems (for example, operating systems and databases) when managing the control attributes of the objects being accessed.

Every object in the CORBA system is fundamentally equivalent to every other object within its natural grouping constructs. However, the only two grouping constructs available are:

❑ The set of all objects executing under a single ORB

❑ The set of all objects implementing a single IDL interface

Recognizing that these two constructs are too restrictive for most applications, the designers of the CORBA security service used a very flexible construct from the standard ORB interoperability architecture – the **domain**. The CORBA security service identifies three types of security-related domain:

761

❑ **Security policy domain** – defines the scope over which a security policy is enforced

❑ **Security technology domain** – defines the scope over which a set of common security mechanisms are used to enforce the security policies

❑ **Security environment domain** – defines the scope within which the ORB environment exhibits certain characteristics (such as the linking encryption of all network connections would relieve the CORBA security service of responsibility for ensuring message confidentiality)

A complete solution for managing the CORBA security service would require services to manage the three aspects of the security policy domains:

❑ The security policy domains as first-class objects, including the ability to create, destroy, and establish relationships between them

❑ Member objects of domains, including the ability to transfer objects between domains

❑ The policies enforced within each domain, including the ability to specify, and then associate, each policy with the appropriate domains

We're ready to implement a custom security solution using the CORBA security services provided by Inprise VisiBroker 4.5.1, which will help us to understand how to implement a custom security solution for EAI using industry standard security protocols such as SSL and certificates.

We want to understand how a generic security infrastructure might be built – one that would allow the underlying applications to use a common authentication and authorization mechanism.

Custom Security Using CORBA

Our example will implement a custom security solution for a CORBA-based application. We'll authenticate a client on the server in two ways; first we'll use a secure SSL connection and certificates, then we'll perform username/password-based authentication.

To compile and run this example you'll need to install Inprise VisiBroker and Borland Security Service – we used versions 4.5.1 and 4.5 respectively. Trial versions of both these applications are available from http://www.borland.com/downloads/.

Our example uses two interfaces; `Account` to get a customer account and `AccountManager` to query the amount of balance in that account. The following IDL (`Customer.idl`) describes these interfaces:

```
module Customer {
  interface Account {
    float accountBalance();
  };

  interface AccountManager {
    Account getAccount(in string name);
  };
};
```

Use the IDL-to-Java tool that ships with VisiBroker to generate the required code:

```
i1d2java Customer.idl
```

Next, we need to implement these interfaces. First we implement the `Account` interface we defined:

```
public class AccountImpl extends Customer.AccountPOA {

  private float _balance;

  public AccountImpl(float balance) {
    _balance = balance;
  }

  public float accountBalance() {
    return _balance;
  }
}
```

Then we implement the `AccountManager` interface we defined:

```
import org.omg.PortableServer.*;
import com.inprise.security.CORBAsec.CurrentHelper;
import com.inprise.security.CORBAsec.*;
import com.inprise.security.ssl.*;
import java.security.Principal;
import java.util.*;

public class AccountManagerImpl extends Customer.AccountManagerPOA {
```

The `getAccount()` method identifies the user using the CORBA security `Current` object and obtains a SSL connection using ciphers. It can also use username/password-based authentication. If the account is not available then it creates an account and provides a random balance for it:

```
public synchronized Customer.Account getAccount(String name) {
  name = null;
  com.inprise.security.CORBAsec.Current current = null;
  try {
    current = CurrentHelper.narrow(
                  _orb().resolve_initial_references("SecurityCurrent"));
  } catch(Exception e) {
    System.out.println("Could not obtain get the security current");
    e.printStackTrace();
    System.exit(-1);
  }

  try {
    com.inprise.security.ssl.Current sslCurrent =
                            (com.inprise.security.ssl.Current) current;
    System.out.println("\nCipher: " +
      CipherSuite.toString(sslCurrent.getNegotiatedCipher(this._this())));
```

```
        System.out.println("Trusted:" +
                           sslCurrent.isPeerTrusted(this._this()));
      X509Cert[] chain = sslCurrent.getPeerCertificateChain(this._this());
      printCertChain (chain);
    } catch(org.omg.CORBA.BAD_OPERATION  e) {
      e.printStackTrace();
      System.out.println("SSL Connection not available");
    }

    try {
```

Print out the identity of the client that initiated the connection:

```
      Principal princ = current.getDelegatedPrincipal();
      name = princ.getName();
      System.out.println("Received a request from: " + princ.toString());

      if (princ instanceof UPprincipal) {
        System.out.println("Using username/password scheme");
        String[] groups = ((UPprincipal)princ).getGroups();
        if (groups != null) {
          for (int i = 0; i <groups.length; i++)
            System.out.println(groups[i]);
        } else {
          System.out.println("User does not belong to a group");
        }
      } else if (princ instanceof PKprincipal) {
        System.out.println("Using public key scheme");
        printCertChain (((PKprincipal)princ).getCertChain());
      } else {
        System.out.println("Improper public key scheme");
      }
    } catch (org.omg.CORBA.BAD_OPERATION e) {
```

If we catch this exception then probably no user information has been sent:

```
      name = "Unidentified User";
      System.out.println("Received request from User :" + name);
    }
```

Look up the account and if no account is available then create a new account and give it a random balance:

```
    Customer.Account account = (Customer.Account) _accounts.get(name);
    if(account == null) {
      float balance = Math.abs(_random.nextInt()) % 100000 / 100f;
      AccountImpl accountServant = new AccountImpl(balance);
```

Activate the account on the default POA (which is the root POA for this servant):

```
try {
  account = Customer.AccountHelper.narrow(
            _default_POA().servant_to_reference(accountServant));
} catch (Exception e) {
  e.printStackTrace();
}
```

Print out the account information and save it to a `Dictionary`:

```
System.out.println("Account Created " + name + "'s account: " +
                   account);
_accounts.put(name, account);
  }
  return account;
}
```

The `printCertChain()` method is used to print out the certificate chain of certificates used by the server:

```
private void printCertChain (X509Cert[] chain) {
  if (chain !=null) {
    for(int i = 0; i < chain.length; i++) {
      System.out.println("Displaying Certificate[" + i + "]:");
      System.out.println(chain[i]);
```

Find the trusted certificate:

```
      if(chain[i].isTrustpoint( )) {
        System.out.println("Certificate " + i + " is a trustpoint");
      }
    }
  } else {
    System.out.println("No certificate available");
  }
}

private Dictionary _accounts = new Hashtable();
private Random _random = new Random();
}
```

We implement the server with the security service, which creates an SSL connection and installs the certificates:

❏   The server initializes the ORB and sets the properties in order to use security and to install the SSL listeners.

❏   The server gets the `SSL.Current` instance by invoking the `ORB.resolve_initial_references()` method, passing `SecurityCurrent` as the argument

❏   The server creates a seed for initializing the required random number generator

❏   The server sets the certificate chain and private key using the instance of the `SSL.Current` object

❏   Then the server instantiates the servants and keeps them alive forever

`InitServer` initializes the CORBA security service and the ORB uses `Server` to instantiate and publish the servant:

```
import java.util.*;
import com.inprise.security.ssl.*;
import com.inprise.security.util.RandomSeedGenerator;
import com.inprise.vbroker.orb.ORB;

public class InitServer
  implements com.inprise.vbroker.interceptor.ServiceLoader {
```

Initialize the ORB and get the `SSL.Current` object:

```
public void init(org.omg.CORBA.ORB o) {
  final ORB orb = (ORB)o;
  Current current = null;
  try {
    current = CurrentHelper.narrow(
                   orb.resolve_initial_references("SecurityCurrent"));
  } catch (org.omg.CORBA.ORBPackage.InvalidName e) {
    System.out.println(e);
    e.printStackTrace();
    System.exit(-1);
  }
```

Generate a seed for the random number generator:

```
RandomSeedGenerator generator = new RandomSeedGenerator();
byte[] seed = generator.getSeed();
current.setPRNGSeed(seed);
seed = null;
```

Set the certificate chain (ordered from user to CA):

```
byte[][] certificates = {
  user_cert_1.getBytes(),
  user_cert_2.getBytes(),
  ca_cert.getBytes()
};

byte[] privateKey = encrypted_private_key.getBytes();
```

Set a certificate chain and an encrypted private key:

```
current.setPKprincipal(certificates, privateKey,"Wrox$$$");

com.inprise.security.trust.Trustpoints tpo =
                                   current.getTrustpointsObject();

byte[][] temp_list = new byte[1][];
temp_list[0] = ca_cert.getBytes( );
```

```
        tpo.addLocalTrustpoints(temp_list);
    }

    public void init_complete(org.omg.CORBA.ORB orb) {   }
    public void shutdown(org.omg.CORBA.ORB orb) {   }
```

We don't show the values of these strings, as their actual values are unimportant (they are, of course, fully implemented in the code available from http://www.wrox.com/):

```
    private static String user_cert_1 =        //.. Certificate 1  ..//
    private static String user_cert_2 =        //.. Certificate 2  ..//
    private static String ca_cert =            //.. CA Certificate ..//
    private static String encrypted_private_key = //.. Private key   ..//
}
```

Next we'll implement our `Server` class:

```
import org.omg.PortableServer.*;

public class Server {

    public static void main(String[] args) {
        try {
```

We initialize the ORB, obtain the reference to the POA, create policies for the POA, and create a POA with the right policies:

```
            org.omg.CORBA.ORB orb = org.omg.CORBA.ORB.init(args,null);
            POA rootPOA =
                    POAHelper.narrow(orb.resolve_initial_references("RootPOA"));
            org.omg.CORBA.Policy[] policies = {
              rootPOA.create_lifespan_policy(LifespanPolicyValue.PERSISTENT)
            };
            POA myPOA = rootPOA.create_POA("customer_poa",
                                      rootPOA.the_POAManager(), policies );
```

Create the servant, create an ID for it and then activate it:

```
            AccountManagerImpl managerServant = new AccountManagerImpl();
            byte[] managerId = "CustomerManager".getBytes();
            myPOA.activate_object_with_id(managerId, managerServant);
```

Activate the POA:

```
            rootPOA.the_POAManager().activate();
            System.out.println("customer_poa is ready.");
```

The ORB waits for requests:

```
        orb.run();
    } catch (Exception e) {
        e.printStackTrace();
    }
  }
}
```

The `server.properties` file configures a server to accept both username/password and certificate identities from clients. This is required for certificate completion when the server completes the client's certificate using its trustpoint repository:

```
vbroker.orb.dynamicLibs=com.inprise.security.Init,InitServer
vbroker.se.iiop_tp.scms=iiop_tp,ssl
vbroker.se.iiop_tp.scm.iiop_tp.listener.type=Disabled-IIOP
vbroker.security.peerAuthenticationMode=request_and_trust
vbroker.security.trustpointsRepository=Directory:trustpoints
vbroker.security.enableAuthentication=true
vbroker.security.passwordBackEnd=FileDB
vbroker.security.FileDB.file=pdbfile
```

To enable username/password authentication we set `requireAuthentication` to `true`:

```
vbroker.orb.dynamicLibs=com.inprise.security.Init
vbroker.se.iiop_tp.scms=iiop_tp,ssl
vbroker.se.iiop_tp.scm.iiop_tp.listener.type=Disabled-IIOP
vbroker.security.enableAuthentication=true
vbroker.security.requireAuthentication=true
vbroker.security.allowGuestUser=false
vbroker.security.passwordBackEnd=FileDB
vbroker.security.FileDB.file=pdbfile
```

The usernames and passwords are maintained in a file named `pdbfile`, which is a flat file. When the server is initialized it reads the username and password data from the specified file and uses this information to authenticate clients. The `pbeadmin` utility provided by VisiBroker can be used to create and administer this database.

We can create the user we require for this example by running the following commands:

```
pbeadmin -create wrox pdbfile
pbeadmin -admin wrox -file pdbfile addgroups eai
pbeadmin -admin wrox -file pdbfile adduser pclare 49ers eai
```

Next, we need to implement the client, which creates an SSL connection and installs the certificates:

❏ The client initializes the ORB in the usual way, and sets the properties so it can use the security service

❏ The `SSL.Current` instance is obtained by invoking the `ORB.resolve_initial_references()` method, passing `SecurityCurrent` as the argument

- ❑ The client creates a seed to initialize the required random number generator
- ❑ The client sets the client's certificate chain and private key using an instance of `SSL.Current`
- ❑ Then the client binds to the `Customer.AccountManager`, which establishes the SSL connection; and the `Current` object is used to retrieve the manager server's certificates

We implement the client as:

- ❑ `InitClient` – to initialize the CORBA security service using certificates
- ❑ `InitClientUP` – to initialize the CORBA security service using username/password authentication
- ❑ `Client` – which uses the remote object and then the servant

First `InitClient`:

```
import java.util.*;
import com.inprise.security.ssl.*;
import com.inprise.security.util.RandomSeedGenerator;
import com.inprise.vbroker.orb.ORB;

public class InitClient implements com.inprise.vbroker.interceptor.ServiceLoader {

  public void init(org.omg.CORBA.ORB o) {
    final ORB orb = (ORB)o;
    Current current = null;
    try {
      current = CurrentHelper.narrow(
        orb.resolve_initial_references("SecurityCurrent"));
    } catch (org.omg.CORBA.ORBPackage.InvalidName e) {
      System.out.println(e);
      e.printStackTrace();
      System.exit(-1);
    }
```

Generate a seed for the PRNG:

```
RandomSeedGenerator generator = new RandomSeedGenerator();
byte[] seed = generator.getSeed();
current.setPRNGSeed(seed);
seed = null;
```

Set the certificate chain (ordered from user to CA):

```
byte[][] certificates = {
  user_cert_1.getBytes(),
  user_cert_2.getBytes(),
  user_cert_3.getBytes()
};

byte[] privateKey = encrypted_private_key.getBytes();
```

Set the encrypted private key:

```
current.setPKprincipal(certificates, privateKey, "Wrox$$$$");

com.inprise.security.trust.Trustpoints tpo =
                                    current.getTrustpointsObject();

byte[][] temp_list = new byte[1][];
temp_list[0] = ca_cert.getBytes( );
tpo.addLocalTrustpoints(temp_list);
}

public void init_complete(org.omg.CORBA.ORB orb) {}
public void shutdown(org.omg.CORBA.ORB orb) {}
```

Again, we're not going to show the details of these strings:

```
private static String user_cert_1 =           //.. Certificate 1  ..//
private static String user_cert_2 =           //.. Certificate 2  ..//
private static String user_cert_3 =           //.. Certificate 3  ..//
private static String ca_cert =               //.. CA Certificate ..//
private static String encrypted_private_key = //.. Private key    ..//
}
```

InitClientUP performs the username/password authentication:

```
import java.util.*;
import com.inprise.security.CORBAsec.*;
import com.inprise.vbroker.orb.ORB;

public class InitClientUP implements
            com.inprise.vbroker.interceptor.ServiceLoader {

  public void init(org.omg.CORBA.ORB o) {

    final ORB orb = (ORB)o;

    Current current = null;
    try {
      current = CurrentHelper.narrow(
        orb.resolve_initial_references("SecurityCurrent"));
    }
    catch (org.omg.CORBA.ORBPackage.InvalidName e) {
      System.out.println(e);
      System.exit(-1);
    }
```

Set the username and password of the client:

```
String username="wrox";
String password="dan";
current.setUPprincipal(username, password);
}

public void init_complete(org.omg.CORBA.ORB orb) {}
public void shutdown(org.omg.CORBA.ORB orb) {}
}
```

Now we can create our `Client` class:

```
import com.inprise.security.ssl.*;
import com.inprise.security.CORBAsec.X509Cert;

public class Client {

  public static void main(String[] args) {
```

Initialize the ORB, obtain the manager ID, and locate the `Customer.AccountManager` using the POA name and servant ID:

```
org.omg.CORBA.ORB orb = org.omg.CORBA.ORB.init(args,null);
byte[] managerId = "CustomerManager".getBytes();
Customer.AccountManager manager =
Customer.AccountManagerHelper.bind(orb, "/customer_poa", managerId);
```

Use `args[0]` as the account name, or a default if none is supplied:

```
String name = args.length > 0 ? args[0] : "Ramesh Nagappan";
```

Request the account manager to get an account and obtain the balance:

```
Customer.Account account = manager.getAccount(name);
float balance = account.accountBalance();

  System.out.println(name + "Customer balance in account is $" +
                     balance);

Current current = null;
try {
  current = CurrentHelper.narrow(
    orb.resolve_initial_references("SecurityCurrent"));
}    catch(Exception e) {
  System.out.println("Could'nt obtain the security current");
  e.printStackTrace();
  System.exit(-1);
}
```

Get information from the SSL layer:

```
try {
  com.inprise.security.ssl.Current sslCurrent =
                          (com.inprise.security.ssl.Current)current;
  System.out.println("\nCipher:  " +
  CipherSuite.toString(sslCurrent.getNegotiatedCipher(manager)));
```

Check that the peer is to be trusted:

```
System.out.println("Peer Trusted:"+sslCurrent.isPeerTrusted(manager));

X509Cert[] chain = sslCurrent.getPeerCertificateChain(manager);
for(int i = 0; i < chain.length; i++) {
```

Print the certificate chain of the server:

```
System.out.println("Certificate[" + i + "]:");
System.out.println(chain[i]);
```

Finally, get the trusted certificate:

```
if(chain[i].isTrustpoint( )) {
    System.out.println("certificate " + i + " is a trustpoint");
}
    }
} catch(org.omg.CORBA.BAD_OPERATION e) {
    System.out.println("Unable to get a valid SSL Connection");
}
}
}
```

The `client.properties` file can be configured so that the client can accept either username/password or certificate identities from clients. The following is the `client.properties` file required for a client using certificates obtained from its trustpoint repository:

```
vbroker.orb.dynamicLibs=com.inprise.security.Init,InitClient
vbroker.security.peerAuthenticationMode=require_and_trust
vbroker.security.trustpointsRepository=Directory:trustpoints
```

The following properties file is required for username/password authentication:

```
vbroker.orb.dynamicLibs=com.inprise.security.Init,InitClientUP
```

Running the Example

To compile and run the classes in this example you will need to include the JAR files found in the `lib` directory of your Inprise VisiBroker installation in your classpath. To run the example you'll need to start the VisiBroker Agent (`osagent`), which found in the `bin` directory of your VisiBroker installation.

To start the server, you should run this command:

```
vbj -DORBpropStorage=server.properties Server
```

Then start the client (using certificates):

```
vbj -DORBpropStorage=client.properties Client
```

772

You should see something like this in the client command prompt:

```
C:\WINNT\System32\cmd.exe                                          _ □ ×
Ramesh Nagappan: Balance in account is $265.75

Cipher: SSL_RSA_EXPORT1024_WITH_RC4_56_SHA
Peer trusted: true
Certificate[0]:
----------------------------------------------------------------
SERIAL NUMBER:
4201108534
SUBJECT DISTINGUISHED NAME:
CN=Kevin, OU=Security, O=Inprise, L=San Mateo, S=California, C=US
ISSUER DISTINGUISHED NAME:
CN=Andre, OU=Security, O=Inprise, L=San Mateo, S=California, C=US
ISSUED THE:
Wed Feb 24 20:58:30 GMT 1999
EXPIRATION DATE:
Sat Feb 21 20:58:30 GMT 2009
----------------------------------------------------------------

NO Extension
```

We can see that information about the certificates has been outputted, and a new account has been created with the default name Ramesh Nagappan – the account has been credited with a random balance, in this case $265.75.

Now start the client using username/password authentication and specify the username and password we set in pdbfile:

```
vbj -DORBpropStorage=client.properties Client pclare 49ers
```

We see something like this in the server command prompt:

```
C:\WINNT\System32\cmd.exe - startCustomerServer.cmd                _ □ ×
Cipher: SSL_RSA_EXPORT1024_WITH_RC4_56_SHA
Trusted: false
No certificate available
Received a request from: CN=pclare
Using username/password scheme
GROUP=eai
Account Created pclare's account: Stub[repository_id=IDL:Customer/Account:1.0,ke
y=TransientId[poaName=/,id={4 bytes: (0)(0)(0)(1)},sec=468,usec=6517373071,codeb
ase=null]
```

If we run the client without specifying a username and password:

```
vbj -DORBpropStorage=client_up.properties Client
```

we see from the client command prompt that the default account (Ramesh Nagappan) is used:

```
C:\WINNT\System32\cmd.exe                                          _ □ ×
C:\ProEAI\Ch16>vbj -classpath C:\Inprise\vbroker\lib\migration.jar;C:\Inprise\vb
roker\lib\migration.jar;C:\Inprise\vbroker\lib\vbdev.jar;C:\Inprise\vbroker\lib\
vbjdev.jar;C:\Inprise\vbroker\libvbjorb.jar;C:\Inprise\vbroker\vbsec.jar;C:\Inpr
ise\vbssl.jar; -DORBpropStorage=client_up.properties Client
Ramesh Nagappan: Balance in account is $546.99
```

Kerberos

If we want to provide a variety of net-centric application-based services to multiple users within a secure EAI environment, we need to be able to identify users when they make requests to access specific functionality within the environment.

Many systems use **authentication by assertion**, in which applications assert the identity of the user to the service (which believes what it is told). Most uses of authentication by assertion are based on the origin of the assertion – if it comes from a trusted network address it is believed.

Authentication by assertion can leave systems open to security risks. To avoid these risks we require a stronger form of authentication – one based on cryptography. If we use authentication mechanisms based on cryptography, a listener on the network would gain no information that could be used to fake a user's identity. **Kerberos** is the most commonly used authentication technology that enables single sign-on support for multiple applications.

The Kerberos Authentication Service

Kerberos is a network authentication protocol created by the Massachusetts Institute of Technology (MIT). MIT makes a free-source implementation of Kerberos available at http://web.mit.edu/kerberos/www/. Commercial implementations of Kerberos are also available from many OS and application software vendors.

> **Kerberos is designed to provide a strong authentication service for distributed application frameworks and client/server applications using secret-key cryptography.**

Kerberos is a distributed authentication service that allows a client application process running on behalf of a user principal to prove its identity to an application server (and vice versa). Then, the client and server can securely encrypt all their compunctions – without having to further prove their identity.

How Kerberos Works

Kerberos enables authentication by providing a layer of security with encrypted communications between applications or services anywhere on the Internet and irrespective of firewall locations. Kerberos maintains a database of clients (which can be both users and services) and their password credentials, known as the **Key Distribution Center (KDC)**:

❑   The KDC creates a **ticket-granting ticket (TGT)** for the client

❑   The TGT is encrypted using the *client's* password as the key

❑   The encrypted TGT is sent to the client

❑   If the client is who it claims to be it will be able to decrypt the TGT using its password

❑   The client can then use the decrypted TGT to provide proof of its identity

The TGT has a finite lifetime and expires at a specified time. Once the TGT has expired the client can obtain an additional TGT. The requesting and granting of these tickets is (like other authentication processes) transparent to the user.

The TGT is valid only for a finite period and expires at a specified time; the client is also able to obtain additional tickets, which give permission for specific services. The requesting and granting of these additional tickets is transparent to the user.

> *For further details of how Kerberos works you should refer to*
> *http://www.microsoft.com/windows2000/techinfo/howitworks/security/kerberos.asp and*
> *http://www.sun.com/software/solaris/pam/.*

Cross-Realm Authentication

An application may span multiple networks, in which case it would not be practical for all users to be registered with a single authentication service. Multiple authentication servers will be used, each responsible for a subset of the users and servers in the system. Such a subset is known as a **realm**. If a realm is replicated, users will need to be registered with more than one authentication server.

> **Cross-realm authentication allows a principal to prove its identity to a server that is registered in a different realm.**

To prove its identity to a server in a remote realm, a Kerberos principal first obtains a TGT for the remote realm from its local authentication server, which means that the principal's local authentication server must share a cross-realm key with the verifier's authentication server. The principal uses the ticket-granting exchange to request a ticket from the verifier's authentication server. This server will detect that the TGT was issued in a foreign realm, and will look up the cross-realm key. This cross-realm key will be used to verify the validity of the TGT. The server will then issue a ticket and a session key to the client. The name of the client, which is embedded in the ticket, includes the name of the realm in which the client was registered.

From version 5 on, Kerberos supports multiple application sign-on and cross-realm authentication, which allows keys to be shared hierarchically between child and parent. The list of realms that are transited during multiple-application, cross-realm authentication is recorded in the ticket. The verifier makes the final decision if the path that was followed should be trusted (shortcuts through the hierarchy are also supported and can improve the performance of the authentication process).

The Generic Security Services API

The **Generic Security Services (GSS) API** (developed by the Internet Engineering Task Force (IETF)) provides a generic authentication and secure messaging interface that supports pluggable security mechanisms. The GSS API is designed to insulate developers from the underlying security mechanisms by allowing the development of application authentication using a generic interface. Indeed, GSS version 2 is defined in a language-independent format.

> **The generic nature of the GSS API allows applications to use different security mechanisms, without having to make any changes to the application itself.**

The JGSS API is part of J2SE 1.4. It provides Java bindings for the GSS, which allows Java developers to create uniform access to security services over different authentication mechanisms – including Kerberos. You can find more information about the JGSS API at http://java.sun.com/j2se/1.4/docs/guide/security/index.html.

> **I expect that JGSS will emerge as the standard API to use for single sign-on authentication – particularly in EAI.**

Comparing JGSS with JSEE and JAAS

Although the JGSS API shares many features with JAAS and the JSSE API, particularly with regard to client-server authentication and data encryption and integrity, it has some features not present in the Java security model. We need to be aware of the differences between the two models so that we can choose the right API to use in a given situation:

❑   The JGSS API contains support for Kerberos as the key authentication mechanism, which allows the creation of applications that provide **single sign-on support**. The JSSE API does not support a Kerberos-based cipher suite – it supports Transport Layer Security (TLS) only.

❑   The JGSS API is a token-based API that relies on the application to handle communication. This allows application to use the transport protocol of its choice to transport the tokens generated by the JGSS API. JSSE supports a socket-based API and so only allows applications to use sockets.

❑   By using Kerberos, both the JGSS API and JAAS allow clients to delegate their credentials to server applications deployed in a multi-tier environment.

❑   The JGSS API is token-based and allows the selection of encryption type, which allows applications to intersperse plain text and cipher-text messages. The JSSE API and JAAS do not support this feature.

Using the JGSS API

The JGSS API is available (in the `org.ietf.jgss` package) as part of J2SE 1.4 and contains a number of useful classes:

❑   `ChannelBinding` – encapsulates the concept of caller-provided channel-binding information

❑   `GSSManager` – serves as a factory for other important GSS API classes and also provides information about the supported authentication mechanisms

❑   `MessageProp` – a utility class used within the per-message `GSSContext` methods to convey per-message properties

❑   `Oid` – represents a universal **Object Identifier** for authentication mechanisms

> *The Kerberos V5 mechanism is identified by the OID* `{iso(1) member-body(2) United States(840) mit(113554) infosys(1) gssapi(2) krb5(2)}` *(that is,* `"1.2.840.113554.1.2.2"`*)*.

The Kerberos version 5 GSS API is available as the default instance of `org.ietf.jgss.GSSManager`. The `GSSManager` class gets an instance of the underlying authentication mechanism and is responsible for invoking them, for example:

```
GSSManager manager = GSSManager.getInstance();
```

`GSSManager` is also a factory class for the most important interfaces. It can be used to create an instance of `GSSName`, which encapsulates a single GSS API principal:

```
GSSName gssClientName = manager.createName("wrox", GSSName.NT_USER_NAME);
```

This code gets a `GSSName` representing the principal "wrox". We could also use an overloaded version of the `createName()` method to get a principal that is a service (with a name "ramesh") running in a realm (in this case "wrox.com"):

```
GSSName gssServerName = manager.createName("ramesh@wrox.com",
                                    GSSName.UNIX_HOSTBASED_SERVICE);
```

`GSSContext` encapsulates the GSS API security context and provides the security services that are available over the context. It has a `createContext()` method that returns a security context that knows the peer it must communicate with, as well as its authentication mechanism (in this case Kerberos):

```
GSSContext secContext = manager.createContext(peerName,
                                    krb5Oid,
                                    clientCreds,
                                    GSSContext.DEFAULT_LIFETIME);
```

`GSSCredential` encapsulates the GSS API credentials for an entity and has a `createCredential()` method that acquires a credential (in this case on the client), for example:

```
GSSCredential clientCreds = manager.createCredential(
                                    gName,
                                    6*3600,
                                    desiredMechs,
                                    GSSCredential.INITIATE_ONLY);
```

We could also acquire a credential on the server:

```
GSSCredential serverCreds = manager.createCredential(
                                    sName,
                                    GSSCredential.INDEFINITE_LIFETIME,
                                    desiredMechs,
                                    GSSCredential.ACCEPT_ONLY);
```

Building a JGSS Client

Let's look at how we could build a JGSS client, using Kerberos as the underlying authentication mechanism:

```
import org.ietf.jgss.*;
import java.net.Socket;
import java.io.IOException;
import java.io.DataInputStream;
import java.io.DataOutputStream;

public class JGSSClient {

   public static void main(String[] args)
       throws IOException, GSSException  {
```

Obtain the command-line arguments:

```
if (args.length < 3) {
   System.err.println("Usage: java <options> Login JGSSClient " +
                      " <gssServer> <gssHostName> <port>");
   System.exit(-1);
}

String gssServer = args[0];
String gssHostName = args[1];
int port = Integer.parseInt(args[2]);
```

Connect to the host server using a socket:

```
Socket socket = new Socket(gssHostName, port);
DataInputStream inStream = new DataInputStream(socket.getInputStream());
DataOutputStream outStream =
                    new DataOutputStream(socket.getOutputStream());
System.out.println("Connected to server " + socket.getInetAddress());
```

Use the `Oid` representation of the Kerberos V5 mechanism:

```
Oid krb5Oid = new Oid("1.2.840.113554.1.2.2");
```

Get the default instance of the `GSSManager`:

```
GSSManager manager = GSSManager.getInstance();
```

Create a `GSSName` out of the server's name:

```
GSSName serverName = manager.createName(gssServer, null);
```

Create a `GSSContext` for mutual authentication with the server:

```
        GSSContext context = manager.createContext(serverName, krb5Oid, null,
    GSSContext.DEFAULT_LIFETIME);
```

Set the desired optional features on the context:

```
    context.requestMutualAuth(true);
    context.requestConf(true);
    context.requestInteg(true);
    byte[] token = new byte[0];
```

Loop while the context is established:

```
    while (!context.isEstablished()) {
```

The token is ignored on the first call:

```
        token = context.initSecContext(token, 0, token.length);
```

Send a token to the server created by `initSecContext`:

```
    if (token != null) {
      outStream.writeInt(token.length);
      outStream.write(token);
      outStream.flush();
    }
```

If the client is done after establishing the context then read a token:

```
    if (!context.isEstablished()) {
      token = new byte[inStream.readInt()];
      inStream.readFully(token);
    }
    }

    System.out.println("Context Established! ");
    System.out.println("Client is " + context.getSrcName());
    System.out.println("Server is " + context.getTargName());
```

Client and server were authenticated to each other:

```
    if (context.getMutualAuthState()) {
      System.out.println("Mutual authentication took place!");
    }
    byte[] messageBytes = "Hello World using GSS !\0".getBytes();
    MessageProp prop =  new MessageProp(0, true);
```

Encrypt the data and send it across:

```
token = context.wrap(messageBytes, 0, messageBytes.length, prop);
System.out.println("Will send wrap token of size " + token.length);
outStream.writeInt(token.length);
outStream.write(token);
outStream.flush();
```

Allow the server to decrypt the message, calculate a MIC on the decrypted message, and send it back to us for verification:

```
token = new byte[inStream.readInt()];
System.out.println("Will read token of size " + token.length);
inStream.readFully(token);
context.verifyMIC(token, 0, token.length, messageBytes, 0,
                  messageBytes.length, prop);
System.out.println("Verified received MIC for message.");
System.out.println("Exiting...");
context.dispose();
socket.close();
  }
}
```

Next, we'll create the JGSS server, again using Kerberos as the underlying authentication mechanism:

```
import org.ietf.jgss.*;
import java.io.*;
import java.net.Socket;
import java.net.ServerSocket;

public class JGSSServer {

  public static void main(String[] args)
    throws IOException, GSSException {
```

Obtain the command-line arguments:

```
if (args.length != 1) {
  System.err.println("Usage: java JGSSServer <Port>");
  System.exit(-1);
}

int Port = Integer.parseInt(args[0]);
```

Establish a `ServerSocket` using a port:

```
ServerSocket ss = new ServerSocket(Port);
```

Get the default instance of the `GSSManager`:

```
GSSManager manager = GSSManager.getInstance();
```

Listen for incoming client connections:

```
while (true) {
   Socket socket = ss.accept();
   DataInputStream inStream =
           new DataInputStream(socket.getInputStream());
   DataOutputStream outStream =
           new DataOutputStream(socket.getOutputStream());

   System.out.println("Got connection from client " + socket.getInetAddress());
```

Create a GSSContext to receive the incoming request from the client:

```
GSSContext context = manager.createContext((GSSCredential)null);
```

Loop while the context is established:

```
byte[] token = null;

while (!context.isEstablished()) {
   token = new byte[inStream.readInt()];
   token = context.acceptSecContext(token, 0, token.length);
```

Send a token to the peer if one was generated by acceptSecContext:

```
if (token != null) {
   outStream.writeInt(token.length);
   outStream.write(token);
   outStream.flush();
}
}

System.out.print("Context Established! ");
System.out.println("Client is " + context.getSrcName());
System.out.println("Server is " + context.getTargName());
```

Client and server were authenticated to each other:

```
if (context.getMutualAuthState()) {
   System.out.println("Mutual authentication took place!");
}
```

Create a MessageProp:

```
MessageProp prop = new MessageProp(0, false);
```

Read the token:

```
        token = new byte[inStream.readInt()];
        System.out.println("Will read token of size " + token.length);
        inStream.readFully(token);
        byte[] bytes = context.unwrap(token, 0, token.length, prop);
        String str = new String(bytes);
        System.out.println("Received data \"" + str +
                        "\" of length " + str.length());
        System.out.println("Confidentiality applied: " + prop.getPrivacy());
```

Generate a MIC and send it to the client:

```
        prop.setQOP(0);
        token = context.getMIC(bytes, 0, bytes.length, prop);
        outStream.writeInt(token.length);
        outStream.write(token);
        outStream.flush();
        System.out.println("Closing connection " + socket.getInetAddress());
        context.dispose();
        socket.close();
      }
    }
  }
```

Again, in order to execute this code you will need to install a Kerberos realm and a Kerberos Key Distribution Center as we discussed earlier.

Single Sign-On

To access heterogeneous applications in an EAI environment, users typically have to sign on to multiple applications, which often require different usernames and authentication information. Maintaining authentication information from multiple application sources so that it can be accessed in a coordinated manner (in order to maintain the integrity of security policy enforcement) can become a complex task for the EAI security administrator. It is also makes things more difficult for the user as they have to remember when to use the many different usernames, passwords, and authentication procedures.

Single sign-on (SSO) authentication provides a generic mechanism in which a single user authentication and authorization will permit a user to access all the underlying applications seamlessly and in compliance with their security policies. SSO defines one master access key for all authorized applications and system resources.

> **Single sign-on allows the maintenance of a single user account that enables access to multiple applications and resources.**

SSO allows developers to adopt security standards and mechanisms such as Kerberos and the GSS API; or to implement a commercial security infrastructure that addresses all the application-level security requirements in an EAI environment.

The X/Open Group has developed a specification for developing single sign-on (code-named XSSO). It is available at http://www.rdg.opengroup.org/public/tech/security/sso/index.htm. To enable SSO functionality it requires:

- An end user application agent that allows users to identify themselves and view the settings for the underlying application

- An authentication and authorization service for the end user; these services should be available to all applications and systems

- Support for applications that use a variety of different security mechanisms, such as MVS RACF (IBM), Kerberos, DCE (X/Open), Microsoft, Novell, UNIX, and PKI

- A single point of user registration and password synchronization implemented across many applications and platforms

Accordingly, XSSO defines these SSO implementation strategies:

- **Single-Point User Registration and Administration –** to enable a unique SSO user account management interface for all underlying applications and systems, the SSO implementation must provide a generic solution for managing users across multiple platforms and applications. This includes the creation, deletion, and modification of user accounts as well as the setting of user-specific attributes and access policies for individual accounts.

- **Password Synchronization –** the SSO is required to synchronize a username/password to recognize the usernames and passwords of the underlying applications and services from disparate systems that each user needs to access. The user signs on to the single sign-on client with a single username/password and then the system takes over and automatically supplies the different passwords to the individual applications as they are accessed. This fulfills the SSO functionality because there is only one user ID and password, which are used for all applications, services, and systems.

- **Support for Industry-Standard Security Mechanisms –** standardization of a particular mechanism within the enterprise will allow the organization to achieve single sign-on support, particularly when using Kerberos, DCE, and PKI.

Some of the most common issues that need to be considered before implementing SSO are:

- The administrative workloads caused by the maintenance of SSO infrastructure

- Problems arising from password synchronization

- The potentially partial implementation of SSO technology because of incompatibility with existing security services

- The lack of interoperability between available solutions because of the propagation of security context

Commercial SSO Solutions

Three of the most popular security infrastructure applications used to provide secure platforms to manage all applications, particularly for e-business-based EAI applications are:

❏ **Netegrity SiteMinder** – available from http://www.netegrity.com/products/
SiteMinder is a security infrastructure solution that provides secure application and portal management capabilities that are designed to enable e-businesses to centralize authorization, authentication, and single sign on across all e-business based resources including the Internet, corporate extranets and Intranet applications.

❏ **EnTrust Entelligence** – available from http://www.entrust.com/entelligence/
Entelligence provides an integrated solution to secure both internal and Internet applications providing a single security layer which encompasses the enterprise's entire set of enhanced security needs including identification, privacy, verification, and security management.

❏ **IBM Tivoli Security Management** – available from http://www.tivoli.com/products/
Tivoli Security provides a full-fledged single sign-on security infrastructure to e-business resources for centralized security management and access control allowing consistent enforcement of security and privacy policies providing centralized enterprise risk management.

Netegrity SiteMinder has the greatest market share, so we'll take a closer look at it.

Netegrity SiteMinder

Netegrity SiteMinder integrates with web server products to provide authentication and access authorization features. It also enhances the performance, scalability, and manageability of the security infrastructure. It does this by replacing the basic authentication mechanism built into the HTTP protocol and Access Control Lists (ACL) used by web servers, with a centrally managed policy-based user authentication and access authorization.

SiteMinder supports a variety of different authentication mechanisms, including: passwords, passwords over SSL, two factor tokens, X.509 certificates, smart cards, method chaining, and form-based authentication.

The Infrastructure of SiteMinder

The major components of a SiteMinder security infrastructure are:

❏ Web and application server agents

❏ The policy server

❏ Policy and user stores

❏ The SiteMinder API

To perform user authentication and resource access authorization, the SiteMinder **agent** (a listener application installed in the HTTP server) intercepts all HTTP requests submitted to the web servers for authentication. SiteMinder agents are available for most web and application servers. The agents also support standard CGI environments.

The agent sends the user's credentials to the SiteMinder **policy server**, which caches the information. SiteMinder agents can then make calls to the underlying web server API and use the required user authentication mechanism. If we have a multi-platform web server implementation, we need to use one of the web servers, and an agent installed on it, to perform the authentication; the other servers use the login session established by the primary server.

The policy server provides services for the authentication, authorization, and auditing of users. The policy server provides centralized access to authorization policy management and implementation. When SiteMinder agents process a request for authentication or authorization, they use the policy server to access the required policies.

After authentication, the SiteMinder agent creates a cookie that contains user-specific information in an encrypted format. It is not possible for the user to modify or update these details and the secret key used for encryption is periodically regenerated as a symmetric cipher secret key.

Authentication, access authorization, and single sign-on are integral parts of the security of EAI-based applications. Figuring out how to scale these services to extra large size is also important, when such systems need to be scaled. For instance, if dozens of web servers are deployed and initialized all at the same time, a single policy server initially serving the requests from agents may get overwhelmed. Also, on an extra large system, even with caching, the load on the policy server can be significant. The answer lies in the deployment of multiple policy servers, and configuration of agents to enable load balancing.

If the user authenticates to a primary web server, and then the business logic wishes to redirect the user to another web server, SiteMinder decrypts the cookie and the agent managing the other server sets the privileged access credentials. This means that all the web servers in the same single sign-on group require access to each other's secret key.

SiteMinder uses a RDBMS or LDAP to store policies and users. LDAP is usually used as the user account store, which means that it is often convenient to use LDAP for policy store as well. The final part of the SiteMinder infrastructure is the SiteMinder API, which is used to develop custom agents.

The Policy Server periodically regenerates the secret key used for cookie encryption, and distributes it to all of the web server agents in the same single sign-on group. The interval of the key regeneration is a configurable parameter, as well as the length of the key.

J2EE Component Integration

SiteMinder allows the authorization or denial of access to resources for the user on each HTTP request. This decision is based on the information contained in the HTTP request, user profile, and policy rules. This means that it is possible to provide access control for individual URLs – even for a web page generated by a servlet. Indeed, SiteMinder agents can make authorization decisions at the level of an EJB running in an EJB container.

Using SiteMinder to integrate EJB and servlet access control allows the flexible, centralized, and delegated administration of policies.

Non-Java Component Integration

SiteMinder also provides Java, C, and C++ APIs, which allow developers to build custom agents for both web- and non-web-based applications. It is also possible to share user and policy stores with non-web-based applications by using policy servers for authorization.

SiteMinder provides policy management, web agent, authentication, authorization, event, and tunnel service APIs. The Policy Management API is useful for developing custom user interfaces, or customizing certain procedures such as encryption key management.

785

Summary

In this chapter we studied the various security mechanisms and management strategies available for implementing secure EAI applications. We discussed the use of security models provided by Java and CORBA, and their relevance to EAI implementation. We also looked at Kerberos, an emerging industry standard for open network authentication technology.

In particular, we looked at:

❑   The Java and CORBA security models

❑   How to use the Java Authentication and Authorization service

❑   The J2EE infrastructure security and how to propagate the security context through all the logical tiers

❑   How to implement a custom security solution using the CORBA security service

❑   Kerberos and the Java GSS API

❑   Single sign-on authentication in EAI and a commercial solution

In the next chapter, we'll examine the general guidelines we should follow, and the technology we can use, to integrate the presentation tier using the J2EE platform.

17

Presentation Integration

Presentation integration is the final phase in EAI, and should be applied after the data level and business level integration phases have been achieved. Presentation integration results in an integrated system with a unified presentation layer through which users can access the functionality of the integrated system. As they will use the newly developed presentation layer, they should not be aware of the diversity of existing applications that are executing in the background. The presentation layer also accesses the functions through common interfaces, provided by business tier higher-level virtual components, developed in the business method level integration phase. Therefore, the presentation layer is essentially decoupled and unaware of the details of existing applications. This makes the presentation layer flexible and enables the relatively easy re-engineering of existing applications and their replacement with newly developed components, as we discussed in Chapter 9.

In this chapter we will look at the guidelines and the technology choices that we have for implementing the presentation integration in the J2EE platform. In the second half of the chapter we will focus on JavaServer Pages (JSP) and servlets for building web-based presentation layer. We will cover the following areas:

❑ Objectives of presentation integration and design principles of user interfaces

❑ Different types of user interfaces

❑ The concept of enterprise portals

❑ Prerequisites for presentation integration and how it fulfills the multi-tier goal

❑ The role of transactions and security in presentation integration

❑ Presentation tier analysis and design

❑ An overview of servlets and JSP pages, and the differences between the two

❑ Different web component tier architectures

❑ Presentation tier patterns

❑ Options for supporting different types of clients

Objectives of Presentation Integration

The objective of presentation level integration is to provide a common, unified presentation layer – a user interface for the entire integrated information system. The user interface is the software that allows human users to interact with the information system. The only access that the typical user has to the information system is through the user interface. Therefore its objective is to make the information system as user-friendly as possible.

This recommendation is easy to make, but it can be difficult to achieve a high standard of usability in practice. Therefore, in this chapter we will focus on the activities, steps, and technologies that we can use in J2EE platform to develop usable user interfaces. To measure usability, we will focus on users trying to perform a range of tasks, using a certain user interface. We will consider the following four aspects:

❑ **Effectiveness**
   Indicates how effectively a user can perform a range of tasks using the user interface. A very similar criterion is **productivity**, which tells us how fast a user can perform tasks.

❑ **Learnability**
   Indicates how much training and practice users require to efficiently use the user interface to the information system.

❑ **Flexibility**
   Indicates how effective the user interface can be adapted to changes in the tasks or environment.

❑ **Attitude**
   Indicates how the users feel when using the system. Do they like the system and find it rewarding? or conversely do they find it tiring or frustrating?

To measure usability of a user interface, there are two common approaches:

❑ **Performance test** measures the speed and accuracy of certain tasks, performed by the users

❑ **Attitude test** measures user satisfaction and user perception of a user interface

Achieving better usability of a user interface is connected with adapting it to the way users work and think. Adapting the user interface to the users requires a lot of effort in all stages of presentation layer development, which increases cost. Therefore the decision regarding how much effort we should invest in user interface development must weigh the cost against the potential benefits.

> We should adapt the user interface to suit the users, rather than trying to adapt users to fit the user interface.

Greater usability of user interfaces has clear advantages to the business – better usability enables users to achieve tasks more productively and we can therefore conclude that user interface usability is directly related to the productivity of users.

The user interface should be designed with the focus on the users. To fulfill this goal, the user interface designers should identify who the users are, what task will they perform, and what their usability requirements are. End users should play an active role in the design of user interfaces, and the user interfaces should reflect their thinking. This is particularly important in presentation integration, because it aligns the integrated information system with the business processes in the company, which is one of the objectives of integration.

Such a user-focused approach might seem obvious but real-world experiences suggest that not many developers actually use this method. Often the user interfaces are designed as add-ons to the functions of the application that only allows users to invoke these functions. This is a consequence of the typical development procedure. We specified the activities of the integration process in Chapter 4, but it is worth reminding ourselves here:

❑ *Requirements specification, where standard business requirements connected with the functionality of the information system are specified*

❑ *Analysis, design, and implementation of the functionality of the information system*

❑ *Design of the user interface on top of the information system functionality, to allow users to invoke functions*

Following this approach the user interface will provide support for all functions, but these will be fragmented and the user will often have to invoke several of them to get a business task done. This will make such user interfaces more difficult to learn, less productive, and result in poor attitude of users towards the systems.

Having defined the usability, we will look at some principles that make user interfaces usable.

Design Principles of Usable User Interfaces

The design principles presented here are a result of many years of research on user interface design and are focused towards designing user interfaces for integrated information systems. We will address the following principles:

❑ **User interfaces should reflect business tasks and processes**
Following this principle places users in control over the information system. It enables users to accomplish tasks using a sequence of steps that they would naturally perform. Ideally the users could define the sequence themselves, which will make the user interface flexible for changes.

A user interface that follows this design principle will not limit the users to some choice of correct steps, usually made by the developers who are not fully familiar with the business tasks. Such an interface would also prevent the users from invoking several distinct operations on different locations in order to get the job done. The user interface should provide clear information about the current state of the information system and the possible actions that the user can perform. Ideally, users should be able to leave the user interface and return later to the same state where they left.

❑ **Simplicity should not compromise usability of functions**
User interfaces should be simple and straightforward to use. A well-organized user interface should support all tasks of the users. Basic functions should be apparent immediately. Advanced functions may be less obvious. Functions should be included only if they are really needed (and not because they may sound fancy). We should keep the number of actions to a minimum while still allowing users to accomplish their tasks. This will improve the learnability and productivity of users, thereby making the user interface more usable.

❑ **Prior knowledge of users should be taken into consideration**
Users of the integrated information system will have had a lot of experience in using the existing applications. Concepts and techniques they have learned can be applied to new user interfaces as well. A good new user interface will allow users to build on prior knowledge and experience. This will allow them to start quicker and make progress faster. This should not, however, compromise the usability of the user interface. Therefore, the new user interface should build on the good characteristics of user interfaces of existing applications and should improve on the others.

❑ **User interface controls should be made obvious and intuitive to use**
We should use real-world representations and vocabulary in the user interface. From the perspective of users, this will give the user interface a familiar look and feel, making it more intuitive to learn and use, thus improving the usability. The user interface controls should be clearly visible and their functions identifiable. We should not rely on graphical representations too much. These should provide reminders for users to understand their roles and relationships. Users should be able to invoke controls directly.

❑ **Users should be able to customize**
Different users have different needs, so they should be able to customize their user interface to reflect them. Customization helps to make the user interface feel comfortable and familiar. Customizing to personal needs is called personalizing a user interface and, indeed, personalization leads to higher productivity and user satisfaction. The personalization information should be made available to the users irrespective of the computer or the location from which they access the information system.

❑ **Actions should be predictable and reversible**
User actions should produce results that users expect. To achieve this, the designers must understand the users' tasks, goals, and their mental model. Users should feel confident in exploring. This can be achieved if they can undo the results of the action anytime. Users feel more comfortable with interfaces in which their actions do not cause irreversible consequences. Actions should provide equal results irrespective of when the user invokes them. Actions should also be available to users all the time.

❑ **Alternate interaction techniques should be supported**
Users should be able to choose the most appropriate interaction method. User interfaces should be flexible enough to accommodate a wide range of user skills, interactions, and usage environments. This requires support for different interaction devices. Each of them is optimized for certain users. Users should be allowed to switch between methods to accomplish a single interaction. Providing different interaction techniques recognizes different user abilities. This includes disabilities as well as user preferences and work environments.

❑ **User interfaces should make users feel the progress**
Users should be able to see the progress and assess the current state always. Any action that a user invokes should provide feedback immediately. Delays lower the confidence of users. Users should always work with up-to-date information. Information should be updated immediately, or refreshed as soon as possible, so that users are not making incorrect decisions or assumptions. This is particularly important when multiple users are working on the same information simultaneously. This requirement might be difficult to achieve, particularly in web-based user interfaces. If it cannot be achieved, the users should be notified.

❑ **Adequate help should be provided**
User interfaces should protect users from errors as much as possible. They should also provide help, either automatically or upon request. This includes visual cues, lists of choices, reminders, wizards, and other aids. Humans are much better at recognition than recall. Users should therefore never have to rely on their own memory for something the information system already knows. If the information is in the information system in any form, it should be presented to the user. User interfaces should also provide two-way communication, which includes confirming and clarifying the requests. The communication should be interactive, should present relevant information, access to related information and context-sensitive help. The help should provide instructions following this maxim: users know what they want to accomplish, but sometimes they find it difficult to express their desires using the user interface.

❑ **User interfaces should have good visual design**
The visual design of the user interface should support the stated design principles and support the communication. The purpose of visual design is to support the user interface usability and should be an integral part of the design process. The result should be an intuitive and familiar representation of the user interface. Therefore, we should eliminate visual elements that do not contribute directly to visual communication. We should address visual hierarchy through understanding the importance of users' tasks. Important aspects can be made more visible, using relative position, contrast, color, and size appropriately.

Types of User Interfaces

Now that we are familiar with the design guidelines for user interfaces it is time to ask questions concerning what types of user interfaces will be interesting to us. User interfaces have come a long way from terminal command and character-based user interfaces to graphical and web-based user interfaces. The development goes in several directions towards intelligent and adaptive user interfaces and will open many new opportunities in the future.

For now we will look at the two major types of user interfaces:

❑ **Graphical user interfaces (GUIs)** – or user interfaces that take over full control of the client screen or window

❑ **Web-based user interfaces** – or user interfaces that use markup languages for presentation

GUIs take over full control of the client device screen, or at least the windows in which they are executing. Today, support for GUIs is provided by operating systems, or as a graphical add-on (shell). Applications typically use elements of GUIs provided by the operation system, but they can also add their own elements. GUIs provide a rich graphical functionality and good responsibility of the user interface to the user input. Its control of the client GUI is usually tightly coupled with the client device, such as desktop or handheld computers. They have to be developed for each client type separately. Graphical user interfaces usually require a lot of code and have to program complex GUI APIs. Therefore they are often called **fat clients**.

793

Web-based user interfaces, on the other hand, give up full control over the user interface appearance. They use markup languages, such as HTML or Wireless Markup Language (WML), to describe the user interface. For final representation they share this responsibility with the client software that is responsible for presenting the markup – usually web browsers. Web-based user interfaces have to generate markup language, which is usually simpler than programming complex GUI APIs. Therefore they are called **thin clients**.

Web-based user interfaces are not directly dependent on the GUI provided by the underlying operating system, and are therefore much more independent of the client device. This opens up the possibility to support a diverse range of different client devices without requiring redeveloping the user interface for each client device, which saves time and effort. Web-based user interfaces place different demands on user interface navigation. Through a web browser the user can always influence the navigation (for example back and forward buttons).

Markup languages provide more and more functions that make web-based user interfaces more GUI-like. However, the major architectural difference remains: web-based user interfaces require two tiers, the client tier, where the web browser (or similar application that interprets the markup) is running on the client device, and the web component tier, where the markup (for example HTML) is prepared through communication with the back-end components. On the other hand, graphical user interfaces always communicate directly with the back-end components.

Let us now focus our discussion on the J2EE platform and look at how graphical and web-based user interfaces are supported there.

Graphical User Interfaces (Fat Clients) in J2EE

Graphical user interfaces in the J2EE platform are developed as applications, which are deployed on the client tier. There are several possibilities for fat clients:

❑ Usually GUI applications are developed as Java applications

❑ GUI applications can also be applets, executing within web browsers, but using GUI elements

❑ GUI applications can also be developed in other programming languages (such a C++, Delphi, and so on)

The common characteristic of GUI fat clients is that they interact with the back-end components directly. Typically they will interact with components on the business logic tier. For this they will use standard J2EE technologies and protocols. The most important are:

❑ IIOP for fat clients using RMI-IIOP or CORBA

❑ JMS interface for asynchronous access using MOM

Fat clients use IIOP and JMS for communication with the business logic tier usually from inside a company's networks (intranets). Unfortunately, firewalls and other security mechanisms usually do not allow us to use these protocols when accessing the information system from outside, meaning the Internet. We have discussed this in Chapter 3 and Chapter 11.

The following figure shows fat clients and their interaction with the business logic tier:

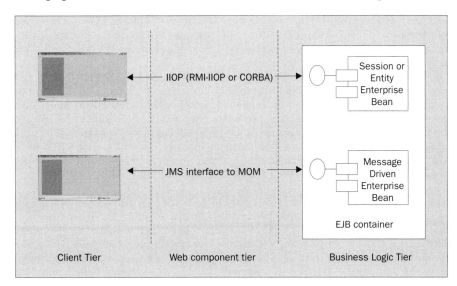

Technically, fat clients might interact with the EIS tier directly too. For this they can use additional protocols, such as JDBC to access databases directly, or proprietary protocols to access existing applications. However, accessing the EIS tier directly breaks the tier separation rules that we defined in Chapter 3 and is therefore not recommended, as we will see also a little later in this chapter.

Using Java for developing GUI applications deserves special attention. The fact that Java is platform and operating system independent changes the way in which graphical user interfaces are developed in J2EE.

The Java platform cannot rely directly on the GUI of a certain operating system.

Rather, it offers GUI services itself and either maps these to the actual operating system on which the application is executing or takes over the responsibility for presenting (drawing) the GUI elements. For this the Java platform provides the Java Foundation Classes/Swing.

This additional layer means that GUI interfaces in Java applications and applets often have not offered the same performance as GUIs developed in other programming languages, which have used GUIs of a certain operating system directly. However, the latest releases of JFC/Swing have managed to solve almost all problems regarding performance.

GUI applications or fat clients also have the disadvantage that they have to be installed in the client computer, which often requires the setting up of different parameters or supporting products, particularly middleware products. The changes in the fat clients then require reinstallations, which increases the maintenance costs and is not really flexible enough, particularly if we would like to allow the access to certain functions to be public.

The Java platform has addressed this problem with two technologies. First Java applets provide a possibility to automatically transfer an applet from the web server (web component tier) to the client tier. The applet can then execute inside the web browser. The fact that browsers were not very quick in supporting the latest versions of the Java platform and, even more importantly, the fact that an applet could not get access to the whole window and all GUI elements, made applets less practical for full-featured GUI user interfaces.

The second approach, which addresses the problem of installing applications on the client tier, is Java Web Start, a new application deployment technology, which makes it possible to launch full-featured Java applications from a web browser. The procedure of installation and setup are automated, which simplifies the deployment and solves maintenance problems. Applications started with Java Web Start running independent of the web browser (although they may be started from the web browser), which means that they can display rich GUI interfaces and that we can even shut down the web browser after we have started the application. Java Web Start will be a part of JDK version 1.4.

GUI fat clients are most commonly used for clients that will spend a considerable amount of time using a certain application, and clients that can be identified, so that the client application can be installed on their computer. These will most likely be users inside a company, executing in the trusted internal network. Users from inside the company will use the information system a lot, therefore they will make use of the advantages of GUI clients, such as rich graphical interfaces, low latency (that is, good responsiveness), additional verification of user entry, 'intelligent' assistance, better control over the layout and formatting, richer navigation, and asynchronous notification of changes. GUI user interfaces will be more useful for them and will outweigh the disadvantages, such as the development and installation overhead.

The development of rich graphical user interfaces is a complex topic that requires the knowledge of related libraries, in our case JFC/Swing. On the other hand, GUI development is a well-known area that is comprehensively covered in many books. A complete review of developing GUI clients is somewhat beyond the scope of this chapter. The reader is encouraged to look into the related literature, for example, the book *Professional Java Custom UI Components*, from Wrox Press, ISBN 1-861003-64-1.

Web-based User Interfaces (Thin Clients) in J2EE

Web-based user interfaces are developed as web components in the J2EE platform and deployed on the web component tier. Web components in J2EE platform can be developed as servlets or JSP pages.

Web components are extensions of the web server. They format the user interface using a markup language (such as HTML, or a vocabulary of XML – XHTML, WML, and so on). Web components generate the markup from their interaction with the business logic tier, where they invoke the operations on the components, such as EJBs and other business logic tier components. Web components use the same protocols as GUI fat clients to communicate with the business logic tier:

- ❑   IIOP for web components using RMI-IIOP or CORBA
- ❑   JMS interface for asynchronous access using MOM

Technically, web components might interact with the EIS tier directly too. For this they can use additional protocols, such as JDBC to access databases directly, or proprietary protocols to access existing applications. Accessing the EIS tier directly, however, breaks the tier separation rules that we defined in Chapter 3 and is therefore not recommended, as we will see a little later in this chapter.

As we have mentioned before, web-based thin clients do not control the client device directly. They use the web server functionality to transfer the markup to the client tier, typically over HTTP or HTTPS (HTTP over SSL). Markup is then presented on the client tier using an application such as a web browser.

Thin clients are therefore partitioned between the client tier and the web component tier. The client tier is relatively simple and does not require us to install any components specific to the application or information system we are using. However, we do have to provide a web browser on the client tier, and to use the latest functions of web technologies usually an up-to-date version of the web browser is required.

The following figure shows a schematic representation of the web-based thin clients in the J2EE integration architecture:

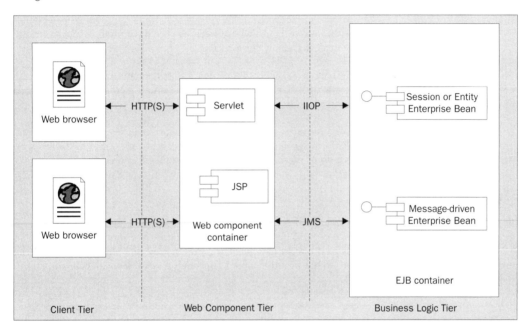

The web component tier is usually located inside the company network (intranet). Therefore, it can use the IIOP and JMS to access the business logic tier without problems connected with firewalls (which usually block these protocols), as we will see later in this chapter. The content (as markup) that is delivered to clients uses HTTP or HTTPS, which can pass through firewalls without problems. Web components are centralized on server computers; as such, the changes and modifications are much easier to maintain. They only have to be deployed on the web component tier.

Web-based user interfaces are particularly suitable when we have to support different devices (platforms, operating systems) on the client tier and we do not want to make additional effort to develop GUI clients for each device separately. They are very appropriate for clients where we do not want or cannot afford to install applications on their devices. Therefore, they are suitable for anonymous clients, which can access some functionality over the web browser. Web-based interfaces are also appropriate for business-to-business (B2B) and business-to-consumer (B2C) interactions, as we will see in Chapter 18.

The disadvantages of web-based clients compared to GUI clients include the following:

❑ The graphical interface is not as rich because the final layout is controlled by the web browser and is therefore not completely the responsibility of the information system

❑ There is not as much possibility to control the flow of the application because users can always use the web browser navigation buttons for example

❑ Higher latency, because the client tier has to communicate with the web component tier

❑ Not all input validation can be done on the client tier because some data is required that can only be accessed from the web component tier

❑ There are fewer possibilities for intelligent assistants, wizards, and so on

❑ Asynchronous notification is more difficult (where refreshes are most often used, because the web component tier cannot call the client tier directly)

The latest developments in markup languages, such as XHTML 1.0 (Extensible Hyper Text Markup Language), the use of XML together with XSLT, attempt to solve the mentioned problems and make web-based user interfaces more comparable to GUI clients.

In the last few years, web-based user interfaces have become the predominant way to build modern presentation layers. In the J2EE platform servlets and JSP pages form a powerful duo for building web-based thin clients. We will discuss both of these technologies later in this chapter.

Enterprise Portal

In EAI, the objective of the presentation tier is to provide a common, unified, and highly usable user interface that will support business tasks and processes. The presentation tier should also provide access to relevant information as easily as possible. In Chapter 1 we emphasized that one of the major reasons for EAI is for access to information, so the portal-oriented approach is worth considering when building the presentation tier.

> **A portal is a single entry point for the user that offers a range of services and information resources.**

IBM specifies portals as Personalization, Organization, Resources, Tracking, Access and Location. Today the word portal is used in many different contexts, including Internet portals, intranet portals, extranet portals, and enterprise portals. We will focus our discussion on enterprise portals.

Enterprise portals have two major objectives:

❑ Integration and aggregation of the business applications presentation tier into a unified user interface, which accesses the business logic through well-defined interfaces. This way the portal centralizes access to different applications and offers a uniform view on different integrated applications that look like one large integrated application.

❑ Integration and aggregation of different types of information, the source of which can be inside or outside the company. This way they deliver up-to-date information, which is important for decision making.

One of the major features of enterprise portals is **personalization**. Personalization on one hand provides information and choices for tasks that are adapted to a particular user. On the other hand, to be able to adapt to the user, they have to gather information about the users. Personalization can be achieved in two ways. One is explicit personalization, where the user has to define which information and which tasks they would like to access. Second is implicit personalization, where the user is not directly aware that the portal is trying to adapt to the way the user works. This requires that the system implements collaborative filtering techniques, which trace and audit the way the user works and try to gather as much information as possible about the user.

Enterprise portals are usually developed using a web-based user interface approach. So, in the J2EE platform the appropriate technologies are the same as for web-based clients: servlets and JSP pages. The fact remains that a portal will usually be very large, have a lot of different options and functions, and will require a lot of time and effort to develop.

Instead of using basic technologies, companies can adopt a portal server, which already provides the basic functionality of enterprise portals. A portal server however has to be adapted to the needs of the company and its integrated information system. Such modification is usually much quicker and the resulting enterprise portal is more robust because it builds on already proven solutions. A large number of portal servers currently on the market support J2EE, so they are a perfect fit into the J2EE integration architecture. Portal servers are a relatively new technology; at the time of writing the most important J2EE-related enterprise portal servers include:

- ❑ BEA WebLogic Portal (http://www.bea.com/products/weblogic/portal/index.shtml)
- ❑ BroadVision InfoExchange Portal (http://www.broadvision.com)
- ❑ Computer Associates Jasmine Portal (http://ca.com/products/jasmineii_portal/)
- ❑ IBM Enterprise Information Portal (http://www-4.ibm.com/software/data/eip/)
- ❑ iPlanet's Portal Server (http://www.iplanet.com/products/iplanet_portal/home_portal.html)
- ❑ Oracle 9iAS Portal (http://www.oracle.com/ip/deploy/ias/portal/index.html)
- ❑ Woolamai.com Personalized Enterprise Information Portal (http://www.woolamai.com/ie.html)

We can see that the major J2EE application server vendors, such as BEA, IBM, Oracle, and others have recognized the importance of enterprise portals and offer portal servers as a part of their application server family of products. Portal servers will play a major role in the development of presentation tier integration. In this book, we do not cover particular products, so we will not go further into the details of portal servers. Rather we will look at the technologies that the portal servers use underneath, such as servlets and JSP pages. Understanding these technologies will allow us to become familiar with and understand different portal servers.

Before looking at the presentation tier technologies we will take a quick look at the prerequisites of presentation tier integration and discuss some security- and transaction- related issues.

Presentation Integration Fulfills the Multi-tier Goal

Irrelevant of whether we build GUI, web-based user interfaces, or enterprise portals, we have to understand that presentation integration is not simply about building the new presentation tier on top of existing applications. A simple extension of existing applications with modern graphical or web-based user interfaces would have several drawbacks:

❑ The functionality of existing applications stays the same. It is only presented in a new user interface, which just gives the applications a nicer look and feel.

❑ Such extension focuses on a single application only, so it does not solve the initial problem, where users have to switch between different applications to get a certain job done.

❑ Even if we extend existing applications with user interfaces that spawn over more than one existing application, such user interfaces would incorporate a lot of logic. They would have to know which existing applications to connect to and how to invoke functions on them. Due to the diversity of existing applications, which we have identified in previous chapters, this would make the user interfaces very complex and difficult to manage.

❑ User interfaces that are tied to certain existing applications directly are inflexible for changes and replacements, as shown in the figure below. If we modify or replace one of the existing applications with a new generation application, we have to modify the user interface and the way they interact with the back-end applications. The direct interaction of user interfaces with existing applications is shown in the next figure:

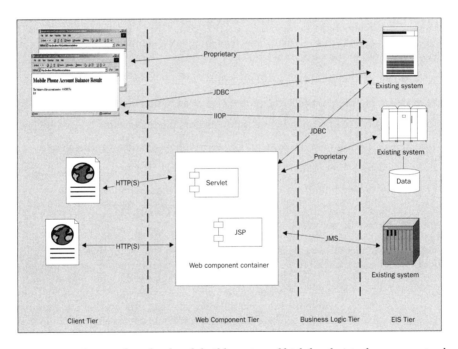

Presentation integration, on the other hand, builds on top of high-level virtual components, developed in business method level integration phase. Higher-level virtual components expose business oriented interfaces, though which they enable clients (user interfaces) to use this functionality on a high abstraction level. The fact that higher-level virtual components communicate with lower-level virtual components, wrappers, and APIs of existing applications, is hidden from the clients.

> **Presentation integration is not simply an extension of existing applications with graphical or web-based user interfaces. Rather, it is the development of the complete presentation layer of top of the business level integration.**

For presentation integration to be successful we should have done the business level integration first, which is the major prerequisite. Business level integration has provided a foundation through which we have performed the following important steps in the integration:

❑   We have defined a global architecture of the integrated information system

❑   We have implemented the functionality of the integrated information system through reuse of existing applications

❑   The functionality of the integrated system is available through high-level business interfaces, exposed by virtual components

❑   Virtual components are presented in J2EE-compliant component technologies

❑   The fact that the existing applications implement the functionality of virtual components is hidden from the client (user interface) so they should be unaware of which existing systems are in the back

Thus, business method level integration does not bring any visible changes to regular users – they still have to use existing applications through their existing user interfaces. In other words, they still use "old applications". The fact that business level integration provided common high-level virtual components, through which functions of the integrated information system are accessible, has not resulted in a direct, visible benefit to users.

The presentation integration phase is therefore a crucial task, which will allow users to actually see the results of the integrated information system. Presentation integration adds the client and web component tiers and therefore exploits the multi-tier integration architecture that we have defined in Chapter 3. Therefore, the presentation integration phase should not be delayed – we should make sure that it is addressed in early iterations of the integration process, as described in Chapter 4.

The architecture of the integrated information system after the presentation integration phase has been accomplished is shown on the figure below. We can see that the client and web component tier access the higher-level virtual components on the business logic tier:

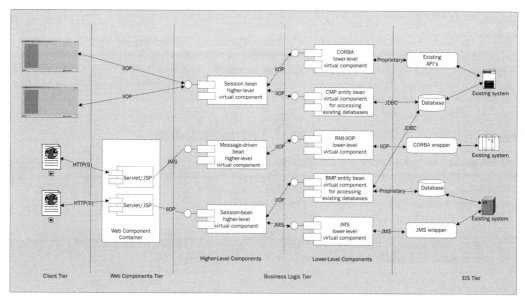

> **The presentation layer built on top of virtual components is unaware of the details of existing applications – it is unaware of the fact that existing applications are reused.**

The presentation layer uses the exposed business interfaces of high-level virtual components on the business logic tier that have been designed anew, and therefore aligns cleanly with the integrated information system.

This also means that such a presentation layer is highly flexible. We can make changes to existing applications and to components on the business logic tier. As long as we leave the component interfaces on the business logic tier components unchanged, the presentation layer remains unchanged too. This is the reason why component interfaces have a crucial role in multi-tier architectures and should be defined very carefully, after the analysis and design of the integrated system, and not in an ad hoc manner.

The fact that component interfaces are the "least common denominator" for interaction between tiers also means that we can replace and re-engineer existing applications and replace them with new developments without influencing the presentation layer or the other applications that interact with the replaced existing applications through these interfaces.

Pragmatic Selection and Prioritizing of User Interfaces to Renew

Developing the new presentation layer for the integrated information system is a huge task. The development of user interfaces should be addressed iteratively (as with all other phases – refer to Chapter 4 for more details). This means that the business level and presentation level integration will be interlaced. We will not first completely finish the business level integration but will proceed in iterative cycles.

To control the iterative development better it makes sense selecting the user interfaces and prioritizing them on a "most wanted" basis. We should then implement the most needed interfaces first. Usually these interfaces will provide the functionality that could not be accessed before integration. That way we will be able to quickly deliver solutions for the most necessary requirements.

Usually the least urgent user interfaces will be those that do not require any integration between applications, that is, functionally the same user interfaces that have already been provided by existing applications. Such user interfaces, supporting tasks like data entry, which have been adequately supported by existing applications already, should be low on our priority list. Sometimes, when the resources and time do not allow, we might even consider leaving these user interfaces as they are.

Presentation Integration and Transactions

Although the newly developed presentation tier accesses the functionality of the existing application through virtual components, it brings together the operations of different existing applications. These different existing applications need to be updated as a part of a single operation. To guarantee consistency, such operations are best performed inside transactions.

> **If we have followed the design guidelines from previous chapters, we should have delegated the transaction management to the business logic tier.**

We have designed high-level virtual components, which model business processes and are naturally executed inside a transaction. In other words, we have provided component interfaces to business logic, where business methods are transaction boundaries.

Neither the web component tier nor the client tier is responsible for starting and ending transactions. Their management is done on the business logic tier, using programmatic or declarative transaction management. Managing transactions from the business logic tier has several advantages:

❑ It simplifies the design of the presentation layer considerably

❑ It does not require the transferring of the transaction contexts between the client or web component tier and business logic tier

❑ It improves performance, because it shortens the duration of transactions

For more information about transaction management have a look at Chapter 3 and Chapter 15.

Security Considerations in Presentation Integration

With the development of the new presentation layer, the information and functionality of the integrated information system becomes more easily accessible. Therefore, we have to pay attention to the security questions, irrespective of the type of user interface we've chosen. Obviously this will depend on the security policy of the company and its structure.

To address security we will have to use security mechanisms. The Java platform provides the Java Authentication and Authorization Service (JAAS) that provides access to security mechanisms (for more information, refer to Chapter 3 and Chapter 16). Security mechanisms in J2EE can be performed programmatically or declaratively. With the former approach, the application components have to provide the necessary code, whereas with the latter approach we mark the application components at deployment and specify the required security mechanisms that have to be performed. The responsibility for performing security mechanisms is then taken over by the container and/or application server. J2EE application servers provide security functionality completely outside of the application components.

In the presentation level integration phase we will have to consider the security mechanisms relevant to the presentation layer, that is, for the client and the web component tiers. As we have seen before, the presentation layer will access the functionality through higher-level virtual components on the business logic tier. Therefore, the presentation layer will use the security defined for higher-level virtual components. The question thus becomes how to integrate the presentation and business logic tier security. Notice that the issues of achieving security on the business logic tier, and integration with the security mechanisms of existing applications, have been discussed in Chapter 16.

To address the presentation layer security and possible integration with business logic tier security we will look at the following security mechanisms:

❑ **Authentication** – a mechanism where the parties involved in an interaction prove that they are the ones they claim to be

❑ **Authorization** – a mechanism to control the access and limit it to the resources that a party is allowed to access

❑ **Communication channel protection** – uses mechanisms to protect communication ways between parties, for example with encryption

❑ **Auditing** – a mechanism for capturing and storing the information about related events that are significant for security

Authentication

Authentication is the mechanism by which the parties involved in communication prove that they are acting on behalf of a specific user or system. Authentication is often performed in two steps. First, based on a password, or some other secret information, an **authentication context** is created. This stores the identity and can create proofs of identity. Second, the authentication context is used to perform authentication of all involved entities.

It is very useful to use authentication when the user first accesses the information system. Once the user is authenticated, the following steps should be based on his role and level in the information system. Such authentication is often referred to as "single sign-on". A logical place to implement authentication is therefore in the presentation layer.

The important question now becomes how we can control the access to the authentication context, and how we propagate it to the business logic tier. Possibilities include the following variations:

❑ After a user is authenticated the authentication context is made available to other trusted components (for example, those that are part of the same application)

❑ The caller can delegate the authentication context to the called component

❑ All processes that have been started by the user who performed the authentication inherit access to the authentication context

The propagation of authorization context, particularly between tiers, introduces a certain overhead. Therefore it is desirable to set up so-called trusted environments in which the components can communicate without authentication. Such environments are called **protection domains**.

In J2EE, the container provides the boundary on which the authentication is performed when outside callers try to access the components inside the container. However, the container boundaries are not always the same as the protection domain boundaries. This makes it possible to gather the web component tier and business logic tier into a single protection domain. This scenario, where the web component tier trusts the business logic tier, is shown on the next figure:

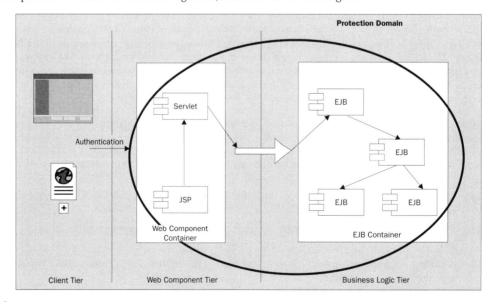

The authentication in J2EE is based on users, realms, and groups. Users represent people that use the information system. A realm is a collection of users that are authenticated in the same way. J2EE supports two realm types: default and certificate. Default realm is used to authenticate all clients except web clients. Web clients have to use the certificate realm. Users of the default realm can belong to a group. A group is a category of users that share a certain role, for example customers, employees, and so on.

In the J2EE architecture a client typically has to go through the container boundaries to get access to web or EJB components. In this case the container performs the authorization. The container can do it in different ways. If it performs it when the client first accesses a protected resource then it makes lazy authentication.

The J2EE web container can support four authentication mechanisms:

❑ **HTTP basic authentication** – the web container makes the authentication based on the username and password obtained from the client. The problem is that the username and password are sent over the wire as plain text, which is not very secure.

❑ **Form-based authentication** – similar to HTTP basic authentication, but it enables that the developers to customize the user interface for authentication presented by web browsers. It shares the same disadvantages as basic authentication.

❑ **HTTPS mutual authentication** – bases the authentication on X.509 certificates that the client and the server exchange to establish their identities. For certificate exchange an SSL-protected channel is used.

❑ **HTTP digest authentication** – is similar to HTTP basic authentication. However, the client does not send the username and password to the server, but rather sends a message digest along with its HTTP request message. The client calculates the digest with a one-way hash algorithm that it applies to the HTTP request message and the password. The web container performs the same algorithm and compares both digests. This way the password is not sent over the wire.

Note that the first three mechanisms are required, whereas the fourth is optional and might not be supported in all J2EE application servers. Hybrid mechanisms that feature HTTP basic, form-based, or digest authentication over SSL can also be supported by J2EE application servers.

Authorization

After users have been authenticated, they will access components on the business logic tier of the integrated information system. Not all authenticated clients will be allowed to access all components or their methods. To limit and control this access we will use authorization.

Authorization mechanisms control the access and limit the interactions of the clients with the components to enforce integrity, confidentiality, and availability constraints. Containers in the J2EE architecture are the authorization boundaries, which exist inside the authentication boundaries. Authorization is always performed after successful authentication. For incoming calls the container checks the security attributes against the authorization permissions.

> **Defining the authorization constraints is the most difficult security issue.**

When designing the authorization rules and selecting the protected resources, we have to ensure consistency. We have to make sure that authorization is performed at each entry point where a component might be accessed.

Fortunately, authorization will not have to be addressed in the presentation integration phase only. The presentation layer will rely on the business logic components, for which we have defined the authorization constraints in the business level integration phase (for more information refer to Chapter 16).

Still, it is necessary to perform some authorization on the web component tier, particularly for limiting the visibility of the choices in the user interfaces according to each user authorization constraints. Authorization for web components, as well as business logic components, in J2EE can be implemented in different levels of granularity. It can specify the authorization permissions on a component level or on a method level. Method level granularity enables fine-grained control over who is allowed to invoke certain methods and who is not. Authorization permissions are usually specified as access control lists for each component.

There are two possibilities how to specify the authorization permissions in J2EE – programmatic and declarative authorization. With the declarative authorization the access control lists in J2EE are defined in terms of permissions, where the actual component deployers have to specify who can do what. The access control permissions are specified in the deployment descriptor. The deployment descriptor defines the security roles, which are logical privileges, and associates them with components, from which actual permissions to access components are derived. The container will allow access to methods of components only if the authorization has been performed successfully.

A web or business logic component can also utilize programmatic authorization and perform additional controls before it actually executes the request. For this it has access to the security context. The web components have to use the `HttpServletRequest.isUserInRole()` method, where the EJB components can access this information with the `EJBContext.isCallerInRole()`. With these methods the components can figure out whether a privilege has been granted to the client. To use these methods the roles have to be specified in the deployment descriptor.

Communication Channel Protection

In addition to authentication and authorization, we also have to consider the communication channel protection mechanisms. Clients almost always execute in untrusted environments and need to be protected. This is particularly true for web-based clients, where the data is transferred over the Internet. This does not mean that communication channel protection is not significant for GUI clients. But, because they usually execute inside company's intranets, they might not be exposed to the possible attacks as much as web-based clients.

There are three main types of possible attacks to messages transferred between tiers:

❏   Messages can be monitored to acquire confidential information

❏   Messages can be captured and reused as they are, for the benefit of the attacker

❏   Messages can be intercepted and modified to change their purpose and then forwarded to the recipients

An effective way to prevent these attacks is the communication channel protection, which ensures that communication between parties is not being intercepted, modified, or tampered with in any other way, so communication is kept confidential.

In presentation level integration the most important communication will be between the clients and the higher-level virtual components. GUI clients will access the virtual components on the business logic tier directly, using IIOP or JMS. Web-based clients will first interact with the web components (such as servlets or JSP pages) using HTTP. Web components will interact with the virtual components on the business logic tier using IIOP or JMS.

A common way to achieve protection of all mentioned protocols is through the use of the Secure Sockets Layer (SSL) protocol, originally developed by Netscape. It is now universally accepted for authenticated and encrypted communication between clients and servers. The SSL protocol runs above the TCP/IP protocol and below higher-level protocols, such as HTTP, IIOP, JMS protocols used by MOM, and other protocols, such as SOAP, or LDAP as shown in the following figure:

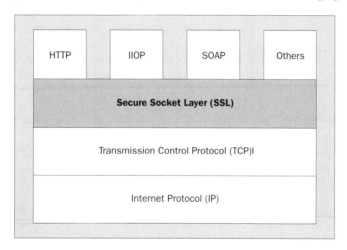

SSL achieves communication channel protection with encryption. All data sent between the client and server is encrypted by the sending software and decrypted by the receiving software. In addition SSL protects messages from being altered in transit. This guarantees a high level of confidentiality.

For encryption, the SSL protocol uses a variety of different cryptographic algorithms and key exchange algorithms, such as Data Encryption Standard (DES), Digital Signature Algorithm (DSA), Key Exchange Algorithm (KEA), Message Digest (MD5) algorithm developed by Rivest, and RSA, a public-key algorithm for both encryption and authentication, developed by Rivest, Shamir, and Adleman.

The client and the server may support different cryptographic algorithms, depending on factors such as which version of SSL, company policies regarding encryption, and government export restrictions on cryptographic software. SSL versions 2.0 and 3.0 therefore support overlapping sets of cryptographic algorithms. When a particular client and server make the SSL handshake, they identify the strongest cryptographic algorithm they have in common and use it for the SSL session.

In addition to communication channel protection, encryption SSL also provides client and server authentication with the use of public-key cryptography and certificates.

Auditing

Auditing is a procedure where we capture and store the information about related events that are significant for security. With this information we can identify users and systems that are responsible for their actions. Although it can also be used when we need to track what users do over the course of a session, auditing is particularly useful after security breaches when we want to identify what exactly has happened and who was allowed to use the system.

The auditing should be performed by the component deployers or system administrators and should be powerful enough to provide different auditing options, like auditing events where some constraints have or have not been satisfied, like auditing of all events for instance. Audition should not require that the developers or integrators develop additional code. Rather, it should be provided by the infrastructure that can be configured by system administrators.

The J2EE specification currently does not require, but only recommends, that the J2EE application servers provide support for auditing. Existing EIS might implement auditing and we have to get a clear understanding regarding what, how, and when it has been audited. Only then will this information will be useful to solve security-related questions.

Firewalls and Demilitarized Zone

A common approach to protect the company intranet from unauthorized access from outside is by using firewalls. Firewalls are a set of related programs that, together with the defined security policies, monitor and prevent outsiders from accessing the resources in the intranet. It also controls what outside resource the users from inside the company have access to.

Firewalls work closely with network router programs, because they examine network packets. A firewall is often installed in a specially designated computer separate from the rest of the network so that no incoming request can get directly at network internal resources.

Companies often use more than one firewall to protect their networks.

> **A demilitarized zone (DMZ) is a configuration of multiple firewalls that add layers of security between the Internet and a company's intranet where critical data and business logic reside.**

The DMZ is particularly suitable for multi-tier architectures and aligns well with the multi-tier J2EE integration architecture. A typical DMZ configuration has an outer firewall between the public Internet and the web component tier (where the web servers and web components reside), and an inner firewall between the web component and business logic tiers. The components that provide access to information system functions and data are located behind the inner firewall. The area between the two firewalls gives the DMZ configuration its name. Additional firewalls can further safeguard access to components and databases.

The figure below shows a typical configuration of two firewalls:

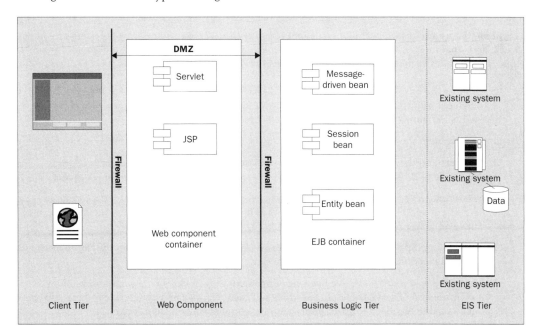

The advantage of using a DMZ is heightened security. Its drawbacks are the more complex administration and maintenance that it incurs.

Now that we have become familiar with the objectives of the presentation tier integration phase and related security issues, let us take a look at the analysis and design activities.

Analysis and Design of the Presentation Tier

Usable user interfaces (as we have defined them in the first section) for the integrated information system require a lot of effort to develop. Developing them cannot be done in an ad hoc style, but should follow the same activities that we have followed in the other integration phases.

In Chapter 4 we defined the integration process, and we saw that integration usually proceeds in four phases (data, application interface, business method, and presentation levels). For each phase we also defined eight technical activities, as shown in the following figure. In this section we will focus on the **problem domain analysis** and **design** activities for the presentation integration phase, the complete procedure of which is shown below:

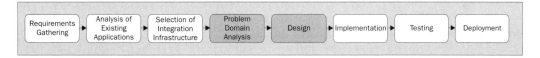

Implementation, testing, and deployment will be addressed in the next sections of this chapter, where we will address servlets and JSP pages.

Fulfilling the user interface usability goals first requires that we understand who the users are, how they work, and what their tasks are. In other words we should attempt to "step into their shoes". When analyzing and designing the presentation tier we should:

❑ Define the business goals that we would like to achieve with the new user interfaces. This includes defining who the users will be, what their prior knowledge is, what productivity is expected, how much time they will have for learning, and so on.

❑ Understand the users and involve them in the user interface design as much as possible.

❑ Understand the tasks the users do, but also assess any alternative scenarios in order to optimize performance of a certain task. Users should be included in this assessment.

❑ Design the user interfaces in terms of user experience. Such designs should be done in teams, where, in addition to the code developers and layout designers, users are included too and have an active role.

❑ Evaluating different user interface designs is very important and not too difficult because users generate feedback early if we show them design prototypes.

❑ After the user interfaces have been developed we should make continual observations where we listen and observe the users and their satisfaction with the user interfaces. From this we can get valuable feedback for user interface improvement in later iterations.

First let's look at the analysis of user interfaces.

User Interface Analysis

The goal of analysis in user-centric user interface development is to develop user interfaces that will fit the users as best as possible. Therefore in the user interface analysis we will have to consider questions such as who the users are, what their usability requirements are, and which tasks they perform with the integrated information system. The user interface analysis will therefore be done in two large steps:

❑ Definition of usability requirements

❑ Modeling user tasks

Both of these steps have several sub steps, shown schematically in the diagram opposite:

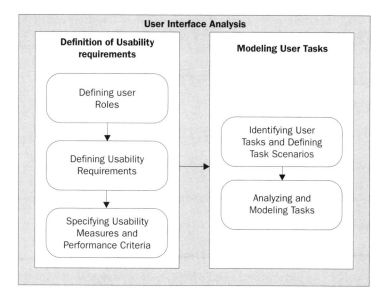

Although the steps are shown as a sequence they do not necessarily need to be performed one-by-one.

Indeed, if we facilitate an iterative development approach, we will usually need to go over these steps several times and not always in a sequential order. We'll take a closer look at these steps in the following sections.

Defining User Roles

Defining the user roles is the first step in the user interfaces analysis. As we have mentioned several times already, we will have to identify which users will use the integrated presentation tier. The best approach is to group these users into roles. In each role there will usually be several users. However, a single user might also have more than one role. The first step will therefore be to define user roles. We have to be careful to include all roles, also those less obvious. Here we can help ourselves with the requirements specification, where we have defined use cases and identified actors. User roles and actors should be the same. For more information on use cases and the requirements specification refer to Chapter 4.

We will also have to describe each user role. This description will differ from the description of actors, because here we will want to know what the users do and how they feel about doing this. We should meet with users and gather their opinions about existing applications and how they would like to work with the integrated information system. We should write a specification for each user role.

Defining Usability Requirements

After we are familiar with the user roles we should identify the usability requirements. We should focus on questions such as how can a user interface contribute to the effectiveness and productivity of the organization (and the employees), how can it help reduce errors and overheads, and how would the users like to access the information that has not been provided by existing applications.

811

We should also rate the performance of tasks that users will perform, allow error rates for intermediate users, the possible learning time for new users and the retention over time. We should also consider the subjective satisfaction. All these factors will influence how we will design the user interface.

Specifying Usability Measures and Performance Criteria

For all usability requirements we should define what will be measured, how they will be measured, and the worst acceptable levels for the integrated information system. Defining this early enough is critical for assessing the user interface usability in the later stages of the development. If we specify the usability requirements strictly, then we will be able to assess how successful we have been. However, we have to be aware that it will be difficult (or even impossible) to measure some usability requirements of every iteration.

We should also define the current performance level of usability requirements provided by existing applications (we will actually measure them if possible). If we also specify how existing applications performed on these requirements, we will be able to assess how much better the integrated information system is.

Identifying User Tasks and Defining Task Scenarios

Next we should identify the tasks that the users will perform. To define the tasks we should observe users at work and discuss their activities with them to classify tasks correctly. We should analyze the business processes and the events that trigger human activities (such as reaching the end of the month, the arrival of an order or a payment, and so on).

Then we should define the common task scenario that includes all possible variations of the same task, performed by different users (humans). We should not forget to supplement these task scenarios with exceptional situations and how they are handled. Defining scenarios has several benefits because scenarios are more representative than simple tasks from each individual user, which makes prototyping more realistic.

Analyzing and Modeling Tasks

After we have identified user tasks and defined the scenarios we should analyze and model them, we should gather the relevant information about each task, such as duration, how often they are performed, how many errors can be introduced, and so on. We should rank the tasks by their priority, where the tasks with a higher volume, and time-critical tasks, usually get the higher priorities.

We analyze and model user tasks to aid the UI design process later. Therefore we should divide the tasks into relevant subtasks and rank their priorities to get a task hierarchy. This will increase the complexity considerably, therefore we should not go into too many details, but we should also not stop too early. Clearly, to judge accurately and adequately for each case we need experience.

Once we have a stable task hierarchy, we should consider possible conditions that might arise during performing a certain task. These conditions can be that input information is missing or it is incorrect; how could the task be interrupted to perform something that is more urgent; what happens if a user makes an error, and so on. For each of these we should consider additional subtasks to provide the most pleasant experience to the users. With this analysis we will also get a feeling of the complexity of real-world, every day activities, which are often much more complicated that the first simplified models.

With the models of user tasks we have completed the user interface analysis activity and we should proceed to the user interface design.

User Interface Design

In the user interface design activity, we will define the model of the user interface as it will be implemented, tested, and deployed. Therefore in this phase, we have to ensure that the system behavior is comprehensible and intuitive to the users, that the user experience with the UI layout and design is satisfactory, and that the design model used for implementation is accurate enough.

To achieve the stated goals we will perform the UI design in three main steps, each of which has several substeps, as shown in the following figure (again, although the steps are shown as a sequence they do not necessarily need to be performed in turn):

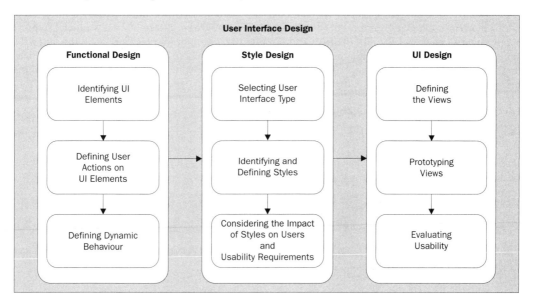

With reference to the previous figure, in the next few sections we'll examine each stage in the user interface design process.

Identifying UI Elements

First, we will identify the UI elements with the information gathered in the analysis, particularly from the task model. For additional information we can look at the class, object, component, and data models that we have developed in the problem domain analysis and design in previous integration phases. Finally, we might get additional information by talking to the users.

The main source of information will be the task model from UI analysis. We will discuss tasks and subtasks with the people who perform them. We have to primarily identify what is created or changed by the tasks. Elements will usually be the noun or noun-phrases mentioned by people. After selecting the initial set of elements we should review it. We should consider the following questions for each identified element:

❑   Does the element exist in the business world?

❑   Do the users interact with the element to perform a task?

❑   Does the element gather the related information needed to perform a task?

❑   Is the element related to system concepts that should be invisible to the users?

❑   Is the element an artifact of the existing applications and can it be made redundant in the newly developed integrated system?

After we have identified the relevant elements we should combine them, add suitable names, and analyze relationships between them.

Defining User Actions on UI Elements

After we have identified the elements we should identify and define the actions that users will need to perform on the elements. Examples of actions might be `calculate`, `print`, `send`, `add`, and so on. The actions on user elements should be identified from the description of user tasks, done in the UI analysis. We will also define some common tasks for all elements (such as help, reposition, and so on). Notice that the whole process is iterative, so we will be able to add actions in several iterations. Identifying and defining all of them at once is usually very difficult.

For each defined action we should specify:

❑   Name

❑   Description

❑   Required inputs before action can be performed (if any)

❑   Effects on UI elements

❑   Outputs from action (if any)

Element actions describe the behavior of elements in the system. They are connected with the elements, so we should also build the element-action matrix.

Defining Dynamic Behavior

For each element we should specify any relevant dynamic behavior with the following:

❑   Observation of actions and focusing on whether they can be invalid

❑   How actions depend on the previous state of elements

❑   Whether there are any limitations in which sequence the actions can occur

If there is state-dependent behavior we might consider modeling it using, for example, UML state chart diagrams.

Selecting User Interface Type

After we have functionally described the UI we should select the type of user interface that we will implement. Basically we will choose between a GUI user interface and a web-based user interface. We might also consider developing the user interface as enterprise portal, using one of these types (user interface types and the enterprise portals were discussed in the first section of this chapter).

Identifying and Defining Styles

Styles define the style standards that we will use for the whole presentation tier of the integrated information system. The objective of this step is to define a standard style for the user interface look and feel, to select a style that enhances usability and is appropriate for user tasks (and users). The definition of styles also depends on the type of user interface we will use. Definition of styles is an activity that requires graphical design experience and human factors expertise. Therefore this step will most likely be done by graphical designer specialists, and not by IT professionals.

Considering the Impact of Styles on Users and Usability Requirements

After we have defined the styles for the UI we should consider the impact of the styles on the users and the usability requirements that we have defined earlier in the UI analysis. It will depend on the characteristics of users and tasks which style will be most suitable for them. We will have to consider their prior knowledge, which can lower the training effort for using the new styles and we should consider the type of control that we want to provide to the user. To assess the styles that we have defined and to improve them we might review the styles of existing applications and the styles of similar integrated information systems in other companies.

After we have assessed the impact of styles on users and usability requirements, we can select a certain style that fits best to the requirements and users. Then we are ready to define the views.

Defining the Views

In this task we will design the user-visible views of the user interface and their behavior. The product of this task should be the UI design, on the basis of which developers will be able to implement it in the technologies appropriate for a certain type of UI. We have already discussed the appropriate technologies for UI development in J2EE in the first section of this chapter.

The design should specify all possible views (refer to Model View Controller pattern in a later section of this chapter) of the presentation layer. These views will be specified as UML class diagrams that will include the relevant technology classes, such as classes defined in servlets, JSP pages, or Swing.

Prototyping Views

The integrated presentation layer will most likely be very large and complex. Therefore before implementing it we should implement prototypes, which help us to measure and improve the usability of user interfaces, according to the usability requirements, measures, and performance criteria previously defined in UI analysis. The implementation of prototypes also provides feedback on the validity of task models, element and action identification, and selection of styles.

It is not necessary to build the prototypes using the same technologies that will be used for the final implementation of user interfaces. We might consider using a prototyping or a Rapid Application Development (RAD) tool. First, prototypes might even be built on paper. If we develop web-based interfaces we can also prototype the user interfaces using a web design tool.

Evaluating Usability

After the prototypes, at the final implementation of the user interface, we should evaluate the usability. The objectives of evaluation usability are to identify the usability problems, to assess whether the user interfaces satisfy the usability requirements and how usable the user interfaces are in practice for the users. Usability evaluation frequently uncovers usability problems not noticed during the development. The usability evaluation of final user interfaces might identify usability problems, not noticed on evaluating prototypes.

Usability evaluation also provides the information on which we can base the decision whether the user interface development is finished or whether new iterations should be started to improve the identified imperfections. For the usability evaluation we will use requirements and performance criteria specified in the UI analysis stage. If these have been applied to the existing applications too, then we will have information with which we will be able to compare the new presentation tier and demonstrate the improvements.

With the usability evaluation we have concluded the UI analysis and design. In the next section we will focus on J2EE technologies for implementation of user interfaces. First we will look at servlets.

Servlets

Java servlets are J2EE web component tier technology appropriate for the implementation of web-based user interfaces. Servlets are components that extend the functionality of a web server. Instead of returning static content to the client, the web server invokes a servlet (a Java program similar to an applet), which can dynamically generate the content (an HTML page, for example). A servlet can communicate with the EJB tier and invoke operations on business logic components. It can also access a database and other EIS systems directly, however we should avoid this approach because it breaks the tier separation rules, and makes servlets too complicated.

The web container on the web component tier invokes a servlet based on an HTTP request. The web container forwards the request to the servlet, which processes it and generates the content dynamically. The web container then transmits the response back to the web server and finally to the client.

In this sense servlets are comparable to the Common Gateway Interface (CGI) and other proprietary web server extensions, such as NSAPI and ISAPI. However, servlets have several advantages, particularly over CGI, because they provide a rich programming model based on the Java platform and Java programming language. Servlets are long lived and do not require spawning separate processes for each request, in contrast to CGI, where each request requires a separate process. Servlets can be tightly integrated with web servers. If they are implemented as in-process web containers then they execute in the same process as the web container, which speeds up the performance further. Therefore, servlets can provide better performance and scalability than CGI solutions. Similar to other Java-based solutions, servlets are fully portable between platforms and web servers – that is, those that support the Java Servlet API Specification, currently in version 2.3.

Servlets are not the only web components supported by J2EE. The other possibility is JSP pages, which we will cover a little later in this chapter. It is worth noting that servlets and JSP pages are complementary technologies. Servlets are more appropriate for processing, such as calling components on the business logic tier (and more appropriate to perform the Controller function of the MVC pattern, which we will introduce later in the chapter). JSP pages are more appropriate for generating markup (HTML or XML) (and therefore perform the View function of MVC). This separation is not absolutely strict, but it makes sense to follow it.

Here we will show the basic steps in developing simple servlets that will use services provided by the business logic tier components. This section does not cover servlets in detail; for more information, take a look at *Professional Java Servlets*, ISBN 1-861005-61-X, or *Professional Java Server Programming J2EE 1.3 Edition*, ISBN 1-861005-37-7, both available from Wrox Press.

The Servlet API

The Servlet API is specified in two Java extension packages as part of J2EE:

❑ `javax.servlet` – in this package we can find protocols, independent classes, and interfaces. The Servlet API can also be used with protocols other than the HTTP, such as SOAP.

❑ `javax.servlet.http` – contains classes and interfaces specific to HTTP protocol, which simplifies the development of HTTP servlets.

The classes and interfaces provided in the Servlet API have the following responsibilities:

❑ **Servlet implementation classes and interfaces** – includes two interfaces: `Servlet` and `SingleThreadModel`, and two classes: `GenericServlet` and `HttpServlet`. To develop servlets we have to implement the `Servlet` interface. The web container then invokes these methods to process requests directed to servlets and to control their life cycle. In most cases we will not implement the `Servlet` interface directly, but will rather extend from one of the two mentioned classes that already provide basic implementations for the methods. Most likely we will extend from `HttpServlet` to implement an HTTP servlet. To support other protocols we will extend the `GenericServlet` class. We will implement the `SingleThreadedModel` marker interface to guarantee that no two threads will execute concurrently in the servlet's service method.

❑ **Servlet configuration interface** – `ServletConfig` provides access to configuration parameters connected with the deployment of the servlet.

❑ **Servlet Exception classes** – `ServletException` and `UnavailableException`. Through these exceptions servlets notify the container of exceptional states.

❑ **Requests and Response interfaces and abstract classes** – provide a means to access the low-level input and output streams associated with the client connection.

❑ **Session Tracking** – enables grouping of related requests and overcomes the disadvantages of HTTP protocol, which is stateless.

❑ **Servlet Context interface** – allows sharing data among servlets and accessing the web container.

❑ **Servlet Collaboration interface** – provides methods for a servlet to invoke other web components, that is, other servlets, JSP pages, or even static resources.

❑ **Filtering** – provides ways to monitor and adapt client requests and responses.

❑ **Cookies** – provide a way to store client-dependent data directly on the client.

❑ **Other utility features** – gathered in the `http.HttpUtils` class, which have been deprecated in Servlet API version 2.3 and moved to the request interfaces.

HttpServlet Class

To develop a HTTP-based servlet, we will typically extend the `HttpServlet` class, which provides HTTP specific implementation of the `Servlet` interface. The `HttpServlet` class provides the following methods:

❑ HTTP request methods in form of `doXXX()` methods (listed below). With the implementation of these methods we implement the functionality of servlets.

❑ Overloaded service methods `service()` that manage requests and responses for servlets. Default implementation is provided, which we should use in most cases.

❑ The `getLastModified()` method that provides a means of caching servlet output for a certain amount of time.

Let us have a closer look at the HTTP request methods:

```
protected void doGet(HttpServletRequest request, HttpServletResponse
                     response) throws ServletException, IOException

protected void doPost(HttpServletRequest request, HttpServletResponse
                      response) throws ServletException, IOException

protected void doHead(HttpServletRequest request, HttpServletResponse
                      response) throws ServletException, IOException

protected void doDelete(HttpServletRequest request, HttpServletResponse
                        response) throws ServletException, IOException

protected void doOptions(HttpServletRequest request, HttpServletResponse
                         response) throws ServletException, IOException

protected void doPut(HttpServletRequest request, HttpServletResponse
                     response) throws ServletException, IOException

protected void doTrace(HttpServletRequest request, HttpServletResponse
                       response) throws ServletException, IOException
```

To develop the servlet, we have to determine which methods our servlet will support, and implement the corresponding methods. In most cases these will be:

❑ `doGet()`

❑ `doPost()`

❑ `doHead()`

❑ `doDelete()`

❑ `doPut()`

The `doOptions()` and `doTrace()` methods are already implemented in the `HttpServlet` class and generally never need to be overridden.

Developing a Simple Servlet

We will develop a simple servlet for the cell phone operator example integration project that we introduced in Chapter 4, and discussed in Chapters 9 to 12. Here, the servlet will call the session EJB that we developed in Chapter 12, to calculate the balance in a cell phone account. The required sequence will be the following:

❑ The user will be asked for the cell phone account number.

❑ The servlet will locate the `CheckBalanceHome` home interface and invoke a `create()` method to get the remote component interface.

❑ The servlet will then invoke the `calculateBalance()` method on the `CheckBalance` session bean and display the result.

Remember that in Chapter 12 the EJB has contacted the RMI-IIOP virtual component (developed in Chapter 11), which contacted the existing application. We will therefore implement a relatively complex interaction, where the HTML client, on the client tier, will use HTTP to interact with the servlet on the web component tier. Our servlet will interact with session EJB on the business logic tier. The session EJB will call an RMI-IIOP virtual component, which will interact with the existing application on the EIS tier. This is shown in the following figure:

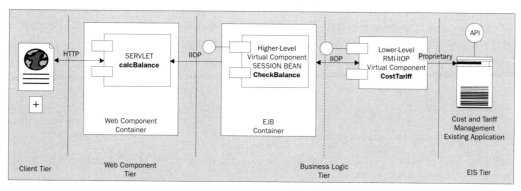

We will start developing our example by writing the HTML form.

Writing the HTML Form

To obtain the necessary parameters from the user we will build a simple HTML form, in which the user will enter the required data. Note that the HTML form presented here is for demonstration purposes, a production system would probable use more complex forms.

A very simple form (`calcBalance.html`) for entering the cell phone account number is presented in the following listing:

```
<html>
<!-- calcBalance.html -->
<head>
  <title>
  Simple web-based user interface
  </title>
</head>
  <body>
    <h1>Cell Phone Account Balance Check</h1>
    <hr><br>
    <form action="./calcBalance" method="POST">
    Account number:
    <input type="Text" name="accNo" align="left" size="20">
    <p>
    <input type="Submit" name="submit" value="Check Balance">
    </form>
  </body>
</html>
```

819

We can see that the form uses POST to submit the data to the servlet. Which servlet will be called is specified in the action declaration of the form (calcBalance in our case). Notice that in real-world examples we would have to do input validation. A common approach to do the general input validation on the client side (such as no account number or number too long/short) is using a script in HTML (possibility is JavaScript) that executes on the client side inside the web browser. Doing general input validation on the client improves the responsiveness of the user interface. But input validation on the client alone is not sufficient, because it cannot check whether the account number is valid, for example. Therefore additional validation would have to be implemented in the servlet. For our example we will not implement any JavaScript, but in the servlet we will check for the account number and allow only one number to demonstrate how to redirect the flow with exceptions.

Developing the Servlet

We will develop a simple servlet that will use HTTP for communication with the client. Therefore we will define the CalculateBalance class, which will extend the HttpServlet class:

```
import javax.servlet.ServletException;
import javax.servlet.http.HttpServlet;
import javax.servlet.http.HttpServletRequest;
import javax.servlet.http.HttpServletResponse;

import javax.rmi.PortableRemoteObject;
import java.util.Properties;

import javax.naming.Context;
import javax.naming.InitialContext;

import java.io.PrintWriter;
import java.io.IOException;

// Import component and home interface of the EJB we'll be accessing
import session1.CheckBalance;
import session1.CheckBalanceHome;

public class CalculateBalance extends HttpServlet {
```

First we will implement the init() method. This method is invoked exactly once when the servlet is initialized. In this method we will connect to the CheckBalanceHome session bean remote home interface. All clients will use the home interface to create their session bean instances. Therefore, it makes sense to do the connection only once and not for each client separately, because it speeds up the performance.

To connect to the CheckBalanceHome session bean home interface we will use the JNDI name eaiSS-CheckBalanceHome, as used in the Chapter 12 example. We will also have to store the reference to the home interface in a private attribute:

```
// Attribute to store the reference to EJB home
private CheckBalanceHome home = null;

// We will acquire the connection to the EJB
// once at the initialization of the servlet
public void init() throws ServletException {
```

```
        try {
          // Define the initial naming context
          // Notice that this is specific to BEA WebLogic
          // and should be modified when used with other app servers
          Properties h = new Properties();
          h.put(Context.INITIAL_CONTEXT_FACTORY,
                      "weblogic.jndi.WLInitialContextFactory");

          // Create the new initial context
          Context ctx = new InitialContext(h);

          // Bind to EJB home interface
          home = (CheckBalanceHome)PortableRemoteObject.narrow(
                  CheckBalanceHome)ctx.lookup("eaiSS-CheckBalanceHome"),
                                          CheckBalanceHome.class);

        } catch(Exception e) {
          throw new ServletException("Exception", e);
        }
      }
```

Next, because we have specified POST in HTML form to submit requests, we will have to implement the doPost() method. In the doPost() method we will do the following:

❑   Extract the account number parameter

❑   Check whether the account number is valid

❑   Create a new session bean instance

❑   Invoke the calculateBalance() method on the CheckBalance session bean

❑   Generate the result that will be displayed on the client

First, we will extract the account number for the request and convert it to integer. As mentioned before, for the purposes of demonstration we will limit the valid account numbers to a single number (41629827). Therefore we will check if the client has entered this number. If not we will raise a user-defined exception: WrongAccNoException. We will declare this exception a little later:

```
    protected void doPost(HttpServletRequest req, HttpServletResponse res)
              throws ServletException, IOException, WrongAccNoException {

      // Get the account number parameter from HTTP request
      String accNoS = req.getParameter("accNo");
      int accNo = (new Integer(accNoS)).intValue();

      // Check the value of accNo
      // Notice that this example allows a single number only
      if (accNo != 41629827)
        throw new WrongAccNoException();
```

Next we will declare a variable to store the balance, create a session bean instance, invoke the corresponding method on the session bean and remove the session bean instance:

821

```
        double balance = 0;

        // Invoke the method on the EJB
        try {
          // create a new session bean instance
          CheckBalance cb = home.create();

          // Invoke the method
          balance = cb.calculateBalance(accNo);

          // Remove the session bean instance
          cb.remove();

        } catch(Exception e) {
        throw new ServletException("Exception", e);
        }
```

Finally we will generate the output. The output will be presented in the client web browser, so we have to generate the HTML in which we will print the account balance:

```
        // Get the writer for the HttpServletResponse res
        PrintWriter out = res.getWriter();

        // Define the content type to text/html
        res.setContentType("text/html");

        // Output the result
        out.println("<html><head><title>");
        out.println("Simple web-based user interface");
        out.println("</title></head><body>");
        out.println("<h1>Cell Phone Account Balance Result</h1><hr>");
        out.println("<p>The balance of the account number: " + accNo +
                    " is:");
        out.println(balance);
        out.println("</p>");
        out.println("</body></html>");

        out.close();
    }
  }
```

With this, we have finished our simple servlet. However, we still have to define our exception, the WrongAccNoException. We will simply extend the ServletException without adding any new functionality. We however could not use the ServletException directly, because the ServletException can be thrown for different reasons, not only for the wrong account number. The definition of the WrongAccNoException.java is shown here:

```
    import javax.servlet.ServletException;

    public class WrongAccNoException extends ServletException {
    }
```

To provide a user-friendly output, we will map this exception to a special HTML page, which will be shown when this exception is raised. We will define this mapping in the deployment descriptor a little later. Here's the simple HTML page that will handle the exception (we'll name it `calcBalanceError.html` in the source code package):

```
<html>
<!-- calcBalanceError.html -->
<head>
  <title>
  Simple web-based user interface
  </title>
</head>
  <body>
    <h1>Cell Phone Account Balance Check</h1>
    <hr><br>
    The entered account number is not valid.<br>
    <a href="calcBalance.html">
    Please click here to reenter the account number
    </a>
  </body>
</html>
```

Before we can test our servlet, we have to write the deployment descriptor, compile the code, create the web component and deploy it to the application server.

Deployment Descriptor

The deployment descriptor for web components has a similar function to the EJB deployment descriptor in that it specifies the necessary data to deploy the application. The deployment descriptor is an XML file and should have the name `web.xml`. The most necessary information that we have to specify is the servlet name (`calcBalance`) and the name of the class where the servlet is implemented (`CalculateBalance`). Notice that the servlet name has to be equal to the name we are referring to in the HTML form.

Let's write the deployment descriptor for our example:

```
<?xml version="1.0"?>

<!DOCTYPE web-app PUBLIC "-//Sun Microsystems, Inc.//DTD Web Application 1.2//EN"
"http://java.sun.com/j2ee/dtds/web-app_2_3.dtd">

<web-app>

  <servlet>
    <servlet-name>calcBalance</servlet-name>
    <servlet-class>CalculateBalance</servlet-class>
  </servlet>
```

We should also specify how the servlet name maps to the URL pattern. For our case we will use the same name for both (`calcBalance`):

```
    <servlet-mapping>
       <servlet-name>calcBalance</servlet-name>
       <url-pattern>calcBalance</url-pattern>
    </servlet-mapping>
```

Next we will specify how to handle `WrongAccNoException`. We will map the exception to the `calcBalanceError.html` file:

```
    <error-page>
       <exception-type>WrongAccNoException</exception-type>
       <location>/calcBalanceError.html</location>
    </error-page>
```

Finally, we will specify the entry page, which will show up when a client enters the URL pattern that we have defined previously. The entry page for our example will be the first HTML file that we have defined, the one that includes the form to enter the account number (`calcBalance.html`):

```
    <welcome-file-list>
       <welcome-file>calcBalance.html</welcome-file>
    </welcome-file-list>

  </web-app>
```

Next we have to compile and build the example.

Building the Example

First we have to compile the source files, using `javac`, and then pack the necessary files for the web components (servlets) to a Web Application Archive (WAR) file (with extension `.war`). In our case, we will create the `calcBalance.war` with the following directory structure:

```
.\calcBalance.html
.\calcBalanceError.html
.\WEB-INF\
         web.xml
         classes\
                 CalculateBalance.class
                 WrongAccNoException.class
                 session1\
                         CheckBalance.class
                         CheckBalanceHome.class
```

Note that we have to place the `calcBalance.html` and the `calcBalanceError.html` files in the root of the `.war` file. In the folder `WEB-INF` we place the deployment descriptor `web.xml`. We create a subfolder, `classes`, where we store our compiled servlet class, `CalculateBalance.class` and the exception class `WrongAccNoException.class`. We also need the remote home and component interfaces of the `CheckBalance` session bean (from Chapter 12). Remember, in Chapter 12 we developed the bean in the `session1` package, so we have to store the corresponding interface class files in the `session1` subfolder.

To create the WAR file run the following command from the `build` directory:

```
jar cv0f calcBalance.war *.*
```

Running the Example

Finally we can deploy our web application and test the servlet. We should deploy the application corresponding to the instructions of the application server we use. Here we use BEA WebLogic, with which deployment is achieved simply through the **server console**. First, select **Applications** under the **Deployments** header, then choose **Install a new Application**.... Now browse for the `calcBalance.war` file (in our case, it is found under the `%BOOK_HOME%\Ch17\Servlet\` directory) and upload it to the server.

Before we can run the example, we have to make sure that:

❑   The `CheckBalance` session bean, developed in Chapter 12 is deployed.

❑   The RMI-IIOP virtual component developed in Chapter 11 is running, together with `tnameserv`, the CORBA Naming Service. To start these we can use the following commands:

To start the servlet, we should start our web browser and enter the following address: http://host_name/calcBalance. Note that host_name will depend on the application server and configuration that we use. If we test the example with WebLogic on the local computer, we can use the following address: http://localhost:7001/calcBalance. We should get the following output, at which point we can enter the account number `41629827`:

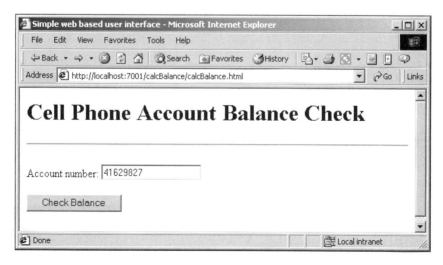

After we have entered the account number we should press the Check Balance button, and see the following response:

We can also observe that the EJB has actually been called if we look at the application server output, and that the RMI-IIOP virtual component has been communicated.

The user might, however, enter a wrong account number. Then the servlet will throw the WrongAccNoException exception. The mapping to the calcBalanceError.html, which we have defined in the deployment descriptor, means that the browser will show the following HTML file:

Although our example is relatively simple, it demonstrates a complex invocation from a web-based user interface all the way to the existing application. Next we will turn our attention to using JSP pages to achieve presentation integration.

JavaServer Pages

JavaServer Pages (JSP) is another J2EE web component tier technology, appropriate for the development of web-based user interfaces. To understand the need for JSP pages let us first consider servlets and their associated disadvantages. We have seen that servlets are developed in the Java programming language. In the servlet that we've developed in the previous section we had to generate the HTML markup inside the servlet using the following code:

```
    ...
      // Output the result
      out.println("<html><head><title>");
      out.println("Simple web-based user interface");
      out.println("</title></head><body>");
      out.println("<h1>Cell Phone Account Balance Result</h1><hr>");
      out.println("<p>The balance of the account number: " + accNo +
                  " is:");
      out.println(balance);
      out.println("</p>");
      out.println("</body></html>");
    ...
```

Generating HTML markup code from servlets is not very nice because we mix Java and markup, and we have to modify to servlet source code, recompile it, create the WAR archive and redeploy it to the application server for every small change.

Obviously it would be much easier if we could write markup pages and include some directives that would execute a certain function. Instead of writing relatively complex Java servlets for creating dynamic pages, we would have to write simply a HTML page and embed directives to provide dynamic content.

JSP pages are the answer to this problem – they can be developed like web pages, but can also include Java code. Code is included within certain markups in the HTML. Remember, JSP pages are developed as markup, so they are very well suited to provide the presentation of data (the View part of the MVC pattern which will be introduced later). However, JSP pages are not particularly well suited to perform processing logic.

Be aware that there is a functional overlap between JSP pages and servlets. We will see later that the best way to select the appropriate solution is to think of servlets as controllers, and JSP pages as view components from MVC. That way they become complementary technologies. Soon we will show how to develop the web client for our example with JSP pages, but first let's get a little more familiar with JSP technology.

How to Write JSP Pages

Java code is included between <% and %> tags in the JSP pages. There are three different JSP tags that we can use:

- ❏ **Scripting elements** – let us insert Java code into the JSP pages.

- ❏ **Directives** – affect the structure of the JSP, but do not generate output.

- ❏ **Actions** – specify runtime behavior of JSP pages. JSP already defines standard actions, through which we can use JavaBeans, for example. We can define our own tags, which are known as custom tags.

When writing JSP pages we also have to follow some rules. Particularly we have to be aware that tags are case-sensitive, which, although we are used to this with Java, is easily forgotten in JSP pages, because they include case-insensitive HTML.

Scripting Elements

Scripting elements allow us to include Java code in JSP pages. We can include the following constructs:

- ❑ **Declarations**
  Declarations are blocks of code, where we define variables and methods. These are initialized with the initialization of the JSP and are visible in the whole JSP. The declarations have to be placed between the `<%!` and `%>` tags. The code included between the tags is typical Java code. The variables and methods, defined as declarations, are then called from various points in the JSP.

- ❑ **Scriptlets**
  Scriptlets are also blocks of code, but they execute during the processing of the JSP. They are pieces of Java code, placed between `<%` and `%>` tags, which execute in the same order in which they are written in the JSP. Code written as a scriptlet can be broken into several parts, between which we place HTML or other markup. We switch between code and the markup with the tags.

- ❑ **Expressions**
  Expressions are provided for shorter notation for Java expressions that output results to the client. Expressions are evaluated when processing client requests. They are converted to strings and outputted and should be written between `<%=` and `%>` tags.

Directives

Directives influence the generation of servlets, which is performed when JSP pages are translated to servlets. Directives are included inside `<%@` and `%>` tags and influence the whole JSP page in which they are declared. There are three directives that we can use:

- ❑ `page` directive – specifies a number of important attributes, including language, possibility to import packages, definition of the buffering model, thread safety, content type, and so on.

- ❑ `include` directive – provides the possibility to include the content of another JSP page in the current page. The syntax is:

  ```
  <%@ include file="Filename" %>
  ```

- ❑ `taglib` directive – enables the use of custom tags defined in tag libraries.

Actions

We have already mentioned that JSP defines several standard actions, so we'll provide a quick overview of these standard actions. Custom actions or custom tags provide a powerful mechanism to extend the functionality of actions (refer to JSP-related literature for more information on custom tags).

Actions have to be placed between `<jsp:action_name attributes>` and `</jsp:action_name>` tags. They are processed by the translation of JSP pages to servlets, where action tags are replaced with corresponding code.

The standard action tags, defined by JSP, are:

- ❑ `<jsp:useBean>`
- ❑ `<jsp:setProperty>`

- ❏ `<jsp:getProperty>`

- ❏ `<jsp:param>`

- ❏ `<jsp:include>`

- ❏ `<jsp:forward>`

- ❏ `<jsp:plugin>`

We have already seen that markup and Java code are mixed inside JSP pages. If not used carefully, this can lead to maintenance problems and unreadable JSP pages, so we have to think about which code to put directly in the JSP pages. For the more complex code, possibly for code that will be used by more JSP pages, we can use the standard action tag `<jsp:useBean>`.

The `<jsp:useBean>` tag enables us to use code from a JavaBean and use the code from the JSP with the `<jsp:setProrerty>` and `<jsp:getProperty>`.

> **The** `<jsp:useBean>`**tag, together with** `<jsp:setProperty>` **and** `<jsp:getProperty>` **standard action tags are appropriate for implementing the Business Delegate pattern in JSP pages.**

To locate or instantiate a new JavaBean we use the `<jsp:useBean>` tag, which we then assign to a variable. Generally we will instantiate a JavaBean with the following tag:

```
<jsp:useBean attributes>
  body
</jsp:useBean>
```

Inside the body we will typically initialize and configure the bean by setting properties. If we do not need the body, we can use a shorter form:

```
<jsp:useBean attributes />
```

There are several parameters that can or must be specified. We have already mentioned that we have to assign a variable. We assign the variable with the id attribute. It has to be a case-sensitive name that identifies the object.

We also have to specify the scope in which the bean will be visible. The following values for scope attributes are permitted:

- ❏ page – the bean is associated with a particular request and page

- ❏ request – the bean is associated with a particular request

- ❏ session – the bean is associated with a particular session with the client

- ❏ application – the bean is associated with the whole web application – all JSP pages within the web application

829

The next attribute is `class` and specifies the class name in which the JavaBean is implemented. Then we have the optional `beanName` attribute, where we specify the name as supplied to the `instantiate()` method.

Finally, we can optionally specify the `type` attribute, which specifies the type of scripting variable that will be created. The default value is the same as `class` attribute. However, sometimes we would like to specify a superclass or an interface instead.

When we deploy the web application we have to put the required JavaBean class or classes in the `WEB-INF\classes` or `WEB-INF\lib` subdirectories. The JavaBean will be searched in the `CLASSPATH` too.

To use JavaBeans we have included in JSP pages we will need to use the following standard action tags:

❑   `<jsp:setProperty>` to set the bean properties

❑   `<jsp:getProperty>` to access the bean properties

With the `<jsp:setProperty>` tag we can set the bean properties from the client request object or through expressions. To set all properties from the `Request` object we can use a single action tag:

```
<jsp:setProperty name="beanId" property="*"/>
```

However, we have to name the request parameters in the same fashion as bean properties. If we don't want to set all properties we can set them one by one, but they still have to have the same names:

```
<jsp:setProperty name="beanId" property="propertyName"/>
```

If the property names and the request parameters names are not the same we can use the following syntax to set them:

```
<jsp:setProperty name="beanId" property="propertyName"
                 param="parameterName"/>
```

If, however, we want to set the property through evaluation of an expression, then we can use the following:

```
<jsp:setProperty name="beanId" property="propertyName" value="…"/>
```

To access the bean properties we can use the `<jsp:getProperty>` tag. The syntax is relatively simple:

```
<jsp:getProperty name="beanId" property="propertyName" />
```

With this tag the property is accessed, converted to string, and outputted to the output stream.

Before we present an example using these standard action tags, let's have a quick look at the other less important action tags.

We can use the `<jsp:param>` action tag to define additional parameters as pairs: name, value. It is used with the next three action tags. The `<jsp:include>` provides a mechanism to include other static or dynamic resources in the JSP at the time of processing the client request. The `<jsp:forward>` makes it possible to forward the request to other JSP pages, servlets, or static resources. The `<jsp:plugin>` provides a mechanism to include Java applets within JSP pages. For detailed explanations of these tags, look into related literature, for example the *Professional JSP 2nd Edition* from Wrox Press.

Developing a JSP to Access EJB Tier Components

To demonstrate how to use JSP pages to build a presentation layer for integration, we will develop a JSP page that will access the same `CheckBalance` session bean for calculating the balance of a cell phone account, as we have done in the previous section where we developed a servlet.

We will implement a JSP page that will invoke a relatively complex interaction, where the HTML client on the client tier will use HTTP to interact with the JSP page on the web component tier. The JSP page will use a JavaBean to interact with the session EJB on the business logic tier. The session EJB will call an RMI-IIOP virtual component, which will interact with the existing application on the EIS tier. This is shown in the following figure:

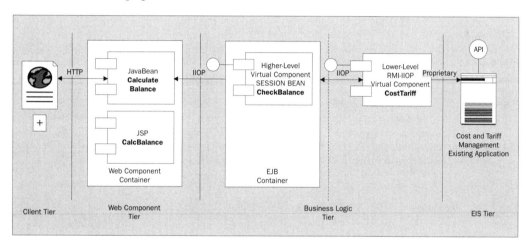

We will first create a JavaBean that will provide two properties: the account number and balance. Balance will be read-only, which means that only the getter method will be implemented. We will then use this bean to access the information about balance from the JSP page.

The JavaBean

Let us first develop the JavaBean, which we will name `CalculateBalance`. We will start with the usual declarations:

```
package jspbean;

import javax.servlet.ServletException;
import javax.servlet.http.HttpServlet;
import javax.servlet.http.HttpServletRequest;
import javax.servlet.http.HttpServletResponse;

import javax.rmi.PortableRemoteObject;
import java.util.Properties;

import javax.naming.Context;
import javax.naming.InitialContext;
```

```
import java.io.PrintWriter;
import java.io.IOException;

// Import component and home interface of the EJB we'll be accessing
import session1.CheckBalance;
import session1.CheckBalanceHome;


public class CalculateBalance {
```

We will then declare two attributes. In one we will store the reference to `CheckBalanceHome`. In the other we will store the account number:

```
private CheckBalanceHome home = null;
private int accountNo = 0;
```

Then we will define the constructor. In the constructor we will obtain the initial reference and resolve the name in JNDI (using our original name: `eaiSS-CheckBalanceHome`) to get a reference to the home interface. Doing this in the constructor improves the performance of the bean if shared among JSP pages. If the bean is stateless then we could create the instance in the constructor too; however, in our example we decided to create the bean instance in the getter method. This does not matter in our case because of the bean scope, which we will define later. To signal that the connection to the session EJB could not be established, the constructor will throw the ServletException (note that the JSP which will call this JavaBean is translated to the servlet – as are all JSP pages):

```
// We will acquire the connection to the EJB
// once at the initialization of the bean
public CalculateBalance() throws ServletException {
  try {
    // Define the initial naming context
    // Note that this is specific to BEA WebLogic
    // and should be modified when used with other app servers
    Properties h = new Properties();
    h.put(Context.INITIAL_CONTEXT_FACTORY,
                 "weblogic.jndi.WLInitialContextFactory");

    // Create the new intial context
    Context ctx = new InitialContext(h);

    // Bind to EJB home interface
    home = (CheckBalanceHome)PortableRemoteObject.narrow(
          ctx.lookup("eaiSS-CheckBalanceHome"), CheckBalanceHome.class);

  } catch(Exception e) {
    throw new ServletException("Exception", e);
  }
}
```

Next we will define the getter and setter method for the `accountNo` property. In the setter we will check for the correct account number (`41629827`). If not we will invoke the `WrongAccNoException`, which is a user-defined exception that extends the `ServletException` (similar as we have done in the servlet example). We will define the `WrongAccNoException` a little later:

```
public void setAccountNo(String accNo) throws WrongAccNoException {
    try {
        accountNo = (new Integer(accNo)).intValue();

        // Check the value of accNo
        // Notice that this example allows a single number only
        if (accountNo != 41629827) {
            throw new WrongAccNoException();
        }
    } catch(Exception e) {
        throw new WrongAccNoException();
    }
}

public String getAccountNo() {
    return Integer.toString(accountNo);
}
```

Finally we will define the getter method for balance:

```
public String getBalance() throws ServletException {
    if (home == null) {
        return "N/A";
    } else {
        double balance = 0;
        try {
            // create a new session bean instance
            CheckBalance cb = home.create();

            // Invoke the method
            balance = cb.calculateBalance(accountNo);

            // Remove the session bean instance
            cb.remove();

        } catch(Exception e) {
            throw new ServletException("Exception", e);
        }
        return Double.toString(balance);
    }
}
```

With this we have finished the development of the JavaBean. We also need to declare the
WrongAccNoException:

```
package jspbean;

import javax.servlet.ServletException;

public class WrongAccNoException extends ServletException {
}
```

Next we will write the necessary HTML form.

HTML Form

After developing the bean, we have to provide the user interface components. First we will define the corresponding HTML form, which will be very similar to the servlet example. However, note that we have specified a JSP in the `action` attribute. This HTML file should be named `calcBalance.html`:

```
<html>
<head>
  <title>
    Simple web-based user interface
  </title>
</head>
  <body>
    <h1>Cell Phone Account Balance Check</h1>
    <hr><br>
    <form action="./calcBalance.jsp" method="POST">
      Account number:
      <input type="Text" name="accountNo" align="left" size="20">
      <p>
      <input type="Submit" name="submit" value="Check Balance">
    </form>
  </body>
</html>
```

We also need to write the HTML file that will be used to report the wrong account number – when the `WrongAccNoException` exception is thrown (we'll name this file `calcBalanceError.html`):

```
<html>
<head>
  <title>
  Simple web-based user interface
  </title>
</head>
  <body>
    <h1>Cell Phone Account Balance Check</h1>
    <hr><br>
    The entered account number is not valid.<br>
    <a href="calcBalance.html">
    Please click here to re-enter the account number
    </a>
  </body>
</html>
```

The JSP Page

Finally we have to define the `calcBalance.jsp` file. In this file we will provide the output to the client, which has been in the servlet scenario generated by the servlet. We will use the corresponding standard action tags to access the JavaBean. First, we will specify that we will use the `jspbean.CalculateBalance` JavaBean (developed previously) and the mapping between JavaBean properties and HTML form properties. Then we will provide the necessary HTML markup, from where we will access the JavaBean properties `accountNo` and `balance`.

The code for the JSP, which should be stored in the `calcBalance.jsp` file, is shown below:

```
<jsp:useBean id="calcBalanceBean" scope="page" class="jspbean.CalculateBalance">
  <jsp:setProperty name="calcBalanceBean" property="accountNo"/>
</jsp:useBean>

<html>
  <head>
    <title>
    Simple web-based user interface
    </title>
  </head>
  <body>
    <h1>Cell Phone Account Balance Result</h1>
    <hr>
    <p>The balance of the account number:
    <jsp:getProperty name="calcBalanceBean" property="accountNo"/>
    is:
    <jsp:getProperty name="calcBalanceBean" property="balance"/>
    </p>
  </body>
</html>
```

The next step is to write the deployment descriptor.

Deployment Descriptor

The deployment descriptor (`web.xml`) for the JSP example is very simple. We have to specify the mapping of the `jspbean.WrongAccNoException` to the `calcBalanceError.html` file and the initial HTML file (`calcBalance.html`):

```
<?xml version="1.0"?>

<!DOCTYPE web-app PUBLIC
    "-//Sun Microsystems, Inc.//DTD Web Application 2.3//EN"
    "http://java.sun.com/dtd/web-app_2_3.dtd">

<web-app>
  <error-page>
    <exception-type>jspbean.WrongAccNoException</exception-type>
    <location>/calcBalanceError.html</location>
  </error-page>
  <welcome-file-list>
    <welcome-file>calcBalance.html</welcome-file>
  </welcome-file-list>
</web-app>
```

Web Application Archive

Before we can test our web application we have to compile the source code using `javac`. Then we have to build the `.war` archive with the following directory structure and corresponding files:

```
.\calcBalance.jsp
.\calcBalance.html
.\calcBalanceError.html
.\WEB-INF\
        web.xml
        classes\
                jspbean\
                        CalculateBalance.class
                        WrongAccNoException.class
                session1\
                        CheckBalance.class
                        CheckBalanceHome.class
```

Again we use the `CheckBalance.class` and `CheckBalanceHome.class` files from the EJB we developed in Chapter 12, and we can build the `calcBalance.war` archive with the following command:

```
jar cv0f calcBalance.war *.*
```

Deploying and Running the Example

After we have created the web application archive we should deploy it to whichever application server we are using and, again, before we can run the example we have to make sure that:

❏   The `CheckBalance` session bean, developed in Chapter 12 is deployed to the application server

❏   The RMI-IIOP virtual component, developed in Chapter 11, is running, together with the Naming Service (`tnameserv`), as shown in the previous example

To start the example with WebLogic on a local machine we can again use the URL http://localhost:7001/calcBalance. Then we should enter the account number 41629827 and press the button to get the following result:

The result is very similar to the servlet example. However, take a look at the address line, where you can see that the JSP has actually been invoked. As with the servlet example, we can observe the call on the application server to the EJB container and the RMI-IIOP virtual component. Additionally, if we enter the wrong account number we get the same error response that we saw with the servlet example.

836

With this example we have seen how to develop a web-based client using JSP pages. We have also gained a basic understanding of how using servlets to do this compares to the JSP approach. Next we will look at some guidelines on how to choose between servlets and JSP pages.

Choosing Between Servlets and JSP Pages

When developing the presentation tier using servlets and JSP pages, we should put some effort into designing the user interfaces and defining a sound architecture. The important point is to make the correct decisions for when to use servlets and when to use JSP pages. Inappropriate usage introduces many problems and makes them very hard to maintain.

The major problem is using JSP pages containing too many code scriptlets, mixed with markup, or servlets that generate markup as part of their methods. When the presentation tier evolves past a certain point and additional developers and layout designers join the team, it is important to separate the jobs and the responsibilities of both. Developers should be responsible for the content generation, while layout designers do the graphical layout of the interfaces. With this separation we should separate the technologies too. Developers should deal mainly with servlets and JavaBeans. Layout designers should deal with JSP pages. It is inappropriate if the layout designer has to use servlets and deal with the Java source code, which they are not familiar with. A similar problem is if the developer has to search through markup to locate the correct piece of code included in a JSP page.

For some scenarios servlets are the only choice, for example, generating binary content. They are also much better for implementing control logic. However, we should not duplicate the control logic we already have in session or message-driven beans.

Sometimes we do not know in advance what we would like to display. Then using servlets is appropriate, because it can generate, or even better, forward the request to other servlets, JSP pages, or static resources. In addition, servlets are better for processing in general and can forward the request to a JSP to display of the results.

JSP pages, on the other hand, are much better for writing and displaying markup. Generating markup from servlets is not "user-friendly" and introduces maintainability problems. JSP pages with limited included code are much easier to maintain and read. It is a good idea to put the necessary code in corresponding JavaBeans and use them to form JSP pages, as we have seen in our example.

Web Component Tier Architectures

When using servlets and JSP pages for developing web-based presentation layers we can choose between two different architectures:

❑　JSP/ servlet-centric designs – also referred to as page-centric designs. Here we make direct requests to a servlet or JSP page, which produce the results through communication with the business logic components, either directly or through JavaBeans. We have demonstrated this approach in our examples.

❑　Front controller designs or dispatcher designs. Here we make the initial request to a controller servlet or JSP, which forwards the requests to other servlets, JSP pages, or JavaBeans. Look at the Model View Controller and Front Controller pattern in the *Presentation Tier Patterns* section of this chapter for more information.

JSP/ Servlet-Centric Design

Although we have become familiar with this design through the examples developed in the previous sections, let us recapitulate it. The basic approach of this architecture is that the client interacts with a JSP or servlet, which embeds the code for interaction with business logic tier components directly or uses JavaBeans for communication with business tier components. Therefore, we talk about two variations of the JSP/servlet-centric design:

❑   The JSP/servlet view design

❑   The JSP/servlet view design with a JavaBean

The JSP/servlet view design is shown on the UML interaction diagram below. We can see that the client interacts with the JSP or servlet, which embeds the code to do the business processing (for example through calling business logic tier components):

The main advantage of this approach is that it is easy to develop. We have shown this approach in the servlet example. There are however several disadvantages, particularly when the requirements are growing. This approach namely leads to large amounts of markup (HTML for example) code embedded in servlets or in large amounts of scriplet code embedded in JSP pages. This reduces reusability and makes maintainability very difficult. Software developers and web layout designers have to use the same components to do their work. The layout designers are forced to cope with Java code, which they may not understand, and vice versa.

The JSP/servlet view design with a JavaBean solves the problem of mixing markup code with Java code. It delegates code related to communication with business logic components to the JavaBean. In the figure below we can see that the JavaBean is inserted between JSP/servlet and the business processing:

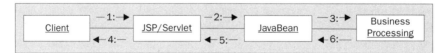

Still this design does not satisfy some requirements, such as providing a controller that would perform some preprocessing, like doing validation of input parameters and redirecting the flow in dependence to the input. This is solved with front controller design.

Front Controller Design

With the front controller design the separation of view and controller roles (refer to MVC pattern in the next section) is more cleanly implemented. Here servlets are used for process-intensive tasks, while JSP pages are used to generate content (views). The front controller is implemented as a servlet that is in charge of request processing and manages the flow of execution which it directs to other web components, particularly JSP pages and JavaBeans. With this design there is no processing logic inside JSP pages.

Depending on the implementation we have two variations of front controller design:

❑ Front controller view design

❑ Front controller service to workers design

In the front controller view design the controller implemented as servlet takes over the usual services such as authentication and the flow of execution. The servlet delegates the request to JSP pages, which invoke the business processing through JavaBeans, similar to the JSP/servlet view with JavaBean design. The front controller view design is shown in the figure below:

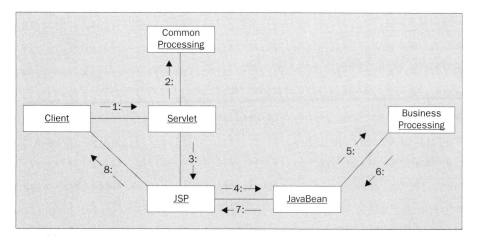

This approach, however, still has the drawback that the JSP pages need to invoke business processing themselves by calling JavaBeans. Therefore they require that the code for calling JavaBeans and for receiving the results be embedded in JSP pages.

This problem is solved by front controller service to workers design, shown in the figure below:

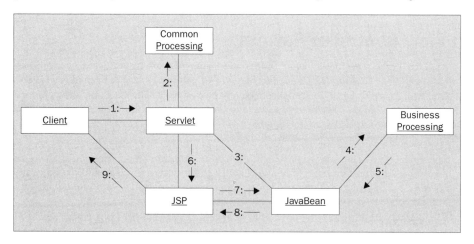

We can see that with this approach the servlet does not invoke the JSP directly, but first invokes the JavaBean, which contacts the business processing components. After business processing is finished, the servlet invokes the JSP, which now only has to access the pre-populated JavaBean. JSP does not have to invoke JavaBeans for business calls, which reduces the amount of code that has to be embedded in JSP pages.

The front controller service to workers design facilitates the cleanest separation of view and controller roles. It puts all processing Java code to servlets and leaves the number of scriplets in JSP pages to a minimum. JSP pages only have to access the JavaBeans for obtaining the results. This improves reusability and maintainability considerably, so this is the preferred design for large web-based user interfaces.

After becoming familiar with J2EE web components and architectures, we will look at the important presentation tier patterns, which will help us to better understand the proposed architectural designs.

Presentation Tier Patterns

When designing the presentation tier it is a good idea to follow proven design patterns. A complete discussion of presentation tier patterns is outside the scope of this chapter, but we can present two general patterns that should be applied to GUI and web-based clients. These are:

❏   Model-View-Controller pattern

❏   Business Delegate pattern

We will also mention some very relevant J2EE web component tier patterns, suitable for web-based clients:

❏   Intercepting Filter

❏   Front Controller

❏   View Helper

❏   Composite View

More information on J2EE patterns can be found at
http://developer.java.sun.com/developer/technicalArticles/J2EE/patterns/ or in the book *Core J2EE Patterns: Best Practices and Design Strategies*, ISBN 0-13-064884-1, from Prentice Hall.

Model View Controller Pattern

When we talk about the presentation layer and the development of user interfaces (both web-based and GUIs) we cannot avoid the Model-View-Controller (MVC) pattern. Although this pattern is relatively old – it has been with us since the 1970s – it has effectively proved its usefulness. Particularly, in modern platforms like J2EE the MVC pattern fits cleanly into the multi-tier architecture of today's applications.

The objective of MVC is the separation of components into three types:

❏   The **model** represents persistent data in the application. Model components manage and transform all persistent data, no matter how they are stored. They should not have any knowledge about the presentation nor the control of the data. Therefore, model components are not concerned with the presentation and user interface issues.

❏   The **view** is responsible for presentation of data, managed by the model. The view components produce visual representation of the data and show it to the users. The view interacts with the model directly.

❑ The **controller** component is responsible for the user interaction with the data, managed by the model and presented by the view. It provides a means to apply the changes to the data in the model or the presentation of these data through the view.

In other words, the MVC pattern clearly separates the roles. It was designed with the objective to simplify the development of systems that had to present the same data in several different ways. In particular, presenting the same data in different ways is the challenge of modern information systems because data here has to be presented in different contexts and on different clients. The development of such systems is simplified with the MVC pattern because model, view, and controller are treated separately, which simplifies changes to parts of the system.

The MVC pattern is appropriate for building GUI clients as well as web-based clients. It can easily be mapped to the technologies provided by J2EE platform:

❑ **Model** – is implemented by components on the business logic tier, particularly entity beans and virtual components that access existing applications.

❑ **View** – for web-based clients the corresponding technology is JSP pages with the support of servlets; for GUI clients the view is taken over by the GUI applications.

❑ **Controller** – suitable technologies for controller are particularly business logic components, such as session and message-drive beans. The role of controller can be taken over by servlets or GUI applications too. The choice will depend of the requirements and the architecture of the application.

The MVC pattern with model, view, controller, their relations, and the corresponding J2EE technologies is shown in the figure below:

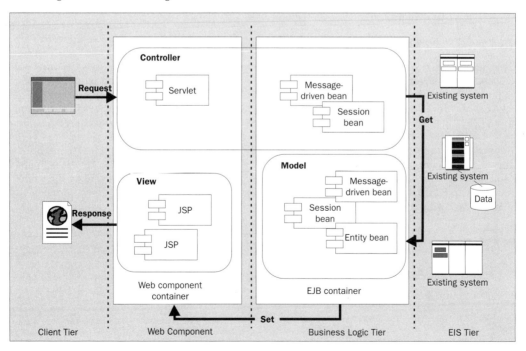

The Business Delegate Pattern

The Business Delegate pattern can be applied to both GUI and web-based clients. From both types of clients (GUI applications or servlets and JSP pages with JavaBeans) we will call the components on the business logic tier. In the previous sections we developed a servlet and a JSP/JavaBean that called the EJB session bean on the business logic tier.

Presentation tier components, which include web components (thin clients) and GUI fat clients, will interact with different EJB components. In Chapter 2 we defined the J2EE integration architecture and defined that we will not just have EJBs on the business logic tier. Rather, we have introduced the term virtual components, which include the following possibilities through which we achieve integration with existing applications:

❑   Session beans

❑   Entity beans

❑   Message-driven beans

❑   CORBA distributed objects

❑   RMI-IIOP distributed objects

❑   JMS-compliant components

These components facilitate two different access mechanisms:

❑   **Synchronous** access through RMI-IIOP or a CORBA ORB for session and entity beans and RMI-IIOP and CORBA distributed objects

❑   **Asynchronous** MOM access through JMS: message-driven beans and JMS components

The important fact is that we access all synchronous and asynchronous components in the same way. Clients are not directly aware how the EJB tier component is implemented. This is particularly important for integration. We can, for example, use a CORBA wrapper to access an existing application. However, over time we will want to replace the existing application and will reimplement it using EJBs.

If we preserve the same interface for the EJB as we did with CORBA, we will not need to modify the clients. All synchronous mechanisms use the same `component.method()` syntax. However, there are some small differences in obtaining initial references. To get the initial references and do the name binding with RMI-IIOP, which includes session and entity beans and RMI-IIOP objects, we have to write the following code:

```
...
Context ctx = new InitialContext();

MyComponentHome MyHome = (MyComponentHome)PortableRemoteObject.narrow(
                ctx.lookup("MyComponentHome"), MyComponentHome.class);
...
```

However, if we use CORBA directly we have to use the following to obtain the reference:

```
...
ORB orb = ORB.init(args, null);

org.omg.CORBA.Object objRef = orb.resolve_initial_references("NameService");
NamingContext ncRef = NamingContextHelper.narrow(objRef);

NameComponent nc = new NameComponent("MyComponentHome", "");
NameComponent path[] = {nc};
MyComponentHome MyHome = MyComponentHomeHelper.narrow(ncRef.resolve(path));
...
```

In real-world examples we will be faced with further differences. Often we will have to provide properties for obtaining the correct initial context, and so on.

When we develop a large number of clients we will see these snippets of code everywhere. Therefore, if we decide to change the implementation we will have to modify the code in many different places. It would be a good idea if we could further reduce the coupling between the presentation tier and the business logic tier. We can achieve this with the Business Delegate pattern.

The idea is very simple: we should gather all the details of remote communication with business logic tier components and provide a client-side abstraction. Instead of using the code above directly, we could gather it into a JavaBean. Such a bean would then abstract the connection to the remote components, with use of home interfaces, and provide the same or similar interface to the remote component interface of the business logic tier components. The client (servlet, for example) will not have to worry about naming, lookup, and similar. We can also implement the handling of remote exceptions in the business delegate, which will simplify the client even more. In addition, we can handle failures in an efficient way in business delegates.

The Business Delegate pattern is schematically shown in the next figure. We can see the client that uses the business component over the business delegate. The business delegate uses the lookup service for locating and creating the business component. After that it forwards the requests:

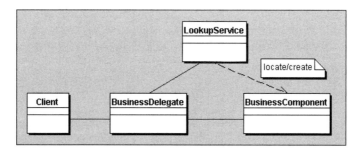

Business delegates are usually implemented as proxies or adapters (see the corresponding patterns in the book *Design Patterns*, ISBN 0-201-63361-2, from Addison-Wesley). You may ask yourself why you should develop another intermediate layer, particularly if you have already designed the architecture using the Distributed Façade pattern. In this case, the mapping between the façade and business delegate will in most cases be one to one. The answer is because of reduced coupling, which will bring benefits in the future.

843

The benefits of the business delegate are that it reduces coupling, improves manageability, it can implement failure recovery and thread synchronization, it can handle remote exceptions, it hides remoteness and exposes simpler, uniform interfaces to the client. Business delegate can, for example, be used for caching results and reducing the number of remote method invocations. It can be perfectly combined with the EJB smart stubs (stubs that provide additional functionality for remote method invocations) strategy, where the business delegate can make use of the smart stubs transparent to the clients. For more information about smart stubs refer to Chapter 15 of the book *Professional EJB*, ISBN 1-861005-08-3, from Wrox Press.

Next we will look at the presentation tier patterns related to the J2EE web component tier.

Web Component Tier Patterns

MVC and Business Delegate patterns are applicable to GUI and web-based clients. The importance of the web-based clients dictates that we will take a brief look at some patterns related to the J2EE web component tier. We will discuss the Intercepting Filter, Front Controller, View Helper, and Composite View patterns.

Intercepting Filter

The requests that web components receive from different clients often need to be preprocessed and post processed. In pre processing, the request is checked whether it passes checks, such as: does the client have a valid session, has the client been authenticated, does the request violate any constraints, and so on. Some of these checks influence the flow of the further interaction and some transform the incoming data flow.

Implementing these checks in each web component would be very difficult to manage because we would have a lot of redundancy. Therefore, we would like to build a flexible mechanism that allows us to add and remove these pre- and post-processing components.

The solution is to use the Intercepting Filter pattern, which enables us to create pluggable filters which process the requests and responses without requiring changes to the core request processing code of web components. The filters intercept the incoming requests and outgoing responses and do pre processing and post processing on them. These filters can be added or removed without influencing other filters or web components.

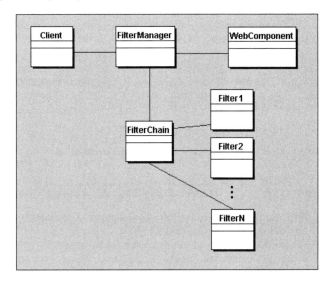

The next figure schematically shows the Intercepting Filter pattern. Between the client and the target web component we have the filter manager that manages a chain of filters, which can be added or removed:

The advantages of the Intercepting Filter pattern are primarily the centralized control with filters that are loosely coupled to web components, which improves reusability of filters and web components. The configuration of filters is highly flexible without influencing the target web component. The drawback is that the communication between filters can require a lot of time and can become inefficient, particularly if large amounts of data have to be transferred between the filters.

Front Controller

Often it is advantageous if we can control and coordinate the processing of each client across multiple requests. We would need a centralized access point for web component request handling. To achieve this we can use the Front Controller pattern.

The Front Controller pattern uses a controller as the initial point of contact for handling a client request. The controller invokes the necessary operations to handle the request, such as authentication, authorization, delegation to appropriate web component for providing view, and so on.

A schematic of the Front Controller is shown below. It shows a client which uses the controller to delegate the requests to the web components such as servlets or JSP pages:

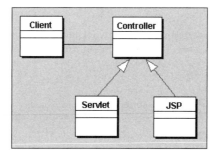

The major benefit is the centralized control, provided by the controller. The controller is a central place where services are handled. This improves manageability, reusability, and security.

View Helper

Developing the presentation layer is difficult. Even more difficult is to keep it up-to-date with the changes to the business logic tier components. The major problem is that component access and presentation formatting are mixed inside a single web component. This makes the system less flexible, difficult to maintain, and less suitable for reuse.

The solution is to create a view (from the MVC pattern) for formatting the presentation layout and to delegate the component access logic to helper classes. The view should be implemented using JSP pages, the helper classes like JavaBeans. The JSP pages should delegate the requests to JavaBeans using custom tags. JavaBeans also store the intermediate data used in view and serve as business data adapters. We have demonstrated this approach in the JSP example in an earlier section of this chapter.

The next figure represents the View Helper pattern:

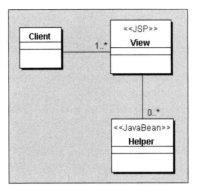

This pattern promotes role separation, as defined by the MVC, and therefore improves application partitioning, reusability, and maintainability.

Composite View

Sophisticated web-based user interfaces, particularly for large integrated information system, or if developed as enterprise portals, present a lot of content from different sources. For this they use multiple views that form a single user interface. Therefore we have to find a solution to easily combine these views into a composite whole.

The Composite View pattern provides a solution to combine atomic views into a composite view. Each component that implements a certain atomic view can be dynamically included into the composite view. The layout can be managed independently of content. The Composite View pattern is shown in the next figure:

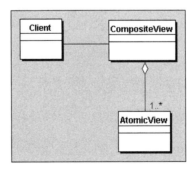

This pattern has several advantages. It improves flexibility and enhances modularity, reusability, maintainability, and manageability. However, this pattern is not without a performance drawback. Generating composite views out of many atomic views may slow performance.

Supporting Different Types of Clients

JSP pages and servlets provide strong technologies for the web component tier and for the development of presentation layers. The examples also show how to use these technologies relatively easily to generate user interfaces. However, the demonstrated examples are focused on web clients using HTML and web browsers. In the last few years the requirements have changed somewhat and today information systems have to support different types of clients, like palmtop computers, cell phones (over WAP using WML), and so on.

When using the approach where the content for web-based clients is generated directly in HTML, to support different types of clients we will have to implement additional web components (JSP pages/servlets) that will generate other markup languages (WML, for example). This will add complexity to the development and maintenance. New types of clients emerge almost every day, so it would also be beneficial to have a flexible architecture that could support different types of clients without too much effort.

Such a flexible solution would generate the presentation layer content in a universal, client-independent format (such as XML) and then use a technique to map this universal format to a client-specific format, for example, eXtensible Stylesheet Language (XSL). Unfortunately, J2EE currently does not provide a mechanism that would do the mapping to different types of clients automatically. However, this function will be provided to .NET developers, so it is a safe bet that the next version of J2EE will provide something similar in the future.

For now the best solution in J2EE is to use XML, XSL, and related technologies. Instead of generating the output of JSP/servlets in HTML, these should generate them in XML format. XML does not specify the formatting, therefore we have to provide style sheets and use XSL to transform the XML to the corresponding formats, suitable for presentation, which includes:

- ❑ Markup languages: HTML, XHTML, WML, and other XML vocabularies.
- ❑ Other non-markup formats: like PDF, PostScript, and so on.

To do the transformations we will use XSL, or more precisely:

- ❑ XSL for Transformations (XSLT) to convert XML to other markup formats, including XHTML, HTML, and so on.
- ❑ XSL Formatting Objects (XSL FO) to generate other formats, such as PDF, PostScript, amongst others.

Java provides APIs that ease the manipulation of XML documents. The basic and most important API is the Java API for XML Processing (JAXP). This is in version 1.1 at the moment and provides support for:

- ❑ XML parsing
- ❑ DOM (Document Object Model) Level 2
- ❑ SAX (Simple API for XML) 2.0
- ❑ XSLT 1.0 (so-called TrAX – the Transformation API for XML)

We can see that JAXP provides the necessary functionality. Other important JAX* APIs are in development within the Java Community Process, including:

❑ Java Architecture for XML Binding (JAXB)

❑ Long Term JavaBeans Persistence

❑ Java API for XML Messaging (JAXM)

❑ Java API for XML-based RPC (JAX-RPC)

❑ Java API for XML Registries (JAXR)

❑ JDOM

We'll see the application of some of these technologies in the next chapter.

Summary

In this chapter we discussed what is meant by presentation level integration. First we defined the objectives of the presentation level integration phase. We identified the good design practices and the types of clients. We saw that our choices for front-end integration are between graphical user-interface based application (fat) clients and web-based (thin) clients. Both have their advantages and disadvantages, and we also identified the technologies that the J2EE provides for both – JFC/Swing and JSP/servlets for GUI and web-based clients, respectively.

Then we discussed enterprise portals as single entry points to the integrated information system. We saw that presentation integration is not simply an extension of existing applications with a graphical or web-based user interface. Rather it is the development of a unified presentation layer for the complete integrated information system.

We saw that presentation level integration builds on business level integration fulfilling the objective of the multi-tier integration architecture that we set in Chapter 2. Presentation level integration provides several advantages that ease the development and maintenance of an integrated information system. The coupling between tiers is based on interfaces, so the approach also enables the painless replacement of existing applications without influencing other parts of the integrated system. We then discussed the support for transactions and security and we saw that the security of integrated systems deserves much attention.

Next we discussed the process of presentation tier development. We focused on the user interface analysis and design activities where we presented the necessary steps that should be performed for effective analysis and the design of the presentation layer.

Then we focused on the implementation technologies, particularly on web-based clients and became familiar with both J2EE technologies for the web component tier – servlets and JSP pages. We developed example web-based user interfaces to access a business logic component on the EJB tier and identified the advantages and disadvantages of both.

We discussed the web component tier architectures and saw that for smaller projects we can use the JSP/servlet-centric design, whereas for larger projects we should use the front controller design, which separates the view and controller roles more cleanly, thus improving the reusability and maintainability.

We also studied the presentation tier patterns. We covered two important patterns that can be applied to all types of clients: the Model View Controller pattern and the Business Delegate pattern. Then we studied four patterns specific to the web component tier: Intercepting Filter, Front Controller, View Helper, and Composite View patterns. Finally, we discussed and identified the technologies for supporting different types of clients.

In the next chapter we'll expand our integration horizons and look at how we can integrate our enterprise systems (in the shape of our newly integrated information infrastructure) with other enterprises of our business partners.

18

Web Services for B2B Integration

So far in this book, we have mainly been concerned with constructing an integration architecture to integrate a range of existing applications within our own enterprise. However, as we mentioned early in the book, this can been seen as merely the first step to integrating the enterprises of different organizations. Therefore, in this chapter, we are going to explore **web services**, which enable business services (potentially implemented using any technology) to be accessed over a network using open standards such as XML and HTTP.

Many manufacturing, financial, retail, and transport companies have long used **Electronic Data Interchange (EDI)** to produce quotes, orders, invoices, and shipping notices – to varying degrees of success. However, EDI is an expensive and complex technology to implement, which meant that EDI was restricted to large companies that can afford the network setup and running costs. Most small-to-medium-sized companies ignored EDI, which meant that they ignored e-business in general – until the Web came along.

The Web provides businesses with a cheap way to make their services available – but most business applications were never designed to be able to communicate with one another, let alone to be used over the Internet. In addition, business applications that use proprietary interfaces to transmit messages will be unable to penetrate most corporate firewalls.

In this chapter we're going to look at how we can provide a way for businesses to expose their business applications over the Internet, including:

❑   How to create services that can be made available

❑ How to let other businesses know that your services exist and are available

❑ How to access services that have been made available

To demonstrate this, we'll build some example web services to implement supply chain management for a fictional company.

Web Services

In order to be able to collaborate, communicate, and conduct business globally we require:

❑ A standard mechanism for describing an organization's business services, business processes, and the associated information model

❑ A mechanism by which organizations can register and store their business services so that they can be shared and reused

❑ Standard definitions for common business transactions

❑ A common data-interchange format

❑ A transport mechanism for exchanging messages in a reliable, secure, and transport-protocol-independent way

❑ Mechanisms for organizations to discover the required business services

❑ A mechanism that allows two or more organizations to negotiate on business terms, and to collaborate with each other before commencing business transactions

What is a Web Service?

Web services are built using open standards (such as SOAP) and accept requests from other systems. These requests are sent using lightweight, vendor-neutral communications technologies, which facilitate implementation-neutral business collaborations. There are three main participants in web services, the **service provider**, the **service requestor**, and the **service registry**.

The service provider is the owner of the business service and publishes the service using **Web Services Description Language (WSDL)** to a **Universal Description, Discovery, and Integration (UDDI)** registry.

> **WSDL is used to describe web services. UDDI provides a common registry in which information about web services is stored.**

The service requestor is an application that requires a certain functionality to complete a business process. The service registry is a naming service to which service providers can publish descriptions of their web services.

All three of these participants must be able to interact with one another, which means that there are three types of interaction. A service provider must be able to **publish** its web service to the service registry; the service requestor must be able to **find** a particular web service from the service registry; and a service requestor must be able to **bind** with a web service once it has been found.

Where are Web Services Used?

The **e-marketplace** is a business model within which companies can communicate, collaborate, and conduct business. Many industries have announced e-marketplaces and many vendors are preparing to provide software and services for them.

> **An e-marketplace is a web-based community in which buyers and sellers conduct business.**

Some e-marketplaces are aiming to provide features such as supply-chain planning, execution, and other collaborative capabilities. These will provide a common platform on which to conduct business. Of course, to build an e-marketplace we need to integrate the diverse software systems of different vendors – we can do this by using web services.

Consider a Business-to-Consumer (B2C) site for books and electronic products. It accepts credit cards so it needs to be able to validate the credit card – it requires a business process that can perform this validation. The site (playing the role of service requestor) can search a UDDI registry and find all the credit card validation services listed within it. The site can then select a service, get the information it needs to build a SOAP request, and send that request to invoke the service. The site will only need to look up the service in the registry once, as the information can then be cached for future use.

EAI and Web Services

Many EAI solutions, although effective, are expensive to implement and maintain. Web services promise to achieve many of the same goals – only faster and cheaper. Web services use SOAP (discussed in the next section) as the transport protocol, which is predominantly used over the HTTP protocol. This means that any company connected to the Internet can access the web service. There is no additional cost involved as there is in setting up an EDI network. As the messages are sent over HTTP, they can travel through firewalls without interference – unlike using RMI (or other proprietary technologies), which requires a new listener port to listen for the socket request.

Technologies such as CORBA, COM, and EJB are not easily made web-enabled or accessible from different clients. Web services allow us to deploy any such component as a service that is easily available via a network. Components on a wide variety of platforms can have their functionality exposed as web services in a consistent manner.

Importantly, web services enjoy industry-wide support. Business leaders such as Microsoft, Sun Microsystems, and IBM are all committed to web services. Standards groups are rapidly developing XML schemas for many kinds of business functions.

Before we can start to use web services to integrate our components, we need to understand better the technologies that underpin them – specifically SOAP, WSDL, and UDDI.

Simple Object Access Protocol

The **Simple Object Access Protocol (SOAP)** is a lightweight XML-based protocol that enables the exchange of structured and textual information in a distributed environment. Essentially, it works by describing a messaging format for machine-to-machine communication. SOAP enables the creation and invocation of web services over the Internet based on an open infrastructure.

The SOAP specification is at release 1.1 at the time of writing, released as a joint effort by IBM and Microsoft. SOAP was submitted to the W3C organization to become a standard and is currently evolving into the 'XML Protocol' standard. See http://www.w3.org/TR/SOAP/ for the latest information on SOAP, and http://www.w3.org/2000/xp/ for more information on XML Protocol-related activities at W3C.

At its core, SOAP is a transport-independent messaging protocol using one-way messages (though they can obviously be combined into request/response sequences). It is worth noting that it is not actually defined what the receiver of a SOAP message does with this message.

Structure of a SOAP Message

SOAP consists of three elements:

❑ **SOAP Envelope**
Defines what is in a message, who the message recipient is, and whether the message is optional or mandatory. The name of this element is the reason why a SOAP message is often referred to as a 'SOAP envelope'.

❑ **SOAP Encoding Rules**
A set of rules for exchanging instances of application-defined data types.

❑ **SOAP RPC Representation**
Defines a convention for representing remote procedure calls and responses.

SOAP can be used in combination with a variety of existing Internet protocols and formats including HTTP, SMTP, and MIME, and can support a wide range of applications from messaging systems to RPC.

A typical SOAP message, in this case to request information from a fictional stock quotation server, is shown below:

```
<IVORY:Envelope xmlns:IVORY="http://schemas.xmlsoap.org/soap/envelope/"
        IVORY:encodingStyle="http://schemas.xmlsoap.org/soap/encoding/">

  <IVORY:Body>
    <m:GetLastTradePrice xmlns:m="Some-URI">
      <symbol>DIS</symbol>
    </m:GetLastTradePrice>
  </IVORY:Body>
</IVORY:Envelope>
```

As seen from the snippet above, a SOAP message is encoded using XML. SOAP defines two standard namespace URIs that uniquely identify the contained elements: one for the envelope and the other for the encoding rules. A SOAP message must not contain a Document Type Definition (DTD); likewise, it should not contain any processing instructions. SOAP is a stateless protocol – there is no context information passed with messages (unless, of course, we add it manually). The SOAP message above simply defines a method called `GetLastTradePrice` that takes a stock symbol as parameter.

There is also no guaranteed delivery of messages – SOAP messages are not transactional. For some environments, however, these things are needed. Thus, SOAP should be implemented over other transport protocols, which therefore provide these additional levels of functionality.

The consumer of a web service would create a SOAP message (as seen before), embed it in an HTTP POST request, and send it to the web service for processing, as shown below:

```
POST /StockQuote HTTP/1.1
Host: www.stockquoteserver.com
Content-Type: text/xml;
charset="utf-8"
Content-Length: nnnn
SOAPAction: "Some-URI"

   ...
   SOAP Message
   ...
```

The web service processes the message, executes the requested operation, and returns the result to the client as another SOAP message. The message for our stock quote example now contains the requested stock price, as follows:

```
<SOAP-ENV:Envelope
        xmlns:SOAP-ENV="http://schemas.xmlsoap.org/soap/envelope/"
        SOAP-ENV:encodingStyle="http://schemas.xmlsoap.org/soap/encoding/"/>
    <SOAP-ENV:Body>
      <m:GetLastTradePriceResponse xmlns:m="Some-URI">
        <Price>34.5</Price>
      </m:GetLastTradePriceResponse>
    </SOAP-ENV:Body>
</SOAP-ENV:Envelope>
```

The message may be returned to the client as an HTTP response and will contain the appropriate HTTP header at the top of the message. As can be seen, in this message we are telling the client that the response from its call to GetLastTradePrice is 34.5; if the client had made requests to more methods, the response would contain more return values.

Interoperability

The major goal in the design of SOAP is to allow for an easy creation of interoperable distributed web services by providing easy access to objects. Since the services can be described in XML, it is a lot easier than comparable descriptions implemented in the RMI, CORBA, or EJB architectures.

Although the SOAP specification does not enforce a specific style of how data is encoded into XML content, SOAP does define a default encoding style (see example above) that works for most simple cases. The encodingStyle attribute allows us to define our own style for encoding, or we can simply extend the SOAP default style. Consequently, messages created by different applications may differ in the level of conformity to the specification – resulting in some non-interoperable applications.

We should also note that a valid XML document may not necessarily be a valid SOAP message, and similarly a valid SOAP message may not be a conformant SOAP message. In simple terms, this means that a SOAP message, though it is a conformant XML message, may not strictly follow the SOAP specification. To test for the conformance, third-party tools may be used. One such tool called SOAP Message Validator is developed by Microsoft and is available at http://www.soaptoolkit.com/soapvalidator/. Using the validator, you can test any SOAP code for conformance to the SOAP 1.1 specification.

Implementations

SOAP technology was developed by DevelopMentor, IBM, Lotus, Microsoft, and Userland. More than 50 vendors have currently implemented SOAP. The most popular implementations are by Apache, which is an open-source Java-based implementation, and by Microsoft, within their .NET platform. The two implementations have a few discrepancies that make applications developed using the two technologies non-interoperable.

Web Services Description Language

Web Service Description Language (WSDL) is used to describe services as a set of endpoints operating on messages containing either document-oriented, or procedure-oriented information.

> Just as IDL defines the interface for a CORBA component in a language-independent way, WSDL uses XML to define the interface for a web service.

For every web service, a service interface description is generated in WSDL. The service requestors can then use this WSDL to understand how to invoke the functionality of a web service, and to understand the results.

WSDL documents are divided into two types: **WSDL service interface documents** and **WSDL service implementation documents**. A WSDL service interface document is reusable. It is used to define generic sections of messages: the descriptions of the data to be exchanged, along with collections of operations. A WSDL service implementation document defines a concrete network deployment of a message, including the address of the SOAP server that will handle the request.

The root element of every WSDL document (both interface and implementation) is `<definitions>`. The root element of an interface document has four child elements:

- ❏   `<types>` – in which application-specific data types are defined

- ❏   `<message>` – in which the data to be communicated is defined

- ❏   `<portType>` – in which the abstract set of operations supported by one or more endpoints is described

- ❏   `<binding>` – in which the protocol and data format for a particular port type is described

The root element of an implementation document contains one child element:

- ❏   `<service>` – in which a collection of related endpoints is described

WSDL documents also contain an `<import>` element, which is used to import an interface document into an implementation document. This allows the same interface document to be used in multiple implementation documents.

Let's look at a simple example, in which we will develop a credit card validation service. We will need to create two classes: `CreditValidationService`, which will perform the actual validation; and `Customer`, which will represent a customer whose card is to be validated. Our `Customer` class is nothing more than a simple JavaBean, with attributes for first name, last name, age, and credit card number.

CreditValidationService is also very simple. It contains a single method that checks if a customer's credit card number and name match values we hard code into the class:

```
public class CreditValidationService {
  public boolean validateCreditCard(Customer customer) {
    int creditCardNumber = customer.getCreditCardNumber();
    String name = customer.getFirstName() + "."+ customer.getLastName();
    return ((creditCardNumber == 12312312312) &&
           (name.equalsIgnoreCase("stephen.mitchell")));
  }
}
```

Our next task is to represent this service using WSDL. Later on we will use the Web Services Tool Kit (WSTK) from IBM to generate WSDL for web services for us. For now, we'll create the WSDL by hand, in order to better understand it. We (like the WSTK) will create two files: the WSDL service interface document, and the WSDL service implementation document (named CreditValidation_Service-interface.wsdl and CreditValidation_Service.wsdl respectively).

The WSDL Service Interface Document

Each WSDL file contains a target namespace, which declares a namespace to which all names declared in the WSDL document belong:

```
<?xml version="1.0" encoding="UTF-8"?>
<definitions
  name="CreditValidation_Service"
  targetNamespace="http://www.wrox.com/CreditValidationService-interface"
  xmlns="http://schemas.xmlsoap.org/wsdl/"
  xmlns:soap="http://schemas.xmlsoap.org/wsdl/soap/"
  xmlns:tns="http://www.wrox.com/CreditValidationService-interface"
  xmlns:types="http://www.wrox.com/CreditValidationService-interface/types/"
  xmlns:xsd="http://www.w3.org/2001/XMLSchema">
```

We need to describe the data types for the input and output parameters. In our example, we have one input parameter – a customer. This is of type Customer, which is not one of the basic data types provided by XSD. Accordingly, we need to generate an XML schema to define our customer data type in WSDL documents. WSDL contains a <types> element, which is used to describe the XML schemas for the input and output parameters. As our output parameter is a Boolean (which is a type provided by XSD), we don't need to define a schema for it:

```
<types>
  <xsd:schema
    targetNamespace="http://www.wrox.com/CreditValidation-interface/types/"
    xmlns="http://www.w3.org/2001/XMLSchema/">
    <xsd:complexType name="Customer">
      <xsd:sequence>
        <xsd:element name="firstName" type="xsd:string"/>
        <xsd:element name="lastName" type="xsd:string"/>
        <xsd:element name="creditCardNumber" type="xsd:string"/>
        <xsd:element name="age" type="xsd:int"/>
      </xsd:sequence>
    </xsd:complexType>
  </xsd:schema>
</types>
```

Now that we have all our data types defined, we can define the input and output parameters. Our credit card validation service requires an input parameter of type `Customer` for its `validateCrediCard()` operation. The `<message>` element is used to define the parameters for each operation. Each `<message>` element consists of a `<part>` element that corresponds to either input or output parameters. We define the object of type `Customer` as an input parameter as follows:

```
<message name="InvalidateCreditCardRequest">
  <part name="meth1_inType1" type="types:Customer"/>
</message>
```

Notice that the `type` attribute with the value `types:Customer` in `<part>` refers to the XML schema (`<xsd:complexType name="Customer">`) that we defined for `Customer`. The return type for the output parameter of the `validateCrediCard()` method is defined as follows:

```
<message name="OutvalidateCreditCardResponse">
  <part name="meth1_outType" type="xsd:boolean"/>
</message>
```

The `<message>` element contains a `name` attribute, which is used to define the method name. The sub-element, `<part>`, also contains a `name` attribute, which is used to define the parameter name and a `type` attribute, which is used to define the parameter type.

Our next step is to define the operations (or methods) of the validation service. WSDL contains a `<portType>` element that we can use to define one or more operations using `<operation>` elements. The `<operation>` element can have `<input>`, `<output>`, and `<fault>` subelements. The `message` attribute in each `<input>` and `<output>` element refers to the `<message>` element that we just defined:

```
<portType name="CreditValidation_Service">
  <operation name="validateCreditCard">
    <input message="tns:InvalidateCreditCardRequest"/>
    <output message="tns:OutvalidateCreditCardResponse"/>
  </operation>
</portType>
```

Finally, we need to define the binding information, which specifies details such as the transport mechanism, transport protocol, and the deployed service name. The `<binding>` element has a `<soap:binding>` subelement, which has `style` and `transport` attributes. The `style` attribute is used to determine the serialization of the message on the wire. When it is set to `"document"`, the `<message>` element defines document formats rather than function signatures. The `transport` attribute refers to a namespace, which in this case signifies that the HTTP SOAP protocol is to be used:

```
<binding name="CreditValidation_ServiceBinding"
         type="tns:CreditValidation_Service">
  <soap:binding style="rpc"
                transport="http://schemas.xmlsoap.org/soap/http"/>
```

The `<soap:operation>` element contains a `soapAction` attribute that refers to the target web service (in this case `urn:creditvalidation-service`). The `soapAction` attribute is required for HTTP binding but should not be present for non-HTTP binding. SOAP 1.1 states that `soapAction` is used to identify the 'intent' of the message:

```
    <operation name="validateCreditCard">
      <soap:operation soapAction="urn:creditvalidation-service"/>
      <input>
        <soap:body
           encodingStyle="http://schemas.xmlsoap.org/soap/encoding/"
           namespace="urn:creditvalidation-service"
           use="encoded"/>
      </input>
      <output>
        <soap:body
           encodingStyle="http://schemas.xmlsoap.org/soap/encoding/"
           namespace="urn:creditvalidation-service"
           use="encoded"/>
      </output>
    </operation>
  </binding>

</definitions>
```

That completes the WSDL service *interface* definition. Our next task is to define the WSDL service *implementation* document.

The WSDL Service Implementation Document

As with the service interface document, the first part of the service implementation document contains the namespace attributes:

```
<?xml version="1.0" encoding="UTF-8"?>
<definitions
   name="CreditValidation_Service"
   targetNamespace="http://www.wrox.com/CreditValidationService"
   xmlns="http://schemas.xmlsoap.org/wsdl/"
   xmlns:interface="http://www.wrox.com/CreditValidationService-interface"
   xmlns:soap="http://schemas.xmlsoap.org/wsdl/soap/"
   xmlns:types="http://www.wrox.com/CreditValidationService"
   xmlns:xsd="http://www.w3.org/2001/XMLSchema">
```

We can import the WSDL service interface document into the WSDL service implementation document using the `<import>` element:

```
<import location="http://localhost:8080/wrox/wsdl/CreditValidation_Service-
interface.wsdl"
        namespace="http://www.wrox.com/CreditValidationService-interface"/>
```

A service is defined as a set of `<port>` elements. Each `<port>` element consists of a `<soap:address>` element to define the exact location of the service using the `location` attribute:

```
<service name="CreditValidation_Service">
  <documentation></documentation>
  <port binding="interface:CreditValidation_ServiceBinding"
        name="CreditValidation_ServicePort">
```

```
        <soap:address location="http://localhost:8080/soap/servlet/rpcrouter"/>
    </port>
</service>

</definitions>
```

Both the service interface and service implementation details could be defined in a single WSDL document. However, by separating the service interface from the service implementation, it is possible to standardize a set of operations. Each provider can then differentiate from another provider by simply providing application-specific details in the service implementation document.

A vertical industry, such as banking, could standardize a set of operations by defining abstract WSDL documents for functions common to all banks. Each bank is then free to define its own implementation-specific protocol, serialization, and encoding values – without duplicating work already done.

This separation between interface and implementation also means that it is easy to integrate a new web service that provides new functionality with existing services.

Universal Description Discovery and Integration

The Java Naming and Directory Interface (JNDI) provides an interface for access to a registry, in which we register (or bind) objects by giving them a unique name (JNDI name), which is used as an identifier. Applications access the objects using the object's JNDI name. As JNDI interfaces are defined using Java, it cannot be used in applications built using other technologies. In addition, JNDI uses RMI, and is not designed to access registry objects using SOAP over HTTP.

What we need is an interface (similar in functionality to JNDI) that we can use to publish and query web services from a registry. This registry could be global and freely accessible via the Internet, or private and used solely within a particular enterprise. **Universal Description Discovery and Integration (UDDI)** plays the role of JNDI for web services. It provides Publish and Inquiry APIs to access business services in the UDDI registry.

> **UDDI is an XML-based technology that enables the storage of information about business services in a registry. It allows service requestors to search and locate the business services that they need.**

UDDI defines basic data type structures that are used to store the details of a business service. UDDI defines a registry with publish and inquiry interfaces. This registry can be global or local to an enterprise. A global registry is meant for use by many different service requestors. For example a group of businesses could maintain a global registry to which service providers can publish their business entities and services using the Publish API. Enterprises can also maintain registries local to the organization; these can be used to store those business services that should be used within the enterprise only.

The Architecture of UDDI

The information provided by a UDDI registry is arranged in three ways – **white pages**, **yellow pages**, and **green pages**. White pages and yellow pages are analogous to the methods used for storing information in telephone directories.

White pages contain information such as the name of a business along with contact information. Yellow pages contain information categorized by industry. This is done using industry codes such as the North American Industry Classification System (NAICS), product codes such as Universal Standard Products and Services Classification (UNISPC), business identification codes such as D-U-N-S number, and geography codes such as ISO 3166. Yellow pages provide this core classification information to service requestors to use as a starting point to find business services.

Green pages contain technical information about business services, including pointers to the URL where a service is located, and information about how to bind to the service.

The Core Components of UDDI

UDDI version 2.0 contains five data structure types that represent classification information. Each structure is defined in XML and contains data fields that are used to provide business and technical descriptions. They are:

- ❏ `businessEntity` – information about the web service provider that published the service
- ❏ `businessService` – descriptive information about a particular web service
- ❏ `bindingTemplate` – technical information about the service entry and point and construction specification
- ❏ `tModel` – meta data about a web service
- ❏ `publisherAssertion` – information about the relationship between two parties, asserted by one or both

`businessEntity` is the root of a UDDI registry structure and can contain multiple `businessService` entries. A `businessService` entry represents a family of technical services and can contain more than one `bindingTemplate` entry, which provides technical information about a service. A `bindingTemplate` entry provides references to multiple `tModel` entries, which represent arbitrary data structures.

WSDL and UDDI are mapped to each other. The WSDL service implementation document is mapped to the `businessService` entry, and each `<port>` element within the document is mapped to a `bindingTemplate` entry. The WSDL service interface document is mapped to a `tModel` entry.

tModel

The `tModel` structure specifies technical information such as wire protocols, interchange formats, and interchange sequencing rules, which we use to bind with the service. The `<tModel>` element contains `<name>`, `<description>`, `<overviewDoc>`, and `<categoryBag>` subelements. The value of the `<name>` element maps to the value of the target namespace we specified in the WSDL service interface WSDL document. The value of the `<description>` element is derived from the `name` attribute of the `<definitions>` element we defined in the WSDL service interface document. For example:

```
<?xml version="1.0"?>
<tModel tModelKey="">
  <name>http://www.wrox.com/CreditValidation-interface</name>
  <description xml:lang="en">
    Standard WSDL service interface definition for CreditValidation_Service.
  </description>
```

The <overviewURL> element provides the URL for the service. This value is derived from the location of the WSDL service interface document. In our example the value of the name attribute in the <binding> element is appended to the location URL with a # symbol. This symbol is required when there is more than one <binding> structure in the WSDL service interface document. In such cases, we must define one <tModel> element for each <binding> element in the service interface document:

```
<overviewDoc>
  <description xml:lang="en">
     WSDL Service Interface Document
  </description>
  <overviewURL>
     http://www.wrox.com/wsdl/CreditValidation_Service-
     interface.wsdl#CreditValidation_ServiceBinding
  </overviewURL>
</overviewDoc>
```

A <tModel> element contains a **category bag**, which contains category information. A category is an identifier based on some predefined taxonomy. <keyedReference> elements are added to the category bag to indicate the type that is being registered:

```
<categoryBag>
   <keyedReference tModelKey="UUID value"
                   keyName="uddi-org:types"
                   keyValue="wsdlSpec"/>
   <keyedReference tModelKey="UUID value"
                   keyName="Credit Card Validation Service"
                   keyValue="522320"/>
</categoryBag>
</tModel>
```

The <categoryBag> element allows businessEntity, businessService, and tModel structures to be categorized according to classification schemes.

You can find more information on UDDI registry elements at
http://www.uddi.org/pubs/DataStructure-V2.00-Open-20010608.pdf.

bindingTemplate

The <bindingTemplate> element contains data that describes the technical characteristics of the given service implementation and refers to one or more tModel structures. Each bindingTemplate has a single logical businessService parent, which in turn has a single logical businessEntity parent. Each bindingTemplate has a unique bindingKey, the associated serviceKey, the accessPoint, and tModelInstanceDetails.

The accessPoint contains an attribute, URLType, to facilitate searching for entry points associated with a particular type of entry point. The URLType can be mailto, http, https, ftp, or even a fax or phone number:

```
<?xml version="1.0"?>
<bindingTemplate bindingKey="" serviceKey="">
  <accesssPoint URLType="http">
```

```
          http://www.wrox.com/creditvalidationservice
      </accessPoint>
      <tModelInstanceDetails>
        <tModelInstanceInfo tModelKey="[tModel Key for Service Interface]">
          <instanceDetails>
            <overviewURL>
              http://www.abc.com/wsdl/CreditValidation_Service.wsdl
            </overviewURL>
          </instanceDetails>
        </tModelInstanceInfo>
      </tModelInstanceDetails>
    </bindingTemplate>
```

The <overviewURL> element points to the location of the WSDL service implementation document (in this case CreditValidation_Service.wsdl). The <accessPoint> is set from the location attribute of the <port> element defined in the WSDL service implementation document. The <accessPoint> element contains the URLType attribute that indicates the protocol used. The <bindingTemplate> element contains one <tModelInstanceInfo> element for each tModel that it references.

businessService

This structure represents the service that a business offers. It contains a unique key that represents the service, the name of the service, and the bindingTemplate structures that hold the technical information. For example:

```
<businessService businessKey="..." serviceKey="...">
  <name>StockQuoteService</name>
  <description xml:lang="en">
    Credit Card Validation Service
  </description>

  <bindingTemplates>
    <bindingTemplate bindingKey="" serviceKey="">
      <accesssPoint URLType="http">
        http://www.wrox.com/creditvalidationservice
      </accessPoint>
      <tModelInstanceDetails>
       <tModelInstanceInfo tModelKey="[tModel Key for Service Interface]">
        <instanceDetails>
          <overviewURL>
            http://www.abc.com/wsdl/CreditValidation_Service.wsdl
          </overviewURL>
        </instanceDetails>
       </tModelInstanceInfo>
      </tModelInstanceDetails>
    </bindingTemplate>
  </bindingTemplates>

  <categoryBag>
    <keyedReference tModelKey="UUID:DB77450D-9FA8-45D4-A7BC-04411D14E384"
                    keyName="Stock market trading services"
                    keyValue="84121801"/>
  </categoryBag>

</businessService>
```

businessEntity

The <businessEntity> structure is the top-level data structure; it contains descriptive information about a business or entity.

The businessEnitity structure specifies a UUID for a web service. To query any web service we need a unique identifier (just as we need a unique JNDI name for EJBs in J2EE applications). Web services use a UUID (which is a DCE 128-bit identifier) as the identifier for a particular web service.

> **The service registry provider (the UDDI operator) generates a UUID when we publish a business entity or a business service.**

The businessEntity element contains information about the company, including contact details. The first part contains information about the UDDI operator:

```xml
<?xml version="1.0" encoding="utf-8" ?>
<businessDetail generic="1.0"
  xmlns="urn:uddi-org:api"
  operator="www.ibm.com/services/uddi" truncated="false">
  <businessEntity
    authorizedName="1000001N4F"
    operator="www.ibm.com/services/uddi"
    businessKey="business key for wrox">
    <discoveryURLs>
```

In our example, the <discoveryURL> element points to the UDDI test registry provided by IBM:

```xml
    <discoveryURL useType="businessEntity">
http://www3.ibm.com/services/uddi/testregistry/uddiget?businessKey="UUID"
    </discoveryURL>
  </discoveryURLs>
  <name>WROX,Inc.</name>
  <description xml:lang="en">
   Leading Publishers
  </description>
  <contacts>
    <contact>
      <personName>David John</personName>
      <phone>1-415-234-5678</phone>
      <email>davidJM@wrox.com</email>
      <address>
        <addressLine>456 market street</addressLine>
        <addressLine>San Francisco</addressLine>
        <addressLine>94102</addressLine>
        <addressLine>CA</addressLine>
        <addressLine>U.S.A</addressLine>
      </address>
    </contact>
  </contacts>
```

The `<keyedReference>` element is added to the category bag to indicate the type that is being registered:

```
    <categoryBag>
      <keyedReference
        tModelKey="UUID value"
        keyName="NAICS: Credit card processing" keyValue="522320">
      </keyedReference>
    </categoryBag>
  </businessEntity>
  </businessDetail>
```

publisherAssertion

The `<publisherAssertion>` element allows large enterprises or market places to make their relationships visible in their UDDI registrations. For example:

```
<publisherAssertions generic="2.0" operator= "www.ibm.com/services/uddi"
      authorizedName="Steve" xml:ns= "some namespace"
   <publisherAssertion>
     <fromKey>some key value</fromKey>
     <toKey>some key value</toKey>
     <keyedReference tModelKey= "uuid value" keyName= "ABC Co"
           keyValue= "parent-child">
     </keyedReference>
   <publisherAssertion>
<publisherAssertions>
```

UDDI and SOAP

The `bindingTemplate` data structure has an `accessPoint` element that provides the URI of the SOAP listener and the URN name of the deployed service. The URN name refers to the `ID` value of the service that is specified at deployment. The URN name is used to set `TargetObjectURI` for the `org.apache.soap.rpc.Call` object in the SOAP client.

A SOAP request is built by using the URI and URN to invoke the service. The publish and inquiry APIs provided by UDDI use SOAP over HTTP as their default transport mechanism.

The UDDI API specification defines a collection of XML requests and their responses that make the API programming-language neutral. UDDI defines two types of APIs, the Publish API and the Inquiry API. Using the Publish API, service providers can register a provider's information and their services in the UDDI registry. The Inquiry API provides interfaces to find a business service, the `tModel` information, and binding template information.

> *You can find more information on the specification and API documentation at*
> *http://www.uddi.org/pubs/ProgrammersAPI-V2.00-Open-20010608.pdf.*

The Publish API

Using the Publish API, we can create new entities, as well as modify and delete existing entities. The Publish API provides methods to change business entities, business service entities, and also `tModels`. Invoking the methods in the Publish API requires authorization and so is usually done by providing username and password credentials for every request.

A service provider is required to register with a UDDI operator before it can publish their business entities and services. To restrict unauthorized access to business services for any modification only an authorized user can modify a service published in the UDDI registry. Accordingly, all publish requests are executed over the HTTPS protocol.

There are methods that are used to save each of the data structure types: save_business(), save_service(), save_binding(), save_tModel(), and set_publisherAssertions(). Each of these methods accepts as input the authInfo and one or more corresponding structures. They all require username and password credentials so that authorization can be performed. The Publish API also contains methods to delete each of the data structures: delete_business(), delete_service(), delete_binding(), delete_tModel(), and delete_publisherAssertions(). All these methods accept the corresponding authToken and UUID key as input parameters.

The Publish API also provides two get methods: get_authToken() and get_registeredInfo(). The get_authToken is used to get an authentication token from a UDDI operator. It accepts a username and password as input parameters and returns an AuthToken, which can be used for authentication in subsequent calls. The get_registeredInfo() method is used to get a summary of information about businessEntity and tModel keys. It accepts an authInfo (which contains the authentication token) as an input parameter and returns a list of abbreviated business information.

The Inquiry API

The Inquiry API provides three forms of query that follow the needs of software (traditionally) used with registries.

The Browse Pattern

The Browse pattern involves starting with some broad information, performing a search, finding general result sets, and then selecting more specific information that can be used to drill down.

The Inquiry API accommodates the Browse pattern by way of find_xx() API calls. The API provides one find method for each data structure type. A find_business() call can be invoked with any information that is available, and returns a businessList structure. This result contains overview information (keys, names, and descriptions) derived from the registered businessEntity information, and matching the name fragment provided.

If we spot the business we are looking for within this list, we can drill down into the corresponding businessService information, to look for particular service types (for example, purchasing or shipping) using the find_service() API call. Similarly, if we know the technical fingerprint (tModel signature) of a particular software interface and we want to see if the business we've chosen provides a web service that supports that interface we can use the find_binding() inquiry message. Each of the find method calls accepts an optional findQualifiers element that is used to alter the default search behavior; for example "sortByNamesDesc" or "exactNameMatch".

The Drill-Down Pattern

Once we have a key for one of the four main data types, it can be used to get more information about a specific data instance. The Inquiry API provides get_xx() methods to get more information about any of the data types by passing the key as input parameter. The API provides get_businessDetail(), get_serviceDetail(), get_bindingDetail(), get_tModelDetail(), and get_businessDetailExt() (to get the extended information of a businessEntity).

The Invocation Pattern

The `bindingTemplate` data obtained from the UDDI registry represents specific details about an instance of a given interface type, including the location at which a program starts interacting with the service. The calling application or program should cache this information and use it to contact the service at the registered address whenever the calling application needs to communicate with the service instance. However, problems can arise when a remote service is moved without any knowledge on the part of the callers. Such moves occur for a variety of reasons – server upgrades, disaster recovery, service acquisition, or business name changes.

When a call that is using cached information fails, the proper behavior is to query the UDDI registry for fresh `bindingTemplate` information. If the data returned is different from the cached information, the service invocation should automatically retry the invocation using the fresh information. If the result of this retry is successful, the new information should replace the cached information. By using this pattern with web services, a business that uses a UDDI operator site can automate the recovery of a large amount of partner information.

Automatic Business Intelligence Using ebXML

Many organizations are developing standards and frameworks that are based on the Internet as the medium for conducting businesses. Web services, which we have discussed already, are one such example; **Electronic Business XML (ebXML)** is another.

> **ebXML defines a set of specifications that enables enterprises to conduct business over the Internet.**

ebXML is a global standard sponsored by the United Nations Center for Trade Facilitation And Electronic Business (UN/CEFACT) (http://www.unece.org/cefact/) and Organization for the Advancement of Structural Information Standards (OASIS) (http://www.oasis-open.org/). ebXML defines a set of specifications that enable a modular electronic business framework. The vision of ebXML is to enable a global electronic marketplace in which enterprises of any size and in any geographical location can meet and conduct business with each other through the exchange of XML messages.

ebXML defines core libraries and business libraries for business processes. It also provides **Collaboration Protocol Profiles (CPPs)** for enterprises to publish the services they offer (and their capabilities), and **Collaboration Protocol Agreements (CPAs)** for business partners to agree on before they execute business transactions. The CPP and CPA allow interoperability between trading partners.

Collaboration Protocol Profile

Trading partners are required to publish their capabilities, business services, and to make agreements through a **Trading Partner Agreement (TPA)** to collaborate and conduct business transactions. The ebXML specification defines an XML-based standard infrastructure for defining a company's profile, known as a Collaboration Protocol Profile (CPP), which is designed to capture all the information required to make business transactions. It provides the following information:

❑   General information about an agreement, for example the expiry date of the agreement

867

- ❏ The Organization's contact information and D-U-N-S number (a nine-digit string assigned by Dun and Bradsheet)

- ❏ Details about communication protocols

- ❏ Information about security properties, including certificates, signature algorithms, and protocols for ensuring secure interchange of information between trading partners

- ❏ The role of a participating trading partner, for example "buyer" or "seller"

- ❏ Information about common interfaces, and the business process schemas for business transactions, such as a purchase order

- ❏ Information about message reliability, including information on retries, retry interval, the degree of reliable messaging (once and only once, or best effort), detection and discarding of duplicate messages, and time duration of persistent storage

- ❏ Additional information such as a reference to a legal document

Collaboration Protocol Agreement

The ebXML specification also defines a common profile of both trading partners known as a Collaboration Protocol Agreement (CPA), which describes the agreement between two companies on technical characteristics that define features, services, and processes in the electronic business relationship between them.

A CPA is based on the capabilities common in the CPPs of both participating companies. The CPA defines the start date and time for the collaborative business between the participants. A CPA also defines the concurrent conversation limit for the number of conversations between the parties processed at any time. Like CPP, CPA also provides certificates and digital signatures and the protocols to ensure the secure interchange of information. The transport protocol, message routing, and security protocol information required for the conduction of business will be decided based upon the capabilities of both the partners and would be specified in the CPA.

ebXML Transactions

There are three functional phases that a company must go through to become operational with ebXML:

- ❏ An **implementation phase** creates the basic ebXML complaint systems

- ❏ A **discovery-retrieval phase** learns the capabilities of trading partners

- ❏ A **runtime phase** covers the exchange of ebXML messages

Implementation Phase

A trading partner or organization that wishes to conduct business via ebXML must first acquire the ebXML specification as well as the core and business libraries. The next step is to implement the ebXML standards by either building a new system, or by building on top of an existing legacy system. Once the system is built, the organization publishes its profile in the ebXML repository for other organizations to discover. This profile, written in ebXML, is the CPP.

Discovery and Retrieval Phase

An organization that is looking to conduct business must search the global ebXML registry for the business services it requires. An ebXML registry is similar to a UDDI registry. Companies publish their CPPs in an ebXML registry. Any organization that requires a business service looks into the CPPs of other organizations in the registry. Once the required CPP is discovered, it is retrieved and information about the organization's capabilities and business services are extracted from it.

If organization A supports the business processes that organization B is interested in (and their transport mechanisms and security arrangements are compatible) a discussion must take place among the decision makers of both organizations. Both organizations must form an agreement, the CPA, which is derived from their CPPs.

Runtime Phase

Once the CPA is completed, the organizations can commence ebXML transactions. In this phase, ebXML messages are exchanged between trading partners using the ebXML messaging service.

ebXML and Web Services

The ebXML specification defines a programming model to help organizations design their applications by integrating technologies such as SOAP, WSDL, and UDDI within a standard specification. We'll discuss each core component of web services and its role in ebXML to get more understanding of how this works.

The ebXML Message Service and SOAP

The ebXML message service specification is designed for use by businesses that require a secure, reliable exchange of electronic business information with their partners, suppliers, and customers.

The ebMXL message service is a set of layered extensions on SOAP 1.1, which means that it provides extensions for security and reliability that are not addressed directly by the SOAP 1.1 specification. An ebXML message contains a soap message container and zero or more payload containers.

The `<SOAPHeader>` element contains three elements specific to ebXML: `<MessageHeader>`, `<TraceHeaderList>`, and `<Signature>`. The `<MessageHeader>` element provides data on the basic identity of the parties such as `From`, `To`, `CPAId`, `ConversationId` and `Version` information. The `<TraceHeaderList>` element is required if a message needs multiple hops to go from the sending to the receiving party. The `<TraceHeaderList>` element provides the order of these hops from one message service handler to the next. The `<Signature>` element provides information on digital signatures to verify the identity of the message senders.

The `<SOAPBody>` element contains three elements: `<Manifest>`, `<StatusData>`, and `<ErrorList>`. The ebXML message introduces a `<Manifest>` element with each message, which contains references to each payload object along with schema location and version information about the payload.

To guarantee reliable message delivery, the ebXML message service provides positive acknowledgement and persistent storage mechanisms. Like SOAP, the ebXML message service also supports a wide variety of communication protocols (including HTTP, SMTP, and FTP). ebXML is also capable of supporting payloads of any type (such as XML, EDI transaction, and binary data).

*You can find more information about the ebXML messaging service at
http://www.ebxml.org/specs/ebMS.pdf.*

CPP and WSDL

WSDL provides binding and service information. CPP not only provides this information, but also the role of an organization in the context of a particular service, as well as information about error handling and failure scenarios. We saw earlier how CPP provides information about the duration of agreement, the role of a participating organization, the communication protocols, the security properties, and the business transactions. Simply put, CPP is a superset of WSDL.

The ebXML Registry Service and the UDDI Registry

Service providers publish their web services in a UDDI registry. Similarly, ebXML defines a registry and repository service, in which CPPs, CPAs, core components, and other ebXML-related documents are stored. The discovery of a business that provides services and the downloading of its CPP will be done via the ebXML registry service. A business described in the ebXML registry/repository can then be published in UDDI to allow other partners to locate it. Organizations can use UDDI to inquire about businesses in the UDDI registry and those entries can then be used to reference ebXML web services in the ebXML registry.

We define a `tModel` key for the ebXML registry; the `uuid` value refers to the ebXML registry:

```
<tModel tModelKey="uuid value">
  <name>ebXML RegRep</name>
  <description lang="en">ebXML conformant registry/repository</description>
  <overviewDoc>
    <description lang="en">EbXML Reg/Rep Specification</description>
    <overviewURL>
      http://www.ebxml.org/project_teams/registry/private/Registry.dtd
    </overviewURL>
  </overviewDoc>
  <categoryBag>
    <keyedReference tModelKey="uuid:C1ACF26D-9672-4404-9D70-39B756E62AB4"
    keyName="uddi: A specification " keyValue="specification"/>
    <keyedReference tModelKey="uuid:C1ACF26D-9672-4404-9D70-39B756E62AB4"
    keyName="uddi: An XML specification " keyValue="xmlSpec"/>
    <keyedReference tModelKey="uuid:C1ACF26D-9672-4404-9D70-39B756E62AB4"
    keyName="uddi: Using SOAP messages " keyValue="soapSpec"/>
  </categoryBag>
</tModel>
```

Then the `tModel` key is referred to by a `<bindingTemplate>` element. The `<businessService>` element to be published in the UDDI registry contains this `<bindingTemplate>` element. Accordingly, the `accesspoint` should point to the ebXML registry:

```
<businessService serviceKey="">
  <name>Some business service name </name>
  <description lang="en">
     The service description goes here </description>
  <bindingTemplates>
```

```
      <bindingTemplate bindingKey="">
        <accessPoint URLType="http">
          "url to point to ebXML regisgry/repository"
        </accessPoint>
        <description lang="en">
          Use your Web Browser to search the World
        </description>
        <tModelInstanceDetails>
          <tModelInstanceInfo
           tModelKey="uuid value">
            <description lang="en">ebXML RegRep</description>
          </tModelInstanceInfo>
        </tModelInstanceDetails>
      </bindingTemplate>
    </bindingTemplates>
  </businessService>
```

Portals

Many web sites are evolving into portals as they begin to offer more interactivity and decision support systems, providing basic search capability, links to other related sites, and the capability to send and receive messages.

> **A portal is a single interface or entry point to access different enterprise applications, databases, workflows, and processes via an intranet or the Internet.**

Portals transform raw data from diverse sources into useful information tailored to a single user, and therefore require a high level of system integration. Portals must be able to manage data from the enterprise, its customers, and its trading partners; this can be done using EAI. A portal must be able to:

❑   Access heterogeneous resources in a common platform

❑   Authenticate against a wide variety of security systems

❑   Authorize the user across various applications based on his role and responsibilities

❑   Index a wide variety of contents

❑   Render a wide variety of services in a common web format

Portals can be broadly classified as one of four types:

❑   **Enterprise or Corporate Portals**
    Provide building blocks called portlets (a component that provides specific functionality) via the Web. This allows the combination of heavily used components from different systems in one place. So, in one web page, corporate portal users can find all the corporate tools and Internet services they use most, as well as viewing personalized information about their customers, products, and markets.

❑ **Employee Portals**
Enable employees to access all of a business' processes, systems, and databases needed to carry out their jobs. These portals are used within an enterprise and are designed to provide the employee with a single interface that they can use to access business services, company new lines, information on department meetings, and e-mail services.

❑ **Customer Portals**
Provide a single entry point for information about products, services, catalogs, orders, and invoices for each customer.

❑ **Decision Processing Portals**
Provide access to business intelligence, online analytical processing (OLAP), and knowledge management.

Portals can be vertical or horizontal. Vertical portals are applications designed for a specific functional area such as ERP, business intelligence, or CRM. They offer a deep experience within a specific domain. Horizontal portals provide a single interface that integrates content and applications from a broad range of systems.

Imagine that we need a portal that integrates diverse applications running on heterogeneous platforms. To integrate data and services from other applications, we would create a portal that used portlets. As an example, we might require:

❑ **A search portlet** – provides search functionality and is provided by a third-party vendor.

❑ **A myPage portlet** – to access personal e-mails, bank accounts, stock quotes, and so on. The bank account application could be a legacy application; the stock quotes application could be hosted on a Microsoft platform; the weather application could be hosted on a UNIX platform.

❑ **A business portlet** – provides business functionality such as sales orders, inventory, and other CRM systems.

❑ **A discussion portlet** – allows the discussion of projects by team members.

❑ **A news portlet** – provides the company newsletter and other information, which might be Microsoft Word documents, PDF files, or HTML documents.

To access all this from a single portal, we need to have interfaces to all the applications. Then we can fetch the data and transform it as per our needs. This might very well involve accessing applications behind firewalls or third-party systems. We also need to decide on a payload format for message exchange and the transport protocol. These integration issues will need to be repeated whenever we add a new portlet to our portal.

> **Since web services are built on open standards, there is no need to build and learn proprietary technologies for integrating diverse applications.**

If these services are exposed as web services, then the integration process is always the same:

❑ Searching for the service in a UDDI or ebXML registry

❑ Retrieving the WSDL document(s) and extracting the binding and service information

❑ Building a SOAP request to invoke the service

❑   Receiving the SOAP response and transforming it accordingly

There are many tools available that facilitate web services deployment, publishing to and inquiring from UDDI registries, generating WSDL documents, and building SOAP requests. For example, CapeConnectThree from CapeClear – you can find more information at http://www.capeclear.com.

Only One Interface

Organizations have two types of web services, those published on the Internet (a public service) to enable collaborative business, and those intended for internal use (a private service).

Often, a service will consist of a series of sequenced activities, each of which could be available as a separate web service. However, only one web service will be exposed to the user. This hides the complex business services from the user. The practice of exposing a single interface for a particular business transaction is known as "**only one interface**".

Imagine a buyer service, a seller service, and a credit card validation service. The credit card validation service is an enabling service (a service that can be used by many applications doing electronic business) for credit card validation processing. Once an order for items is received, the seller service triggers a workflow with the following activities:

1. Invoke and execute the credit validation service before processing the order

2. Once the order is checked and found to be acceptable, the seller service checks the availability of the items in the inventory (we'll assume that the inventory has enough in stock of the ordered items and this activity is executed by the inventory service)

3. An invoice is generated and the items are sent for shipping – this is done using the invoice service

4. There is also a customer service and a status-tracking service, which will send a notice to the buyer once the items are shipped and keeps track of those items while they are in transit

The inventory, invoice, and customer services are specific to the organization so they are published as private services in the organization's private registry. The organization exposes only one interface – the seller service – to trading partners and customers.

We'll assume that our organization uses J2EE for all its applications, and that services are implemented either as JavaBeans or as EJBs. However, they are implemented on different platforms at different locations, all connected via the intranet. A private service can invoke one or more web services when executing its business process:

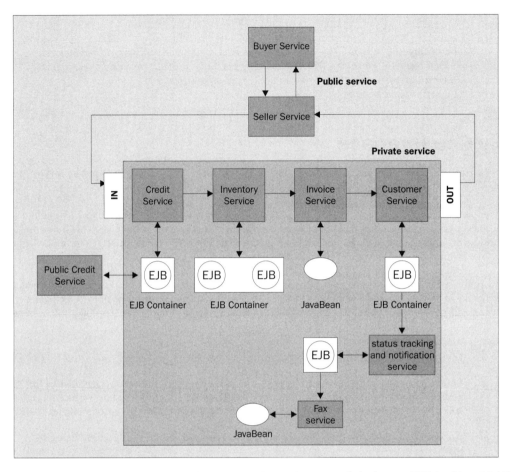

The seller service first invokes the credit service. The credit service (which is an EJB) builds a SOAP request to invoke the public credit service. Once the response is received, the EJB invokes the inventory service by building the required SOAP request. The inventory is implemented by a session bean, which uses one or more entity beans for checking the availability of items in the inventory database. If inventory has the items of the required quantity, the next activity will be to ship the item for delivery and generate an invoice.

The customer service uses a status-tracking and notification service, which in turn uses a fax service for communicating with the customers.

This chain of a web service invoking other web services comes in very handy when the services are implemented in heterogeneous platforms comprising different languages. In large organizations, it is common to have services on various platforms that all use different databases.

JAX Pack

As Java programmers, we obviously expect to have some Java APIs to facilitate the tasks of publishing and querying web services, building SOAP requests, parsing SOAP responses, and other XML structures. Two of the APIs from the JAX Pack are intended to provide easy handling of XML documents by providing parsing functionality and also functionality for modifying an XML document, adding elements and attributes to XML documents. Other APIs are provided as a layer to wrap the implementation details of web services standards, SOAP, WSDL, and UDDI.

There are **document-oriented** APIs that consist of JAXP and JAXB; and there are **procedure-oriented** APIs that consist of JAXM, JAXR, and JAX-RPC. As well as providing flexibility to the Java programmer, these APIs follow industrial standards set by W3C and OASIS.

You can find more information on JAX in Chapters 6, 7, and 8.

Using the JAX APIs

The following diagram shows an overview of how the JAX APIs are used in building web services:

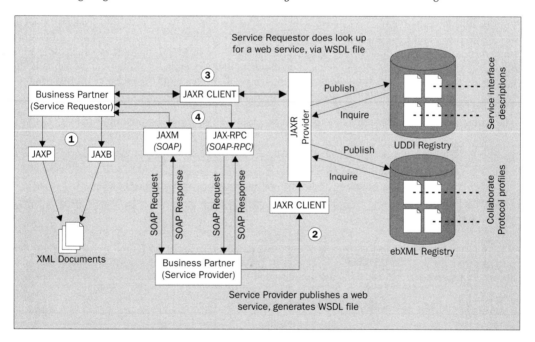

1. JAXP and JAXB provide interfaces to work with XML documents.

2. A service provider uses JAXR to publish business entities, services, and business templates in the registry. JAXR provides a common interface for different global registries.

3. A service requestor uses JAXR to query information about business services.

4. JAXM and JAX-RPC are used for message exchange between the trading partners. Generating SOAP requests, marshaling, un-marshaling, and encoding activities are performed by JAX APIs.

Building and Using Web Services with Java

We've discussed the concepts of web services, the main players, and the core components. Now, we're ready to build a sample supply-chain demo application using Java.

Defining the Application

The supply chain demo application consists of three players:

❏ The manufacturer – Delivers the finished goods to consumers

❏ The supplier – Supplies products to the manufacturer

❏ The consumer – Purchases finished goods from the manufacturer

For our supply chain demo application, we have a manufacturer, ABC, Inc. (Applications, Businesses, and Customers), and a supplier, JITS, Inc. (Just In Time Supply). ABC has software applications that are implemented on diverse platforms ranging from Windows NT to Mainframes. Most of its applications are not exposed to the Internet. After realizing opportunities available from B2B commerce, ABC has decided to make their applications web-enabled. They will do this by providing accessibility via the Internet using HTTP so that business can be conducted in a collaborative way.

The functionality that ABC wants to expose on the network (both Internet and intranet) is:

❏ A Request For a Quote (RFQ) functionality – which involves generating a RFQ and sending it to many suppliers

❏ An Inventory functionality – to look at the inventory of various warehouses

❏ A Catalog Upload functionality – which allows the suppliers to dynamically add products to ABC's catalog of products

JITS, the supplier, is also in the process of exposing its business services on the Internet. For our demo purpose we consider that JITS wants to expose its product catalog service so that manufacturers can access the catalog of products. The functionality that JITS wants to expose is:

❏ A Catalog functionality – to view the catalog of products

We will implement these functionalities and expose them as web services.

Web Services Provided by the Manufacturer

Let's examine the functionality provided by the services required by ABC. We'll develop these services using Java, deploy the services, and then publish the services in a UDDI registry.

The Request For Quote Service

ABC generates RFQs for products from its existing suppliers and new suppliers. The RFQ service has the following functionality:

- ❑ Generate a new RFQ
- ❑ Publish the RFQ as a Topic using the Java Messaging Service (JMS) – suppliers who subscribed to the topic then receive the RFQ
- ❑ Suppliers can also receive the RFQ via the Internet

The Inventory Service

The Inventory Service has the following functionality:

- ❑ View products in the inventory
- ❑ Add a new product to the inventory
- ❑ Update the quantity of an existing product in the inventory

The Product Catalog Upload Service

The Product Catalog service has the following functionality:

- ❑ Suppliers can dynamically add new products to ABC's catalog of products
- ❑ New suppliers can dynamically upload their products to ABC's catalog of products

Web Services Provided by the Supplier

JITS, the supplier for our demo application requires a catalog service. We will be developing, deploying, and publishing this service.

The Catalog Service

The Catalog service has the following functionality:

- ❑ Browsing the product catalog

The Architecture of the Application

The following architecture diagram shows how the manufacturer communicates with the suppliers using web services. The message is exchanged as an XML document:

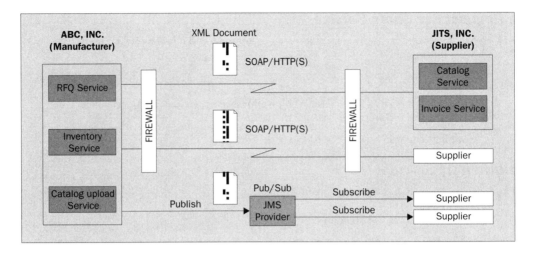

Design Decisions

We need to discuss some of the decisions taken in implementing the supply-chain demo application.

Using XML for Data Representation

All the information used for message exchanges is represented as XML, which allows data from legacy systems and applications to be sent via the Internet to other applications for data exchange without having to standardize the back-end technologies. Since any business transaction can be represented in XML, it lends itself to transmitting everything from RFQs, purchase orders, product catalogs, to invoices; and because of its extensibility, trading partners can accommodate industry-specific data for the message exchange.

XML enables the definition of business-specific structures as XML schemas. Many enterprises started building proprietary XML structures that are tailored to their applications for performing business transactions, which led to duplication of structures for business processes. To avoid this unnecessary work, XML structures are defined by standard bodies like ebXML (http://www.ebXML.org) and RosettaNet (http://www.rosettanet.org), which are working to develop XML standards.

> **Our focus is not to explore standardized structures, other than to stress the importance of open standards usage in facilitating easy integration, so we will not develop or use any in our example.**

There are efforts to define standard XML structures for business processes, transport, and security protocols. These will make it easier to integrate with new trading partners dynamically. We saw when we looked at ebXML how specifications exist for messaging and collaboration protocols.

Implementing Services Using JavaBeans

In our example, all the services are implemented using JavaBeans. In real applications the services could (and most likely would) be implemented using many different technologies: C++, COM, or EJBs. We will use JavaBeans in order to keep the code at a minimum so we can concentrate on the overall process.

Required Software

You'll need a variety of tools, APIs, and applications to create, deploy, and run the example application:

- ❏ BEA WebLogic 6.1 – from http://www.bea.com/products/weblogic/server/index.shtml
- ❏ Tomcat 4 – from http://jakarta.apache.org/tomcat/index.html
- ❏ Apache SOAP 2.2 – from http://xml.apache.org/soap/index.html
- ❏ IBM's Business Test Registry – from http://www-3.ibm.com/services/uddi/
- ❏ IBM's UDDI4J – from http://oss.software.ibm.com/developerworks/projects/uddi4j
- ❏ IBM's Web Services Toolkit 2.4 – from http://www.alphaworks.ibm.com/tech/webservicestoolkit/
- ❏ **JDOM API** (we used beta 7) – from http://www.jdom.org/
- ❏ **MySQL** (we used version 3.23) – from http://www.mysql.org
- ❏ **MM.MySQL JDBC Driver** (we used version 2.0.6) – from http://www.mysql.org/

However, we're not actually going to take you through every step of building and running the application. Rather our intention is to provide you with a guide to the steps you need to take if you are going to build, publish, and use web services. We'll concentrate on the steps that you will reuse time and again, so that you can apply the concepts in your applications. You can find the complete code in the download for this chapter from http://www.wrox.com.

Creating the Database

This is the SQL script for the creation of tables required for the example:

```sql
CREATE DATABASE abcdb;
USE abcdb;

CREATE TABLE rfq_table (rfqid CHAR(10) NOT NULL PRIMARY KEY,
                        rfqname VARCHAR(25) NOT NULL,
                        orgnizationname VARCHAR(25) NOT NULL,
                        rfqdate CHAR(10) NOT NULL,
                        creator VARCHAR(25) NOT NULL,
                        submissiondate CHAR(10) NOT NULL,
                        status CHAR(10) NOT NULL,
                        index IDX_RFQ_STATUS (STATUS)
                        );

CREATE TABLE rfq_product_table (rfqid CHAR(10) NOT NULL,
                        productid CHAR(10) NOT NULL PRIMARY KEY,
                        productname VARCHAR(25) NOT NULL,
                        quantity INT NOT NULL,
                        index IDX_RFQ_RFQID (RFQID)
                        );
```

```
CREATE TABLE inventory_table (productid CHAR(10) NOT NULL PRIMARY KEY,
                             productname VARCHAR(25) NOT NULL,
                             quantity INT NOT NULL
                             );

CREATE TABLE product_catalog_table (productid CHAR(10) NOT NULL PRIMARY KEY,
                                    productname VARCHAR(25) NOT NULL,
                                    unitprice DOUBLE(8,2) NOT NULL
                                    );

CREATE TABLE db_metadata_table (databaseid INT NOT NULL PRIMARY KEY,
                                databaseurl VARCHAR(40) NOT NULL,
                                dbname CHAR(15) NOT NULL,
                                tablename CHAR(15) NOT NULL,
                                dbuser CHAR(10) NOT NULL,
                                dbpassword  CHAR(8) NOT NULL
                                );

CREATE TABLE supplier_info_table (supplierid CHAR(10) NOT NULL PRIMARY KEY,
                                  suppliername VARCHAR(25) NOT NULL,
                                  password CHAR(8) NOT NULL,
                                  databaseid INT NOT NULL,
                                  );

CREATE DATABASE jits;
USE jits;

CREATE TABLE PRODUCT_CATALOG_TABLE (productid CHAR(10) NOT NULL PRIMARY KEY,
                                    productname VARCHAR(25) NOT NULL,
                                    unitprice DOUBLE(8,2) NOT NULL
                                    );
```

Though the schema can be definitely improved by applying normalization, we have purposefully made the schema simple and straightforward to avoid any complexity in the SQL queries.

If you want to use this example application you'll need to populate the database with some sample data.

Creating the Web Services

We have four web services to create and publish. We'll begin by developing and publishing the manufacturer's services, before moving onto the supplier's.

Creating the RFQ Service

The RFQ service is implemented as a simple JavaBean. ABC internal users will use the RFQ service to generate a new RFQ. The RFQ service can either publish the RFQ using JMS or send it as an XML request using a service proxy to invoke a suppliers service, with upload functionality, in the supplier's system.

When a new RFQ is created, its status remains OPEN till the submission date is over. Then the status will be marked as CLOSED.

The RFQ service makes use of the following helper classes:

- ❑ DBHelper – to get a database connection object
- ❑ JMSHelper – to send messages using the Java messaging service
- ❑ XMLBuildHelper – to build XML structures
- ❑ XMLParseHelper – to parse XML structures

Creating the Helper Classes

All services use a database helper class for connecting to the database:

```
package com.abc.helper;

import java.sql.*;

public class DBHelper {

  public void static {
    try {
      Class.forName("org.gjt.mm.mysql.Driver");
    } catch(Exception e){}
  }

  public Connection getConnectionObject(){
    Connection con = null;
    try {
      con = DriverManager.getConnection(
```

You'll need to set the username and password for your system:

```
      "jdbc:mysql://localhost:3306/ABCDB", "username","password");
    } catch (Exception e) {
      System.err.println("Unable to create a connection object");
    }
    return con;
  }
}
```

We need a context factory for accessing objects from the JNDI. WebLogic 6.1 provides the
WLInitialContextFactory for accessing the JMS administered objects and EJB beans using JNDI interface:

```
package com.abc.helper;

import java.util.*;
import javax.naming.InitialContext;
import javax.naming.NamingException;
import javax.transaction.*;
import javax.naming.*;
import javax.jms.*;

public class JMSHelper {

  private final static String JNDI_FACTORY =
                              "weblogic.jndi.WLInitialContextFactory";
```

We assume that the administered objects, `ABCTopicConnectionFactory` and `ABC-RFQ` are already defined using the WebLogic Administrator console:

```
private final static String JMS_TOPIC_FACTORY =
                                "ABCTopicConnectionFactory";
private final static String TOPIC = "ABC-RFQ";
```

Then, we initialize the connection factory by making a look up in the context and create a connection object:

```
private TopicConnectionFactory tConnectionFactory;
private TopicConnection tConnection;
private TopicSession topicSession;
private TopicPublisher publisher;
private Topic topic;
private TextMessage msg;
private InitialContext ictx = null;
```

We need to get the initial context to look up the JNDI for the administered objects. Since we are using the WebLogic implementation of JMS, the values for `INITIAL_CONTEXT_FACTORY` and `PROVIDER_URL` were set accordingly:

```
private InitialContext getInitialContext() throws NamingException {
   String url = "http://localhost:7001";
   Hashtable env = new Hashtable();
   env.put(Context.INITIAL_CONTEXT_FACTORY, JNDI_FACTORY);
   env.put(Context.PROVIDER_URL, url);
   return new InitialContext(env);
}
```

In the constructor, we initialize the connection factory object by referring the same to the administered object via a JNDI lookup. Then a connection object is obtained from the connection factory:

```
public JMSHelper() throws JMSException,NamingException {
   ictx = getInitialContext();
   tConnectionFactory =
               (TopicConnectionFactory) ictx.lookup(JMS_TOPIC_FACTORY);
   tConnection = tConnectionFactory.createTopicConnection();
   tConnection = tConnectionFactory.createTopicConnection();
```

A session object is created from the connection object. The parameter `false` indicates that the session is non-transacted and the acknowledgement mode `session.AUTO_ACKNOWLEDGE` indicates that the session automatically acknowledges the client's receipt of message:

```
topicSession = tConnection.createTopicSession(false,
                                Session.AUTO_ACKNOWLEDGE);
}
```

Then, the message is published on the specified topic:

```
public void publish(String message, String topicName)
  throws JMSException,NamingException {
  topic = (Topic) ictx.lookup(topicName);
  publisher = topicSession.createPublisher(topic);
  msg = topicSession.createTextMessage();
  msg.setText(message);
  publisher.publish(msg);
}
}
```

We use a helper class to build XML structures:

```
package com.abc.helper;

import java.util.*;
import java.io.*;
import java.sql.*;

import org.jdom.Element;
import org.jdom.Document;
import org.jdom.output.XMLOutputter;

import com.abc.beans.*;

public class XMLBuildHelper {
  public static String buildRFQXML(Vector vRFQ) {
    Element eRoot = new Element("message");
    Document doc = new Document(eRoot);

    Element eRFQ = new Element("RFQ");
    eRoot.addContent(eRFQ);

    Element eHeader = new Element("header");
    eRFQ.addContent(eHeader);
```

You can see that the code loops through the `Vector vRFQ` to retrieve the `RFQDataBean`. Then, we fetch the RFQ information using get methods and build the XML structure. The value for the element is set using the `setText()` method of the `Element` class provided by JDOM:

```
for(int i = 0; i < vRFQ.size(); i++) {
  RFQDataBean rfqbean = (RFQDataBean)vRFQ.elementAt(i);

  Element eOrg = new Element("organizationName");
  eOrg.setText(rfqbean.getOrganizationName());
  eHeader.addContent(eOrg);
```

You'll need to do the same for `rfqName`, `rfqId`, `rfqDate`, `creator`, `SubmissionDate`, and `static` elements:

```
...

Element eBody = new Element("body");
eRFQ.addContent(eBody);

Element ePList = new Element("ProductList");
eBody.addContent(ePList);
```

An RFQ is raised for one or more products. So we need to get the `Product` objects of type `ProductBean` from `RFQDataBean` and then build the XML structure:

```
Vector vProducts = (Vector)rfqbean.getProducts();

for(int j = 0; j < vProducts.size(); j++) {
  ProductBean product = new ProductBean();
  product = (ProductBean)vProducts.elementAt(j);

  Element eProduct = new Element("product");
  ePList.addContent(eProduct);

  Element eName = new Element("name");
  eName.setText(product.getProductName());
  eProduct.addContent(eName);

  Element eQty = new Element("quantity");
  eQty.setText("" + product.getQuantity());
  eProduct.addContent(eQty);
  }
}
```

Finally, the document object is passed to the `getXMLString()` method to get a string representation of XML document. The `getXMLString()` is a wrapper method and uses the `XMLOutputter` object provided by JDOM. The `outputString()` method defined in `XMLOutputter` accepts the `Document` object as an input parameter and returns a string representation of the same:

```
    String xml = getXMLString(doc);
    return xml;
  }

private static String getXMLString(Document doc) {
  String xmlRequest = null;
  try {
    XMLOutputter output = new XMLOutputter();
    xmlRequest = output.outputString(doc);
  } catch(Exception e){System.out.println(e);}
  return xmlRequest;
  }
}
```

We also use a helper class to parse XML structures. Here we will be doing the opposite to what we did earlier in the `XMLBuildHelper` class. This time, we need to build a vector of `RFQDataBean` objects that contains a vector of `ProductBean` objects by parsing the XML request string. We use a SAX parser to parse the XML structure. The `SAXBuilder` class from JDOM provides the functionality to parse XML structures:

```
package com.abc.helper;

import java.util.*;
import java.io.*;

import org.jdom.output.*;
import org.jdom.*;
import org.jdom.input.*;

import com.abc.beans.*;

public class XMLParseHelper {

    private static SAXBuilder saxBuilder = new SAXBuilder();

    public static Vector getRFQVector(String xmlRequest) throws Exception {
        Vector vRFQ = new Vector();
        Vector vProducts = new Vector();
        RFQDataBean rfqbean = new RFQDataBean();
        Document doc = saxBuilder.build(new StringReader(xmlRequest));
        Element root = doc.getRootElement();
```

We build the XML structure for RFQ:

```
        Element eRFQ = root.getChild("rfq");
        Element eHeader = eRFQ.getChild("header");
        rfqbean.setOrganizationName(
        eHeader.getChild("organizationName").getTextTrim());
        rfqbean.setRFQName(eHeader.getChild("rfqName").getTextTrim());
        rfqbean.setRFQId(eHeader.getChild("rfqId").getTextTrim());
        rfqbean.setRFQDate(eHeader.getChild("rfqDate").getTextTrim());
        rfqbean.setCreator(eHeader.getChild("creator").getTextTrim());
        rfqbean.setSubmissionDate(
                        eHeader.getChild("submissionDate").getTextTrim());
        rfqbean.setStatus(eHeader.getChild("status").getTextTrim());
        Element eBody = root.getChild("body");
        Element eProductList = eBody.getChild("productList");
        List lProduct = eProductList.getChildren("product");
        Iterator iterator = lProduct.iterator();
```

Using `Iterator`, we loop through the XML structure to get all the products and then build the XML structure:

```
        while(iterator.hasNext()) {
            ProductBean product = new ProductBean();
            Element eProduct = (Element)iterator.next();
```

```
        product.setProductId(eProduct.getChild("productId").getTextTrim());
        product.setProductName(
                            eProduct.getChild("productName").getTextTrim());
        product.setQuantity(
                Integer.parseInt(eProduct.getChild("quantity").getTextTrim()));
        vProducts.addElement(product);
      }
      rfqbean.setProducts(vProducts);
      vRFQ.addElement(rfqbean);
      return vRFQ;
    }
  }
```

We use a simple JavaBean with getter and setter methods to capture the RFQ information. The RFQDataBean class has attributes named OrganizationName, RFQName, RFQId, RFQDate, Creator, SubmissionDate, and Status. It also contains a vector that contains instances of ProductBean. The ProductBean class is a JavaBean to represent the product information.

We have discussed all the helper classes and the JavaBean classes required for RFQ service. Now, it's time to look the service itself. The RFQ service supports three types of functionality:

❑ Generate a new RFQ – Capable of generating a new request for a quote

❑ Get all open RFQ – Gets all the RFQ with status OPEN

❑ Get all RFQ – Gets all the RFQs regardless of status

The RFQService constructor creates a java.sql.Connection using the getConnectionObject() method of the DBHelper class. A java.sql.Statement object is created from the Connection object:

```
package com.abc.services;

import java.util.*;
import java.sql.*;

import com.abc.helper.*;
import com.abc.beans.*;

public class RFQService {

  DBHelper dbhelper = new DBHelper();
  Connection con = null;
  Statement stmt = null;

  public RFQService() throws Exception {
    con = dbhelper.getConnectionObject();
    stmt = con.createStatement();
  }
```

All our service classes will create java.sql.Connection and java.sql.Statement objects in the constructor.

Generating a New RFQ

The RFQ service uses JMS for the message exchange. Since there will be more than one supplier interested in receiving the RFQ, we use the Publish/Subscribe model to publish our RFQ using the ABC-RFQ topic.

The generateRFQ() method accepts the RFQ information as an input parameter (message) of type java.lang.String. The message is a XML structure and is parsed using the helper class, XMLParseHelper to build a Vector (vRFQ) of RFQ data beans (RFQDataBean). The XMLParseHelper is a simple JavaBean that uses the JDOM API to parse an XML structure:

```java
public void generateRFQ(String message) throws Exception {
  Vector vRFQ = new Vector();
  vRFQ = XMLParseHelper.getRFQVector(message);
  insertNewRFQ(vRFQ);
  publish(message, "ABC-RFQ");
}
```

Once vRFQ is created, the generateRFQ() method invokes a private method, insertNewRFQ(), to insert the RFQ information in the RFQ_TABLE in the database. The insertNewRFQ() method is designed to insert more than one RFQ. The method first creates PreparedStatement objects. It then fetches the RFQDataBean objects from vRFQ and extracts various values from RFQDataBean objects and enters them in RFQ_TABLE and RFQ_PRODUCT_TABLE:

```java
private void insertNewRFQ(Vector vRFQ) throws Exception {
  PreparedStatement stmt = con.prepareStatement(
                        "INSERT INTO rfq_table VALUES(?,?,?,?,?,?,?)");
  PreparedStatement stmt1 = con.prepareStatement(
                        "INSERT INTO rfq_product_table VALUES(?,?,?,?)");
  for(int i = 0; i < vRFQ.size(); i++) {
    RFQDataBean rfqbean = (RFQDataBean)vRFQ.elementAt(i);
    stmt.setString(1, rfqbean.getRFQId());
    stmt.setString(2, rfqbean.getRFQName());
    stmt.setString(3, rfqbean.getOrganizationName());
    stmt.setString(4, rfqbean.getRFQDate());
    stmt.setString(5, rfqbean.getCreator());
    stmt.setString(6, rfqbean.getSubmissionDate());
    stmt.setString(7, rfqbean.getStatus());
    stmt.executeUpdate();

    Vector vProducts = rfqbean.getProducts();
    for(int j = 0; j < vProducts.size(); j++) {
      ProductBean productbean = (ProductBean)vProducts.elementAt(i);
      stmt1.setString(1, rfqbean.getRFQId());
      stmt1.setString(2, productbean.getProductId());
      stmt1.setString(3, productbean.getProductName());
      stmt1.setInt(4, productbean.getQuantity());
      stmt1.executeUpdate();
    }
  }
}
```

Once the new RFQ is inserted in the database, the generateRFQ() method invokes a private publish() method that publishes the RFQ information as an XML message using the topic name ABC_RFQ. The publish() method uses the JMSHelper class, which does the job of creating the connection and session objects and publishing the topic:

```
private void publish(String message, String topicName) throws Exception {
   JMSHelper jmshelper = new JMSHelper();
   jmshelper.publish(message,topicName);
}
```

Get All Open RFQ

This functionality retrieves all the RFQs with OPEN status from the RFQ_TABLE in the database:

```
public String getOpenRFQ()throws Exception {
   String sql = "SELECT * FROM rfq_table WHERE status='OPEN'";
   String response = fetchRFQ(sql);
   return response;
}
```

The getOpenRFQ() method uses the private method fetchRFQ() to get all the RFQs from RFQ_TABLE. The private method fetchRFQ() actually does the job of retrieving all the RFQ information from the database, builds the vector of RFQDataBeans, and invokes the buildRFQXML() method of XMLBuildHelper to get the XML representation of the RFQ vector:

```
private String fetchRFQ(String sql) throws Exception {
   ResultSet rs = stmt.executeQuery(sql);
   Vector vRFQ = new Vector();

   while (rs.next()) {
      RFQDataBean rfqbean = new RFQDataBean();
      rfqbean.setOrganizationName(rs.getString("organizationname"));
      rfqbean.setRFQName(rs.getString("rfqname"));
      rfqbean.setRFQId(rs.getString("rfqid"));
      rfqbean.setRFQDate(rs.getString("rfqdate"));
      rfqbean.setCreator(rs.getString("creator"));
      rfqbean.setSubmissionDate(rs.getString("submissiondate"));
      rfqbean.setStatus(rs.getString("status"));

      Vector vProducts = new Vector();
      String sql1 = "SELECT * FROM rfq_product_table WHERE rfqid='" +
                     rfqbean.getRFQId()+"'";
      ResultSet rs1 = stmt.executeQuery(sql1);
      while (rs1.next()) {
         ProductBean p = new ProductBean();
         p.setProductName(rs1.getString("productname"));
         p.setProductId(rs1.getString("productid"));
         p.setQuantity(Integer.parseInt(rs1.getString("quantity")));
         vProducts.addElement(p);
      }
      rfqbean.setProducts(vProducts);
      vRFQ.addElement(rfqbean);
   }

   String xmlResponse = XMLBuildHelper.buildRFQXML(vRFQ);
   return xmlResponse;
}
```

Get All RFQ

The getAllRFQ() method provides functionality to retrieve all the OPEN and CLOSED RFQs from the database:

888

```
public String getAllRFQ()throws Exception {
   String sql = "SELECT * FROM rfq_table";
   String response = fetchRFQ(sql);
   return response;
}
```

We have finished developing our RFQ service, so we're ready to build and deploy it. So, compile the helper and bean classes, remembering to include `jdom.jar` in your classpath (for the `XMLBuildHelper` class).

Deploying the RFQ Service

We'll use the Apache SOAP implementation to deploy the RFQ service. We'll be using Tomcat 4 as the servlet container to execute `rpcrouter`, which is responsible for routing the requests to the relevant deployed services and invoking the specified methods in the deployment wizard.

> *Make sure that you have `jdom.jar` available for Tomcat to use. One way to ensure that it is available is to place it in the `%CATALINA_HOME%\common\lib` directory.*

To deploy our `RFQService`, we need to use the Apache SOAP Admin tool available at http://localhost:8080/soap/admin/. The Admin tool allows us to deploy a service, list the deployed services, and delete deployed services. Select Deploy and enter the values shown:

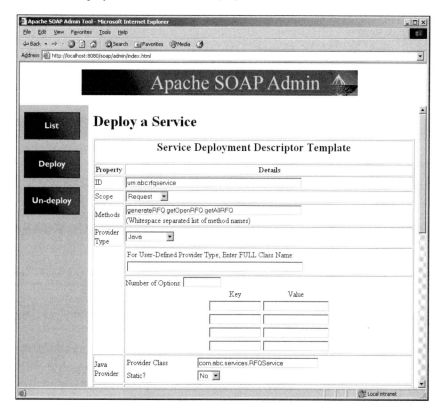

You need to set the ID to `"urn:abc:rfqservice"`; **Methods** to `"generateFRQ getOpenRFQ getAllRFQ"`; and **Provider Class** to `"com.abc.services.RFQService"`. You can use the default values for everything else. Click on the **Deploy** button at the bottom of the page. You will see a window confirming that our service has been deployed. If you now click on the **List** button all the deployed services will be listed. If you follow the urn:abc:rfqservice link you'll see details of our service:

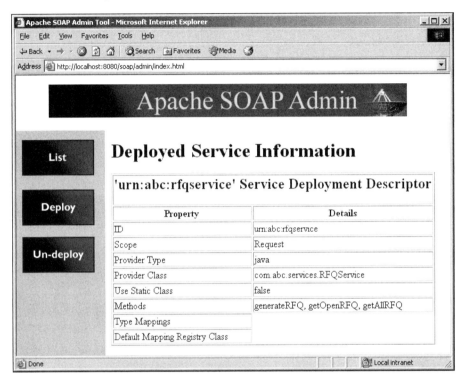

Generating WSDL for RFQ Service

For generating the WSDL files, we will use IBM's Web Services Tool Kit (WSTK) 2.4. We could of course generate the documents by hand but using the tool is a lot easier. Once you have installed the toolkit you should run the **wsdlgen** script in the `bin` directory of the installation. You should select the default option of **Java Class** in the resulting window and click the **Next** button. You will see the following window:

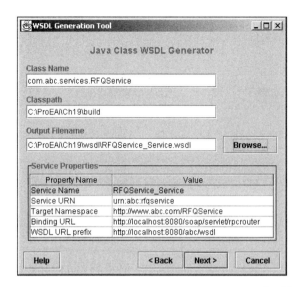

We set the **Class Name** to `com.abc.services.RFQService`; we set the **Classpath** to the location of our compiled classes; we set **Output Filename** to the location we want the WSDL files. We also need to set a number of service-specific properties. We set **Service Name** to `RFQService_Service`; we set **Service URN** to `urn:abc:rfqservice`; we set **Target Namespace** to `http://www.abc.com/RFQService`; we set **Binding URL** to `http://localhost:8080/soap/servlet/rpcrouter`; and we set **WSDL URL prefix** to `http://localhost:8080/abc/wsdl`.

Once all the values are entered, click on **Next**. A window will pop up showing all the methods in that class. As it shows all the inherited methods, this list can be quite large. We need to select the methods we want to make accessible over the network. For `RFQService`, we select `generateRFQ()`, `getOpenRFQ()`, and `getAllRFQ()`:

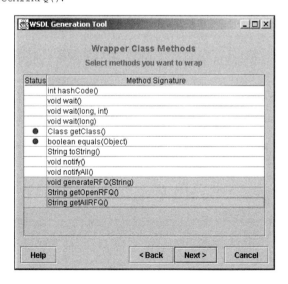

The red dot in the status column means that the method contains complex data types that the WSDL generator may not be able to recognize. If you select an operation with a red dot and continue with the generation process, you will need to modify the WSDL manually to support the operation. In our services, none of the operations have red dots.

Then click on Next. A window will appear to confirm your choice. Now click on Finish. The WSDL files are generated; if you look in the directory we specified, it should contain the following two WSDL files:

❑   `ABC_RFQ_Service-interface.wsdl` – This file contains the `<message>`, `<portType>`, and `<binding>` parts of a WSDL description that describe the interface to the web service

❑   `ABC_RFQ_Service.wsdl` – This file defines the `<service>` part of a WSDL description and imports `ABC_RFQ_Service-interface.wsdl`

We could have many `*Service.wsdl` files for a single `*interface.wsdl` file, and search a registry such as UDDI for one or more implementations of a particular interface description.

If we open the service interface definition file, `ABC_RFQ_Service-interface.wsdl` we can see that the value of `soapAction` is same as that of the Service URN ID that we set in the SOAP deployment wizard:

```
<operation name="generateRFQ">
  <soap:operation soapAction="urn:abc:rfqservice"/>
  ...
</operation>
```

The service information, specified by the `<service>` element, is not included in this WSDL file. It is defined in the service implementation file, `ABC_RFQ_Service.wsdl`. This WSDL file also imports the service interface WSDL file using the `<import>` element:

```
<import
   location="http://localhost:8080/abc/wsdl/ABC_RFQ_Service-interface.wsdl"
   namespace="http://www.abc.com/RFQService-interface">
</import>
```

For our example, we have used `http://localhost:8080/` as the base URI to specify the `rpcrouter` class and location of WSDL files. In real applications, the base URI would map to the name of the enterprise, for example:

```
<import
    location="http://www.abc.com/wsdl/ABC_RFQ_Service-interface.wsdl"
    namespace="http://www.abc.com/RFQService-interface">
</import>
```

The service implementation document also defines the port details and the location of the service listener, in our case, the `rpcrouter` servlet class:

```
<service name="RFQ_Service">
  <documentation>
    IBM WSTK V2.4 generated service definition file
  </documentation>
```

```
    <port binding="interface:RFQ_ServiceBinding"
        name="RFQ_ServicePort">
      <soap:address location="http://localhost:8080/soap/servlet/rpcrouter"/>
    </port>
  </service>
```

Publishing in the UDDI Registry

We'll use the **UDDI Business Test Registry** from IBM for publishing web services of both the manufacturer and supplier. It can be found at https://www-3.ibm.com/services/uddi/testregistry/protect/registry.html. Once you've registered you'll be able to register businesses and services.

We could publish our web services programmatically using the Publish API we discussed earlier. However, we will use the web-based GUI provided by the IBM UDDI Business Test Registry. You might want to investigate publishing services programmatically if you have a large number of web services that need to be published to different UDDI registries.

We need to create a new business named "ABC, Inc." and give it a business locator (which describes the type of business ABC is in) of NAICS 33411. You can also add contact details (although they aren't required for our example). The UDDI registry will generate a unique business key, which is used for query purposes:

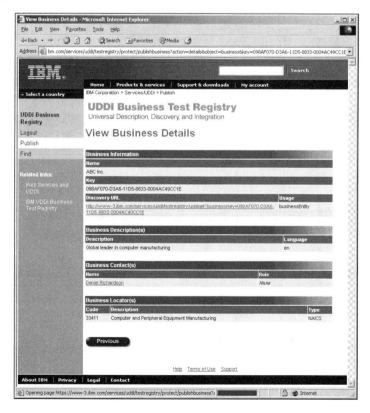

Then we need to register our RFQ service. Use the **Add a new Service Type** wizard to register the service. Set the name of the service to `RFQ_service`, and set an access point with a **Service Type** of `http` and an **Address** of `localhost:8080/soap/servlet/rcprouter`. We can also add a description of the web service if we wish. When we've finished we can view the details of the registered service:

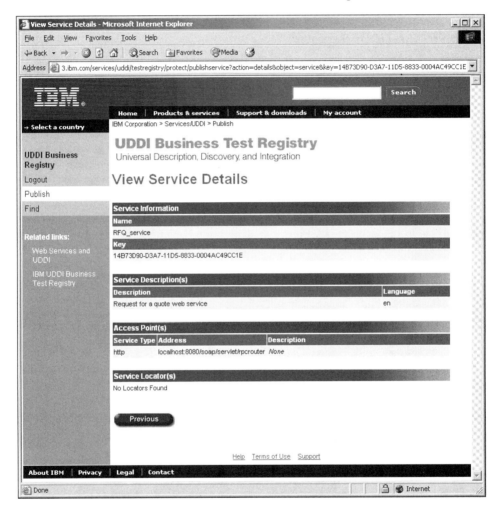

The Inventory Service

The employees of ABC use the inventory service to view products, add new products, and update the quantity of existing products in the inventory. This service also makes use of the helper methods we created earlier. The Inventory service provides functionality to get all the products, the details of a particular product, update the quantity of an existing product and add a new product to the inventory:

```
package com.abc.services;

import java.sql.*;
import java.util.*;

import com.abc.beans.*;
import com.abc.helper.*;

public class InventoryService {

  private final static String TABLE_NAME = "inventory_table";
  DBHelper dbhelper = new DBHelper ();
  Connection con = null;
  Statement stmt = null;

  public InventoryService() throws Exception {
    dbhelper = new DBHelper();
    con = dbhelper.getConnectionObject();
    stmt = con.createStatement();
  }
```

Get All Products

The Invoice service provides functionality to get all the products from the inventory. The getAllProducts() method retrieves the products result set from the inventory table and constructs a vector of products. XMLBuildHelper is used to get the XML representation of the products:

```
public String getAllProducts() throws Exception {

  String sql = "SELECT * FROM inventory_table";
  ResultSet rs = stmt.executeQuery(sql);
  Vector vProducts = new Vector();
  while(rs.next()) {
    ProductBean product = new ProductBean();
    product.setProductName(rs.getString("productname"));
    product.setProductId(rs.getString("productid"));
    product.setQuantity(rs.getInt("quantity"));
    vProducts.addElement(product);
  }
  String xmlResponse = XMLBuildHelper.buildProductListXML(vProducts);
  return xmlResponse;
}
```

Get The Product Details

The Invoice service provides a method to get particular product details. The getProductDetails() method takes the productId as the input parameter to query the inventory table. The result set we obtain returns the product details in XML form. We construct a ProductBean object and add it to the vector of products. The reason for adding the single product is that the buildProductListXML() method of XMLBuildHelper accepts vProducts as an input parameter. You could also overload the buildProductListXML() method to accept both Vector and ProductBean:

895

```
public String getProductDetails(String productId) throws Exception {
   String sql= "SELECT * FROM inventory_table WHERE productid ='" +
            productId+"'";
   ResultSet rs = stmt.executeQuery(sql);
   Vector vProducts = new Vector();
   while(rs.next()){
      ProductBean product = new ProductBean();
      product.setProductName(rs.getString("productname"));
      product.setProductId(rs.getString("productid"));
      product.setQuantity(rs.getInt("quantity"));
      vProducts.addElement(product);
   }
   String xmlResponse = XMLBuildHelper.buildProductListXML(vProducts);
   return xmlResponse;
}
```

Update Quantity of an Existing Product in Inventory

The Invoice service provides functionality to update the quantity of an existing product in the inventory. The code is quite simple:

```
public void updateQuantity(String productId,
                       int quantity) throws Exception {
   String sql= "UPDATE " + TABLE_NAME + "SET quantity=" + "?" + "WHERE" +
            "productid=" + "?";
   PreparedStatement stmt1 = con.prepareStatement(sql);
   stmt1.setInt(1, quantity);
   stmt1.setString(2, productId);
   stmt1.executeUpdate();
}
```

Add a New Product to the Inventory

The Invoice service provides functionality to add a new product to the inventory. The `productName`, `productId`, and `quantity` are passed as the input parameters. The `addProduct()` method requires the product ID, name, and quantity as input parameters:

```
public void addProduct(String productId,
                    String productName,
                    int quantity) throws Exception {
   String sql = "INSERT INTO " + TABLE_NAME + " VALUES(?, ?, ?)";
   PreparedStatement stmt1 = con.prepareStatement(sql);
   stmt1.setString(1, productId);
   stmt1.setString(2, productName);
   stmt1.setInt(3, quantity);
   stmt1.executeUpdate();
}
```

We could also define the method to take the `ProductBean` as the input parameter. In that case the SOAP client program would require a definition of the `BeanSerializer` for the `ProductBean`.

The input parameters are not passed as an XML structure, rather we used the actual data types. Since the input parameters for our demo are the basic data types supported by SOAP, we use the exact data types to avoid the overhead of building and parsing the XML structure. It may not be the case with real applications, as the parameters required for adding a new product may be many.

Although we have hard coded the SQL queries by specifying table names, it will not be the same with real applications. In real applications, such services would be capable of dynamically generating SQL queries by taking the location and other details as input. The inventory service might even make internal calls to other services.

We see here how the concept of "Only One Interface" is applied. Enterprises can publish only one generic inventory web service. This inventory service may call one or more web services (internally) by using a service proxy manager. The service proxy manager may even call an adapter controller, which updates various databases using adapters. As shown in the following diagram, ABC can have web services to access inventories of different departments and locations. ABC may have some of the inventory information residing in legacy databases and the only way to access them is through adapters. The service proxy manager is capable of invoking the adapters using the adapter controller.

ABC can also provide the accessibility to inventory details to all of its suppliers with whom it has agreed to conduct business by defining Trading Partner Agreements (TPAs):

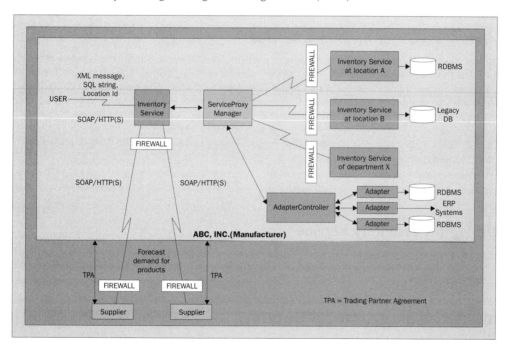

A large company could rely on hundreds of internal and external suppliers for the components it needs to build its products. To automate the supply chain process, we need to integrate its system with many suppliers. If the supplier's applications are built on proprietary technologies and run on legacy systems, then the integration will be a difficult (and expensive) project.

We need a technology that allows us to access the functionality provided by these applications using the Internet or intranet. That technology should be able to provide accessibility to applications running behind firewalls. It should also provide security and easy integration. Based on the discussions we had so far, we could realize that for the above requirements web services is the best fit as a technology for integration.

Enterprises that already have defined contracts and TPAs with the suppliers can provide access to its inventory details through the Inventory service so that suppliers can forecast the requirements of products much in advance to supply the same. This way a supplier can ensure timely delivery of their products to the manufacturer. To provide restricted access, we can bind our service to use HTTPS so that authentication from the suppliers is required. Since web services are built on open standards, even new suppliers can have immediate access to the manufacturer's services after forming TPAs. There is no issue of integrating with proprietary technologies; just having the systems connected to the network is sufficient for invoking the service.

Deploying the Inventory Service

We need to deploy the Inventory service in the same way we deployed the RFQ service. Enter the following values for the web service using the Apache SOAP deployment tool. You need to set the ID to `"urn:abc:inventoryservice"`; Methods to `"getAllProducts getPRoductDetails addProduct updateQuantity"`; and Provider Class to `"com.abc.services.InventoryService"`.

Generating WSDL for Inventory Service

Generate the WSDL files for the inventory service using WSTK as we did for the RFQ service. This time we set the Class Name to `com.abc.services.InventoryService`; we set the Classpath to the location of our compiled classes; we set Output Filename to the location we want the WSDL files. We also need to set a number of service-specific properties. We set Service Name to `Inventory_Service`; we set Service URN to `urn:abc:inventoryservice`; we set Target Namespace to `http://www.abc.com/InventoryService`; we set Binding URL to `http://localhost:8080/soap/servlet/rpcrouter`; and we set WSDL URL prefix to `http://localhost:8080/abc/wsdl`.

Two WSDL files will be generated: `ABC_Inventory_Service-interface.wsdl` and `ABC_Inventory_Service.wsdl`.

Publishing the Inventory Service

In the same way that we published the RFQ service to the UDDI registry, we publish the inventory service. Use the Add a new Service Type wizard, this time setting the service name to `Inventory_service`.

Product Catalog Upload Service

ABC provides a service for its suppliers to dynamically upload new products into ABC's catalog of products. The only constraint is that the product catalog that needs be uploaded should confirm to that of open standards like RosettaNet and ebXML. As shown in the diagram below, using the Product Catalog Upload service suppliers can upload new products into manufacturer's product catalog:

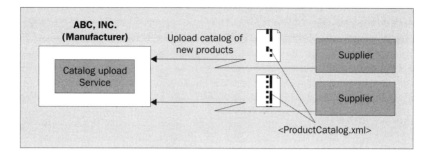

The transport mechanism is SOAP and HTTPS as shown in the previous diagram, in order to restrict access from un-authorized sources. The suppliers will be given a supplier ID and password once the TPA is completed between ABC and the suppliers.

Suppliers can add new products to the manufacturer's catalog of products using the catalog upload web service. The Upload Product Catalog service also uses XMLParseHelper to parse the input XML structure to build a Vector of product objects of type ProductBean.

The getProductVector() method parses the XML request using JDOM's SAXBuilder. Once we get the list of products, we iterate through it to build the vector of product objects:

```
public class XMLParseHelper {
   ...
   private static SAXBuilder saxBuilder = new SAXBuilder();

   public static Vector getProductVector(String xmlRequest)
     throws Exception {
     Vector vProducts = new Vector();
     Document doc = saxBuilder.build(new StringReader(xmlRequest));
     Element root = doc.getRootElement();
     Element eBody = root.getChild("body");
     Element eProductList = eBody.getChild("productList");
     List lProduct = eProductList.getChildren("product");
     Iterator iterator = lProduct.iterator();
     while(iterator.hasNext()) {
       ProductBean product  = new ProductBean();
       Element eProduct = (Element)iterator.next();
       product.setProductId(eProduct.getChild("productId").getTextTrim());
       product.setProductName(
                         eProduct.getChild("productName").getTextTrim());
       Double DUnitPrice = new Double(
                            eProduct.getChild("unitPrice").getTextTrim());
       double dUnitPrice = DUnitPrice.doubleValue();
       product.setUnitPrice(dUnitPrice);
       vProducts.addElement(product);
     }
     return vProducts;
   }
   ...
}
```

Uploading the Catalog of Products

The Upload service requires authentication. On successful authentication, the `authenticate()` method returns a database ID, which is used by the Upload service to map to the database that the supplier wants to upload products to:

```
package com.abc.services;

import java.sql.*;
import java.util.*;

import com.abc.beans.ProductBean;
import com.abc.helper.XMLParseHelper;
import com.abc.helper.DBHelper;

public class ProductCatalogUploadService {

  DBHelper dbHelper = new DBHelper();
  Connection con = null;
  Statement stmt = null;

  public ProductCatalogUploadService() throws Exception {
    con = dbHelper.getConnectionObject();
    stmt = con.createStatement();
  }

  private int authenticate(String supplierId, String password)
      throws Exception {
    int databaseId = 0;
    String sql = "SELECT databaseid FROM supplier_info_table WHERE " +
                 "supplierid='" + supplierId + "'" + "AND password='" +
                 password + "'";
    ResultSet rs = stmt.executeQuery(sql);
    while(rs.next()) {
      databaseId = rs.getInt("databaseid");
    }
    return databaseId;
  }
```

Using the database ID, the service will fetch the database meta data information such as the database URL, table name, and user credentials:

```
  public String uploadProductCatalog(String xmlProductCatalog,
                                      String supplierId,
                                      String password) throws Exception {
    String databaseURL = null,
    tableName = null,
    dbUser = null,
    dbPassword = null;
    int     databaseId = 0;

    if((databaseId = authenticate(supplierId, password))!= 0) {
      String sqlSelect = "SELECT * from db_metadata_table WHERE " +
                         "databaseid=" + databaseId;
      ResultSet rs = stmt.executeQuery(sqlSelect);
      while(rs.next()){
        databaseURL = rs.getString("databaseurl");
        tableName = rs.getString("tablename");
```

```
            dbUser = rs.getString("dbuser");
            dbPassword = rs.getString("dbpassword");
        }
```

The `XMLParseHelper` object parses the XML structure and returns a vector of product objects:

```
        Vector vProducts = new Vector();
        vProducts = XMLParseHelper.getProductVector(xmlProductCatalog);
```

Then, a new `java.sql.Connection` object is created using the database URL and user credentials:

```
        Connection conn1 = DriverManager.getConnection(databaseURL,
                                        dbUser,
                                        dbPassword);
```

A `java.sql.PreparedStatement` object is created for inserting the new products into the catalog:

```
        PreparedStatement stmt1 = conn1.prepareStatement(
                        "INSERT INTO " + tableName + " VALUES(?,?,?)");

        for(int i = 0; i < vProducts.size(); i++) {
            ProductBean product = new ProductBean();
            product = (ProductBean)vProducts.elementAt(i);
            stmt1.setString(1, product.getProductName());
            stmt1.setString(2, product.getProductId());
            stmt1.setDouble(3, product.getUnitPrice());
            stmt1.executeUpdate();
        }
        return "CATALOG UPLOADED";
    } else {
        return "INVALID USERCREDENTIALS";
    }
  }
}
```

Deploy the Catalog Upload service

Deploy the Catalog Upload service using the Apache Soap implementation as we did before. Enter the following values for the web service using the Apache SOAP deployment tool. You need to set the ID to "`urn:abc:cataloguploadservice`"; Methods to "`UploadProductCatalog`"; and Provider Class to "`com.abc.services.ProductCatalogUploadService`".

Generating WSDL for the Catalog Upload Service

Generate the WSDL files for the Catalog Upload service using WSTK in the same way we did before. This time we set the Class Name to `com.abc.services.ProductCatalogUploadService`; we set the Classpath to the location of our compiled classes; we set Output Filename to the location we want the WSDL files. We also need to set a number of service-specific properties. We set Service Name to `CatalogUpload_Service`; we set Service URN to `urn:abc:cataloguploadyservice`; we set Target Namespace to `http://www.abc.com/CatalogUploadService`; we set Binding URL to `http://localhost:8080/soap/servlet/rpcrouter`; and we set WSDL URL prefix to `http://localhost:8080/abc/wsdl`.

Again, two WSDL files will be generated: `ABC_ProductCatalogUpload_Service-interface.wsdl` and `ABC_ProductCatalogUpload_Service.wsdl`.

Publishing the Upload Service

Publish the catalog upload service in the IBM Test UDDI registry in the same way we published the RFQ service. This time set the name of the service to `Product_Catalog_Upload_service`.

Services Provided by the Supplier

JITS (the supplier) provides a catalog service to browse the catalog of products. Although not covered in our application, JITS may also deploy the invoice service as a web service, which would be capable of generating invoices (similar to the generation of RFQs in RFQService by ABC).

The Catalog Service

The Catalog service provides the functionality to view the supplier's (JITS) product catalog. This facilitates the manufacturers to view the suppliers' product catalog. In cases where a supplier gets parts for its products from other suppliers, this catalog service will allow the supplier's suppliers to browse the products to get information about the parts required. The employees of JITS can also use the catalog service to browse the products:

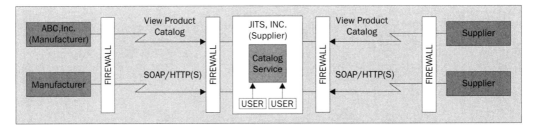

The Catalog service provides functionality to browse the catalog of products. This functionality is implemented in the `CatalogService` class:

```
package com.jits.services;

import com.jits.helper.*;
import com.jits.beans.*;

import java.sql.*;
import java.util.*;

public class CatalogService {

    DBHelper dbhelper = new DBHelper();
    Connection con = null;
    Statement stmt = null;

    public CatalogService() throws Exception {
        con = dbhelper.getConnectionObject();
        stmt= con.createStatement();
    }
```

The Catalog service (`CatalogService` class) defines the method, `getProductCatalog()` for retrieving the product catalog from the database. The query string is executed using the private data member, `stmt`, of type `Statement` object. Then it iterates through the result set to construct a `Vector` of product objects of type `ProductBean`:

```
public String getProductCatalog() throws Exception {
    String sql = "SELECT * FROM product_catalog_table";
    ResultSet rs= stmt.executeQuery(sql);
    Vector vCatalogProducts = new Vector();

    while(rs.next()) {
      ProductBean product = new ProductBean();
      product.setProductName(rs.getString("productname"));
      product.setProductId(rs.getString("productid"));
      product.setUnitPrice(
                    new Double(rs.getString("unitprice")).doubleValue());
      vCatalogProducts.addElement(product);
    }
```

The `XMLBuildHelper` class is used to get the XML representation of product catalog:

```
    String xmlResponse =
                    XMLBuildHelper.buildProductCatalogXML(vCatalogProducts);
    return xmlResponse;
  }
}
```

Deploying the Catalog Service

Again, we need to deploy the catalog service using Apache SOAP deployment. Enter the following values for the web service using the Apache SOAP deployment tool. You need to set the ID to "`urn:jits:catalogservice`"; Methods to "`getProductCatalog`"; and Provider Class to "`com.jits.services.Catalogservice`".

Generating WSDL for the Catalog Service

Generate the WSDL files for the inventory service using WSTK in the same way we did before. This time we set the Class Name to `com.jits.services.CatalogService`; we set the Classpath to the location of our compiled classes; we set Output Filename to the location we want the WSDL files. We also need to set a number of service-specific properties. We set Service Name to `Catalog_Service`; we set Service URN to `urn:jits:catalogservice`; we set Target Namespace to `http://www.abc.com/CatalogUploadService`; we set Binding URL to `http://localhost:8080/soap/servlet/rpcrouter`; and we set WSDL URL prefix to `http://localhost:8080/jits/wsdl`.

Two files will be generated: `JITS_Catalog_Service-interface.wsdl` and `JITS_Catalog_Service.wsdl`.

Publishing the JITS Business Entity

We need to publish the JITS business entity and the services in UDDI registry. We need to create a new account for JITS. Create a business entity named "JITS, Inc." and set the category code to the NAICS code 334119 (for "Monitors, computer peripheral equipment, and manufacturing").

903

Publishing the Catalog Service

Publishing the catalog service is similar to that of publishing the RFQ service – just set the service name to `"Catalog_service"` instead.

Creating a Client Application

Let's develop a client application to access the RFQ service provided by ABC:

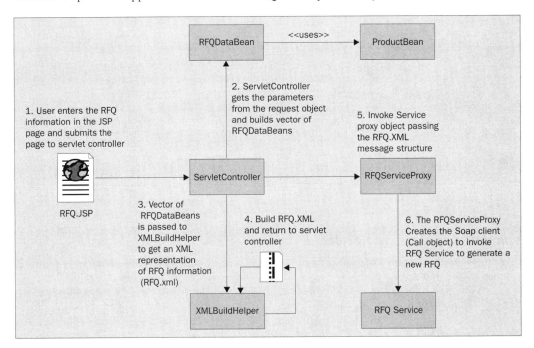

To build the application we'll use Model-View-Controller (MVC) -based Model-2 architecture, in which a servlet is used as the controller and all requests from the view (a JSP page) will be directed to the controller. The model will be represented by JavaBeans, which will execute the business logic.

The User Interface

We use JSP to build the graphical user interface, which consists of a `header.html` file to represent the company logo and an `RFQ.jsp` file to capture RFQ information. A form asks the user for details of the RFQ, including RFQ name, ID, and creator; the product name, ID, and quantity; and the submission date. A hidden input parameter called `action` is created to define the action to be taken. The value of action parameter in `RFQ.jsp` is `"RFQ"`. This allows the servlet controller to decide what action should be taken for the request:

```
<form method="POST" action="./servlet/Controller">
   ...
   <input type="hidden" name="action" value="RFQ" size="3">
   ...
</form>
```

The complete code for RFQ.jsp and the rest of the application can of course be found in the code download.

This form is submitted to the servlet controller.

The Servlet Controller

ServletController retrieves the value of the hidden input parameter, action from HttpServletRequest:

```
package com.client.controller;

import java.io.*;
import java.util.*;
import java.net.URL;
import javax.servlet.*;
import javax.servlet.http.*;
import javax.naming.Context;
import javax.naming.InitialContext;

import com.client.beans.RFQDataBean;
import com.client.beans.ProductBean;
import com.client.helper.XMLBuildHelper;
import com.client.serviceproxy.RFQServiceProxy;

public class ServletController extends HttpServlet{

  public void doPost(HttpServletRequest req, HttpServletResponse res)
    throws IOException, ServletException {

    System.out.println("in servlet");
    if((req.getParameter("action")).equals("RFQ")) {
```

If the value of action is 'RFQ' then the corresponding if block is executed to create a vector of RFQDataBeans:

```
    RFQDataBean rfqbean = new RFQDataBean();
    rfqbean.setOrganizationName("ABC,INC.");
    rfqbean.setRFQName(req.getParameter("rfqName"));
    rfqbean.setRFQId(req.getParameter("rfqId"));
    rfqbean.setRFQDate("" + new Date());
    rfqbean.setCreator(req.getParameter("Creator"));
    rfqbean.setSubmissionDate(req.getParameter("mm") +
                              req.getParameter("dd") +
                              req.getParameter("yyyy"));
    rfqbean.setStatus("OPEN");

    ProductBean p1 = new ProductBean();
    p1.setProductName(req.getParameter("product1"));
    p1.setProductId(req.getParameter("productId1"));
    p1.setQuantity(Integer.parseInt(req.getParameter("qty1")));

    ProductBean p2 = new ProductBean();
```

```
        p2.setProductName(req.getParameter("product2"));
        p2.setProductId(req.getParameter("productId2"));
        p2.setQuantity(Integer.parseInt(req.getParameter("qty2")));

        System.out.println("rfq name :"+rfqbean.getRFQName()+ "\n Id :" +
                           rfqbean.getRFQId() +
                           "\n creator:" +rfqbean.getCreator() +
                           "\n submission date: " +
                           rfqbean.getSubmissionDate());

        System.out.println("productName: " + p1.getProductName() +
                           " Id :" + p1.getProductId() + " qty: " +
                           p1.getQuantity());
        System.out.println("productName: "+p2.getProductName()+
                           " Id :" + p2.getProductId() +
                           " qty: "+p2.getQuantity());

        Vector vProducts = new Vector();
        vProducts.addElement(p1);
        vProducts.addElement(p2);
        rfqbean.setProducts(vProducts);

        Vector vRFQ = new Vector();
        vRFQ.addElement(rfqbean);
```

The `ServletController` then uses `XMLBuildHelper` to create the XML representation of RFQ information:

```
        String xmlRFQ = XMLBuildHelper.buildRFQXML(vRFQ);
        System.out.println(xmlRFQ);
```

Finally, the service proxy object is used to create the SOAP request:

```
        RFQServiceProxy.invokeService(xmlRFQ);
      }
    }
}
```

`RFQServiceProxy` is a proxy class used for invoking the RFQ service. First we need to create a URL object by specifying the location of the servlet responsible for handling all soap requests. We know that in the Apache SOAP implementation, all SOAP requests will be handled by `rpcrouter`:

```
package com.client.serviceproxy;

import java.util.*;
import java.net.*;

import org.w3c.dom.*;
import org.apache.soap.util.xml.QName;
import org.apache.soap.*;
import org.apache.soap.encoding.soapenc.*;
import org.apache.soap.rpc.*;
```

```
public class RFQServiceProxy {

   public static String invokeService(String message) {
     String response = null;
     URL url = null;
     try {
       url = new URL("http://localhost:8080/soap/servlet/rpcrouter");
     } catch (java.net.MalformedURLException me) {
       System.err.println("Exception not a valid URL");
       System.exit(1);
     }
```

Then, we need to create the `Call` object and setup the URI of the target object, the method name to be invoked, the encoding style, and the input parameters required for the method:

```
Call call = new Call();
call.setTargetObjectURI("urn:abc:rfqservice");
call.setMethodName("generateRFQ");
call.setEncodingStyleURI(Constants.NS_URI_SOAP_ENC);
Vector params = new Vector();
params.addElement(new Parameter("xmlRequest",
                        String.class,message, null));
call.setParams(params);
```

And then we invoke the service by executing the `invoke()` method provided by the `Call` object. This method returns an `org.apache.soap.rpc.Response` object, which contains the result that is returned by the `gererateRFQ()` method:

```
try {
   Response resp = call.invoke(url,"");
```

If the method invocation succeeds, then the `generatedFault()` method returns a `false` value:

```
if(!resp.generatedFault()) {
   Parameter ret = resp.getReturnValue();
   response = (String)ret.getValue();
}
```

If the method invocation results in an error, the actual fault is retrieved and displayed and the value of response string is set to `rejected`:

```
else {
   Fault fault = resp.getFault ();
   System.out.println("Sorry! the call failed: ");
   System.out.println("Fault Code= " + fault.getFaultCode());
   System.out.println("Fault String= " + fault.getFaultString());
   response = "rejected";
}
} catch (SOAPException e) {
```

```
        System.err.println("Caught SOAPException (" +
                        e.getFaultCode() + "): " +
                        e.getMessage());
    }
    return response;
  }
}
```

web.xml

The `<servlet>` element indicates the mapping between a servlet name and the actual servlet class. You can see that the `<servlet-name>` has the value, "`Controller`"and is mapped to the `<servlet-class>`, "`com.abc.controller.ServletController`":

```
<?xml version="1.0" ?>

<!DOCTYPE web-app PUBLIC
        "-//Sun Microsystems, Inc.//DTD Web Application 2.3//EN"
        "http://java.sun.com/dtd/web-app_2_3.dtd">

<web-app>
  <servlet>
    <servlet-name>Controller</servlet-name>
    <servlet-class>com.client.controller.ServletController</servlet-class>
  </servlet>
```

To direct all requests from the JSP page to the controller, we specify mapping between `<url-pattern>` and `<servlet-name>`:

```
  <servlet-mapping>
    <servlet-name>Controller</servlet-name>
    <url-pattern>/servlet/*</url-pattern>
  </servlet-mapping>
</web-app>
```

By doing this, all request URLs with a `.jsp` extension from the client application will be directed to the `ServletController`.

Summary

This chapter provided a basic introduction to web services and ebXML, and also explained the importance of using web services in enterprise application integration. We discussed the flexibility, portability, data exchange mechanism suitability, security features, and ease of implementation of web services.

We saw how web services help in A2A, B2B, and B2C integration by providing:

❑ Portable data representation (XML)

❑ A message transport mechanism (SOAP) built using XML as the data representation format

❑ A transport mechanism that uses protocols such as HTTP, SMTP, and FTP

❑ XML structures to represent business services, processes, protocols, and binding information (WSDL)

❑ Interfaces for publishing, and querying, as well as a means to represent business entities and services in a global registry (UDDI)

❑ A definition of a language-, platform-, and location-independent technology to make applications accessible via a network

Index

913

R

S

Y

Notes

Notes

Notes

Notes

p2p.wrox.com
The programmer's resource centre

A unique free service from Wrox Press
With the aim of helping programmers to help each other

Wrox Press aims to provide timely and practical information to today's programmer. P2P is a list server offering a host of targeted mailing lists where you can share knowledge with four fellow programmers and find solutions to your problems. Whatever the level of your programming knowledge, and whatever technology you use P2P can provide you with the information you need.

ASP Support for beginners and professionals, including a resource page with hundreds of links, and a popular ASP.NET mailing list.

DATABASES For database programmers, offering support on SQL Server, mySQL, and Oracle.

MOBILE Software development for the mobile market is growing rapidly. We provide lists for the several current standards, including WAP, Windows CE, and Symbian.

JAVA A complete set of Java lists, covering beginners, professionals, and server-side programmers (including JSP, servlets and EJBs)

.NET Microsoft's new OS platform, covering topics such as ASP.NET, C#, and general .NET discussion.

VISUAL BASIC Covers all aspects of VB programming, from programming Office macros to creating components for the .NET platform.

WEB DESIGN As web page requirements become more complex, programmer's are taking a more important role in creating web sites. For these programmers, we offer lists covering technologies such as Flash, Coldfusion, and JavaScript.

XML Covering all aspects of XML, including XSLT and schemas.

OPEN SOURCE Many Open Source topics covered including PHP, Apache, Perl, Linux, Python and more.

FOREIGN LANGUAGE Several lists dedicated to Spanish and German speaking programmers, categories include. NET, Java, XML, PHP and XML

How to subscribe
Simply visit the P2P site, at http://p2p.wrox.com/

wrox

Programmer to Programmer™

Wrox writes books for you. Any suggestions, or ideas about how you want
information given in your ideal book will be studied by our team.
Your comments are always valued at Wrox.

Free phone in USA 800-USE-WROX
Fax (312) 893 8001

UK Tel.: (0121) 687 4100   Fax: (0121) 687 4101

Professional J2EE EAI – Registration Card

Name _____

Address _____

_____

_____

City _____ State/Region _____

Country _____ Postcode/Zip _____

E-Mail _____

Occupation _____

How did you hear about this book?

☐ Book review (name) _____

☐ Advertisement (name) _____

☐ Recommendation _____

☐ Catalog _____

☐ Other _____

Where did you buy this book?

☐ Bookstore (name) _____ City_____

☐ Computer store (name) _____

☐ Mail order_____

☐ Other _____

What influenced you in the purchase of this book?

☐ Cover Design ☐ Contents ☐ Other (please specify):

_____

How did you rate the overall content of this book?

☐ Excellent ☐ Good ☐ Average ☐ Poor

What did you find most useful about this book? _____

_____

What did you find least useful about this book? _____

_____

Please add any additional comments. _____

_____

What other subjects will you buy a computer book on soon?

_____

What is the best computer book you have used this year?

_____

Note: This information will only be used to keep you updated
about new Wrox Press titles and will not be used for
any other purpose or passed to any other third party.

wrox

Programmer to Programmer™

Note: If you post the bounce back card below in the UK, please send it to:

Wrox Press Limited, Arden House, 1102 Warwick Road,
Acocks Green, Birmingham B27 6HB. UK.

Computer Book Publishers

NO POSTAGE
NECESSARY
IF MAILED
IN THE
UNITED STATES

BUSINESS REPLY MAIL

FIRST CLASS MAIL   PERMIT#64   CHICAGO, IL

POSTAGE WILL BE PAID BY ADDRESSEE

**WROX PRESS INC.,
29 S. LA SALLE ST.,
SUITE 520
CHICAGO IL 60603-USA**